CW00919652

ANGLO-SAXON ENGLAND
AND THE CONTINENT

MEDIEVAL AND RENAISSANCE
TEXTS AND STUDIES
VOLUME 394

Essays in Anglo-Saxon Studies
Volume 3

ANGLO-SAXON ENGLAND AND THE CONTINENT

Edited by

Hans Sauer and Joanna Story
with the assistance of Gaby Waxenberger

ACMRS
(Arizona Center for Medieval and Renaissance Studies)
Tempe, Arizona
2011

Published by ACMRS (Arizona Center for Medieval and Renaissance Studies)
Tempe, Arizona
© 2011 Arizona Board of Regents for Arizona State University.
All Rights Reserved.

Library of Congress Cataloging-in-Publication Data

Anglo-Saxon England and the continent / edited by Hans Sauer and Joanna
Story with the assistance of Gaby Waxenberger.
        p. cm. -- (Medieval and Renaissance texts and studies ; v. 394) (Essays in
Anglo-Saxon studies ; v. 3)
    A selection of papers presented at the twelfth conference of the International
Society of Anglo-Saxonists in Munich, August 1-6, 2005.
    Includes bibliographical references and index.
    ISBN 978-0-86698-442-3 (alk. paper)
    1. English literature--Old English, ca. 450-1100--History and criticism-
-Congresses. 2. Civilization, Anglo-Saxon, in literature--Congresses.
    3. Civilization, Anglo-Saxon--Historiography--Congresses. I. Sauer, Hans.
II. Story, Joanna, 1970- III. Waxenberger, Gabriele, 1956- IV. International
Society of Anglo-Saxonists. Meeting (12th : 2005 : Munich, Germany)
V. Title.
    PR176.A64 2011
    829.09--dc22

                                                                        2011010062

Cover Image
Bishop Willibald of Eichstätt (c.700–787)
Sculputure by Loy Hering in the Cathedral of Eichstätt, reproduced by permission of the
Cathedral Museum at Eichstätt, photograph by Ingeborg Limmer.

∞
This book is made to last. It is set in Adobe Caslon Pro,
smyth-sewn and printed on acid-free paper to library specifications.
Printed in the United States of America.

TABLE OF CONTENTS

Abbreviations

AASS	Acta Sanctorum
AION	*Annali dell'Instituto Orientale di Napoli*
ANQ	*American Notes and Queries*
ASC	*Anglo-Saxon Chronicle*
ASE	*Anglo-Saxon England*
ASPR	The Anglo-Saxon Poetic Records
BAR	British Archeological Reports
BCS	Walter de Gray Birch, *Cartularium Saxonicum*, 3 vols. (London, 1885–1893)
BEASE	*The Blackwell Encyclopaedia of Anglo-Saxon England*, ed. Michael Lapidge, John Blair, Simon Keynes, and Donald Scragg (Oxford, 1999).
Bede, *HE*, ed. Colgrave and Mynors	Bede's *Ecclesiastical History of the English People*, ed. Bertram Colgrave and R.A.B. Mynors (Oxford, 1969).
BHL	Bibliotheca Hagiographica Latina
BL	British Library
BN	Bibliothèque Nationale
ca.	circa
Cameron	Angus Cameron, "A List of Old English Texts," *A Plan for the Dictionary of Old English*, ed. Roberta Frank and A. Cameron (Toronto, 1973), 25-306.
CBA	Council for British Archeology
CCCC	Cambridge, Corpus Christi College
CCSL	Corpus Christianorum Series Latina
chap.	chapter
CLA	*Codices Latini Antiquiores*
CPG	*Clavis Patrum Graecorum*
CPL	*Clavis Patrum Latinorum*
CSASE	Cambridge Studies in Anglo-Saxon England
CSEL	Corpus Scriptorum Ecclesiasticorum Latinorum
d.	died
DB	Domesday Book

DOE	*The Dictionary of Old English*, ed. Angus Cameron et al., Fascicles A–F on CD-ROM, version 1.0 (Toronto, 2003)
ed.	edited by
edn.	edition
EEMF	Early English Manuscripts in Facsimile
EETS	Early English Text Society
o.s.	Original Series
s.s.	Supplementary Series
EHR	*English Historical Review*
ELL	*English Language and Linguistics*
esp.	especially
FF	Folklore Fellows
GenB	Genesis B (the OE version of the OS Genesis)
HBS	Henry Bradshaw Society
HE	see Bede, *HE*
Hel	*Heliand*
IE	Indo-European
Ker	N.R. Ker, *Catalogue of Manuscripts Containing Anglo-Saxon* (Oxford, 1957 [repr. 1991])
km	kilometer(s)
m	meter(s)
m²	square meter(s)
MGH	Monumenta Germaniae Historica
DD Mer	Diplomata Merovingica
DD Kar	Diplomata Karolingorum
Merov.	Merovingicarum
rer. Germ.	rerum Germanicarum
rer. Merov.	rerum Merovingicarum
SS	Scriptores
MHG	Middle High German
ModG	Modern German
MRTS	Medieval and Renaissance Texts and Studies
Och Slav	Old Church Slavonic
OE	Old English
OED	*The Oxford English Dictionary*, ed. J.A.H. Murray et al., 2nd edn. by J.A. Simpson and E.S.C. Weiner, 20 vols. (Oxford, 1989).
OHG	Old High German
Old Lith	Old Lithuanian
ON	Old Norse
OS	Old Saxon

PASE	*Prosopography of Anglo-Saxon England*
PG	*Patrologia Graeca*, ed. J.P. Migne (Paris, 1857–1887)
PL	*Patrologia Latina*, ed. J.P. Migne (Paris, 1844–1865); Supplemental Series, ed. A. Hammon and L. Guillaumin (Paris, 1958-1974)
s.	saeculo
s.a.	sub anno
SASLC	*Sources of Anglo-Saxon Literary Culture*
S	Peter H. Sawyer, *Anglo-Saxon Charters: An Annotated List and Bibliography*, Royal Historical Society, Guides and Handbooks 8 (London, 1968).
VatG	Vatican Genesis (fragment of the Old Saxon Genesis)
vol., vols.	volume, volumes

List of Illustrations

INTRODUCTION

Hans Sauer and Joanna Story

The present volume contains a selection of papers presented at the twelfth conference of the International Society of Anglo-Saxonists (ISAS) in Munich, 1–6 August 2005. The general theme of the conference was 'England and the Continent' (modelled on Wilhelm Levison's *England and the Continent in the Eighth Century* [Oxford, 1946]), and this is reflected in the title of this volume, *Anglo-Saxon England and the Continent* and, of course, in its contributions, which concentrate on this theme.

From its very beginning to its very end, Anglo-Saxon England was always in close contact with the Continent. To mention just some of the most important events, friendly ones as well as hostile: the Angles, Saxons, and Jutes (and perhaps also Frisians) who started to defeat the Celtic Britons and to conquer and to settle Britain from 449 onwards (according to Bede, *HE*) came from what is today northern Germany and western Denmark; Christianity was mainly introduced by missionaries from Rome who arrived in 597, led by S. Augustine; Theodore, a monk of Greek origin, became archbishop of Canterbury in 669 and together with Hadrian also established an important school there; Scandinavian Vikings attacked England from 793 onwards and began to settle in its eastern and northern parts (the Danelaw) in the later ninth century; King Alfred (d. 899), after he had come to an agreement with the Vikings, assembled helpers from England and Wales as well as from the Continent in order to get his educational program and his translations started; the Benedictine Reform (Monastic Revival) in the second half of the tenth century followed Continental models; the renewed Viking and Danish attacks in the late tenth and early eleventh centuries led to the rule of Danish kings over England (Swein Forkbeard 1013 –1014 and Cnut 1016–1035); the Normans who put an end to Anglo-Saxon England in 1066 came ultimately also from Scandinavia but immediately from Normandy in northwestern France. Literature traveled from the Continent to England, too: the *Beowulf* story, for example (or at least part of it), must have come to England from Denmark long after the Anglo-Saxon settlement (see the contribution by J. D. Niles); *Genesis B* came to England probably in the ninth century (see the contribution by A. N. Doane).

But relations were by no means one-sided. There was a lot of intermarriage between royal and aristocratic houses on both sides of the Channel; Christian Anglo-Saxons traveled to Italy and to Jerusalem from the sixth to the eleventh centuries on ecclesiastical business or on pilgrimage or to do trade, and also brought manuscripts to Italy such as the Vercelli Book or the Codex Aminatinus (see the contributions by R. Aist, R. Marsden, and D. Pelteret); mainly in the eighth century Anglo-Saxon missionaries such as Boniface, Willibald, and Willehad, and also women such as Hugeburc and Leoba, in their turn Christianized large parts of what is Germany today (see, e.g., the contributions by J. Palmer and B. Yorke); Anglo-Saxon scholars such as Bede and Alcuin were famous on the Continent and their works are preserved in a large number of Continental manuscripts; Alcuin was even invited by Charlemagne in 781 to join the circle of scholars at court and he died as abbot in Tours in 804 (see the contribution by L. Sinisi).[1]

The contributions assembled in this volume cover many different aspects of the mutual relationship between England and the Continent. Most of them combine a description of the evidence with its interpretation, and some offer theories and hypotheses which might not be generally accepted but which will certainly stimulate further discussion. In the following paragraphs, we give a brief outline of their contents and their main arguments, also pointing out the interrelations and parallels between some of them. The paper by Helmut Gneuss provides a general survey of research; John Hines deals with the home life of the Anglo-Saxons. John D. Niles, Alger N. Doane, and Thomas Bredehoft discuss aspects of Old English poetry (*Beowulf, Genesis B,* Old Saxon influence on other OE poems) whereas Angelika Lutz analyzes the Celtic influence on the Old English language. James Palmer and James Roberts investigate questions of Anglo-Saxon identity with relation to the Continent, especially Saxony; Rodney Aist and Barbara Yorke (as well as James Palmer) look at saints' lives and their relevance as historical sources (Willibald; Leoba; Willehad). Richard Marsden and David Pelteret explain the relationship of the Anglo-Saxons with Italy. Lucia Sinisi and Catherine Clarke offer interpretations of Anglo-Latin poems (by Alcuin and Abbo of Fleury). Nicholas Brooks explains the Continental models for cathedral reform at Canterbury in the early ninth century; Michael Hare interprets a recently discovered wall-painting at Deerhurst which probably dates from the tenth century; Debby Banham shows how Continental medical texts were introduced into England in the eleventh century.

---

[1] In connection with the conference, an exhibition of manuscripts showing Anglo-Saxon influence on Germany, especially Bavaria, was presented; see Hans Sauer, ed., *Angelsächsisches Erbe in München/Anglo-Saxon Heritage in Munich* (Frankfurt am Main, 2005); Hans Sauer, "Angelsächsisches Erbe in München / Anglo-Saxon Heritage in Munich," *ShelfLife: The Bulletin of the Research Group on Manuscript Evidence* 1 (2006): 24–31.

1. **Helmut Gneuss** provides a broad survey of the current state of Anglo-Saxon studies as well as achievements in the past and fruitful areas for future research, concentrating on linguistic and philological aspects. He discusses a number of current projects, e.g. the *DOE* (*Dictionary of Old English*), *SASLC* (*Sources of Anglo-Saxon Literary Culture*), *Fontes Anglo-Saxonici*, and *PASE* (*Prosopography of Anglo-Saxon England*). He states that several important critical editions, detailed studies of single manuscripts, and investigations of the Old English language have been published, but that more work needs to be done in all of these areas. Existing grammars of Old English, for example, will have to be revised in the light of all the available manuscripts. Other desiderata are an inventory of copies of Old English texts made since the sixteenth century, and comprehensive surveys of Old English word-formation and of the etymology of the Old English vocabulary. He also points to the numerous areas where there is still uncertainty (in spite of a lot of scholarly discussion), mentioning, for example, problems such as the dating of Old English poetry (including *Beowulf* — see the contribution by J. D. Niles), the origin of the Old English dialects (did the differences already exist on the Continent or did they develop in England? — see the contribution by A. Lutz), the relation and mutual intelligibility of Old English and Old Norse, the use of Latin (but not of Old English) in the liturgy, the Anglo-Saxon influence on the Continent, including the insular script, and the recent debate about a Carolingian calendar based on insular sources.

2. **John Hines** discusses aspects of the home life of the Anglo-Saxons, ranging from the aristocracy to peasants and slaves, and compares it to Continental developments. He uses mainly archaeological evidence from excavations, but also takes literary texts (including Old English poetry) into account. He looks at the recently discovered (in 2003/4), very elaborate Prittlewell chamber grave, an aristocratic (or even royal) burial which shows that the Sutton Hoo burial with its splendor was not an isolated case. The prince was buried with weapons as well as with equipment for hospitality such as drinking-horns. Hines moves on to the symbolic interpretation of burials, and then to the stability or rather instability of houses — because they were made of wood, their life-span was relatively short. He also explains the concept of the labile settlement, which was subject to change and translocation. Stable sites on the other hand were often connected with the church and were seats of bishops. Ownership of the land was very important in Anglo-Saxon England. Hines also points out that the kin-group was the fundamental social structure in Anglo-Saxon England; later it was replaced by feudal structures. *Familia* in Anglo-Saxon England, however, meant 'household' rather than 'family' in the modern sense.

3. **John D. Niles** points out the importance of the excavation of two large halls at Lejre (Gammel Lejre) on the island of Zealand, Denmark, because Lejre is often taken to have been the seat of the (fictitious) Danish kings (the Skjöldungs or Scyldingas) who play an important role in the first part of *Beowulf*. He explains the dualistic character of the landscape where the halls were situated,

xiv   Introduction

namely open fields and grassland (symbolic of culture and humanity) on one side and a dead-ice hinterland (symbolic of nature and inhuman beings) on the other side, and assumes that this situation could easily give rise to a story of hall-haunting by a monster. Starting from this, he provides a new hypothesis about the evolution of the *Beowulf* story in six conceptual stages (some of which may have occurred simultaneously): 1. Part I, the haunting of the hall of the Scyldings, arose in Denmark, perhaps even at Lejre. 2. It was developed into a two-troll plot. 3. It was brought to England during the Viking period (i.e. some time after the mid-ninth century); the subsequent additions were made in Anglo-Saxon England. It survives in England and in Iceland (in the *Rolfs saga kraka*), but not in Denmark itself. 4. Part II, the dragon episode and the hero's death were added. 5. The story was turned into a poem. 6. The poem was endowed with a religious meaning.

4. The Old English poem *Genesis B* (*GenB*), which was later inserted into the Old English poem *Genesis A* (both are transmitted in Oxford, Bodleian Library, Junius 11), is closely based on the Old Saxon Genesis poem—part of the latter still exists in a Vatican manuscript (*VatGen*), so that some passages of the Old Saxon and the Old English version can be directly compared. *Genesis B* is often regarded as a transcription or transliteration of the Old Saxon poem, rather than a translation. Similarly to J. D. Niles, who reconstructs the development of *Beowulf* through several stages (see above), **Alger N. Doane** postulates that *Genesis B* evolved through a number of stages. He assumes that around 900 a group of collaborators transcribed the Old Saxon Genesis into Old English, and that later Anglo-Saxon scribes and readers then tried to naturalize the text, but succeeded only partly—this can be seen from various anomalies in the Old English *Genesis B*. In Doane's opinion the original collaborators included some of King Alfred's helpers who had come from the Continent, especially Grimbald and John "the Old Saxon", whose role he discusses. He discusses also several instances of subtle changes, misunderstandings, and mistakes on all levels (vocabulary, syntax, meter, cultural background) that occurred during the process of adapting the Old Saxon text into Old English, or, to put it differently, during transposing it from one intertext into another. Doane also endorses the opinion that an illustrated copy of the Old Saxon Genesis must have circulated in Anglo-Saxon England around 900, which can be seen from some peculiarities of the pictures in Junius 11.

5. **Thomas A. Bredehoft** argues that *Genesis B* is not the only Old English poem to show Old Saxon influence. According to him at least four others, namely *The Dream of the Rood*, the poetic *Solomon and Saturn*, *The Battle of Finnsburg*, and *The Metrical Preface to Wærferth's Translation of Gregory's Dialogues*, were also influenced by Old Saxon poetry. He shows that these poems have metrical features that are rare or even unmetrical in Old English verse, but common and metrical in Old Saxon poetry. He postulates a scansion system different from the one developed by Sievers, and rather follows the system developed by Geoffrey Russom. Bredehoft bases his argument mainly on verse types that are unmetri-

cal or rare in Old English (but not in Old Saxon) as well as the use of anacrusis. As additional pieces of evidence of Old Saxon influence on *The Dream of the Rood*, Bredehoft points out some parallels of vocabulary and phrasing between this poem and the *Heliand*, especially in the depiction of the crucifixion. He also finds some verbal parallels between *Solomon and Saturn* and *Heliand*. In an appendix, he outlines his metrical principles.

6. Although the West-Saxon dialect of Old English is related to the Continental Old Saxon dialect, both dialects also show a number of differences. **Angelika Lutz** argues that some of the structural peculiarities of West-Saxon are due to early Insular Celtic influence on early Old English (West-Saxon); she assumes that they result from a large-scale language shift of Insular Celtic speakers from Celtic to (pre-)Old English. She discusses a number of older as well as more recent theories about the relationship of the Celtic Britons to the Anglo-Saxons and points out their weaknesses. It is often assumed that the defeated Britons were put to death or to flight by the victorious Anglo-Saxons or turned into slaves; this was seen as the reason why there has been little lexical influence of British Celtic on Old English. Lutz points out, however, that typically a superstrate language (in this case Old English) contributes mainly the vocabulary, whereas a substrate language (in this case British Celtic) contributes morphologic and syntactic features. As signs of Celtic influence on Old English morphology and syntax she mentions (a) the twofold present tense of the verb 'to be' in West-Saxon (*ic bēo—ic ēom* etc.) and (b) the progressive form (*they were fighting* vs. *they fought*). These features are peculiar to (Old) English and do not exist in other Germanic languages. But whereas the twofold present of 'to be' was later lost, the progressive was grammaticalized only in Modern English. As lexical and semantic evidence she adduces the fact that Old English *wealh* means 'foreigner, Briton, Celtic person' as well as 'slave, British or Celtic slave' which seems to show that the slaves of the early Anglo-Saxons were typically of Celtic origin. This is also true of related words such als *wiln* 'female slave'—the female house-slaves of Celtic origin could have influenced the language of their masters' children.

7. In the eighth century, Anglo-Saxon missionaries Christianized in Frisia and Saxony, while the Franks (Carolingians) conquered these areas. **James Palmer** explores issues of identity and authority that arose from this situation. He asks how far there was a sense of relatedness between the missionaries and the Frisians and Saxons, a kind of symbolic association and a concept of *Germanitas*. He looks at two saints' lives from the ninth century, Altfrid of Münster's *Vita Liudgeri* and the anonymous Bremen *Vita Willehadi*. Liudger died in 809; he was a Frisian who founded several churches, e.g. in Dokkum, Münster, and Werden. Altfrid thus commemorates a predecessor, and he apparently envisaged Münster and Werden between Carolingian and Northumbrian cultural traditions, with the courts of Alchred of Northumbria and of Charlemagne cooperating. A similar perspective apparently also applied to the *Vita Willehadi*. Willehad, who died in 789, was a Northumbrian who became the first bishop of Bremen. Palmer also

takes into account later developments, such as the division of the Carolingian empire in 843.

8. **James Roberts** is also concerned with questions of Anglo-Saxon identity by looking at the correspondence of Æthelweard and Matilda. Æthelweard (d. ca. 998) was an important *ealdorman* in late tenth-century England, and possibly also the compiler of the Latin *Chronicon Æthelweardi*, which is largely based on the *Anglo-Saxon Chronicle*. Matilda was abbess of Essen 973–1011. Both were related, ultimately descending from the West-Saxon king Æthelwulf (839–58); Matilda was also a descendant of Edith, the daughter of Edward the Elder (899–924), who married the future German ruler Otto I. In the prologue to the *Chronicon*, the relation and exchange of letters between Æthelweard and Matilda are mentioned. Roberts assumes that their common concern probably was to obtain information about their family history. In view of this, Roberts finds it strange that in the *Chronicon* the role of the saintly king Oswald of Northumbria (d. 642) is much reduced as compared to the *Anglo-Saxon Chronicle*, although the cult of Saint Oswald was widespread not only in England, but also in Ottonian Germany, and Roberts offers several possible explanations for this neglect of Oswald.

9. The Anglo-Saxon missionary St. Willibald (700–787), prior to becoming the first bishop of Eichstätt (741–787), spent almost twenty years in the Mediterranean area: he stayed in Rome (720–723), Jerusalem (724–726), Constantinople (727–729), and Monte Cassino (729–739). Many years later, in 778, he dictated his experiences, especially in Jerusalem, to his relative, the nun Hugeburc, and his report has been preserved in Hugeburc's *Vita Willibaldi*. **Rodney Aist** discusses mainly the sites of Jerusalem mentioned in Willibald's description, especially the Church of the Holy Sepulchre and the place where the Holy Cross was found—he points out that the cross was twice connected with Willibald's recovery from a severe illness. According to Aist, Willibald also stresses the importance of perseverance: those who overcome all the obstacles during their arduous pilgrimage will in the end reach (the heavenly) Jerusalem. But contrary to the common view of Jerusalem as the center of the world, for the elderly bishop Willibald Jerusalem was a distant place at the edge of his geographical experience.

10. Leoba (d. 782), a relative of Boniface, was born in England but spent the greater part of her life in Germany; she was the founder and abbess of the nunnery at Tauberbischofsheim and was buried at Fulda. The main source for her life is the *Vita S. Leobae*, written by the German monk Rudolf of Fulda in 836–838. **Barbara Yorke** investigates how far Rudolf describes Anglo-Saxon customs and how far Frankish reality or ideals. More generally, she discusses to what extent his work was influenced by earlier models, especially the conventions of the saint's life, and how far it can be used as a historical source. She emphasizes that Rudolf also used information based on oral traditions about Leoba from people that still knew her; but even those were shaped by the traditions of hagiography. She illustrates this from the description of several incidents which show the intermingling of historical facts with their Christian and monastic interpretation, and

furthermore the effects of good story-telling. She also compares Rudolf's account with other extant historical sources.

11. The Codex Amiatinus is the oldest surviving complete Latin Bible and thus also the earliest witness of the Vulgate text. It was copied at the monastery of Wearmouth-Jarrow under Abbot Ceolfrith around 700 and sent to Rome in 716. By the early eleventh century it was at the monastery of San Salvatore, Monte Amiata; in the later sixteenth century it was in Rome again and was used for a new edition of the Vulgate. Today it is in Florence, Biblioteca Medicea Laurentiana, as codex Amiatino 1. **Richard Marsden** discusses in some detail the history of this codex, including its use in Rome in the sixteenth century, as well as a number of the corrections and additions to the text, especially those made in Italy.

12. **David Pelteret** brings together a wealth of evidence as well as hypotheses about the journeys of Anglo-Saxons to Italy, not only to Rome but also to places such as Pavia, Lucca, Monte Sant' Angelo, and elsewhere. He sketches the journeys of well-known figures such as the controversial and deposed bishop Wilfrid (ca. 634–709), who traveled to Rome several times, for the last time in ca. 704. He also discusses some of the practicalities of traveling such as which route to choose, how and where to spend the night, the speed of travel, the dangers of traveling, and where to stay in Rome, and looks at the different but sometimes overlapping motivations of the travelers (ecclesiastical business, pilgrimage, trade). Furthermore he points to runic and non-runic inscriptions as well as coins left by Anglo-Saxons in Italy, and discusses the relevance of the cult of St. Mary and of St. Michael to Italy and to Anglo-Saxon England.

13. Apart from many other works, Alcuin (ca. 735–804) wrote ca. 150 poems. **Lucia Sinisi** provides an interpretation of one of them, the poetic epistle *Cartula perge cito trans pelagi aequora cursu*, which is named from its first line (it has no title in the manuscript). Alcuin probably wrote it around 780, i.e. not long before he moved from York to the court of Charlemagne. It is transmitted in one manuscript only (now Paris, BN, lat. 528, fols. 132rv) which was, however, copied at Saint-Denis around 800, i.e. still during Alcuin's lifetime. Sinisi gives a close reading of the poem and also places it into its literary tradition. Alcuin addresses his own poem (which he sends on a journey from England to Saint-Denis)—thus following a widespread tradition which goes back to classical antiquity. He describes in detail the journey of the poem, mentioning in a kind of frame technique all the stops on the way and the important people the poem is going to meet and how to best address them. The stops are: 1. mouth of the Rhine; 2. Utrecht; 3. Dorestad; 4. Cologne; 5. Echternach; 6. the residence of bishop Beornrad; 7. the court of Charlemagne; 8. Mainz; 9. Speyer; 10. Saint-Denis; from there, the *cartula* begins its homeward journey. Sinisi notes particularly close parallels to Sidonius Apollinaris' *Propempticon ad libellum*, and assumes that the poem was intended to give instructions to a young man, probably one of Alcuin's pupils, who carried an official letter or a book to Charlemagne—but

while the poetic epistle remains, we do not know which letter or book it was intended to accompany.

14. A close reading and an interpretation of another Latin poem is offered by **Catherine A. M. Clarke**. Abbo of Fleury (ca. 945/50–1004) spent two years at Ramsey abbey (985–987). Although he once described his time in England as an exile, he also wrote a short poem (14 lines) as a panegyric in praise of Ramsey in a kind of hermeneutic style, which is transmitted in different manuscript contexts. Clarke points out that Abbo offers a variation on the theme of the (monastic) *locus amoenus*: he describes Ramsey as a cultivated island among the wilderness of the fens, and employs an imagery of light and its reflection in the sky and in the water. He also uses astronomical imagery. Clarke compares this with astronomical texts, and also looks at later texts.

15. **Nicholas Brooks** states that bishops in the Latin west often sought to reform their cathedral clergy by imposing upon them a kind of monastic discipline, including communal living, thus blurring the contrast between contemplative monks and pastoral clergy. His main question is whether the cathedral reform at Christ Church Canterbury by Archbishop Wulfred (805–832) was inspired by Continental models, especially by the reforms of Chrodegang of Metz (742/47–766) and the subsequent efforts of Charlemagne, Benedict of Aniane, and Louis the Pious, or whether it was a parallel but independent effort. Whereas for the Continental reform rules survive, e.g. the *(Enlarged) Rule of Chrodegang* (which was later also translated into Old English), the main witness to Wulfred's reform are charters, especially a charter from 813 (S 1265), which Brooks interprets in detail. All the reformers mentioned drew on the Benedictine rule, but contrary to it allowed the cathedral canons to retain private property which, however, was eventually to remain in the community. Brooks illustrates this from the property owned by the priest Werhard, a kinsman of Wulfred. He answers his initial question by stating that Wulfred's reform was probably influenced by the Continental reforms, and like these was intended for canons, not for monks. The relevant charters are edited in an appendix.

16. **Michael Hare** discusses an Anglo-Saxon wall-painting at St. Mary's Church, Deerhurst (Gloucestershire), which is fairly high up in the church and probably for that reason was discovered only in 1993 and first analyzed in 2002. This is an important addition to the small corpus of Anglo-Saxon wall-paintings. The painting, which probably dates from the tenth century, shows a (probably male) figure with a halo and a book in his right hand. This type of figure was common throughout the Middle Ages, but the identity of the Deerhurst figure is difficult to establish. According to Hare it represents a saint rather than Christ. From its position high up in the church Hare concludes that Deerhurst Church originally must have had an upper floor from which this (and perhaps also a parallel) painting could be viewed. To put the Deerhurst painting into context, Hare compares it with Anglo-Saxon manuscript illustrations and also with Continental churches, e.g. St. Emmeram in Regensburg (Germany) and St. Peter in

Beho (Belgium). But there are still many problems of interpretation; for example, the liturgical function of the painting is unclear.

17. In Anglo-Saxon England there existed—in contrast to the Continent—a number of medical or medicobotanical texts in the vernacular, i.e. in Old English. As **Debby Banham** points out, however, from the middle of the eleventh century onwards the number of vernacular texts decreased, whereas the number of Latin medical texts increased, and their contents and structure also changed. The texts containing the 'new medicine' (sometimes also described as 'Salernitan'), for example, refer to the four humors, cite authorities, and give measurements; on the whole they are more sophisticated. Banham also tackles the question of how 'the new medicine' came to England, and looks specifically at the manuscript London, BL, Sloane 1621, probably written at Bury, and perhaps connected with the medical practitioner Baldwin of Bury (abbot 1065–1097).

Our thanks go to the contributors and their patience with us, and, of course, to the people who helped to prepare the manuscript for publication, especially Gaby Waxenberger, Zora Gnädig, Gabi Gaina and Elisabeth Kubaschewski, they go also to Todd Halvorsen and Roy Rukkila at the Arizona Center for Medieval and Renaissance Studies for seeing the volume through the press and making many useful suggestions.

Postscript

Since the original compilation of this volume two new and exciting archaeological discoveries have been made that are especially important for themes discussed by John D. Niles and James Roberts:

1. A new round of excavations undertaken at Lejre during the summer of 2009 revealed the existence of additional Viking-Age structures, including one building that, at 60 metres in length, is the largest yet known from prehistoric Denmark. These discoveries await publication and analysis.

2. Recent excavations in the cathedral at Magdeburg revealed the tomb of Edith (Eadgyth) (died 946). She was the daughter of Edward the Elder and half-sister of Athelstan, who arranged her marriage to the German King and Emperor Otto I in 930. Isotopic analysis of the tooth enamel has confirmed that the remains in the tomb are indeed those of Otto's Anglo-Saxon queen. The analysis shows that she spent her childhood in southern England; the results from this skeleton are quite different to those derived from people known to have been brought up in the region of Magdeburg. Her bones are thus the earliest known of any member of a royal English dynasty.

Anglo-Saxon Studies:
Past, Present, and Future

Helmut Gneuss

I must begin with an apology for my title, which—as I admit—I had chosen somewhat rashly when I was invited to deliver this plenary lecture, and at a time when I was still uncertain what I might venture to offer our Society, meeting for the first time in Germany. Please consider my title then as a makeshift, not as an example of Munich megalomania. However, I do want to say something about the past, the present, and the future of our studies, common concerns and interests, although I will have to concentrate on fields where I am at home—especially books, texts, and language—being keenly aware, of course, that, at a time when the call for 'the interdisciplinary approach' has almost developed into a fashion, it is the members of the International Society of Anglo-Saxonists who have truly and with great success practised and promoted this approach for many years, as is amply documented in the contributions, annual bibliographies, and reviews of research in the two periodicals *Anglo-Saxon England* and *Old English Newsletter*, and—to name just two distinguished series—in the volumes of the Cambridge Studies in Anglo-Saxon England and the Old English Newsletter Subsidia. I will presently return to these and other important achievements.

In talking of these, and in looking at the situation of our subject (or rather, at what I am able to judge and assess), it is my express aim to emphasize that important work is still before us, and it is my hope to provide appropriate encouragement to undertake such work. This reminds me of a delightful passage in Dorothy Whitelock's Inaugural Lecture at the University of Cambridge in 1958, where, considering a host of then recent Anglo-Saxon studies, she noted,

> I could not help recalling with a somewhat wry amusement how, when Professor Chadwick suggested that I should undertake research [this must have been in 1924], I was afraid that before I could get going there would be nothing left to do.[1]

---

[1] Dorothy Whitelock, *Changing Currents in Anglo-Saxon Studies* (Cambridge, 1958), 2; repr. as no. I in eadem, *History, Law and Literature in 10th–11th Century England* (London, 1981).

Hans Sauer and Joanna Story, eds., *Anglo-Saxon England and the Continent*. With the assistance of Gaby Waxenberger. Essays in Anglo-Saxon Studies, vol. 3. MRTS 394. Tempe: ACMRS, 2011.   [ISBN 978-0-86698-442-3]

Looking into the annual bibliographies and the lists of work in progress now, eighty years later, I dare to quote from an excellent book on Roman grammar—certainly also of interest to Anglo-Saxonists—by an American classicist who states unequivocally: "The subject is rich, and there is much work to be done."[2] That, I think, is also our situation, in all our fields, and it applies to the literary historian and the textual critic just as to the archaeologist or the numismatist—to mention just those four—if I am not mistaken.

It would be tempting but risky to try to paint a picture of the general situation of our subject, of its disciplines especially in the Arts faculties of the universities. For this depends to a large extent on the policies and means of individual universities or—in Europe—on government policies concerning higher education, and on research assessment, and we might all be in a position to tell our stories of promising progress, but also of deplorable developments. In these days of reforms (or what are supposed to be reforms) and of economies, medieval studies will, it seems, frequently be among the subjects that have to defend their status and work, or even their existence. Of the reforms now so energetically proposed in some places let me just mention the view (apparently a peculiarly German idea) that research work in the humanities, particularly Ph.D. work, should be based on, or linked to, an organized group of researchers, a collective, as if an individual scholar could not be expected to succeed in writing a good book unless she or he be a member of an intellectual *kolkhoz*.

But now to Anglo-Saxon studies. I have the word 'Past' in my title, because our studies can look back on a remarkable history of scholarship, and because it is gratifying to note that there has been an increasing interest in this history, marked by studies and by editions like those of Humfrey Wanley's and George Hickes's letters,[3] while numerous, well-written entries in the new *Oxford Dictionary of National Biography* and two excellent bibliographies now provide an up-to-date reference network.[4] Although all this may seem of exclusively antiquarian interest, its practical usefulness should not be ignored. It is well known that some important Old English texts, or versions of such texts, survive only in modern copies by Francis Junius and others; but Junius's reliability as a copyist,

---

[2] Robert E. Kaster, *Guardians of Language: The Grammarian and Society in Late Antiquity* (Berkeley and Los Angeles, 1988), xii.

[3] *Letters of Humfrey Wanley, Palaeographer, Anglo-Saxonist, Librarian 1672–1726*, ed. P. L. Heyworth (Oxford, 1989); *A Chorus of Grammars: The Correspondence of George Hickes and his Collaborators on the Thesaurus linguarum septentrionalium*, ed. Richard L. Harris, *Publications of the Dictionary of Old English* 4 (Toronto, 1992).

[4] *The Oxford Dictionary of National Biography*, ed. H. C. G. Matthew and Brian Harrison, 60 vols. (Oxford, 2004); Carl T. Berkhout, "Anglo-Saxon Scholarship," http://www.u.arizona.edu/~ctb/ [literature up to 1996]; Simon Keynes, *Handbook* [see n. 7 below], sections S 1–155.

combined with his role as a textual critic, has only very recently been properly examined. Manuscript material of the antiquaries of the sixteenth to nineteenth centuries is copious, and more textually relevant transcripts may turn up; the recent discovery and edition of the nineteenth-century tracing of an Old English prayer otherwise unknown is a good example.[5] Even an early printed edition has been overlooked until now.[6]

An inventory of all early transcripts, made since the sixteenth century, of manuscripts with Old English and early Anglo-Latin texts and glosses is, I think, a desideratum, and I wonder if ISAS could help in setting up an archive covering the lives and work of Anglo-Saxonists in more recent times, either holding the papers and, perhaps, annotated books left behind by them, or collecting and providing information on where (and under what legal restrictions) such papers and books can be consulted. Even in our times, the so-called 'information age', information (not only that stored in computers) may get lost very quickly, and can we not imagine researchers who very soon might want to study notes or drafts left behind by John Pope, René Derolez, or Patrick Wormald?

This brings me to the 'Present' of my title. My aim, as I said, is to show that our subject is full of rewarding tasks and opportunities, by pointing out some of the achievements, especially of the last ten or twenty years. Even my necessarily subjective selection should result in an impressive array, including models of what can be done, e.g. with various kinds of texts, or for projects in progress which can still be joined. Once again, I apologise for staying within the fields with which I am familiar, and I apologise above all for including just some examples of words and works, and not others, which in no way implies a value judgement. As I refer mainly to widely-known books and projects, I will have to mention names and titles only rarely; they are all in the footnotes.

First of all, there are two handbooks that are distinguished by their comprehensive scope as well as the fact that they will admirably serve experienced scholars, research students, and undergraduates, and they are also distinguished because nothing of the kind had been previously available. One is the *Blackwell*

---

[5] Kees Dekker, "Francis Junius (1591–1677): Copyist or Editor?," *Anglo-Saxon England* 29 (2000): 279–96; Rebecca Rushforth, "The Barrow Knight, the Bristol Bibliographer, and a Lost Old English Prayer," *Transactions of the Cambridge Bibliographical Society* 13 (2004): 112–31.

[6] The fragmentary homily on the Deposition of St. Augustine of Canterbury in CCCC 162, p. 563 (Ker, *Catalogue*, no. 38 art. 55; Cameron B.3.3.2), was apparently first printed by Hildegard Tristram, "Vier altenglische Predigten aus der heterodoxen Tradition" (Ph.D. diss., Freiburg University, 1970), Appendix 1, 428, with notes. But it had previously been edited, together with a Modern English translation, by Elizabeth Elstob, *An English-Saxon Homily on the Birthday of St. Gregory: Anciently Used in the English-Saxon Church* (London, 1709), Appendix, 33–34, an edition overlooked by Richard Wülker, *Grundriss zur Geschichte der angelsächsischen Litteratur* (Leipzig, 1885) and others.

Encyclopaedia of Anglo-Saxon England, concise but authoritative, up-to-date and skilfully edited. The other work, first published in 1985 (then with 41 pages) and now in its twenty-second edition (2006), with 285 pages, plus maps, illustrations, and genealogies, is the annually updated, professionally and entertainingly annotated bibliography by Simon Keynes, now entitled *Anglo-Saxon England: A Bibliographical Handbook for Students of Anglo-Saxon History*; it is compiled and updated single-handedly, and, in spite of its subtitle covers every aspect of Anglo-Saxon studies. Other historical disciplines, like those concerned with early medieval France or Germany, can only dream of such an invaluable guide.[7]

Let us look at Old English texts. Some important ones had been available in print for a long time, yet were only insufficiently understood. Now, at last, we are fortunate to have reliable, critical texts with expert commentaries of one of our classics, Ælfric's *Catholic Homilies*, and of that difficult and idiosyncratic *Handbook* by Byrhtferth,[8] and now, long after the pertinent discovery was made by Julius Zupitza, we have at last a printed edition (with English translation) of that abbreviation of Priscian's *Institutiones grammaticae* that served Ælfric as a model for what may have been the most successful 'bestseller' in Anglo-Saxon times, his Latin Grammar.[9] I will refer to the first critical (though partial) edition of Alfred's *Cura Pastoralis* later on.

I will return to the study of the Old English language later, but must, at this point, say a word about two indispensable works on words. One is of course the *Dictionary of Old English*. This pioneering undertaking, introducing into historical lexicography tools and methods unheard of till the 1970s, was sadly and severely afflicted by personal and scholarly tragedies, above all the untimely deaths of its founding and early editors, Angus Cameron and Ashley Amos, and yet, as we all know, this demanding project went on and has made admirable progress, with about 40% of the entries now 'in print' or in finished drafts,

[7] *The Blackwell Encyclopaedia of Anglo-Saxon England*, ed. Michael Lapidge, John Blair, Simon Keynes, and Donald Scragg (Oxford, 1999); Simon Keynes, *Anglo-Saxon England: A Bibliographical Handbook for Students of Anglo-Saxon History*, 7th edn., ASNC Guides, Texts, and Studies 1 (Cambridge, 2006), 1st edn. 2000, preceded by fifteen editions under the title *Anglo-Saxon History: A Select Bibliography* (1985–1999) [henceforth Keynes, *Handbook*].

[8] *Ælfric's Catholic Homilies: The First Series. Text*, ed. Peter Clemoes, EETS s.s. 17 (London, 1997); *The Second Series. Text*, ed. Malcolm Godden, EETS s.s. 5 (London, 1979); *Introduction, Commentary and Glossary*, by Malcolm Godden, EETS s.s. 18 (Oxford, 2000); *Byrhtferth's Enchiridion*, ed. Peter Baker and Michael Lapidge, EETS s.s. 15 (Oxford, 1995).

[9] *Excerptiones de Prisciano: The Source of Ælfric's Latin-Old English Grammar*, ed. David W. Porter, Anglo-Saxon Texts 4 (Cambridge, 2002); see also Helmut Gneuss, "The First Edition of the Source of Ælfric's *Grammar*," *Anglia* 123 (2005): 246–59. For Zupitza's discovery see *Archiv für das Studium der neueren Sprachen und Literaturen* 79 (1887): 88–89.

thanks to the commitment of the staff, and to the scholarly energy and optimism of Toni Healey. I do hope that ISAS will be able to continue supporting this great project. The other work is the *Thesaurus of Old English*, innovative and unique, the first onomasiological dictionary and—as far as I can see—the only one of an early Germanic language, serving to solve a wide range of philological problems, even the restoration of lost or damaged texts.[10]

Achievements and exemplary work must be reported from other fields, again selectively. Anglo-Latin texts of the Anglo-Saxon period have at last found the interest and treatment they deserve: it is Michael Lapidge who was and is foremost among the scholars working in this field; his recent, monumental *Cult of St Swithun*—to mention only one of his numerous editions and studies—is a model of what is needed for a proper appreciation of Latin (and Old English) texts by Anglo-Saxon authors, and of their later medieval tradition.[11] Significant progress has also been made in the study of liturgical texts and books written in England, especially in the form of carefully edited, annotated, and indexed editions published by the Henry Bradshaw Society, as in the two volumes of the *Leofric Missal*, now seen as a genuine English manuscript, while Rebecca Rushforth's *Atlas of Saints in Anglo-Saxon Calendars*[12] and the first volume of *Sources of Anglo-Saxon Literary Culture* (*SASLC*) provide a secure foundation for all future hagiographical work.

As is well-known, *SASLC* is one of the two collaborative landmark projects, supplementing each other, that will eventually furnish a complete and reliable record of the Latin works—classical, patristic and medieval—known at

---

[10] *Dictionary of Old English*, ed. Angus Cameron, Ashley Crandell Amos, and Antonette diPaolo Healey: *A–G* (Toronto, 1986–2007); *H* is in preparation. For this, for the *Dictionary of Old English Corpus* and other related and important publications, see Keynes, *Handbook*, A 86–87. Jane Roberts, Christian Kay, and Lynne Grundy, *A Thesaurus of Old English*, 2 vols., King's College London Medieval Studies 11 (London, 1995); 2nd edn., Costerus New Series 131 (Amsterdam, 2000).

[11] *The Cult of St Swithun*, Winchester Studies 4 (Oxford, 2003). There is now a complete bibliography of Michael Lapidge's groundbreaking work in *Latin Learning and English Lore: Studies in Anglo-Saxon Literature for Michael Lapidge*, ed. Katherine O'Brien O'Keeffe and Andy Orchard, 2 vols. (Toronto, 2005), 2: 395–406.

[12] *The Leofric Missal*, ed. Nicholas Orchard, 2 vols., HBS 113–114 (London, 2002); Rebecca Rushforth, *An Atlas of Saints in Anglo-Saxon Calendars*, ASNC Guides, Texts, and Studies 6 (Cambridge, 2002), now revised as *Saints in English Calendars Before A.D. 1100*, HBS 117 (London, 2008). More editions of Anglo-Saxon liturgical manuscripts and of the numerous fragments now known are needed. More fragments are still being found; for those now at the Riksarkivet in Stockholm, see the contributions by Michael Gullick and K. D. Hartzell in *Medieval Book Fragments in Sweden: An International Seminar in Stockholm 13–16 November 2003*, ed. Jan Brunius (Stockholm, 2005). K. D. Hartzell, *Catalogue of Manuscripts Written or Owned in England up to 1200 Containing Music* (Woodbridge, 2006) is now indispensable.

any time to Anglo-Saxons. The other great project, now far advanced, is *Fontes Anglo-Saxonici*, in the form of an online database, and on CD-ROM, with its admirably meticulous documentation of the sources of Anglo-Saxon (i.e. English and Latin) texts.[13] Finally, for all those engaged in editing or studying Anglo-Latin texts, there is now the definitive handbook for sorting out any problems they may have with the language, so often differing from classical Latin, the five-volume *Handbuch zur lateinischen Sprache des Mittelalters* by Peter Stotz.[14]

Our knowledge of early English history has been greatly advanced in recent years. The Collaborative Edition of the *Anglo-Saxon Chronicle*, with individual volumes for each of the manuscripts, is now complete, and of the Anglo-Saxon Charters series, a new edition, arranged by archive, eleven volumes have appeared,[15] and more are forthcoming or in preparation. Personal names in Anglo-Saxon England have been studied in great detail and for a long time by historical linguists, especially in Scandinavia, whereas for the persons bearing those names, historians so far had only one comprehensive handbook, Searle's *Onomasticon Anglo-Saxonicum*, with brief entries, now dated and "to be handled with care" (Keynes). What historians have really needed is a biographical register of all persons who have left some trace of their existence. For the years up to 1042, this is now available in *PASE*, the *Prosopography of Anglo-Saxon England*, a project begun in the year 2000, in the form of an online database containing biographical entries of all persons who lived in Anglo-Saxon England and are known from literary or documentary sources.[16] Incidentally, in this context it

---

[13] *Sources of Anglo-Saxon Literary Culture, Volume One: Abbo of Fleury, Abbo of Saint-Germain-des-Prés, and Acta Sanctorum*, ed. Frederick M. Biggs, Thomas D. Hill, Paul E. Szarmach, and E. Gordon Whatley (Kalamazoo, 2001); *Fontes Anglo-Saxonici*: http://fontes.english.ox.ac.uk, and Peter Jackson, "20th Annual Progress Report," *Old English Newsletter* 38, no. 3 (Spring 2005): 34–35; see also Keynes, *Handbook*, A 50.1–2, and now Michael Lapidge, *The Anglo-Saxon Library* (Oxford, 2006), esp. the Appendices and the "Catalogue of Classical and Patristic Authors and Works Composed before AD 700 and Known in Anglo-Saxon England," 275–342.

[14] Peter Stotz, *Handbuch zur lateinischen Sprache des Mittelalters*, 5 vols. (Munich, 1996–2004); for the lexicography of Anglo-Latin see 1: 213–17.

[15] *The Anglo-Saxon Chronicle: A Collaborative Edition*, ed. David Dumville and Simon Keynes (Cambridge, 1983–2004); for volumes and editors see Keynes, *Handbook*, B 42–50. *Anglo-Saxon Charters* (Oxford, 1973-); for volumes published, forthcoming, and in preparation, see Keynes, *Handbook*, B 342, and B 321 for the 'Electronic Sawyer,' a revised and updated version of P. H. Sawyer, *Anglo-Saxon Charters: An Annotated List and Bibliography* (London, 1968).

[16] William George Searle, *Onomasticon Anglo-Saxonicum* (Cambridge, 1897). For *PASE* and its continuation for 1042–1100, *PASE II*, see Keynes, *Handbook*, A 295.

may perhaps not be out of place to mention a remarkable publishing venture: a one-volume paperback edition of the complete Domesday Book in translation.[17]

It is clearly impossible here to do justice to all the essential and outstanding contributions to Anglo-Saxon studies in the recent past. Thus, characterising developments in art history, archaeology, and numismatics must be left to the experts. But one field in which remarkable progress has been made should finally be mentioned, and that is palaeography and the study of manuscripts. Although discoveries are still being made now and then, it seems safe to say that we now have a fairly good idea of what survives in manuscripts or manuscript fragments from Anglo-Saxon England, including what was imported and what was exported,[18] and a good idea, too, of how far dates and places of origin or provenance of books can be determined. There seems no need to list the well-known names of the scholars to whom we owe this knowledge, but as much of our work necessarily depends on good reproductions, let me just mention that, unfortunately, the magnificent *Early English Manuscripts in Facsimile* series, now with 28 volumes, has come to an end; but by now twelve volumes (sixteen in 2008) of the *Anglo-Saxon Manuscripts in Microfiche Facsimile* have appeared,[19] and so we can expect that every small library and individual scholar may sooner or later have a complete set of facsimiles of everything in Old English (except documentary records) on their shelves, an exciting prospect, undreamed of not so long ago. The digitized images of Anglo-Saxon manuscripts that are becoming available in increasing numbers on the websites of the great libraries must also be mentioned as helpful research tools for manuscript studies in the electronic age.

With regard to tasks for future research, I believe that studies of individual manuscripts, especially composite books, will remain useful and rewarding, no matter whether this is in the form of an article, a monograph, or a collection of essays by specialists, and it is to be hoped that manuscripts mainly or wholly in Latin will find the same attention as those mainly in Old English. Outstanding recent examples of such work are the studies of the *Book of Cerne* and the

---

[17] *Domesday Book: A Complete Translation*, ed. Ann Williams and G. H. Martin, Penguin Classics (London, 2003).

[18] For surviving books, and for the libraries, see Helmut Gneuss, *Handlist of Anglo-Saxon Manuscripts: A List of Manuscripts and Manuscript Fragments Written or Owned in England up to 1100*, MRTS 241 (Tempe, AZ, 2001), and idem, "Addenda and Corrigenda to the *Handlist of Anglo-Saxon Manuscripts*," *Anglo-Saxon England* 32 (2003): 293–305, further Addenda are in preparation; Lapidge, *The Anglo-Saxon Library*; *The Cambridge History of the Book in Britain*, vol. 1, ed. Richard Gameson, forthcoming.

[19] For manuscript studies and palaeography see Keynes, *Handbook*, B 760–814, and now the bibliography in Jane Roberts, *Guide to Scripts Used in English Writings up to 1500* (London, 2005), 257–75. For Early English Manuscripts in Facsimile see Keynes, *Handbook*, B 813. *Anglo-Saxon Manuscripts in Microfiche Facsimile*, ed. Phillip Pulsiano and A. N. Doane, 16 vols. published (Binghamton, NY, 1994–1996; Tempe, AZ, 1997–2008), in progress; on this series see Gneuss in *Anglia* 126 (2008): 134–41.

Lindisfarne Gospels by Michelle Brown, and a collection of pioneering articles dealing with the Durham *Liber Vitae*, unaccountably badly neglected until now.[20]

And it is in manuscript studies that discoveries can still be made, and this often enough with implications reaching beyond an individual book or fragment. When in a Paris manuscript of mainly Christian Latin poetry, an eleventh-century Old English gloss to a line from Ovid (together with Latin scholia) is found, and this is the only Old English in the book, why should we not suspect that similarly concealed glosses could still turn up elsewhere? Or when an eleventh-century English flyleaf with a fragment from a commentary on Donatus's *Artes* turns up, which so far was only known from a continental copy, we can assume that the study of Latin grammar from various sources had not at all ceased with the publication and distribution of Ælfric's work. Again, the discovery of bilingual homiletic fragments at Taunton has led to the realization that in Anglo-Saxon England a type of homiliary was known and used that differed essentially from the types known until now in the collections of Paulus Diaconus, of Ælfric and others.[21]

Allow me now to deal somewhat more fully with Old English, i.e. the language, as an example of what has been achieved, and what still can and needs to be done. It is not a popular subject among Anglo-Saxonists, in spite of all the work in this field that our annual bibliographies record. As to its future, some may think that a more theoretical approach should be adopted, while others feel that we already know and have all that is required for our work, e.g. in preparing editions and analysing texts. It has been clear for quite a long time that we need two types of handbook or grammar with differing aims: the introductory book, which provides students with the essentials of the language, covering phonology and inflexions, ideally also syntax and vocabulary. There is an ever-increasing number of such books—not always as competent as one could wish—and there is, perhaps, general agreement on what they should offer.[22]

[20] Michelle P. Brown, *The Book of Cerne: Prayer, Patronage and Power in Ninth-Century England* (London, 1996), and eadem, *The Lindisfarne Gospels: Society, Spirituality and the Scribe* (London, 2003); *The Durham 'Liber Vitae' and its Context*, ed. David Rollason, A. J. Piper, Margaret Harvey, and Lynda Rollason (Woodbridge, 2004).

[21] Paris gloss: Birgit Ebersperger, *Die angelsächsischen Handschriften in den Pariser Bibliotheken* (Heidelberg, 1999), 164; the fragment from the so-called Einsiedeln Commentary on Donatus will be published by Rebecca Rushforth; Homiliary: Mechthild Gretsch, "The Taunton Fragment: A New Text from Anglo-Saxon England," *Anglo-Saxon England* 33 (2004): 145–93, and Helmut Gneuss, "The Homiliary of the Taunton Fragments," *Notes and Queries* 250 (2005): 440–42.

[22] It is obvious that there are limits to what the introductory book can and should offer, but what is offered should at least be reliable and competent. Yet we find that *dōm* is said to be a new noun formed from *dēman*, and similarly *lufu* from *lufian*, *full* from *fyllan*, and *gōd* from *gōdian*—but on the same page *lufian* is said to be derived from the

The second type is the comprehensive handbook, covering all periods and dialects of Old English in detail, as far as they are known; if we leave out of account, for the time being, syntax and the various aspects of the vocabulary, we have to think of the works by Luick, Campbell, Sievers-Brunner, and Hogg.[23] No serious study of Old English, no editorial work seems feasible without them. Of course, they are reference works the scope, methods, and arrangement of which should be known to *all* those who have occasion to consult them (which, unfortunately, is not always the case).[24] However, they are books to be consulted as authorities, or at least guides, not books to be learned by heart—which reminds me of my teacher of medieval German, Helmut de Boor, who used to explain the difference between the student and the professor by saying that there is this difference *not* because the professor knows more, but because he or she knows where to find the information ("er weiß, wo's steht").

I have just used the term 'authority' but must now come back to my intention to talk about future tasks. I need hardly stress that it is desirable to incorporate important work published in the last forty or fifty years into the standard grammars mentioned above, especially the older ones. But let me draw your attention to another point that appears to have escaped notice so far. When you look into our standard grammars, you will find certain dialectal varieties of Old English covered in great detail: the Northumbrian of the Lindisfarne Gospels, the presumed Mercian of the Vespasian Psalter, the Early West Saxon in the Hatton manuscript of the *Cura Pastoralis*, the language of the few texts considered Kentish. *Late* West Saxon forms and spellings are of course fully treated, but what about the basis of this treatment? Consider the work with the widest distribution of all Old English prose texts throughout the eleventh century, Ælfric's *Catholic Homilies*. Of the twenty surviving copies containing the complete collection, or one of the two series, or at least a substantial number of the homilies, fourteen were written towards the end of the tenth century or in the eleventh. It is obvious that they should provide invaluable evidence for the spellings, sounds, and inflexions of what the grammarians call 'Late West-Saxon'—apart from scattered forms of other dialects. Also, if we believe that from the tenth century onwards a late Old English written standard developed, then all these manuscripts would greatly

---

older noun *lufu*—and all this (and more) in Richard Hogg, *An Introduction to Old English* (Oxford, 2002), 104. Cf. n. 31 below.

[23] Karl Luick, *Historische Grammatik der englischen Sprache* (Leipzig, 1914–1940); A. Campbell, *Old English Grammar* (Oxford, 1959); Karl Brunner, *Altenglische Grammatik: Nach der Angelsächsischen Grammatik von Eduard Sievers*, 3rd edn. (Tübingen, 1965); Richard M. Hogg, *A Grammar of Old English, Volume 1: Phonology* (Oxford, 1992).

[24] For an example of what has become possible in our days, see Mechthild Gretsch, "The Fonthill Letter: Language, Law and the Discourse of Disciplines," *Anglia* 123 (2005): 667–86, at 686 n. 76, discussing the 'philology' of Lisi Oliver, *The Beginnings of English Law* (Toronto, 2002).

contribute to what we know about such a standard, whether and where it was a reality, how rigorously it was followed, how much room was left for variants.

But consider how much of all this was accessible at the time our standard grammars (Hogg's excepted) were written: all they could consult was Thorpe's meritorious edition (1844–1846) of one early manuscript, Cambridge, University Library Gg.3.28, admittedly an excellent copy, but not more. All this has changed with the appearance of the masterly edition of the *Catholic Homilies* by Peter Clemoes and Malcolm Godden, but even here there had to be limits to what a critical apparatus could take; a variant reading that is of no consequence for the sense or interpretation of a passage, or for our understanding of the transmission of a text, may justifiably not have been recorded, and yet may still be of interest to the linguist. Or take another example: King Alfred's version of Pope Gregory's *Regula Pastoralis*, preserved in five copies, together with a seventeenth-century copy of an early manuscript almost completely destroyed in the Cotton fire of 1731 and the binder's fire at the British Museum in 1864.[25] When our standard grammars were written, Henry Sweet's edition of the earliest manuscript, Oxford, Bodleian Library, Hatton 20, and the seventeenth-century copy of London, Cotton Tiberius B.xi were available and used, but four other, more or less complete copies were known but had not been edited or collated; only in the 1970s was a Swedish edition of one of these printed, and now, at last, a thorough study of the language of all four, based on a printed partial edition, has appeared.[26]

It would seem indispensable to review what our standard grammars have to say about the most widely transmitted variety of Old English in the light of texts, or copies of texts, not so far utilized by these grammars. Work in this field, approaching the problem from different angles, has recently been done at the University of Manchester, and is in progress at the University of Göttingen; a first report on the Göttingen project has appeared.[27] What I have just

---

[25] For these disastrous events see now Andrew Prescott, " 'Their present miserable state of cremation': The Restoration of the Cotton Library," in *Sir Robert Cotton as Collector: Essays on an Early Stuart Courtier and his Legacy*, ed. C. J. Wright (London, 1997), 391–454.

[26] *King Alfred's West-Saxon Version of Gregory's Pastoral Care*, ed. Henry Sweet, 2 vols., EETS o.s. 45, 50 (London, 1871–1872); *The Pastoral Care edited from British Museum MS. Cotton Otho B.ii* by Ingvar Carlson, 2 vols., vol. 2 completed by Lars-G. Hallander et al., Stockholm Studies in English 34, 48 (Stockholm, 1975–1978); Carolin Schreiber, *King Alfred's Old English Translation of Pope Gregory's 'Regula Pastoralis' and its Cultural Context: A Study and Partial Edition According to All Surviving Manuscripts Based on Cambridge, Corpus Christi College 12*, Texte und Untersuchungen zur Englischen Philologie 25 (Frankfurt am Main, 2003).

[27] Language in manuscripts of Ælfric's works: Manchester: "The MANCASS C11 Database": <http://www.arts.manchester.ac.uk/mancass/C11database/data>. Göttingen: Mechthild Gretsch, "In Search of Standard Old English," in *Bookmarks from the Past:*

suggested about the revision of our standard grammars may not lead to revolutionary results, but will, I hope, provide a more realistic and reliable picture of the linguistic situation in England, especially in the eleventh century.

There is another problem that needs to be considered when we aim at such a realistic picture; this concerns dialectal traces in late Old English manuscripts that may well provide valuable evidence for a dialect otherwise not so well known. I am thinking in particular of late Kentish in the tenth and eleventh centuries. For our grammars, this is the dialect represented (not in pure form) in parts of London, British Library, Cotton Vespasian D.vi from St Augustine's, Canterbury. The *Kentish Hymn*, the *Kentish Psalm*, and the twelve hundred Kentish glosses, mainly interlinear, are found in the manuscript. But there are not a few manuscripts whose Late West-Saxon is interspersed with Kentish forms, which does not seem surprising when one thinks of the importance and productivity of the scriptoria at Canterbury and Rochester. In a preliminary search, I found thirty such manuscripts, and there may well be more — a source that should not be ignored by our grammars.[28]

There are other desiderata in language studies that one might mention, but let me just refer to the increasing interest in, and work on, Old English texts written or copied in the twelfth century. This is a most welcome development, and helps us to understand that the role of written English in the twelfth century seems to have been underestimated until now. In this connection, it appears most unfortunate that we have no comprehensive grammar of Early Middle English (and not of Late Middle English either) that would provide us with a framework for identifying retention, modernization, or innovation of linguistic features of the vernacular in the period; so let us hope for Margaret Laing's promised *Atlas of Early Medieval English*, for which we already have her excellent catalogue of texts.[29]

Studies in Early English Language and Literature in Honour of Helmut Gneuss, ed. Lucia Kornexl and Ursula Lenker, Texte und Untersuchungen zur Englischen Philologie 30 (Frankfurt am Main, 2003), 33–67, and now also eadem, "A Key to Ælfric's Standard Old English," in *Essays for Joyce Hill on her Sixtieth Birthday*, ed. Mary Swan, Leeds Studies in English n.s. 37 (Leeds, 2006), 161–77.

[28] Kentish and Kentish traces: Ursula Kalbhen, *Kentische Glossen und kentischer Dialekt im Altenglischen: Mit einer kommentierten Edition der altenglischen Glossen in der Handschrift London, British Library, Cotton Vespasian D.vi*, Texte und Untersuchungen zur Englischen Philologie 28 (Frankfurt am Main, 2003); Helmut Gneuss, "Origin and Provenance of Anglo-Saxon Manuscripts: The Case of Cotton Tiberius A.III," in *Of the Making of Books: Medieval Manuscripts, their Scribes and Readers: Essays Presented to M.B. Parkes*, ed. P. R. Robinson and Rivkah Zim (Aldershot, 1997), 13–48, at 47–48.

[29] *Rewriting Old English in the Twelfth Century*, ed. Mary Swan and Elaine M. Treharne, Cambridge Studies in Anglo-Saxon England 30 (Cambridge, 2000); Margaret Laing, *Catalogue of Sources for a Linguistic Atlas of Early Medieval English* (Cambridge, 1993). For the new Research Project "English Manuscripts 1060 to 1220," see www.le.ac.uk/ee/em1060to1220.

Let me stay for another moment with language, this time with the vocabulary of Old English. I have already referred to the *Dictionary of Old English*, a great work, which in its final form will consist of about 30,000 entries based on nearly four million tokens—a foundation unrivalled by the transmission of any of the early Germanic languages. Now for very many years, together with the other members of the International Advisory Committee, I have had the task—or rather, the pleasure—to look through the draft entries of the *DOE*; indeed, I think I have seen all of them, and I hasten to add that for many years now have come to feel that very little remains for me to do: the so-called drafts are usually in a state in which they should go straight to the printer, or rather, to the electronic wizard responsible. However, whenever a problem remained, for the lexicographers and for me, it usually turned out to be connected with questions of word-formation or etymology, and it is exactly these two disciplines that are badly in need of reliable and comprehensive treatments, which must replace or integrate special studies and earlier books now dated or unsatisfactory.

Thus for Old English etymologies, we have Holthausen's work, useful only really for readers with a sound knowledge of Germanic and Indo-European philology, while more comprehensive works—like the *OED* and the excellent etymological Supplement by Calvert Watkins in *The American Heritage Dictionary* (I mention just these two; there are others) —cover only that part of the Old English vocabulary that has survived until our days.[30] Similarly, there is a considerable number of studies on special aspects of Old English word-formation, but much remains to be done and cleared up. I have singled out the two fields of etymology and word-formation, although we know that, here in Bavaria as it happens, two of our colleagues (Alfred Bammesberger and Hans Sauer) are preparing or planning the respective handbooks. Yet, as anybody knows who has looked for specific answers in one of these fields, there seems to be plenty of room and opportunities for studies of word histories or word-formation patterns that could form contributions on which the larger handbooks might build. An excellent example is Klaus Dietz's paper, just published, on prefixes in Old English.[31]

---

[30] Ferdinand Holthausen, *Altenglisches etymologisches Wörterbuch* (Heidelberg, 1934; 2nd edn. with supplementary bibliography, 1963); Calvert Watkins, "Indo-European Roots," in *The American Heritage Dictionary of the English Language*, 4th edn., ed. Joseph P. Pickett (Boston, 2000), 2020–55.

[31] Klaus Dietz, "Die altenglischen Präfixbildungen und ihre Charakteristik," *Anglia* 122 (2004): 561–613. Until Hans Sauer's comprehensive work becomes available, see Dieter Kastovsky, "Word-formation," in *The Cambridge History of the English Language, Volume 1: The Beginnings to 1066*, ed. Richard M. Hogg (Cambridge, 1992), 355–400. Knowledge of word-formation in Old English appears to be imperfect even among philologists: cf. n. 22 above, and John Walmsley, "How the Leopard Got its Spots: English Grammatical Categories, Latin Terms," in *Inside Old English: Essays in Honour of Bruce Mitchell*, ed. idem (Oxford, 2006), 248–67, where (at 261) the author identifies an affix

Let me finish this subject by referring to a more general or practical issue, the use of Old English for various types of text. Apparently there were no restrictions on such use, and this is exactly what gives Old English language and literature their prominent position among the vernaculars spoken and written in Europe before the twelfth century, with texts in practically any subject composed in, or glossed in, or translated into, Old English: history, theology, philosophy, law, documents, grammar, medicine. But there is one field, richly documented in Anglo-Saxon manuscripts, in which Old English has no place, and that is the liturgy of Mass and Office. I leave it to specialists to find pertinent regulations by councils and in decretals concerning the language of the liturgy in the Roman Church. The subject, however, is of considerable interest, as among the ca. 1250 surviving manuscripts and manuscript fragments from Anglo-Saxon England in the period up to 1100, more than 200 are books, or come from books, for Mass, Office, and special services directed by bishops. To these should be added more than eighty Gospel books or fragments of such books, so that nearly a quarter of our manuscript evidence, ranging from the seventh to the late eleventh century, consists of liturgical books—and they are all, without exception, in Latin, as everywhere in the West since the fourth century.

This seems notable because it has occasionally been suggested that certain elements in Anglo-Saxon church services may have been said or sung in the vernacular. But look at what we have, conveniently recorded and discussed by David Dumville: interlinear glosses, rubrics, directions for private devotions, entries in calendars (with names of the months, chronological and other information), computus material, penitential texts, confessional and private prayers—all of these are clearly not liturgical texts in the strict sense. However, there are two texts, or types of texts, that might conceivably have found their way into the all-Latin services: the West-Saxon Gospels (or other English versions of Gospel or Epistle texts), and the Old English homilies, notably those in Ælfric's collections. This is not the place for a detailed consideration of their use and function; let us just note that there is no evidence for *liturgical* recitation of passages or pericopes of the Gospels in Old English, having *replaced* the Latin text, while an Old English homily, even if read out somewhere during Mass, would not be an integral and requisite part of the liturgy, nor is there any indication that such a homily would have replaced a Latin homily in the Office of Nocturns.[32]

-igen in OE *un - declin - igen - lic* (faulty for *undeclinigendlic*, Ælfric's *Grammar* 223.1) and considers *wordes gefera* (= *adverbium*, Ælfric's *Grammar* 223.2–3) a compound.

[32] David Dumville, *Liturgy and the Ecclesiastical History of Late Anglo-Saxon England: Four Studies* (Woodbridge, 1992), 127–32; Ursula Lenker, "The Rites and Ministries of the Canons: Liturgical Rubrics to Vernacular Gospels and their Functions in a European Context," in *The Liturgy of the Late Anglo-Saxon Church*, ed. Helen Gittos and M. Bradford Bedingfield, HBS Subsidia 5 (London, 2005), 185–212; Roy Michael Liuzza, "Who Read the Gospels in Old English?," in *Words and Works: Studies in Medi-*

At the beginning of a century, and after more than four centuries of Anglo-Saxon studies, it is certainly appropriate to take stock of what has been achieved, of what we know, and of how we expect to continue our work. At the same time, I wonder if it may not also be appropriate, and instructive, to note, or at least exemplify, what we do *not* know, or where facts are uncertain and views controversial, where we can describe, but not explain. The limitations of work and results in all our fields are of course conditioned by the limitations, or total lack, of evidence, by the need to draw conclusions from what survives in some form, and the risk of having to revise or rewrite established views and books, as happened after the excavations at Sutton Hoo, or after, late in the nineteenth century, the Codex Amiatinus had been found to be a genuine English, Northumbrian production of the late seventh or early eighth century (see also the contribution of Richard Marsden in this volume).

For a few examples of gaps and uncertainties in our knowledge, allow me to return to texts and language. The large and impressive corpus of Old English poetry has been intensively studied for a long time, but for most of its texts the date of origin is disputed, especially, of course, the date of *Beowulf*, with suggestions ranging over nearly four centuries. But so far, no incontestably safe criteria for dating Old English poetic texts seem to have been found.[33] Similarly, the question of the original dialects of the poetry has met with controversial answers,[34] while literary historians are painfully aware of the accidental character of the transmission and preservation of their texts, and of the complete loss of what must have been a substantial oral tradition.

Again, we may ask in vain why the written prose vernacular—mainly in translations and adaptations—played such an outstanding role in Anglo-Saxon

---

eval English Language and Literature in Honour of Fred C. Robinson, ed. Peter S. Baker and Nicholas Howe (Toronto, 1998), 3–24; Milton McC. Gatch, *Preaching and Theology in Anglo-Saxon England: Ælfric and Wulfstan* (Toronto, 1977), esp. chap. 5.

[33] The debate continues. See R. D. Fulk, *A History of Old English Meter* (Philadelphia, 1992), 381–92, and Dennis Cronan, "Poetic Words, Conservatism and the Dating of Old English Poetry," *Anglo-Saxon England* 33 (2004): 23–50, and the sceptical comment by Eric Stanley in *Notes and Queries* 250 (2005): 270 n. 7. The work by Ashley Crandell Amos, *Linguistic Means of Determining the Dates of Old English Literary Texts* (Cambridge, MA, 1980) and the essays in *The Dating of Beowulf*, ed. Colin Chase (Toronto, 1981), remain important. See also John D. Niles, "On the Danish Origins of the *Beowulf* Story," in this volume.

[34] For recent views, see Malcolm R. Godden, "Literary Language," in *The Cambridge History of the English Language* 1: 490–535, at 496–98; David Megginson, "The Case Against a 'General Old English Poetic Dialect'," in *Prosody and Poetics in the Early Middle Ages: Essays in Honour of C. B. Hieatt*, ed. M. J. Toswell (Toronto, 1995), 117–32; Franz Wenisch, "On the Dialectal Provenance of Old English Verse," in *Tangenten: Literatur und Geschichte*, ed. Martin Meyer, Gabriele Spengemann, and Wolf Kindermann (Münster, 1996), 166–79.

England, at any rate from the ninth century onwards. It is tempting to adopt the traditional view, recently again expressed, that these prose texts were made "because hardly a soul in the whole country, even those whose business required it, could adequately understand Latin."[35] This is as King Alfred saw it, but this was not the situation all the time and everywhere; most of our surviving manuscripts are in Latin (only about 170 out of 1250 manuscripts written up to 1100 are entirely or mainly in Old English, or are continuously glossed in Old English or contain bilingual glossaries), while the numerous Old English homilies were clearly meant to be read to audiences that were in no way required to understand Latin.

Another field marked by doubts and problems is that of the Old English dialects. Were they imported, or did they develop only after the immigration period in Britain? Different views have been held, not surprisingly, with no written transmission of English for several centuries after the beginning of the settlements, and so without safe evidence on which to build. But Michael Korhammer's discovery that certain dialectally differing features in Old English correspond with such features in different manuscripts of the Old Saxon *Heliand* (after the recent discovery of a fragment of the poem at Straubing in Bavaria) affords us a chance of reviewing this debated issue; in any case, is it likely that the immigrants from the Continent would have entered Britain speaking a more or less uniform language?[36]

There is another question connected with the dialects, and one that so far has not been answered and perhaps cannot be answered at all; it concerns scribes and scriptoria, mainly in Anglo-Saxon monastic houses: would the members of these communities, and so their scribes, usually have grown up in the region or dialectal area in which the house was situated? And would monks, nuns, and clerics stemming from other parts of the country adopt, or copy, dialectal peculiarities, or traces of these? Occasional south-eastern forms in late texts from Canterbury and Rochester may be interpreted either way. The problem might deserve an examination of manuscripts whose place of origin can be safely determined. But since it has recently been shown that heterogeneous dialect forms in a text or a gloss could well reflect political, social, and linguistic reality, this problem has become even more complicated.[37]

---

[35] Liuzza, "Who Read the Gospels in Old English?," 7.

[36] Michael Korhammer, "Altenglische Dialekte und der *Heliand*," *Anglia* 98 (1980): 85–94, but see also Hans F. Nielsen, "The Straubing *Heliand*-Fragment and the Old English Dialects," in *Language Contact in the British Isles: Proceedings of the Eighth International Symposium on Language Contact in Europe, Douglas, Isle of Man, 1988*, ed. P. Sture Urland and George Broderick (Tübingen, 1991), 243–73. Thomas E. Toon, "Old English Dialects," in *The Cambridge History of the English Language* 1: 409–51, has nothing to say about the problem.

[37] Mechthild Gretsch, "The Junius Psalter Gloss: Its Historical and Cultural Context," *Anglo-Saxon England* 29 (2000): 85–121, and eadem, "Winchester Vocabulary and

As is well known, our knowledge of English dialects in late Anglo-Saxon England is limited because of the spread of a type of language standardized in spellings and inflexions, and obviously based on a south-western dialect. This supra-regional language was written or copied in scriptoria all over the country (Canterbury, Worcester, Ramsey, York). But how did it spread? Was there a council's decree, a bishop's recommendation, or was the usage of a highly respected religious and intellectual center, perhaps of Winchester *and* Canterbury, voluntarily and readily adopted as a model? We cannot be certain, just as we do not know why, since the late tenth century, and again throughout the country, a code of handwriting was followed which recommended or prescribed the use of Caroline minuscule for Latin texts, and insular minuscule for everything in Old English, including proper names in Latin texts (but not for the copy of the Old Saxon *Heliand* written in England, London, British Library, Cotton Caligula A.vii), and all this although the Caroline script could have been easily adapted for writing English texts and glosses.

There is still the knotty problem of English and Norse in England, and their mutual intelligibility, recently reviewed by Matthew Townend, and the fictitious Anglo-Norse 'Creole' in the Midlands invented by Patricia Poussa.[38] But I must make an end with things we do not know. One of my reasons for referring to them is the fact that 'Histories of the English Language' (as opposed to those of Old English literature) appear to present our knowledge of the language in the Anglo-Saxon centuries in a far too optimistic light.

I have so far tried, though not systematically, to deal with various aspects of Anglo-Saxon studies mainly in the fields of books, texts, and language, and so I may owe you an apology for an omission. This concerns new directions and theories in literary and cultural studies and what they can do (or cannot do) to further our understanding of Anglo-Saxon life and letters. I do not claim to know this

---

Standard Old English: The Vernacular in Late Anglo-Saxon England," *Bulletin of the John Rylands University Library of Manchester* 83 (2001): 41–87. For the related problem of local dialects and written language in early monastic scriptoria in Germany see now Wilhelm Braune, *Althochdeutsche Grammatik I: Laut- und Formenlehre*, 15th edn. rev. by Ingo Reiffenstein (Tübingen, 2004), 5 n. 2.—As for recent work on Old English dialects, I refrain from commenting on the publications of Peter Kitson, on account of his doubtful methodology and a measure of arrogance and insolence unparalleled in scholarly work; see e.g. "On Margins of Error in Placing Old English Literary Dialects," in *Method and Data in English Historical Dialectology*, ed. Marina Dossena and Roger Lass (Bern, 2004), 219–39. For some of Kitson's serious shortcomings, see Gretsch, "Winchester Vocabulary and Standard Old English," 23 n. 99.

[38] Matthew Townend, *Language and History in Viking Age England: Linguistic Relations between Speakers of Old Norse and Old English*, Studies in the Early Middle Ages 6 (Turnhout, 2002); Patricia Poussa, "The Evolution of Early Standard English: The Creolization Hypothesis," *Studia Anglica Posnaniensia* 14 (1982): 69–85. See also the contribution of Niles in this volume.

subject well, but it certainly needs extensive treatment, and I wonder if it could be considered for sessions in a future ISAS meeting.

There remains, at last, the subject indicated by the theme of this Conference, a subject that, in a sense, is also of local interest. We are here meeting in the (metropolitan) diocese of Munich and Freising. It was formed in 1818, but is largely identical with the ancient bishopric of Freising. Now this is one of the four Bavarian dioceses founded or reorganized by St. Boniface in 739: Freising, Regensburg, Passau, and Salzburg (with Eichstätt following slightly later), and this explains also why there are two cathedral churches, in Freising and Munich. So my subject is obvious: the Anglo-Saxon mission, and its contribution to the ecclesiastical organisation of Bavaria, Franconia, and Hesse — one of the important events of English and European history.

Once again, manuscripts provide a wealth of evidence of the impact of this mission — and some of the problems: when it is uncertain whether a book in insular script was written (a) in England, or (b) by an Anglo-Saxon in a continental scriptorium, or (c) by a German scribe trained by Anglo-Saxons in such a scriptorium. There are plenty of such doubtful cases recorded in Lowe's *Codices Latini Antiquiores* — presumably all based on Bernhard Bischoff's work and expertise. In any case, we have a full record of scribal work on the Continent under insular influence for the eighth century in *CLA*, and we now have also a record of ninth-century work of this type in Bernhard Bischoff's Catalogue of books and fragments of this period edited by Birgit Ebersperger, with the final, third, volume in preparation. This is important, because in some places, especially Fulda, insular script was employed well into the ninth century, when elsewhere, with certain exceptions, Caroline minuscule was superseding earlier types of handwriting.[39]

In this field, too, work is continuing. More manuscript material may be found. When I had an opportunity, several years ago, to see about three hundred manuscript fragments used from the sixteenth century onwards as wrappers for the records of administrative centres in the principality ('Fürstentum'; earlier a county) of Schwarzburg-Sondershausen in Thuringia, uncatalogued and virtually unknown until 2004, I found an impressive, though not well-preserved,

---

[39] For the English mission and the manuscript evidence see Keynes, *Handbook*, E 1–23; Bernhard Bischoff, *Latin Palaeography: Antiquity and the Middle Ages*, trans. Dáibhí Ó Cróinín and David Ganz (Cambridge, 1990), esp. 93–95; E. A. Lowe [and Bernhard Bischoff], *Codices Latini Antiquiores*, 11 vols. and Supplement (Oxford, 1934–1971; vol. 2 2nd edn. 1972); Bernhard Bischoff, *Katalog der festländischen Handschriften des neunten Jahrhunderts (mit Ausnahme der wisigotischen)*, ed. Birgit Ebersperger, 2 vols. (Wiesbaden, 1998–2004): the final third volume is in preparation. See now the excellent treatment of the subject by Michael Lapidge, *The Anglo-Saxon Library*, 77–90, and his edition of "Eighth-Century Inventories of Latin Books from the Area of the Anglo-Saxon Mission in Germany," and list of "Surviving Eighth-Century Manuscripts from the Area of the Anglo-Saxon Mission in Germany," 148–66.

bifolium from a Latin Bible, or Old Testament, written in the 820s or 830s in insular minuscule, possibly at Fulda. From Fulda also, or another Anglo-Saxon center on the Continent, come the fragments of the earliest copy of Bede's metrical *Vita* of St. Cuthbert, of which only recently three leaves were found in the archives of the City of Munich.[40] An exhibition of representative examples of continental manuscripts in insular handwriting, or containing works by insular authors, chosen from the thousands of medieval manuscripts held by the Bayerische Staatsbibliothek, has been arranged for this ISAS meeting.[41]

There are other weighty issues and topics in the field of Anglo-Saxon spiritual and intellectual influence on the Continent. I mention the recent dispute over a calendar: the late Professor Arno Borst of the University of Konstanz, a distinguished medievalist, in a much-acclaimed work postulated that a new 'Reichskalender' which became highly influential had been elaborated in 789 at the Abbey of Lorsch, based on sources supplied to Lorsch from the court of Charlemagne. But Paul Meyvaert has pointed out that Borst's key manuscript (Berlin, Staatsbibliothek Preussischer Kulturbesitz, Phillipps 1869, ca. 840, from Prüm) had an exemplar with a heavy layer of hagiography pointing unmistakably to northern England, and more specifically to York, and that it went back to a calendar circulating together with Bede's *De temporum ratione*. The complicated issue can be followed in Meyvaert's article in *Analecta Bollandiana*;[42] suffice it to say that here is another important example of what the Continent owed to Anglo-Saxon learning.

I have, on the whole, until now deliberately refrained from controversial issues, although they are there: not only the disputes of scholars, but also eminently practical matters, like the ever-increasing size, variety, and dogmatism of

---

[40] *Bestandskatalog zur Sammlung Handschriften- und Inkunabelfragmente des Schlossmuseums Sondershausen*, ed. Gerlinde Huber-Rebenich and Christa Hirschler (Sondershausen, 2004), 56: MS. Lat. bib. 1; Helmut Gneuss and Michael Lapidge, "The Earliest Manuscript of Bede's Metrical *Vita S. Cudbercti*," *Anglo-Saxon England* 32 (2003): 43–54.

[41] An exhibition catalogue has appeared: *Anglo-Saxon Heritage in Munich: Anglo-Saxon Manuscripts, Scribes and Authors from the Collections of the Bavarian State Library in Munich*, ed. Hans Sauer, with contributions by Birgit Ebersperger, Carolin Schreiber, and Angelika Schröcker (Frankfurt am Main, 2005). The exhibition of 2005 was again shown at the Staatsbibliothek Bamberg in 2008, with additional manuscripts from the Bamberg library.

[42] Arno Borst, *Die karolingische Kalenderreform*, MGH Schriften 46 (Hannover, 1998); Paul Meyvaert, "Discovering the Calendar (*Annualis Libellus*) Attached to Bede's Own Copy of *De Temporum Ratione*," *Analecta Bollandiana* 120 (2002): 5–64. See now also D. A. Bullough, "York, Bede's Calendar and a Pre-Bedan English Martyrology, " *Analecta Bollandiana* 121 (2003): 329–55. Arno Borst, *Der Streit um den karolingischen Kalender*, MGH Studien und Texte 36 (Hannover, 2004), does not invalidate Meyvaert's arguments.

style-sheets (which, of course, do have a useful function), or like the question of the language of published work: is such work if not in English still read, and by how many?

But as I had hoped that I might encourage future scholarly work, even by mainly pointing to achievements of the recent past, I felt that there is one issue that deserves to be considered. It is about editions, and I owe the idea of mentioning them here to a recent article by Paul Szarmach. Now editing texts is not popular everywhere, perhaps is even thought to be a dry if not pedantic business. But I want to plead, together with Paul, *for* editions, and to emphasize what they mean, what they have to offer to the community of scholars and students, even to the 'common reader,' and how much work, commitment, and competence has to go into establishing a text, investigating its history and transmission, and providing readers with all they need to understand and appreciate what is before them. Let us join then in trying to convince deans, colleagues, and academic committees that editing is a demanding task, not just 'service', and that a good edition is always a secure basis for assessing the qualities of a future university teacher. And there is still considerable scope in the field, as Andy Orchard has so convincingly demonstrated.[43]

Editing is not, of course, the only means of qualifying for an academic career. There are many more, and demanding tasks among them. Just let us remember that "the subject is rich, and there is much work to be done," and if directed and carried out with circumspection, sound knowledge, and an awareness of what is and will remain essential, we need not fear, in Anglo-Saxon studies, what in a recent article by Colin MacCabe[44] was deplored as "the amount of wasted labour involved in the production of unread academic work."[45]

---

[43] Paul E. Szarmach, "Editions of Alfred: The Wages of Un-influence," in *Early Medieval English Texts and Interpretations: Studies Presented to Donald G. Scragg*, ed. Elaine Treharne and Susan Rosser, MRTS 252 (Tempe, AZ, 2002), 135–49, at 149; Andy Orchard, "Re-editing Wulfstan: Where's the Point?," in *Wulfstan, Archbishop of York: The Proceedings of the Second Alcuin Conference*, ed. Matthew Townend, Studies in the Early Middle Ages 10 (Turnhout, 2004), 63–91.

[44] Colin MacCabe, "The Next Stage of Socialism: Privatising the Universities," *Critical Quarterly* 47 (2005): 179–83, at 181.

[45] The text of this lecture remains essentially as it was delivered on 1 August 2005 in Munich, but the bibliographical references have been supplemented and updated. No alterations or additions were made after October 2008.

No Place Like Home?
The Anglo-Saxon Social Landscape
from Within and Without

John Hines

1. Introduction

Dorothy Whitelock's rightly respected volume in the Pelican History of England series, *The Beginnings of English Society*, appeared in 1952 and was manifestly
designed to complement (and compliment) Sir Frank Stenton's Oxford History of
England volume, *Anglo-Saxon England*, the first and second editions of which had
been published in 1943 and 1947 respectively. While Stenton provided a magiste-
rial political and constitutional overview of history, full of dates and details of the
reigns, achievements, and fates of kings, and emphasizing above all his belief in
the significance of the free peasantry at the root of English social development,
Whitelock sought to portray the conditions and experiences of history: "what can
be learnt about the ways of life of the English."[1] Yet there is little in her book on so
basic an aspect as the home life of these people: barely nine pages of rather trusting
summary of what a blend of administrative, archaeological, and literary sources
suggest could have been the experience of "life in a nobleman's hall."[2] It may indeed
appear that the mundane and quotidian realities of domestic life, especially as
experienced by the humbler mass of the population of Anglo-Saxon England, lack
celebration in Anglo-Saxon culture. Our sources thus leave this field little known
to us; inevitably, then, even less is it appreciated.

It may seem incongruous if not ostentatiously contrary to contribute to a volume on *Anglo-Saxon England and the Continent* an essay seeking to highlight precisely this domestic topic, the horizons of which would seem so very limited. It
can be proposed, however, that this is in fact a particularly good example of how

---

[1] Dorothy Whitelock, *The Beginnings of English Society*, 2nd edn. (Harmondsworth,
1954), 7.

[2] Whitelock, *Beginnings*, 86–95.

Hans Sauer and Joanna Story, eds., *Anglo-Saxon England and the Continent*. With the assistance of Gaby Waxenberger. Essays in Anglo-Saxon Studies, vol. 3. MRTS 394. Tempe: ACMRS, 2011.   [ISBN 978-0-86698-442-3]

practical and local aspects of Anglo-Saxon cultural life were deeply interconnected with far larger and wider historical processes. Not least of importance, in
relation to early medieval cultural history generally, is the fact that an exploration
of the intimacy of mundane life in the context of the great historical narrative
confronts us with the inverse of the direction of developments in an all-pervasive
top-down relationship, governed by powerful institutions and movements such as
kings and the church. What we read is a tale of consistent responses to common
experiences and conditions that cumulatively moved the lives and perceptions of
people of this era over very wide areas, both in England and on the Continent,
towards similar outcomes. Local autonomy and agency in governing how people
lived in those conditions prove to be essential factors in the account.

2. The Prittlewell Chamber-Grave

We may not be starting at the humbler end of the social scale but will still begin
appropriately by rectifying the misapprehension that the home was symbolically
insignificant in Anglo-Saxon culture. A remarkable archaeological discovery
was made in the winter of 2003–2004, at the edge of the modern park over
the site of the early twelfth-century Benedictine Prittlewell Priory, now within
Southend-on-Sea, Essex. This was a 'princely burial'—a description that should
be taken simply as a label expressing the exceptional wealth of the grave goods
interred with the deceased. This is the most important single burial find since
that of the Sutton Hoo mound 1 boat grave in August 1939, and indeed stands
in the next rank of social wealth to Sutton Hoo along with a handful of other
princely burials—at Broomfield, also in Essex, and Taplow, Buckinghamshire.[3]

---

[3] Other possible candidates for inclusion in this category are known, but in these
cases the burials have survived in too damaged a state for us to be sure: particularly
Coombe (Kent), discussed by Hilda R. Ellis Davidson and Leslie Webster, "The Anglo-
Saxon Burial at Coombe (Woodnesborough), Kent," *Medieval Archaeology* 11 (1967):
1–41; Asthall and Cuddesdon (Oxon), discussed by Tania M. Dickinson and George
Speake, "The Seventh-Century Cremation Burial in Asthall Barrow, Oxfordshire: A
Reassessment," in *The Age of Sutton Hoo*, ed. Martin Carver (Woodbridge, 1992), 95–130
and Tania M. Dickinson, *Cuddesdon and Dorchester-on-Thames, Oxfordshire: Two Early
Saxon 'Princely' Sites in Wessex* (Oxford, 1974); Caenby (Lincs.) discussed by E. Jarvis,
"Account of the Discovery of Ornaments and Remains, Supposed to be of Danish Origin, in the Parish of Caenby, Lincolnshire," *The Archaeological Journal* 7 (1850): 36–44,
and R. L. S. Bruce-Mitford, *The Sutton Hoo Ship-Burial*, 3 vols. (London, 1975–1983), 2:
207. However it is crucial to recognize the real distinction in the quantity and elaborate
nature of the grave goods deposited between the definitive cases listed in the text and
the merely "rich" barrow burials of the seventh century. Cf. John Shepherd, "The Social
Identity of the Individual in Isolated Barrow Cemeteries in Anglo-Saxon England," in
Space, Hierarchy and Society: Interdisciplinary Studies in Social Archaeological Analysis, ed. B.

FIGURE 2.1. Reconstruction of the princely chamber grave at Prittlewell, Essex (Museum of London site-code EX-PRO 03).

Copyright Faith Vardy and Museum of London Archaeology Service (MoLAS); reproduced by kind permission.

The Prittlewell tomb was constructed as a wooden chamber, with a planked floor, walls, and ceiling. Of immense value to us is the fact that the gaps between the planks of these relatively loose structures allowed the local sandy soil to infiltrate and fill up the chamber to a considerable extent, so that most of the deposit remained precisely in situ as the chamber itself rotted away and collapsed.[4]

What made this discovery at Prittlewell particularly surprising, perhaps paradoxically, was the fact that the archaeologists were on site precisely because they already knew there were Anglo-Saxon burials of this date in Prittlewell Park.[5] The fact is that we should not then have expected this sort of princely burial to occur in such direct association with what otherwise looks like a fairly

---

C. Burnham and J. Kingsbury, BAR International Series 59 (Oxford, 1979), 47–79; Sam Lucy, *The Anglo-Saxon Way of Death* (Oxford, 2002), 97–103, 146–52.

  [4] Museum of London Archaeology Service, *The Prittlewell Prince: The Discovery of a Rich Anglo-Saxon Burial in Essex* (London, 2004).

  [5] William Pollit, "The East Saxons of Prittlewell," *Transactions of the Southend-on-Sea District Archaeological and Historical Society* 2 (1932): 89–102; Susan Tyler, "The

normal cemetery of the late sixth to later seventh centuries. It is true that a larger burial ground of the late sixth century has now been found at Sutton Hoo,[6] but it is not contiguous to the royal grave mounds and can validly be considered separate. Of further especial interest and importance in the case of Prittlewell is the fact that it is not really the most personal equipment and adornments with which the dead man was buried that identify him as of exceptional rank. Certainly the gold artefacts—the buckle and the two foil crosses—are very special indeed. The crosses betoken a Christian allegiance, and are unique in England although paralleled in contemporary, early Christian Germanic burials on the Continent.[7] A Roman and Byzantine type of spoon, inscribed with a cross and some Latin legend in the bowl, is also of a definite if not fully explained Christian character, and is again paralleled on the Continent.[8] The buckle is a startlingly plain example of this type in gold.[9] This fact, however, is very much consistent with a positively emphatic lack of ostentation in this man's personal accoutrements: certainly something unusual in relation to the norms of his time. The armament he was buried with is that of a fully equipped warrior, a powerful and respected man in his community: two spears, a shield, and a sword. But again, unlike Sutton Hoo, and (albeit to a lesser extent) Broomfield and Taplow, this is not outstanding display equipment.[10] The assemblage belongs within the top layer of the normal range of weapon-combinations; it does not stand above it. In fact, the spearheads, sword, and shield-boss are very similar indeed in type to those in several other graves at Prittlewell.

There are two features of the Prittlewell burial, however, that confirm its place in an exceptional category of structure and furnishing, and so imply the equally exceptional social status of the deceased interred here rather than mere prominence within contemporary society. One of these is the quantity and quality of the equipment for hospitality in the assemblage: drinking-horns, turned wooden bowls, a bronze Byzantine flagon, and glass vessels; iron- and bronze-bound wooden tubs; and various copper-alloy bowls, be they for hand-washing or holding foodstuffs or

---

Anglo-Saxon Cemetery at Prittlewell, Essex: An Analysis of the Grave-Goods," *Essex Archaeology and History* 19 (1988): 91–116.

[6] Martin Carver, *Sutton Hoo: A Seventh-Century Princely Burial Ground and its Context* (London, 2005), esp. 483–86 and 495, fig. 220.

[7] W. Hübener, ed., *Die Goldblattkreuze des frühen Mittelalters* (Baden, 1975).

[8] Horst Wolfgang Böhme, "Löffelbeigabe in spätrömischen Gräbern nördlich der Alpen," *Jahrbuch des Römisch-Germanischen Zentralmuseums Mainz* 17 (1970): 172–200; D. A. Sherlock, "Zu einer Fundliste antiker Silberlöffel," *Bericht der Römisch-Germanischen Kommissions* (1973): 203–11; Bruce-Mitford, *Sutton Hoo*, 3.1: 143–45.

[9] Sonja Marzinzik, *Early Anglo-Saxon Belt Buckles (Late 5th to Early 8th Centuries A.D.): Their Classification and Context*, BAR British Series 357 (Oxford, 2003), 49–50 and pls. 127–30.

[10] Heinrich Härke, *Angelsächsische Waffengräber des 5. bis 7. Jahrhunderts* (Cologne, 1992), 104–13, esp. Taf. 9.

both.[11] To these we could add the lyre, a musical instrument for group entertainment, although this is not actually quite such an exclusive item of grave goods: we have a number of examples, not all in exceptional graves.[12] The second distinguishing feature is the construction of a large planked chamber for the interment of both the body and the grave goods. Although this type of structure can be paralleled on a smaller scale at Spong Hill in Norfolk in a burial of the earlier sixth century,[13] the chamber takes its place amongst a range of ways in which the graves of especially important individuals—men far more frequently than women, not surprisingly—were made to stand out with special forms and structures. Other wooden chambers are either known or at least inferred in a small number of additional cases.[14] There had been a chamber constructed over the ship that was covered by the barrow of mound 1 at Sutton Hoo.[15]

One of the shared characteristics of the Anglo-Saxon princely graves is the exceptional wrought-iron artefacts they contain. There are examples of elaborate cauldron chains and the cauldrons themselves. The Sutton Hoo 'standard' is esoteric, and while it is impossible to state with confidence what exactly its function was, one has to be obstinately sceptical not to accept that it is likely to have been some item of symbolic regalia.[16] Comparable in the Prittlewell burial is a tall iron stand with a bowl for a lamp on the top. Although special—in fact unique amongst known finds—this is an item of practical, probably interior, equipment which underlines the point that what was reconstructed within the Prittlewell tomb was a version of a lived-in building. That building, of course, was not a personal home anything like as we would conceive of such a thing, but the open hall: practically, in fact, the only type of dwelling structure known in England at this

---

[11] The burial assemblage at Taplow included 3 iron- and copper-alloy bound wooden buckets or tubs, 2 large bronze bowls—one of them a vast cauldron, 4 glass claw-beakers, at least 2 large drinking horns, and 2 wooden cups; that at Broomfield 2 drinking horns, 2 wooden cups, 2 glass cups, 2 iron-bound wooden tubs—one of them huge, and an iron cauldron; Sutton Hoo mound 1 contained very much more of the same: Bruce-Mitford, *Sutton Hoo*, vol. 3.

[12] Graeme Lawton, "The Lyre from Grave 22," in *The Anglo-Saxon Cemetery at Bergh Apton, Norfolk*, ed. Barbara Green and Andrew Rogerson, East Anglian Archaeology 7 (Gressenhall, 1978), 87–98; idem, "Report on the Lyre Remains from Grave 97," in *The Anglo-Saxon Cemetery at Morning Thorpe, Norfolk*, ed. Barbara Green, Andrew Rogerson, and Susan G. White, East Anglian Archaeology 36, 2 vols. (Gressenhall, 1987), 12, 166–71.

[13] Grave 40: Catherine M. Hills et al., *The Anglo-Saxon Cemetery at Spong Hill, North Elmham: Part III: Catalogue of Inhumations*, East Anglian Archaeology 21 (Gressenhall, 1984), 91–94.

[14] Lucy, *Way of Death*, 102.

[15] Carver, *Sutton Hoo*, 177–99.

[16] Bruce-Mitford, *Sutton Hoo*, 2: 403–21.

period.[17] The provision for substantial hospitality in this hall reflects the exceptional size and composition—in terms of privilege and value—of this prince's implied household: but to introduce here the notion of 'public' space would be as inappropriate as any idea of a 'private' home. This was a space for an initiated elite; we can be quite sure that open access to a leader such as this was carefully controlled, both physically and procedurally. It is possible that the separate sleeping quarters or *būr* could be found in settlement contexts at this date, be that in the form of ancillary buildings or partitioned-off spaces within halls—in which case we ought rather to see the Prittlewell chamber as a conflation of two space-functions in one. Ideally, though, as we know, every acknowledged need was met in the hall. Complementary manifestations of the symbolic evocation of the home in the grave in seventh-century England occur in the burial of other furniture in graves, such as the folding stool of Prittlewell, and several bed-burials, all but one the graves of adult women. It is also in this phase that women's domestic activities in the form of the crafts of spinning and weaving come to be regularly represented in the collections of grave goods.[18]

Without pretending that we can fully or certainly identify the ideas, both conscious and subconscious, that are expressed in these varieties of burial rite, some of the symbolism is so direct that it poses little difficulty of explication. If there was a concept of an afterlife, which may or may not have been Christian, it is hardly surprising that it should be represented in terms of familiar human life here: with the same social distinctions and gender roles, and including the most essential of all elements of material culture, namely, a place to live. The introduction of a means of transport, the ship in a few cases, implies a sense of burial as a rite of passage. This is probably how we should also interpret the considerable number of burials of men and women with horses, especially in cremation cemeteries.[19] The symbolic meaning of the bed-burials would appear to have

---

[17] Helena Hamerow, *Early Medieval Settlements: The Archaeology of Rural Communities in North-West Europe 400–900* (Oxford, 2002), 12–51.

[18] Helen Geake, *The Use of Grave-Goods in Conversion-Period England, c. 600–c. 850*, BAR British Series 261 (Oxford, 1997), 34–35, 58–62; but compare Nick Stoodley, *The Spindle and the Spear: A Critical Enquiry into the Construction and Meaning of Gender in the Early Anglo-Saxon Burial Rite*, BAR British Series 288 (Oxford, 1999), 35, 38. Stoodley suggests that the burial of textile-working equipment was equally common throughout the period from the later fifth to the late seventh century. The comprehensive observations made in the course of the ongoing English Heritage-funded research project "Anglo-Saxon England, c. 580–720: The Chronological Basis" (Queen's University, Belfast, and Cardiff University), however, agree with Geake's conclusions this respect, as summarized in the text here.

[19] Chris Fern, "The Archaeological Evidence for Equestrianism in Early Anglo-Saxon England, c. 450–700," in *Just Skin and Bone? New Perspectives on Human-Animal Relations in the Historical Past*, ed. Aleksander Pluskowski, BAR International Series 1410 (Oxford, 2005), 43–71.

been to portray worldly death as transitional; the grave as a place of sleep or rest, from which one might arise. There is in fact a noticeable correlation in England between bed-burial and other forms of overtly Christian symbolism,[20] and it is not impossible that this form of grave represents a seventh-century adaptation of traditional funerary practices to the new religion.

These various contemporary expressions of an explicit concept between life and death reflect, on the one hand, the presence of a sense of an afterlife, and at the same time reflect upon the fundamental relationship between life and death. The imposition of domestic symbolism upon funerary ritual in the seventh century need not be interpreted as evidence for a completely new consciousness of the home having emerged by that juncture—as if such a thing had been lacking, or was simply unimportant, hitherto. What it must reflect, though, is a new mind-set and new social and cultural circumstances in which analogies between the cosmos and the life beyond and the practicalities of life on earth began to be expressed in a very explicit way.

3. House and Home: Stability and Change

In her contribution to the multidisciplinary round-table discussion "Cædmon's World," at the International Congress on Medieval Studies, Kalamazoo, in May 2005, Faith Wallis presented a brilliant study of Cædmon's Hymn from the perspective of a historian of science and religion.[21] She found particular significance and symbolism in the image of the created world as a building:

> hē āērest scop aelda barnum
> heben til hrōfe . . .

> ['First of all He created for the children of mankind / Heaven as a roof . . .']

As developed in the ensuing debate in that meeting, this image proved to be a basis for a far more problematic conceptualization of stability and change than one might initially expect. Undoubtedly one can find an element here of the proverbial notion of things being as "safe as houses," just as elsewhere in Old English literature. However, as Chris Loveluck's discussion of the settlement site at Flixborough in the same session showed—a seventh- to tenth-century site, possibly monastic during one period of its history—the normal timber buildings

---

[20] George Speake, *A Saxon Bed Burial on Swallowcliffe Down* (London, 1989), esp. 124–26.

[21] Faith Wallis, "Cædmon's Created World and the Monastic Encyclopedia," in *Cædmon's "Hymn" and Material Culture in the World of Bede*, ed. Allen J. Frantzen and John Hines (Morgantown, WV, 2007), 80–110.

of this period had to be replaced, and were usually moved, every few decades.[22]
Tantalizingly familiar though the idea of monumental architecture as a symbol
of stability may appear, in Anglo-Saxon England we are dealing with an historical context in which the average life-span of both people and buildings was much
shorter than we are used to. In both cases, anything much over half-a-century
was unusually long-lived. The conceptual stability of the built environment could
not have subsisted in an utter fixity that excluded the renewal and replacement
of the subject; rather—and indeed much more interestingly—it was based upon
an apprehension of the regularity and dependability of a material world that was
at the same time largely organic, and the elements of which went through life-
cycles remarkably similar to our own human ones.

This has some further thought-provoking consequences, when we try to
comprehend how the world may have been seen in Anglo-Saxon England. Sheer
familiarity with change and replacement in such circumstances is likely to have
reduced the salience of those changes in perception. If something is going on all
the time, it tends not to be noticed, or at least to attract less attention and thought.
People were, of course, being born and dying all the time, and one would hardly
claim that the transience of human life was something that Anglo-Saxon people
were barely aware of as a result. Rather, the analogy between human life and
material culture reveals a vital distinction in cognitive categories: that people
really did have individual identity, which existed in one form—and was indeed
subject to existentialist modification—during the person's earthly life; according to Christian belief there was also a real and individual eternal afterlife for
all. Buildings could also have their own identity—expressed in their names as
so-and-so's hall, "Heorot," and so on—but they did not have that individuating
spirit of life. Thus any individual building could be replaced, and in its current
form continued to be *that* building: hall, church, whatever.[23] In the present context the point to be stressed is that in circumstances of constant and ubiquitous
change, it can be very difficult indeed to perceive that things are developing

---

[22] Hamerow, *Settlements*, 104–6; C. P. Loveluck, "A High-Status Anglo-Saxon Settlement at Flixborough, Lincolnshire," *Antiquity* 72 (1998): 146–61; idem, "Cædmon's
World: Secular and Monastic Lifestyles and Estate Organization in Northern England,
AD 650–900," in *Cædmon's "Hymn" and Material Culture in the World of Bede*, ed. Frantzen
and Hines, 150–90; idem, *Excavations at Flixborough*, 4 vols. (Oxford, 2007–2008).

[23] Besides the well-known literary examples of named halls in Old English literature—Finnsburh and Heorot—and a relative profusion in Old Norse, we may note
Bede's reference to Yeavering, a site that was repeatedly rebuilt but abandoned by his day,
as "uilla regia qua uocatur adgefrin" (Bede, *HE* 2.14). However, the English historical
evidence of names being passed on between successive buildings is inevitably most copious in respect of church dedications. It is frustrating that the many charter references we
have to the archaeologically excavated site at Cheddar relate only to the middle phase (ca.
930–1000) of its archaeological sequence.

in any particular direction. Some people in Anglo-Saxon England—perhaps many—were aware of a different past, represented for them once again by the settlement archaeology of Roman masonry ruins: expressed most graphically in *The Ruin*. That, however, is quite different from a consciousness of teleological change in the present. It is only too likely that modern historians and archaeologists will see processes and developments taking place in Anglo-Saxon England, processes of which the agents of those changes had no particular idea of the purpose, or even any sense of change at all. They might have perceived only maintenance and renewal.

It lies beyond reasonable question that the most fundamental issues governing the conditions in which people lived and worked in Anglo-Saxon England were the control of land—which increasingly came to mean the ownership of land—and the organization of farming. These were the foundations of wealth and security. We have to substantiate this insight into Anglo-Saxon culture from the historical and documentary sources: beginning with charters of the later seventh century and then reflected in increasing, and changing, detail down to the great *Domesday Book* of 1086/87. Although it was a comprehensive survey of a kind, the Domesday Inquisition was primarily concerned with lordship over landholdings and with the economic returns that could be expected from them. To this end, its records do provide some idea of the settlement units in the various districts and counties, the manor houses and vills, but the Domesday commissioners were thoroughly indifferent to the actual form any settlement took. Only by inference can we decide that in some areas the records concern dispersed individual homesteads, even for peasant farmers; in other cases compact villages.[24]

At the same time, it is a striking feature of *Domesday Book* that the records depend fundamentally on terms representing the house and home to describe the social structure of William's England. The terms *bordarius* and *cottarius* represent a considerable group (possibly two different types) of peasants. The roots of both terms are words meaning 'a humble house': medieval Latin *borda*, Old French *borde*, in the former case, and Old English *cot* in the other. In the same way, the Old English legal tract *Rectitudines Singularum Personarum*, probably a few decades earlier,[25] refers to one type of peasant as the *kotsetla* and another as *gebūr*, again a term based upon a root meaning 'dwelling'. Both of these classes were taxed according to their possession of a home, owing a *hearth-penny* to the church each Easter. Moving higher up the social scale, our firmest evidence of the widespread establishment of

---

[24] F. W. Maitland, *Domesday Book and Beyond* (Cambridge, 1897); C. W. Dyer, "Dispersed Settlements in Medieval England: A Case Study of Pendock, Worcestershire," *Medieval Archaeology* 34 (1990): 97–121; idem, *Making a Living in the Middle Ages: The People of Britain 850–1520* (New Haven and London, 2002), 91–99.

[25] Felix Liebermann, *Die Gesetze der Angelsachsen*, 3 vols. (Halle a. S., 1903), 1: 444–53; P. D. A. Harvey, "*Rectitudines Singularum Personarum* and *Gerefa*," *English Historical Review* 108 (1993): 1–22.

(at least) key features of the system we know as 'manorial' appears in wills of the late tenth and earlier eleventh centuries, which repeatedly refer to the *heafod-botl* or 'chief homestead.' At the top of that scale, maxims tell us bluntly "cyning sceall on healle."[26] Within the inter-related economic and social landscapes of later Anglo-Saxon England, there can, therefore, be no doubt of the conceptual centrality of the place and category of residence, and the right to residence, in defining and embodying an individual's social identity.

From one standpoint, we could say that this sort of aggregated historical evidence helps us to understand emotive uses of the home as a topos in Old English poetry: for instance when Breca, having proved a better swimmer (or rower) than Beowulf, makes his way to his

swæsne ēþel,

. . .
freoðoburh fægere,   þær hē folc āhte,
burh ong bēagas. (lines 520, 522–523)

To his 'dear homeland . . . the fine secure house, where he had his people, a home and rings.' As I translate these lines, I would argue that the etymological sense of *burh* as 'enclosure, fortified place' is now very distant, and that the term primarily signifies just 'a homestead.'[27] Of definite date and context, in *The Battle of Maldon*, Leofsunu of Stourmere announces that he will not return home with his lord who lies dead on the battlefield to face reproach there:

> Ne þurfon mē embe Stūrmere stedefæste hæleð
> wordum ætwītan, nū mīn wine gecranc,
> þæt ic hlāfordlēas hām siðie . . . (lines 249–251)

> ['Around Stourmere, steadfast warriors will have no cause to reproach me in words, now my lord is fallen, that I should travel home a lordless man . . .']

Shortly before, Ælfwine the Mercian had likewise declared that he would not seek his own land, where the thegns would condemn him in these circumstances (lines 211–224). For the warrior echelon of society, the home was where a man's reputation would be preserved, be it good or bad: a mirror-image of the relationship between home and funerary monument as expressed by the Prittlewell chamber-grave.

---

[26] *Maxims II*, 28b. The sentence is completed in the following half-line "bēagas dǣlan," 'a king must share out rings in the hall,' but the maxim is part of a long sequence stating both where certain characters, objects, or creatures should be found together with what behaviour is expected of them (lines 16–49).

[27] Kenneth Cameron, *English Place Names* (London, 1961), 112–15; *DOE*, s.v. *burh*.

This ideological valorization of the home was every bit as evident in the neighbouring areas of the Continent. Robert Fossier, attempting to characterize a key feature of social and economic history on the Continent in the period across the fulcrum of the Middle Ages from the tenth to thirteenth centuries, writes of what he describes as a significant shift in family structures, which he attributes to the late ninth and tenth centuries:

> The lineage . . . crumbles, breaks up and forgets itself. We are now confronted by the "house" (*Haus, maison, domus*), with a simple direct line of descent. Everything suggests that this simple structure, based on the nuclear family, formed gradually within the lineage [= kin-group; clan; ancestral family], and that if the latter disappeared before the millennium it was as a result of this internal subdivision.[28]

The essence of Fossier's argument is that the house and home was in the foreground as a conceptual focus of social identity and relationships precisely as, and indeed *because*, a Europe in which extended kindreds had been at the heart of social identity, loyalty, and security was giving way to a feudal Europe in which political loyalty and contractual allegiance allowed ambitious and powerful men to assemble and control ever greater resources of manpower and land. In its own way, this in fact represents yet another twist and version of the "birth of the individual" hypothesis, for, as H. M. Chadwick saw eighty years ago, a system whereby one's identity, rights, and duties were genetically predetermined by birth into a certain kin-group at the very least appears to be fundamentally anti-existentialist and anti-individualistic.[29]

We can dispute the presentation of these distinctions, contrasts, and conflicts primarily as chronological strata falling into a smooth, systematic evolutionary sequence that saw the demise of what is clearly conceived (in old-fashioned anthropological terms) as a 'primitive' state of society in which the kin-group was fundamental, and its replacement by a more advanced society (which was a crucial stage in the formation of the nation-state, in which political units could be created voluntarily out of a combination of power and consent). At the very heart of an alternative view must lie the historical and linguistic evidence for the existence of the hide, certainly from as early as the second half of the seventh century in England: the *terra familiae*, 'land of a family,' as it then appears in the Latin documents. The key point here is that, although the term 'family' might

---

[28] Robert Fossier, "Rural Economy and Country Life," in *New Cambridge Medieval History*, vol. 3, *c. 900–c. 1024*, ed. T. Reuter (Cambridge, 1999), 27–62, at 31–32: the words in square brackets are my addition; Robert Fossier, *La société médiévale* (Paris, 1991), and idem, "Les structures de la famille en occident au moyen âge," in *Congrès international des sciences historiques: Rapports* (Bucharest, 1980), 2: 115–32.

[29] H. M. Chadwick, *The Heroic Age* (Cambridge, 1926), 344–65.

appear to defer to the dominance of kinship, the Latin term *familia* cannot mean 'family' in the way we could all too easily imagine by thinking of things in our own terms. It is, of course, to be translated 'household' rather than 'family,' and certainly it signifies nothing like the nuclear family centered on parents and children of the modern notion.[30] There is, simply, no known word in Old English for a nuclear family unit of that kind: that is, one referring solely to the close relationship between this small group of individuals. The nearest terms we have are words such as *hīrēd, hīwisc*, derivatives of the Germanic root **hīwa*, which again means a 'household' rather than being purely personal and relational.[31] The word *home* itself is another deep cognate, with parallels in Sanskrit *kṣemas* and other Indo-European languages showing an extremely deep stability of meaning.[32] This underlines the significance of the point made just above, about the conceptual consequences of life expectancy. Life was transitory. There were always very real threats: sickness or age or violence, as a poet put it.[33] No social unit was more intrinsically *un*-stable than the nuclear family, with high infant mortality on top of everything else.[34] Under an exogamous system, many women had to be relative strangers within their immediate households.[35] Growth and change would have been highly salient in these small social units. It can consequently be no surprise that it was the material, external structure of the household that defined it, not an abstract unity determined by the relationships between the transient and changing individuals within.

It is at the same time fair to characterize a particularly regular, systematic, and evolutionary view of these aspects of early medieval social and economic development as a 'Continental perspective'—perhaps better a 'Continentalist' perspective. With the benefit of Carolingian polyptychs ('account books') of the late eighth and ninth centuries and further records of church landholdings from subsequent centuries, together with our knowledge of the Roman legal system regarding property, it is possible not only to trace a larger and more detailed historical sequence on the Continent than in England, but also to identify certain shared developments in agrarian settlement and economic history—for

[30] P. W. Glare, ed., *The Oxford Latin Dictionary* (Oxford, 1982), s.v. *FAMILIA*, 1–4. See now Eric G. Stanley, "The *familia* in Anglo-Saxon Society: 'household' rather than 'family, home life' as Now Understood," *Anglia* 126 (2008): 37–64; *Familia and Household in the Medieval Atlantic Province*, forthcoming from MRTS.

[31] Julius Pokorny, *Indogermanisches Etymologisches Wörterbuch* (Bern, 1959), s.v. 1. *KEI-*.

[32] D. H. Greene, *Language and History in the Early Germanic World* (Cambridge, 1998), 102–3.

[33] "adl oþþe yldo oþþe ecghete": *The Seafarer*, line 70.

[34] Sally Crawford, *Childhood in Anglo-Saxon England* (Stroud, 1999), esp. 75, 109–14.

[35] T. Malim and J. Hines, *The Anglo-Saxon Cemetery at Edix Hill (Barrington A), Cambridgeshire*, CBA Research Report 102 (York, 1998), 303–17; compare Christine Fell, *Women in Anglo-Saxon England* (Oxford, 1984), 74–75.

instance the regular practice of crop-rotation—earlier on the Continent than in the English sources.[36] The identification of such a Continentalist perspective is also justified because knowledge and understanding of developments of these kinds on the Continent have been employed by some scholars, not unreasonably, as a basis for postulating what may have been going on in England where direct evidence is far less substantial or clear.[37] Of course such a 'Continentalist' position need not take the form of merely assuming that things were essentially the same; nonetheless, it leaves the problem of how we can test and justify adequately the application of such analogical reasoning when it is used where the empirical evidence is weak.

What may be proposed as the most interesting and useful aspect of the Continentalist perspective on the social and economic aspects of Anglo-Saxon settlement history could in fact, in effect, be the inverse of such an assumption. The regularity of the historical patterns postulated for the Continent is itself far from certain. Regional variation on the Continent was indisputably considerable, and long-term historical and locally specific roots running back into the Roman period are persistent factors underlying that range of variation. This phenomenon is widely recognized in areas that are clearly separate, such as France, southern Germany, and Italy, but has also been identified in micro-regions in all of those lands.[38]

In central France, for instance, where the classic manorial 'bipartite' system of demesne land alongside tenanted holdings can be identified as early as the mid-eighth century, there are signs that such a system went through a process of partial shrinkage and retreat by the ninth century.[39] A new system, one that is regarded as characteristic of the high medieval agrarian society and economy, had indeed been introduced, but that system was as yet far from stable in practice and in physical realization. An important factor in the settlement and agrarian history of this period both in England and on the Continent was the effective

---

[36] The literature on these issues is of course copious. Convenient and relevant overviews specifically connected to studies of the Anglo-Saxon situation can be found in Hans-Jürgen Nitz, "Settlement Structures and Settlement Systems of the Frankish Central State in Carolingian and Ottonian Times," and Helmut Hildebrandt, "Systems of Agriculture in Central Europe up to the Tenth and Eleventh Centuries," in *Anglo-Saxon Settlements*, ed. Della Hooke (Oxford, 1988), 249–73, 275–90 respectively.

[37] Georges Duby, "Medieval Agriculture 900–1500," in *The Middle Ages*, ed. Carlo M. Cipolla (London, 1972), 175–220, and Timothy Reuter, "Introduction: Reading the Tenth Century," in *New Cambridge Medieval History*, vol. 3, 1–24, at 14–15, both identify and discuss this problem as a serious issue, and yet seem unable themselves to break entirely free from the Continentalist perspective as an influential factor in their essays and reconstructions overall.

[38] This is amply demonstrated in Chris Wickham, *Framing the Early Middle Ages: Europe and the Mediterranean, 400–800* (Oxford, 2005).

[39] Adriaan Verhulst, "Economic Organisation," in *New Cambridge Medieval History*, vol. 2, *c. 700–900*, ed. Rosamond McKitterick (Cambridge, 1995), 481–509, at 498.

colonization, for more intensive exploitation, of lands that may have been formerly pasture, woodland, or waste; this created satellite settlements and landholdings, and, in particular, encouraged the settlement of semi-free peasants who had a real interest in working hard and doing well in this situation. There is an obvious systemic logic in this set of circumstances; it encouraged a change in taxation practices, whereby the primary entity from which tax was collected, the *man-sis*, became a house rather than the whole estate; and concomitantly, the greater material definition of such key buildings by enclosing them, in an ostensibly defensive manner, with a moat.[40] But the relationships producing such changes are only associable with increasing fixity in settlement pattern and steady economic growth in a very long-term view indeed: those gradual historical processes were largely irrelevant to the reality of life as it was experienced at the time.

4. Home Thoughts

Returning to the illustrative example of the Prittlewell burial chamber, it is consequently not just a matter of considering in archaeological terms the structure and the assemblage of artefacts within it, although such an approach is, undoubtedly, sufficient to reveal to us the fact that domestic space had a symbolic meaning and value that was being reflected in a new way in the seventh century. As we have just seen, the historical and a linguistic context add significantly to our ability to understand the terms in which contemporary people may have thought about the Prittlewell burial. We do not have directly contemporary vernacular literature from the first half of the seventh century, although we can reasonably extrapolate from later Old English poetry to enrich our understanding yet further. The Prittlewell burial, however, is an *exceptional* archaeological monument. Can the archaeology of real Anglo-Saxon houses and homesteads add anything further to this picture, or must our exploration of the symbolic importance of the Anglo-Saxon home rely on creative and imaginative transformations of or reactions to mundane facts that are untypical of the actual settlement evidence itself?

The relevant archaeological evidence is certainly profuse, not least because of the intrinsic mutability of the sites already noted. We now have evidence from hundreds of occupation sites to consider, many of them accessible because settlement has shifted so much from time to time that many formerly built-over sites have lain largely undisturbed under soil, crops, and grass for centuries since.[41] We also find that the requisite rebuilding of timber structures every few decades

---

[40] Christopher Loveluck, "Rural Settlement Hierarchy in the Age of Charlemagne," in *Charlemagne: Empire and Society,* ed. Joanna Story (Manchester, 2005), 230–58.

[41] Andrew Reynolds, "Boundaries and Settlements in Later Sixth- to Eleventh-century England," in *Boundaries in Early Medieval Britain,* ed. David Griffiths, Andrew Reynolds, and Sarah Semple, Anglo-Saxon Studies in Archaeology and History 12 (Oxford, 2003), 98–136, esp. 98–99.

enables us to look at sequences of development within settlement sites: developments, as noted above, of which we are likely to be much more aware than anyone responsible for them could have been. A nice example is the site of Bishopstone in Sussex, where on Rookery Hill a Roman-period native farmstead (that is, not a romanized villa) seems to have survived to about AD 400. After that, the site shows no signs of activity for several decades, until in the second half of the fifth century a community using an entirely Germanic material culture re-occupied the site, alongside but not re-using the Romano-British features.[42]

The small early Anglo-Saxon village or hamlet upon Rookery Hill has some detectable phases of development of its own, but there is no evidence here to indicate that its life extended much longer than a century—in other words, beyond the sixth century into the seventh. This site was excavated from 1967 to 1975. More recent work at Bishopstone, the excavation phase of which has just finished, has identified late Anglo-Saxon settlement features adjacent to the church which itself contains a considerable amount of surviving Anglo-Saxon fabric. The occupation in this area can certainly be dated to the tenth century; it may well go back into the ninth. We see buildings of new types here: the familiar post-in-trench halls; and also the rather rarer aisled buildings that were coming into use in the very late Anglo-Saxon period. There is evidence, in the form of both detritus and tools, for metalworking, agriculture, and textile production in this settlement—just as one would expect. One of the more puzzling features is a substantial, deep-cellared structure, which has been identified speculatively as a possible example of the bell-house required of the homesteads of those of thegnly status in the Wulfstanian provisions *Geþynco*.[43] Yet this later settlement is on the opposite side of the valley to Rookery Hill where the earliest Anglo-Saxon settlement was situated. There is a little, as yet unverified, evidence of intermediary settlement from a third site to the south of the surviving church.

The mobile and dynamic nature of Anglo-Saxon settlement found expression in several different forms. At the well-studied early sites of Mucking in Essex and West Stow, Suffolk, we are familiar with the concept of the labile settlement, which seems to drift across the landscape as farmsteads were replaced and developed.[44] A point of particular interest at West Stow that has only recently started to receive the attention it merits is the introduction of area-partition, through fencing, at a relatively late stage in the site's history. Despite the obvious practical need for enclosures to protect and control stock and poultry at any phase of settlement, there are no convincing examples of such features known from

---

[42] Martin Bell, "Excavations at Bishopstone," *Sussex Archaeological Collections* 115 (1977): 192–241; Gabor Thomas, "Bishopstone: In the Shadow of Rookery Hill," *Current Archaeology* 196 (2005): 184–90.

[43] Liebermann, *Gesetze*, 1: 456–58; Patrick Wormald, *The Making of English Law: King Alfred to the Twelfth Century*, vol. 1: *Legislation and its Limits* (Oxford, 1999), 391–94.

[44] Hamerow, *Settlements*, 93–99.

before the later sixth or seventh century, even though we certainly have earlier settlements.[45]

Changes in the character of a site did not always mean a change in location. This is particularly well illustrated for us by two sites at which, for at least some stages of their history, a special ecclesiastical character can be claimed: North Elmham in Norfolk, believed to be the minster site of the East Anglian see of Dommoc from the late seventh century to ca. 870, and again from the 950s to until after the Norman Conquest when the bishop's seat was moved to Thetford; and Flixborough, in Lincolnshire, where, on the basis of distinctive finds and the special diet of the inhabitants implied by the bone assemblage retrieved, monastic status is proposed for certain phases of a multi-period site that was occupied from the seventh century to the tenth (Fig. 2.2, see page 40).[46] The evidence we know from North Elmham begins within the putative episcopal phase in the early ninth century (Period I). Here, occupied plots are separated by ditches, two of which appear to define a droveway or lane. One of these plots had a large hall, eventually extended to nearly twenty meters in length, at which point it had a new structural style, the hipped roof, and a separate cookhouse. In the late ninth century, this was superseded by another large hall constructed directly over one of the earlier boundary ditches, and subsequently joined by an L-shaped building to form a courtyard (Period II). After that, in the eleventh century, we find that the area was divided up again, now occupied by small, apparently humble, simple post-built structures, often only about five meters by six, although one superior example was double that size and had an internal partition (Period III). These seem to be peasant houses and barns, with a hierarchy visible even among these cottages.

No single site, however, can be imagined to have been economically and socially so self-sufficient and independent that it developed in isolation. These sites were always part of a regional settlement pattern, and, perhaps most importantly, functioned within regional and even national economies.[47] There need be no doubt that one general feature and explanation of the developments in the settlement pattern in England across the Anglo-Saxon period was the intensification of production, not least in the case of the expansion of settlement into hitherto marginal areas, such as uplands or coastal wetlands.[48] Denser settlement could succeed there when the overall economic system supported the sort of specialization implied by sites like Simy Folds in County Durham where

---

[45] Reynolds, "Boundaries."

[46] Peter Wade-Martins, *Excavations in North Elmham Park 1967–1972*, East Anglian Archaeology 9, 2 vols. (Gressenhall, 1980); Loveluck, "High-Status Settlement," "Cædmon's World," and *Flixborough*.

[47] David M. Hinton, *Gold and Gilt, Pots and Pins* (Oxford, 2005), esp. 7–170.

[48] Della Hooke, *The Landscape of Anglo-Saxon England* (London, 1998), esp. 170–95.

iron-production was the principal subsistence basis.[49] The viability of such sites depended upon a system of economic exchange, whether through an effective open market or one controlled entirely within what is known as the 'multiple estate' with its complementary resources supporting an estate center. In terms of the relative flourishing of the two systems, it may be noted that it is believed that the Scandinavian conquest and settlement of the north, with the consequent breakup of large ecclesiastical multiple estates, greatly accelerated the process of specialization and economic growth in that region.[50]

If, then, the manor is not just a local economic and fiscal center but is, just as significantly, a house of this emergent kind that was becoming involved in external dealings and was thus historically and economically distinct from the 'multiple estate center,' one key element in the ill-defined process known as 'manorialization' must be economic liberalization: that is, the growth of profit-motivated, commercial, exchange through bargaining at fairs or in market towns—the latter indisputably a new feature of tenth- and eleventh-century England, and elsewhere in Europe.[51] Within the whole emergent feudal society and culture, the social changes that accompanied this liberalization were by no means limited to the thegnly and yeomanry ranks who emerged as the lords of the manors. This was also the period of the extensive, if scarcely truly liberating, form of social emancipation that saw slavery rapidly disappear in western Europe, to be replaced by feudal serfdom.[52] But even while we can acknowledge the genuine relatedness of these facts of social and economic history on the one hand, and the settlement archaeology on the other, and recognize that real and major changes did take place across western Europe, including not only England but eventually also Wales, Scotland, and Ireland as well, we should not feel that we ought to try to compress the explanation of these changes into a single determinative scheme. The fact is that we can see, if we are prepared to look seriously at what relevant evidence is available to us (which means historical, linguistic, archaeological, and literary evidence alike), that the issues and the distinctions, and therefore all of the factors that eventually coalesced and brought this process of historical development to fruition, existed centuries before.

---

[49] Denis Coggins et al., "An Early Medieval Settlement Site in Upper Teesdale, Co. Durham," *Medieval Archaeology* 27 (1983): 1–26; Denis Coggins et al., "Simy Folds: Twenty Years On," in *Land, Sea and Home*, ed. John Hines, Alan Lane, and Mark Redknap, Society for Medieval Archaeology Monograph 20 (Leeds, 2004), 325–34.

[50] D. M. Hadley, *The Northern Danelaw: Its Social Structure, c. 800–1100* (London and New York, 2000), esp. 197–215.

[51] John Schofield and Alan Vince, *Medieval Towns*, 2nd edn. (London and New York, 2003), 21–26; P. Johansen, "Merchants, Markets and Towns," in *New Cambridge Medieval History*, vol. 3, 64–94.

[52] David A. E. Pelteret, *Slavery in Early Medieval England* (Woodbridge, 1995).

Indeed, even the best evidence we have for classic manorialism in the late Anglo-Saxon period is of elements that represent the high medieval system in the abstract, not even in any convincingly embryonic form. At only one site, Faccombe Netherton in Hampshire, has a known manor house of the tenth and eleventh centuries been excavated showing what we can start to identify as characteristic manorial features: an enclosure that is at least defensive in style, and a little stone-walled building.[53] However, the structure that must be the manor house recorded in *Domesday* as having been held *Tempore Regis Edwardi* directly of the king by a man named Lang, was a classic timber Anglo-Saxon hall.[54] It was completely rebuilt soon after the Norman Conquest, and successive manor houses stood on this site until the fourteenth century. In fact even this continuity of site is quite exceptional. A comparable building has been excavated at Sulgrave, Northamptonshire, which may have been the manor held by Giles de Picquigny there in 1086–1087: but according to the Northamptonshire *Domesday* three other men were the resident tenants of his four hides of land at Sulgrave, where there had been four individual tenants *Tempore Regis Edwardi*, and archaeologically this manor house itself was superseded by minor buildings by the late eleventh century.[55] This discontinuity does not just represent the insecurity of the late Anglo-Saxon landowning classes in face of the Norman Conquest. Even with the carefully planned peasant tofts like those at North Elmham, of which we find specimens from the tenth century onwards, it is again only at one known site, West Cotton in Northamptonshire, that we have excavated examples that continue unbroken from the late Anglo-Saxon period through the Conquest and into the high and late Middle Ages.[56] The predominant picture, by contrast, is one of the elements that we are given to regard as having evolved steadily and logically into the classic medieval manorial system and feudal village existing in a generically inchoate state well into the eleventh century—a situation that we can treat as quite characteristic of both England and the Continent almost throughout the Early Middle Ages.

---

[53] J. R. Fairbrother, *Faccombe Netherton: Excavations of a Saxon and Medieval Manorial Complex*, 2 vols. (London, 1990). At the Prebendal Manor House, Nassington, Northants, archaeological investigations have demonstrated how a *mansis* in the possession of King Cnut originated as a relatively simple Middle and Late Anglo-Saxon building and was successively rebuilt and enlarged into a major later medieval and early modern manor complex: Anon., "Nassington: The Prebendal Manor," *Current Archaeology* 197 (2005): 248–55.

[54] Hampshire Domesday, fol. 39v.

[55] Northamptonshire Domesday, fol. 227r; Brian K. Davison, "Excavations at Sulgrave, Northamptonshire, 1960–76," *The Archaeological Journal* 134 (1977): 105–14.

[56] Cf. Stephen Parry, *Raunds Area Survey: An Archaeological Study of the Landscape of Raunds, Northamptonshire 1985–94* (Oxford, 2006), 172–77.

The Prittlewell burial has been used in this discussion as an illustration of how inseparable the domestic experience was from a mind-set that also encompassed metaphysical ideas about human life, thus finding its place in a coherent spectrum of material culture along with funerary practices. Whoever actually was buried at Prittlewell—a prince, possibly even a king, of the East Saxons—he was in a real sense a predecessor of Byrhtnoth, the ealdorman of Essex killed at Maldon in 991: the elegy for whom has also proved useful illustrative evidence in this discussion. It may help to encapsulate the ideas and connexions that have been discussed in this paper to reflect upon the posthumous treatment and veneration of Byrhtnoth's body as a further instructive vignette. His headless body was reportedly retrieved from the battlefield by the monks of Ely and entombed in their abbey, where it was re-interred beneath a carved effigy, reportedly in 1154.[57] The absence of the head—an absence that was itself a token of martyrdom—was emphasized by the provision of a ball of wax in its place. There were also monuments outside the tomb: the wall-hanging commissioned by his widow, Ælfflæd, and the literary eulogies of the *Vita Oswaldi*, from Ramsey, and *The Battle of Maldon*, followed later by *Liber Eliensis* and medieval historians such as John of Worcester. The fictive but symbolic account in the *Liber Eliensis* has the significant anecdote of how Byrhtnoth, a patron and benefactor of several religious houses, sought support from Ramsey and Ely immediately before the battle of Maldon, but received it only from Ely.[58] Ely, then, was true—but true in its *dealings* with its lord—not simply blindly and devotedly subservient. Just as was the case with the other, minor heroes of Maldon, of all the houses Byrhtnoth might have thought to have been his own, Ely was, as a result of its support before the battle, the one that maintained his renown and to which he came bodily home in death:

Uton wē hycgan   hwær wē hām āgen
ond þonne geþencan   hū wē þider cumen

['Let us think where we might have a home
And then consider how we may get there']

These words are found towards the end of *The Seafarer* (lines 117–118). The sentiment, and in particular the variability implied by those two subjunctives, were indeed deeply embedded in the Anglo-Saxon experience.

---

[57] Elizabeth Coatsworth, "Byrhtnoth's Tomb," in *The Battle of Maldon, AD 991*, ed. D. G. Scragg (Oxford, 1991), 279–88.

[58] Janet Fairweather, trans., *Liber Eliensis* (Woodbridge, 2005), 2.62.

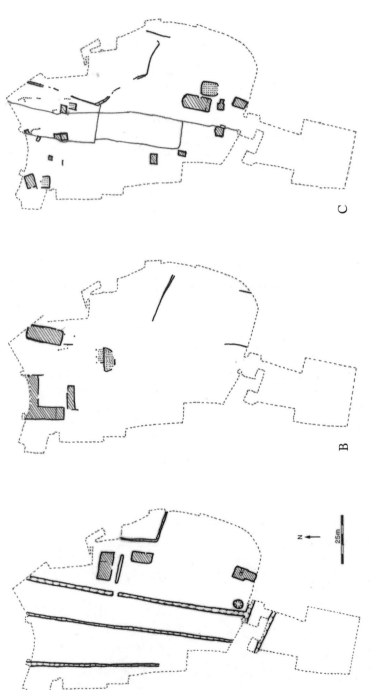

Figure 2.2. Successive settlement layouts in the excavated area of North Elmham Park, Norfolk. Redrawn after Wade–Martins, *North Elmham*: (a) Period I, at phase 2: early to mid-ninth century; (b) Period II, at phase 3: late tenth century; (c) Period III, at phase 2: mid-eleventh century. Ditches, fences, and one well are shown; shaded buildings are probable houses, stippled buildings probable structures for storage or working areas, with at least one open side. For scale and orientation, see (a).

ON THE DANISH ORIGINS
OF THE *BEOWULF* STORY

JOHN D. NILES

1. Introduction

It is now twenty years since the remains of a massive hall dating from the late Germanic Iron Age and the Viking Age (ca. AD 680–1000) were discovered just west of the village of Gammel Lejre, on the island of Zealand, Denmark.[1] Scholars concerned with *Beowulf* have now had some time to digest that interesting fact. If the opportunity has not been seized upon as yet, this period of inertia may have less to do with the less-than-lightning-like pace of advances in medieval studies in general than with the idiosyncratic tendency of many Anglo-Saxonists

---

[1] These excavations were undertaken in 1986–1988. They were reported by Tom Christensen in his book *Lejre—Syn og Sagn* (Roskilde, 1991) and his article "Lejre Beyond Legend—The Archaeological Evidence," *Journal of Danish Archaeology* 10 (1991): 163–85. The former study is now included in English translation in J. D. Niles, *Beowulf and Lejre* (Tempe, AZ, 2007), 13–101. For the sake of simplicity, I speak of "the hall" when referring to what Christensen calls Houses III and IV at Lejre, or Houses III, IVa, and IVb; the archaeological record here is a complex one that involves several stages of rebuilding and repair. Similarly, when speaking henceforth of Gammel Lejre, I will refer to it simply as "Lejre," ignoring the fact that a more modern village of that name is located about 1 km to the south, at the local railway station. — A short illustrated version of the present essay was presented, under the title *"Beowulf* and Lejre: The Continental Connection," at the biennial meeting of ISAS held in Munich in 2005, and I am grateful to many persons in attendance on that occasion for their comments. Some maps and illustrations that were used then appear in J. D. Niles, "Beowulf's Great Hall," *History Today* 56:10 (October 2006): 40–44; in addition, numerous maps and illustrations are included in *Beowulf and Lejre*, passim, and so there is no need to include such materials here. I am grateful to Tom Christensen and Marijane Osborn for their invaluable contributions to that book and for their expert advice on many matters. Neither of them is responsible for any claims made here, however.

Hans Sauer and Joanna Story, eds., *Anglo-Saxon England and the Continent*. With the assistance of Gaby Waxenberger. Essays in Anglo-Saxon Studies, vol. 3. MRTS 394. Tempe: ACMRS, 2011.   [ISBN 978-0-86698-442-3]

to be looking the other way when something arresting is happening somewhere other than in Britain.

The shock felt in many quarters just now, however, is that renewed excavations undertaken at Lejre during the summers of 2004–2005 have uncovered the remains of a second hall.[2] This hall, built at a spot about half a kilometer north of the other one, is of comparable size but earlier date, for as far as can be told at present it was built ca. AD 550. The relevance of this discovery to *Beowulf* studies needs no belaboring, for the whole first part of that poem is set at the hall of the Scylding kings during a period that, while unspecified in the poem, has been taken to be roughly the early sixth century AD.[3] As for the Scylding kings of *Beowulf*, they are universally acknowledged to be equivalent to the far-famed Skjöldung kings of Danish tradition; and in Old Norse and medieval Latin sources, the Skjöldung dynasty is firmly localized at Lejre.[4]

What might be called the missing link of *Beowulf* studies has therefore now been found—and found in duplicate. For many years, informed persons have localized the action of the first part of that poem at Lejre, near the modern city of Roskilde, on the basis of what Saxo Grammaticus and other medieval authorities have to say about the location of the chief seat of the Skjöldungs.[5] The *Beowulf* poet, however, makes no mention of Lejre or any other specific place in Denmark when speaking of the Scyldings' hall. Until now, moreover, the absence of archaeological evidence confirming that Lejre was an important settlement during this period of prehistory has left room for doubt regarding the location of the

---

[2] The only report published as yet is T. Christensen, "A New Round of Excavations at Lejre (to 2005)," in Niles, *Beowulf and Lejre*, 109–26.

[3] At p. xxxi and p. xxxviii of his introduction to *Beowulf and The Fight at Finnsburg*, 3rd edn. with 1st and 2nd supplements (Lexington, MA, 1950), Fr. Klaeber assigns approximate hypothetical dates to the Danish, Geatish, and Swedish kings who figure in the action of the poem; his dates range from AD 445 to 545.

[4] Texts and modern English translations of the chief medieval sources that speak of Lejre as the home of the Skjölding kings are gathered together (excerpted where necessary) in Niles, *Beowulf and Lejre*, 295–387. These sources are the eddic-style Old Icelandic lay known as *Grottasöngr*, difficult to date; the anonymous Latin *Chronicon Lethrense*, difficult to date, but perhaps of the late twelfth century; Sven Aggesen's *Brevis historia regum Dacii*, a Latin chronicle of the late twelfth century; the anonymous Old Norse *Skjöldunga saga*, as known chiefly from Arngrímur Jónsson's sixteenth-century Latin paraphrase; Saxo Grammaticus' great Latin *Gesta Danorum*, of the late twelfth or early thirteenth century; excerpts from Snorri Sturluson's *Ynglinga saga* and *Skáldskaparmál*, two Old Icelandic works of the early thirteenth century; and the Old Icelandic *Hrólfs saga kraka*, usually dated to the early fifteenth century.

[5] Thus Klaeber, *Beowulf and The Fight at Finnsburg*, xxxvii; also, with more detailed discussion, R. W. Chambers, *Beowulf: An Introduction to the Study of the Poem*, 3rd edn. (Cambridge, 1959), 16–20.

hall the poet names "Heorot."[6] The tendency among specialists during the past fifty years or so has therefore been to let the matter drop.

That situation has now changed, and the significance of these new finds should be evaluated. This task is not as straightforward as one might think. At no other major settlement pertaining to the Iron Age and the Viking Age in southern Scandinavia is there evidence of two halls having been built on separate but closely related sites, the second in succession to the first. This fact calls for explanation, both for its own historical interest and in relation to *Beowulf* studies. In addition, only at Lejre does one find evidence of a great cremation mound having been built up in close proximity to an Iron Age or Viking Age hall. The presence at Lejre of the mound named Grydehøj, which has now been C¹⁴ dated to the period ca. AD 630–650, needs to be factored into whatever thinking takes place concerning the two halls that once stood here.[7]

2. On the Semantics of Size

What is impressive about these monuments at Lejre is first of all their size. Although size might seem to be so self-evidently an aspect of a hall or a cremation mound as not to be worth dwelling upon, one should not forget that during this period even more than today, the perceived worth of an item (a torque, a retinue, a ship, a building) tended to be in direct ratio to its size.

If one looks at the whole of southern Scandinavia during the Germanic Iron Age and the Viking Age, only two halls have been discovered of a size comparable to the ones at Lejre, which measured about 47 m and 48.5 m in length, respectively. These are, first, the hall built at Gudme, a major cult center on the neighboring island of Funen, during the period AD 350–500 (ca. 47 m in length), and, second, the hall built at the military stronghold of Tissø, near the west coast of Zealand, in the late tenth century (ca. 48 m in length).[8] The width

---

[6] Attempts by modern scholars to localize the action of the first part of *Beowulf* either at Lejre or elsewhere are reviewed by Marijane Osborn, "The Lejre Connection in *Beowulf* Scholarship," in Niles, *Beowulf and Lejre*, 287–93. The name *Heorot* occurs only in *Beowulf* (with variant spellings) and in *Widsith*.

[7] Harald Andersen, "Hovedstaden i riget," *Nationalmuseets Arbejdsmark* (Copenhagen, 1960), 13–35; Steen Wulff Andersen, "Lejre—skipssætninger, vikingegrave, Grydehøj," *Aarbøger for Nordisk Oldkyndighed og Historie* (1993): 7–142. An English translation of excerpts from the former study is included in Niles, *Beowulf and Lejre*, at 129–38; an English-language summary of the latter study is included at 143–57.

[8] Lars Jørgensen, "From Tribute to the Estate System, 3rd–12th Century," in *Kingdoms and Regionality: Transactions from the 49th Sachsensymposium 1998 in Uppsala* (Stockholm, 2001), 73–82, evaluates these three Danish sites in relation to one another, with bibliography. The most up-to-date and authoritative survey of Danish prehistoric archaeology is Jørgen Jensen, *Danmarks Oldtid*, 4 vols. (Copenhagen, 2001–2004); of particular

of these halls is also important to take into account, for a difference of only a few meters in width can produce a significant difference in height and interior volume. The hall at Gudme, the first and second halls at Lejre, and the hall at Tissø measured respectively 10 m, 7.5 m, 11.5 m, and 12.5 m in breadth at their midpoint, which was their widest point since each of these buildings was slightly tapered toward its gable ends. To put these numbers into perspective, the houses in the well-known late tenth-century military camp at Trelleborg in southwestern Zealand measured close to 30 m long by 8 m wide.[9] The seventh-century hall at Yeavering, Northumberland, which is the largest such building known from early Anglo-Saxon England, measured close to 25 m long by 12 m wide.[10]

As for the mound named Grydehøj, it is badly eroded today. When new, however, it is estimated to have measured 36–40 m in diameter and 4–5 m in height. The funeral pyre that was kindled there is estimated to have covered 380 m² of ground. While larger funeral mounds than this are known from elsewhere in Europe (e.g. at Old Uppsala in Sweden, and there are many examples from the region of the steppes),[11] this was an impressive monument to set beside a Danish hall, or for some Danes to have set a great hall beside. The only mounds built in southern Scandinavia during the late Germanic Iron Age that are comparable to Grydehøj in size are a pair located at Slots Bjergby near Slagesle, west Zealand; but the larger of these, the one named Galgehøj ('Gallows Hill,' measuring 50 m across and 5 m high), was not made from scratch at that time but was built on top of a prehistoric barrow of earlier date, so the comparison is not a true one.[12]

The upshot of these remarks is that each of these structures built at Lejre was a major statement inscribed upon the land. Structures like these could only have been built by important people, or in honor of important people, though today we have no way of knowing who those people were. The semantics of these monuments is written in large bold font, even if the script is hard to read.

---

relevance to the present chapter are his vol. 3: *Ældre Jernalder* (2003) and vol. 4: *Yngre Jernalder og Vikingetid* (2004).

[9] Steen Wulff Andersen, *The Viking Fortress of Trelleborg* (Slagelse, 1996), provides a guide to this brief-lived but impressive site, together with information about the system of fortresses of which it formed one part.

[10] The basic guide to this complex site is Brian Hope-Taylor, *Yeavering: An Anglo-Saxon British Centre of Early Northumbria* (London, 1977).

[11] Renate Rolle, *Die Welt der Skythen* (Luzern, 1980); *The World of the Scythians*, trans. F. G. Walls (Berkeley, 1989). Pages 19–54 (of the English edition) in particular are relevant to the question of the influence of the mound culture of the steppes on northern Europe. See recently Walter Pohl, "The *Regia* and the *Hring*: Barbarian Places of Power," in *Topographies of Power in the Early Middle Ages*, ed. Mayke de Jong and Frans Theuws (Leiden, 2001), 439–66, and, especially, Lotte Hedeager, "Scandinavia and the Huns: An Interdisciplinary Approach to the Migration Era," *Norwegian Archaeological Review* 40 (2007): 42–58.

[12] Jensen, *Danmarks Oldtid*, 4: 191–92.

When, therefore, the *Beowulf* poet speaks of King Hrothgar as building 'the biggest of halls' (*healærna mæst*, 78a), 'the best of halls' (*húsa sēlest*, 146a, 285b, 658b, 935a) 'one that the children of men have heard of ever since' (*þone yldo bearn æfre gefrūnon*, 70)[13] we can be sure that the members of his audience would have thought of those words as having some possible truth value. The Scyldings did live in a place where the greatest hall of its era had stood (or, to be precise, the *fictional* Scyldings were *attributed* life in such a hall, for we must not be fooled into thinking of these literary and legendary figures as having flesh-and-blood reality). Likewise, when the fictive hero Beowulf, having sacrificed his life for his people, is buried in a mound that is 'high and broad' (*hēah ond brād*, 3157b) after his corpse has been consumed by 'the biggest of funeral pyres' (*bǣlfyra mǣst*, 3143b), such statements would have had the ring of truth about them for anyone who knew anything about Lejre. In the old pagan days referred to in this poem, pyres were kindled and mounds were built for great kings and heroes: anyone who had visited Lejre would have seen a very large mound of that kind there. Of course we all know that in the poet's narrative account, Beowulf is not a Dane and his pyre is located in the land of the Geatas, wherever that shadowy people might be thought to have lived[14]—but still, the cluster of monuments at Lejre lends verisimilitude to the ensemble of themes in the poem.

3. The Role of the Vikings in Britain in the Dissemination of Danish Legends

As is well known, the action of *Beowulf* is set almost entirely in Scandinavia. The setting of the first part of the poem is Denmark during what modern scholars have called the Migration Age, or the Heroic Age, or simply the late Germanic

---

[13] Quotations of *Beowulf* in the present chapter are from *Klaeber's Beowulf and The Fight at Finnsburg*, 4th edn., ed. R. D. Fulk, Robert E. Bjork, and J. D. Niles (Toronto, 2008). In the third of the three quotations just given, however, MS *þone* is restored for editorial *þon[n]e*, and the translation is adjusted accordingly; this is in keeping with a suggestion made by Fred C. Robinson in *The Editing of Old English* (Oxford, 1994), 47–52, though my translation of that line differs from his.

[14] Although this topic cannot be taken up here, I address it in a chapter titled "Anglo-Saxon Heroic Geography: How (on Earth) Can It Be Mapped?" in J. D. Niles, *Old English Heroic Poems and the Social Life of Texts* (Turnhout, 2007), 119–40. There I also address (at 140) a question that is not raised in the present article but that might occur to some readers; namely, why, if Zealand was an important place in late ninth-century Denmark, does Ohthere, King Alfred's informant about the geography of that region, not mention it? In brief, the answer is that Ohthere does mention it (under the name *Sillende* in the Old English Orosius), but this reference has been misconstrued by most modern scholars as referring to the southeast of Jutland.

Iron Age. Much is said (or alluded to) here and there in the poem about the dynastic affairs of the Scylding family of kings.

The Danes had reasons to care about these people. The English did not, apparently, until such time as appreciable numbers of Danes had settled in Britain, bringing stories of the Skjöldungs with them.[15] The means by which story materials of this kind made their way across the North Sea have sometimes been discussed inconclusively in the past, and now is an appropriate time to reopen that topic.[16]

By the late tenth century, one or more versions of the Old English poem we know as *Beowulf* existed in oral tradition and/or script. By this same time, many people of Danish descent were living in the eastern regions of Britain. Having migrated into Britain after various Viking chieftains had ravaged the land and after either those warlords or their compatriots had established centers of power in Yorkshire, Lincolnshire, and East Anglia, Danish settlers had established farms, villages, and towns in these areas in the midst of a native English-speaking population. During the tenth century, even after the three main parts of the Danelaw were absorbed into the single kingdom of England, Scandinavian influence in these parts remained strong. The North Sea routes between Denmark and the east coast of Britain would have remained open, while Danish merchants

---

[15] The earliest mention of Scyld occurs in four manuscripts of the *Anglo-Saxon Chronicle* under the year 855 (the obit for King Alfred's father, King Æthelwulf). This annal is now believed to have been part of the original Alfredian compilation of the *Chronicle*, dating from ca. 890–892. The presence of Scyld (spelled *Scyldwa*, *Sceldwea*, or otherwise) in this genealogy almost certainly represents an Anglo-Saxon appropriation of Danish traditions. Alfred's biographer Asser (ca. 893) also mentions Scyld (spelled *Sceldwea*) in his version of the West Saxon royal genealogy, as does Æthelweard, the author of the late tenth-century *Chronicon*, who uses the spelling *Scyld* as in *Beowulf*. Information about these sources is given in Alexander M. Bruce, *Scyld and Scef: Expanding the Analogues* (New York, 2002), particularly in his chap. 3: "Scyld and Scef in English Genealogies of the Anglo-Saxon Period" (31–41). They are discussed by Alexander Callander Murray, "*Beowulf*, the Danish Invasions, and Royal Genealogy," in *The Dating of Beowulf*, ed. Colin Chase (Toronto, 1981), 101–11, and Audrey Meaney, "Scyld Scefing and the Dating of *Beowulf*—Again," in *Textual and Material Culture in Anglo-Saxon England*, ed. Donald Scragg (Cambridge, 2003), 23–73 (an augmented reprint of an article published in 1989).

[16] Some topics of possible interest will have to be ignored here. These include the questions of why Lejre developed into a place of importance in central Denmark; how it came to pass that legends of the Skjöldung kings were localized at Lejre and not elsewhere; what the political relationship may have been between Lejre and other Danish central places of the period AD 500–1000; how Grydehøj fits into this picture; and what relation, if any, there is between the unusual Ice Age landscape at Lejre and the *Beowulf* poet's eerie description of Grendel's mere. I deal with these questions in my main contribution to *Beowulf and Lejre* (169–233).

based in Ribe, Hedeby, York, London, and other urban centers are likely to have visited ports here and there in Britain, not just in the Danelaw.[17]

Stories generally move with people; they do not waft through thin air.[18] To the extent that people were crossing between Denmark and Britain during the period beginning ca. AD 835 and continuing well into the tenth century, conditions were favorable for the dissemination of Danish cultural elements of all kinds into Britain. During this period, bilingualism would have been common (especially among merchants). Intermarriage between the two populations surely took place, though the extent of it is hard to ascertain. On occasion, English kings patronized Danish skalds and/or took on Danish retainers.[19] All these bilingual settings provided opportunities for cultural exchange. To the extent that Danes of Denmark, Anglo-Danes, and English-speaking inhabitants of Britain were talking with one another, stories can easily have moved back and forth between these groups. Early-daters of *Beowulf* may wish to point out that Danish lore and story materials could have traveled into Britain at an earlier time, as well. True. Still, as R. I. Page has documented with many specific examples,[20] it was during the Viking period that conditions were especially favorable for cultural commerce of this kind. Before the first Viking raids occurred in 793 there is no

---

[17] Still authoritative in his treatment of this period is H. R. Loyn, *The Vikings in Britain*, 2nd edn. (Oxford, 1994), first published 1977. For recent perspectives see *Cultures in Contact: Scandinavian Settlement in England in the Ninth and Tenth Centuries*, ed. Dawn M. Hadley and Julian D. Richards (Turnhout, 2000) and *Vikings and the Danelaw*, ed. James Graham-Campbell et al. (Oxford, 2001). An invaluable study of linguistic interactions is Matthew Townend, *Language and History in Viking Age England* (Turnhout, 2002).

[18] This premise underlies the modern science of folktale research, including research of the historic-geographic kind that forms the basis of Antti Aarne and Stith Thompson, *The Types of the Folktale*, FF Communications 184 (Helsinki, 1961), now superseded by Hans-Jörg Uther, *The Types of International Folktales: A Classification and Bibliography*, 3 vols., FF Communications 284–286 (Helsinki, 2004).

[19] Roberta Frank, "Skaldic Verse and the Date of *Beowulf*," in Chase, *The Dating of Beowulf*, 123–39.

[20] R. I. Page, "The Audience of *Beowulf* and the Vikings," in Chase, *The Dating of Beowulf*, 113–22, cites many examples of Anglo-Danish contacts in circumstances where something other than hostility was involved. He takes ca. 835 as the time when "Viking invasions began in earnest" (113), and so I use that date here as a convenient marker even though interchanges between Anglo-Saxons and Danes are more frequent and meaningful during the second half of the ninth century and later. Page emphasizes that English hostility to the Danes was to some extent based on religion rather than ethnicity (118–19), and thus was subject to diminishment as the Danes in Britain converted to Christianity. He also notes that during the first part of the tenth century, as the English kings gradually won control of the Danelaw, "the distinction between Danish settler and Anglo-Saxon must have weakened" (121); in other words, the two populations were merging.

direct evidence of a Scandinavian presence in Britain unless one goes back to the period of the initial fifth- and sixth-century migration of the Angles and other Germanic-speaking peoples from the Continent—and the main period of those migrations surely predates both the development of the Skjöldung legend-cycle and the building of the first hall at Lejre.

As for Lejre, although it was important in the Neolithic period and the Bronze Age, archaeological evidence suggesting that it had any significance in the Iron Age before ca. 550 is lacking. By the time of the ninth-century Viking expansion into Britain, however, it had become an important regional center. Although one can only speculate on this point, it was perhaps a royal center as well, whether for kings of Zealand or for kings of what can perhaps be called Denmark, if it is licit to speak of a nascent Danish kingdom at so early a date.[21] Thietmar of Merseburg, writing in the early eleventh century, speaks of Lejre as formerly having been *caput istius regni* 'the capital of this realm'—that is, Denmark,[22] while Sven Aggesen, writing somewhat later about Lejre's period of greatness, speaks of it as *tunc famosissima regis* [. . .] *curia* 'the king's most famous residence at that time',[23] for what these two reports are worth.

If Lejre was an important place during the centuries leading up to the end of the first millennium, it is not unreasonable to think that during the tenth-century period when *Beowulf* was evidently in circulation, there were people in Britain who had with their own eyes seen its Viking Age hall and the mound now called Grydehøj. Other people might have heard at second hand of Lejre's hall, and they might also have heard of its predecessor, the Iron Age hall that had once stood a short walk away.

To speak about "conditions for the dissemination of Danish cultural elements" is one thing, however. To speak about the actual transfer of stories about the Skjöldungs to Britain is another. That more specific topic now deserves brief attention.

Whether tales about the heroic deeds and sufferings of the ancient Skjöldung line of kings ever circulated widely in Anglo-Saxon England cannot now be known. The fame of those legendary figures eventually became so widespread in northern Europe, however, as to lend plausibility to that thought. Legends of the Skjöldungs had become a foundational aspect of Danish cultural and national identity by the end of the twelfth century, by which time Sven Aggesen, Saxo Grammaticus, and the anonymous authors of the *Chronicon Lethrense* and the *Skjöldunga saga* had written or were writing their respective accounts of the deeds of those kings. How

---

[21] Ulf Näsman, "The Ethnogenesis of the Danes and the Making of a Danish Kingdom," *Anglo-Saxon Studies in Archaeology and History* 10 (1999): 1–10.

[22] *Die Chronik des Bischofs Thietmar von Merseburg*, ed. Robert Holtzmann (Berlin, 1935), 23.

[23] *Scriptores Minores Historiæ Danicæ*, ed. M. Cl. Gertz, 2 vols. (Copenhagen, 1917–1922), 1: 94–141, at 96.

old these legends were by that time remains a mystery,[24] but when the *Beowulf* poet alludes to the future destruction of the Scyldings' hall (82b–85) as a result of a feud involving Hrothgar's son-in-law Ingeld (2020–2069a), he does so in an oblique manner that suggests that his audience was already familiar with the gist of this feud: namely, that Ingeld was the son of Froda, who had been killed by (or had killed?) Hrothgar's older brother Healfdene.[25] The author of *Widsith* refers to the outcome of this feud as well:[26]

> Hroþwulf ond Hroðgar heoldon lengest
> sibbe ætsomne suhtorfædran,
> siþþan hy forwræcon wicinga cynn
> ond Ingeldes ord forbigdan,
> forheowan æt Heorote Heaðobeardna þrym.   (45–49)

> ['Hrothwulf and Hrothgar maintained their mutual bonds of peace and kinship for a very long time after they destroyed the race of Vikings and forced Ingeld's vanguard into submission, hewed down at Heorot the glory of the Heathobards.']

One imagines that this poet's intended audience, too, was supposed to know the gist of this story: namely, that Ingeld, taking up his father's feud despite his marriage to Hrothgar's daughter, mounted a fierce attack on the Skjöldungs' hall but was soundly defeated. If a modern reader is somewhat amused to notice the cultural appropriation whereby, in this poem from the Exeter Book, Hrothgar and Hrothwulf are bent on destroying Vikings when the Danes of the Anglo-Scandinavian period doubtless thought of Ro and Rolf, the counterparts of these two figures, as great progenitors of Vikings, this is a typical wrinkle among the ethnic reconfigurations of this era.

What I wish to take up now in greater detail, though, is the process by which the long, complex Old English poem that we call *Beowulf* may have emerged out

---

[24] Not to be taken lightly, though I do not in the end find it convincing, is the suggestion made by Frank that "the Scyldings and their legends may have been an Anglo-Danish innovation" ("Skaldic Verse and the Date of *Beowulf*," 129). What Frank does successfully show in this article is that there is no need to think of these legends as having great antiquity; that Anglo-Danish contacts contributed a good deal to their dissemination; and that Scandinavian skalds, some of whom found patronage in Britain, were important intermediaries in this process.

[25] These are the *Beowulf* poet's forms of the latter two names; the Danish forms are *Ro* and *Haldan*, respectively. There is no agreement in the various sources concerning who killed whom in the earlier stage of this feud, though in *Beowulf* it is Ingeld's father who is killed.

[26] *The Exeter Book*, ed. George Philip Krapp and Elliott Van Kirk Dobbie, ASPR 3 (New York, 1936), 150–51. The *Hroþwulf* of *Widsith* corresponds to Danish *Rolf* (Old Norse *Hrólfr*).

of much simpler source materials. Granted, this question involves much speculation. The process by which the poem's constituent elements evolved into the
unique form that they have in London, BL, Cotton Vitellius A.xv can only be
inferred from a few points of light in the midst of a very large expanse of black-
ness. Still, this topic is worth addressing in response to the recent discoveries at
Lejre, where archaeology has illuminated a good deal more ground than before.

4. On Oneness and Twoness, and on Gold and Silver

At the risk of stating the obvious, the first thing that strikes one as interesting
about the halls at Lejre is that there are two of them. Oneness represents unity,
singularity, indivisibility. Oneness basks in its oneness. Twoness introduces the
dynamics of opposition. With two halls there is the possibility of a there and a
here, a then and a now, a them and an us. When two halls are built very close
to one another in different eras, there is the potential for dialogue between the
centuries, and legendary history can progress.

Though I see no way of proving this point, it seems to me a reasonable
hypothesis that the Skjöldung kings, for whom no real claims of historicity can
be made,[27] are very largely the invention of people dwelling in or around the second hall at Lejre who looked back at the people who had dwelled in the first hall,
which would not have been forgotten, and thought of them as pertaining to a lost
heroic world. The physical presence of the mound Grydehøj at Lejre could have
stimulated such induced memories. For anyone living in the Viking Age, that
earlier sixth- and seventh-century world could easily have seemed like an Age of
Gold—quite literally so, when one considers the amount of pure gold that was in
circulation in Scandinavia at that time, some of it wrought into exquisite material
objects that may have still been visible on occasion as heirlooms.

Heorot is literally gilded, the *Beowulf* poet states (it is *goldfāh*, 308a). Its roof
is gilded (926b–927a), and its mead-benches too are adorned with gold (*golde
geregnad*, 777a). Thereby endowed with an almost preternatural light, the hall
shines over many lands: *līxte se lēoma ofer landa fela* (311). Likewise, the people
pertaining to the era depicted in the poem exhibit moral qualities that shine
with an almost superhuman glow. Heorot is to any ordinary large building as

---

[27] Here, though it is inessential to my reasoning, I accept in its general features the
argument made by Niels C. Lukman, *Skjoldunge und Skilfinge: Hunnen- und Herulerkönige
in ostnordischer Überlieferung*, Classica et Mediaevalia Dissertationes 3 (Copenhagen,
1943) that some of the personal names of the Skjöldung kings are of Hunnish or Herulian
origin. The implication of that argument is that the fame of several prominent members
of these latter tribes, circulating in Scandinavia, stimulated the growth of a cycle of legends concerning the "Skjöldungs," or 'sons of Skjold' (that latter name, 'Shield,' being an
obvious invention).

Hrothgar is to any actual king and ring-giver, or as Beowulf is to any flesh-and-blood hero, or as Grendel is to any ordinary killer. Everything in the world of *Beowulf* is larger or more magnificent or more horrible than life—and this is what is meant when one speaks of a heroic poem, or of the heroic imagination.

The cycle of legends about the Skjöldung kings and their doomed fortress becomes explicable when one entertains the idea that these legends emerged in retrospect, when people who lived at Lejre in a later age began telling tales about what had once taken place at that same place, when people like the great person who was cremated at Grydehøj (whoever that person was) walked this very ground.

When one thinks of that later Viking period, what one is struck by is how much it resembles an Age of Silver. Not literally, of course. Halls and other buildings were not constructed of silver joists and beams. But not merely metaphorically, either. Silver was the basic currency for the Vikings;[28] it was their gold standard, if a paradox will be forgiven. Silver coins and hack silver were apparently exchanged on an equal footing on the basis of weight. The quantity of silver coins minted in Anglo-Saxon England that came into Scandinavian hands during the late ninth, the tenth, and the early eleventh centuries cannot easily be estimated, but it was huge. When, about the year 890, some Danes of the Viking period rebuilt their hall at Lejre from the bottom up, shifting it very slightly in position as they did so,[29] what paid for this work of reconstruction was surely a surplus of silver. Some of this wealth may even have come from Britain, for some of the Vikings' best successes had taken place recently in that island.[30]

So the dynamic quality of twoness at Lejre had to do not only with then and now, there and here, them and us, but also with gold and silver. Speaking in practical terms, the men and women of old tied their social knots in gold, in a gift economy, while the men and women of later times did their dealings in silver, in a mercantile economy. Metaphorically, the contrast of gold and silver has to do with the difference between ideals in their golden state and ideals in their silver state, once the metal of virtue has become subject to tarnishing. An awareness of this contrast, imposed in diachronical terms upon the past, has always been a driving force in the generation of heroic legends.

---

[28] This topic is treated by Birgitta Hårdh, *Silver in the Viking Age*, Acta Archaeologica Lundensia, series in 8°, 25 (Stockholm, 1996).

[29] See Christensen, "Lejre Beyond Legend," and idem in Niles, *Beowulf and Lejre*. The distinction is between House III and House IV, two stages of construction on the same site.

[30] The near coincidence of the year 890, an approximate date obtained through C[14] testing of some of the remains of timbers used for the reconstruction of the Viking Age hall at Lejre, with the dates associated with the consolidation of the Danelaw (878) and the treaty between Alfred and Guthrum (between 886 and 890), will not go unnoticed.

5. On a Gentle Landscape and a Not-So-Gentle One

A second point of interest about the Lejre settlement also has to do with oppositional dynamics, this time figured in spatial terms. Each of the two halls at Lejre
occupied a similar position relative to the surrounding topography, in that each
was situated in the midst of some gentle fields that directly abut an inhospitable
hinterland known to specialists in Ice Age geology as a dead-ice landscape.[31] The
open fields are amenable to agriculture, animal husbandry, horse racing, and so
forth. The dead-ice hinterland is not. The open fields directly overlook several
stream valleys (the valleys of Lejre River, Kornerup River, and the smaller brook
known as Hjorterende) that once ran with a supply of fresh water.[32] The dead-ice
hinterland is dotted with stagnant pools, bogs, and marshes interspersed among
hillocks, some of which are densely wooded. In its oppositional qualities, the
physical topography of the Lejre area is thus amenable to stories featuring the
dualistic clash of two separate realms (call them culture and nature) inhabited by
two different sorts of creatures (call them men and monsters).[33]

The dualistic character of the landscape at Lejre cannot fail to make an
impression on a person who sets out for a walk in this area, especially if one
progresses from the gentle area nearby the former hall sites to the less hospitable
area that one enters no more than a kilometer away to the west. The transition from cultivated fields to narrow paths threading through woods and by the
banks of lakes and pools is quite distinct. In addition, the dualistic quality of
this landscape shows up clearly when one studies the geographical distribution
of prehistoric remains in this area. If you were to draw up a map plotting all the
evidences of prehistoric settlement in the Lejre region—and the map will show
quite a lot of such evidence, going back to the Stone Age—they form a kind of

---

[31] Axel Schou, "The Landscapes," in *Atlas of Denmark: Text and Photographs*, ed.
Niels Nielsen (Copenhagen, 1949), 1: 33–34. Much information about the landscape
at Lejre and its evolution is included in *Lejreområdet—dets landskab og historie, frem-
tidig planlægning og pleje* (Copenhagen, 1985), a publication of the Fredningsstyrelsen
(Department of Conservation).

[32] The waterways in this region have been channeled and diverted in modern times,
and it is difficult to reconstruct their exact ancient character. The two halls were built in
obvious proximity to these river valleys, however.

[33] When considering the landscape at Lejre, one must take into account (as in the
previous note) that its appearance today differs from its appearance a thousand or fifteen
hundred years ago. Fields can be cleared and then can revert to nature again. Lakes
can be dammed, streams diverted, woodlands felled, and marshes drained, and all these
things have happened at Lejre. Still, the basic contours of the land here remain much as
they have been since the end of the last Ice Age, and the local ecologies of this region are
not without continuity over time (see n. 31 above).

horseshoe pattern enclosing the dead-ice landscape on three sides.[34] Prehistoric people built monuments and houses to the north of the dead-ice zone (where there are numerous Bronze Age barrows), to the east of it (where there are three Stone Age mounds, several Bronze Age barrows, the two halls, Grydehøj, and the village of Gammel Lejre), and to the south of it (another area dotted with Bronze Age mounds), but for a period of some thousands of years, very few traces of human settlement can be found in the middle of this zone. While deeply inhospitable to normal human use, this region is a natural haven for wildlife. The dead-ice landscape directly west of Lejre is a farmer's nightmare but a hunter's paradise. With the least breath of imagination, a person comfortably situated in a settlement at Lejre could imagine this backwoods area as being populated by creatures hostile to humankind.

Moreover, the ground close by the two hall sites at Lejre is a landscape of the dead. It has been so at least since the Neolithic period, when the people who lived in this area built the mounds now named Harald Hildetandshøj, Ravenshøj, Pilehøj, and other funeral monuments in this area. During the Bronze Age especially, enough tumuli were built in the neighborhood of Lejre to confirm its character as a mound landscape. Later on, when unknown persons living in the sixth century AD decided to build a great hall at this site (probably in imitation of the hall that had previously stood at the cult center of Gudme, 100 kilometers to the west), they must have done so not just because Lejre was located in a strategically central position among the Danish territories, but also because the landscape here had already been sacralized. It was already a place of power, even though the civilizations that had built those ancient mounds had long since been superseded. It is not by accident that the first of the two halls constructed at Lejre was built right into the side of a Bronze Age mound—an arresting example of the perceived importance of the past in the past.[35]

6. Beowulf *and* Hrólfs saga kraka

When one takes the topography at Lejre into account, then, one can scarcely be surprised that stories of hall hauntings came to be associated with this place. When a dead-ice landscape easily identified with what is wild and inhuman directly adjoins a hall representing an ideal of civilization, then we have the ingredients of a good scare story. This is especially true seeing that when one looks about the Lejre area in practically any direction, what one sees is a funeral

---

[34] See *Lejreområdet—dets landskab og historie*, the maps on 29 (*Stenalder*), 31 (*Bronzealder*), and 33 (*Jernalder*).

[35] For discussion of insular examples of this phenomenon see Howard Williams, "Monuments and the Past in Early Anglo-Saxon England," *World Archaeology* 30 (1998): 90–108. The theme of this issue of that journal is "The Past in the Past."

mound: a house of the dead. For the first hall at Lejre to have been built right
against a Bronze Age barrow was an open invitation for storytellers to exercise
their talents.

Still, it is a curiosity of the legendary history of the Skjöldungs that of all the
medieval authors who wrote about them, only two—the *Beowulf* poet and the
author of the late Old Icelandic *Hrólfs saga kraka*—speak of the haunting of these
kings' hall. It almost seems as though anyone living in medieval Europe who
knew anything at all about ancient Scandinavia knew about the Skjöldungs, and
yet the theme of the hall of those kings being attacked by one or more malignant
creatures is found only in these two sources.

This seems to me a problem that needs addressing, for it has a direct bearing
on an important question regarding the evolution of the *Beowulf* story. Did the
story of the haunting of the Skjöldungs' hall migrate from Denmark to Britain
(and also to Iceland), or was this essential ingredient of the *Beowulf* story a later,
insular development? The existence of *Hrólfs saga kraka* is crucial to note in this
connection, for if that saga did not exist in addition to *Beowulf*, this question
would be unanswerable.[36]

There are in essence three possibilities: (a) The *Beowulf* poet and the author
of *Hrólfs saga kraka* made up such a tale independently of each other. Or, (b) the
later Icelandic author was influenced by the earlier Anglo-Saxon author (or by
the tradition of *Beowulf* in Britain) and developed his plot accordingly. Or, (c) the
story of the haunting of the Skjöldungs' hall was part of an original Danish legend complex, and yet it survived only on the periphery of Scandinavia (in Britain
and Iceland) and not in Denmark itself, where other stories about the Skjöldungs
took precedence over this one and eventually drove it out.

Counting against the first of these options is the improbability that two
similar stories whose action is situated at the same place, the hall of the Skjöldungs in Denmark, should have developed independently of each other. There
are enough points of resemblance between *Beowulf* and *Hrólfs saga kraka* to confirm that these narratives derive from a common tradition.[37] One example is

---

[36] The saga has recently been ably translated by Jesse L. Byock, *The Saga of King Hrolf
Kraki* (London, 1998), with introductory notes on "Skjold and the Skjoldung Dynasty:
The Legendary Past," "Archaeology and the Legendary Hleidargard," "*The Saga of King
Hrolf Kraki* and *Beowulf*," and "Beowulf and Bodvar Bjarki: The Bear Warriors" (xiv–
xxviii). Byock was quick to note the importance of the 1986–1988 excavations at Lejre; a
few of his references to Lejre now need updating, however.

[37] Still convincing is Chambers' discussion of this point in *Beowulf: An Introduction*,
54–61. A helpful review of this and nearly all questions relating to *Beowulf* and its Scandinavian analogues is offered by Theodore M. Andersson, "Sources and Analogues," in *A
Beowulf Handbook*, ed. Robert E. Bjork and John D. Niles (Lincoln, NE, 1997), 129–34.
Since Andersson is cool on this particular parallel (131–33), however, I have wanted to
make clear my agreement with Chambers. Cf. the similar view of Tom Shippey in his

the ursine characteristics of the hero (the bear-like Beowulf on the one hand, the bear's son Böðvarr Bjarki on the other).[38] Another is the fact that both protagonists depart from what philologically, at least, is the same homeland (in Old English, the land of the *Geatas*; in Old Icelandic, the land of the *Gautar*) on their way to the land of the Skjöldungs, where each hero provides notable service at the king's hall, freeing it from the depredations of one or more monstrous creatures. The existence of such conspicuous common threads in the design of these two works can scarcely be a matter of coincidence.

Counting against the second option is a different kind of improbability. This is the extremely slim chance that either *Beowulf* or its English tradition, assuming there was such a tradition, had any influence on Icelandic authors. *Beowulf* did not have the status of Bede or the Bible. Although, as is well known, no few Old Icelandic parallels to the action of the poem's Danish episodes have been cited by now in the critical literature, there is no convincing evidence that the Anglo-Saxon poem itself was known in Iceland.[39]

"Afterword" to *Beowulf and Lejre* (at 476–77). Andersson follows Larry D. Benson, "The Originality of *Beowulf*," in *The Interpretation of Narrative: Theory and Practice*, ed. Morton W. Bloomfield (Cambridge, MA, 1970), 1–43 (at 15–19)—who in turn follows Oscar L. Olson, *The Relation of the Hrólfs Saga Kraka and the Bjarkarímur to Beowulf* (Chicago, 1916), esp. 13–20—in discounting the value of *Hrólfs saga kraka* as a parallel to *Beowulf* on the grounds that the Icelandic saga is a late witness to the story and, moreover, one that is embellished by other influences. Benson makes much of the fact that Saxo Grammaticus, writing in about the year 1200, has nothing to say about the role of Biarco (a heroic figure corresponding to Böðvarr bjarki) in delivering the Skjoldungs' hall from monstrous or bestial enemies, or about Biarco's arrival from Gautland. In this regard as in others, however, it is easy to overemphasize Saxo's authority in providing what Benson calls "the earliest form of the Bjarki story" (Benson, "Originality," 17). It stands to reason that narrative elements that turn up in a late Icelandic saga, when they coincide with the gist of what is said in *Beowulf* (a much earlier witness than Saxo), may reflect the original form of a story once in circulation in northern lands. What Saxo writes in his polished Latin history may represent a different form of the story, and not necessarily the most authoritative one.

[38] Technically speaking, Böðvarr is a were-bear's son, in that his father is a bear who formerly had human form. This is all weird and strange and typical of this saga.

[39] The saga containing the closest Icelandic analogues to certain features of *Beowulf*, namely *Grettis saga*, is discussed in typically judicious fashion by Chambers in *Beowulf: An Introduction*, 48–53. I part company with Chambers, however, as regards his belief that a story underlying these two works originated in the ancient homeland of the English, Angeln, from which point it migrated west to Britain and east and north into other Scandinavian territories, and thence to Iceland (51). A point of origin right at the putative home of the Skjöldung kings in Zealand, and hardly at such an early date as Chambers assumes, seems more likely. Chambers wrote his analysis of this question when the overwhelming critical consensus was that *Beowulf* was composed in the seventh or early

These negative considerations lend greater credence to the third possibility, the idea that the story of the haunting of the Skjöldungs' hall came to be attached to the cycle of legends about those kings at an early stage, and in Denmark. Consistent with this view is the fact that *Beowulf*, however one dates it, is (together with *Widsith*) one of the two earliest recorded sources that tell about this dynasty. Even if it is an insular poem that reflects an English perspective and doubtless distorts some things (from a Danish point of view), it is a primary witness to the Skjöldung legend cycle as that cycle existed at an early stage of its development.

As I have already suggested, an additional reason to suspect that a story about the haunting of the Skjöldungs' hall was part of a primitive legend of Lejre is that the landscape at Lejre is conducive to this type of storytelling. Anyone of the late Iron Age or the Viking Age who visited either of the two halls at Lejre and who stepped outside for awhile at nightfall would have seen the outlines of barrows against the sky and, to the west, would have seen the sun set behind two rather prominent hills that mark the edge of the dead-ice landscape. It is a most natural thing, in an environment like this, for a person to fear what might emerge from such a hinterland, or for storytellers to play with the idea that once upon a time, ancestral figures living in a hall *just like this one* suffered horribly from the ravages of some creature of the dark.

We seem here to be in the presence of what has been called the conservatism of the periphery: the phenomenon that some things are better preserved in colonies, where people tend to keep a tenacious hold on certain elements of their cultural property, than in the home country, where new trends are all the go.

7. The Evolution of the *Beowulf* Story: A Conceptual Model

I therefore suggest that the Danish origins of the *Beowulf* story should be sought out at the point where two different legend-types converge. The first of these — more properly a legend complex than a simple legend — concerns the heroic deeds and tragic sufferings of the Skjöldung line of kings from the arrival of their founding figure, Scyld, to the death of the last of them, Rolf Krake.[40] The second legend relating to the Skjöldungs, a simpler one, concerns the haunting of

---

eighth century. Today, there is reason to wonder if even the core legend of the haunting of the Skjöldungs' hall arose at that early a date.

[40] I discuss the probable character of the core legendary history of the Skjöldungs in "Was There a 'Legend of Lejre?'," in *Beowulf and Lejre*, 255–65. Granted, Saxo writes of a seemingly endless succession of kings who lived after Rolf, several of whom are associated with Lejre. Much of Saxo's prose, however, is best taken as filling in the blanks of a history of Denmark that he wished to present in complete form, even where sources were lacking.

their hall by a horrible creature of the wasteland (or by two such creatures) and of the deliverance of that hall by a hero who comes from overseas.

There was no need for these two legends to marry, but marry they did, before divorcing at a later stage. I have shown grounds for supposing that this fusion of elements pertains to the early stages of this legend cycle, before stories of the Skjöldungs were disseminated to Britain and Iceland and before the story of the haunting of their hall was forgotten (as far as can be known) in Denmark. As for when the haunt story faded out in Denmark, no date can be ascribed to that development, but no learned Danish authors seem to have been talking about monsters attacking the Skjöldungs' hall by the late twelfth century, when Saxo and others wrote about those rulers in a manner animated more by Danish patriotism than by an interest in swamp things.

How much else pertaining to *Beowulf*, in addition to some grand and tragic legendary history and a horrible hall-haunting monster or two, is likely to have originated in Denmark?

Not much else, in my view. The following paragraphs set forth what seems to me a plausible concept regarding how either a single English poet, or a succession of English storytellers and/or poets, transformed a scare story set in the time of the earliest kings of the Danes into one of the more complex and accomplished works of the world's imaginative literature.

The model set forth below is meant as no more than a conceptual summary of this process. Its relative chronology and overall teleology seem to me fairly secure. Anyone who is familiar with scholarly controversies about the origins and date of *Beowulf*, as well about the difficulty of pinning dates on oral traditions, will readily understand that the absolute chronological value of any of its stages is a matter of great uncertainty. In particular, I make no claim to know how many poets touched on the theme of *Beowulf*—if any did—before the author of the one extant text took it up. Nor am I sure to what extent that author was schooled in clerical modes of writing as opposed to oral modes of composition—nor do I know if that person thought of these categories as oppositional, as so many modern critics seem to do. In short, no one should be so intrepid these days as to claim knowledge of just how and when this poem evolved into its extant form. Better schemes than the following one will perhaps be proposed as knowledge of this period increases. Of one thing we can be sure, however. By one means or another, more probably in incremental fashion rather than all at once, what must have started as a fairly simple narrative was transformed into a long, complex, sophisticated poem.

1. The seed is planted. The gist of Part I of *Beowulf*, which tells of the haunting of the great hall of the Skjöldungs and its deliverance by a hero who is not a Dane,[41] arose at the place where all early authorities locate the seat of power of

---

[41] Since in both English and Icelandic sources, the hero who saves the Danes is ascribed what is in essence the same tribal identity, this ethnic identification must be

those kings: at Lejre in Zealand, where the remains have been found of a succession of halls (dating from the period ca. AD 550–1000) whose rulers must have dominated that region. A plausible scenario (though it is only that) is that persons associated with the second hall at Lejre told such stories about the inhabitants of the first hall, now long dead, with everything touching upon that earlier era now transfigured by the imagination. In a manner analogous to legends of the ancient Ynglings in Sweden and legends of the ancient Volsungs in Norway, legends concerning the ancient Skjöldung kings who had once ruled from Lejre would have helped to confirm the prestige and authority of the actual rulers of Zealand and Denmark at a later time.

2. *The story takes on a two-troll form.* The tale of the haunting of the hall of the Skjöldung kings took on the form of a two-troll type of story whereby the death of one deadly marauder incites the malevolence of a second, more dangerous one. Since in both English and Icelandic sources the hero has ursine characteristics that include superhuman strength, and since this is a feature of the internationally-known folktale known as "The Bear's Son," which often has a two-troll plot, the story of the haunting of the Skjöldungs' hall seems to have been drawn into the bipartite "Bear's Son" mode at an early stage of development, perhaps even from the start, in a fusion of folkloric and legendary materials.[42]

3. *The story migrates to Britain.* Once stories about the Skjöldungs and the haunting of their hall were in circulation during the Viking period (even if these narratives originated earlier), there was nothing to hinder their migration across the North Sea to Britain. The period of active Danish settlement in the eastern

---

considered part of the primitive form of the tale. Why the Geatas/Gautar are honored in this way remains a mystery, though an answer is surely to be sought in the shifting ethnic alliances and syntheses of southern Scandinavia during the first millennium. Perhaps, once the Geatas/Gautar were absorbed politically by their neighbors, they were ripe for exploitation as a source for heroic legend, just as (in my suggested scenario) heroic legends about the Skjöldungs could have been cultivated once the real people who had inhabited the earlier hall at Lejre were dead and their hall was dismantled.

[42] The term "two-troll" story was introduced by Peter A. Jorgensen, "The Two-Troll Variant of the Bear's Son Folktale in *Hálfdanar saga Brönufóstra* and *Gríms saga loðinkinna,*" *Arv: Journal of Scandinavian Folklore* 31 (1975): 35–43. It was taken up by J. Michael Stitt, *Beowulf and the Bear's Son: Epic, Saga, and Fairytale in Northern Germanic Tradition* (New York, 1992). The connection between *Beowulf* and the "Bear's Son" type of tale (also referred to now as Type 301, "The Three Stolen Princesses") was developed systematically by Friedrich Panzer, *Studien zur germanischen Sagengeschichte, I: Beowulf* (Munich, 1910) and was helpfully analyzed by Chambers, *Beowulf: An Introduction,* 62–68. On the basis of this folktale analogue and the Icelandic saga analogues mentioned above, Andersson concludes that "there is [. . .] ample evidence of a Scandinavian monster story with which *Beowulf* is closely associated" ("Sources and Analogues," 134). He surmises that this monster story is more germane to the origins of *Beowulf* than is the legendary history about the Skjöldungs.

parts of Britain is a likely time for this to have occurred, although other scenarios cannot be ruled out.[43] What came to Britain, it seems, was not a set of miscellaneous legendary materials, but rather a coherent setting and cast of characters (the Skjöldungs' hall and a nearby hinterland, a Geatish/Gautish hero, and a pair of monsters) as well as the basic plot with which readers of the first part of *Beowulf* are familiar. These elements had fused with some well-known dynastic history regarding the Skjöldungs. There is no evidence to suggest that this story was yet versified, however, or that it had taken on any specific linguistic form.

4. *The dragon episode and the hero's death are added.* At some unknown stage — it is impossible to say when, but there is no sign that this development took place anywhere other than in Anglo-Saxon England — the dragon fight was added on to the two-troll story, thus giving the story more ample proportions and providing the hero with a suitable death in his own homeland. The idea of the hero having a great cremation funeral might, or might not, have been encouraged by reports concerning the mound named Grydehøj at Lejre; there is no point in trying to find a direct connection here, however. In any event, the story came to feature a hero whose life pursues a complex trajectory: someone who is not just an indomitable warrior in his youth, but also a tragic figure who meets his death as the result of a desperate venture late in life. This narrative development could have taken place simultaneously with stage 5 and/or stage 6 summarized below.[44]

5. *The story becomes a poem.* The story came into the hands of one or more poets who versified it in the elaborate manner that is characteristic of Old English alliterative verse. The genealogy of the Scylding kings took on the specific sequence it has in this poem, if this had not happened before.[45] Danish personal names were

---

[43] In his Afterword to *Beowulf and Lejre* (469–79), Tom Shippey argues that groups of Scandinavians may have migrated to Britain after the fifth- and sixth-century Conquest but before the Viking Age, leading to a peaceful merging of Scandinavian and Anglo-Saxon populations and to the synthesis of their cultures. Similar arguments are developed by John Hines, *The Scandinavian Character of Anglian England in the Pre-Viking Period*, BAR British Series 124 (Oxford, 1984), and Sam Newton, *The Origins of Beowulf and the Pre-Viking Kingdom of East Anglia* (Cambridge, 1993).

[44] The presence of a flying dragon-like beast in chap. 23 of *Hrólfs saga kraka* complicates things somewhat. This creature, however, is a monster afflicting the Skjöldungs' hall, and hence is a structural counterpart to Grendel. In this saga there is no separate episode involving the hero's return to his homeland to fight a dragon at a later date. The handling of the dragon episode in *Beowulf* must be considered a uniquely English development. This is essentially the position to which Christine Rauer is led in her book *Beowulf and the Dragon: Parallels and Analogues* (Cambridge, 2000), where, after analyzing numerous parallels, she concludes: ". . . Study of the text's analogues and speculation on its literary sources can only help to highlight the uniqueness of *Beowulf*" (142).

[45] A collation of some of these genealogies is given as an appendix to Christensen, *Lejre — Syn og Sagn*, 93, reprinted with some changes of spelling in Niles, *Beowulf and Lejre*, 93–94.

anglicized. The name *Grendel* was added, drawn from native English traditions of monsters haunting desolate regions.[46] The names *Beowulf* and *Heorot* were added as well, together with the names of many supporting characters who are unattested elsewhere, e.g. *Wealhtheow, Unferth* (MS *Hunferth*), *Hygd, Freawaru,* and *Wiglaf.* Figures known from various historical or pseudo-historical sources were enlisted as well (e.g. *Offa, Hengest, Eormanric*). Many details relating to Swedish dynastic history of the period of *Ongentheow* (Old Norse *Angantýr*) and his descendants were introduced, and the tragic death of King *Hygelac* (Latin *Higlacus* and other spellings) in the Rhineland, known from several sources, was developed into a leitmotif.[47] Characters were filled out, speeches added, and descriptive passages introduced or expanded; some incidents were drawn out to epic proportion, while others were presented in a kaleidoscopic manner. An elegiac tone came to permeate what was now, in its last part, the tale of "the fall of the house of Beowulf." Again, this stage could have taken place simultaneously with stage 4 above and/or stage 6 below.

6. *The poem is endowed with religious meaning.* Most significantly, the whole story was reconceived in terms consistent with Christian lore and doctrine. Some biblical learning was introduced relating to the Creation, the Flood, and Cain and Abel. The young hero of the poem (now the nephew of King Hygelac, the famous giant), though himself unaware of the true nature of his role, came to be represented as an agent of divine will, while Grendel (now descended from Cain) came to embody satanic evil.[48] Given the extent to which Christian thinking pervades the narrative, it is best not to think of the story's conversion to Christianity as a separate stage in its evolution, but rather as a natural result of the process by which the core story was reimagined as soon as it began circulating in Anglo-Saxon England.

---

[46] *Beowulf and its Analogues,* trans. G. N. Garmonsway and Jacqueline Simpson (New York, 1971), 301–2, includes modern English translations of a cluster of Anglo-Saxon charters in which the names "Grendel's Pit," "Grendel's Mere," and similar ones appear. For excerpted OE texts and translations see "Appendix A: Parallels" of *Klaeber's Beowulf,* 4th edn., at 293–94.

[47] Prominent allusion to the death of Higlacus in the Rhineland is made in the *Liber Monstrorum,* which is thought to be of eighth-century Anglo-Saxon origin; Gregory of Tours and an anonymous Frankish chronicler also refer to this event (see *Klaeber's Beowulf,* 311–12, 310–11, respectively; Garmonsway and Simpson, *Beowulf and its Analogues,* 112–13). Andy Orchard discusses this and other connections between the *Liber Monstrorum* and *Beowulf* in his *Critical Companion to Beowulf* (Cambridge, 2003), 133–36.

[48] An authoritative study of the *Beowulf* poet's Christian vocabulary and thematic repertory is Fr. Klaeber, "Die christlichen Elemente im *Beowulf,*" *Anglia* 35 (1911): 111–36, 249–70, 453–82; 36 (1912): 169–99, trans. Paul Battles, *The Christian Elements in Beowulf,* Old English Newsletter Subsidia 24 (Kalamazoo, 1996).

Somewhere in the latter part of this process (stages 4, 5, and 6, which are thought of as conceptual stages rather than chronological ones), we are in the presence of the *Beowulf* poet. Perhaps this person based his work on that of previous English poets who had developed their own versions, now lost, of a story of a great troll-slayer and dragon-fighter. Perhaps there were no such precedents.[49] Conceivably, the poet perfected his creation over a lifetime of many years, though no more than one textual record of it has survived. The lack of allusions elsewhere in the literature of Anglo-Saxon England (or anywhere else, for that matter) to a hero named *Beowulf* fighting a monster named *Grendel* points in the direction of a relatively short tradition for the poem in its developed form. Perhaps it is not going too far to think of *Beowulf* as, in large measure, the creation of a single, talented, innovative person who was wholly at home in the time-tested medium of heroic verse, and who chose to compose a long work set in ancient Scandinavia in a style suggestive of an antique oral tradition.

8. Conclusion

In sum, analysis of the archaeological evidence from Lejre, coupled with a new look at the constituent elements of *Beowulf* and its analogues, lends plausibility to a somewhat different picture of *Beowulf* than has been offered before. While bringing out the uniqueness of this English poem, this view also makes something more substantial out of its Danish origins. It also puts into rather high relief the probable role of ethnic Danes in bringing the story across the North Sea in its primitive form.[50]

---

[49] The pertinent remarks of Benson, "The Originality of *Beowulf*," are meant to be provocative on this score.

[50] The possible role of Anglo-Danish contacts in the evolution of *Beowulf* has been discussed in various ways since Levin L. Schücking, "Wann entstand der *Beowulf*? Glossen, Zweifel und Fragen," *Beiträge zur Geschichte der deutschen Sprache und Literatur* 42 (1917): 347–410 (esp. at 399–408). Although not well received in its time, this study anticipates current interest in Anglo-Scandinavian milieux and the making of *Beowulf.* Note in this connection Nicolas Jacobs, "Anglo-Danish Relations, Poetic Archaism, and the Date of *Beowulf*: A Reconsideration of the Evidence," *Poetica* [Tokyo], 8 (1978): 23–43, and Murray, "Beowulf, the Danish Invasions, and Royal Genealogy"; Meaney, "Scyld Scefing and the Dating of *Beowulf*—Again"; Page, "The Audience of *Beowulf* and the Vikings"; and Frank, "Skaldic Verse and the Date of *Beowulf*." Because of constraints of space, I must forego discussing the arguments of Kevin Kiernan, *Beowulf and the Beowulf Manuscript*, 2nd edn. (Ann Arbor, 1996; first published 1981), to the effect that *Beowulf* was composed during the reign of King Cnut, and Newton, *The Origins of Beowulf*, to the effect that it was composed in East Anglia before the coming of the Vikings.

In this new picture, some Danes who lived at (or who were accustomed to visiting) the Viking Age settlement at Lejre entertained themselves and their guests with stories about ancestral kings who had once ruled in that same area. These kings, the largely fictive Skjöldungs, were said to have lived in splendor at an earlier hall built in this same locale in a former golden age, though not without suffering troubles that arose both from internecine and intertribal warfare and from the depredations of a monstrous creature or two. These intertwined stories about the Skjöldungs probably traveled to Britain after the mid-ninth century in the company of Danish warriors, merchants, and/or settlers. There, most likely after Scyld was annexed to the West Saxon royal genealogy (ca. 890?), a story along these lines was transfigured by a gifted English poet who versified it in heroic style, endowing it with philosophical depth and religious meaning. Somewhere in Britain this poem was written down in an authoritative text, perhaps as a result of intelligent patronage that may have had some influence on the poem's character.[51] Around AD 1000 that text was copied out by two scribes, not terribly well, in the unique recorded version that can be read today.

This is the picture that I offer up here for contemplation, at any rate. I am aware of its incompatibility with certain alternative accounts of the origins of *Beowulf* that have been given in the critical literature, sometimes on linguistic or paleographical grounds.[52] I am also aware that a huge number of questions having to do with the apparent making of *Beowulf* during the period ca. AD 890–990—and by the middle of that period, by my guess—remain unanswered here. Whether my account will strike anyone else as reasonable or useful I cannot say; and whether, even if it seems reasonable or useful now, it will stand the test of time and live up to future discoveries is anyone's guess.

---

[51] This is the direction of my argument in J. D. Niles, "Understanding *Beowulf*: Oral Poetry Acts," *Journal of American Folklore* 106 (1993): 131–55, reworked as chap. 4 ("Oral Poetry Acts") of *Homo Narrans: The Poetics and Anthropology of Oral Literature* (Philadelphia, 1999), 89–119. In the present discussion, I have wished to avoid controversies regarding the oral versus literary mode of composition of *Beowulf*. Regardless of whether patronage operates in an oral context or a literary one, it can shape the character of a work.

[52] Not in any way to be slighted, for example, are the conclusions of R. D. Fulk, *A History of Old English Meter* (Philadelphia, 1992), who argues on phonological/metrical grounds for Anglian composition before 825 at the latest, and Michael Lapidge, "The Archetype of *Beowulf*," *ASE* 29 (2000): 5–41, who argues on paleographical grounds for an eighth-century exemplar for the extant text. Both these studies, however, involve methodologies that have been challenged; see E. G. Stanley, "Paleographical and Textual Deep Waters: <a> for <u> and <u> for <a>, <d> for <ð> and <ð> for <d> in Old English," *ANQ* 15 (2002): 64–72 (on Lapidge's claims), and Roberta Frank, "A Scandal in Toronto," *Speculum* 82 (2007): 843–64 (on both Lapidge's and Fulk's claims).

THE TRANSMISSION OF *GENESIS B*

A. N. DOANE

This essay explores the idea that *Genesis B* received its present form of existence in a multi-stage process. The first stage involved a cooperative effort by a
team of collaborators, some of whom were familiar with the input language and
poetic intertext of Old Saxon but who did not know West Saxon or the Old
English poetic intertext well, and some of whom were familiar with the receptor
language and poetic intertext of West Saxon, but perhaps uncomfortable with
the Continental poem. The resultant text was a word-for-word translation, virtually an interlinear gloss, of the Old Saxon *Genesis* negotiated by a team. At
later stages Anglo-Saxon scribes and readers made various efforts to improve and
naturalize the text.

   Such a situation required translation which initially proceeded on the basis
of interdialectal calquing, a process which drew the words from one intertext
and set them in motion in another without adjusting for the effects of intercul-
tural reception. Therefore misreading and revision, semantic slippage and ad hoc
repair were the fate of this text from its first Englishing in the early West Saxon
period until it was copied into the extant manuscript, Oxford, Bodleian Library,
Junius 11. It is the system generally assumed to have been used to translate most
extant Anglo-Saxon poems from Anglian to West-Saxon. The method left the
text open to retranslation as readers encountered linguistic, stylistic, and conceptual puzzles. At later stages, Anglo-Saxon scribes and readers made various
efforts to incorporate into new copies improvements and 'naturalizations' of the
text. The total effect can be studied obliquely via various anomalies and also
directly via the brief overlap of the Old Saxon *Genesis* and *Genesis B.*

   In his Preface to the *Pastoral Care*, Alfred says:

> Then I recalled how the Law was first composed in the Hebrew language,
> and thereafter, when the Greeks learned it, they translated it into their own
> language, and all other books as well. And so too the Romans, after they
> had mastered them, translated them all through learned interpreters into
> their own language. Similarly all the other Christian peoples turned some
> part of them into their own language.

Hans Sauer and Joanna Story, eds., *Anglo-Saxon England and the Continent.* With the assistance of Gaby Waxenberger. Essays in Anglo-Saxon Studies, vol. 3. MRTS 394. Tempe: ACMRS, 2011.   [ISBN 978-0-86698-442-3]

Keynes and Lapidge, whose translation this is, offer the thought that King Alfred might have known the Old Franconian prose translation of a Gospel harmony, and/ or the Old Saxon *Heliand*, a Gospel harmony in alliterative verse, and/or the Rhenish Franconian metrical/rhyming Gospel harmony by Otfrid of Weissenburg.[1]

While not the 'Law,' strictly, all these German Gospel works were made in the ninth century and all reflect an Italian-type of *Diatessaron* circulating in the Carolingian ambit. It is less likely that Alfred knew the prose harmony or Otfrid's (neither had wide currency even in Germany), but it is quite possible he knew, or at least knew of, the *Heliand*, since an English recopying of that lengthy alliterative poem, a copy nearly complete and faithfully reproducing its dialect and Carolingian minuscule handwriting, is preserved in London, BL, Cotton Caligula A. vii (s. x^2).[2] The place of origin and medieval provenance of the Cotton manuscript is unknown, but its decoration, though sparse, may indicate Canterbury or Winchester. It certainly attests that a genuine Carolingian copy existed in England at some earlier point. Beyond speculation is the knowledge that in England in the late ninth and tenth century there did exist a copy of the companion piece to the *Heliand*, the Old Saxon *Genesis* which is indeed a vernacular foreign-language version of the 'law.'[3]

There is in the Vatican an early ninth-century computus manuscript, Vatican, Pal. Lat. 1447, which, besides *Heliand* excerpts, contains in blank spaces several episodes from an Old Saxon Genesis poem, including one passage that is substantially identical to twenty-six lines of the Old English *Genesis B*, preserved in Oxford, Bodleian Library, Junius 11 as an interpolation into the long Anglo-Saxon poem, *Genesis A*. Eduard Sievers long ago showed that by its style, versification, and vocabulary *Genesis B* had to be a translation from an Old Saxon poem, and this was subsequently confirmed by the discovery and publication of the Vatican Genesis fragments by Zangemeister and Braune.[4] In the 1970s Barbara Raw convincingly demonstrated that the core of the picture cycle in Junius 11 also went back to a Carolingian original, to wit, an illustrated copy of the Old Saxon Genesis, since in their details the Junius pictures illustrate not *Genesis A*

---

[1] Simon Keynes and Michael Lapidge, eds., *Alfred the Great: Asser's 'Life of King Alfred' and other Contemporary Sources* (London, 1983), 295–96; the citation from the "Preface" to the *Pastoral Care* occurs on 125–26.

[2] Facsimile in *Anglo-Saxon Manuscripts in Microfiche Facsimile*, vol. 1, ed. A. N. Doane (Binghamton, 1994).

[3] For the statements made in this paragraph, besides Keynes and Lapidge, *Alfred the Great*, see also A. N. Doane, ed., *The Saxon Genesis* (Madison, 1991), 3–4, 44–45, 51–52.

[4] Eduard Sievers, *Der Heliand und die angelsächsische Genesis* (Halle, 1875); Karl Zangemeister and Wilhelm Braune, eds., "Bruchstücke der altsächsischen Bibeldichtung aus der Bibliotheca Palatina," *Neue Heidelberger Jahrbücher* 14 (1894): 205–94.

but the Old Saxon Genesis.[5] This is proved by the picture of Enoch on p. 60 of Junius 11 illustrating a detail of an episode not preserved in *Genesis B*, and corresponding to nothing in *Genesis A*, the text ostensibly being illustrated by this picture. The picture is of Enoch triumphing over the Antichrist and corresponds to the climax of the Vatican Genesis's second episode (as arranged in editions): in the Junius manuscript it is placed in relation to Enoch's translation into heaven described in *Genesis A*, but apparently was so puzzling to the compiler of the exemplar of Junius 11 (or perhaps to the makers of Junius 11 itself) that a second Enoch picture was supplied on the facing leaf, showing Enoch being raised into heaven by angels on the model of an Ascension of Christ.[6] We might call the Antichrist/Enoch picture an interpix, an illustrative fragment from another archive which has accidentally become associated with a text it was not intended to illustrate: as such, it is analogous to many of the intertexts which have found awkward company in the present text of *Genesis B*, and for the same reason, a casual mixing of archives, followed by attempts to make sense of them in their new contexts. Details aside, what Junius 11 attests to is the earlier presence in England of an illustrated Old Saxon Genesis. These two pictures also illustrate how the original text and pictorial program were altered in subsequent copies to fit later circumstances and understandings.

Once in England, the *Heliand* and the *Genesis* may have existed together as a two-volume set, since both extant English copies (Cotton and Junius) share some common floral and zoomorphic design elements. We can go further and say that at least the *Genesis* was in England by the late ninth or early tenth century because *Genesis B* shows, amidst its preponderance of distinct late West-Saxon forms, a significant smattering of early West-Saxon forms (ca. 900).[7] The linguistic evidence indicates a fairly straightforward development of the text: the poem began to be transcribed into Old English about 900 and received a number of subsequent copyings in environments which maintained a West-Saxon standard as it was gradually remodeled into the text we now have. There are no Anglian forms (apart from a few conventional poetic forms such as *waldand*).[8] Which brings us back to Alfred, and to the question of what his international and multicultural team of scholars

---

[5] Barbara Raw, "The Probable Derivation of Most of the Illustrations in Junius 11 from an Illustrated Old Saxon *Genesis*," *Anglo-Saxon England* 5 (1976): 187–207. Recently, Catherine Karkov, *Text and Picture in Anglo-Saxon England*, CSASE 31 (Cambridge, 2001), 9, attempts to cast doubt on Raw's hypothesis, but does not rigorously confront her arguments.

[6] Illustrations in Junius 11 that are mentioned in this paper can be consulted conveniently in Thomas H. Ohlgren, *Anglo-Saxon Textual Illustrations* (Kalamazoo, 1992), 558–59, and in *A Digital Facsimile of Oxford, Bodleian Library, MS. Junius 11*, ed. Bernard J. Muir, software, Nick Kennedy (Oxford, 2004) [CD–ROM].

[7] See B. J. Timmer, *The Later Genesis Edited from Ms. Junius 11* (Oxford, 1948), 19–42.

[8] Doane, *Saxon Genesis*, 47–49.

first abbot, places his birth at Thérouanne, about thirty miles east of Boulogne;[15] and he spent the majority of his life in the monastery of St. Bertin in St. Omer. Stevenson therefore supposed that if he was a native of the St. Omer area:[16]

> [he] would speak a mixed Frankish and Saxon dialect, the former unaffected by the Old High German sound-shift. His difficulties would be somewhat greater than John's in understanding and speaking English, but they could not have been very great. It is even possible that his native tongue was little more removed from English than Old Saxon, for St. Omer adjoins a portion of Picardy (that round Boulogne) that seems to have been settled by Saxons who were related to the conquerors of Britain even more closely than the old Saxons.

Bately, on the other hand, is not at all convinced that Grimbald spoke a Germanic dialect, because Thérouanne was in his day right on the border between Romance and Germanic language areas (he may have spoken both); his house, St. Bertin's, was itself in the Flemish area (if that term may be used for a period so early), but many of its denizens were probably Romance-speaking.[17] On the other hand, as there is direct evidence that Grimbald was specifically requested by Alfred to be sent by his bishop, Fulco of Rheims, to assist the translation projects, it seems unlikely someone unable to negotiate in a dialect comprehensible to English speakers would have been tagged.[18]

At any rate, the king mentions as being among the personnel of his translation staff an array of contemporary vernacular speakers: an Englishman of Mercia, a Welshman, a Fleming, and perhaps a Saxon, if John was not a Romance-speaking Frank. If work on the Old Saxon Genesis did begin in Alfred's circle, Asser would seemingly have been of no use.[19] At first sight one can plausibly find the combination of necessary linguistic skills in Plegmund plus John or Plegmund plus Grimbald; but Plegmund is almost certainly ruled out as his native dialect was Anglian and, as I already indicated, there is no Anglian layer in

---

[15] In the earliest *vita* of Grimbald (probably s. x[1]), ed. J. B. L. Tolhurst, *The Monastic Breviary of Hyde Abbey, Winchester*, vol. 4, HBS 78 (London, 1939), fols. 288r–290v, the place of his birth is called "urbs Morinorum," which "was a recognized circumlocution for Thérouanne"; see Philip Grierson, "Grimbald of St. Bertin's," *English Historical Review* 220 (1940): 529–61, at 530, n. 2.

[16] W. H. Stevenson, ed., *Asser's Life of King Alfred*, new impression ed. Dorothy Whitelock (Oxford, 1959), 311.

[17] Bately, "Grimbald," 4–10.

[18] Grierson, "Grimbald," 547–50; the letter of Fulco to Alfred is translated in Keynes and Lapidge, *Alfred the Great*, 182–86.

[19] Stevenson conjectured that Asser may have spent some time on the Continent and picked up some Germanic dialect(s), but even if the first were true it would not make the second likely (see Bately, "Grimbald," 2–3).

Genesis B; John may or may not have been a Saxon. There is some evidence that both were interested in (Latin) poetry of the monastic type,[20] and they may have thought that the combination of biblical subject matter, Germanic customs, and moral precepts in the Old Saxon *Genesis* made it a good candidate to include in the project of vernacular texts.

Of John and Grimbald, Grimbald is the more interesting, as he undoubtedly grew up in a mixed dialect area. Long before the concepts of national languages or even of dialect came into being, people's inflections, pronunciation, speech melodies, and vocabularies would have differed slightly from village to village and area to area, and over wider areas there would be spectrums and blendings.[21] There would not have been clear boundaries between dialects or associations of dialects with ethnicities. The key distinction would have been broad and practical, Romance vs. Thiudisc. If Grimbald did speak a blend of north-west Franconian and southern Low-German, the poetic brand of Old Saxon would have been somewhat at the extreme edge of the spectrum for him, but probably within his grasp: for him its strangeness might have arisen as much from its simply being in written form as from any dialectal particularities.[22] Presumably the difficulties would have come in finding words in English Saxon.

Certainly native English speakers could have made out most of the Saxon *Genesis* and guessed about other parts, but they would have wanted to consult an expert. But, in return, the expert would have needed help in determining what the English word or form would be. If not Grimbald and his peers, whoever did this project must have comprised a similarly diverse group, working towards the end of the ninth or beginning of the tenth centuries within a West-Saxon linguistic environment. Such a committee approach to translation would have entailed a consensus word-by-word technique, depending heavily on cognates, just as we find in *Genesis B*. In the initial phase of Englishing the *Genesis*,

---

[20] Michael Lapidge ascribes two brief Latin acrostic poems to John the Old Saxon ("Some Latin Poems as Evidence for the Reign of Athelstan," *Anglo-Saxon England* 9 [1981]: 61–98, at 81–83; the poems are translated in Keynes and Lapidge, *Alfred the Great*, 192). Grimbald may have imported the volume of Prudentius, CCCC MS 223, a ninth-century manuscript from St. Bertin's (Grierson, "Grimbald," 553).

[21] See Tim Machan, *English in the Middle Ages* (Oxford, 2003), 96–104, on the pre-history of 'dialects.' In sociolinguistic terms, we might think of Grimbald's German existing in a 'diglossic' rather than 'bilingual' environment.

[22] And it was for just such readers as Grimbald for whom the Old Saxon poems were intended, for it should be kept in mind that the language of the *Heliand* and *Genesis* was itself an artificial 'universal' *Schriftsprache* for all the Germanic-speaking parts of the empire, composed as it was — to put it simply — of High German vocalic elements and Low German consonants; see Erik Rooth, "Über die Heliandsprache," in *Fragen und Forschungen im Bereich und Umkreis der Germanischen Philologie: Festgabe für Theodor Frings zum 70. Geburtstag* (Berlin, 1956), 40–79, repr. in *Heliand*, ed. Eichhoff and Rauch, 200–46.

Anglo-Saxons and speakers of low-German dialects would have brought their respective competencies to bear, for it is unlikely that any individual at that time was equally at home in both Old and Anglo-Saxon; this would account for the curiously mixed and incomplete — in fact, half-baked — nature of the language and style of *Genesis B*, in many places amphibiously placed as neither Old Saxon nor Old English, in other places ambiguous as to whether Old Saxon or the Old English sense is operational. The poem, after an initial and partial translation, in its subsequent recopyings no doubt continued to be spottily translated, updated, revised by any number of puzzled, intrigued, or exasperated scribes. This process continued into Junius 11 itself, where a couple of modernizations of words and forms have been written between the lines, apparently as preparation for another revised copy.[23]

So it is not strictly correct to speak of a translation in the first place. What we have is a transcription or transliteration from one dialect to another, not unlike a transcription of an Old English text from Northumbrian to West-Saxon. True, the dialectal gap is greater in this case, but Old English and Old Saxon would have been mostly mutually intelligible, and if the project in the initial phase involved several speakers of the two dialects cooperating, the difficulties of understanding could have been resolved or minimized. Of course certain elements, such as personal pronouns, inflections, and certain idioms, were translated in the proper sense, since there was no equivalent in the receptor language, but satisfaction, not perfection, must have been the goal: to make a new text which was intelligible to English speakers, or at least which seemed so to the original workers, not a perfect image of the original. At every further copy further changes must have been made. The result is, as everyone notes in reading, a kind of hybrid, with intelligible but Saxon syntax, words that, although meaningful, occur nowhere else in Old English, beside downright confusions that mislead us from the intended sense of the original.

So we find pure or modified Old Saxon spellings, even after intermediate recopyings, such as *gien[g]* 626, *genge* 834, *scēne* 467, *scēonest* 704 (OE *gēong*, WS *sciene, scȳne*); pure OS words like *geongordom, landscipe* remain; they remain because they were transparent in meaning, even if not English. Tics of syntax, such as the repeated objective use of *his*, slip through. Whole phrases are neither flesh nor fowl, for example, *Genesis B* 330, 361 *fyre to botme* ('fire at the bottom'?) which is a shift for the Old Saxon phrase *ina ferne te boðme* (as at *Hel* 2510, cf. 3358) 'the abyss of Hell' (*fern* < Lat. *infernum*).[24] In most cases, one can only

---

[23] The manuscript is usually dated in the first quarter of the eleventh century, and the revision process was still going on at the time of the copying of Junius 11: at *Genesis B* (*GenB*) 259 *wende* and *hebban*, both Saxon forms, have been altered by a corrector to *awende* and *ahebban* to make them more Anglo-Saxon.

[24] Michael J. Capek, "The Nationality of a Translator: Some Notes on the Syntax of *Genesis B*," *Neophilologus* 55 (1971): 89–96, at 91. That this is right is guaranteed by the

speculate as to how the Anglo-Saxon audience would have received such features, whether for them the poem as a whole had an 'exotic' or 'German' cast. Besides these, are cases of 'pure' English, for example, words for God shared with *Genesis A* but not in the Old Saxon corpus: *stiðferhð cyning, metod mancynnes, drihten ure,* as well as stretches that seem freely recomposed.

In one case we can more than speculate and see that the translation led to serious misunderstanding. *Genesis B* 327b-329a runs:

> hie hyra gal beswac,
> engles oferhygd,   noldon alwaldan
> word weorþian.

gal is a transcription of a cognate Saxon word, *gel,* which does not occur often in Old Saxon: in the *Heliand* it is said that Jesus will not take up earthly rule and the son of God fled *gelero gilpquidi* (*Hel* 2896), not exactly 'prideful boasts,' but 'vain' or 'foolish' declarations, 'thoughtless speeches.' Other occurrences *gel-hert, gel-modig,* show that the emotion is not pure pride, but delusion or disbelief; one occurrence (*Hel* 3928 *gel-mod*) is in a context where 'pride' is the appropriate meaning, as the context is with other words clearly connoting pride: *wlanca, gelp mikil, hosca*), so that semantically the Old Saxon word ranges from 'foolish exaltation' to 'delusion' to 'pride.' In any case, given the context and knowing the Old Saxon meaning, the *Genesis B* passage must be translated something like:

> Their foolish exaltation deceived them,
> (as well as) the angel's [Satan's] pride, they would not honor
> the command of the Ruler.

The lesser devils were misled (1) by their own personal foolishness, (2) by the prideful suggestions of their leader; this is both good theology and good psychology. But of course in normal Old English the predominant sense of *gal* is not 'pride' but 'luxuria,' 'lust,' a meaning generally supported by the etymology of the word.[25] It does not share the special semantic development that took place

---

context in each place: 330b–331a *fyre to botme / on þa hatan hell,* where *hell* has the Old Saxon, not Old English inflection, and 361b–362a *fyre to botme, / helle þære hatan.* In the first instance, the follow-up verse mirrors the syntax of the *Saxon* form (locative) and is probably exactly word-for-word Saxon (cf. *Hel* 2510b–2511a *ferne te boðme / an thene hêten hel*), while in the second, the follow-up verse is reinterpreted according to the appearance of the OE calque as destinative. It suggests the translator is learning as he goes. All quotations of the *Heliand* are from Otto Behaghel, ed., *Heliand und Genesis,* 8th edn. (Tübingen, 1965).

[25] Cf. Gothic *gailjan* 'delight,' ON *geiligr* 'pretty,' OHG, MHG *geil* 'gay,' OHG *geilen* 'make happy,' ModGerm *geil* 'lewd,' 'exciting, fascinating,' OldLith *gailas* 'passionate,' Och Slav *(d)zělo* 'very,' Irish *gealt* 'mad,' IE **ghoilo-s* 'violent, unrestrained; gay,

in Old Saxon: indeed several passages of Old English specifically distinguish *gal* from *superbia*, for example, the *Liber Scintillarum*: "superbia mentis et luxuria carnis ['pride of mind and lust of the flesh'] . . . þæt is ofermodignysse modes and galnysse flæsces."[26] Thus, even if the original project hosts understood the Old Saxon meaning correctly and read it into their Old English version, as Hans Schabram argues,[27] some readers did not, as we can see by the illustrations. On the opening pp. 16–17 are two depictions of the fall of the devils into Hell: in a cognate picture, a sort of frontispiece in several registers on p. 3, the devils are shown plain from the waist down, in fact they seem to be wearing tights or panty-hose. However, on pp. 16–17, in what is in effect a repetition of p. 3, they are naked, and several of them have distinct and elaborate male genitalia.[28] But not Satan 'who was not deceived.' Our passage, 'their *gal* deceived them,' occurs immediately overleaf from the illustration, on p. 18, and must have influenced the English illustrator, who, reading the text as he received it, naturally thought that the devils were suffering from sexual frenzy. The translator has allowed the reader to invent a new theological trope: the angels fell from heaven not for aiming too high, but for aiming too low.

This is a rare confirmable instance in *Genesis B* of the ungrammaticality that must have often arisen for its original readers from a too-literal technique of translation: a word has been taken from its proper 'sociolect' (the *Heliand/Genesis* poetic style-corpus) where it is embedded in a web of received intertexts (in this case 'pride → pride') and slotted into another 'sociolect' (the Old English poetic style-corpus) creating an intertextual gap or tear ('pride → lust').[29] This textual feature must have been invisible to the scribe/translator/writer (let's call

---

happy': Samuel Berr, *An Etymological Glossary to the Old Saxon Heliand*, European University Papers, Series 1, German Language and Literature 33 (Berne and Frankfurt a. M., 1971), 152; perhaps cognate with Lat. *hilaris* (*OED*, s.v. *gole³*).

[26] *Defensor's Liber Scintillarum with an Interlinear Anglo-Saxon Version*, ed. E. W. Rhodes, EETS o.s. 93 (Oxford, 1889), 88; see also A. N. Doane, "Interdialectics and Reading in *Genesis B*, " in *Of Pavlova, Poetry and Paradigms: Essays in Honour of Harry Orsman*, ed. Laurie Bauer and Christine Franzen (Wellington, 1993), 112–22, at 114–15.

[27] Hans Schabram, "Die Bedeutung von *gâl* und *gâlscipe* in der ae. *Genesis*," in *Beiträge zur Geschichte der deutschen Sprache und Literatur* (Tübingen, 1960), 82, 271–72.

[28] Illustrations in Ohlgren, *Anglo-Saxon Textual Illustrations*, 528, 536, 537, and in Muir and Kennedy, *MS Junius 11* (CD–ROM).

[29] "Intertext," coined about thirty years ago by Julia Kristeva, is now often loosely used. I intend it somewhat technically, following Michael Riffaterre's concept; he distinguishes "intertext" from "source," "analogue," or "influence," as "a corpus of texts, textual fragments, or textlike segments of the sociolect that shares a lexicon and, to a lesser extent, a syntax with the text we are reading (directly or indirectly) in the form of synonyms or, even conversely, in the form of antonyms": "Intertextual Representation: On Mimesis as Interpretive Discourse," *Critical Inquiry* 11 (1984): 141–62, at 142. That is, the sociolect is a tempering corpus of texts, actually and/or conventionally associated,

him Grimbald for the sake of the argument), immersed as he was in the original intertext, but, given the nature of reading, the gap causes a purposive re-reading on the part of the Anglo-Saxon illustrator, who alters the received Carolingian picture in order to make it conform with his own world of intertexts and whose activity can be regarded as normative for the Anglo-Saxon reader in general.

Presumably great stretches of *Genesis B* could be back-translated into *Heliand*-ese if one wished to take the trouble. Any large-scale attempt would be quixotic, but it is interesting to take note of the subtle changes which occur in a transfer of even a small segment of the Old English back into a simulacrum of the Old Saxon intertext. Here is *Genesis B* (297b–299a), a moral comment following the first introduction of Satan's pride, which is easily transcribed word-for-word into grammatical Old Saxon poetry (vowel length is marked in both versions for metrical reasons):[30]

	297b	swā dēð monna gehwilc
þe wið his waldend		winnan ongynneð,
mid māne wið þone		mǣran drihten.

	*297b	sō duot monna gihuuilīc[31]
the wið his uualdande		uuinnan biginnit,
mid mēnu wid thana		mārean drohtin.

Word-for-word as it is, the meter of the 'Old Saxon' is subtly different, due to different morphological patterns:[32]

297b	298a	298b	299a
GenB: 3B*1b	a1c / 1A*1a		1A*1c(2A1a)
*OS: +1A*2	d1c / 1A*1a		1A*1c(2A1a)

In *297b the addition of a half-stress at the end of the line (*gihuuilīc* vs. *gehwilc*) requires 1A* type with anacrusis, a pattern common in *Heliand*, e.g. 2732a *that that*

---

that forms a language background out of which texts are produced and before which texts are received.

[30] From this point on, quotations will be identified with the markers *OS (hypothetical Old Saxon reconstruction); *GenB* Genesis B, *VatG* Vatican Genesis, i.e., the Old Saxon *Genesis*, following the usage in Doane, *Saxon Genesis*.

[31] So I transcribe conservatively for the sake of the argument: it would be more regular OS style to write *so duot alloro monna gihuuilic*, though this would merely lengthen the prelude of the verse, not change its metrical structure (cf. *Hel* 3216 *huo scal allaro manno gehuilic*). Here and in following discussions the prototypes of the *OS lines and *Heliand* examples are drawn from the materials in E. H. Sehrt, *Vollständiges Wörterbuch zum Heliand und zur altsächsischen Genesis*, 2nd edn., Hesperia 14 (Göttingen, 1966), *ad loc.*

[32] Here and in the following, the metrical analysis is based on that in Doane, *Saxon Genesis*, 65–88, esp. 72–75 and the metrical tables, 437–64.

erlo gehuilic, 4595b *antsuok thero manno gehuilic*, etc.; once in *VatG*, 312b *uuard thero burugeo giuuilic*.[33] Verse *298a gains a final syllable because in Old Saxon the prepositional phrase requires a dative rather than an accusative, and this results in a d1 type. The morphological variants are automatically compensated for in the metrical systems of each dialect. It is notable that in the hypermetrical verse 299a/*299a, the most obviously Saxon line in the passage, the scansion is identical in both cases.

There are further subtle effects from a literary, readerly standpoint. The Old Saxon may be translated:

> 'So does every man
> who against his Ruler   undertakes to strive,
> with sin against the holy Lord.'

The comment is tropological and has a literal kernel: 'He who struggles against God is like Satan.' It must be read against the intertext it refers to, which, as far as is known, consists exclusively of the artificial sociolect of the *Heliand* and *Genesis*. In this intertext *uualdand* and *drohtin* refer exclusively to the Christian God or Christ (cf. the frequent compound *uualdand-god* in *Heliand* and *Genesis*) and their semantic equivalence is reinforced by their relation in apposition.[34] Presumably, low-German-speaking translators, working word-by-word, would have been aware of this intertextual background. I suppose one could argue that the restriction of the Old Saxon connotations is a result of the biblical, ecclesiological subject matter of the two poems. That, however, is not merely accidental, but a necessary condition of the artificial and restricted intertext, which had little other extension. The other so-called Old Saxon texts as collected, for example, by Wadstein and Gallée[35] are so spread in time (mostly rather later than the poetry), dialect, geography, genre, and register as to hardly constitute part of the intertext for poetry.

On the other hand, once left to float among English readers conditioned to a different intertext, whatever corpus of Old English verse and prose was current, the meaning of the English version shifted startlingly, for in the Old English literary intertext *wealdend* and *dryhten* are polysemous, equally susceptible of referring to human or divine masters.[36] The seeds of this doubling of the reading are already in the OS word *mari*, which has at one extreme the meaning 'holy,'

<hr/>

[33] In *Saxon Genesis*, 464, I analyze this verse as 3B*1c but such would require elision and reduction of stress, which seems unlikely in OS.

[34] There is one apparent exception, *Hel* 3424, where *drohtin* refers to a human master, in the Parable of the Vineyard, but of course the master is parabolically God.

[35] Elis Wadstein, ed., *Kleinere altsächsische Sprachdenkmäler*, Niederdeutsche Denkmäler 6 (Norden and Leipzig, 1899); J. H. Gallée, ed., *Altsächsische Sprachdenkmäler* (Leiden, 1894).

[36] This scarcely needs documentation; it is interesting to note an incidentally similar usage to our passage in the *Laws of Wihtræd* 9: "gif esne ofer dryhtnes hæse þeowweorc wyrce an sunnan æfen efter hire setlgange . . . LXXX scillinga se drihtne gebete"; 'If a

but which also often modifies neutral or non-human words (*erðe*, *Hiericho*, etc.) and at an extreme, *Barrabas* (*Hel* 5400), where it means 'notorious.' Nevertheless, the lack of polysemy in OS *drohtin* would seem to obviate its potential as an intertextual trigger in this case. In the readerly environment, then, the sentence as it actually occurs at *Genesis B* 297b–299a contains puns arranged chiastically and doubles its tropological force:

> 'The same does every man
> who strives against   his master/Ruler,
> with sin/offence, (strives) against the holy Lord / known master.'

In the Old English, the kernel meaning doubles complexly: 'he is like Satan who strives against his lord and who strives against his lord strives against God.'[37]

The preceding has reversed the actual process of 'translation.' Fortuitously, the process can be studied directly, because twenty-six lines of the two texts happen to coincide.[38] A comparison of the two passages shows that the original method consisted of a morpheme-by-morpheme transcription of the Saxon, which was deflected by accidental and inevitable circumstances. Wider deviations may be due to the original translators' awareness of differences between Saxon and English or because of interventions by an English collaborator, or by English revisors at later times; probably all of these are working in the final text we have. Here are the most important factors:[39]

Accidental differences arising because of variants in the exemplars of the two texts, e.g.:

> *VatG* 16b gisuuerek upp *dribit*
> *GenB* 807b gesweorc up *færeð*;
> ['darkness drives/fares upward']

> *VatG* 18a ferid *ford* an gimang
> ['it fares forth all at once']
> *GenB* 809a færeð *forst* ongemang.
> ['fares frost all in a mass']

---

servant against the command of the 'lord' does work after sunset [on Sunday eve] . . . he must pay 30 shillings to (his) lord' (cited, *DOE*, s.v. *dryhten* 1.b).

[37] Given the premise of this paper, the intertextual corpus relevant to the ur-version of *Genesis B* ought to be restricted to texts current in the Alfredian ambit, including the Alfredian prose, texts with running interlinear glosses, and such of the poetic tradition as was available in written form. As the poem was recopied and, presumably, revised in the course of the tenth century, the intertext would have expanded as more texts were created.

[38] *VatG* 1–26, *GenB* 791–817a, see Doane, *Saxon Genesis*, 232–35, 229, and discussion, 55–64.

[39] See Doane, *Saxon Genesis*, 56.

A couple of times, but fewer than one might expect, a foreign word having no equivalent or totally misleading in Old English is replaced; there are only three clear instances:

> *VatG* 17a Kumit haglas *skion*,
> *GenB* 808a cymeð hægles *scur.*
> ['there comes a cloud/shower of hail']

OS *skio* probably means 'cloud' or 'cloudy sky.' OE *scēo* occurs only once, in Riddle 1.41 ('cloud'?); probably the translators were not familiar with it. *Genesis B*'s *scur* cannot represent the exemplar, as in OS *skur* means only 'protection,' not 'weather-showers.'[40]

> *VatG* 13b thero uuaron uuit er beðero *tuom*
> ['there were we two free of both (sc. hunger and thirst)']

OE *tōm*, 'lacking, free of,' is another word so rare (it occurs once in poetry, *Christ* 1210) that the translators probably did not know it as an English word. However, in this case, the avoidance of the Old Saxon word has caused one of the rare circumlocutions, one Old Saxon line becoming two feeble Old English ones, perhaps an instance of later recomposition:

> *GenB* 803b-804a/b   þæs wit begra ær
>   wæron orsorge   on ealle tid
>   ['so as we both once
>   were sorrow-free at all times']

The most striking of the vocabulary changes, occurring together, it seems to me betoken later recomposition:

> *VatG* 12b-13a   Nu *thuingit* mi giu hungar endi thrust
>   bitter *balouuerek.*
> *GenB* 802b-803a   nu *slit* me hunger and þurst
>   bitre *on breostum*

OS *thwingan*, 'oppress,' 'force,' is in its nominal form a common word in the *Heliand*, so common that its traces show up three times in *Genesis B*, and each time a different type of effort has been made to revise it away. So it seems clear that this is a case of later rewriting.[41] Probably the change from the transparent

---

[40] See Doane, *Saxon Genesis*, 305.

[41] See *Hel* 2145, 5169, *hard helligithuing*, 'fierce hell-force.' *GenB* 696b has *hellgeþwin*, with a letter, probably *g* erased after *n*, the scribe perhaps attempting to remodel to *-gewin(n)*, certainly not tolerating the word as it stood in his copy. At *GenB* 317a is *sum heard gewrinc* ('a hard twist' [?], 'torture'); Sisam was right in seeing Old Saxon *githuing*

bitter bealuweorc is part of the same later revision. Surprisingly, *bealuweorc* is not recorded in Old English. Probably it is avoided here, or as I think, revised out at a later time, not because it meant nothing but because it seemed to mean 'a bad deed done against one' rather than 'a bad deed one does.'[42]

A change which implies perhaps a later stage of revision, since it shows a pretty exact knowledge of the nuances of Old English, is *VatG* 11b *uuardon* represented by *GenB* 801b *warian*; OE *warian* means the same thing as OS *wardon* (weak class II), 'beware,' whereas the exact etymon, OE *weardian*, means 'keep,' 'defend.'[43]

At the same time, a couple of words that are rare, or used in a sense that is somewhat forced in Old English, remain:

1a/791a *gimarakot* / *gemearcod* 'designated', also at *GenB* 363, 395, 591, 595, 459,

2a/792a, 10a/800a *sið* / *sið* 'fate',

18b/809b *firinum kald* (intensifier 'evilly cold, damned cold') / *fyrnum ceald* ('very cold'), also at *GenB* 316, 832.

The greatest number of deliberate changes seem to be made in order to reduce the syllable-rich Old Saxon lines down to something approximating Old English poetic rhythm, with the effect that hypermetrics are converted into normal verses or the number of syllables in preludes is reduced; it seems reasonable, since it is so consistent and pervasive, that it was part of the original program of translation, perhaps the main device for domesticating the text. The symptoms are:

1. Incidental reduction of syllables in Old English lines because of morphological differences between Old English and Old Saxon, e.g. *VatG* 2a *unkaro selbaro sið*, *GenB* 792a *uncer sylfra sið*. This is the only pure and direct example (where no words are omitted or changed), but it is a general tendency within

---

behind this word, but wrong in suggesting it be so emended, since the word had obviously been deliberately altered away from that form; see A. N. Doane, "*Genesis B* 318a: *sum heard gewrinc*," *Philological Quarterly* 56 (1977): 404–7.

[42] A variation which is hard to assess is *VatG* 22a *ni [t]e sk[erema], ni te scura* ('neither for protection nor shelter'), *GenB* to *scursceade*; the OS is a reconstruction, though a likely one (see Doane, *Saxon Genesis*, 63, 304); the OE has been drastically remodeled, reducing the curiously doubled structure of the OS hypermetric, a1b(1A*1b), to a simple d3a type.

[43] The change of *VatG* 14v *liahta* 'light,' to *GenB* 805b *lande* is prose, since in OS poetry *liahta* does mean 'life, home in the world' (see Sehrt, *Vollständiges Wörterbuch zum Heliand und zur altsächsischen Genesis*, s.v. *lioht*, 2: 'Leben, Welt, Erde'); this sense is preserved in *GenB* 258, 310, suggesting that the variant at *GenB* 805b is an isolated later revision.

the line throughout the poem and automatically brings the translation closer to normal Old English meter.

2. Reinforcing this inevitable tendency, the translation restricts redundant function words:

		a1e
VatG 1a Uuela that thu nu eua habas, quað adam		(2A1a)
['Alas that you now, Eve, have, quoth Adam']		
GenB 791a hwæt, þu eue hæfst		3B1a
['Lo, you Eve have']		

VatG 11a that uuit hunk sulic uuiti		a1e
['that we two for us such punishment']		
GenB 801a þæt wit unc wite		a1c
['that we two for us punishment']		

VatG 14b efto hu sculun uuit an thesum liahta uuesan		3B1j
['or how will we two in this light exist']		
GenB 805b oððe on þys lande wesan		3B1d
['or how on this land exist']		

3. Pushing this line of development further, an Old Saxon word is replaced with a shorter Old English equivalent:

VatG 5b   this uuas alloro lando *sconiust*
                 ['this was of all lands the most beautiful']
GenB 795b   ac þis is landa *betst*.
                 ['but this is best of lands']

Not all changes lead to simplification:

VatG 2b nu maht thu sean thia suarton hell		3B1e
['now you can see that black hell']		

GenB 792b gesyhst þu nu þa sweartan helle		a1e (2A1a)
['do you now see that black hell']		

In order to avoid the stressed infinitive (the infinitive not being stressed in Old Saxon) and the illegal pattern x/x/x, *GenB* 792b adopts a light hypermetric (and so in an elegant manner actually avoids extra weight). This change suggests metrical sophistication on the part of the adapter and strikes me as a product of later revision. However that may be, it is undeniable that heavy verses still predominate in *Genesis B*, as measured by normal Old English prosodic standards.

Another evident change in the overlapping passages is the way the syntax of the original has been rewritten in several places, somewhat to the detriment of the translation. The tendency of the changes is away from the paratactic style of the Old Saxon original, towards longer, smoother hypotactic syntactical runs that are found in the fully developed Old English classical style. An overall jaggedness of style, a stark, contrastive, paratactic technique of opposing scenes, characters, and statements, marks the Old Saxon text. The tendency of the Anglo-Saxon version is to smooth this out using hypotaxis. This is consonant with the metrical changes towards a more Anglo-Saxon standard. For example,

> *VatG* 4b-5b   nis heƀanriki
> gelihc sulicaro lognun.   thit uuas alloro lando sconiust.
>   ['heaven-realm was not
> like such flames. That was of all lands the most beautiful.']

> *GenB* 794b-95b   nis heofonrice
> gelic þam lige   ac þis is landa betst.
>   ['heaven-realm was not
> like that fire but this is the best of lands.']

The Old English smoothes over the opposing sentences with an *ac* clause, bringing the opposition into a familiar stylistic structure.

> *VatG* 21b-24a   nis unk hier uuiht biuoran,
> ni [t]e sk[erema], ni te scura.   unk nis hier scattas uuiht
> te meti gimarcot.   uuit ebbiat unk giduan mathigna god,
> uualdand, uureda[n].

>   ['There is nothing here before us,
> neither shelter nor protection.   For us here there is not any money
> appointed for food.   We two have made mighty God,
> the ruler, angry.']

> *GenB* 812b-15a   nis unc wuht beforan
> to scursceade   ne sceattes wiht
> to mete gemearcod   ac unc is mihtig god,
> waldend, wraðmod.

>   ['There is nothing before us
> for protection-shade,   nor any money
> appointed for food   but to us is mighty God,
> the ruler, wrath-minded.']

The Old Saxon version is a series of inexorable drum-beats, 'here there is nothing . . . here there is not . . .'. The Old English tones it down for the sake of smooth grammar, avoiding the repetitions and again employing the formula of a following *ac* contrastive clause. More significantly, the Old English loses the sense of self-blame ("uuit ebbiat unk giduan mahtigna god") in favor of an inscrutable, angry, and vengeful God. Yet the Old English does keep the one element that a more alert translation might have omitted (or explained): the odd need of money in Eden. Readers of *Genesis B* always note this as a droll and quaint item. But the cultural code of the Old Saxon *Genesis* is consistent in presenting Adam and particularly Eve as disloyal vassals,[44] Satan as a tribal leader torn between comitatus and imperial throne, Cain as a disaffected landholder, Abraham as a loyal court vassal,[45] and the Sodomites as shadowy types of heretics and devils:[46] in the Saxon version, the action is systematically contemporized so that it reflects the ideology of the emerging imperial system against the old pre-feudal tribal society. These cultural intertexts are not part of the Old English poetic tradition, and in the English version they are mere remainders that must be made sense of as best a reader can.

Indeed, there is a lot of such semantic and cultural slippage in the passage from the original imperial, courtly milieu to an environment that was still prefeudal and, insofar as it was intellectual at all, monastic. Many of the cultural references could have meant little or nothing to an Anglo-Saxon audience, lay or clerical, though it might have seemed self-evident to translators hailing from the continent. In the Adam and Eve sections, the elaborate byplay surrounding the references to God's *boda*, his messenger, retains an ironic sting because the trope of 'false messenger,' 'angel as messenger,' and so forth, cannot be lost. But the political specifics and contemporary point are flattened out. The devilish *boda*, whom Adam rejects because he has no 'insignia' (*tacen*), whom Eve accepts because she recognizes his 'uniform' (*gearwa*), who has recently been with his Lord (God) and who will report back to his Lord (sc. Satan), plays on the specifically Carolingian institution of the *missus dominici*, the imperial functionary sent out by the emperor to see that his commands are obeyed throughout his dominions. On a more specific level, but in the same vein, Adam and Eve must *dom forlætan* (632) when they disobey God. This is glossed by Timmer 'give up glory,' and indeed, the Anglo-Saxon audience doubtless so understood it. But this truism is not what the Old Saxon meant. In Saxon *dom* means 'choice,' and the privileges and obligations that flow from it. In the Old Saxon *Genesis* the formula *selbas dom* (self-judgement) carries feudal rather than heroic connotations. Abra-

---

[44] Cf. *GenB* 708a, she had *holdne hyge*. But her loyalty is not as she insinuates, to Adam or God, but to her new lord, the devil; see Doane, *Saxon Genesis*, 146, and for the following two instances, see Doane, *Saxon Genesis*, 123, 154–55.

[45] Ute Schwab, "Proskynesis und Philoxenie in der altsächsischen Genesis-Dichtung," in *Text und Bild: Aspekte des Zusammenwirkens zweier Künste in Mittelalter und früher Neuzeit*, ed. Christel Meier und Uwe Ruberg (Wiesbaden, 1980), 231–40.

[46] A. N. Doane, "Towards a Poetics of Old Saxon: Intertextuality and the Sodom Episodes in *Heliand* and *Genesis*," in *Medieval German Literature*, ed. A Classen, Göppinger Arbeiten zur Germanistik 507 (Göppingen, 1989), 1–19, at 15–16.

ham says to the three angels who appear to him, sent out as royal agents, *bodan*, by God the king (277), "quat that he im selbas duom/ gaui sulicas guodas/ so im god habdi/ farliuuen an them landa," 'he said that he would give to them judgement according to any of [the king's] goods such as God had granted to them in that district.' So what the first people give up is their prelapsarian freedom from the compulsions of the contemporary system of vassalage.

Through the tenth century scribes continued to copy and anglicize the text and formed a kind of critical Anglo-Saxon audience of a text that became less and less Old Saxon in succeeding copies. As readers, these scribes and correctors tried to make something of the words presented. Acceptance of literal interdialectal transcriptions of the *gel/gal* type may show understanding, or fuzziness, but there were limits to what could be tolerated. The scribes participated in constructing the sense, more anxious to achieve a usable text in the present than to recover or preserve something of doubtful or obsolete meaning. Keeping in mind a kind of stereoscopic view of the text as it travels down a relative narrow cultural channel of transmission reminds us of how vernacular texts in general were changed to remain usable. The Old Saxon original text was created about 840 by imperial fiat and distributed in deluxe copies throughout the Carolingian realms in an artificial atmosphere of domination of Franks over Saxons, intended to teach the latter a lesson of obedience to ecclesiastical and feudal lords and magnates. It seems probable that several learned and multicultural scholars made the original transcription in the late ninth century but left much to be desired. The Anglo-Saxon monks who continued to use and copy this text neither knew the original program of the Saxon poet nor had they the insider information of the first transcribers; with no political or cultural program in mind, they thus dealt with the text as best they could, and refashioned it bit by bit in accord with their linguistic, ecclesiological, and homiletic habits of thought, rather far removed from the world of the original makers and audiences.

OLD SAXON INFLUENCE ON OLD ENGLISH VERSE: FOUR NEW CASES

Thomas A. Bredehoft

1. Introduction

As is well known, Eduard Sievers' hypothesis that the Old English *Genesis B* (*GenB*) was a translation from Old Saxon was spectacularly confirmed in 1894 by the discovery of portions of an Old Saxon *Genesis* in the Vatican library (*VatG*), fortuitously including a partial overlap with the Old English version.[1] There is little likelihood, it seems, of further such remarkable manuscript discoveries, although it is my intention in this essay to argue that at least four additional Old English poems (*The Dream of the Rood, Solomon and Saturn, The Battle of Finnsburh,* and *The Metrical Preface to Wærferth's Translation of Gregory's Dialogues*) also show unmistakeable marks of the influence of Old Saxon verse.[2] Such a possibility, of course, has radically important implications for our understanding of Anglo-Saxon literary

---

[1] The proposal of an Old Saxon origin for *Genesis B* was made in Eduard Sievers, *Der Heliand und die angelsächsische Genesis* (Halle, 1875); the account of Sievers' deduction and the discovery of the Vatican Genesis fragments is admirably clear in A. N. Doane, ed., *The Saxon Genesis* (Madison, 1991), 7–8. See also idem, "The Transmission of *Genesis B*," in this volume. Possible influence from Old Saxon has also been hypothesized for the Old English poem *Christ III*, as summarized and discussed in Roland Zanni, *Heliand, Genesis, und das Altenglische* (Berlin, 1980); I want to thank Jane Roberts for calling my attention to the discussion of *Christ III* and possible Old Saxon influence.

[2] I am not aware that an Old Saxon origin or Old Saxon influence has been proposed before for *Solomon and Saturn, Finnsburh,* or *The Metrical Preface*; Robert D. Stevick, "The Meter of *The Dream of the Rood*," *Neuphilologische Mitteilungen* 68 (1967): 149–68, at 163–64, however, has noted the similarity between *The Dream of the Rood*'s hypermetric verses and those seen in *Genesis B*, although he ultimately backed off from the possibility of direct influence, stating that he had "no intention . . . of implying that 'The Dream of the Rood' should be understood as having meter imitative of that translation of biblical paraphrase from Old Saxon. There is simply not enough evidence to connect the independent Old English short poem with continental Saxon verse" (my ellipsis).

Hans Sauer and Joanna Story, eds., *Anglo-Saxon England and the Continent*. With the assistance of Gaby Waxenberger. Essays in Anglo-Saxon Studies, vol. 3. MRTS 394. Tempe: ACMRS, 2011.   [ISBN 978-0-86698-442-3]

history, and this new understanding of these poems strongly suggests that Anglo-Saxonists would do well to consider much more carefully how literary influences between England and the Continent operated during the ninth century. Such a reconsideration, however, lies beyond the scope of the present essay, which must concern itself primarily with the evidence itself.[3]

In the case of all four poems, the evidence for Old Saxon influence (either as a result of direct translation or possibly by other means) is primarily, but not exclusively, metrical in nature.[4] Each of these poems, as I will show, is characterized by a variety of metrical features that are either plainly unmetrical or rare in Old English verse in general, but common and metrical in Old Saxon. Nevertheless, there also appear to be important differences between the characteristic metrical forms of the four poems, and so I will examine them separately. First, however, it is necessary to briefly summarize the metrical perspective that will enable me to make the comparison between Old English and Old Saxon verse.

2. Old English and Old Saxon Meter: A Comparison

Traditionally, studies of both Old English and Old Saxon meter have generally built upon the foundational work of Eduard Sievers, although in my opinion Sieversian metrics hinders our understanding of the meter in some ways. It is especially important to note that Old Saxon verse departs in some ways from the basic Sieversian paradigm quite radically. To give only a single example, Old Saxon verses such as *Hel* 1983a, "thea ic hîr an thesumu berge uppan," 'that I here up on this mountain,' can hardly be scanned within the Sievers system at all.[5] Most frequently, such verses are treated as Type A with anacrusis—here including seven syllables, but with up to ten seemingly allowed.[6] Such treatment is strikingly at odds with the general treatment of anacrusis in Old English, where

---

[3] I hope to undertake a consideration of the literary implications of Old Saxon influence on Old English verse in a future work.

[4] The survival of the Old Saxon *Genesis* makes its direct translation into *Genesis B* demonstrable; it is at least possible that the poems considered here were influenced indirectly, by *Genesis B* itself, or by other, no-longer-extant, translations. Of the poems under consideration here, *The Metrical Preface*, which is closely associated with Alfred's court, may have been composed by one of Alfred's Old Saxon helpers, writing in Old English, but with an Old Saxon sense of metrical form; see below.

[5] Verses from the *Heliand* will be cited from *Heliand und Genesis*, ed. Otto Behaghel and Burkhard Taeger, 9th edn. (Tübingen, 1984). Throughout, translations are my own.

[6] Seiichi Suzuki, *The Metre of Old Saxon Poetry: The Remaking of Alliterative Tradition* (Cambridge, 2004), 405, scans 1983a as Type A1 with seven syllables of anacrusis. A similar scansion is used by Dietrich Hofmann, *Die Versstrukturen der altsächsischen Stabreimgedichte Heliand und Genesis*, 2 vols. (Heidelberg, 1991). Geoffrey Russom, *'Beowulf' and Old Germanic Metre* (Cambridge, 1998), 149, n. 67, scans 1983a as type

restrictions on the number, types, and placement of syllables in anacrusis are well known.[7] Occasionally, such verses are treated as light hypermetric verses, even though they almost always occur outside of hypermetric clusters and generally fail to appear in the a-line in hypermetric clusters.[8] To make this type of verse fit into Sieversian scansion, then, metricists have allowed anacrusis that is so radically different from its Old English analogue that we must question whether it is even the same phenomenon in the first place.

As this kind of example suggests, the problem lies not in the verse type itself (which is clearly formulaic in Old Saxon as the *Heliand* and *Genesis* examples attest)[9] but in the Sieversian scansion system itself. In order to understand the metricality of such verses, we must adopt an alternative scansion system. In this essay, I will employ a scansion system for Old Saxon (elaborated in some detail in the Appendix) based upon the system I used to describe classical Old English meter in *Early English Metre*.[10]

From this perspective, the basic differences between Old English and Old Saxon meter (both of which appear to descend from a common West Germanic ancestor) derive from linguistic processes affecting Old Saxon.[11] Specifically, Old Saxon underwent a process of de-syncopation that had the effect of adding unstressed syllables to a wide variety of Old Saxon root words.[12] According to the

---

Sx/Sx (corresponding to Type A) with anacrusis, noting however that "the frequency of double alliteration [in such verses] remains low."

[7] In brief, anacrusis in Old English is usually understood as being limited to two syllables in the a-line (one syllable in the b-line), demanding of double alliteration in general, and largely (although by no means exclusively) associated with verbal prefixes and the negator.

[8] Doane, *Saxon Genesis*, 464, scans the similar *VatG* 297a, "an enum berge uppan," 'up on a mountain,' as hypermetric, type a1c(2A1a), although the verse does not appear in a hypermetric cluster. Russom, *Old Germanic Metre*, 152 (and n. 81) indicates the inappropriateness of such a scansion, writing "the first foot of an a-verse appearing in a hypermetrical cluster will contain a stressed alliterating word." Verses from the Old Saxon *Genesis* (*VatG*) will be cited from Doane, *Saxon Genesis*.

[9] Additional verses with "berge uppan" or "gibirgi uppan" and varying numbers of initial unstressed syllables also occur at *Hel* 2686a, 2895a, 2901a, 4739a, and 4983a, confirming that the verses in question belong to an Old Saxon formula.

[10] Thomas A. Bredehoft, *Early English Metre* (Toronto, 2005).

[11] While the two traditions share a number of formulas likely to have been inherited from a West Germanic ancestor tradition, each tradition is also characterized by many formulas not attested in the opposite tradition, suggesting relatively independent development of the two traditions.

[12] Suzuki, *Metre of Old Saxon*, 12–13 discusses the restoration of syncopated vowels (which are understood to have been originally syncopated in West Germanic). The process of vowel epenthesis involving svarabhakti vowels (discussed by Suzuki, *Metre of Old Saxon*, 13–22) also increases syllable numbers, but it appears not to involve a met-

logic of the word-foot formalism developed by Geoffrey Russom,[13] such changes would have resulted in an increased number of metrical foot forms, including metrical feet of the form Sxsx (and the like), patterned on (ideally syncopated) B (Sxs) and C (Ssx) feet—where the new foot (which we can call a D foot) is clearly based on the old foot, but expanded by a single unstressed syllable.[14] *Hel* 1983a clearly makes use of such a foot (following an unstressed light foot), and we can scan it straightforwardly (according to the principles outlined in the Appendix) as Type xD: xxx/(xxxx)Sxsx. Other key differences between Old English and Old Saxon meter also derive from directly analogous de-syncopated foot forms.

This analysis of the metrical similarities and differences that characterize Old English and Old Saxon meter makes it possible to trace Old Saxon influence in Old English poems far more precisely than a Sievers-based analysis has allowed. Specifically, in the four poems under discussion in this essay, we find a wide variety of verses (and types of verse) that are unmetrical or exceptional in Old English verse, but perfectly typical (and clearly metrical) in Old Saxon. In each case, the number and variety of problematic verses in these poems that can be understood by hypothesizing influence from Old Saxon is large enough to make the probability of such influence very high. Further, in several cases, the

---

rical change, as resolution would normally count the resulting disyllables as metrical monosyllables, as noted by Eduard Sievers, *Altgermanische Metrik* (Halle, 1893), 151. Frequently, discussions of the metrical peculiarities of Old Saxon begin with discussion of Old Saxon's weakened phonological stress; see Suzuki, *Metre of Old Saxon*, 11 and Irmengard Rauch, *The Old Saxon Language: Grammar, Epic Narrative, Linguistic Interference* (New York, 1992), 90, but while this stress weakening clearly had phonological consequences, Old Saxon meter continues to make use of three metrically distinct stress levels, as in Type E (Ssx/S) verses. The effects of de-syncopation, then, appear to be the most powerful influence on the meter.

[13] See Geoffrey Russom, *Old English Meter and Linguistic Theory* (Cambridge, 1987) for a full exposition of word-foot formalism as applied to the meter of *Beowulf*. In brief, Russom's analysis divides metrical verses into two metrical feet, each of which is patterned on the stress contour of a single word. The analysis given in Bredehoft, *Early English Metre*, takes Russom's word-foot formalism as a starting point.

[14] The clearest demonstration of how desyncopation adds syllables to metrical feet may lie in B-Type feet, as in the following verses:

> *Elene* 1031a: þurh þa halgan gesceaft   xx/Sxxs
> ['through the holy creation']
> *Heliand* 4064a: thurh thiu hêlagon giscapu   xx/Sxxxs
> ['through the holy shaping/decree']

Here the long (five-syllable, counting the resolved sequence as a single metrical syllable) B foot is literally a de-syncopated version of the Old English Sxxs foot. Verses from Old English will be cited by line number from the appropriate volume of the ASPR, unless otherwise noted.

hypothesis can clarify lexical or other issues in these poems as well. In the following sections, I shall examine each poem in some detail.

3. Old Saxon Features in *The Dream of the Rood*

Metricists, usually employing a Sieversian perspective, have often underplayed or failed to recognize the numerous ways in which the meter of *The Dream of the Rood* departs from the standards of classical Old English verse, both at the level of individual verse types and at the level of distributional patterns. Three types of evidence must be addressed: types unmetrical in Old English, types rare in Old English, and the use of anacrusis. I will take each type of evidence in order.

3.1. Verses unmetrical in Old English.

Although *The Dream of the Rood* is only 156 lines long, five of its verses are clearly unmetrical in Old English:

33a: gefæstnodon me þær feondas genoge   xsxx/(xx)Sx/(x)Sx
    ['numerous enemies there fastened me']
48a: Bysmeredon hie unc butu ætgædere   Sxxx/(xx)Sx/(x)Sx
    ['they disgraced us both together']
60b: Genamon hie þær ælmihtigne god   xsx/(xx)Ssxx/S
    ['they seized there almighty God']
86a: æghwylcne anra   Ssx/Sx
    ['each of those ones']
153a: anwealda ælmihtig   Ssx/Ssx[15]
    ['almighty Lord']

The last two of these verses are unmetrical because they begin with an Ssx foot, which is allowed as an initial foot in Old English only in inverted E Type verses.[16]

---

[15] The scansions given here reflect scansion of these verses according to Old Saxon meter, not Old English.

[16] Old Saxon verses of the form Ssx/Sx (with or without extrametrical syllables between the feet) are relatively common: there are several dozen examples in the *Heliand*, including a number with secondary stress on the s position (e.g., *Hel* 956b, 1068b, 1718a, 2321a, 2492a, 2724a, 3290b, 3928a, 4093a, 4337a, 4795a, and 5102a) and (more often) those with a long syllable on the s position; see also *VatG* 93a; and *GenB* 321a, 633b, and 740a. Old Saxon Ssx/Ssx verses include *Hel* 473a, 480a, 668a, 4812a and *VatG* 135a (not including verses with a proper name in the first foot); none of these Old Saxon examples shows secondary stress on the s-position in the first foot, but such verses would likely have been metrical. The lists in this note (and similar subsequent notes) are not necessarily exhaustive, but are intended only to demonstrate that the forms indicated are, indeed, well attested in and characteristic of Old Saxon poems.

Verse 33a is unmetrical in Old English because anacrusis is disallowed before Sxx feet, since (in Old English) anacrusis is always formed by analogy to s-feet, none of which have two unstressed syllables after the stress.[17] Verses 48a and 60b have four-syllable feet (Sxxx and Ssxx, respectively) that are excluded from classical Old English verse (the only allowed four-syllable foot being Sxxs).[18] All five verses, however, can clearly be understood as metrical, de-syncopated forms, analogous to metrical Old English forms that have been augmented by a single unstressed syllable attached to a stressed position. Four of the five clearly have precise metrical analogues in surviving Old Saxon verse. Only 153a, "anwealda ælmihtig," fails to have a precise parallel (with secondary stress in the first foot) in Old Saxon, although it seems likely that this verse would also have been acceptable in Old Saxon.

A further verse type that is unmetrical in Old English generally but common in Old Saxon involves what I have labelled s-feet, verse-initial feet patterned on and usually filled by finite verbs. In Old English the longest s-foot has two

---

[17] For anacrusis in Old English, see Bredehoft, *Early English Metre*, 43–46. As noted in the Appendix to this essay (section 8), however, s-feet of the forms xsxx and xxsxx are indeed allowed in Old Saxon. Thus, in Old Saxon, we would expect anacrusis to be possible before Sxx feet, and examples before finite verbs, non-finite verbs, and non-verbs are not difficult to find. Although not a hypermetric verse, Old Saxon "gimarcode mahtig," 'mighty one accomplished' is clearly formulaic (using a finite verb on an xsxx foot), appearing in *Hel* 1514a, 2792a, and 4780a. For a clear example with a non-finite verb, see *Hel* 2140a; with an adjective, see *Hel* 3275a.

[18] Russom excludes other four-position feet from his formalism either because Old English foot forms are not allowed to overlap verse forms (Russom's rule 12: *Linguistic Theory*, 26–27) or by their simple non-presence in *Beowulf*; following Russom, my analysis of Old English verse in *Early English Metre* also made no use of these four-position feet. In Old Saxon, both these forms are metrical, de-syncopated forms. For an Old Saxon verse-initial foot of form Sxxx, see *Hel* 611a; for verses with an Ssxx foot (and an especially clear parallel to *Dream* 60b), see *Hel* 903a, "up te them alomahtigon gode," 'up to the almighty God' (scanned as Sx/(x)Ssxx/S) — this verse from the *Heliand*, of course, is identical to *GenB* 544a, "up to þam ælmihtegan gode" ; see also *VatG* 188a, 199b. Note that some of the verse forms and foot forms under discussion here are also metrical in late Old English verse, as described in *Early English Metre*. However, late Old English forms appear only in the middle tenth century and later, too late to have influenced Old Saxon verse. It is likewise impossible for late Old English verse to have influenced *The Dream of the Rood*: late Old English makes no use of hypermetric verses, and thus could not possibly account for verses 33a, 48a, and 60b, all of which appear in hypermetric clusters. Further, the four-syllable verb [.]ismæræ[..]u (= *bysmeredon* in the *Dream*), 'disgraced' appears in the Ruthwell Cross inscription, which is almost certainly too early to have been influenced by late Old English forms. In short, the forms of late Old English verse cannot be invoked to explain these anomalous forms, which must be seen as unmetrical in a classical Old English poem like the *Dream*.

unstressed syllables before the verb, making the following examples from *The Dream* anomalous:

34b: þæt he me wolde on gestigan	xxxsx/Sx/Sx
['that he wished to climb upon me']	
49b: siððan he hæfde his gæst onsended	xxxsx/(x)Sx/Sx
['after he had sent off his spirit']	
107a: þæt he þonne wile deman	xxxxs/Sx
['that he then will judge']	

The finite verbs in these verses (here, forms of *willan* and *habban*) are impossible to scan on s-positions, and are (in my analysis) unmetrical in Old English as a result.[19] Old Saxon, on the other hand, regularly allows up to four unstressed syllables at the beginning of s-feet, and verbs in these positions are not anomalous in Old Saxon.[20]

3.2. Verses rare in Old English.

One further practice of the *Dream*-poet involves metrical forms that are relatively rare in Old English, but frequent in Old Saxon. As such the following verses offer support to the possibility that the *Dream* was influenced by the practices of Old Saxon poets:

79a: þæt ic bealuwara weorc	xx/Sxxs
['that I the work of evil-dwellers']	
84b: Forþan ic þrymfæst nu	xxx/Sxs
['therefore I glorious now']	
98a: se ðe ælmihtig god	xx/Sxxs
['he who almighty God']	
130b: ond min mundbyrd is	xx/Sxs
['and is my protection']	

---

[19] This line of argument, of course, depends on my own analysis of these finite verbs as being generally restricted to s-feet when occuring before the first S-foot of a clause (see Bredehoft, *Early English Metre*, 24–25, 39–47). Most other metrical systems simply treat non-alliterating finite verbs as purely unstressed elements, and thus in most metrical accounts, the number of unstressed syllables that precede them is irrelevant. But such an analysis fails to account for the data sufficiently: most classical Old English poems clearly exclude finite verbs (other than forms of *wesan* and *weorþan*) preceded by more than two unstressed syllables: in all of *Beowulf*, *Andreas*, and *Elene*, for example, there is only one such example (*Andreas* 303b), which falls in an unclustered hypermetric line. Treating non-alliterating finite verbs as unstressed particles simply cannot explain such a distribution, and so s-foot formalism seems to give a superior account of such verbs.

[20] I count 125 examples in the *Heliand*; see also *VatG* 25b, 57a, 58b, 66b, 83b, 99a, and so on, as well as *GenB* 286b, 391a, 394b, 396b, 400b, 405a, and 603a.

In these examples, we see the second elements of compounds that fall in the dip
of B Type verses, a position rare, but not unparalleled, in Old English poems.[21]
Although the occasional appearance of this feature in Old English poems makes
this evidence less than conclusive, the verses collected here do add to the likelihood that the forms of Old Saxon verse have influenced what we see in the
Dream, since the otherwise remarkable clustering of these rare forms in a poem
as short as the *Dream* can be accounted for easily by the hypothesis of Old Saxon
influence.

3.3. Anacrusis.

In *Early English Metre*, my use of s-feet allowed a fairly precise articulation of
the relationship between the phenomenon known as anacrusis and finite verbs
in Old English: unstressed syllables may appear before alliterating finite verbs,
when such verbs are scanned on s-feet (xs, xxs, xsx, and xxsx), before non-finite
verbs scanned (through a scanning mismatch) on identical feet, or before other,
typically stressed words by analogy to s-feet.[22] In *Beowulf*, as we would expect
from such an account, the number of anacrustic syllables preceding finite verbs
far surpasses the number preceding other types of words: seventy-eight percent
of verses in *Beowulf* with anacrusis have s-feet with finite verbs. Further, anacru-

---

[21] Compare Russom, *Linguistic Theory*, 35 (who limits the occurrence of the phenomenon to compounds with "reduced stress") and Bredehoft, *Early English Metre*, 46.
Examples are very numerous in the *Heliand*. For a fairly close parallel to *Dream* 130b,
see *Hel* 1242b, "endi mundburd gihêt," 'and commanded protection,' for a parallel to the
seemingly problematic co-alliteration of -*wara* and *weorc* in *Dream* 79a, see *Hel* 4182b,
"the imu tôuuard uuas," 'that was coming toward him.' For other examples, see also *VatG*
25b and *GenB* 661a and 730b. Of all the metrical differences between Old English and
Old Saxon, the tolerance for secondary stress in the dip of a B foot is the difference most
likely to be related to Old Saxon's reduced phonological stress, as such reduced stress
might have minimized the difference between secondary stress and no stress in such an
environment.

[22] For clarity's sake, I will point out that this sentence essentially defines anacrusis
as any unstressed syllables occurring before an alliterating stress in the first foot. Some
metricists, on the other hand, follow Bliss in suggesting that some verses included in this
definition do not feature anacrusis, such as *Beowulf* 1027a, "ne gefrægn ic freondlicor,"
'I have not heard tell of a more friendly,' compare the scansion of 1027a as type d1d in
A. J. Bliss, *The Metre of Beowulf*, 2nd edn. (Oxford, 1962), 146. Bliss, operating on the
assumption that a finite verb accompanied by unstressed syllables at the beginning of
a clause was itself a Kuhnian "unstressed sentence particle," understands such verbs as
unstressed whether they alliterate or not, but such a conclusion seems incorrect to me,
and I believe it is precisely the unstressed syllables before -*frægn* in this verse (and other
syllables like them) that allow us to understand the appearance of anacrustic syllables
before non-finite verbs, nouns, and so on.

sis is quite rare in most Old English verse; to use *Beowulf* as a touchstone text once again, we see anacrusis in only 1.3 percent of its verses.

TABLE 1: Anacrusis in Old English and Old Saxon poems.

Poem	Frequency of Anacrusis	Percent of Anacrusis Not Linked to Finite Verbs
Beowulf	1.3%	22%
Meters of Boethius	0.7%	61%
Heliand	8.0%	74%
Old Saxon *Genesis*	6.1%	76%
Genesis B	6.3%	78%
Dream of the Rood	9.3%	52%
Solomon and Saturn	3.0%	43%

As Table 1 shows, however, *The Dream of the Rood* uses anacrusis much more frequently than *Beowulf* (in 9.3 percent of its verses)[23] and uses it before non-finite verbs, nouns, and adjectives slightly more than half the time.[24] These numbers have more in common with the numbers seen in the *Heliand* and the Old Saxon *Genesis (VatG)* than with classical Old English poetry as seen in *Beowulf*, where the association between anacrusis and finite verbs remains relatively strong.[25]

The metrical evidence presented so far makes, I believe, a strong case for the probable influence of Old Saxon verse forms on *The Dream of the Rood*, but the metrical forms of at least two additional verses can also be better understood if we hypothesize some sort of influence from Old Saxon. These are the following:

---

[23] Anacrusis appears in the *Dream* in twenty-nine verses: 2b, 7a, 14a, 16a, 17a, 23a, 25a, 30a, 31a, 33a, 39a, 40b, 46a, 49a, 53a, 61a, 63a, 64a, 67a, 75a, 83a, 102a, 122a, 125a, 131a, 133a, 141a, 149a, and 150a.

[24] Anacrusis not associated with finite verbs appears in the *Dream* in the following fifteen cases: 2b, 7a, 14a, 16a, 17a, 23a, 30a, 49a, 53a, 102a, 125a, 131a, 141a, 149a, and 150a.

[25] I include numbers for *The Meters of Boethius* in Table 1 since their composition must date to around 900, roughly contemporary with the translation of *GenB*. The *Meters* data show that anacrusis in Old English was probably no longer so closely linked to finite verbs by that time, but the frequency of anacrusis appears to be even lower than in *Beowulf*. For the purposes of comparing Old English to Old Saxon practice, then, the frequency of anacrusis appears to be the most important number. Although my scansion system is different and leads to somewhat different results, see Patricia Bethel, "Notes on the Incidence and Type of Anacrusis in *Genesis B*: Some Similarities to and Differences from Anacrusis Elsewhere in Old English and Old Saxon," *Parergon* n.s. 2 (1984): 1–24.

10a: fægere þurh forðgesceaft   Sx/(x)Sxs
      ['fair by pre-ordained creation']
133a: gewiton of worulde dreamum   xs/(x)Sxsx
      ['passed from the joys of the world']

The first of these, "fægere þurh forðgesceaft" appears within a cluster of hypermetric lines, although it is apparently too short in the second foot, which ought
to be structured like a normal verse with two S-feet.[26] The metrical problem,
however, is immediately resolved by transposing the troublesome word into its
Old Saxon cognate *forthgiskefti*.[27] Such a possibility is reinforced by the apparent
meaning of the word in the *Dream*; Swanton glosses *forðgesceaft* as 'creation, that
which is pre-ordained.'[28] Bosworth-Toller identifies only the senses 'creation' and
'the future' for the word, but gives the sense 'decree of fate' for the Old Saxon
giskefti.[29] In short, if Swanton's gloss is correct, the word seems to have an exceptional Old English sense in the *Dream*, having to do with destiny or fate. But that
sense is precisely what we would expect from the Old Saxon word. If this word's
appearance in *The Dream of the Rood* is understood as a transliteration from Old
Saxon, the metrical and the definitional issues are both resolved at once.

In the second example, verse 133a, "gewiton of worulde dreamum," appears
to be a hypermetric a-line within a long series of normal verses, a circumstance
that is somewhat unusual in Old English but perhaps not unprecedented. But
once again, if we understand the verse as transliterated from Old Saxon, the
scansion as given above is unexceptional for an Old Saxon sD verse.[30] Both of
these examples, then, provide additional support for the possibility of Old Saxon
influence on *The Dream of the Rood*, perhaps even at the level of direct translation
from an Old Saxon original.

---

[26] *The Dream of the Rood* and the *Heliand* generally use Type 1 hypermetric rules,
described in Bredehoft, *Early English Metre*, 51–55.

[27] Specifically, the metrical issue is that Sx/(x)Sxs should be a normal verse in Old
English, not a hypermetric verse. But in both Old English and Old Saxon, Sx/(x)Sx/Sx is
an extremely common form of hypermetric verse.

[28] *The Dream of the Rood*, ed. Michael J. Swanton, rev. edn. (Exeter, 1996), 143.

[29] *An Anglo-Saxon Dictionary Based on the Manuscript Collections of the Late Joseph
Bosworth*, ed. T. Northcote Toller (Oxford, 1898), s. v. *forðgesceaft* and *gesceaft*. The *DOE*
reads, for the word's second definition, 'future (state/condition/destiny),' although it
appears that the verse from the *Dream* is the only real support for the idea of destiny.

[30] Type sD will normally feature an s-foot, followed by a long foot of the form Sxsx
or Sxxsx. Although these verses formally overlap hypermetric types, I believe they are
best understood in Old Saxon as normal verses. The following examples all fail to fall
in (or even near) hypermetric clusters: *Hel* 954a, 1096a, 1512a, 1561a, 4265a, 4986a (all
a-line examples with double alliteration, as in the verse from the *Dream*); see also *VatG*
20a and 233b and *GenB* 792b and 811a.

3.4. Vocabulary and phraseology.

As a final bit of evidence, we can note the ways in which the *Heliand* (in particular, its account of the crucifixion) has long been seen as a useful intertext for understanding various parts of *The Dream of the Rood*'s remarkable vision, as well as its terminology. Both poems, of course, are well known for their depictions of Christ as *dryhten* 'lord', but a simple listing of other similarities that Swanton and Cook point out in their editions of the Old English poem is illuminating. First, Swanton somewhat cryptically suggests that the specific sense of *guma* 'man' in line 49 is unparalled in Old English verse, although it is seen in the *Heliand*'s crucifixion passage in line 5743.[31] Further, both poems note (as a somewhat surprising detail) that the corpse (or its limbs) cooled on the cross: "hræw colode" (*Dream* 72b); "is lithi cuolodon" (*Hel* 5702b).[32] Swanton, in his note on the end of line 67, "sorhleoð galan," 'to sing a sorrowful song' remarks that "The OS *Heliand* 5741–4 contains a similar note of lamentation," although without noting that 5741b describes the mourners as *griotandi* 'weeping', which echoes the probable correct reading of *Dream* 70a: *[g]reotende*.[33] Finally, Cook suggests that the passage from the *Heliand* about how much of creation spoke of Christ's death (5674b–5677a) stands as a useful parallel to *Dream* 55b–56a, although both appear to derive ultimately from Gregory the Great.[34] Although these verbal parallels are not especially numerous, some are quite close, and when taken together with the metrical evidence presented above, the possibility that the *Heliand* may have influenced *The Dream of the Rood* certainly seems worth considering.

In short, there is a surprisingly extensive amount of evidence to suggest that *The Dream of the Rood* was, if not translated directly from Old Saxon, influenced by Old Saxon's characteristic metrical forms and habits, and possibly even directly influenced by the depiction of the crucifixion seen in the *Heliand*. We see verses in the *Dream* that are unmetrical in Old English (but metrical in Old Saxon), metrical practices that are atypical of Old English in general (e.g., frequent anacrusis), and lexical items that seem to have Old Saxon roots, as well as verbal parallels between the *Dream* and the *Heliand*'s account of the crucifixion. These features occur in a significant number of the *Dream*'s lines, and I can think of no competing hypothesis that would account for the variety and extent of the evidence.

---

[31] Swanton, *Dream*, 121. Cook, in *The Dream of the Rood*, ed. A. S. Cook (Oxford, 1905), 30, makes a similar comment: "so *Hel.* 5743: 'thes gumen grimman dod,' and elsewhere, but not in OE. poetry." Cook's references to biblical passages such as John 19:5 suggest that the specific sense referred to by Swanton and Cook is the use of *guma* in reference to Christ.

[32] Noted by Cook, *Dream*, 35.

[33] Swanton, *Dream*, 128. Swanton prefers to read *[h]reotende* in line 70 for the manuscript's *reotende*, although *[g]reotende* makes as good sense and suits the alliterative pattern of the line far better. The ASPR prints *greotende*.

[34] Cook, *Dream*, 31.

Yet it has often been suggested that the Ruthwell Cross's inclusion of verses corresponding to those in the *Dream* must mean an early date of composition for the poem, indeed a date before the conversion of the Continental Saxons: the most commonly accepted date for the Ruthwell Cross is given by Page as "the first half of the eighth century."[35] Nevertheless, it is important to note that the appearance of *bismærædu* in the runic inscription suggests either the influence of Old Saxon or else a metrical anomaly on the Cross. 'Underdotting' one of the vowels to make this troublesome four-syllable word into a more tractable trisyllable seems inappropriate, as the often-remarked phonetic precision of the Cross's *fuþorc* suggests a special attempt on the part of the carver to achieve phonetic accuracy, as it also implies that the text was not simply transliterated into runes from a Latin-letter text: it may have been inscribed from memory or via recitation. Other features of the Cross inscription might also be usefully compared to Old Saxon practice, including the incidence of anacrusis (5 examples; 24% of verses) and anacrusis not associated with finite verbs (two examples, 40%). It is at least plausible that the inscription, too, shows signs of Old Saxon influence.

Further, recent arguments suggest that it may be possible to date the runic inscription as later than the rest of the Cross; a tenth-century date for the Cross's version of the *Dream* would allow us a mechanism for explaining the metrical anomaly and the other features, which are otherwise very nearly inexplicable on an early (and hence presumably conservative) Old English monument. Note that Page writes, regarding the runes' layout on the Ruthwell Cross: "So odd does [the layout] appear that I incline to think it may not be part of the original design for the cross, and to wonder if these runes were added by a later carver who had less command over the space he had to fill. But this is a heretical view and not shared by art historians."[36] E. G. Stanley, working also from a position that sees the runes as a later addition, has re-examined the language of the text, suggesting that "one might say that to seek the date of the inscription in the ninth century has nothing against it, and that on the whole I think it less unlikely that the text is of the second half of the ninth century and perhaps later, than of the first half or even earlier."[37] Such a date well suits the argument presented here,

---

[35] R. I. Page, *An Introduction to English Runes*, 2nd edn. (Woodbridge, 1999), 145.

[36] Page, *English Runes*, 147.

[37] E. G. Stanley, "The Ruthwell Cross Inscription: Some Linguistic and Literary Implications of Paul Meyvaert's Paper 'An Apocalypse Panel on the Ruthwell Cross'," in *A Collection of Papers with Emphasis on Old English Literature*, Publications of the Dictionary of Old English 3 (Toronto, 1987), 384–99, at 396. In a recent essay, Patrick Conner has suggested a tenth-century date for the Ruthwell poem: "The Ruthwell Monument Runic Poem in a Tenth-Century Context," *Review of English Studies*, n. s. 59 (2007): 25–51. For the conventional position of an early date for all of the Ruthwell texts, see Éamonn Ó Carragáin, *Ritual and the Rood: Liturgical Images and the Old English Poems of the* Dream of the Rood *Tradition* (London, 2005).

and the recognition of the likelihood of Old Saxon influene on the *Dream* adds additional support for a late dating of the Ruthwell inscription. The next section addresses the equally compelling case for Old Saxon influence in the poetic *Solomon and Saturn*.

4. Old Saxon Features in *Solomon and Saturn*

The most noticeable formal feature of the poetic *Solomon and Saturn*—its frequent use of extrametrical speech indicators, "Salomon cwæð" 'Solomon said' and "Saturnus cwæð" 'Saturn said'—can be directly compared to the widespread use of similar phrases in extrametrical positions in both the *Heliand* and the Old Saxon *Genesis*.[38] This feature, very unusual in Old English but common in Old Saxon, stands as one piece of evidence to support the possibility of Old Saxon influence in *Solomon and Saturn*, but the case is strengthened (as with *The Dream of the Rood*) by the variety and frequency with which verses that are anomalous or unmetrical in *Solomon and Saturn* can be understood as echoing metrical Old Saxon forms. We can take the various types of metrical issues in the same order as above.

4.1. Verses unmetrical in Old English.

As in *The Dream of the Rood*, a significant number of verses from *Solomon and Saturn* are simply unmetrical in Old English, as listed here:

21a: Unlæde bið on eorþan ['is wretched on the earth']	Ssx/(xx)Sx
34b: frean ælmihtigum ['Lord almighty']	S/Ssxx
57a: wuldorlicne wlite ['marvelous beauty']	Sxsx/S
180b: middangeardes ræswan ['leader of middle-earth']	Sxsx/Sx
232a: hafað tungena gehwylc ['each of the tongues has']	s/Sxxxs

---

[38] There are dozens or hundreds of examples (with pronouns) in the *Heliand*; "quað he" ['he said'] also appears after Old Saxon *Genesis* 37b, 43a, 58b, 177b, 207a, 213a, 219b, and so on (see also *GenB* 278a). Some differences should be noted: in *Solomon and Saturn*, the speech markers generally precede the quoted speech and appear between full lines; in Old Saxon practice, the speech markers generally seem to appear after the first half-line of speech and to come at the end of either the a-line or the b-line. Note that "quað aðam" ['said Adam'], with the proper noun, appears after Old Saxon *Genesis* 1a, perhaps the closest analogue to what we see in *Solomon and Saturn*. Compare also "quad Hiltibrant" 'said Hiltibrant' after *Hildebrandslied* 30a, 49a, and 58a; cited from F. Klaeber, ed., *Beowulf and the Fight at Finnsburh*, 3rd edn. (Boston, 1950).

236b: and hiera winrod lixan	xxx/Sxsx
['and its joy-rood shine']	
260b: hie ðæs wære cunnon	xx/Sxsx
['they know the protection of that']	
261a: healdað hine niehta gehwylce	sx/(xx)Sxxsx
['holds him each night']	
289a: gegangan geara gehwelce	(x)Sx/Sxxsx
['go each year']	
351a: Unlæde bið and ormod	Ssx/(xx)Ss
['is wretched and despairing']	
432b: ðonne we on geflitum sæton	xxx/(xx)Sxsx
['when we sat in conflict']	
434a: meðelcwidas mengdon	Ssx/Sx
['joined in formal speeches']	
448b: Ac tohwan drohteð heo mid us	xxx/Sxxxs
['but why does she dwell among us']	

Three of these (21a, 351a, and 434a), of course, feature Ssx feet in A Type verses, a type also seen in the *Dream*.[39] The rest involve four- and five-syllable feet (including Sxxxs, an extra-long B Type foot), all of which are unmetrical in Old English, but acceptable in Old Saxon. Indeed, most of the specific types given here, I believe, have fairly close parallels in Old Saxon.[40] Further, there are a large number of verses in this poem that feature finite verbs preceded by three or four syllables:

> 84a: And se ðe wile geornlice (also 43a, 234a, 353a, 357b, and 388a)
> ['and he who wishes eagerly']
> 440a: and hwæðre him mæg wissefa (also 166a, 259a, 340a, and 453b)
> ['and yet the wise-minded may']

Once again, the existence of Old Saxon s-feet structured as xxxs and xxxxs (and so on) provides a clear analogue to these otherwise troublesome verses. Two verses, however, have an additional metrical anomaly that can also be paralleled in Old Saxon. They are:

---

[39] For Ss in the second foot of an A Type verse beginning with Ssx (parallel to *Solomon and Saturn* 351a), see for example, *Hel* 2712a. The likelihood that *Caldeas* 'Chaldeans' should be scanned as Ssx in *Solomon and Saturn* is indicated in verses 176b and 207b; thus, verses 20b and 194b should probably be added to the list of those scanned as Ssx/Sx, although I leave them out of consideration here on the possibility that the word might be variably scanned.

[40] Parallels to verses of type Ssx/Sx are listed above. Close metrical parallels to *Solomon and Saturn* 34b, 57a, 180b, 232a, 236b, 261a, 289a, and 448b can be found in *Hel* 951b, 468a, 16a, 520a, 2110a, 5566b, 5892a, and 2381b, respectively.

393b: Ne mæg don unlæde swa   xs/(x)Sxxs
    ['the wretched may not do so']
453b: oðer him ongan wyrcan ðurh dierne cræftes   xxxxs/(xxx)Sx/Sx
    ['or began to work against him through secret arts']

Both verses show infinitive verbs that are apparently scanned as unstressed, following finite verbs scanned as stressed (on s-feet). Such a situation is clearly anomalous in Old English, but is clearly paralleled in Old Saxon.[41]

Finally, a handful of additional troublesome verses should probably also be listed here:

103a: Wendeð he hiene ðonne under wolcnum   sx/(xxxxxxx)Sx
    ['he moves himself then under the skies']
204a: Wat ic ðonne gif ðu gewitest   sx/(xxxxx)Sx
    ['I know then if you travel']
274a: Nyste hine on ðære foldan   sx/(xxxxx)Sx
    ['knew him not on the earth']
464a: aweorp hine ða of ðam wuldre   xs/(xxxxx)Sx
    ['threw him then from the glory']

In each of these cases, the extrametrical element between the s-foot and the S-foot consists of five or more syllables. I suggested in *Early English Metre* that the maximum in Old English for such syllables was four; five or six such syllables are relatively common in Old Saxon, and seven (as in *Solomon and Saturn* 103a) certainly also occurs.[42]

---

[41] An especially close analogue is in the Old Saxon *Genesis* 2b, "nu maht thu sean this suarton hell," 'now you can see the dark hell', scanned as xsx/(xx)Sxs, with the infinitive *sean* placed in the extrametrical x position.

[42] Bredehoft, *Early English Metre*, 24, 27. *Solomon and Saturn* 103a should, in fact, probably be scanned as sxx/(xxxxxx)Sx; Old Saxon allows sxx as an s-foot, and treating the subject pronoun as part of the s-foot is, in fact, very common in both Old English and Old Saxon. Such a scansion would allow the extrametrical portion of the verse to remain most clearly within Old Saxon norms. For an example, however, of seven extrametrical syllables after the first foot (in this case, in a hypermetric verse) see *Hel* 5917a. Of course, most previous metrical theories place no firm limits on how many unstressed syllables can occur in such verses, but I believe the limit of four is a firm one in classical Old English verse; my point here, of course, is that *Solomon and Saturn* departs from the standards of classical Old English verse, and that it does so in ways that can be accounted for by the hypothesis of Old Saxon influence. Also, *Solomon and Saturn* 8a, "Swylce ic næfre on eallum þam fyrngewrytum," 'such as I never in all the ancient writings' shows nine syllables before a B-Type second foot, exceeding the classical Old English theoretical maximum I hypothesized in *Early English Metre* of a four-syllable x-foot plus four extrametrical syllables (Bredehoft, *Early English Metre*, 27 and n. 24). This verse too, then, can be seen as utilizing an Old Saxon pattern.

4.2. Verses rare in Old English.

As in *The Dream of the Rood*, B-verses with the second element of the compound in the dip also appear in *Solomon and Saturn*:

98a: ðonne hine on unðanc. ᚱ r. [43]
  ['Then him angrily r']
113b: læteð foreweard hleor
  ['lets the cheek go forward']
393b: Ne mæg don unlæde swa
  ['the wretched may not do so']

While not unparalleled in Old English, these verses once again contribute to the larger pattern of metrical anomalies in the poem that can be accounted for by the hypothesis of Old Saxon influence.

4.3. Anacrusis.

The frequency of anacrusis in *Solomon and Saturn* (3.0 percent) is lower than in *The Dream of the Rood*, but notably larger than in *Beowulf* and *The Meters of Boethius*. [44] Nearly half of the cases of anacrusis (thirteen of thirty: forty-three percent) do not involve finite verbs, which is not too dissimilar from *The Dream of the Rood*'s fifty-two percent. [45] As with the *Dream*, *Solomon and Saturn* seems to fall into a middle region between the norms for Old English and those for Old Saxon on these criteria, although perhaps not quite so far towards the Old Saxon side. But again, the direction in which this poem departs from the norms of Old English does seem to point towards the possibility of Old Saxon influence.

---

[43] As is clear from the alliteration of the Pater Noster letters in *Solomon and Saturn*, they are to be given the phonetic value of the names of the Roman letters, not the names of the runes. Verse 98a should be scanned then, as xx/(xxx)Sxs, with double alliteration; the rune remains unpronounced, despite its presence in CCCC 422 (no runes are present in CCCC 41's record of *Solomon and Saturn*).

[44] Anacrusis appears thirty times in *Solomon and Saturn*: 18a, 27b, 31a, 42a, 56a, 69a, 107b, 161a, 176a, 181a, 207a, 212a, 240a, 241a, 284a, 289a, 296a, 297a, 303a, 304a, 307a, 321a, 338a, 358a, 405a, 458a, 459a, 464a, 479a, and 503a. I leave out of my count here verse 334a, which appears to feature anacrusis, but since it is not paired with a b-line, it seems of doubtful value in this count; note also that I scan line 459 as a single hypermetric a-line, paired with 460a to make a full line; 460b, then, remains unpaired, perhaps as the third verse in a triplet, as *f*-alliteration continues.

[45] Anacrusis not associated with finite verbs appears in *Solomon and Saturn* 27b, 31a, 56a, 69a, 107b, 176a, 181a, 207a, 212a, 289a, 358a, 458a, and 479a.

4.4. Vocabulary.

As with *The Dream of the Rood*, however, the case for influence from Old Saxon does not rest on metrical evidence alone. At least two words are used in *Solomon and Saturn* that are rare (at best) in Old English verse but which might relate to Old Saxon. The first is *hulic* 'of what sort' from line 53, a fairly unusual word in Old English, although the spelling suggests the Old Saxon interrogative pronoun, *huilic* or *huuilic* 'of what sort'.[46] Just as notable is *Solomon and Saturn*'s use of the word *feðerhoman* 'feather covering' in line 151a. This compound appears four times in Old English verse: here, twice in *Genesis B* (417a and 670a), and once in *The Phoenix* (l. 280a).[47] It also appears twice in the *Heliand* (1669a and 5798a). Outside of *Solomon and Saturn*, then, it is clearly a rare word in Old English verse, but a word used in Old Saxon—and presumably brought from that source into *Genesis B*. It seems likely that (at least before Ælfric's time) *feðerhoman* may have been perceived as primarily an Old Saxon, rather than Old English, word.

Finally, it is also worth considering the way in which at least one scholar has seen a literary connection between *Solomon and Saturn* and Old Saxon poetry. G. Ronald Murphy's translation of the *Heliand* contains an appendix on magic in the *Heliand*, including discussion of "the introduction of the *Pater Noster* as a secret runic mystery."[48] In such a context, *Solomon and Saturn*'s discussion of the power of the Pater Noster's letters seems to be a striking analogue, and Murphy writes that "It might be helpful to know if the West Saxon *Solomon and Saturn* is contemporaneous with the *Heliand*," although he ultimately hypothesizes a seventh-century origin for the poem and suggests that it may have influenced the *Heliand*.[49] *Solomon and Saturn* should probably be dated to the ninth century, and it very probably post-dates the *Heliand*, so we should probably see the Pater Noster section of *Solomon and Saturn* as expanding on the *Heliand*'s notion of the power of the Pater Noster, replacing the magic of runes with the magic of roman

---

[46] The *Solomon and Saturn* example is the lone example of *hulic* in the ASPR, as J. B. Bessinger, ed., *A Concordance to the Anglo-Saxon Poetic Records*, programmed by Philip H. Smith, Jr. (Ithaca, 1978) indicates. The closely-related Old Saxon pronoun for 'such' is often written *sulic*. The simplest explanation for the use of the rare Old English word in *Solomon and Saturn* may be a misreading or misinterpretation of the Old Saxon pronoun *huilic* as *hulic* rather than the more normal transliteration *hwilc*.

[47] The *DOE* also shows that the word was later used by Ælfric at least four times; Ælfric also used the participle form (or extended *bahuvrihi* adjective) *(ge)feþerhamode* 'feathered' at least three times. The noun *feþerhoma* is also used in the *Prose Solomon and Saturn*; see *The Poetical Dialogues of Solomon and Saturn*, ed. Robert J. Menner (New York, 1941), 170.

[48] G. Ronald Murphy, S. J., *The Heliand: The Saxon Gospel* (Oxford, 1992), 205.

[49] Murphy, *The Heliand*, 217–18, quotation at 217.

letters.[50] Such a reading, of course, makes perfect sense if the poem is aimed at relatively new converts in Saxony in the ninth century; it is less obvious how it might have functioned in the context of the long-established Christianity of late ninth-century Wessex.[51]

5. Old Saxon Features in *The Battle of Finnsburh*

Although *Finnsburh* is short and fragmentary, a number of verses seem more typical of Old Saxon than Old English. Verse 24a, "'Sigeferþ is min nama,' cweþ he," ["'Sigeferth is my name," he said'] features the extrametrical "cweþ he" so prevalent in the *Heliand*, and the parallelism between the Old English usage and the Old Saxon is in this case even closer than that described above in relation to *Solomon and Saturn*.[52] Further, the following verses are unmetrical or unusual in Old English:

---

[50] Although dating *Solomon and Saturn* is difficult (as with most Old English poems), some of its metrical features do appear to indicate a date in (or after) the late ninth century to the poem's appearance in Old English. The appearance of Type 3 hypermetric rules is one bit of evidence; Type 3 rules (and Type 2 rules as well) are probably best understood as modifications to the 'classical' hypermetric system seen in Type 1 rules; the use of Type 2 rules in *The Meters of Boethius* suggest that such modifications must have been happening at least by the end of the ninth century; see Bredehoft, *Early English Metre*, 51–57. Likewise, *Solomon and Saturn* uses two separate words to fill out the two stresses of verses of type xx/Ss (*Solomon and Saturn* 287a and 406a); this development is either Alfredian (see R. D. Fulk, *A History of Old English Meter* [Philadelphia, 1992], 252) or else derived from Old Saxon, i.e., after the presumable date of the *Heliand*; there are two examples of the relevant type xx/Ss in *Hel* 3805a and 5879a. Although not noted above, the use of this verse type may, in fact, be one more bit of evidence of influence from Old Saxon. Patrick P. O'Neill, "On the Date, Provenance, and Relationship of the 'Solomon and Saturn' Dialogues," *ASE* 26 (1997): 139–68, at 164 summarizes "evidence that links the Dialogues in language and content with King Alfred's Old English translations."

[51] One additional consequence of this investigation is worth noting. In *Solomon and Saturn*, the evidence that supports an Old Saxon origin lies in both parts of the poem; indeed, I have treated the poem as a unified whole. The primary evidence for not doing so, it seems, has been a perception of difference in content, along with the fact that *Solomon and Saturn II* begins with a fresh line of capital letters in CCCC 422 (see Dobbie, ASPR 6: li); the division into fitts or songs, of course, is well attested in both the *Heliand* and the Old Saxon *Genesis* (see Doane, *Saxon Genesis*, 27–28), and what modern readers have seen as a major break between the sections of *Solomon and Saturn* may simply be an internal break of the sort regularly seen in other Old Saxon works. On rather different grounds, Kathryn Powell, "Orientalist Fantasy in the Poetic Dialogues of *Solomon and Saturn*," *ASE* 34 (2005): 117–43 has also recently argued for a shared perspective between the two parts.

[52] See the discussion above. Dobbie's note on this verse is especially relevant in this context: "The words ["cweþ he"] are certainly extrametrical, and are without parallel in

2b: ne her draca ne fleogeð   xx/Sxsx
     ['nor does a dragon fly here']
13a: ða aras mænig goldhladen ðegn   xxs/(xx)Sxxs
     ['then many a gold-laden thane arose']
14b: drihtlice cempan   Ssx/Sx
     ['lordly warriors']
39a: ne nefre swan*as* hwitne medo[53]   (xxx)Sx/Sxs or xxx/Sxxxs
     ['nor never warriors white mead']

From an Old English perspective, 2b has unacceptable disyllabic anacrusis in the b-line, but the verse would be a perfectly acceptable xD verse in Old Saxon. Verse 13a has the second element of a compound in the dip of a B Type verse, and 14b has an initial Ssx foot in Type A.[54] If Klaeber's version of 39a is correct, it features trisyllabic anacrusis, which is unmetrical in Old English, but acceptable in Old Saxon.[55]

Several other issues should be noted. First, although Richard Marsden notes that the "intrusive *u* in *buruhðelu* (30) and *Finnsburuh* (36)" might be typically late West Saxon forms, it may be worth noting that both words would also be typical Old Saxon forms, resulting from vowel epenthesis.[56] Doane, discussing *Genesis B*, line 240a, suggests that *Finnsburh* 17b, "hwearf him on laste," 'he followed on the track,' shows a rare Old English reflexive use of this verb, though such usage is seen three times in *Genesis B* and at least once in the *Heliand*.[57] Finally, in reading "[H]næf hleoþrode ða" in 2a, Klaeber cites only *Hel* 4824b, "Uuerod sîðode thô," as a precise metrical parallel. Taking all these cases together, at least four,

---

Anglo-Saxon poetry, although such indications of speaker are frequently found in the Old Saxon Heliand" (ASPR 6: 134).

[53] Verses from *Finnsburh* are quoted from Klaeber, ed., *Beowulf*, 245–47; in 39a, the ASPR emends to "ne nefre swetne medo" on metrical grounds. Hickes' text, "Ne nefre swa noc hwitne medo" is clearly problematic.

[54] A second anomaly in verse 13a also has analogues in Old Saxon: the treatment of *mænig* 'many' as unstresssed. By my count, forms of Old English *monig* appear in the *ASPR* 259 times, only five of which are unstressed. This verse from *Finnsburh* is one example, and the examples from *Durham* 20 and *Maldon* 282 clearly belong to the late Old English verse tradition; *Maldon* 282 is one of *Maldon*'s rhyming lines, and *mænig* may therefore be stressed. The other examples are *Descent into Hell* 62a and *Meters of Boethius* 11, 44a. By contrast, forms of Old Saxon *manag* are unstressed (for example) in *Hel* 14b, 733b, 1225b, 2335b, 2349b, and 4888a, as well as *VatG* 317b. This feature of *Finnsburh* 13a, then, may also point to Old Saxon influence.

[55] Alternatively, as shown, Klaeber's version of 39b could also be scanned as xxx/Sxxxs, as a long xB type with a fully stressed word in the dip, as in *Hel* 1471a. Either way, then, the verse seems to be metrically authorized by comparison to Old Saxon.

[56] Richard Marsden, *The Cambridge Old English Reader* (Cambridge, 2004), 287. For discussion of vowel epenthesis, see Suzuki, *Metre of Old Saxon*, 15.

[57] Doane, *Saxon Genesis*, 256 (citing *Hel* 5339a).

and possibly as many as nine, verses in this forty-eight-line poem may show Old Saxon influence. Even if only four verses are especially clear, the proportion of the whole is similar to that seen in *The Dream of the Rood*, and the exceptional use of "cweð he" in *Finnsburh* 24a makes the idea of Old Saxon influence as possibly explaining other verses in this poem seem especially likely.

6. Old Saxon Features in the Metrical Preface to Wærferth's Translation of Gregory's Dialogues

The *Metrical Preface* itself is only twenty-seven lines. Of these, at least five verses are plainly unmetrical from the perspective of classical Old English verse. As before, these can simply be listed:

1b: teonð mid rihtum geðance	s/(x)Sxxsx
['troubles with right thought']	
3a: gastlices lifes	Ssx/Sx
['of spiritual life']	
5a: to ðam heofonlican hame	xx/SxxSx
['to the heavenly home']	
19b: gemearcude siendon	(x)Sxx/Sx
['are marked']	
27a: oððe he iorðcyninga ær[58]	xxx/Sxxxs
['or he previously of earthly kings']	

1b is acceptable in Old English only if scanned as a hypermetric verse, which is possible, although this verse is paired with a normal a-line. Verse 3a shows an Ssx foot in the first position of an A Type verse. Verse 5a might be scanned as featuring disyllabic anacrusis, which is allowable in the a-line, although (once again) Old English anacrusis is disallowed before trisyllabic initial feet. Verse 19a features a similar problem.[59] Verse 27a has three syllables between the alliterating elements of an xB Type verse; Old English, of course, allows only two unstressed syllables in B feet. Further, the placement of the secondary element of a compound (-*cyninga*) in the dip of a B verse is rare in Old English, although occasionally allowed.[60]

---

[58] Verses from this poem are cited from David Yerkes, "The Full Text of the Metrical Preface to Wærferth's Translation of Gregory," *Speculum* 55 (1980): 505–13, as this edition offers a more correct text than the ASPR.

[59] As noted above, Old Saxon *gimarcode* is used in the *Heliand* with anacrusis three times, in the formula *gimarcode mahtig* (*Hel* 1514a, 2792a, and 4780a).

[60] A particularly close parallel from the *Heliand* might be noted: *Hel* 159a, "Thô uuarð that heƀencuninges bodon." Although not featuring double alliteration, this verse otherwise seems a very close parallel.

Several other issues deserve mention. Line 20, "and þæt him god ællmihtig" appears anomalous as it stands; Yerkes, like Dobbie, prints it as a single unpaired half-line. Unpaired half-lines are rare but do appear occasionally in Old English (especially, as here, if they share alliteration with an adjacent line), but line 20 would be unmetrical in Old English unless scanned as an unpaired hypermetric half-line: possible but out of the ordinary. Line 26, "þara þe he sið oððe ær fore secgan hyrde," however, is troublesome because Dobbie's lineation gives us an exceptional expanded D verse with four syllables in anacrusis.[61] Dobbie makes no comment on the metrical problem other than to note that Holthausen had omitted *fore* for metrical reasons.[62] Although syntactically problematic, we might be tempted to shift *fore* to the b-line, in order to regularize verse 26a, but the result is a b-line with disyllabic anacrusis, which is, of course, unmetrical in Old English (although scannable as xD in Old Saxon). Again, the central metrical difficulties enountered in the poem can all be accounted for by the hypothesis of Old Saxon influence.

The idea of influence from Old Saxon is especially intriguing in this case, as the *Metrical Preface* is clearly associated with an Alfredian-era translation, and Alfred is well known to have engaged European and even Old Saxon scholars in his literary program (specifically, John the Old Saxon). Doane's suggestion that the translation of the Old Saxon *Genesis* (*VatG*) in *Genesis B* took place "about 900" hints that it, too, may have been associated with Alfred and his Saxon helper or helpers.[63] In short, Alfred's court appears to fit both the time of the *Metrical Preface*'s composition and to provide a mechanism for how Old Saxon features might be found in an Old English composition.

Besides the metrical evidence for Old Saxon influence, we might also note that Sisam, in addressing the lengthy debate about which bishop is claimed to have commanded the writing of the manuscript[64] (or its exemplar), describes the German scholars Keller and Wülker as interpreting the Old English word *bysene* in line 23 as meaning 'command' or 'commission.'[65] It is useful to quote the passage from the poem in full:

and eac swa his beahgifan,   þe him ðas bysene forgeaf,
þæt is se selesða   sinces brytta
Ælfryd mid Englum   (23–25a)

['And likewise also his ring-giver, who gave him this *bysene*, who is the best of treasure-givers, Alfred among the English.']

---

[61] Compare *Hel* 5549a.

[62] Dobbie, ASPR 6, 203.

[63] Doane, *Saxon Genesis*, 54. See also the article by Doane in this volume.

[64] London, British Library, Cotton Otho C. i, vol. 2 (probably Worcester, s. xi in.)

[65] Kenneth Sisam, "Addendum: The Verses Prefixed to Gregory's Dialogues," in idem, *Studies in the History of Old English Literature* (Oxford, 1953), 225–31, at 227.

Whoever the bishop is whose speaking voice we hear here, Sisam reads *bysene* as necessarily meaning 'copy-text,' as it usually does in Old English. Thus, Sisam's reading of the poem understands the translation of the *Dialogues* as having been by Wærferth, but takes the writing of these introductory verses as by Wulfsige, who had apparently been employed by Alfred to make an extra copy of the work. Sisam's logic is apparently accepted by Keynes and Lapidge, who title the poem "Bishop Wulfsige's Preface."[66]

But along the way, Sisam, in supporting his contention that *bysene* must mean 'copy-text' and cannot mean 'commission,' includes the following commentary on this word:

> Now English *bysen* means either "example" or "exemplar," not "commission". The etymological sense "command" or the like is recorded only from *Genesis B*, where recent editors suggest influence of Old Saxon *anbusan*, "command". . . As all four examples in *Genesis B* alliterate with *b*, they may point to an unrecorded Old Saxon form without prefix corresponding to OE *bysen*.[67]

Although Sisam brings up this information from *Genesis B* only to dismiss it, the likelihood discussed here is that the *Metrical Preface* shows lexical evidence of influence from Old Saxon. Thus we must consider much more carefully than Sisam did the very real possibility that *bysen* here does, in fact, mean 'command' or 'commission,' just as it does in *Genesis B*. This poem, too, then, may show lexical support for the possibility of Old Saxon influence, in addition to the metrical evidence.[68]

7. Conclusions

In the cases of all four of these poems, I believe, there is substantial metrical evidence to support the possibility that they were influenced by the forms of Old Saxon verse. These poems regularly feature diagnostic foot forms (such as Sxsx or Ssxx) and verse types (such as Ssx/Sx) that are unmetrical in Old English, but metrical in Old Saxon. Individual poems often have additional specific forms that are likewise unmetrical in

---

[66] Simon Keynes and Michael Lapidge, trans., *Alfred the Great: Asser's 'Life of King Alfred' and Other Contemporary Sources* (Harmondsworth, 1983), 187.

[67] Sisam, "Verses Prefixed," 227; ellipsis mine.

[68] It is not clear, of course, why Wulfsige (if he is indeed the author of the *Metrical Preface*, as Sisam argued) might have been influenced by the forms and possibly the vocabulary of Old Saxon verse. It might be possible to suppose that Wulfsige, like Alfred himself, employed an Old Saxon scholar to help with his literary work, or (perhaps more simply) Wulfsige may have been influenced directly by the example of *Genesis B*, which (as noted above) seems to have been an Alfredian-era translation. Sorting out these possibilities, however, may well prove to be impossible.

Old English, but metrical in Old Saxon (Sxxx: *Dream*; anacrusis before Sxx: *Dream*, *Preface*; Sxxsx: *Solomon, Preface*; Sxxxs: *Solomon, Preface*). Further, *The Dream of the Rood* and *Solomon and Saturn* use anacrusis with a frequency beyond what seems typical of Old English; both of those poems also allow finite verbs in clause-openings to appear after three of four unstressed syllables; and all four poems allow the second elements of true compounds to fall in the dip of B Type verses. The extrametrical use of speech markers in *Solomon and Saturn* and *Finnsburh* is also difficult to explain from an Old English perspective, but common in Old Saxon practice. In short, there are a large number of features in these poems that are unusual at best in Old English, but typical of Old Saxon. By far the most economical explanation for the metrical anomalies in these four poems is the hypothesis of Old Saxon influence.[69] But, in addition, as I have discussed above, there are occasional lexical and contextual features in these poems that have their clearest analogues in surviving Old Saxon poems. The variety and extent of the features of these works that can be explained by the hypothesis of Old Saxon influence is simply too great to ignore—unless an alternative hypothesis can be found to account for them.[70] In short, I believe the likelihood of Old Saxon influence on all four poems is high, and it may even suggest that one or more of the poems was translated directly from Old Saxon, although perhaps less mechanically than *Genesis B* seems to have been.

In the end, the metrical, lexical, and contextual similarities described here among *The Dream of the Rood*, *Solomon and Saturn*, *The Battle of Finnsburh*, *The Metrical Preface*, and Old Saxon greatly clarify at least some aspects of our understanding of these poems and their place in Anglo-Saxon literary culture. Like *Genesis B*, these poems stand as evidence for a remarkable and underappreciated degree of cross-cultural interchange between the Anglo-Saxons and their Continental cousins during the ninth century. The ninth century, of course, culminating with Alfred's reign and his literary translation and education program, is a period for which our specific knowledge of Old English literature sometimes seems distressingly lacking. The identification of Old Saxon influences lying behind these four very different Old English poems, however, offers the possibility of broadening our

---

[69] While virtually all of the features under discussion do occur as isolated examples in many other Old English poems, my point is simply that the dense accumulation of Old Saxon-like metrical patterns in these four poems is unlikely to have been caused by scribal transmission or the metrical idiosyncrasies of an Old English poet ignorant of Old Saxon. It is precisely the clustering of Old Saxon-like features in these poems that demands an explanation.

[70] Lest it begin to seem like one can find these features of Old Saxon influence wherever one looks for them, I will simply point out that none of these features apppear in either *Waldere* or in the *Metrical Preface* or *Epilogue to the Pastoral Care*, although these poems are clearly the closest Old English analogues to *Finnsburh* and *The Metrical Preface to Wærferth's Translation*. The four poems I have considered in this essay truly do stand out from the bulk of Old English verse in their unusual metrical practices.

understanding of ninth-century Old English verse as well as how literary activity in the period related to Old Saxon literary activity.

8. Appendix: Old Saxon Meter and "s-foot" Formalism

8.1. In *Early English Metre*, I offered a new interpretation of classical Old English meter intended to clarify the role of finite verbs in verse-initial position. The key innovative component of my scansion system involved what I called "s-feet," which were feet patterned on the syllabic structure of Old English finite verbs, and which were marked as secondary in terms of alliteration. The value of such feet, I argued there, was the way in which they clarified certain troubling features of Old English verse, especially alliteration patterns, anacrusis, and the distribution of unstressed syllables.

In this Appendix, I extend "s-foot" formalism to Old Saxon verse. At the same time, however, I believe the analysis offered here will also clarify some of the most troubling features of Old Saxon verse, which departs in significant ways from the standards of Old English verse, which have (unfortunately) dominated the study of Old Saxon verse from Sievers' day right up to the present. Old Saxon, however, as is widely acknowledged, differs linguistically from Old English in the restoration of vowels previously syncopated in West Germanic, and the metrical consequences of this difference have been poorly understood. In brief, the de-syncopation of vowels had the effect of making a number of Old Saxon words differ from their Old English cognates by the addition of one unstressed syllable. The key differences between Old English and Old Saxon verse stem primarily from these unstressed syllables. But once such a difference is recognized, s-foot formalism can be very readily adapted to Old Saxon verse, and the remainder of this Appendix presents a very brief but relatively detailed description of Old Saxon meter, paralleling my description of classical Old English meter in *Early English Metre*.

8.2. Three principles can be taken as basic; these principles are essentially identical to those for Old English, and should probably be understood as inherited from West Germanic.

P1. Alliteration (the repetition of initial sounds of stressed syllables) generally links Old Saxon verses (sometimes called half-lines) into lines. All initial vowels are considered to alliterate with one another, and the clusters 'sk-', 'st-', and 'sp-' count as separate alliterators and do not alliterate with one another or with 's-'.

P2. Each normal metrical verse (half-line) is formed by the combination of two metrical feet.

P3. Old Saxon feet are generally patterned on the stress patterns of Old Saxon words.

As in Old English, there may be exceptions in Old Saxon to all three of these principles, but they nevertheless remain the basic constituents of the metrical system. Three additional kinds of rules, however, need to be specified to account for actual Old Saxon verses: a description of what sorts of metrical feet exist, and rules for how they combine into metrical verses, and how verses combine into lines. The key differences from Old English verse lie in the rules for Old Saxon metrical feet, as described below.

8.3. Old Saxon Foot Structure Rules

FS1. Resolution. Resolution is a principle of syllabic equivalence in which a short, stressed syllable plus a following unstressed syllable is metrically equivalent to a long stressed syllable. For purposes of syllable counting, a resolved sequence can be counted as a single syllable (although it remains, phonologically, two).

FS2. Foot-forms: S-feet, s-feet, and x-feet. Metrical feet in Old Saxon differ from Old English feet in significant ways. Fully stressed feet (S-feet) are very probably patterned on existing Old Saxon lexical items, although it is, perhaps, more straightforward to derive them from Old English metrical feet supplemented by the addition of unstressed syllables corresponding to syllables deriving from de-syncopation. Such a process results in the following list:

OLD ENGLISH S-FEET	OLD SAXON S-FEET
S	S
Sx, Ss (A feet)	Sx, Ss (A feet)
Sxs, Sxxs (B feet)	Sxs, Sxxs, Sxxxs (B feet)
Ssx, Sxx (C feet)	Ssx, Sxx, Sxxx (C feet)
	Sxsx, Ssxx, Sxxsx, Sxsxx (D feet)

The long Type B and C feet are innovative in Old Saxon, as are the D feet. Geoffrey Russom has suggested the existence of a rule for Old English that disallows individual feet from overlapping the pattern of a complete verse. No such rule applies in Old Saxon.

Unlike Old English, Old Saxon s-feet cannot be simply derived from Old Saxon finite verbs, because even a brief glance at Old Saxon shows that finite verbs in verses may be preceded by up to four unstressed syllables, even though this number cannot be derived from Old Saxon verbal prefixes. Nevertheless, the evidence is clear, and the following s-feet are (in principle) available in Old Saxon:

OLD SAXON s-FEET

s, sx, sxx

xs, xsx, xsxx

xxs, xxsx, xxsxx

xxxs, xxxsx, xxxsxx

xxxxs, xxxxsx, xxxxsxx

As in Old English, verses with anacrusis (unstressed syllables preceding an alliterating stress in the first foot) either feature s-feet or are modelled upon them;
thus anacrusis in Old Saxon may involve up to four syllables, but no more; in
the b-line, anacrusis is probably still generally limited to one syllable, but with
scattered examples of two. Note also that feet such as xsxx suggest that Old
Saxon anacrusis may appear before trisyllabic words, although it is prohibited
from doing so in classical Old English.

In Old English, x-feet are limited to four syllables and the longest s-foot is
four syllables. It may be the case that Old Saxon may use x-feet of up to seven syllables, as that is the maximum length of an s-foot. Certainly, x-feet up to six syllables are used in Old Saxon, but I will treat seven as the theoretical maximum.

OLD SAXON X-FEET
x, xx, xxx, xxxx, xxxxx, xxxxxx, xxxxxxx

These feet, too, are not always patterned on individual words.

The number of metrical feet in Old Saxon is far larger than the number
available in Old English. But this circumstance accounts for one of the most
obvious differences between the two traditions: the greater average length of Old
Saxon verses.

8.4. Old Saxon Foot Combination Rules: Old Saxon metrical feet combine into
normal verses according to the following rules.

> *FC1. Minimal size.* All metrical, non-hypermetrical verses must have at
> least four metrical syllables (a resolved sequence is counted as one metrical
> syllable). Resolution is blocked or suspended if it would drop the number
> of metrical syllables below four or if it would change the class of the verse
> (see below).

> *FC2. Extrametrical elements.* Up to seven extrametrical syllables may appear
> between metrical feet, although there seem to be additional constraints
> operative in certain specific types. As in Old English, the limit on extra-
> metrical syllables appears to be limited by the size of available x-feet.

> *FC3a. Normal verses.* Normal verses end with an S-foot of at least two syl-
> lables. B-feet are excluded from the first foot.

FC3a in Old Saxon differs from the corresponding Old English rule. In Old
English, Ssx is also excluded from the first foot; the logic for allowing Ssx
(and D-feet) in the first foot in Old Saxon will be addressed below (under Rule
FC3b).

By far the majority of Old Saxon verses are normal verses as defined here. The final foot form of normal verses determines their basic type, and thus we can label verses according to the following scheme:

A Type verses end with	Sx, Ss
B Type verses end with	Sxs, Sxxs, Sxxxs
C Type verses end with	Ssx, Sxx, Sxxx
D Type verses end with	Sxsx, Ssxx, Sxxsx, Sxsxx

The rule that resolution is blocked if it would change the class of a verse (FC1) applies to prevent Type C from shifting to Type A when the s position of a C foot is filled by a short syllable with secondary stress. It may be the case that some of the D Types might be better characterized as C (or even B), but one advantage of the labels given here is to identify as D Types those types which are unique to Old Saxon and unmetrical in Old English. Previous metrical accounts of Old Saxon have generally identified D Type verses either as verses with anacrusis or as hypermetric verses.

Since initial feet may be x-feet, s-feet, or S-feet, we can thus list the twelve basic varieties of normal Old Saxon verse:

Initial foot type	Second foot type	Verse types
x	A	xA, sA, SA
s	B	xB, sB, SB
S	C	xC, sC, SC
	D	xD, sD, SD

FC3b. Inverted verses. Verses corresponding to Sieversian E verses are inverted. In classical Old English, such verses always begin with a trisyllabic compound foot and end in a foot of form S, but in Old Saxon, desyncopation seems to have allowed the final foot to appear as either S or Sx. We thus find the following inverted verse types in Old Saxon:

CS: Ssx/S, Ssx/(x)S, and Ssx/(xx)S
CA: Ssx/Sx (extrametrical syllables allowed between the feet)
DS: D-foot/S
DA: D-foot/Sx

A small but significant number of verses indicate that Old Saxon inverted verses allowed at least two extrametrical syllables, as opposed to the limit of one found in Old English. Also, while CA and DA verses apparently derived from inverted verses, Old Saxon poets may have felt that they were also like A Type verses, thus allowing them to have more than two extrametrical syllables (cf. *Hel* 432a, 1454a, and so on).

8.5. Old Saxon Verse Combination Rules: Verse combination rules specify how metrical verses combine into full lines.

>*VC1. Alliteration.* Alliteration links the first two S-positions of the two verses in a line.

>*VC2. Double Alliteration.* Double alliteration is generally required (with some exceptions) in a-lines with two S positions. Where double alliteration is not required it is always optional in a-lines with more than one stressed (S or s) position.

The requirement for double alliteration is suspended for full-verse compounds, verses with semantic doublets or proper names, and, somewhat surprisingly, many verses with compound feet filled by groups of words, rather than single compounds. That is, Old Saxon poets seem to have treated compounds as especially clearly marked for alliteration, but allowed even heavy types to use single alliteration if they did not feature a compound.

>*VC3. Exclusions.* Types xA and sA are excluded from the b-line.

8.6. Old Saxon Hypermetric Rules: Old Saxon appears to most closely follow Type 1 hypermetric lines, which can be succinctly described according to the following additional rules.

>*HFC1. Hypermetric verses have three feet, rather than two.* The final two feet must be S-feet and they must generally combine according to the rules for normal SS verses. The first foot of a hypermetric verse must be at least two syllables.

>*HFC2. Extrametrical syllables.* Extrametrical syllables may appear before the second foot, the third foot, or both, although those falling between the final two feet are limited by the same constraints as suit normal SS verses (e.g., if the final two feet are Ssx and S, then at most two extrametrical syllables are allowed).

>*HVC1. Hypermetric a-lines and b-lines.* Old Saxon hypermetric a-lines generally have an initial s-foot or S-foot; Old Saxon hypermetric b-lines generally have an initial x-foot or s-foot.

>*HVC2. Alliteration.* Alliteration links the first S-positions in the two halflines. Double alliteration is generally mandatory in the a-line.

>*HVC3. Pairing.* Old Saxon hypermetric verses must generally be paired with one another, but may occasionally be paired with normal verses, especially in hypermetric clusters.

8.7. Additional Remarks: Although the preceding has been brief, it has given the basic rules of Old Saxon meter, although for scansion purposes, a number of additional observations also need to be made.

As in Old English, the final word of a verse is always stressed. The basic type of a verse is generally determined by this rule, and a number of verses can only be properly scanned by recognizing the effects of this rule.

Finite forms of *uuesan* and *uuerðan* are always scanned as x syllables. Occasionally in Old Saxon, other finite or non-finite verbs must also be scanned as x-syllables, but in general, this is only to be done when no other scansion is possible.

The second elements of compounds frequently appear in scansion as x-syllables. This may be related to Old Saxon's relatively weak phonological stress, which allows secondary stress to be 'demoted' to unstress relatively easily. This scansion applies primarily in the dip of B feet (and, less often, D feet) and when anacrusis appears to precede Ssx feet, which (by this rule) are to be scanned as Sxx or sxx.

Why is West-Saxon English Different from Old Saxon?

Angelika Lutz

1. Possible Reasons for Differences between West Saxon and Old Saxon

According to Bede, members of three Germanic tribes left their homelands in regions that today form parts of northern Germany and Denmark and gradually conquered those parts of Britannia that today constitute the heartlands of England.[1] If Bede's *Historia Ecclesiastica* is basically correct, the Saxons came from an area which can be roughly equated with modern Lower Saxony and conquered large parts of southern Britannia. West Saxon texts preserve a Low German variety of West Germanic which is closely related to that in Continental Old Saxon texts such as *Heliand* and *Genesis*. Yet, at the same time, the two varieties of Low German exhibit lexical and structural differences of various kinds.[2] Due to the time gap between the Anglo-Saxon Conquest and the earliest attested texts on both sides of the North Sea, these differences may be owing to various causes. The most likely ones are (a) that West Saxon and Old Saxon texts reflect different dialect regions of prehistoric Continental Saxon; (b) that West Saxon features result from dialect mixing, e.g. with Mercian; (c) that Old Saxon features result from dialect mixing, e.g. with Frankish; and (d) that West Saxon

---

[1] Cf. Bede, *HE* 1.15, ed. Colgrave and Mynors, 48–53.

[2] For a convenient overview of the research on Old Saxon see Steffen Krogh, *Die Stellung des Altsächsischen im Rahmen der germanischen Sprachen*, Studien zum Althochdeutschen 29 (Göttingen, 1996). For the relationship between the Old English and Old Saxon *Genesis* poems see *The Saxon Genesis: An Edition of the West Saxon 'Genesis B' and the Old Saxon Vatican Genesis*, ed. Alger N. Doane (Madison, 1991); René Derolez, "*Genesis*: Old Saxon and Old English," *English Studies* 76 (1995): 409–23; and John Hines, "Attitude Problems? The Old Saxon and Old English *Genesis* Poems," in *Language Structure and Variation: A Festschrift for Gunnel Melchers*, ed. Magnus Ljung, Stockholm Studies in English 92 (Stockholm, 2000), 69–90.

Hans Sauer and Joanna Story, eds., *Anglo-Saxon England and the Continent*. With the assistance of Gaby Waxenberger. Essays in Anglo-Saxon Studies, vol. 3. MRTS 394. Tempe: ACMRS, 2011.   [ISBN 978-0-86698-442-3]

features result from language shift by native speakers of Insular Celtic to Saxon. We may well assume different causes for different kinds of divergences between West Saxon and Old Saxon as attested in the texts. Assumption (a), that West Saxon and Old Saxon as recorded in the texts reflect different dialect regions of prehistoric Continental Saxon, receives some support from the evidence of the Straubing fragment of the *Heliand* poem. This fragment contains form words diverging from those in the other manuscript versions, which reflects differences in Old English between West Saxon and Anglian.[3] Assumption (b), namely that insular West Saxon features result from dialect mixing in England from the fifth century onwards, is suggested e.g. by certain traits of early West Saxon spelling that resemble Mercian, and also by Anglian features in late West Saxon poetry.[4] Assumption (c), namely that some Old Saxon features result from dialect mixing on the Continent after the fifth century, is supported by the fact that *Heliand* and *Genesis* seem to represent a more southerly, mixed variety of Old Saxon differing from that of the few prose texts, which suggests that the language of the two poems may have been influenced by Frankish and Old High German as a result of Frankish-dominated Christianization.[5]

Thus, assumptions (a) to (c) may all be valid as causes for some of the differences between West Saxon and Old Saxon. Yet my paper will concentrate on assumption (d), namely that some West Saxon features result from language shift by speakers of Insular Celtic to Saxon. It will become apparent that the Old English evidence for Celtic influence after the Anglo-Saxon Conquest is essentially different from the later English evidence for French influence after the Norman Conquest. My scenario for early Anglo-Saxon England built on this evidence assumes large-scale language shift from Celtic to (pre-)Old English. This scenario, which is built entirely on linguistic evidence, will then be compared with the current competing scenarios built on recent archaeological and genetic evidence.

---

[3] Michael Korhammer, "Altenglische Dialekte und der *Heliand*," *Anglia* 98 (1980): 85–94; Hans Frede Nielsen, "The Straubing *Heliand*-fragment and the Old English Dialects," in *Language Contact in the British Isles*, ed. P. Sture Ureland and George Broderick (Tübingen, 1991), 243–73, and idem, "Ingerid Dal's View on Old Saxon in the Light of New Evidence," in *Language Change and Language Structure: Older Germanic Languages in a Comparative Perspective*, ed. Toril Swan et al. (Berlin, 1994), 195–212, at 200–7.

[4] See Kenneth Sisam, "Dialect Origins of the Earlier Old English Verse," in idem, *Studies in the History of Old English Literature* (Oxford, 1953), 119–39; Alistair Campbell, *Old English Grammar* (Oxford, 1959), §§ 6–17; Thomas Toon, "Old English Dialects," in *The Cambridge History of the English Language*, vol. 1: *The Beginnings to 1066*, ed. Richard M. Hogg (Cambridge, 1992), 409–51.

[5] Cf. Krogh, *Die Stellung des Altsächsischen*, 138–40.

2. The Anglo-Saxon Conquest and the Fate of the Celts: Languages in Contact?

Our two most important historical sources for the Anglo-Saxon and British prehistory of England, Bede's *Historia ecclesiastica gentis Anglorum* (eighth century) and Gildas' *De excidio et conquestu Britanniae* (sixth century),[6] both see the Anglo-Saxons as the winners and the Celts as the losers of a long series of battles. For members of the losing side, Bede describes three types of destiny: flight (to the west or across the sea to Brittany), death, and slavery.[7] Until today, it is widely assumed on linguistic grounds that after the Anglo-Saxon Conquest, there must have been little contact between Anglo-Saxons and Celts, since English exhibits remarkably few Celtic loanwords. An early (1882) explanation for the few lexical loans is found in Edward A. Freeman's *Lectures to American Audiences*:[8]

> The plain fact is that, in utter contrast to the phænomena of Teutonic conquest on the mainland, the Britons were, as a race, exterminated within those parts of Britain which the English occupied while they were still heathens.

In his *Old English History for Children* (1869), Freeman discussed the situation of the Celtic women in that area and drew a link between their assumed fate and the genetic and linguistic consequences:[9]

> The [British] women of course would be made slaves, or they would sometimes be married to their masters. Thus there may doubtless be some little British and Roman blood in us, just as some Welsh and Latin words crept into the English tongue from the very beginning. But we may be sure that we have not much of their blood in us, because we have so few of their words in our language.

---

[6] See Gildas, *The Ruin of Britain and Other Works*, ed. and trans. Michael Winterbottom (London, 1978).

[7] Bede, *HE*, 1.15, ed. Colgrave and Mynors, esp. 52–53.

[8] Edward A. Freeman, *Lectures to American Audiences, I: The English People in its Three Homes* (Philadelphia, 1882), 133. A few years later, Freeman made this comparison with the Continent even more explicit: "Those who thus lived side by side with their conquerors in Gaul, in Spain, in Lombardy, kept their language. Why did those who were in exactly the same case in Britain lose theirs? I answer once more, . . . because in Britain there was a real displacement of one people by another, while in Gaul, Spain, and Italy there was not" (*Four Oxford Lectures: Teutonic Conquest in Gaul and Britain* [Oxford, 1888], 103).

[9] See Edward A. Freeman, *Old English History for Children* (London, 1869), 27. The role of Celtic women is also discussed in *Lectures to American Audiences*, 133.

William Stubbs, in his *Constitutional History* (1871), conceded that "great numbers of Britons may have survived in servile or half-servile conditions," particularly in the west, but then continued:[10]

> ... these probabilities only bring out more strongly the improbability of any general commixture or amalgamation of the races. . . . It is impossible that such a commixture could have taken place without leaving its traces on the language or the religion.

Otto Jespersen, in *Growth and Structure of the English Language* (1905), offered a different explanation for the extremely small number of Celtic loanwords:[11]

> There was nothing to induce the ruling classes to learn the language of the inferior natives; it could never be fashionable for them to show an acquaintance with that despised tongue by using now and then a Keltic word. On the other hand the Kelt would have to learn the language of his masters, and learn it well.

Thus, in contrast to Freeman, Stubbs, and others, Jespersen did not assume a direct link between the number of Celtic loanwords and an assumed number of Celts but related the linguistic evidence to the unequal relationship between winners and losers after the Anglo-Saxon Conquest. According to Jespersen, this contact on unequal terms left practically no trace in the English language whereas Celtic suffered a dramatic loss of speakers over the centuries. More or less explicit versions of both Freeman's and Jespersen's views are also found in various more modern textbooks. Thus, Charles Barber, after a discussion of the remarkably slight influence of Celtic on the Old English lexicon, including place names, attributes "The failure of Celtic to influence Old English to any great extent" (without any further specification) to the fact that "they were a defeated people whose language had no prestige compared with that of the conquerors, and the Anglo-Saxons had settled in such large numbers that there could be no

---

[10] William Stubbs, *The Constitutional History of England* (Oxford, 1874), 67. For discussions of the views of the 19th-century 'Anglo-Saxonists' see Hugh H. MacDougall, *Racial Myth in English History: Trojans, Teutons, and Anglo-Saxons* (Montreal, 1982); Gary D. German, "Britons, Anglo-Saxons and Scholars: 19th Century Attitudes towards the Survival of Britons in Anglo-Saxon England," in *The Celtic Englishes II*, ed. Hildegard L. C. Tristram (Heidelberg, 2000), 347–74, esp. 354–61; and Markku Filppula, Juhani Klemola, and Heli Pitkänen, "Early Contacts between English and the Celtic Languages," in *The Celtic Roots of English*, ed. eidem, Studies in Languages 37 (Joensuu, 2002), 1–26, esp. 3–7.

[11] Otto Jespersen, *Growth and Structure of the English Language*, 10th edn. (Oxford, 1982 [¹Leipzig, 1905]), 35–36.

question of their absorption by the Celts."[12] Albert C. Baugh, in his *History of the English Language*, emphasizes that "the Celts were by no means exterminated except in certain areas" and later on specifies these areas: "In the east and southeast, where the Germanic conquest was fully accomplished at a fairly early date, it is probable that there were fewer survivals of a Celtic population than elsewhere. Large numbers of the defeated fled to the west."[13] Richard Hogg, in *The Cambridge History of the English Language*, merely remarks "that, although relations were sometimes friendly, the fifth- and sixth-century Anglo-Saxons were in this respect as resolutely monolingual as their twentieth-century descendants."[14]

Otto Jespersen was right with regard to the main reason for the few lexical traces of such an unequal contact, but he—just like most later scholars—did not look for structural effects of language shift from Celtic to English. However, in treatments of language contact outside the field of English studies, it has become textbook knowledge that such unequal contacts between two peoples resulting from a conquest have very different effects on the two languages concerned, that of the conquerors (the *superstratum*) and that of the losing side (the *substratum*).[15] The substratum has little lexical effect on the superstratum. Nevertheless, a

---

[12] Charles Barber, *The English Language: A Historical Introduction* (Cambridge, 1993), 101–2.

[13] Albert C. Baugh and Thomas Cable, *A History of the English Language*, 5th edn. (London, 2002), § 54. In Baugh's first edition (New York, 1935), § 55, nothing specific is said about the situation in the Lowlands, and the Anglo-Saxon-Celtic relations in general are characterized as follows: "The relation of the two races was not such as to bring about any considerable influence on English life or on English speech. The surviving Celts were a submerged race. Had they, like the Romans, possessed a superior culture, something valuable to give the Teutons, their influence might have been greater. But the Anglo-Saxons found little occasion to adopt Celtic modes of expression and the Celtic influence remains the least of the early influences which affected the English language."

[14] Richard Hogg, "Introduction," in *The Cambridge History of the English Language*, vol. 1: *The Beginnings to 1066*, ed. idem, 1–25, at 3.

[15] For sufficiently precise definitions of this pair of terms and for clear descriptions of the linguistic effect of a substratum on the superstratum see especially Rudolf E. Keller, *Die deutsche Sprache und ihre historische Entwicklung*, rev. trans. Karl-Heinz Mulagk (Hamburg, 1978), 620 (glossary of linguistic terms); Theo Vennemann, "Bemerkung zum frühgermanischen Wortschatz," in *Studia Linguistica et Philologica: Festschrift für Klaus Matzel zum sechzigsten Geburtstag*, ed. Hans-Werner Eroms, Bernhard Gajek, and Herbert Kolb (Heidelberg, 1984), 105–19, at 105–12; and idem, "Germania Semitica: ⁺*plōg-/*⁺*pleg-*, ⁺*furh-/*⁺*farh-*, ⁺*folk-/*⁺*flokk-*, ⁺*felh-/*⁺*folg-*," in *Deutsche Grammatik—Thema in Variationen: Festschrift für Hans-Werner Eroms zum 60. Geburtstag*, ed. Karin Donhauser and Ludwig M. Eichinger (Heidelberg, 1998), 245–61, at 245–48 [both papers reprinted in Theo Vennemann, gen. Nierfeld, *Europa Vasconica—Europa Semitica*, ed. Patricia Noel Aziz Hanna, Trends in Linguistics: Studies and Monographs 138 (Berlin, 2003) as nos. 1 and 19 and supplied with abstracts in English]; Sarah Grey Thomason and Terrence Kaufman, *Language Contact, Creolization, and Genetic Linguistics* (Berkeley, 1988), 68–69, 116–18.

substratum language may exert far-reaching structural influence on the super-stratum, i.e. on its phonology, morphology, and syntax, if many speakers of the substratum abandon it for the superstratum, i.e. in case of large-scale language shift. By contrast, the superstrate language may have far-reaching effects on the lexicon of the substratum, if the substratum survives, and the lexical effects of the Norman Conquest on English demonstrate that this applies particularly to military, legal, and administrative terms, which reflect the change of power.[16]

There are a number of studies that leave no doubt that in terms of struc-ture, many characteristic features of Modern English result from Celtic influ-ence whereas Old English preserves many Germanic structures largely intact.[17] Very recently, however, some authors have gone so far as to claim that compared to later stages of English, Old English is practically free from Celtic influence and that the emergence of the Celtic structures in later English was made pos-sible by the breakdown of the Anglo-Saxon power structures after the Norman Conquest. This view is presented most explicitly in a recent paper by Hildegard Tristram.[18] Tristram claims that written Old English represents the language of

---

[16] See Angelika Lutz, "When Did English Begin?," in *Sounds, Words, Texts and Change: Selected Papers from 11 ICEHL, Santiago de Compostela, 7–11 September 2000,* ed. Teresa Fanego and Elena Seoane (Amsterdam, 2002), 145–71, at 148–50. That this applies cross-linguistically is illustrated by Vennemann, "Bemerkung zum frühgerma-nischen Wortschatz," 105–16. For the low status of British and its large number of for-eign loans, compared to Irish, see Thomas Charles-Edwards, "Language and Society among the Insular Celts 400–1000," in *The Celtic World,* ed. Miranda J. Green (London, 1995), 703–36, at 729–30: "Welsh showed no inhibitions in borrowing from English," and at 735: "Because British had low status by comparison with Latin, Irish and English, it was more subject to external influence." That the number of Celtic loans in English is not quite as small as usually believed is shown by Andrew Breeze, "Seven Types of Celtic Loanwords," in *The Celtic Roots of English,* ed. Filppula et al., 175–81.

[17] See numerous recent papers in *The Celtic Roots of English* and in *The Celtic Eng-lishes I-III,* ed. Hildegard L. C. Tristram (Heidelberg, 1997, 2000, 2003) and *The Celtic Englishes IV: The Interface between English and the Celtic Languages,* ed. Hildegard L. C. Tristram (Potsdam, 2006). For important older studies see n. 31 below.

[18] Hildegard Tristram, "Diglossia in Anglo-Saxon England, or What was Spoken Old English Like?,"*Studia Anglica Posnaniensia* 40 (2004): 87–110. For similarly extreme views see Theo Vennemann, "On the Rise of 'Celtic' Syntax in Middle English," in *Mid-dle English from Tongue to Text: Selected Papers from the Third International Conference on Middle English,* ed. Peter Lucas and Angela Lucas (Frankfurt, 2002), 203–34, at 204, where he states that "written Old English is a pure West Germanic language," and in idem, "Sprachgeburt durch Sprachkontakt: Die Entstehung des Englischen," in *Sprach-tod und Sprachgeburt,* ed. Peter Schrijver and Peter-Arnold Mumm (München, 2004), 21–56, at 49, where he argues for a "Zweiteilung, . . . mit Angelsächsisch als der Phase der germanischen Syntax und Englisch als der Phase der keltisierten Syntax" ('a division into two, . . . with Anglo-Saxon as the phase of Germanic syntax and English as the phase of Celticized syntax'), with a breaking point in the fourteenth century.

the Germanic élite and that the language of the Celtic-influenced lower classes did not make it into the Old English sources:[19]

> The written language was, of course, that of a small powerful elite, ethnically the Anglo-Saxons. . . . In the later period, there must have been a tripartite division of the types of OE: a) the *written* language of the elite the norms of which were carefully maintained (OE$_W$), b) the *spoken* vernacular of the elite (OE$_H$), . . . and c) the *vernacular* of the bulk of the population, which was largely of British and in the Danelaw areas also of Scandinavian extraction (OE$_L$). . . . Of the two types of spoken Old English, only the low variety surfaced after the replacement of the Anglo-Saxon elite by William the Conqueror.

The Indo-Europeanist and Celticist Peter Schrijver, who—like Tristram, Filppula, and others, including myself—generally assumes strong Celtic structural influence on English, claims in another recent paper that the lowland areas, which were affected by the Anglo-Saxon Conquest earliest and most strongly, experienced little direct contact with Celtic, as becomes clear from his summary:[20]

> Germanic settlers that began occupying the North Sea basin from the fourth century onwards from northern Germany and Denmark primarily came into contact with speakers of North Sea Celtic in the British Highland Zone . . . and with speakers of Northwestern Romance in the British Lowland Zone and in the Low Countries, where Saxon, Kentish, Coastal Dutch and Frisian came into being.

Thus, with regard to the Saxons as the most important Low German group that settled the Southern Lowlands, Schrijver assumes that there was hardly any contact with Celtic-speaking Celts but instead with Romanized Celts who spoke Latin though presumably with a Celtic accent and with Celticisms in their syntax. This would mean that our extant West Saxon texts lack obvious Celtic contact features.

[19] Tristram, "Diglossia," 103.
[20] See Peter Schrijver, "The Rise and Fall of British Latin: Evidence from English and Brittonic," in *The Celtic Roots of English*, ed. Filppula et al., 87–110, at 109.

3. Some Linguistic Evidence for Celtic Substratum Influence

3.1. The Twofold Paradigm of the Old English Verb 'to be'

For my assumption of direct substratal Celtic influence on pre-Old English, I consider the twofold present tense of the verb 'to be' the most important piece of structural evidence. In this respect, Old English differs from the other Germanic languages, including Old Saxon, and agrees with the Celtic languages, as the forms of the singular indicative demonstrate:[21]

West Saxon		Cymric		Old Saxon	Old High German	Old Norse	Gothic
bēo	ēom	byðaf	wyf	bium	bim	em	im
bist	eart	byðy	wyt	bist	bist	est	is
bið	is	byð	yw	is(t)	ist	es	ist

The so-called 'habitual' present is expressed by forms with initial *b*- in Old English and Celtic, the so-called 'actual' present by forms with initial vowel, like in Old Norse and Gothic; Old Saxon and Old High German exhibit a mixture of forms with initial *b*- in the first and second persons and with initial vowel in the third person. Most grammars simply mention this twofold paradigm as a feature of Old English as opposed to later stages of English. Hans Krahe and Wolfgang Meid consider it to be an Indo-European feature which is preserved in Italic, Celtic, and Old English but lost in all other Germanic languages, and they suggest that its preservation in Old English may be due to language contact with Celtic.[22]

---

[21] See Campbell, *Old English Grammar*, § 768 (d) for the forms of the Old English dialects; Hans Krahe and Wolfgang Meid, *Germanische Sprachwissenschaft II: Formenlehre*, Sammlung Göschen 780b, 7th edn. (Berlin, 1969), § 98 for the Germanic languages; Johan Hendrik Gallée, *Altsächsische Grammatik: Register von Johannes Lochner*, 3rd edn. (Tübingen, 1993), § 422 for variation within Old Saxon; and J. Morris Jones, *A Welsh Grammar: Historical and Comparative* (Oxford, 1931), § 189 for Cymric.

[22] Krahe and Meid, *Germanische Sprachwissenschaft*, § 97, at 140–41. Campbell, *Old English Grammar*, § 768, at 350, seems to think along the same lines when stating that "The distinction of the pres. indic. tenses *eom* and *bēo* is fairly well preserved in OE." For the difficult functional distinction of the uses of the two paradigms in Old English see Bruce Mitchell, *Old English Syntax*, 2 vols. (Oxford, 1985), 1: §§ 651–54, and Matti Kilpiö, *Passive Constructions in Old English Translations from Latin, With Special Reference to the OE Bede and the 'Pastoral Care'*, Mémoires de la Société Néophilologique de Helsinki 49 (Helsinki, 1989), esp. 94–98. Abbot Ælfric mentions one of the functional distinctions in his chapter *De Verbis anomalis vel inequalibus*, where he equates the Latin present tense *sum* etc. with Old English *ic eom* and the Latin future tense *ero* with Old

Wolfgang Keller was the first to suggest an alternative to preservation of the twofold paradigm in the two languages, namely language shift from Celtic to pre-Old English.[23] After explaining the fact that English exhibits very few Celtic loanwords by referring to German, which contains only few loans from Slavic, as being due to the similarity of those contacts, namely one between serfs (Celts and Slavs) and masters (Anglo-Saxons and Germans), he continued:[24]

> Nicht im Wortschatz, sondern in der Syntax ist der Einfluß der fremd-sprachigen Unterschicht in erster Linie zu spüren, denn es handelt sich für den deutsch sprechenden Slaven ebenso wie für den englisch sprechenden Kelten zunächst um ein Einsetzen der fremdsprachigen Wörter in den Satz der eigenen Sprache, ein wörtliches Übersetzen.

> ['The influence of the lower classes speaking a different language is mostly felt in the syntax and not in the lexicon, since for Slavs speaking German and Celts speaking English means first of all inserting foreign words into the sentences of their own language, translating word by word.']

According to Keller, the twofold present tense was introduced into pre-Old English by the early Britons in the course of acquiring the language of the new rulers of Britain:[25]

> [Die] altenglischen Formen und Funktionen der Wurzel *bheu, die den anderen germanischen Dialekten fremd sind, entstanden im Munde und im Denken von englisch sprechenden Briten.

> ['The Old English forms and functions of the root *bheu, which are alien to the other Germanic dialects, developed in the mouths and minds of English-speaking Britons.']

In Keller's time, this explanation was novel. Meanwhile, however, it has become textbook knowledge in general contact linguistics and is characterized as *imperfect learning* in the course of language shift from the substratum to the superstratum.[26] Keller's insightful account was largely ignored on both sides of the North

---

English *ic bēo*; see *Ælfrics Grammatik und Glossar*, ed. Julius Zupitza, 3rd edn. with a new preface by Helmut Gneuss (Berlin, 2002), 201–2.

[23] Wolfgang Keller, "Keltisches im englischen Verbum," in *Anglica: Untersuchungen zur englischen Philologie = Festschrift für Alois Brandl*, vol. 1 (Leipzig, 1925), 55–66, at 56–60.

[24] Keller, "Keltisches im englischen Verbum," 56.

[25] Keller, "Keltisches im englischen Verbum," 60.

[26] Cf. Thomason and Kaufman, *Language Contact*, 38–43, 49–52, 110–19. For the related but more general term *interference* see Uriel Weinreich, *Languages in Contact: Findings and Problems* (New York, 1953), esp. chap. 2.3 "Grammatical Interference," and Thomason and Kaufman, *Language Contact*, chaps. 2 and 5.

Sea. With regard to textbook accounts written in English, one might excuse this as being due to the fact that it was written in German. Yet when in 1963 a similar explanation was put forward in English by J. R. R. Tolkien,[27] it suffered the same fate.

The assumption that the politically and legally unequal status of the two peoples in early Anglo-Saxon England resulted in large-scale language shift from Celtic to (pre-)Old English is compelling, but its linguistic consequences need to be differentiated for different periods of Celtic-Saxon contact. Initially, the distinction between the two paradigms of 'to be' may have appeared as a Celticism of the lower classes to the Saxon élites, but by the time of the Old English textual sources, almost three centuries after the Anglo-Saxon Conquest, the distinction between the two paradigms of 'to be' was clearly no longer a feature of lower-class speech only, since it was used in prose of all kinds and even in poetry.[28] This suggests early large-scale language shift from Celtic to Old English, and it weakens Tristram's claim that the language of the Anglo-Saxon élite was practically unmixed Low German. Note that in the case of the habitual paradigm with initial *b-*, even the forms were similar in Old English and Celtic. This formal similarity speaks for direct language contact with Celtic and thus possibly weakens Schrijver's assumption of total Romanization of Lowland Britannia by the time of the Anglo-Saxon Conquest.

3.2. The Old English Beginnings of the Progressive Aspect

The second piece of structural evidence for the assumption that some differences between West Saxon and Old Saxon result from language shift by speakers of Insular Celtic to Saxon is the progressive aspect. Unlike the twofold paradigm of 'to be', the progressive was in a very early stage of development in Old English and became fully grammaticalized only in the course of Modern English. My sketch of the discussion, which is based on an excellent recent overview by Markku Filppula,[29] will concentrate on the situation in Old English and early Middle English. The origin of the English progressive is one of the most hotly disputed problems of historical English grammar. Three main types of hypotheses as to its origin have been put forward: two are based on foreign influence, one assumes an independent development which was possibly reinforced by foreign influence.[30]

---

[27] "English and Welsh," in *Angles and Britons: O'Donnell Lectures*, ed. Nora K. Chadwick (Cardiff, 1963), 1–41, at 30–32.

[28] See *DOE* s.v *bēon*.

[29] M. Filppula, "More on the English Progressive and the Celtic Connection," in *The Celtic Englishes III*, ed. Tristram (Heidelberg, 2003), 150–68.

[30] See Filppula, "More on the English Progressive," 151–58; independent development in English was suggested by G. O. Curme, "History of the English Gerund," *Englische Studien* 45 (1912): 349–80, and Gerhard Nickel, *Die Expanded Form im Altenglischen: Vorkommen, Funktion und Herkunft der Umschreibung beon/wesan + Partizip Präsens*

The Celtic hypothesis is mostly favored by Celticists and other linguists with an intimate knowledge of the corresponding structures in various stages and varieties of Celtic.[31] For my purpose, it will suffice to list the strongest linguistic arguments for Celtic influence on the basis of Filppula's well-balanced account and then concentrate on the situation in Old English, with particular reference to West Saxon. The most forceful arguments in favor of Celtic and against Latin and French influence are the following:

1. The progressive aspect, being a grammatical feature just like the Old English twofold paradigm of 'to be', is a typical candidate for substratal influence due to language shifting.

2. The Celtic languages exhibit a progressive aspect as a grammaticalized category at their earliest attested stages and thus antedate the English progressive.[32]

3. In strongly Celticized varieties of Modern English such as Irish English, the use of the progressive extends beyond that of its sphere of usage in Standard English; this extended usage in the Celtic Englishes reflects the more extended use of the progressive in the respective Celtic languages.[33]

4. Scholars who assume Latin influence need to explain why similar contact with Latin did not lead to a similar development in Old High German and Old Saxon.

(Neumünster, 1966). The fundamental study in favor of Latin (and French) influence is Fernand Mossé, *Histoire de la forme périphrastique 'être + participe présent' en germanique: Moyen-anglais et anglais moderne* (Paris, 1938).

[31] Important studies in favor of Celtic influence are Keller, "Keltisches im englischen Verbum," 61–66; Ingerid Dal, "Zur Entstehung des englischen Participium Praesentis auf -*ing*," *Norsk Tidsskrift for Sprogvidenskap* 16 (1952): 5–116; Wolfgang Preusler, "Keltischer Einfluß im Englischen," *Indogermanische Forschungen* 56 (1938): 178–91, and idem, "Keltischer Einfluß im Englischen," *Revue des Langues Vivantes* 22 (1956): 322–50; Heinrich Wagner, *Das Verbum in den Sprachen der Britischen Inseln* (Tübingen, 1959); Bjørn Braaten, "Notes on the Continuous Tenses in English," *Norsk Tidsskrift for Sprogvidenskap* 21 (1967): 167–80; Ingo Mittendorf and Erich Poppe, "Celtic Contacts of the English Progressive?," in *The Celtic Englishes II*, ed. Tristram (Heidelberg, 2000), 122–45; Erich Poppe, "The 'Expanded Form' in Insular Celtic and English: Some Historical and Comparative Considerations, with Special Emphasis on Middle Irish," in *The Celtic Roots of English*, ed. Filppula et al., 237–70, and most recently, Filppula, "More on the English Progressive."

[32] See especially Mittendorf and Poppe, "Celtic Contacts of the English Progressive?," 117–35 on Middle Welsh, and Patricia Ronan, "Periphrastic Progressive in Old Irish," in *The Celtic Englishes III*, ed. Tristram, 129–49 on Old Irish.

[33] Filppula, "More on the English Progressive," 161–66.

As regards the use of the present participle in Old English as opposed to the verbal noun in later English, which is modeled more closely on the nominal Celtic construction, opinions continue to be divided. Several scholars are ready to accept Celtic as the model for the later use of the verbal noun but believe that the Old English construction with the present participle was modeled on Latin, despite the fact that in that case we would have to expect early forms of the progressive also in Old High German and Old Saxon.[34]

Filppula deals with the situation in Old English on the basis of the evidence presented by Ingerid Dal.[35] According to Dal, there is Old English evidence for the use of the present participle and the prepositional construction with -ing/ -ung alongside each other with the same meaning, namely[36]

> 1. in appositional participial position, e.g. *spræc wēpende* : *spræc on wēpinge*;

> 2. as predicate with verbs of motion and stance (*Ruhe*), e.g. *cōm rīdende* : *cōm on rīdinge*;

> 3. as predicate with *bēon*, e.g. *wæs feohtende* : *wæs on feohtinge*;

> 4. as predicate of an object with verbs of perception and feeling, e.g. *geseah hine rīdende* : *geseah hine on rīdinge*.

Dal explains the scarcity of the verbal-noun construction in Old English and early Middle English texts, compared with the participial construction, with the influence of the conservative West Saxon literary tradition, which might have regarded the use of the more obviously Celticized verbal-noun construction as vulgar and therefore as something to be avoided.[37] It is true that the Old English participial construction was less obviously Celtic in form. Yet, in (pre-)Old English when both present and past participles were regularly treated as predicate

---

[34] For this discussion see Braaten, "Notes on the Continuous Tenses in English," 168–73; Nickel, *Die Expanded Form im Altenglischen*, 299–300; and Mittendorf and Poppe, "Celtic Contacts of the English Progressive?" 119. For the English and Celtic verbal-noun construction and its connection with Hamito-Semitic see Theo Vennemann, "Atlantis Semitica: Structural Contact Features in Celtic and English," in *Historical Linguistics 1999: Selected Papers from the 14th International Conference on Historical Linguistics, Vancouver, 9–13 August 1999*, ed. Laurel J. Brinton (Amsterdam, 2001), 351–69, at 353–56.

[35] See Filppula, "More on the English Progressive," 156–57, and Dal, "Zur Entstehung," 29–102.

[36] Filppula, "More on the English Progressive," 156, based on Dal, "Zur Entstehung," 101–2.

[37] Dal, "Zur Entstehung," 113.

adjectives,[38] the present participle possibly offered a more adequate translation for the Celtic progressive in the mouths and minds of (pre-)West Saxon-speaking Britons than in Middle English, when the participles lost their predicative, adjectival character.

With regard to the range of uses of the Old English participial construction, Filppula, referring to Nickel, emphasizes that the progressive was used especially in "vivid descriptions."[39] Nickel illustrated this stylistic prefererence with passages from Alfredian translations, particularly from the Old English *Orosius*, since Nickel's aim was to demonstrate the syntactic and stylistic independence of Old English renderings of Latin texts. But such uses of the participial construction are also found in passages of presumably original Old English prose, as demonstrated by Nickel. Three possibly very early West Saxon occurrences of this use are attested in the Cynewulf and Cyneheard episode entered in the *Anglo-Saxon Chronicle* sub anno 755, which deals with a conflict in the West Saxon royal family—and thus certainly not in a lower-class context.[40] All three occurrences are examples for Dal's construction type 3):

7 þa ut ræsde on hine 7 hine miclum gewundode, 7 hie alle on þone cyning **wærun feohtende** oþ þæt hie hine ofslegenne hæfdon.

['and thereupon he rushed out against him and wounded him severely. Then they all fought against the king until they had slain him.']

7 hiera nænig hit geþicgean nolde. Ac hie simle **feohtende wæran** oþ hie alle lægon butan anum bryttiscum gisle, 7 se swiþe gewundad wæs.

---

[38] In formal terms, this is obvious only in the past participle, which agreed in number and partly also in case and gender with the noun it referred to; see Tauno F. Mustanoja, *A Middle English Syntax, I: Parts of Speech* (Helsinki, 1960), 440; Mitchell, *Old English Syntax*, §§ 33–37, 759–64; and Kilpiö, *Passive Constructions*, 126–35.

[39] See Filppula, "More on the English Progressive," 154, and Nickel, *Die Expanded Form im Altenglischen*, 262–65. For examples from translated texts, Nickel demonstrates the stylistic independence of the Old English renderings in their use of participial constructions and points to similarities of usage with that of the continuous form in Modern English.

[40] *The Anglo-Saxon Chronicle MS A*, ed. Janet Bately, *The Anglo-Saxon Chronicle*: A Collaborative Edition, ed. David Dumville and Simon Keynes, 3 (Cambridge, 1986), 36–67; translation from *English Historical Documents*, vol. 1: *c. 500–1042*, ed. Dorothy Whitelock, with David C. Douglas and Susie Tucker, 2nd edn. (London, 1979), 175–76. For the views that this dramatic episode is based either on an earlier written source or on oral tradition, see Stanley B. Greenfield and Daniel G. Calder, *A New Critical History of Old English Literature*, with a survey of the Anglo-Latin background by Michael Lapidge (New York, 1986), 60 with note 91.

['and not one of them would accept it. But they continued to fight until they all lay dead except for one British hostage, and he was severely wounded.']

7 hie ymb þa gatu **feohtende wæron** oþ þæt hie þærinne fulgon 7 þone ęþeling ofslogon . . .

['and they proceeded to fight around the gates until they broke their way in, and killed the atheling']

Dorothy Whitelock's translation employs the simple past in all three instances, expressing the temporal extension of imperfective *feohtende wæron* with lexical means in two cases ('continued to . . . proceeded to'), but Benjamin Thorpe renders the participial constructions in all three cases with the continuous form ('and they were all fighting . . . but they continued fighting . . . And they then were fighting about the gates').'[41] Nickel points to a number of preferred uses of such participial constructions in the Chronicle and in other texts considered to be relatively independent of Latin, among them their use with imperfective verbs expressing either stance (*sittende, standende, wuniende*) or motion (*ergende, feohtende, winnende*), and to the fact that in most cases the Modern English continuous form would serve as an adequate translation.[42] According to Dal (cited above), both the present participle and the prepositional construction with *-ing/-ung* occur as predicate with verbs of motion and stance in Old English. Together with Dal, I would therefore view the participial construction and the prepositional construction as two alternative or, rather, consecutive attempts at imitating the same Celtic construction type.

The grammatical features adduced as evidence for Celtic influence here so far have been discussed for a long time and repeatedly, but in recent years with the additional support of general, comparative contact linguistics, which presents evidence for substratal influence on the syntax of the superstratum from many different languages. In the following section, I would like to draw attention to lexical and semantic evidence from Old English and particularly from West Saxon.

3.3. Lexical and Semantic Evidence for a Celtic Substratum in West Saxon

The pieces of lexical evidence that can be adduced in support of Celtic substratal influence due to language shift from Celtic to (pre-)West Saxon are not loanwords but Old English designations for Celts and their status by Anglo-Saxons,

---

[41] *The Anglo-Saxon Chronicle, according to the Several Original Authorities*, ed., with a translation, Benjamin Thorpe, vol. 2, "Translation," Rolls Series 23.2 (London, 1861), 43.

[42] Nickel, *Die Expanded Form im Altenglischen*, 133–36. Yet in Old English such participial forms were still only rarely used compared to the simple form in the same types of contexts.

in particular by West Saxons. The following list of related words for 'slave' deriving from 'Celt' is based on David Pelteret's excellent study of slavery in Anglo-Saxon England:[43]

> OE *weale* sb. (f) 'A female Celtic slave.'
> OE *wealh* sb. (m)
>> 1. 'A foreigner.'
>> 2. 'A Briton, a person of Celtic-speaking origin.'
>> 3. 'A slave.'
>> 4. 'A British or Celtic slave.'
> OE *weal-sada* sb. (m) 'A slave-shackle.'
> OE *wilisc* adj.
>> 1. 'Foreign.'
>> 2. 'British, Celtic.'
>> 3. 'Of slave status.'
>> 4. 'British (language).'
>> 5. 'Welsh.'
> OE *wiln* sb. (f) 'A female slave.'
> OE *wiln-incel* sb. (f) 'A little or young slave.'

Before dealing with *wealh* and formally related words, it needs to be emphasized that the most widely-used Old English word meaning 'slave' is *ðēow*, *ðēowa*, with a large number of derivatives.[44] The evidence for all Old English words meaning 'slave' reflects the fact that the institution of slavery was well established in Anglo-Saxon England and that Anglo-Saxons figured as slave owners, as slavers, and as slaves.

---

[43] Cf. David A. E. Pelteret, *Slavery in Early Medieval England* (Woodbridge, 1995), "The Old English Terminology," 319–22, 325–28. Besides Pelteret's book, see also Margaret L. Faull, "The Semantic Development of Old English *wealh*," *Leeds Studies in English* 8 (1975): 20–44, and *A Thesaurus of Old English*, ed. Jane Roberts and Christian Kay, with Lynne Grundy, 2 vols. (London, 1995) 1: 546–47, section 12.01.10.09 'Bondage, slavery.' The meaning 'slave' of *wealh* has been adduced as evidence for the status of the Celts in Anglo-Saxon England before; see e.g. Barber, *The English Language*, 102: "The Old English word *wealh*, which originally meant 'foreigner', came to mean both 'Celt, Welshman' and 'servant, slave', which illustrates both the survival of the Britons among the Anglo-Saxons, and their low status." See also Raymond Hickey, "Early Contact and Parallels between English and Celtic," *Vienna English Working Papers* 4 (1995): 87–119, at 103–4. However, Pelteret's detailed study of the entire word family on the basis of the complete textual evidence allows for a far more precise and differentiated assessment of its historical and linguistic relevance.

[44] Pelteret, *Slavery*, 41–45, 305–16. For its disputed etymology see Friedrich Kluge, *Etymologisches Wörterbuch der deutschen Sprache*, 24th edn., expanded and revised Elmar Seebold (Berlin, 2002), s.vv. *dienen* 'serve', *Diener* 'servant', and *Dirne* 'prostitute'.

The above list of related words for 'slave' deriving from 'Celt' deserves specification in several ways: According to Pelteret, senses (2) of the noun *wealh* and the adjective *wīlisc*, 'Briton' and 'British, Celtic', are most frequently attested in the *Anglo-Saxon Chronicle*, especially in place-names referring to locations predominantly or exclusively inhabited by Britons.[45] By contrast, sense (3) 'slave'

> see[m]s to have been limited to the south of England. In biblical translations it appears only in those composed in the West-Saxon dialect. Thus in the West-Saxon version of Matthew 24: 50 *weales* (*weles*, *wieles*) translates *serui* . . . In the Vespasian Psalter, undoubtedly in the Mercian dialect even though transcribed in Canterbury, *seruus* is always glossed *þiow*; in the Rushworth Gospels the corresponding word is *esne*; and the Lindisfarne Gospels have either *esne*, *ðea*, or *þræl*.[46]

But he emphasizes that the West Saxon evidence is not uniform, as Ælfric's use of *wealh* for 'slave' betrays:[47]

> Ælfric's use of *wealh* . . . seems to have been limited to his earlier writings, and even then its appearance is a rare occurrence . . . it was not in regular use in his vocabulary . . . he eliminated it over a period of time, perhaps because of the possibility of confusing it with sense 2).

The evidence for OE *wiln* 'female slave' (< *wealhin*) tells a different and more straightforward story, as will become apparent from the following quotes from Pelteret's detailed treatment. The first refers to the early date of this derivative, to its uniform sense, and its dialectally limited attestation:[48]

> Since *wiln* displays i-mutation, a phonological change that can be dated to *ca* A.D. 700, the suffix must have been added before then. It is never found in the sense 'Celtic woman' and may have had a wider dialectal distribution than *wealh*, though it still appears to have been a southern word.

Thus the formation of this derivative and its wholesale change of meaning to 'slave' must be dated to the centuries between the Anglo-Saxon Conquest and the

---

[45] Pelteret, *Slavery*, 319–20.

[46] Pelteret, *Slavery*, 320–21. As regards the adjective *wīlisc*, the meaning 'Welsh' is a late Old English development which presumably reflects the consolidation of the political border between late Anglo-Saxon England and Wales. Pelteret states: "Only from the middle of the eleventh century do various versions of the *Anglo-Saxon Chronicle* record *wilisc* several times in this, the sense that has survived into Modern English" (*Slavery*, 326).

[47] Pelteret, *Slavery*, 321.

[48] Pelteret, *Slavery*, 43; see also 327: "Unlike *wealh*, however, the word is never used as any sort of national appellative for the Celts in extant sources. . . . the word always represents *ancilla*."

earliest attested sources, and the textual evidence for *wīln* points to the Southern Lowlands, which were affected by the Anglo-Saxon Conquest earliest and most strongly. Most attestations for the word are from Ælfric's works.[49] *Wīln* needs to be contrasted with the semantically more specific formative *wēale* 'female Celtic slave,' a weak n-stem without i-mutation, presumably a more recent derivative from *wealh* combining senses (2) 'Briton' and (3) 'slave,' which is attested only in two riddles.[50] Whether the etymological relation between *wīln* and *wealh* had become partly obscure by that time is difficult to say.[51]

With regard to the exact contextual meaning of *wīln*, Pelteret notes in his terminological appendix:[52] "In every case where the word appears it seems to refer to legal status, unlike *þeow*, which sometimes denotes a state of spiritual dependance, as in *Godes þeow*." And he quotes an example from Ælfric's homily *On the Epiphany of the Lord*:[53]

> Hit gelimpþ forwel oft þæt on anre tide acenð seo cwen and seo wyln and ðeah geðicð se æðeling be his gebyrdum to healicum cynesetle, and ðære wylne sunu wunað eal his lif on ðeowte.

> ['It happens very often that the queen and the slave bring forth at one time, and yet the prince, through his birth, grows up for the lofty throne, and the son of the slave continues all his life in servitude.']

Pelteret further remarks that "there are several indications that the word was not just used to denote a female slave in general but that it referred more specifically

---

[49] Pelteret, *Slavery*, 328; this contrasts with Ælfric's decreasing use of *wealh* in the sense 'slave' in his later works discussed above.

[50] See Pelteret, *Slavery*, 51–53. The Old English riddle tradition is dated to the 8th century at the earliest. Whereas n-stems, both masculine and feminine, are very productive (for the integration of Latin loans into this pattern cf. Campbell, *Old English Grammar*, §§ 560–61), feminine formations with *-en* (< *-in*) with umlaut had become rare by late Old English; cf. Dieter Kastovsky, "Semantics and Vocabulary," in *The Cambridge History of the English Language*, vol. 1: *The Beginnings to 1066*, ed. Hogg, 290–408, at 389–90.

[51] Both due to its specialized sense and to sound changes; note, however, that the adjective *wīlisc* was likewise affected by i-mutation, compensatory lengthening resulting from intervocalic loss of /h/ and, in late West Saxon, by monophthongisation (see Campbell, *Old English Grammar*, §§ 200, 240–55, 300–1, 318).

[52] Pelteret, *Slavery*, 327.

[53] Pelteret, *Slavery*, 327, referring to *The Sermones Catholici*, 1.7, ed. and trans. Benjamin Thorpe, 10.26–29, 111.25–28. This quote also helps to explain how a girl might have attained the status of a *wīln-incel*.

to one who had a personal relationship with her owner."[54] And he adduces a
quote from Ælfric's *Sermon on Auguries*:[55]

> Ac seo sawl is ðæs flæsces hlæfdige and hire gedafnað þæt heo simle
> gewylde ða wylne, þæt is þæt flæsc to hyre hæsum. þwyrlice færð æt ðam
> huse þær seo wyln bið þære hlæfdian wissigend and seo hlæfdige bið þære
> wylne underðeodd.

> ['But the soul is the flesh's mistress, and it befits her that she should ever
> rule the bondmaid, that is the flesh, according to her command. It fares
> ill with the house where the bondmaid is the ruler of the mistress and the
> mistress is in subjection to the bondmaid.']

The relationship between a female slave and her master is also attested in a law of
Cnut (II Cnut, § 54) presumably devised by Archbishop Wulfstan, "which lays
down penalties for a married man who has sexual relations with his own slave.
The latter is referred to as a *wyln*."[56]

Ælfric and Wulfstan, in their functions as high-ranking men of the church,
were concerned with the moral and legal problems related to Anglo-Saxon masters and their house slaves, and the fact that they addressed such problems in
homilies and laws suggests that they were not dealing with isolated cases. But
what kinds of conclusions can we reasonably draw from this evidence for the
assumption of a Celtic substratum in Wessex? The textual evidence for *wealh*
'slave' and *wīln* 'female slave' suggests that in the Southern Lowlands slaves were
frequently of Celtic origin, at least in early Anglo-Saxon England, and that in
those early times at least the prototypical female slave was of Celtic origin. This
could well have led to the types of substratum influences on the verbal system
discussed above, especially if female house slaves were also recruited from mono-
lingually Celtic enclaves for an extended period of time. It should, however, be
emphasized that in later Anglo-Saxon England, when the term *wīln* had attained
the more general meaning 'female slave,' the use of this word need no longer refer
to a woman of Celtic origin.

Our knowledge of the legal status of the Celts in Anglo-Saxon England is
patchy and uneven. At the time of Ine's laws, slave status appears to have been only

---

[54] Pelteret, *Slavery*, 327.

[55] Pelteret, *Slavery*, 327, with references to Skeat's edition and translation (the latter
emended by Pelteret). In another quote from the same sermon, "Ælfric uses *seo wyln* of a
slave who is elsewhere referred to as *an minra wimmanna*" (327–28).

[56] Pelteret, *Slavery*, 328.

one explicit form of a more general legal inequality for Celts in Wessex,[57] but by Alfred's time the legal status of Celts was no longer specified. Pelteret states:[58]

> The main body of the code indicates that changes had taken place in West-Saxon society since the time of Alfred's predecessor, Ine. The latter's legislation, promulgated between 688 and 694, had recognized that the British were an important ethnic group in Wessex, even though many of them appear to have been slaves. No consideration is given to them in Alfred's laws and one must assume that in some measure they had been integrated into Anglo-Saxon society during the intervening two centuries, even though the process still had some way to go as the South-west had not yet been completely subjugated.

The knowledge of (pre-)Saxon among people of Celtic origin would have been 'imperfect' to various degrees, i.e. characterized by interference from Celtic particularly in their syntax and phonology. As regards female house slaves, influence of their 'imperfect' Saxon on their masters' language, i.e. on that of adult men of higher rank, is doubtful. But as house slaves, they would have been in close contact not only with their masters but, linguistically more important, also with their masters' children.

The West Saxon laws of Ine and Alfred permitted *ceorlas* to own slaves,[59] but it is reasonable to assume that members of the Anglo-Saxon upper ranks of society could afford more slaves than could *ceorlas*. For these reasons, we may expect the language of the Saxon upper classes to have been in closer contact with Celticized forms of Saxon than that of the Saxon farmers. Thus the linguistic conditions for intimate contact between speakers of the Saxon superstratum from the upper ranks and the Celtic substratum may be assumed to have been particularly favorable, at least in early Anglo-Saxon England. For these reasons, Tristram's claim that the language of the Anglo-Saxon élite remained practically unaffected by Celtic for six centuries seems untenable, and it is in fact countered by the West Saxon structural and lexical evidence adduced here.

---

[57] Pelteret, *Slavery*, esp. 32–34, 81–89. See also Charles-Edwards, "Language and Society," 730–31, who draws a parallel between the status of the Britons in early Wessex and that of the Gallo-Romans under Frankish rule: "They had a legal status, but their wergilds were around half those enjoyed by the corresponding Frankish or English rank. . . . the West Saxon noble had a wergild of 1,200 shillings, but the Welsh noble within the West Saxon kingdom had a wergild of 600 shillings. The further use of *wealh* for a slave is only a more extreme expression of the low status accorded to the alien." For the relationship between the Lex Salica and Ine's laws with regard to the rights of Celts see also Patrick Wormald, *The Making of English Law: King Alfred to the Twelfth Century*, vol. 1: *Legislation and its Limits* (Oxford, 1999), 104–6.

[58] Pelteret, *Slavery*, 84.

[59] For their rights as slave-owners see Pelteret, *Slavery*, 84.

Schrijver's reasoning, which is based both on British Latin sources and on the phonology of Old Welsh, is basically sound but seems in need of qualification. Even if the sources for the Southern Lowlands suggest widespread use of Latin in writing in Roman-dominated Britannia, wholesale language shift from Celtic to Latin for the entire British lowland population in the fourth and fifth centuries appears less likely than various degrees of Celtic-Latin bilingualism, most concentrated in the Roman towns and villas. And after the Anglo-Saxon Conquest, it would have been the most Romanized members of the upper classes of the Roman towns and villas who decided to leave the Lowlands, presumably together with some of their dependents, either for the West Country or for Brittany. And it would have been the lower classes, particularly in the rural areas, with little or no knowledge of Latin, who stayed behind because they had little to lose. On the contrary, e.g. as house slaves, they could hope to improve their situation eventually, or at least that of their children, namely by working for their new masters and by learning their language. And in doing so, they gradually transformed the structures of that language due to imperfect learning and to transmitting this form of Saxon to their masters' children. Schrijver, with particular reference to the phonology of Latin, Welsh, and Old English, assumes that pre-Saxon was influenced by a British-Latin substratum. But in my view, the grammatical evidence from West Saxon, especially that of the formally and functionally similar twofold paradigm of 'to be,' can more plausibly be explained as the result of direct Celtic substratum influence on pre-Saxon, and the specifically West Saxon lexical evidence for *wealh* and *wīln* provides information about the legal and socio-cultural situation in which this substratum influence may have operated.

4. The Historical and Archaeological Debate: Population Replacement or Acculturation?

4.1. The Interpretation of the Place-Name Evidence

In a paper of 1993 entitled "Why Aren't We Speaking Welsh?"[60] the place-name expert Margaret Gelling reacted to publications by some historians and archaeologists who criticized earlier interpretations of Bede's *Historia* as evidence for large-scale Anglo-Saxon immigration and instead assumed small-scale military movements of Anglo-Saxon military élites which left the structures of post-Roman Britannia largely intact but eventually resulted in 'acculturation' of the Celtic population to the Anglo-Saxon élites and in language shift to Old English. Before dealing with the historical and archaeological debate in more detail,

---

[60] *Anglo-Saxon Studies in Archaeology and History* 6 (1993): 51–56.

it seems worthwhile to address Gelling's assessment of the place-name evidence and her attempt at an answer to her own question.

With reference to the place-name evidence from the Southern Lowlands, Gelling claims that the numbers of both Germanic settlers and Celts must have been substantial:[61]

> Any rational appraisal of the place-name evidence supports a belief in the continuance of British speech in conditions of peaceful coexistence during at least the first two centuries of the Anglo-Saxon period, but at the same time such an appraisal compels the recognition that the Anglo-Saxons must have settled in great numbers, at any rate in the south and east of Britain, and that they came as farmers, not simply as warlords.

Gelling believes that "the virtual absence . . . of words borrowed from Welsh,"[62] which had led many linguists to assume large-scale population replacement for the Southern Lowlands, is not in agreement with the assumption of a substantial Celtic population in that area, and she ventures a new explanation for the extremely small number of lexical loans from Celtic in Old English:[63]

> Perhaps, though, this is not proof of lack of contact, but rather of community of interests. Both groups were farmers who would be fully equipped with all the words they needed for the things which concerned them in their daily lives. Words are borrowed when people encounter objects or concepts not catered for in their own vocabulary.

It is true that her assumption of "community of interests" helps to explain the particular scarcity of cultural loans from Celtic, compared to cultural loans from various non-European peoples who came under English rule in modern times, as I have tried to make clear elsewhere:[64]

> Lexical borrowing from a substratum language into the superstratum is practically restricted to linguistic contact in a habitat which is alien to the conquerors but familiar to the conquered population, e.g. in colonial North America and Australia between British colonists and indigenous tribes. In

---

[61] Gelling, "Why Aren't We Speaking Welsh?" 51. On the basis of this evidence, she criticizes both the assumption of the "extermination" of the Lowland Celts and Nora Chadwick's alternative assumption that "the Anglo-Saxon occupation of England was a gradual process which involved no change of population on any large scale" (Nora K. Chadwick, "The British or Celtic Part in the Population of England," in *Angles and Britons: O'Donnell Lectures*, ed. eadem, 111–47, at 146).

[62] Gelling, "Why Aren't We Speaking Welsh?" 56.

[63] Gelling, "Why Aren't We Speaking Welsh?" 56.

[64] Lutz, "When Did English Begin?" 163 n. 14. For legal inequality in early Wessex reflected by Ine's laws see above, n. 57.

the British Isles, however, Anglo-Saxon conquerors and subjected Celts "shared" a familiar European habitat.

But Gelling's observation does not help to answer her initial question — "Why aren't we speaking Welsh?", which she herself characterizes as rhetorical but which in my view is a serious linguistic question. This question was implicitly answered decades ago by Otto Jespersen in his discussion of the politically and legally unequal relationship between Anglo-Saxons and Celts after the Anglo-Saxon Conquest cited in more detail above: "There was nothing to induce the ruling classes to learn the language of the inferior natives; . . . On the other hand the Kelt would have to learn the language of his masters, and learn it well."

But unlike Gelling, Jespersen failed to take account of relative numbers of Anglo-Saxons and Celts in the Lowlands, although this is likewise linguistically relevant, not only for the question which of the two languages eventually prevails but also for the relative strength of the effects of language shift on the structures of the superstratum language. The later French superstratum, which resulted from the Norman Conquest of Anglo-Saxon England, did not prevail in the end but only left a strong superstratal imprint on the vocabulary of substratal Middle English; and this has always been attributed to the relatively small size of the French-speaking ruling class.[65] Thus the place-name evidence for substantial numbers of both Saxons and Celts in the Lowlands presented by Gelling helps to understand why even the earliest attested sources exhibit grammatical features that can best be explained as effects of language shift of a very substantial number of native speakers of Celtic to the Saxon superstratum.

However, Gelling's assumption of "peaceful coexistence" is clearly contradicted by the historical evidence from Gildas, Bede, and the *Anglo-Saxon Chronicle* for long series of battles between slowly westward-advancing Anglo-Saxons and retreating Celts.[66] Yet this historical evidence and her place-name evidence do not really contradict each other. After the respective battles, when an area had been subjected to Saxon rule, the new rulers were certainly interested in some kind of peaceful coexistence between Saxon and Celtic farmers within

---

[65] See, e.g., Barber, *The English Language*, 41: "A considerable number of Normans settled in England after the conquest, but they never outnumbered the English in the way the Anglo-Saxon settlers must have outnumbered the Britons, and ultimately French died out in England." The fates of the Germanic superstrates in Normandy and Visigothic Spain likewise provide notable counterexamples to Anglo-Saxon English. See also Donald Winford, *An Introduction to Contact Linguistics* (Oxford, 2003), chap. 2, "Language Maintainance and Lexical Borrowing," esp. 34–36.

[66] See Peter Hunter Blair, *An Introduction to Anglo-Saxon England*, 2nd edn., reset and reissued Folio Society (Cambridge, 1997), chap. I.6, "The Kingdoms of the Southern English."

their territory, as shown by Ine's laws for late seventh-century Wessex.[67] Thus what is lacking in Gelling's picture is a qualification of the conditions for "peaceful coexistence" in the Southern Lowlands; these conditions of legal inequality can be derived from numerous articles of Ine's laws. Under such conditions, the preferred language would have been the Saxon superstratum, even for exchanges between Saxon and Celtic farmers.

4.2. Archaeological Evidence and its Interpretation

One of the foremost proponents of the view that under the military rule of small Anglo-Saxon élites the Celts were eventually 'acculturated' to Anglo-Saxon England is Nicholas Higham. His book *Rome, Britain and the Anglo-Saxons* had a mixed reaction.[68] Thus Catherine Hills pointed to the excavation of Spong Hill as archaeological counterevidence.[69] She assumed an "insular" tendency behind this view and warned:[70]

> The tendency to play down migrations and invasions in favour of long-term indigenous development suits our view of our own past—unconquered since 1066. It may sometimes be an obstacle to understanding that past.

---

[67] See *Die Gesetze der Angelsachsen*, ed. F. Liebermann, 3 vols., 1: *Text und Übersetzung* (Halle, 1903–1916; repr. Aalen, 1960), 89–123. The importance of Ine's laws as evidence for a substantial British population in early Wessex is also pointed out by Bryan Ward-Perkins, "Why Did the Anglo-Saxons Not Become More British?" *EHR* 115 (2000): 513–33, at 523–25.

[68] Nicholas Higham, *Rome, Britain and the Anglo-Saxons* (London, 1992). See also idem, "The Saxon Conquest in Britain: Literary Evidence and the Case for Acculturation in the Formation of Anglo-Saxon England," *Studien zur Sachsenforschung* 11 (1998): 135–44. The collection of articles in *Britons in Anglo-Saxon England*, ed. Nick Higham, Publications of the Manchester Centre for Anglo-Saxon Studies 7 (Woodbridge, 2007) are addressed in A. Lutz, "Celtic Influence on Old English and West Germanic," in *Reevaluating the Celtic Hypothesis*, ed. Markku Filppula and Juhani Klemola, spec. no. of *ELL* 13 (2009): 227–49.

[69] Catherine Hills, review of Higham, *Rome, Britain and the Anglo Saxons*, in *Antiquity* 66 (1992): 988–89, at 989: "I cannot accept that the communities buried in the large cremation cemeteries such as Spong Hill in Norfolk were élites. In these cemeteries there were men, women, children, horses, dogs and cows, all cremated and buried according to the practice common in northern Germany/southern Scandinavia." Helena Hamerow's review (*Early Medieval Europe* 2 [1993]: 172–73) is similarly critical, whereas Della Hooke (*Landscape History* 15 [1993]: 78) comes to the conclusion that "his [i.e. Higham's] suggestions go far to offer a plausible working hypothesis."

[70] Hills, review, 989.

In her recent book, Catherine Hills discusses a wide range of archaeological as well as historical, linguistic, and genetic studies and pleads for a cautious, joint evaluation of different types of evidence.[71]

One such attempt, from the archaeologist's point of view, is Heinrich Härke's contribution to *Celtic Englishes III*.[72] In a careful overview of various types of archaeological research, he adduces evidence both for continuation of earlier agricultural practices and for the introduction of new artefacts of Continental origin in the south and east of England in the fifth century.[73] Drawing on studies combining archaeological and anthropological investigations of male burials, he shows

> that men buried with weapons in the 5th and 6th centuries (48% of male adults) were Germanic immigrants or their descendants, while most men without weapons were Britons[74] [and that]

> [I]n the 7th century, the use of the weapon burial rite as an ethnic symbol ceased, and burial with weapons (23% of male adults in the 7th/early 8th cent.) became the prerogative of an increasingly mixed, Anglo-British elite buried in Anglo-Saxon fashion.[75]

And he concludes:[76]

---

[71] Catherine Hills, *Origins of the English*, Duckworth Debates in Archaeology (London, 2003). Her chapter 3, "Language," does not distinguish between superstratal effects on the lexicon and substratal structural effects.

[72] Heinrich Härke, "Population Replacement or Acculturation? An Archaeological Perspective on Population and Migration in Post-Roman Britain," in *The Celtic Englishes III*, ed. Tristram, 13–28.

[73] Härke, "Population Replacement," 16–20.

[74] Härke, "Population Replacement," 20, based on idem, "Warrior Graves? The Background of the Anglo-Saxon Weapon Burial Rite," *Past and Present* 126 (1990): 22–43.

[75] Härke, "Population Replacement," 20, based on idem, "Changing Symbols in a Changing Society: The Anglo-Saxon Weapon Burial Rite in the Seventh Century," in *The Age of Sutton Hoo*, ed. M. O. H. Carver (Woodbridge, 1992), 149–65. See also Härke's concluding observation in "Early Anglo-Saxon Social Structure," in *The Anglo-Saxons from the Migration Period to the Eighth Century: An Ethnographic Perspective*, ed. John Hines (Woodbridge, 1997), 126–60, at 152: "The shift of burial rite from ethnic affiliation to social differentiation in the seventh century appears to mark a crucial transition: from ethnically divided conquest societies to the formation of early states." This shows that Ine's laws provide at best a last glimpse of the prehistoric situation.

[76] Härke, "Population Replacement," 20–21, with the author's emphases. For a differentiated assessment of the archaeological evidence for Saxon settlements see also idem, "Briten und Sachsen im nachrömischen England: Zum Nachweis der einheimischen Bevölkerung in den angelsächsischen Landnahmegebieten," *Studien zur Sachsenforschung* 11 (1998): 87–119.

These observations also allow a very rough estimate of the ratio of immigrants to natives *among males*: approximately 1 : 1 in 'Anglo-Saxon' settlements of the 5th/6th centuries, plus Britons in enclaves, and a much higher proportion of Britons in the north and south-west of England . . . [and] that the maximum possible immigration in the post-Roman period was about 20% Germanic immigrants of the *female* population.

Härke nevertheless emphasizes that his own model does not reflect a consensus view in Anglo-Saxon archaeology, and he particularly refers to Nicholas Higham's assumption of an Anglo-Saxon immigration of ca. 10,000, less than the Norman influx some five hundred years later. And he further emphasizes that despite widely differing views as to the relative sizes of Germanic and Celtic populations in Anglo-Saxon England, there is consensus

> that acculturation was the key process which turned substantial numbers of native Britons into Anglo-Saxons [and] that this perspective is shared by those (few) archaeologists and historians who understand the linguistic evidence.[77]

One of the scholars mentioned by Härke is Thomas Charles-Edwards, whose insightful views on the status of the Celts in Anglo-Saxon England have been referred to in sections 2 and 3.3 above. In the same article, referring to Hans Wagner's *Das Verbum in den Sprachen der Britischen Inseln*, Charles-Edwards argues:[78]

> If similarities between Welsh and English syntax, for example in the use of auxiliary verbs, are to be attributed to British influence on English, . . . nevertheless the similarity did not emerge until the later Middle Ages.

Wolfgang Keller's seminal article and Ingerid Dal's detailed presentation of the evidence for the Old English beginnings of the progressive aspect are linguistic proof to the contrary. Thus, in my view, the linguistic evidence for large-scale language shift from Celtic to (pre-)Saxon basically agrees with Gelling's assessment of the place-name evidence and with Härke's model based on archaeological and also genetic evidence.

---

[77] Härke, "Population Replacement," 23–24.
[78] Charles-Edwards, "Language and Society," 732 n. 155.

5. The term acculturation: Some concluding remarks
from a linguistic point of view

The choice of language is an important part of the cultural choices of individuals and groups. From the viewpoint of contact linguistics, the term *acculturation*, used widely in recent archaeological and historical research in Britain, appears unnecessarily vague, particularly with respect to the question of what were the cultural choices for the subjected Celts in early Wessex. The study of language contact in the history of English has suffered from a similar kind of vagueness. Until now, textbooks of the history of English largely ignore the results of comparative, general contact linguistics. They still fail to make a clear distinction between cultural borrowing of terms for new concepts from a foreign culture due to its appeal (e.g. from the Latin-based classical and medieval culture) and the results of superstratally forced contact (e.g. the seemingly unnecessary adoption of the French-based legal terminology, which supplanted a pre-existing, highly differentiated Anglo-Saxon terminology as a result of the Norman Conquest).[79] And it is for basically the same reason that many scholars still fail to explain why English borrowed so little from Celtic and, at the same time, overlook essential differences of grammatical structure between English and the most closely-related continental-Germanic languages as well as the similarities of these English structures with those of the Celtic languages.

---

[79] For the linguistic relevance of this distinction for the history of English see Lutz, "When Did English Begin?" 146–56.

Beyond Frankish Authority?
Frisia and Saxony between the
Anglo-Saxons and Carolingians

James Palmer

1. Introduction

In the eighth century, Anglo-Saxon missionaries, monks, and pilgrims traveling to the Continent played a crucial role in the foundation of Christian communities east of the Rhine.[1] Their religious activities fitted well with Frankish plans for expansion and frontier defence. As the Carolingians moved into Frisia and Saxony, Anglo-Saxons helped to bring the North into wider church infrastructures and to harmonize the cultures of the different regions. It seems, at least according to Bede and Boniface, that many Anglo-Saxons were drawn into this situation because they believed they were distantly related to many of the pagan peoples of northern Europe and thus felt a duty to save their souls.[2] But the rhetoric of an ethnically-specific mission was rarely repeated in the Frankish sources which otherwise provide a great deal of information on the missions. In the large number of *vitae* composed about figures such as Boniface, for example, not one mentions the involvement of concepts of *germanitas*. For the Frisians and Saxons themselves, the interrelation of Saxon or Germanic identities was not always dominant. Karl Leyser argued that "relations with England could not be paramount for the ninth-century continental Saxons, because . . . they had to

---

[1] The classic account remains Wilhelm Levison, *England and the Continent in the Eighth Century* (Oxford, 1947). For more recent studies, see Lutz E. von Padberg, *Mission und Christianisierung: Formen und Folgen bei Angelsachsen und Franken im 7. und 8. Jahrhundert* (Stuttgart, 1995), and J. Palmer, *Anglo-Saxons in a Frankish World*, Studies in the Early Middle Ages 19 (Turnhout, 2009). Further context is provided by Joanna Story, *Carolingian Connections: Anglo-Saxon England and Carolingian Francia, c. 750–870* (Aldershot, 2003).

[2] Bede, *HE* 5.9, ed. Colgrave and Mynors, 476; Boniface, *Die Briefe des hl. Bonifatius und Lullus*, no. 46, ed. Michael Tangl, MGH Epistolae Selectae 1 (Berlin, 1916), 74–75.

Hans Sauer and Joanna Story, eds., *Anglo-Saxon England and the Continent*. With the assistance of Gaby Waxenberger. Essays in Anglo-Saxon Studies, vol. 3. MRTS 394. Tempe: ACMRS, 2011.   [ISBN 978-0-86698-442-3]

live with their conquerors, the Franks."[3] While this may have been the case in general, there is enough evidence to suggest that some relationships with England maintained a place in the development of new identities in the North. In this paper I will explore some of the related issues of identity and authority which come out of the Anglo-Saxon missions and the Saxon conquests, asking how communities east of the Rhine dealt with their mixed heritage. In particular, I will focus on two saints' lives associated with Frisia and Saxony in the ninth century, when Carolingian dominance was more or less secure: Altfrid of Münster's *Vita Liudgeri* and the anonymous Bremen *Vita Willehadi*.[4] Passages from these texts raise some important questions about uses of the past and identities in a dramatically changing world.

Identities, like most social structures, are dynamic forces. While they influence the ways in which people may act, they are also subject to being recreated and adapted through human agency.[5] They form part of the cultural capital which empowers individuals to act and to define the social worlds around them.[6] The conceptualisation of identities in these terms helps to understand how they are created and why they are so valuable. In the study of the post-Roman world, such theories have underpinned many aspects of the theories of 'ethnogenesis'.[7]

---

[3] Karl Leyser, "The Ottonians and Wessex," in idem, *Communication and Power in Medieval Europe: The Carolingian and Ottonian Centuries*, ed. Timothy Reuter (London, 1994), 71–104, at 75. On Saxony in the ninth century: Matthias Becher, *Rex, Dux und Gens: Untersuchungen zur Entstehung des sächsischen Herzogtums, 9. und 10. Jahrhundert* (Husum, 1996); Christopher Carroll, "The Bishoprics of Saxony after the First Century of Christianisation," *Early Medieval Europe* 8 (1999): 219–46; Helmut Beumann, "Die Hagiographie 'Bewältigt': Unterwerfung und Christianisierung der Sachsen durch Karl den Großen," in *Cristianizzazione ed organizzazione ecclesiastica delle campagne nell'alto medioevo: espansione e resistenze*, Settimane di Studi del Centro Italiano di Studi sull'Alto Medioevo 28 (Spoleto, 1982), 129–63.

[4] Altfrid, *Vita Liudgeri*, ed. Walter Diekamp, *Die Vitae Sancti Liudgeri*, Die Geschichtsquellen des Bistums Münster (Münster, 1881), 1–53; *Vita Willehadi*, ed. Alain Poncelet, *Acta Sanctorum*, Nov. III (Brussels, 1910), 835–51.

[5] Anthony Giddens, *The Constitution of Society: Outline of the Theory of Structuration* (Berkeley, 1986), 1–37; William H. Sewell, "A Theory of Structure: Duality, Agency and Transformation," *American Journal of Sociology* 98 (1992): 1–29.

[6] The concept of cultural capital was originally set out in Pierre Bourdieu, "Cultural Reproduction and Social Reproduction," in *Knowledge, Education and Cultural Change*, ed. Richard K. Brown (London, 1973), 71–112, to explain the social mobility of those with less economic capital.

[7] For a summary of the debate—held principally between the Vienna School and followers of Walter Goffart—see Andrew Gillett, "Ethnogenesis: A Contested Model of Early Medieval Europe," *History Compass* 4 (2006): 241–60, and the essays in *On Barbarian Identity: Critical Approaches to Barbarian Ethnicity in the Early Middle Ages*, ed. Andrew Gillett, Studies in the Early Middle Ages 4 (Turnhout, 2002).

Ethnic identities are viewed as something constructed and developed, rather than something strictly inherent. My focus in this study is not on the genesis of specific ethnic identities, but rather on the cultural and political significance of the ways in which clusters of local, regional, and supra-regional identities are assumed to relate to each other over time. Large-scale identities, like *Fresones* or *Saxones*, often covered over the political and social disunity of the people to which the names referred.[8] The management of the ways different layers of identity interact is an important aspect of how they generate ideas, conflicts, and institutions. Friction and co-operation between groups is an important part of driving change. For the people who lived in the overlapping worlds of Frisia and Saxony (or at least Westphalia), there were clusters of identities attached to families, political groupings, and religion. The ways in which these could be negotiated were affected by external groups who were trying to encourage or impose a variety of other identities onto the North, be they Christian, Germanic, or simply political factions.

Texts such as saints' lives can play an important role in the negotiation of these identity clusters because they are both products and shapers of the world around them.[9] By providing a perspective on events and ideas, hagiographical and historiographical texts moralized, affirming and denying things as necessary.[10] The cult of saints to which much hagiography pertained is well known for its power to regulate aspects of society. Peter Brown's still-illuminating study characterized cults as having distinct social functions, providing occasion for moral instruction, spiritual patronage and intercession, and social advancement and the accrual of wealth.[11] Stories about the saints, such as those derived from hagiography, furnished the public activities of cultic activity with a mythology of

---

[8] Matthias Becher, *"Non enim habent regem idem Antiqui Saxones:* Verfassung und Ethnogenese in Sachsen während des 8. Jahrhunderts," *Studien zur Sachsenforschung* 12 (1999): 1–31.

[9] Gabrielle Spiegel, "History, Historicism, and the Social Logic of the Text in the Middle Ages," *Speculum* 65 (1990): 59–86. On hagiography in this context, see Patrick Geary, "Saints, Scholars, and Society: The Elusive Goal," in idem, *Living with the Dead in the Middle Ages* (Ithaca, NY, 1994), 9–29. A pertinent recent study is Ian Wood, *The Missionary Life: Saints and the Evangelisation of Europe 400–1050* (Harlow, 2001).

[10] On the moralizing impulse of narrative, see Hayden White, "The Value of Narrativity in the Representation of Reality," in idem, *The Content of the Form: Narrative Discourse and Historical Representation* (Baltimore and London, 1987), 1–25, at 7–24, discussed in relation to hagiographical narratives in Catherine Cubitt, "Memory and Narrative in the Cult of Early Anglo-Saxon Saints," in *The Uses of the Past in the Early Middle Ages*, ed. Yitzhak Hen and Matthew Innes (Cambridge, 2000), 29–66, at 48–49.

[11] Peter Brown, *The Cult of the Saints: Its Rise and Function in Latin Christendom* (Chicago, 1981). For some recent reflections on Brown's work, see *The Cult of Saints in Late Antiquity and the Early Middle Ages*, ed. James Howard-Johnston and Paul Antony Hayward (Oxford, 1999).

recognized truths and an imagined communal past shared through the saint.[12] Even hagiography which was not part of a functioning cult had the potential to operate in such a context, and it still tells us something of the choices and thoughts of the author. Thus saints' lives and cults can often be seen as reflections of social ideals, standards, and structures.[13] It is on such a pedestal that saints become patrons of kingdoms, factions, or families.[14] Through hagiography, it is possible to gain a sense of the negotiation of multiple identities at a local level.

2. Liudger and Willehad

In Frisia and Saxony, the cults of saints emerged from both a missionary and a military background. The conversion of the Saxons once promoted by St. Boniface in the 730s failed to materialize despite the saint's best intentions.[15] In the decades that followed, it was left to the efforts of a new generation of missionaries to follow the Carolingian military campaigns in the North and found the first churches of *Saxonia*. Foremost amongst these were Willehad (d. 789) and

---

[12] On the public use of saints' lives, see Katherine Heene, "Merovingian and Carolingian Hagiography: Continuity or Change in Public and Aims?," *Analecta Bollandiana* 107 (1989): 415–28, and Wolfert S. van Egmond, "The Audiences of Early Medieval Hagiographical Texts: Some Questions Revisited," in *New Approaches to Medieval Communication*, ed. Marco Mostert (Turnhout, 1999), 41–67. On imagined communities see of course Benedict Anderson, *Imagined Communities: Reflections on the Origin and Spread of Nationalism*, rev. edn. (London, 1991).

[13] František Graus, *Volk, Herrscher und Heiliger im Reich der Merowinger: Studien zur Hagiographie der Merowingerzeit* (Prague, 1965); Joseph-Claude Poulin, *L'idéal de sainteté dans l'Aquitaine carolingienne (750–950)* (Québec, 1975); Thomas Head, *Hagiography and the Cult of Saints: The Diocese of Orléans 800–1200*, Cambridge Studies in Medieval Life and Thought, 4th ser., 14 (Cambridge, 1989).

[14] Gabrielle Spiegel, "The Cult of Saint Denis and Capetian Kingship," *Journal of Medieval History* 1 (1975): 43–69; Alan Thacker, "*Pecularis patronus noster*: The Saint as the Patron of the State in the Early Middle Ages," in *The Medieval State: Essays Presented to James Campbell*, ed. J. R. Maddicott and D. M. Palliser (London, 2000), 1–24. On local saints, see the essays in *Local Saints and Local Churches in the Early Medieval West*, ed. Alan Thacker and Richard Sharpe (Oxford, 2002), and Julia M. H. Smith, *Province and Empire: Brittany and the Carolingians*, Cambridge Studies in Medieval Life and Thought, 4th ser., 18 (Cambridge, 1990). On family and hagiography, see Lutz von Padberg, *Heilige und Familie: Studien zur Bedeutung familiengebundener Aspekte in den Viten des Verwandten- und Schülerkreises um Willibrord, Bonifatius und Liudger*, Quellen und Abhandlungen zur mittelrheinischen Kirchengeschichte 83, 2nd edn. (Mainz, 1997).

[15] James T. Palmer, "Saxon or European? Interpreting and Reinterpreting St Boniface," *History Compass* 4 (2006): 852–69.

Liudger (d. 809).[16] Willehad was a Northumbrian who may have come from the same family as the first great Anglo-Saxon missionary, Willibrord (d. 739), and his distant relatives Alcuin of York and Beornrad of Sens.[17] He worked as a missionary in Frisia and Saxony between ca. 770 and 787 with varying degrees of success, before spending the final eighteen months of his life as the first bishop of Bremen in Westphalia. Liudger, whose work overlapped with Willehad's, was a native Frisian from a powerful family who owned lands around Utrecht, in East Friesland, and in Westphalia.[18] As a boy he was taught in Frisia by Boniface's favorite pupil Gregory of Utrecht, and then in York by the great scholar Alcuin,[19] and later he went on to found churches at Dokkum (770s), Münster (793), and Werden (799).[20] The missionary heritage of Willehad and Liudger, combined with their success in establishing new religious foundations, placed them at the forefront of the Christian history of Westphalia and Frisia, helping to define the communities there. It was not, however, until the 840s that these saints were finally commemorated by their former communities.

The purposes of the two *vitae* are, like all texts, dependent on their contexts. Altfrid's is easy to discern from his writing and reputation. He was bishop of Münster between 839 and 849 and was writing, according to the preface of his work, for the monks of Werden.[21] Both Münster and Werden had been founded on family lands by Liudger, who was also Altfrid's uncle.[22] Altfrid's text is concerned with numerous aspects of family and local history: he discusses

---

[16] On Liudger, see Arnold Angenendt, *Liudger: Missionar—Abt—Bischof im frühen Mittelalter* (Münster, 2005). There is no comparable account of Willehad's work.

[17] On Willibrord see Levison, *England and the Continent*, 45–69.

[18] Karl Schmid, "Die Liudgeriden: Erscheinung und Problematik einer Adelsfamilie," in *Geschichtsschreibung und geistiges Leben im Mittelalter: Festschrift Heinz Löwe*, ed. Karl Hauck and Hubert Mordek (Cologne and Vienna, 1978), 71–101.

[19] Jan Gerschow, "Liudger und die angelsächsische Kirche," in *805: Liudger wird Bischof: Spuren eines Heiligen zwischen York, Rom und Münster*, ed. Gabrielle Isenberg and Barbara Rommé (Mainz, 2005), 141–48. On Alcuin now see Donald Bullough, *Alcuin: Reputation and Achievement* (Leiden, 2004).

[20] For Liudger's biography of Gregory, see Liudger, *Vita Gregorii abbatis*, ed. Oswald Holder-Egger, MGH Scriptores 15 (Hannover, 1887), 66–79.

[21] Karl Hauck, "Ein Utrechter Missionar auf der altsächsischen Stammesversammlung," in *Das erste Jahrtausend: Kultur und Kunst im werdenden Abendland an Rhein und Ruhr*, ed. Victor Elbern, 2 vols. (Düsseldorf, 1964), 2: 734–45. On early veneration for Liudger: Karl Hauck, "Apostolischer Geist im *genus sacerdotale* der Liudgeriden: Die 'Kanonisation' Liudgers und Altfrids Bischoffsgrablege in Essen-Werden (Beiträge und Miszellen)," in *Sprache und Recht: Beiträge zur Kulturgeschichte des Mittelalters: Festschrift für Ruth Schmidt-Wiegand zum 60. Geburtstag*, ed. Karl Hauck et al. (Berlin and New York, 1986), 2: 191–219.

[22] Foundation of Werden: Altfrid, *Vita Liudgeri*, 1.21, ed. Diekamp, 25. Foundation of Münster: Altfrid, *Vita Liudgeri*, 1.23, ed. Diekamp, 28.

generations of Liudger's family, gets distracted by other missionary stories such as that of Lebuin, and above all lists all the different locations around Frisia and Westphalia in which Liudger and his family worked.[23] Charlemagne makes regular appearances, for example to confirm the creation of Münster and Werden and also to forbid Liudger from starting a mission to the Danes in 805. The text thus serves to bind together Anglo-Saxon missionary traditions and Carolingian authority through the activities of Liudger and his family. The *Nachleben* of the text illustrates the difficulties of pinning down the meaning of a saint: two further *vitae Liudgeri* based on Altfrid's work were written in Werden, one in the 850s with a more carefully crafted image of Liudger as a holy bishop, and a third shortly after 864 with more emphasis on relics and papal authority.[24] Interest in the Anglo-Saxons' missions remained steady throughout the rewrites, becoming even more pronounced in the *Vita Liudgeri II*.[25]

The context of the *Vita Willehadi* has been open to more dispute. Much rests on whether one believes it is from Bremen or Echternach. The argument for Echternach, first set out by Gerlinde Niemeyer, sees the text as fundamentally separate from Archbishop Anskar of Hamburg-Bremen's *Miracula Willehadi* of 860 on the grounds that there is no cross-referencing.[26] Niemeyer also argued that it is plausibly an Echternach product because there was a cult of Willehad there in the eleventh century. In fact, the first premise does not quite work: not only does the *Miracula* often travel with the *Vita* in manuscripts (from Bremen and Echternach) but there is also no good reason why a collection of posthumous miracles should refer to or borrow from the earlier story of the life. In the eleventh century, Adam of Bremen for one mistakenly believed the two works to have been written by Anskar, such was their perceived coherence.[27] The two texts complement each other well and bear comparison with other *vitae-miracula* developments (the later *vitae Liudgerii* being striking examples). On internal evidence we can pin the text down chronologically: it postdates the death of Bishop Willerich of Bremen in 838, who is described in the past tense, and it appears to

---

[23] Although with a curious reticence about Westphalia: Hauck, "Ein Utrechter Missionar," 741.

[24] On the dates see Diekamp, *Die Vitae*, lii. For an analysis of the different purposes of the texts, see Eberhard Kaus, "Zu den Liudger-Viten des 9. Jahrhunderts," *Westfälische Zeitschrift* 142 (1992): 9–55.

[25] Lutz E. von Padberg, "Die Liudger-Viten in der angelsächsischen Tradition der Missionsarbeit im geistlichen Familienverband," in *Die Vita Sancti Liudgeri: Vollständige Faksimile-Ausgabe der Handschrift Ms.theol.lat.fol. 323 der Staatsbibliothek zu Berlin – Preußischer Kulturbesitz: Text, Übersetzung und Kommentar, Forschungsbeiträge*, ed. Eckhard Freise, Codices Selecti 95 (Graz, 1999), 113–26.

[26] Gerlinde Niemeyer, "Die Herkunft der *Vita Willehadi*," *Deutsches Archiv für Erforschung des Mittelalters* 12 (1956): 17–35, at 18–19.

[27] Adam of Bremen, *Gesta Hammaburgensis ecclesiae pontificum*, 1.13 (14), ed. Bernhard Schmeidler, MGH SS rer. Germ. 2 (Hannover, 1917), 17.

predate the unification of the dioceses of Bremen and Hamburg in 848.[28] These were uncertain times for the community of Bremen, and the preface to the text proclaims that it intends to offer consolation and guidance.

The two *vitae* are revealing in the ways they treat the distant authorities which contributed to the founding of their Christian communities. The things chosen for commemoration by a writer—and through him/her their community—reveal much about the relationship between historical horizons and identities. An intriguing example is the story of Aluberht, an Anglo-Saxon preacher, in Altfrid's text. In the mid-760s, the story went, Aluberht approached Gregory of Utrecht to see if he could be of assistance in preaching in Frisia. Gregory was impressed by the Anglo-Saxon and encouraged him to become a bishop because, after an unsavory incident in which one of his brothers had murdered an uncle of the mayor of the palace, Gregory was prevented from becoming bishop himself.[29] Although the see of Utrecht itself was closely bound to powerful Frankish families, Aluberht decided to travel to his home diocese of York to be consecrated by Archbishop Ælberht.[30] Why this was not conveniently forgotten is a little surprising, given that it tacitly undermined Carolingian authority in Frisia. There was some precedence for Aluberht in the actions of Suidberht of Kaiserwerth. Suidberht was an Anglo-Saxon from Willibrord's circle who, in ca. 690, sought consecration in Britain as bishop to the Boructuars, receiving his commission from the exiled Northumbrian bishop St. Wilfrid, in the absence of any archbishop in Canterbury.[31] The decision perhaps reflects his personal connections and interest in the archiepiscopal authority found within the Anglo-Saxon church but still lacking among the Franks; it was not obviously a deliberate affront to Frankish authority, and he was able to work until Saxon attacks and old age forced him to retire.[32] The infrastructure of the Frankish church was hardly comparable in the 760s, however. When Alberic, Gregory's nephew, was transferred from royal service in Italy to take over the bishopric of Utrecht in 777, he went to the Frankish bishop of Cologne as one might more normally have

[28] Niemeyer, "Die Herkunft," 19–20 was satisfied with this as a date-range even if the text is a product of Echternach.

[29] Boniface, *Die Briefe*, no. 50, ed. Tangl, 83; Matthias Werner, *Adelsfamilien im Umkreis der frühen Karolinger*, Vorträge und Forschungen, Sonderband 28 (Sigmaringen, 1982), 304–13.

[30] *Diplomata maiorum domus regiae*, no. 11, ed. Georg H. Pertz, MGH DD Mer. (Hannover, 1872), 98–99; Boniface, *Die Briefe*, no. 109, ed. Tangl, 235–36; and the dubious charters, *Die Urkunden Pippins, Karlmanns und Karls des Grossen*, nos. 4–5, ed. Engilbert Mühlbacher, MGH DD Kar. 1 (Hannover, 1906), 6–8.

[31] Levison, *England and the Continent*, 57–58; Knut Schäferdiek, "Suidberht von Kaiserwerth," *Düsseldorfer Jahrbuch* 66 (1995): 1–21.

[32] On Suidbert's consecration as a provocative act: Knut Schäferdiek, "Fragen der frühen angelsächsischen Festlandmission," *Frühmittelalterliche Studien* 28 (1994): 172–95, at 192.

expected.[33] Precisely of what or to whom Aluberht was supposed to be bishop is left unsaid by Altfrid. Liudger, writing ca. 800, saw Aluberht as Gregory of Utrecht's *chorepiscopus*.[34] In the York Annals for 767, however, we read *Aluberht ad Ealdsexos ordinatus est episcopus*.[35] Maybe in the days before Charlemagne's campaigns there had been hopes of establishing a quasi-autonomous Saxon diocese, at least from the perspective of the Northumbrians. Altfrid's reticence may stem from his intention, not to elaborate on ecclesiastical order, but to tell the story of Liudger, who followed Aluberht to York and remained there a number of years. The archiepiscopal authority of York in that context was part of the Anglo-Saxon cultural heritage embodied by the *Liudgeriden*. If the stories one tells about a community's past are in some way constitutive of identities, Altfrid saw Werden, Münster, and Utrecht between Carolingian and Northumbrian lines of cultural authority.

Willehad's story began in the same historical context and was similarly preserved in spite of any attempt to re-orientate the Saxons towards Frankish authority. The author of the *vita* relates that Willehad, shortly after being made a priest, heard that the Frisians and Saxons had begun to reject the worship of idols and accept Christianity.[36] It is possible that this news had come from someone like Aluberht, with ecclesiastical interests on both sides of the Channel. Willehad asked permission of King Alchred to leave Northumbria and the king convened a synod—presumably again overseen by Ælberht of York—so that the priest could preach with the *permissus atque licentia* of his bishops. Again the question of commemoration is important. In few comparable *vitae* was it felt necessary to explain under whose authority a saint traveled, except in cases like the *Vita Bonifatii* or *Vita Leobae* where elaborate background stories were integral to the overarching spiritual message. Willehad just could have appeared with no biographical background in the regions that were familiar to the audience, not unlike Aluberht or Lebuin. Moreover, did he really need more than the authority of Charlemagne himself, which he received later, to preach in Saxony? The story of Aluberht and letters from Alchred's court to Bishop Lull of Mainz and Charlemagne suggest a certain co-ordination of efforts in Saxony in the 770s. This is reflected in the number of references to Saxon campaigns in the York Annals which provided a context for the story of Aluberht.[37] Commemoration of these cultural horizons in Saxony might have been aided by the activities of the Northumbrian Willeric of

---

[33] Liudger, *Vita Gregorii abbatis*, chap. 15, ed. Holder-Egger, 79. Altfrid, *Vita Liudgeri*, 1.15, ed. Diekamp, 19. Charlemagne was quick to be generous to Alberic in Utrecht: *Die Urkunden*, no. 117, ed. Mühlbacher, 163–64.

[34] Liudger, *Vita Gregorii abbatis*, chap. 10, ed. Holder-Egger, 75.

[35] York Annals, s.a. 767 = Symeon of Durham, *Historia Regum*, ed. T. Arnold, Rolls Series 75.2 (London, 1885), 3–283, at 43.

[36] *Vita Willehadi*, chap. 1, ed. Poncelet, 842.

[37] Story, *Carolingian Connections*, 95–104.

Bremen (bishop 789–838), particularly as according to Adam of Bremen he found
the Saxons as unwilling to accept episcopal authority as Frankish royal authority
(which probably amounted to much the same thing in their eyes).[38] It is not any
historical veracity which should strike us in these texts; rather, it is the way stories
about Northumbrian heritage were preserved in the contexts of the shifting webs
of cultural associations which characterized the period 770–840.

The use of geography is important within both texts. Accounts of place
define the physical horizons of a saint's cult, so it is important to pay attention
to the hagiographers' interests.[39] In the *Vita Willehadi*, Charlemagne established
the diocese of Bremen to include the regions of "Wigmodia, Laras, Rüstringen
and Östringen, as well as Norden and Wangerland."[40] This is supported by a list
of those who had been martyred following Willehad: "Folcardus the priest and
Count Emmiggus in the district called Laras and Benjamin in Rüstringen; also
the cleric Atrebanus in Ditmarschen Berg and Gerwalus with his company in
Bremen."[41] Earlier Willehad's work in Frisia had been carefully detailed, starting from Dokkum and then moving down the River Lauwers, first in Hunsingo
to the north of modern Groningen, and then in Drenthe to the south. All this
created an association between East Friesland and Willehad that stretched from
Dokkum to the western edge of Bremen's diocese at Norden. These lands, however, soon fell firmly under Liudger's control after the end of Widukind's Saxon
revolt in the 780s. According to Altfrid, Liudger had been given the five districts
of Hugmarch, Hunsingo, Fivelingo, Emsgau, and Federitgau—all of which are
near Groningen—and the island of Bant (only a few miles from Norden) by
Charlemagne before the foundation of Münster and just after the foundation of
Werden.[42] This was then reinforced in the text by time Liudger spent preaching
in the area around Delfzijl in Hunsingo after he had established Werden.[43] The

---

[38] Adam of Bremen, *Gesta*, 1.14 (15), ed. Schmeidler, 18. There are similar comments in the *Vita Willehadi*, chap. 8, ed. Poncelet, 845, which may be Adam's model for
this comment.

[39] See the case of rewriting the *Vita Cuthberti*: Cubitt, "Memory and Narrative,"
39–46.

[40] *Vita Willehadi*, chap. 8, ed. Poncelet, 845.

[41] *Vita Willehadi*, chap. 6, ed. Poncelet, 844: "Folcardum presbiterum cum Emmiggo
comite in pago denominato Leri, Beniamin autem in Ubhriustri, Atrebanum vero clericum in Thietmaresgaho, Gerwalum quoque cum sociis suis in Brema."

[42] Altfrid, *Vita Liudgeri*, 1.22, ed. Diekamp, 25–26: ". . . pervenit eius fama ad aures
gloriosi principis Caroli. Qui constituit eum doctorem in gente Fresonum ad orientali
parte fluminis Labeki super pago quinque, quorum haec sunt vocabula Hygmerthi,
Hunuga, Fivilga, Emisga, Federitga, et unam insulam, quae dicitur Bant." For a late-
ninth-century snapshot of Werden's landholdings, which mirror Altfrid's geographical
settings, see *Die Urbare der Abtei Werden a.d. Ruhr A*, ed. Rudolf Kötzschke, Rheinische
Urbare 2 (Bonn, 1906).

[43] Altfrid, *Vita Liudgeri*, 1.25, ed. Diekamp, 30.

two texts are thus concerned with the same overlapping worlds, although it is not immediately clear from what the hagiographers say why there was such interest in relatively detailed geographical locations of activities in East Friesland.

Altfrid's *Vita Liudgeri* and the *Vita Willehadi* seem to be two texts written within the same windows of time, both concerned with geographical precision and the sources of authority for a range of Christian foundations. Surprisingly, it has not yet been considered whether we are dealing with the kind of "textual argument" that Ian Wood has demonstrated drove the production of much missionary hagiography in the early Middle Ages.[44] In the context of the 840s one might wonder if the need to write about Liudger and Willehad was prompted by the Frankish civil war of 840–843, or more specifically the settlements made in 843 at Verdun.[45] The civil war broke out in part as a result of Emperor Louis the Pious's (ruled 817–840) decision in 838 to change his inheritance plans to include Charles the Bald (d. 877), his only son by his second marriage, alongside the sons from his first marriage. When Louis died in 840, Charles's half-brothers Lothar I (d. 855) and Louis the German (d. 876) engaged Charles in a series of armed conflicts and diplomatic moves to claim what they felt was their rightful inheritance.[46] Charles emerged with the stronger hand and Lothar, the eldest of the three, endeared himself to few except the Saxons. In 843 the three brothers finally came together to carve out a new political geography for the vast Frankish kingdom. Unfortunately, no record of the agreement has survived. Nonetheless, there are records of the division of the Middle Kingdom (later Lotharingia) between Charles and Louis in 870 which give a sense of some of the decisions made.[47] From this and other contemporary sources we can infer that the following things happened which affected Münster and Bremen:

1. Bremen and Münster were placed in East Frankia under Louis the German.

2. They remained to a certain extent subject to the archiepiscopal control of Cologne, which was placed in Lothar's Middle Frankish kingdom along with Werden.

---

[44] Wood, The Missionary Life, esp. xi on his debt to Walter Goffart's *The Narrators of Barbarian History: Jordanes, Gregory of Tours, Bede, and Paul the Deacon* (Princeton, 1988).

[45] On these settlements: François L. Ganshof, "Zur Entstehungsgeschichte und Bedeutung des Vertrags von Verdun (843)," *Deutsches Archiv für Erforschung des Mittelalters* 12 (1956): 313–30; Peter Classen, "Die Verträge von Verdun und von Coulaines 843 als politische Grundlagen des westfränkischen Reiches," *Historische Zeitschrift* 196 (1963): 1–35.

[46] For a convenient account of the disputes, see Janet L. Nelson, *Charles the Bald* (Harlow, 1992), 105–39.

[47] *Annales Bertiniani*, s.a. 870, ed. Georg Waitz, MGH SS rer. Germ. 5 (Hannover, 1883), 110–13.

3. Many of the territories in the north of Friesland, particularly around Groningen and Rüstringen, went to Lothar's kingdom. In fact, in 826 Louis the Pious had granted much land here to the Danish king, Harald Klak, on the occasion of his baptism in Mainz.[48] In 841 Lothar granted further lands around Walcheran to Harald to secure his support during the civil war.[49]

4. Utrecht, too, went to Lothar despite its association with Westphalia through the *Liudgeriden*.

The net result of the 843 division, therefore, was that the lands of the *Liudgeriden* were politically divorced from the lands set down as part of the dioceses of Münster and Bremen in East Friesland.[50] The principles of *affinitas* and *congruentia* intended to govern the division were not adhered to.[51] Here would be a typical cue for a community to start writing about authority and foundation legends, to recreate unity or argue for one's lands back.[52]

The words of Adam of Bremen, writing in ca. 1076, are testament to the difficulties this moment appeared retrospectively to have caused. Adam composed his *Gesta Hammaburgensis Ecclesiae Pontificum* in reaction to the problems of his archbishop, Adalbert, and the wider crises of the reign of Henry IV.[53] The world of Boniface and his heirs provided the bedrock on which Hamburg-Bremen's history could stand. Willehad in particular was prominent, naturally,

---

[48] *Annales regni Francorum*, s.a. 826, ed. Georg Pertz, MGH SS rer. Germ. 6 (Hannover, 1895), 169–70.

[49] *Annales Bertiniani*, s.a. 841, ed. Waitz, 26.

[50] Hauck, "Ein Utrechter Missionar," 743 in reference to the *Vita Liudgeri* only.

[51] Nithard, *Historia*, 4.1, ed. Georg H. Pertz, MGH SS rer. Germ. 44 (Hannover, 1870), 40; Ganshof, "Entstehungsgeschichte," 317–20.

[52] For a similar reaction to 843 by the historian Nithard, who lost lands in the settlement, see Janet Nelson, "Public *Histories* and Private History in the Work of Nithard," *Speculum* 60 (1985): 195–238.

[53] Timothy Reuter's introduction to the 2002 edition of Francis J. Tschan's translation indicates a useful new appendix on Adam in Peter and Birgit Sawyer, *Die Deutschen und das europäische Mittelalter: Die Welt der Wikinger* (Munich, 2002), but I have been unable to consult this work for this essay. On Adalbert, see Horst Fuhrmann, "Studien zur Geschichte mittelalterlicher Patriarchate: der Patriarchatsplan Erzbischof Adalberts von Bremen," *Zeitschrift der Savigny-Stiftung für Rechtsgeschichte, Kanon. Abt.* 41 (1955): 120–70. For recent work on Adam, see Volker Scior, *Das Eigene und das Fremde: Identität und Fremdheit in den Chroniken Adams von Bremen, Helmolds von Bosau und Arnolds von Lübeck*, Orbis mediaevalis 4 (Berlin, 2002), and Henrik Janson, "Adam of Bremen and the Conversion of Scandinavia," in *Christianizing Peoples and Converting Individuals*, ed. Guyda Armstrong and Ian Wood, International Medieval Research 7 (Turnhout, 2001), 83–88.

as the founder of Bremen, here presented as an extension of Bonifatian ideals.[54] The creation of the diocese of Bremen in the story is accompanied by a charter, setting out inviolable boundaries, because "what has happened in the past makes us cautious for the future."[55] In the context of establishing a new diocese this last comment may seem a little odd, but in the context of three hundred years of disputes it makes more sense. The charter was forged at the bidding of Adalbert, and refers to long-running territorial disputes.[56] Any sense of the extent to which these stemmed from the 840s is subsequently unclear in Adam's narrative. He summarized it as follows: "Lothar should possess Rome with Italy and Lotharingia with Burgundy; Louis should rule the Rhine with Germany; Charles, Gaul; Pippin, Aquitaine."[57] There was space to lament the loss of Turholz to Charles' kingdom—something about which Rimbert of Hamburg-Bremen had complained bitterly in the *Vita Anskarii* (ca. 870).[58] Adam's simplified formulation of the 843 divisions reimposed a coherence in the north that had been lost during the original settlements at Verdun.

Returning to the plight of the ninth-century hagiographers, it is notable how little discord there is between Christian territories and rulers in their texts. Liudger and Willehad wander between Frankish and [Anglo-]Saxon worlds with apparent ease, working with the courts of Alchred and Charlemagne happily. Co-operation between the two courts was certainly not unheard of: Alchred, for example, wrote to Charlemagne pledging support for the conversion of Saxony sometime between 771 and 774.[59] Bishop Lull of Mainz, the Mercian successor of St. Boniface, appears to have played a role in facilitating communication, and individuals like the priest Wigbert can be seen in the later

---

[54] Adam of Bremen, *Gesta Hammaburgensis*, 1.11 (12)-13 (14), ed. Schmeidler, 12–17. The reference to Lull's involvement in the foundation in 787 is particularly spurious given that he died in 786.

[55] Adam of Bremen, *Gesta Hammaburgensis*, 1.13 (14), ed. Schmeidler, 16: " . . . quia casus preteritorum cautos nos faciunt in futurum . . ."

[56] On the forgery: Richard Drögereit, "Erzbistum Hamburg, Hamburg-Bremen oder Bremen? Studien zur Hamburg-Bremer Frühgeschichte," *Archiv für Diplomatik* 21 (1975): 136–230, at 175–76. On the wider history of Hamburg-Bremen forgeries: Gerhard Theuerkauf, "Urkundenfälschungen des Erzbistums Hamburg-Bremen vom 9.–11. Jahrhundert," *Niedersächsisches Jahrbuch für Landesgeschichte* 60 (1988): 71–140, esp. 136–37 on Adalbert.

[57] Adam of Bremen, *Gesta Hammaburgensis*, 1.24, ed. Schmeidler, 28: ". . . ut Lotharius maior natu cum Italia Romam, Lotharingiam cum Burgundia possideret, Ludvicus [for Ludovicus] Rhenum cum Germania regeret, Karolus Galliam, Pippinus Aquitaniam."

[58] Rimbert, *Vita Anskarii*, chap. 21, ed. Georg Waitz, MGH SS rer. Germ. 55 (Hannover, 1884), 13–79; James T. Palmer, "Rimbert's *Vita Anskarii* and Scandinavian Mission in the Ninth Century," *Journal of Ecclesiastical History* 55 (2004): 235–56, at 242–43.

[59] Alchred, *Die Briefe*, nos. 121, ed. Tangl, 257–58.

Bonifatian correspondence making sure the missions were promoted widely.[60] But to note that the impression of the *vitae* is historically plausible is to miss the more significant fact that, seventy years later, two writers came to reflect on it at about the same time with apparent independence. There is no cross-referencing between the two *vitae*, although Adam of Bremen later added up the evidence and postulated that Liudger and Willehad had worked together in Echternach.[61] The two *vitae* do present competitive images of the two saints. Altfrid celebrates at length Liudger's foundation of the church at Dokkum where Boniface was martyred.[62] The Bremen *vita*, meanwhile, begins Willehad's missionary exploits with his alleged successes in Dokkum where "he showed himself to be the brightest light in that place."[63] This is quite a boast, and even manages a possible nod to Liudger's claim in his *Vita Gregorii abbatis* that Boniface's arrival in Frankia was *quasi lucifer.*[64] Willehad then preached for a while in the areas around Groningen, according to his *vita*, but it cannot have been much later that, according to Altfrid's *vita*, Charlemagne granted this region to Münster.[65] The agreements at Verdun in 843 among the three Carolingian kings appear to have ridden roughshod over a situation between Bremen and Münster that was already competitive—not that we should imagine it being bitter—leaving neither side particularly happy.

Some hagiographers wrote even more independently of the voice of Frankish authority, notably in the Utrecht *Vita altera Bonifatii*. This tells the story of St. Boniface from a more Frisian perspective than had the earlier eighth-century *Vita Bonifatii* (ca. 760) by Willibald in Mainz. Unfortunately the oldest manuscript, from the fourteenth century, hints at considerable editing along its passage from the ninth century, if not even outright forgery. A note in the manuscript associates the story with Bishop Radbod of Utrecht (899–917), but as Wilhelm Levison showed in his edition of the *Vita*, the author's use of Latin and biblical analogy seems wildly out of step with Radbod's more thoughtful style.[66] If we take the central part of the *Vita altera* as genuine, there are some interesting observations to be made. Firstly, there is not a single mention of the Franks or the Carolingians as their rulers. This need not be taken as a rejection of Carolingian authority, but the *Vita* is further evidence that one could work through the history of Frisia and Saxony without it. Liudger was more than happy ca. 800 to write about the

---

[60] Wigbert, *Die Briefe*, nos. 137–139, ed. Tangl, 275–78.

[61] Adam of Bremen, *Gesta Hammaburgensis*, 1.11 (12), ed. Schmeidler, 13.

[62] Altfrid, *Vita Liudgeri*, chaps. 19–20, ed. Diekamp, 22–24.

[63] *Vita Willehadi*, chap. 2, ed. Poncelet, 843.

[64] Liudger, *Vita Gregorii*, chap. 1, ed. Holder-Egger, 66.

[65] *Vita Willehadi*, chap. 3, ed. Poncelet, 843; Altfrid, *Vita Liudgeri*, 1.22, ed. Diekamp, 25–26.

[66] *Vita altera Bonifatii auctore Radbodo qui dicuntur episcopo Traiectensi*, ed. Wilhelm Levison, MGH SS rer. Germ. 57 (Hannover, 1905), 62–78, at lii–liii.

Frankish kings, although then Frisia could subscribe to an overarching ideology of authority created by Charlemagne to reinforce Christian authority in the region. The particular perspective of the *Vita altera Bonifatii* is all the more surprising because it was written at St. Martin's in Utrecht—an *ecclesiola* which later charters, forged in the twelfth century, claimed Pippin had given to Boniface.[67] This church was not mentioned by either Liudger or Altfrid; they both celebrated the importance of St. Salvator's in the same city, and Altfrid even claimed that Liudger had often slept in the church.[68] The St. Martin's priest thus opted out not only of Carolingian history, but also of the traditions of the *Liudgeriden*. The commemoration of mission in the mid-ninth century can reveal a variety of parallel ongoing discourses.

In the middle of all this, it seems that the Northumbrian court is one of a number of places one could legitimately recall within a historically-constructed discourse. Altfrid and the Bremen cleric could work within the reality of a tripartite Carolingian Empire, but this was not always how it had been or even how it should be. The stories of the *vitae*, of Frisian and Saxon worlds becoming part of Christendom and the Frankish kingdoms, were by their very nature stories of creation and transition, produced by a time of dramatic creation and transition. Systems of power were not fixed. In the 840s, no one could argue that the Northumbrian court could exercise any tangible counter-authority in the region to help Bremen or Münster, but clearly people still remembered the court as a place which had once been a legitimate place of appeal. In part, this was facilitated in both cases by veneration for Alcuin of York, whose *gravitas*, poetry, and hagiographical models litter the texts. Altfrid recalled that Liudger had spent time in York under Alcuin's tutelage and included one of Alcuin's poems celebrating Boniface's martyrdom; the author of the *Vita Willehadi*, meanwhile, seems to have used Alcuin's *Vita Willibrordi*—a text quoted in Liudger's *Vita Gregorii*—as a model.[69] But there is also something deeper about the identities of Frisia and Saxony which must come into play.

3. A 'Brotherhood' of Identities

Fundamentally, the Anglo-Saxon missions to the Continent which established and shaped Bremen and Utrecht had claimed an ethnically-specific ideology. Bede wrote about the origins of the missions, claiming they began with the monk Ecgberht, later famous for converting Iona to Roman practices in 716.[70]

---

[67] See n. 29. For context, see C. van de Kieft, "Bonifatius en het Bisdom Utrecht," *Tijdschrift voor Geschiedenis* 74 (1961): 42–63, 526–32.

[68] Altfrid, *Vita Liudgeri*, 1.18, ed. Diekamp, 21.

[69] Wood, *The Missionary Life*, 91.

[70] Bede, *HE*, 5.22, ed. Colgrave and Mynors, 554.

Ecgberht "knew that there were many peoples living in Germany from whom the Angles and Saxons, who now live in Britain, derived their origin . . . These were the Frisians, Rugians, Danes, Huns, Old Saxons and Boructuars. There are also many others in the same regions who still practice pagan rites, to whom the soldier of Christ proposed to go."[71] It is clear from this and other references in his works that Bede perceived each of these peoples to be distinctive *gentes*, somehow united.[72] But the impression of a kind of brotherhood (*germanitas*) is not as simple as it may appear. The Rugians and Huns are not "Germanic" in the sense we would normally consider, and in general it is hard to sustain any argument about the involvement of anyone from the list in the *adventus Saxonum* except Danes and Old Saxons.[73] But, as James Campbell argued, "[Bede] does not generally write carelessly."[74] We might prefer to see these as peoples who shared a geographical space and interconnected history. Bede's turn of phrase is awkward, but his interest appears to be as much in *Germania* as it is in the *gentes Germanorum*.

From Bede's list, it is important to bear in mind the role the Danes could play in shaping the north. The early recorded history of Denmark suggests strongly that its people were well placed to offer competitive models of association to Frisia and Saxony. The first properly-documented connection comes from 777, when the *Annales regni Francorum* recorded that the Westphalian chieftain Widukind, whose rebellions disrupted the work of Liudger and Willehad, "fled with his companions to Sigifred, king of the Danes."[75] Einhard, writing at the court of Emperor Louis the Pious in ca. 817, commented that King Godefrid I of the Danes (d. 810) "had come to look upon Frisia and Saxony as belonging to him."[76] It was also noted in the *Annales Bertiniani* for 838 that King Horik I (ruled 829–854) demanded that Emperor Louis give Frisia and the Obodrites (a Slavic people who settled in Saxony) to him, although Louis considered the idea ludicrous.[77] A few years later, in 841, King Louis the German of the East

---

[71] Bede, *HE*, 5.9, ed. Colgrave and Mynors, 476.

[72] See Becher, "Verfassung und Ethnogenese," 18–20 on this and the problems of relating it to the impression elsewhere of the Saxons' internal divisions.

[73] Rolf H. Bremmer, "The Nature of the Evidence for a Frisian Participation in the *Adventus Saxonum*," in *Britain 400–600: Language and History*, ed. Alfred Bammesberger and Alfred Wollman (Heidelberg, 1990), 353–71; Schäferdiek, "Fragen," 176–80; Catherine Hills, *Origins of the English* (London, 2003).

[74] James Campbell, "The Lost Centuries: 400–600," in *The Anglo-Saxons*, ed. idem, Eric John, and Patrick Wormald (Harmondsworth, 1982), 20–44, at 31.

[75] *Annales regni Francorum*, s.a. 777, ed. Waitz, 19: ". . . Widichindum . . . qui multorum sibi facinorum conscius . . . ad Sigifridum Danorum regem profugerat."

[76] Einhard, *Vita Karoli*, chap. 14, ed. Georg Waitz, MGH SS rer. Germ. 25 (Hannover, 1880), 12: "Frisiam quoque atque Saxoniam haud aliter atque suas provintias aestimabat."

[77] *Annales Bertiniani*, s.a. 838, ed. Waitz, 16.

Franks reportedly "feared that the Norsemen . . . might unite with the Saxons."[78] There appeared, then, to be some strong political connections between the lands north of the Franks. Ports of Viking-Age Scandinavia, such as Ribe, Hedeby, and Birka, have also yielded much archaeological evidence which suggests that there were flourishing trade routes linking Frisia, Saxony, Denmark, and Sweden.[79] Close social and economic links are attested by Rimbert's *Vita Anskarii* and the *Vita Rimberti* (written ca. 900 in Nienheerse).[80] Whatever political and cultural impositions had been introduced by the Franks and Anglo-Saxons in Frisia and Saxony, they faced influence and competition from the regions further to the north.

The Franks' own place in some kind of Germanic brotherhood is trickier to discern. Bede's *Boructeri* are often thought to be Frankish, but that did not mean that the Franks in general were 'brothers' to the other Germans of the North. In *Beowulf*, with its Anglo-Saxon takes on Scandinavian and Frisian relations, the Franks lurk in the background. When they do appear in the text, it is as an enemy. The *Beowulf* poet traces feelings of enmity back to the raids of Hygelac against the 'Hugas' or 'Francum' and the Frisians.[81] This is an often-discussed extract because it is 'verified' by Gregory of Tours' *Libri Decem Historiae*—or at least suggests the poet had read Gregory, since his work was known to Bede and therefore to others in Britain.[82] The implication of "us wæs a syððan Merewioingas milts ungyfeðe" (lines 2920–2921) is that the ill-feeling had spilt over into the present time, although apparently not the Carolingian present. One implication within this tradition is that martial encounters had created a distance between the Danes, Frisians, and Franks before the Carolingian era. Matthew Innes has shown that 'Germanic' Frankish culture was so intertwined with its Latin and Romance cousins as to create something that was not really isolatable, most famously represented by the legends about the Franks' Trojan origins.[83]

---

[78] Nithard, *Historia*, 4.2, ed. Pertz, 46: "Igitur metuens Ludowicus, ne idem Nortmanni necnon et Sclavi propter affinitatem Saxonibus . . . coniungerent."

[79] For Hedeby, see Herbert Jankuhn, *Haithabu* (Neumünster, 1986); on Ribe, see Stig Jensen, *The Vikings of Ribe*, trans. G. Bibby (Ribe, 1991); on Birka, see *Early Investigations and Future Plans*, ed. Björn Ambrosiani and Helen Clarke, Birka Studies 1 (Stockholm, 1992).

[80] For example: Rimbert, *VA* chaps. 20 and 27 (45, 59); *Vita Rimberti*, chap. 18, ed. Georg Waitz, MGH SS rer. Germ. 55 (Hannover, 1884), 81–99, at 95–96.

[81] *Beowulf*, ed. Bruce Mitchell and Fred C. Robinson (Oxford, 2000), ll. 2910–2922.

[82] Gregory of Tours, *Libri Decem Historiae*, 3.3, ed. Bruno Krusch and Wilhelm Levison, MGH SS rer. Merov. 1 (Hannover, 1951), 99.

[83] Matthew Innes, "Teutons or Trojans? The Carolingians and the Germanic Past," in *The Uses of the Past in the Early Middle Ages*, ed. Hen and idem, 227–49. See also Paul Edward Dutton, "Charlemagne's Mustache," in idem, *Charlemagne's Mustache and Other Cultural Clusters of a Dark Age* (London, 2004), 3–42.

This might explain why, for all Boniface's calls for support and literary allusions to a Germanic 'brotherhood' in letters to the English, he never seems to have suggested to the Franks that mission in the north was their duty too. Although there were arguably shared elements in the cultural clusters by which the groups involved identified themselves, the totality of these clusters did not add up to same-ness. Indeed, Boniface faced great reluctance amongst the Frankish clergy to engage in mission (regardless of whatever had happened in the seventh century), and Liudger too seems to have aimed criticisms at the nobles in his audience for not being supportive enough.[84] For sure there were political reasons — the late Timothy Reuter noted a reticence for expansion in the ninth century — but this initially helped support mission to Denmark as a way of securing borders.[85] It is also striking that, in all the *vitae* written about the Anglo-Saxon missions to the continent in Frankish territories, not once do they mention ethnicity as an influencing factor.

The Franks themselves were fully aware of the dangers and advantages of the politics of identity. On a variety of textual and legal levels, Saxon identity appears to have been suppressed as a result of Frankish invasion.[86] Einhard is often cited as the authority here: he claimed that the Franks' violent subjugation of the Saxons resulted in the two peoples becoming as one as a polity under Christianity, a turn of phrase later echoed by Widukind of Corvey (d. after 973).[87] The key moments of the campaign have been thoroughly discussed. In 774, after years of problems on the Frankish-Saxon borders, Charlemagne's army felled the great shrine of the Irminsul tree and took away many treasures.[88] The Saxons' persistent transgression of peace agreements led first to the imposition of harsh legal measures by the Franks, probably at a general assembly at Paderborn in 777, then in 782 the slaughter of 4,500 Saxon hostages, and finally in 804 Charlemagne ordered the forcible repatriation of Saxons from beyond the Elbe, giving the lands to the Obodrites.[89] Anglo-Saxon missionaries had played a varied role in the background of these campaigns.[90] Willehad was of course

---

[84] Heinz Löwe, "Liudger als Zeitkritik," *Historisches Jahrbuch* 74 (1954): 79–91.

[85] Timothy Reuter, "The End of Carolingian Military Expansion," in *Charlemagne's Heir: New Perspectives on the Reign of Louis the Pious,* ed. Peter Godman and Roger Collins (Oxford, 1990), 391–405, esp. 392–94; Palmer, "Rimbert's *Vita Anskarii,*" 251.

[86] Bonnie Effros, "*De partibus Saxoniae* and the Regulation of Mortuary Custom: A Carolingian Campaign of Christianization or the Suppression of Saxon Identity?," *Revue Belge de Philologie et d'Histoire* 75 (1997): 267–86.

[87] Einhard, *Vita Karoli,* chap. 7, ed. Georg Waitz, MGH SS rer. Germ. 25 (Hannover, 1911), 10. Becher, *Rex, Dux und Gens,* 41–50; Beumann, "Die Hagiographie 'Bewältigt'," 133–35.

[88] *Annales regni Francorum,* s.a. 774, ed. Waitz, 34–35.

[89] *Annales regni Francorum,* s.a. 777, 782, 804, ed. Waitz, 48, 62, 118.

[90] James Palmer, "The 'Vigorous Rule' of Bishop Lull: Between Bonifatian Mission and Carolingian Church Control," *Early Medieval Europe* 13 (2005): 249–76.

active in the mission field, as were Lebuin and the Anglo-Saxon priest Wigbert. Lull of Mainz and Alcuin acted as advisors on various issues. There is little doubt that some Anglo-Saxons back home were interested too, with Charlemagne's campaigns being amongst the few Continental events to be reported in insular annals.[91] But many hagiographical traditions arising from many Saxon centers like Paderborn or Halberstadt did not comment on the Anglo-Saxons in the ninth century, even when discussing Bonifatian foundations such as Fulda and Würzburg.[92] They were more preoccupied with Charlemagne's invasion and the ensuing cultural realignment.[93]

In part the use of saints to reflect particular matrices of identities was made problematic by the Frankish cult of saints. Pierre Riché pointed out that the Franks of the Carolingian period were less interested in new saints than were their predecessors, and Paul Fouracre has argued that this was part of a deliberate attempt to regulate the cult of saints.[94] Recently deceased figures lent themselves far too easily to supporting the politics that they had left behind, becoming post-mortem representatives of particular places or factions. One of the reasons missionaries appear to have been popular Carolingian saints is because they fulfilled a need on the frontiers to provide locally meaningful saints for communities who had little or no Christian past. In practice, even the Bonifaces and Anskars were not widely venerated outside these regions.[95] It is worth observing the influx of older, often Roman saints, into Germany. Einhard himself oversaw the translation of the bones of Saints Marcellinus and Peter to Seligenstadt; Hrabanus Maurus of Fulda brought a great number to Fulda and its surrounding churches; Paderborn received St. Liborius of Le Mans ca. 836; Hamburg, Sextus and Sinicius of Rheims; et cetera.[96] The descendants of *dux* Widukind were involved, for example in 851 when Waltbert had relics of St. Alexander translated to

---

[91] Story, *Carolingian Connections*, 99.

[92] *Translatio s. Librorii*, chap. 5, ed. Georg H. Pertz, MGH Scriptores 4 (Hannover, 1841), 149–57, at 151; *Vita Liutbirgae*, chap. 1, ed. Georg H. Pertz, MGH Scriptores 4 (Hannover, 1841), 158–64, at 158–59.

[93] Beumann, "Die Hagiographie 'Bewältigt'," 143–44, 152–54.

[94] Pierre Riché, "Les Carolingiens en quête de sainteté," in *Les fonctions des saints dans le monde occidental (IIIe–XIIIe s.)*, Collection de l'Ecole Française de Rome 149 (Rome, 1991), 217–24; Paul Fouracre, "The Origins of the Carolingian Attempt to Regulate the Cult of Saints," in *The Cult of Saints in Late Antiquity and the Early Middle Ages*, ed. Howard-Johnston and Hayward, 143–66.

[95] James T. Palmer, "The Frankish Cult of Martyrs and the Case of the Two Saints Boniface," *Revue Bénédictine* 114 (2004): 326–48, at 345–46.

[96] Julia M. H. Smith, "Old Saints, New Cults: Roman Relics in Carolingian Francia," in *Early Medieval Rome and the Christian West: Essays in Honour of Donald A. Bullough*, ed. eadem (Leiden, 2000), 317–39.

Wildeshausen.[97] This is not a context in which it would have been easy to promote new Christian identities within Germany through saints' cults drawn from local resources. Genuine saints were long-dead and preferably Roman, making them less directly representative of the localities expected to engage with them.

There was, however, no obvious suppression of 'Germanic' identities in the ninth-century cult of saints, at least in the hagiography. Lupus of Ferrières wrote the *Vita Wigberti* for the former Saxon mission station of Hersfeld sometime between 836 and 842, opening with an account of the *Angli-Saxones* and their arrival from the northern regions of *Germania* where the Saxons lived.[98] To Lupus, folk migrations provided a kind of historical symmetry with the return peregrinations of Anglo-Saxon missionaries in the eighth century. At Fulda, the *Translatio sancti Alexandri* (ca. 865) likewise set out the connection between the Anglo-Saxons and the Saxons for Waltbert:[99]

> According to ancient tradition, the Saxons came from the Angles living in Britain, and sailed over the ocean to the German coast, intending, as was necessary, to seek a place in which to settle . . . [They fought against Theodoric of the Franks and were settled in Thuringia] . . . South of the Saxons lived the Franks and that part of the Thuringians which had not been touched by the preceding storm of war . . . On the north were the Northmen, a very ferocious people. On the east lived the Obodrites and on the west the Frisians, who had constantly to secure their borderlands either by treaties or by wars against the Saxons who, though peaceful at home and benignly mindful of the welfare of their tribesmen, were excessively restless and troublesome to the settlements of their neighbors.

It seems that concerns over borders drove the construction of this extract.[100] But precisely what these 'ancient traditions' comprised is unclear, with plenty of scope to speculate about oral traditions and misremembered or misinterpreted

---

[97] *Translatio s. Alexandri*, chap. 1, ed. Georg H. Pertz, MGH Scriptores 2 (Hannover, 1829), 674–81.

[98] Lupus of Ferrières, *Vita Wigberti*, chap. 1, ed. Oswald Holder-Egger, MGH Scriptores 15.1 (Hannover, 1887), 37–43, at 37.

[99] *Translatio s. Alexandri*, chap. 1 (674–75): "Saxonum gens, sicut tradit antiquitas, ab Anglis Britanniae incolis egressa, per Oceanum navigans Germaniae litoribus studio et necessitate quaerendarum sedium appulsa est . . . A meridie quidem Francos habentes et partem Thuringorum, quos praecedens hostilis turbo non tetigit . . . A septentrione vero Nordmannos gentes ferocissimas. Ab ortu autem solis Obodritos, et ab occasu Frisos, a quibus sine intermissione vel foedere vel concertatione necessario finium suorum spacia tuebantur. Erant enim inquieti nimis et finitimorum sedibus infesti, domi vero pacati et civium utilitatibus placida benignitate consulentes."

[100] Becher, *Rex, Dux und Gens*, 33; Ian Wood, "Beyond Satraps and Ostriches: Political and Social Structures of the Saxons in the Early Carolingian Period," in *The Continental Saxons from the Migration Period to the Tenth Century: An Ethnographic Perspective,*

textual borrowings. Procopius had written about return migrations from Britain, but these appear to refer to the settlement of Brittany and there is little evidence that Procopius was known in ninth-century Fulda.[101] Maybe the passage simply echoes the Anglo-Saxon missions themselves, with Saxons traveling from Britain to the Rhineland. Perhaps the most significant point, however, is that the Saxons were not really confronting Frankish overlordship at the expense of their English affiliations in the ninth century. Rather, they were dealing with different cultural and political affiliations at the same time. Rudolf, the author of the first part of the *Translatio*, gave a somewhat measured account of the Saxon wars. He noted the *perfidia* of the Saxons, but also avoided comments like Einhard's *quasi una populus* because of its oppressive overtones, while also making the Saxons predestined to receive Christianity.[102] The resulting hotchpotch is a reminder that identities are never stable, coherent and 'given.'

4. Vitae, *germanitas*, and *imperium*

The problems of saints' cults and identities under the Carolingians provide further contexts in which Altfrid and the author of the *Vita Willehadi* worked. Frisian and Saxon identities were among those 'barbarian' ethnicities which became institutionalized and politicized in the post-Roman world.[103] For our two hagiographers, much was naturally framed by ideas of ecclesiastical structure. An example of this comes in the *Vita Liudgeri* when Liudger is described in death as formerly an (or maybe 'the'?) *episcopus Saxonum Fresonumque*.[104] The story in which this is mentioned is revealing. A young man named Adam had killed his brother, Henry, in a brawl and was put in chains and exiled by Bishop Jonas of Orléans (d. 843/4). A year spent praying at the shrine of St. Geretrudis of Nivelles—an important Pippinid saint—released Adam's left arm, but further time spent praying at St. Peter's in Rome was of no benefit, and Adam fell ill. At this point he had a vision directing him to seek out the shrine of Liudger,

---

ed. Dennis Green and Frank Siegmund, Studies in Archaeoethnology 6 (Woodbridge, 2003), 271–90.

[101] Procopius, *History of the Wars*, 8.20, ed. and trans. H. B. Dewing, 7 vols. (Cambridge, MA, 1961–1962), 5: 252–71.

[102] *Translatio s. Alexandri*, chap. 3, 675–76; Beumann, "Die Hagiographie 'Bewältigt'," 144–48.

[103] On the process in general: Hans-Werner Goetz, "*Gens*: Terminology and Perception of the 'Germanic' Peoples from Late Antiquity to the Early Middle Ages," in *The Construction of Communities in the Early Middle Ages: Texts, Resources and Artefacts*, ed. Richard Corradini, Max Diesenberger, and Helmut Reimitz, Transformation of the Roman World 12 (Leiden, 2003), 39–64.

[104] Altfrid, *Vita Liudgeri*, 2.20, ed. Diekamp, 51.

where of course his body and soul were cured. The whole construction is useful to Altfrid's scheme of work because it demonstrates Liudger's posthumous *potentia* as part of a wider matrix of Frankish sanctity of which Nivelles and Rome were representative.[105] By contrast we could compare the more inward-looking *Miracula Willehadi*, in which few miracles occur outside the diocese of Bremen because it was intended to console that area.[106] In taking the audience outside the world of the *Liudgeriden*, the reference to Liudger as *quondam episcopus Saxonum Fresonumque* is a device to bring events back home. A certain combination of ecclesiastical infrastructure and ethnicity thus helped to locate Liudger within the wider world of the Franks.

Similar conjunctions of the Frisians and Saxons are evident in the *Vita Willehadi* as a background to Willehad's work. They are described as *Fresones atque Saxones populi hactenus increduli atque pagani*, who had decided to reject their culture of idols *en masse*. This unity of action, while let down by Willehad's experiences in the mission field, projects an institutional concept of a northern continuum. The very idea that Willehad could be transferred (*transferre*) to these *partes* by the Northumbrian court suggests that the author is not imagining an unstructured world beyond the frontier. Charlemagne's campaigns in the late 770s helped to impose some kind of order, and he was given a diocese (*diocesis*) in Wigmodia which included both *Fresones et Saxones*—prefiguring the centralized unity subsequently created by the *translatio imperii* in 800, which the hagiographer places at the heart of the story as a digression.[107] Empire is the clearest manifestation of lots of smaller identities grouped under one larger banner. Within the word *imperium*, Bede had brought together the disparate peoples of the *gens Anglorum*, and Alcuin had given expression to Charles Martel's hold over Frisia Citerior.[108] From a Frankish perspective, the *Annales Mettenses priores* had described Pippin II as having ambitions in 687 to reassert Frankish authority over the *diversa gentes* who had once been subjected to Frankish dominion.[109] While not being a formal concept of overlordship or *imperium*, the list that

---

[105] On the healing power of shrines, see Brown, *Cult of Saints*, 113–20.

[106] Herwig Röckelein, "Miracles and Horizontal Mobility in the Early Middle Ages: Some Methodological Reflections," in *The Community, the Family and the Saint*, ed. Joyce Hill and Mary Swan, International Medieval Research 4 (Turnhout, 1998), 181–97.

[107] *Vita Willehadi*, chap. 5, ed. Poncelet, 843–44.

[108] Bede, *HE*, 2.5, ed. Colgrave and Mynors, 148–50; Alcuin, *Vita Willibrordi*, chap. 13, ed. Levison, 127. On Bede's much-discussed words see Patrick Wormald, "Bede, the Bretwaldas and the Origins of the *Gens Anglorum*," in *Ideal and Reality in Frankish and Anglo-Saxon Society*, ed. idem, Donald Bullough, and Roger Collins (Oxford, 1983), 99–129; Stephen Fanning, "Bede, *Imperium*, and the Bretwaldas," *Speculum* 66 (1991): 1–26.

[109] *Annales Mettenses priores*, ed. Bernhard von Simson, MGH SS rer. Germ. 10 (Hannover, 1905), 12.

follows—which begins with the Frisians and Saxons—is still as indicative of an ideal political status quo which included the subjugation of neighbours. Liudger, meanwhile, saw things less politically, portraying the various religious activities of the Franks, *Angli*, Frisians, Saxons, Bavarians, Sueves, and more as a parallel movement to the creation of a secular empire.[110] There were a number of possible models in which Frisia and Saxony could be absorbed into the wider political and Christian world.

The problem that the author of the *Vita Willehadi* and Altfrid both faced was that, under Widukind, Frisia and Westphalia had developed into a much more hostile environment.[111] It was impossible for them to portray the attacks on the Christian Franks in anything other than negative terms. But can one create an inclusive cluster of identities which explicitly demonizes one of the parts involved? The *Vita Willehadi*, taking a cue from the letters of Alcuin, talks of the Saxons being coerced (verb *cogere*; adjective *coactus*) into the Christian faith.[112] But despite a flicker of criticism, it is an overwhelmingly positive view of Charlemagne's actions. Altfrid variously criticizes the Saxons for being impious and rough, but never portrays them as anything other than a homogenous enemy.[113] There is no attempt to portray much by way of a transition towards a better state of affairs, no effort to create a bridge between the past and present. Late in the ninth century, the Paderborn *Translatio sancti Liborii* could still praise Charlemagne for "taming [the Saxons] by sword, making them receive the Christian faith, and adding them to the empire" through his hard work.[114] The inclusive religious model in Liudger's *Vita Gregorii* had later found echoes in political ideals.

Altfrid's (re)creation of Liudger's world was also open to the tensions created by the threats of the Danes and certain groups of Saxons, despite any affinities. A dream of Liudger's related by his sister Heriburga described "the sun fleeing across the sea from northern parts, with black clouds following" only after time to return, "smaller and paler than it had been, and chasing the fog across the sea."[115] Here Liudger's dream presented a metaphor for the Viking attacks which would cause so many problems after his death, embedding it in a representation of the

---

[110] Liudger, *Vita Gregorii*, chap. 11, ed. Holder-Egger, 75; von Padberg, *Mission und Christianisierung*, 239–40.

[111] *Vita Willehadi*, chaps. 6 and 8, ed. Poncelet, 844, 845; Altfrid, *Vita Liudgeri*, chap. 1.21, ed. Diekamp, 24.

[112] *Vita Willehadi*, chap. 9, ed. Poncelet, 845; Alcuin, *Alcuini epistolae*, nos. 110–11, ed. Ernst Dümmler, MGH Epistolae 4 (Hannover, 1895), 157–62.

[113] Altfrid, *Vita Liudgeri*, chap. 1.15 and 1.23, ed. Diekamp, 19, 27.

[114] *Translatio s. Liborii*, chap. 2, ed. Waitz, 149: ". . . illos ferro edomitos Christi fidem suscipere fecit suoque addidit imperio . . . ."

[115] Altfrid, *Vita Liudgeri*, chap. 1.27, ed. Diekamp, 32–33.

physical world so familiar to the seaborne Frisians.[116] Altfrid, like the author of the *Vita altera Bonifatii*, was able to note that after the destruction of monasteries, churches, and settlements, the Vikings were chased away and peace restored.[117] Despite the optimism of hindsight—premature, as it transpired—Altfrid said that Liudger was "anxious" to preach to the Danes, although Charlemagne would not allow him. There are a number of practical and literary concerns at work here. One of Altfrid's models was the *Vita Willibrordi* of Alcuin (ca. 796), in which Willibrord had preached in Denmark after failing to evangelize Frisia Ulterior.[118] For both Alcuin and Altfrid, the stories were likely an extension of their own missionary interests.[119] Alcuin, as a Northumbrian with an interest in Bede, possibly thought in terms of the *Historia Ecclesiastica*'s *Germanitas*; but what of Altfrid? His reference to the evangelization of the Northmen came in a stylized account of how Liudger wrote about and conformed to standards of piety set down by Gregory, Alberic, and Boniface (although not the more temporally distant Willibrord).[120] There is no indication of *Germanitas*. But Altfrid did also borrow the phrase *confinium Fresonum et Danorum* from Alcuin and strengthen it by substituting *et* for *atque*.[121] Given that Altfrid was writing after the grant of Rüstringen to Harald Klak in 826, the closeness in the region was probably difficult to ignore. It is further testament to the ways in which demographic and political change within a geographical area can reshape attitudes.

5. Conclusion

In the ninth century there was a range of identities on which Frisians and Westphalians could draw. The previous century had seen Anglo-Saxons proclaiming a sense of unity between those peoples who lived north of the Franks and either

---

[116] See the description of the Frisians in the *Vita altera Bonifatii*, chap. 9, ed. Levison, 68.

[117] Altfrid, *Vita Liudgeri*, chap. 1.27, ed. Diekamp, 33; *Vita altera Bonifatii*, chap. 6, ed. Levison, 66 (regarding Britain).

[118] Alcuin, *Vita Willibrordi*, chap. 9, ed. Wilhelm Levison, MGH SS rer. Merov. 7 (Hannover, 1920), 81–144, at 123–24. Close borrowing occurs in the description of the cult of Fosite: Alcuin, *Vita Willibrordi*, chap. 10, ed. Levison, 124–25; Altfrid, *Vita Liudgeri*, chap. 1.22, ed. Diekamp, 26–27.

[119] For Alcuin, see *Alcuini epistolae*, no. 6, ed. Dümmler, 31. For Altfrid, see the suggestion of Wood, *The Missionary Life*, 115.

[120] Compare with Rimbert, *Vita Anskarii*, chap. 35, ed. Waitz, 66–70.

[121] Altfrid, *Vita Liudgeri*, chap. 1.22, ed. Diekamp, 26; Alcuin, *Vita Willibrordi*, chap. 10, ed. Levison, 124. For similar examples of conjunctions, illustrating a persisting emphasis on *gentes* over territory, see Walter Pohl, "Zur Bedeutung ethnischer Unterscheidungen in der frühen Karolingerzeit," *Studien zur Sachsenforschung* 12 (1999): 193–208, at 199–201.

currently or formerly inhabited *Germania*. Efforts in those years of mission to establish some kind of ecclesiastical structure were commemorated, and offered important affiliations to a sympathetic Christian cultural world. The Bonifaces and Willehads were not entirely synonymous with Frankish overlordship in retrospect, but with a range of concepts and foundation legends on which any community could profitably reflect. Those communities had their own local perspectives which helped in different ways to define horizons. A family like Liudger's could project its history in all directions because members had been supported by the Franks, evangelized by Anglo-Saxons, and educated in Northumbria, all while developing landholdings and interests further east and north than Frisia itself. In a sense its smaller-scale identity could, through its history and landholdings, extend beyond the geographical preconceptions of an ethnic label. Any institutional connection to Anglo-Saxon England was quickly forgotten, if one had ever existed, to be replaced by symbolic associations. What mattered was that the best associations could be maintained and developed as different groups reacted to the changing world around them.

Saint Oswald and Anglo-Saxon Identity in the *Chronicon Æthelweardi*: The Correspondence of Æthelweard and Abbess Matilda

James Roberts

The *ealdorman* of the western provinces of Anglo-Saxon England during the final quarter of the tenth century was Æthelweard. From 993 he was the most senior *ealdorman* in Anglo-Saxon England.[1] His career seems to have lasted until 998 when a final appearance in the witness lists of surviving charters means it is likely that he died soon after. A single record of Æthelweard in the *Anglo-Saxon Chronicle* describes how he and Bishop Ælfheah of Winchester were sent by Æthelred to bring the Norwegian king, Olaf Tryggvason, to Andover prior to his conversion.[2] Æthelweard is recognized chiefly for his association with a late tenth-century Latin chronicle that drew extensively on the *Anglo-Saxon Chronicle*.[3] Known as the *Chronicon Æthelweardi*, the text makes explicit in its prologue that someone called Æthelweard was responsible for its compilation. It continues by describing how Æthelweard's relation, Matilda, had requested from him an

---

[1] Simon Keynes, *The Diplomas of King Æthelred* (Cambridge, 1980), 187–88.

[2] *The Anglo-Saxon Chronicle MS C*, ed. Katherine O'Brien O'Keefe, *The Anglo-Saxon Chronicle: A Collaborative Edition*, ed. David Dumville and Simon Keynes, 5 (Cambridge, 2001), 87.

[3] The connection between the *ealdorman* Æthelweard who appears in the charters and the author of the *Chronicon Æthelweardi* is ultimately based on circumstantial evidence. The text's prologue describes Æthelweard as *consul*, probably intending to imply that he was an *ealdorman*, but no evidence explicitly connects the *ealdorman* of the western provinces with the *Chronicon*. Even if it is accepted that the Æthelweard who appears in the preface to the *Chronicon Æthelweardi* is indeed *ealdorman* Æthelweard, it is not possible to argue with certainty that the *ealdorman* Æthelweard actually composed the text personally. See Æthelweard, *Chronicon Æthelweardi*, ed. Alistair Campbell (London, 1962), xiii. This essay will assume that the *ealdorman* Æthelweard was in some way responsible for compiling the *Chronicon Æthelweardi*, and for convenience the text's author will be referred to as Æthelweard.

Hans Sauer and Joanna Story, eds., *Anglo-Saxon England and the Continent*. With the assistance of Gaby Waxenberger. Essays in Anglo-Saxon Studies, vol. 3. MRTS 394. Tempe: ACMRS, 2011.   [ISBN 978-0-86698-442-3]

account of their family history.[4] Matilda was abbess of Essen from 973–1011 and was descended from Edith, the daughter of Edward the Elder who had married the future German ruler Otto I in 930. This essay will consider what the *Chronicon Æthelweardi* reveals about the links Æthelweard claims to have maintained with his relation in Ottonian Germany and will argue that this contact between Matilda and Æthelweard produced a text that constructed a specific version of Anglo-Saxon identity.

Eighteen badly damaged fragments of an early eleventh-century manuscript of the *Chronicon Æthelweardi* survived the fire in the Cotton Library in 1731, and these constitute the only Anglo-Saxon evidence for the text. The earliest surviving complete witness to nearly all of the *Chronicon Æthelweardi* is a sixteenth-century printed transcription that was produced by Sir Henry Savile and published in 1596.[5] This situation presents numerous problems for attempts to discover whether or not Savile had used the Cotton Otho manuscript, in a less damaged state, to compile his version of the text. Chief among these difficulties is, inevitably, the fact that no medieval manuscript witness survives for most of the *Chronicon Æthelweardi*, and the effect of Savile's editorial methods on the text he produced is equally unclear.[6] While he used a manuscript of the *Chronicon Æthelweardi* that contained a text similar to the one in the Otho manuscript, it is not known whether or not Savile used the Otho manuscript itself. Eric Barker drew attention to chapter headings in the Otho manuscript that are absent from Savile's version of the *Chronicon Æthel-weardi*.[7] Nothing has survived in the Cotton Otho manuscript of the contents

---

[4] *Chronicon Æthelweardi*, ed. Campbell, 1–2. On the identity of Matilda, see R. L. Poole, "The Alpine Son-in-Law of Edward the Elder," in *Studies in Chronology and History*, ed. A. L. Poole (Oxford, 1934), 115–22. Elisabeth van Houts, "Women and the Writing of History in the Early Middle Ages: The Case of Abbess Matilda of Essen and Æthelweard," *Early Medieval Europe* 1 (1992): 53–68, at 60–62.

[5] The manuscript is now split between two codices, London, British Library, Cotton Otho A.x and A.xii (these will hereafter be cited as the Cotton Otho manuscript). For the sixteenth-century printed edition of the *Chronicon* see Henry Savile, *Rerum Anglicarum scriptores post Bedam praecipui* (London, 1596), 473–84. The manuscript fragments are described in N. R. Ker, *A Catalogue of Manuscripts Containing Anglo-Saxon* (Oxford, 1959), 249–50. For an account of the manuscript's history after the fire in the Cotton Library, see Andrew Prescott, "The Ghost of Asser," in *Anglo-Saxon Manuscripts and their Heritage*, ed. Phillip Pulsiano and Elaine M. Treharne (Aldershot, 1998), 255–92.

[6] D. R. Woolf, *Reading History in Early Modern England* (Cambridge, 2000), 55–56, discusses Savile's editorial style.

[7] E. E. Barker, "The Cottonian Fragments of Æthelweard's Chronicle," *Bulletin of the Institute of Historical Research* 24 (1951): 46–61, at 51–53 analyses the similarities between the text in the medieval manuscript fragments and the corresponding text in Savile's version of the *Chronicon*. In the Otho manuscript, the table of contents for the final book of the *Chronicon Æthelweardi* contains chapter headings for the reigns of Edward the Martyr and Æthelred. They survive in *capitula* for the Book Four of the

of these two chapters, but the existence of the headings demonstrates that the relationship between medieval versions of the *Chronicon Æthelweardi* and the sixteenth-century one is not without problems. While it is likely that Savile used a manuscript of the *Chronicon Æthelweardi* that originated in the same manuscript tradition as the surviving Cotton Otho manuscript, we do not know exactly what Savile's manuscript was like.

The *Chronicon Æthelweardi* provides the only surviving evidence that Æthelweard and Matilda were related. The prologue to the text reveals that their relationship was through the West-Saxon king Æthelwulf, who reigned 839–858. Knowledge of Æthelweard's immediate Anglo-Saxon relatives is otherwise limited. It is only from the *Chronicon Æthelweardi* that it is possible to know that Æthelweard was descended from Æthelwulf's fourth son, Æthelred.[8] There were probably three intervening generations, but little further information survives. Significantly, no such information is provided for the reader anywhere in the *Chronicon Æthelweardi* itself. Although she was born and raised in Saxony, Matilda's Anglo-Saxon lineage was through King Æthelwulf's youngest son, Alfred. The *Chronicon Æthelweardi* includes more detailed information about Matilda's Anglo-Saxon descent and describes how Edith, who was the daughter of Alfred's son Edward the Elder, married the future German King Otto I. Information supplied from other sources reveals that Otto I and Edith's son, Duke Liudolf of Swabia, was Matilda's father, and that Matilda later became the abbess of Essen who corresponded with Æthelweard. In an Anglo-Saxon context, therefore, Matilda was the great-granddaughter of Edward the Elder, and the great-great-granddaughter of Alfred.[9]

Æthelweard's links with Matilda are set out in the prologue to the *Chronicon Æthelweardi*. At this, the earliest opportunity, it is revealed that the pair had maintained a close correspondence and that they were acutely aware of their common family:

> Suscepi desiderii mei epistolam, charissima, uestram, et amplexus animotenus scripta non tantum legi sed etiam condidi in thesauro cordis mei. Siquidem altissimi exoro crebrius gratiam dei, ut in hac præsentia incolumem et post migrationem corporis custodiat, ducens ad æterna tabernacula. De notitia equidem communis prosapiæ, generis quoque et migratione, ut ante breuiter per epistolam insinuauimus tibi, nunc cooperante deo ab ipsius principio mundi annalem sumentes ritum, dilucidius explicare oportet, ut et lectoris susurro intuitus et auditoris augmentetur capiendi uoluntas.

Chronicon given on fol. 1 of Cotton Otho A. x but they are not in the *capitula* in Savile's text. Savile's version has, instead, references to chapters on Eadred and Eadwig which are not in the Cotton Otho manuscript.

  [8] *Chronicon Æthelweardi*, ed. Campbell, 2.

  [9] For a family tree showing the relationship between Æthelweard and Matilda, see van Houts, "Women and the Writing of History," 56.

['Most beloved, I have received the letter I desired from you and, having embraced what you wrote in my mind, I have not only read it but set it away in the treasury of my heart. Often I beg earnestly the favor of the most high God that he should keep you safe in this life and, after departure from the body, leading you to the eternal dwellings. As we have previously informed you by letter shortly about what is known of our common family and also about the migration of our people, it is now desirable, with the help of God, employing yearly usage from the beginning of the world itself to offer a clearer exposition, so that attention may be increased by the gentle voice of the reader and the desire of the listener to hear may grow.'][10]

Including the *Chronicon* itself, the production of at least three letters is described in this account of the contact between Matilda and Æthelweard: Matilda sent one, and Æthelweard also wrote to her prior to sending the *Chronicon Æthelweardi*. Although it is not revealed when or how their relationship was first established, it could have been initiated by the receipt of a letter. Equally, however, they could have been made aware of one another through a mutual personal contact. There is no evidence that Æthelweard and Matilda ever met face to face, and contact through an intermediary is possible.[11] In any case Æthelweard requested, from Matilda, further information about Edith's sister who had accompanied her to Germany as a potential wife for Otto. If Matilda had responded with another letter this would mean that a minimum total of four were generated by their contact.[12] Whatever the reality was of the relationship between Æthelweard and Matilda, the prologue to the *Chronicon Æthelweardi* was constructed to show its audience that they communicated regularly and that both parties used the written word as at least a partial medium for maintaining their contact.

Central to understanding the relationship between Æthelweard and Matilda is the issue of what they might have gained from their communication. The concerns which are likely to have shaped Matilda's desire for information from Æthelweard about her family have emerged in studies of the roles played by noble women during the Middle Ages in preserving and transmitting information about

---

[10] *Chronicon Æthelweardi*, ed. Campbell, 1.

[11] In other cases of contact between Anglo-Saxon England and the Continent, for example by Coenwald on behalf of Æthelstan, an individual who is usually an ecclesiastical figure acts as an intermediary. See Simon Keynes, "King Æthelstan's Books," in *Learning and Literature in Anglo-Saxon England: Studies Presented to Peter Clemoes on the Occasion of his Sixty-Fifth Birthday*, ed. Michael Lapidge and Helmut Gneuss (Cambridge, 1985), 143–201, at 198–201.

[12] *Chronicon Æthelweardi*, ed. Campbell, 1: "Alteram etiam subiunxit cuipiam regi iuxta Iupitereos montes, de cuius prole nulla nobis notitia extat" ['The other sister he married to a certain king near the Alps, of whose family we have no detail remaining'].

their families' past.[13] The desire to assemble written records of their families' histories seems to have been felt particularly keenly among women in Ottonian Germany. Among the prominent Ottonian women who commissioned texts that appear to have fulfilled commemorative functions were Queen Matilda I, the wife of Henry I, as well as Gerberga, the abbess of Gandersheim.[14] For Matilda of Essen, the desire to assemble a record of her family's history would have meant that she needed an account of her Anglo-Saxon descent. In this context, the *Chronicon Æthelweardi* can be considered, along with other texts compiled in Ottonian Germany, as a product of the significant role played by women in preserving and transmitting family memory.

The prologue to the *Chronicon Æthelweardi* makes it clear that Æthelweard and Matilda were keen to exchange knowledge about their *communis prosapiæ* ['common family'].[15] An insight into how this process operated emerges from Æthelweard's request for information from Matilda about Edith's sister, who had traveled with her to Germany.[16] Æthelweard requested this information because the passage of time and the geographic distance at which the events took place meant that the details had not been preserved in any of the sources available to him in Anglo-Saxon England. Edith's sister has been the subject of some debate, and Hrotsvit of Gandersheim recorded in the *Gesta Ottonis* that her name was *Adiva* and she was "inferior to Edith in age and merit."[17] The desire to discover and preserve this kind of information about their family is presented as central to Æthelweard and Matilda's correspondence. Matilda's only sibling, Otto, duke of Swabia, had died unexpectedly in 982, and it is around this time that the *Chronicon Æthelweardi* was probably composed.[18] Matilda's interest in preserving the memory of her family was likely to have been sharpened further by her brother's

---

[13] Van Houts, "Women and the Writing of History," 66–67. See also eadem, *Memory and Gender in Medieval Europe 900–1200* (London, 1999), 67–70.

[14] Van Houts, "Women and the Writing of History," 55–59 analyses examples of women's role in the preservation of the past. Abbess Gerberga of Gandersheim requested that Hrotsvit compose the *Gesta Ottonis*, while Widukind of Corvey's *Res Gestae Saxonicae* was dedicated to abbess Matilda of Quedlinburg. Queen Matilda I, the wife of Henry I, is described in the earlier of two accounts of her life as handing to her granddaughter a list of those whose memories must be preserved. These examples illustrate the close association of women with the production of commemorative texts in Ottonian Germany.

[15] *Chronicon Æthelweardi*, ed. Campbell, 1.

[16] The Anglo-Saxon King Æthelstan sent Edith and one of her sisters to Henry I, so that one could be selected to marry Otto: see Karl Leyser, "The Ottonians and Wessex," in idem, *Communications and Power in Medieval Europe: The Carolingian and Ottonian Centuries*, ed. Timothy Reuter (London, 1994), 73–104, at 83–84.

[17] Hrotsvit, "Gesta Ottonis," in *Hrotsvithae Opera*, ed. P. von Winterfeld, MGH Scriptores Rer. Germ. 34 (Berlin, 1902), 201–28, at 207.

[18] L. Whitbread, "Æthelweard and the *Anglo-Saxon Chronicle*," *EHR* 74 (1959): 577–89; van Houts, "Women and the Writing of History," 65–66.

death. His death, without leaving an heir, meant that their family line was set to end. It is possible to see how such issues might have led to anxieties about family memory and might have stimulated the type of long-distance contact which catalyzed the production of the *Chronicon Æthelweardi* in England and its subsequent transmission to Ottonian Germany. From this emerges a context for reading the text whereby both Matilda and Æthelweard were seeking information about their mutual family that could not be found elsewhere.

Anglo-Saxon Identity in Ottonian Germany: The Case of King Oswald

The prologue to the *Chronicon Æthelweardi* reveals that Matilda's family history was linked directly to Anglo-Saxon England and shows that she needed a local contact to provide information about this distant branch of her family.[19] Having established such a link, Matilda received an account of the Anglo-Saxon side of her family that had been constructed in an environment that was geographically and culturally distinct from her own. The *Chronicon Æthelweardi* thus presented an Ottonian audience with a version of the Anglo-Saxon past that had been forged in a specifically Anglo-Saxon context. This combination of circumstances meant that the particular image of Anglo-Saxon "identity" embedded in the text had been influenced not only by the Anglo-Saxon textual and political contexts in which it was compiled but also by the demands of the contemporary contact between Æthelweard and Matilda.

The positive connotations of Anglo-Saxon identity within Ottonian society was an important factor in Henry I's decision to seek an Anglo-Saxon wife for his son. To the Liudolfing family, Edith brought a connection with the Anglo-Saxons' long-established Christian rulership and thus, by association, the Liudolfings' rule acquired a sense of historical authenticity.[20] Traces of the ways that Ottonian writers integrated the Anglo-Saxons and their Christian tradition into their own local histories emerge in the texts that were composed during this period. The *Gesta Ottonis* was composed by Hrotsvit of Gandersheim in around 962 and was commissioned by Otto I's niece, Gerberga, the abbess of Gandersheim, to coincide with Otto's imperial coronation. Hrotsvit gave an account of Edith that described how "public opinion by a unanimous decision rated her the best of all women who existed at that time."[21] In a similar vein, Hrotsvit also reported that Edith had been descended from saintly ancestors. Traditions like this would have boosted her credentials as a potential wife for Otto, adding

[19] Van Houts, "Women and the Writing of History," 68, speculates about other individuals in Anglo-Saxon England with whom Matilda could have maintained contact.

[20] Leyser, "The Ottonians and Wessex," 76–85.

[21] Hrotsvit, "Gesta Ottonis," 207.

saintly virtues to her value as a princess descended from a ruling family with strong royal credentials.

The saintly ancestor with whom Hrotsvit explicitly connected Edith was the "martyred" seventh-century Northumbrian king, Oswald:

> Haec nam versiculis proles quam scriptito regis,
> Haec, inquam, fama cunctis fuerat bene nota:
> Nobilitate potens, primis meritis quoque pollens
> Edita magnorum summo de germine regum;
> Cuius praeclaro facies candore serena,
> Regalis formae miro rutilabat honore;
> Ipsaque perfectae radiis fulgens bonitatis,
> In patria talis meruit praeconia laudis,
> Ut fore iudicio plebis decernitur omnis
> Optima cunctarum, quae tunc fuerant, mulierum.
> Nec mirum, meritis si lucebat bene primis,
> Germen sanctorum quam producebat avorum:
> Hanc tradunt ergo natam de stirpe beata
> Oswaldi regis, laudem cuius canit orbis,
> Se quia subdiderat morti pro nomine Christi.[22]

['For this daughter of a king about whom I repeatedly write in little verses was, I say, by reputation well known to all. Influential because of her nobility and equally so because of her esteemed excellences, she was a descendant of an eminent family of great monarchs. Her calm countenance was one of remarkable sincerity, and she was resplendent with a wondrous charm of queenly bearing. Adorned with a radiance of such exceeding goodness, she merited such a meed of praise in her native land that public opinion by a unanimous decision rated her the best of all women who existed at that time. Little wonder that she was conspicuous for eminent virtues, since she was descended from a family of sainted ancestors. For they say, furthermore, that she was descended from the blessed stock of King Oswald, with whose praise the universe resounds because he submitted himself to death for the name of Christ.']

It is no longer clear whether it was a written source or some form of oral testimony that led Hrotsvit to draw this particular association between Edith and Oswald.[23] According to Bede, Oswald had had a West Saxon wife with whom he

---

[22] Hrotsvit, "Gesta Ottonis," 207.

[23] Patrick Corbet, *Les Saints Ottoniens: Sainteté dynastique, sainteté royale et sainteté féminine autour de l'an Mil*, Beihefte der Francia 15 (Sigmaringen, 1986), 111–14 discusses Hrotsvit's account of Edith's descent. *Edita* (line 4) is possibly a pun on the name *Edita* and the word *edita* 'issue' (from *edere, editum*).

had a son, after which the family line probably died out.[24] In spite of this, some effort has been made to identify a line of descent from Oswald to Edith.[25] The significance of their association is more likely to lie in the Liudolfings' desire to promote a parallel with the contemporary Anglo-Saxon ruling house by exploiting an Anglo-Saxon saint who was well known in Ottonian Germany. This process reflects what has been described as the "propagandist functions" of genealogy.[26] Associating Edith with Oswald effectively enhanced her identity as a representative of an established Christian ruling house. It remains unknown exactly how Hrotsvit became aware of a link between Edith and Oswald of Northumbria, or whether one really existed at all. Even so, it is clear that Hrotsvit sought to demonstrate that Edith, like Oswald, represented a perceived Anglo-Saxon tradition of well-established Saxon rulership within a Christian tradition.

There is some evidence to explain what might have shaped Hrotsvit's decision to link Edith with Saint Oswald. His cult was widely disseminated on the Continent and is likely to have been introduced there by eighth-century Anglo-Saxon missionaries; Oswald is one of only two English saints recorded in an eighth-century martyrology from Echternach and is described as *rex pius Anglorum* in a ninth-century martyrology from Prüm.[27] Oswald's feast day was included in the calendar at Borghorst, alongside an entry noting a feast for Edith.[28] One of the three extant tenth-century sacramentaries from Essen includes Oswald, and it dates specifically to Matilda's time as abbess there in late tenth century.[29] In

---

[24] Bede, *HE* 3.7, ed. Colgrave and Mynors, 232–37. According to Bede, Oswald's wife was the daughter of the West Saxon King Cynegils. On Bede's depiction of Oswald see Robert Folz, "Saint Oswald Roi de Northumbrie: étude d'hagiographie royale," *Analecta Bollandiana* 98 (1980): 49–74, at 49–51.

[25] Dagmar Ó Riain-Raedel, "Edith, Judith, Matilda: The Role of Royal Ladies in the Propagation of the Continental Cult," in *Oswald: Northumbrian King to European Saint*, ed. Clare Stancliffe and Eric Cambridge (Stamford, 1995), 210–29, at 212–16.

[26] David Dumville, "Kingship, Genealogies and Regnal Lists," in *Early Medieval Kingship*, ed. P. H. Sawyer and I. N. Wood (Leeds, 1977), 72–104, at 83, and Ian Wood, "Genealogy Defined by Women: The Pippinids," in *Gender in the Early Medieval World: East and West 300–900*, ed. Leslie Brubaker and Julia H. M. Smith (Cambridge, 2004), 234–56, at 253–54.

[27] Alan Thacker, "*Membra Disjecta*: The Division of the Body and the Diffusion of the Cult," in *Oswald: Northumbrian King to European Saint*, ed. Stancliffe and Cambridge, 98–127, at 115. For the metrical martyrology of Wandelbert of Prüm, see J. Dubois, *Le Martyrologie d'Usuard: Texte et Commentaire* (Brussels, 1965), 57–58.

[28] Gerd Althoff, *Das Necrolog von Borghorst: Edition und Untersuchung* (Münster in Westfalen, 1978), 30. On the extent of the dissemination of Oswald's cult, see Peter Clemoes, *The Cult of St Oswald on the Continent*, Jarrow Lecture 1983 (Jarrow, 1984).

[29] Düsseldorf, University Library MS D. 2, fol. 15. Oswald is not in the two other extant Essen sacramentaries, MSS D. 1, D. 3; See Leyser, "The Ottonians and Wessex," 78–79.

the *Historia Ecclesiastica*, Bede provided an extensive account of Oswald's activities that circulated widely on the Continent, and various sets of chapters from the relevant section of the text (*HE* 3.1–14) were often excerpted from the main text and circulated separately.[30] Ælfric referred to Bede's account of Oswald in the *Life of Oswald* that formed part of his late tenth-century *Lives of Saints*. Of the nineteen extant English calendars from the ninth, tenth, and eleventh centuries, only one fails to note his feast day.[31] Oswald's relics were translated to Gloucester in 909, where it has been suggested that the future King Æthelstan saw their arrival.[32] As a consequence it is clear that, as well as having been widely disseminated on the Continent, Oswald's cult was also thriving in Anglo-Saxon England during the tenth century and had certainly spread beyond its Northumbrian origins.[33]

The speculative connection between Oswald of Northumbria and Edith provides an insight into one of the elements that was active in the Ottonians' construction of Anglo-Saxon identity. The dissemination of the cult demonstrates that it functioned in a wide range of contexts both in Ottonian Germany and in Anglo-Saxon England. Given that the express purpose of Æthelweard's relationship with Matilda was to preserve and record their common family history, Oswald's cult ought to have been something in which their interest in preserving their family's past gave them some degree of investment. It is particularly striking therefore that Oswald of Northumbria is almost completely absent from the *Chronicon Æthelweardi* even though he appears in *Anglo-Saxon Chronicle* MS A, which is the surviving version closest to the one Æthelweard used to compile the

---

[30] Bede, *HE*, 3.6–9, ed. Colgrave and Mynors, 230–45.

[31] The only surviving Anglo-Saxon calendar that does not have an entry for Oswald is the 'Leofric Missal', Oxford, Bodleian Library, MS. Bodley 579. See *The Leofric Missal*, ed. Nicholas Orchard, HBS 113, 2 vols. (London, 2002). See also Clemoes, *The Cult of Saint Oswald on the Continent*, 9.

[32] Recent archaeological evidence from the Anglo-Saxon Minster of St Oswald's, Gloucester, suggests that the translation of Oswald's relics in 909, together with the burials of Æthelred in 911 and Æthelflæd in 918, coincided with the construction of a new, subterranean building at the east end of the church. See Carolyn Heighway and Richard Bryant, *The Golden Minster: The Anglo-Saxon Minster and Later Medieval Priory of St Oswald at Gloucester*, CBA Research Report 117 (York, 1999), 67. On the political significance of the translation of Oswald's relics to Gloucester, see David Rollason, *Saints and Relics in Anglo-Saxon England* (Oxford, 1989), 153–54, and A. T. Thacker, "Chester and Gloucester: Early Ecclesiastical Organization in Two Mercian Burhs," *Northern History* 18 (1982): 199–211, at 207–9.

[33] James Campbell, "Some Twelfth-Century Views of the Anglo-Saxon Past," in idem, *Essays in Anglo-Saxon History* (London, 1986), 209–28, at 216. M. Wood, "The Making of Æthelstan's Empire: An English Charlemagne?" in *Ideal and Reality in Frankish and Anglo-Saxon Society: Studies Presented to J. M. Wallace-Hadrill*, ed. Patrick Wormald (Oxford, 1983), 250–64, at 258.

Chronicon Æthelweardi.[34] The section of MS A which describes Oswald is brief but nonetheless records details of his existence:

(634) AN. .dcxxxiiii. Her Birinus biscep bodude Westseaxum fulwuht.

(635) AN. .dcxxxv. Her Cynegils wæs gefulwad from Birino þæm biscepe in Dorkeceastre, 7 Oswold his onfeng.

(636) AN. .dcxxxvi. Her Cuichelm wæs gefulwad in Dorcesceastre 7 þy ilcan geare forþferde. 7 Felix biscep bodade Eastenglum Cristes geleafan.

AN. .dcxxxvii.

AN. .dcxxxviii.

(639) AN. .dcxxxvix. Her Birinus fulwade Cuþred on Dorcesceastre 7 onfeng hine him to suna.

(640) AN. .dxcl. Her Redbald Cantwara cyning forþferde / he ricsode .xxv. wintra.[35]

AN. .dcxli.

(642) AN. .dcxlii. Her Oswald Norþanhymbra cyning ofslægen wæs.

['(634) In this year, Bishop Birinus preached baptism to the West Saxons.

(635) In this year, King Cynegils was baptized by Bishop Birinus in Dorchester and Oswald stood sponsor to him.

(636) In this year Cwichelm was baptized in Dorchester, and he died that same year, and Bishop Felix preached the faith of Christ to the East Angles.

(637)

(638)

---

[34] Æthelweard's *Anglo-Saxon Chronicle* exemplar was compiled using a text which shared a common ancestor with the one used to produce MS A. See *The Anglo-Saxon Chronicle MS A*, ed. Janet Bately, *The Anglo-Saxon Chronicle: A Collaborative Edition*, ed. David Dumville and Simon Keynes, 3 (Cambridge, 1986), lxxix–lxxxviii; Janet Bately, *The Anglo-Saxon Chronicle: Texts and Textual Relationships* (Reading, 1991), 59–62.
[35] *ASC MS A*, ed. Bately, 28–29. For the purpose of clarity, I have omitted material that was added to this annal by Bately's hand *8c*, who was also responsible for adding material to annals 640, 725, and 748.

(639) In this year Bishop Birinus baptized King Cuthred in Dorchester and also received him as his godson.

(640) In this year Eadbald, king of the people of Kent, died, and he had reigned 25 years.

(641)

(642) In this year Oswald, king of the Northumbrians, was slain.']

This passage appears in a broadly similar form in the *Chronicon Æthelweardi*:

[634] Impletis uero annis sex uenit Byrinus episcopus ad Occidentales Anglos prædicans eis euangelium Christi. Transactusque est numerus annorum ab aduentu in Britanniam de Germania eorum fere centum uiginti. [635] Tum suscepit in tempore illo baptismum Cinegils a Byrino sancto episcopo in oppido quod Dorceastre nuncupatur. [639] Ipse et Cuthrid baptizat post quadriennium in eadem ciuitate, quem et baptisticum filium sumpsit.

7. [648] Deinde impletis annis nouem Cenuualh propinquo suo Cuthride tradidit ex prædiis suis tria millia adiacentia colle qui uulgo dicitur Escesdune.[36]

['[634] Next after a further six years Bishop Birinus came to the West Saxons, preaching to them the gospel of Christ. And a number of years approximately one hundred and twenty was completed since their arrival in Britain from Germany. [635] Then at that time Cynegils received baptism from Birinus the holy bishop in the town that is called Dorchester. [639] And after a period of four years Birinus baptized Cuthred in the same city, and also took him as his godson.

7. [648] Then at the end of nine years Cenwalh gave to his relative Cuthred three thousands from his farmlands adjacent to the highland called in the vulgar tongue Ashdown.']

Comparison of these two passages reveals that they are similar but, as noted above, some of the details present in the *Anglo-Saxon Chronicle* MS A are missing from the *Chronicon Æthelweardi*. This material that is not in the *Chronicon Æthelweardi* relates to Oswald sponsoring the baptism of the West-Saxon King Cynegils, the baptism and death of Cwichelm, Felix preaching to the East Angles, and the deaths of two kings: Rædwald and Oswald himself.

It is surprising that the *Chronicon Æthelweardi* does not contain the material relating to Oswald because these details are in the *Anglo-Saxon Chronicle* MS A and are thus likely to have been in the version of the *Anglo-Saxon Chronicle*

---

[36] *Chronicon Æthelweardi*, ed. Campbell, 19.

that Æthelweard used. Their omission is also odd in light of Æthelweard and
Matilda's connections through Edith, who was associated with Oswald explicitly
in Ottonian texts that circulated during the late tenth century. The first possibility that might explain why Oswald was omitted from the *Chronicon Æthelweardi*
is that the information was removed from Æthelweard's *Anglo-Saxon Chronicle*
source before he used it to compile his own text and it was therefore unavailable
to him. This is possible, but would necessitate the existence of a tradition in the
early circulation and transmission of the *Anglo-Saxon Chronicle* which had deliberately removed Oswald. The circumstances that might have shaped a text in this
way are, however, difficult to account for.

The disappearance of Oswald from the *Chronicon Æthelweardi* might not be
quite as significant in this case as it first appears. Æthelweard did in fact include
a reference to King Oswald in his text. It comes in a list of the eight kings who
ruled all of Britain, which appeared in the entry for 827:

> Nam primus fuit Ælle, rex Australium Anglorum, qui possessor tantæ
> ditionis fuerat ut Ecgbyrht. Secundus fuit Ceaulin, rex Occidentalium
> Anglorum; tertius Æthelbyrht, rex Cantuariorum; quartus Ræduuald, rex
> Orientalium, quintus Eaduuine, rex Northymbriorum; sextus Osuuald;
> septimus Osuueo, frater Osuualdi; post quem octauus Ecgbyrht, cuius
> supra fecimus mentionem.[37]

> ['For the first to be possessor of a jurisdiction as great as that of Ecgbyrht
> was Ælle, king of the South Saxons. The second was Ceawlin, king of the
> West Saxons. The third was Æthelberht, king of Kent. The fourth was
> Rædwald, king of the East (Saxons). The fifth was Edwin, king of the Nor-
> thumbrians. The sixth was Oswald. The seventh was Oswiu, brother of
> Oswald. After him the eighth was Egbert whom we mentioned above.']

To remove Oswald from this passage would have presented specific problems
because it would have required that alterations were made to the numerical
sequence. It would not have been as straightforward to remove Oswald from this
list as it was to leave him out when transcribing the section of the *Anglo-Saxon
Chronicle* for the mid-seventh century that was discussed above. Furthermore,
the appearance of Oswald in this list in the *Chronicon Æthelweardi* indicates that
the saint had not been written out of the version of the *Anglo-Saxon Chronicle*
that Æthelweard used.[38] Had Oswald had been removed from the list of eight
kings, this would have provided a relatively secure indication that Æthelweard
was actively writing King Oswald out of his text. Instead, this inconsistent handling of Oswald in the compilation of the *Chronicon Æthelweardi* conflicts with
expectations of the text that are shaped by its likely Ottonian audience, for whom

---

[37] *Chronicon Æthelweardi*, ed. Campbell, 29.
[38] *ASC MS A*, ed. Bately, 55–56.

the saint was of special interest. It appears that the factors that determined the inclusion or omission of Oswald in the *Chronicon Æthelweardi* depended, to a significant extent, on whether Æthelweard considered it convenient to do so.

Work on the relationship between the *Chronicon Æthelweardi* and the version of the *Anglo-Saxon Chronicle* that Æthelweard used has already shown that some material, present in the source text, was deliberately left out of the *Chronicon Æthelweardi*.[39] It has demonstrated that Æthelweard manipulated his source text and has highlighted his preoccupation with West-Saxon events, leading him to omit material concerning the history of other kingdoms or ecclesiastical issues that were present in the version of the *Anglo-Saxon Chronicle* that he used.[40] In this case, Oswald's omission from the *Chronicon Æthelweardi* may not reveal a particular political or ideological concern. Instead, like the Kentish entries also omitted, it is possible that Æthelweard did not think that Oswald was a subject relevant to the audience for whom he was writing.

In spite of this, it would be difficult to suggest that Æthelweard was unaware of Oswald's cult.[41] He was almost certainly familiar with Oswald from Bede's *Historia Ecclesiastica*; Æthelweard demonstrated his knowledge of Bede's text while composing the *Chronicon Æthelweardi* by using sections of it to supplement the *Anglo-Saxon Chronicle*. The evidence of surviving Anglo-Saxon calendars, discussed above, shows that Oswald routinely appeared in them and that his cult was widely established. Ælfric noted that the patronage of Æthelweard and his son Æthelmær had encouraged him to produce the *Lives of Saints*, which included a Life of Oswald.[42] The wide dissemination of Oswald's cult in Anglo-Saxon England means that Æthelweard is very likely to have been aware of its significance in Anglo-Saxon contexts. As a result, the possibility that Æthelweard chose to omit references to Oswald from the *Chronicon Æthelweardi* strongly implies that

---

[39] E. E. Barker, "The Anglo-Saxon Chronicle Used by Æthelweard," *Bulletin of the Institute of Historical Research* 40 (1967): 74–90, at 78 argues that some information in the *Anglo-Saxon Chronicle* was left out by Æthelweard. Barker's analysis of the relationship between the *Chronicon* and the surviving versions of the *Anglo-Saxon Chronicle* has been contradicted by Janet Bately, who argues that Æthelweard's source was closer to MS A than any of the other surviving manuscripts of the *Anglo-Saxon Chronicle*: see Bately, *Texts and Textual Relationships*, 41–53.

[40] Audrey Meaney, "St Neots, Æthelweard and the Compilation of the Anglo-Saxon Chronicle: A Survey," in *Studies in Old English Prose*, ed. Paul E. Szarmach (New York, 1986), 193–243.

[41] Æthelweard uniquely names the burial place of Æthelred, Lord of the Mercians, as Gloucester, suggesting that he had access to a source of information about contemporary events at Gloucester which would very likely refer to the translation of Oswald's relics.

[42] See Ælfric's prefaces to the *Lives of Saints* in *Ælfric's Prefaces*, ed. Jonathan Wilcox, Durham Medieval Texts 9 (Durham, 1994), 119–21; see also 9 for a summary of the references to the patronage of Æthelweard and his son in Ælfric's writings.

he did not anticipate that such information might have been relevant to the text's intended audience. This creates difficulties for understanding the circulation of the *Chronicon Æthelweardi* in Ottonian contexts where Oswald was closely associated with Anglo-Saxon identity.

The likelihood that Æthelweard left out some but not all references to King Oswald when he composed a text apparently intended for Matilda, abbess of Essen, has several implications. Although the Ottonians valued Oswald as a personification of the combined Christian and Anglo-Saxon royal traditions with which they wanted to link themselves, Æthelweard seems to have been unaware of this. The nature of the correspondence between Æthelweard and Matilda must be reconsidered as a result, considering the possibility that the text's functions were actually quite different to the ones indicated in the prologue. Æthelweard's prologue is constructed to give to a reader the impression that he and Matilda conducted close and extensive correspondence. In this part of the text, Æthelweard promises to illuminate their common family and provides some brief but relevant genealogical information that describes Matilda's descent from Edith and King Alfred. In contrast to this, there is not a single mention of Edith in the text of the *Chronicon Æthelweardi* itself. In this respect, the text fails to do what is expected of it, judging from the claims made in the prologue. Apart from the kings themselves, none of Æthelweard or Matilda's recent family is described in the tenth-century sections of the *Chronicon Æthelweardi*. Æthelweard's own parents are omitted, for example, and so are his children.[43] The treatment of the tenth century in the *Chronicon Æthelweardi* is generally sparse, reflecting the decline in entries in the *Anglo-Saxon Chronicle* at this point. Even so, it is not easy to show how the main text of the *Chronicon Æthelweardi* was of any use to Matilda at all for learning any significant new information about her Anglo-Saxon descent.

The *Chronicon Æthelweardi* may, alternatively, have been intended to acquire its usefulness for an Ottonian audience through more indirect means, by describing the Saxon origins of the Anglo-Saxons.[44] This could be a valid interpretation of how Matilda and Æthelweard perceived their common family. Much of the information in the *Chronicon Æthelweardi* about this came from Bede, however, and was therefore already in circulation on the Continent by the tenth century. As a result Matilda could probably have located it without needing the assistance

---

[43] Æthelweard and his son, Æthelmaer, refounded Cerne Abbey in 987. See Barbara Yorke, "Aethelmaer: The Foundation of the Abbey at Cerne and the Politics of the Tenth Century," in *The Cerne Abbey Millennium Lectures*, ed. Katherine Barker (Cerne, 1998), 15–25, at 23.

[44] For a discussion of how the Saxons' arrival in Britain is presented in the *Chronicon Æthelweardi* see Wojtek Jezierski, "Æthelweardus Redivivus," *Early Medieval Europe* 13 (2005): 159–78, at 162–68.

of a distant relation.[45] It was then, perhaps, important to Matilda that she could show that she had acquired this information from a conspicuously Anglo-Saxon and current source and in an Anglo-Saxon manuscript. In contrast, the most convincing contexts that have emerged for understanding how the *Chronicon Æthelweardi* functioned in Ottonian Germany highlight the role of noble women in preserving the memory of their relatives.[46] To an extent, this interest is borne out by Æthelweard's desire to identify Edith's sister, but the majority of the *Chronicon Æthelweardi* beyond the preface is redundant in this respect. In addition, it appears that Æthelweard might have left out some information available to him, like details about Oswald, which would have been of specific interest to Matilda of Essen.

A number of issues might offer insight into why Oswald was omitted from a text compiled for an Ottonian audience, in spite of his significance in this context. When Matilda requested information from Æthelweard, he could have composed a preface containing the detail she wanted and appended it to a version of the *Chronicon Æthelweardi* which had already been composed for a different function. In this case, Oswald, a person of particular interest to an Ottonian audience, would have been left out because he was not important for the audience for whom the text was initially compiled. If taken to its fullest extent, this hypothesis means that Æthelweard ordered a lightly revised copy of the existing *Chronicon Æthelweardi* for Matilda, because on two occasions within the main text Matilda is addressed by name.[47] It seems conceivable that Æthelweard commissioned a refocused chronicle that permitted the preface to be incorporated into the existing text while the exemplar was retained with two added addresses to its new dedicatee.

Other scenarios could explain this peculiar dislocation between what is known about the text's content and the audience for which it is deliberately articulated. In one of her earlier letters, Matilda may have pointed out to Æthelweard that she already knew enough about Oswald. If Æthelweard then left out information about which he thought Matilda already knew, this might also accommodate the absence of any information about his own immediate family.

---

[45] Many accounts of the links between Anglo-Saxons and Continental Saxons circulated on the Continent. For example, Rudolf of Fulda's account of the translation of Saint Alexander's relics, the *Translatio sancti Alexandri*, describes Saxons migrating from Britain to the Continent. See Bruno Krusch, "Die Übertragung des Heiligen Alexander von Rom nach Wildeshausen durch den Enkel Widukinds 851: Das älteste niedersächsische Geschichtsdenkmal," *Nachrichten von der Gesellschaft der Wissenschaften zu Göttingen aus dem Jahre 1933*, Philologisch-Historische Klasse (Berlin, 1933), 405–36. For discussion of texts that articulated the links between the Anglo-Saxons and the Old Saxons, see Leyser, "The Ottonians and Wessex," 75.

[46] Van Houts, *Memory and Gender in Medieval Europe*, 70.

[47] *Chronicon Æthelweardi*, ed. Campbell, 38, 39.

The omission of seemingly important information that might have supported claims for Matilda's descent from Oswald, as well as the names of recent family members, goes some way to undermining the notion that the *Chronicon Æthelweardi* was intended to preserve family memory. Including these details again could only help to secure their survival. Furthermore, information was commonly repeated during the copying and transmission of medieval texts without any such anxieties. If Matilda had hoped that the *Chronicon Æthelweardi* would function as a lasting record of her family, then reiteration of her descent from Saint Oswald could only have enhanced her own prestige and that of her family and her foundation at Essen. Another possibility is that the text was compiled without an Ottonian audience in mind at all. The only extant manuscript of the *Chronicon Æthelweardi* appears unlikely to have ever left England, so there is no specific evidence beyond the preface to demonstrate that the text circulated among an Ottonian audience. In this case the preface might have been intended to demonstrate, in England and to an Anglo-Saxon audience, a desirable Continental affiliation for its owner.

The last of these suggestions is an hypothetical approach to the surviving evidence of the contact between Æthelweard and Matilda. It nonetheless highlights how much about the function and audiences of the *Chronicon Æthelweardi* remains uncertain. Differences appear to have existed between the preoccupations implicit in the text itself and those shaped by the anxieties about memory and identity that operated in the contexts in which the *Chronicon Æthelweardi* is likely to have circulated. These inconsistencies mean that further consideration of the complex set of concerns which shaped the text's production remains necessary. The example of the contact between Æthelweard and Matilda, as it is demonstrated by the *Chronicon Æthelweardi*, shows that Anglo-Saxon identity did not operate uniformly across Anglo-Saxon England and the Continent, and that it might not have meant the same thing on both sides of Matilda's and Æthelweard's correspondence. As a result, it remains necessary to continue investigating aspects of the authorship, audience, and circulation of the *Chronicon Æthelweardi* in order to grasp more fully the contexts that influenced its compilation and transmission. Strong arguments have been assembled elsewhere that the *Chronicon Æthelweardi* functioned in ways similar to other Ottonian historiographic texts concerned with family memory. In spite of this, the treatment of Saint Oswald in the *Chronicon Æthelweardi* reveals how frequently expectations, encouraged by the text itself and by generic and contextual approaches to understanding it, are unfulfilled. In the context of contact between Anglo-Saxon England and Ottonian Germany, the *Chronicon Æthelweardi* demonstrates the need to continue investigating how the functions of historical writing are constantly reshaped by the relationship between the text and the values and concerns of the environments in which it circulates.

Images of Jerusalem: The Religious Imagination of Willibald of Eichstätt

Rodney Aist

1. Introduction

The life and adventures of Willibald of Eichstätt (700–787), recorded in the *Vita Willibaldi*, expose the student to an impressive number of movements, places, and events associated with eighth-century Christendom.[1] While a summary of Willibald's life is provided below, the present study, rather than focusing upon the accomplishments of the Anglo-Saxon holy man, offers a preliminary investigation into the religious thought and imagination of the Eichstätt bishop, primarily addressing his image of the city of Jerusalem, which he visited in 724–726.

The discussion of Willibald's image of the holy city is divided into two parts. The first section addresses Willibald's descriptions of the holy places of Jerusalem. While each site will be briefly mentioned, the place where the Holy Cross was found will be more extensively discussed, thus providing a short case study on one of the more prominent features of Willibald's image of Jerusalem. Willibald's references to the place of the Holy Cross will be set within the larger context of his personal association with the image of the Holy Cross and will

---

[1] Willibald's biographical information is contained in Hugeburc's *Vita Willibaldi*. The Latin manuscript is Munich, Bayerische Staatsbibliothek, Clm 1086, and dates from the late eighth or early ninth century. The text was edited by O. Holder-Egger, MGH Scriptores 15.1 (Hannover, 1887), 86–106. The Holder-Egger edition also appears in A. Bauch, *Quellen zur Geschichte der Diözese Eichstätt, I: Biographien der Gründungszeit* (Eichstätt, 1962), 11–122, along with notes and a German translation. English translations appear in *The Library of the Palestine Pilgrims' Text Society*, vol. 3, trans. W. R. Brownlow (London, 1887–1897), 1–36 ("The Hodoeporicon of Saint Willibald"), and in C. H. Talbot, *The Anglo-Saxon Missionaries in Germany* (London, 1954), 153–80. J. Wilkinson provides a partial translation of the text in *Jerusalem Pilgrims before the Crusades* (Warminster, 2002), 233–51. References to the text will be abbreviated as *VW* and will follow the pagination of Holder-Egger.

Hans Sauer and Joanna Story, eds., *Anglo-Saxon England and the Continent*. With the assistance of Gaby Waxenberger. Essays in Anglo-Saxon Studies, vol. 3. MRTS 394. Tempe: ACMRS, 2011.   [ISBN 978-0-86698-442-3]

be analyzed in light of other textual sources on the Jerusalem commemorations associated with the Holy Cross legend.

Secondly, the paper will argue that in spite of his one-time intimacy with the city, Willibald viewed Jerusalem as a remote and distant place. This perspective is explicitly expressed in the *Vita Willibaldi*'s description of Willibald's motive for embracing the challenge of the Jerusalem pilgrimage. As Willibald would later remember, his pilgrimage to Jerusalem was an arduous experience, complicated by aspects of culture, religion, and politics as well as by a number of personal hardships, and the distance of Jerusalem was measured by the numerous obstacles that separated the Western pilgrim from the walls of Jerusalem. Willibald's image of Jerusalem as positioned on the eastern peripheral edge of his imagination contrasts significantly with the view of the city as the center of the world. Moreover, although Willibald's description of Jerusalem provides his audience with an eyewitness account of the holy sites, a distinct subtext—that of perseverance—accompanies his story. While the walls of Jerusalem were remote and essentially inaccessible, for those who persevered to the end, the day would come when the faithful would enter Jerusalem by the gates of the new and heavenly city.

2. The Life and Travels of Willibald of Eichstätt

Before considering aspects of Willibald's image of Jerusalem, it is important to provide a summary of his life and travels as well as the contextual background of the *Vita Willibaldi*. Willibald was born in AD 700 in the Anglo-Saxon kingdom of Wessex and was raised as a child oblate in the monastery of Bishop's Waltham. At the age of twenty, Willibald talked his father and younger brother, Wynnebald (701–761), into making a pilgrimage to the tomb of St. Peter in Rome.[2] During the journey, Willibald's father died in the Italian city of Lucca, and after providing a proper burial for him, the pilgrim brothers continued on to Rome, arriving in November 720.[3] Two and a half years later, Willibald, desiring to see the city of Jerusalem, left Rome with at least two of his close companions.[4] From

---

[2] On the popularity of Anglo-Saxon pilgrimage to Rome in the early eighth century, see Bede, *HE*, 5.7, ed. Colgrave and Mynors, 468–73. See also the contribution by D. Pelteret in this volume. For the entire subject see M. McCormick, "Les pèlerins occidentaux à Jérusalem, VIIIe–IXe siècles," in *Voyageurs à Byzance et en Occident du VIe au XIe siècle*, ed. A. Dierkens et al. (Geneva, 2000), 273–90.

[3] A legend later developed around Willibald's deceased father, turning the unnamed Anglo-Saxon landowner into a minor king with the unlikely Norman name of Richard. The tomb of King Richard is in the Trenta Chapel in the basilica of San Frediano in Lucca.

[4] Wynnebald remained in Rome until 739 when he joined the Boniface mission in Germany. In 751, he founded the monastery of Heidenheim, a day's journey from Eich-

there, Willibald traveled to Sicily before taking a ship to Ephesus. He went by foot along the coast of Asia Minor before wintering in Patara. In the spring, he sailed to Cyprus and crossed the island on foot before sailing to Syria.[5]

Shortly afterwards, in the city of Emesa, Willibald and his companions were arrested as spies.[6] The ordeal lasted several weeks, long enough for them to be befriended by a merchant, presumably a local Christian, who brought them two meals a day. On Wednesdays and Saturdays, his son took the prisoners to the bath, and on Sundays, the merchant took them to church and the market, buying them things at his own expense. The pilgrims were also befriended by a Spaniard, whose brother served as a chamberlain to the Saracen king and who was able to arrange an audience with the king.[7] Seeing no harm in the pilgrims, the king provided them with the necessary travel documents, and they continued their journey towards Jerusalem.

Two and a half years later, Willibald left the Holy Land from the port of Tyre, sailing to Constantinople, where he spent two years living in a cell in the Church of the Apostles.[8] His two-year sojourn in Constantinople (727–729) coincided with the outbreak of the first iconoclastic period under Emperor Leo III (c. 680–741). Willibald returned to Italy aboard a ship carrying papal and imperial emissaries.

In the autumn of 729, Willibald joined the recently refounded monastic community of Monte Cassino.[9] He played a significant role in the revitalization of the famous monastery, serving as sacristan, dean, and porter of the monastery for ten years until the autumn of 739 when he was summoned by Pope Gregory III (d. 741) to join his kinsman Boniface (ca. 672–754) in the Anglo-Saxon mission in Germany.[10] Willibald arrived in Bavaria in the summer of 740, where Boniface entrusted Willibald with the area of Eichstätt and immediately ordained

---

stätt, which became the setting of the composition of the *Vita Willibaldi*. Biographical information on Wynnebald is contained in Hugeburc's *Vita Wynnebaldi*, ed. O. Holder-Egger, MGH Scriptores 15.1 (Hannover, 1887), 106–17.

[5] *VW*, ed. Holder-Egger, chap. 92.26–94.10.

[6] The Emesa narrative (*VW*, ed. Holder-Egger, chap. 94.10–95.15) is the longest single episode in the *Vita*, indicating the impact that the events there had upon Willibald's memories of his Holy Land travels.

[7] Willibald's own terminology, including references to the Saracens, will be employed throughout the paper.

[8] On Willibald's sojourn in Constantinople, see *VW*, ed. Holder-Egger, chap. 101.18–29.

[9] *VW*, ed. Holder-Egger, chap. 102.15–35. Monte Cassino was founded by Benedict of Nursia in the first half of the sixth century. The monastery was sacked by the Lombards in 580 and was restored in 718, just eleven years before Willibald's arrival.

[10] On Willibald's audience with Pope Gregory III, see *VW*, ed. Holder-Egger, chap. 102.35–104.26.

him to the priesthood.[11] A year later, in 741, he was ordained by Boniface to the episcopacy,[12] and Willibald served for nearly fifty years as the founding bishop of the diocese of Eichstätt until his death in 787 at the age of 87.[13]

3. The *Vita Willibaldi*: The Reflections of an Elderly Bishop

Approximately nine years before his death, on 23 June, 778, a Tuesday, Willibald sat down at the age of seventy-eight with his younger relative Hugeburc in the monastery of Heidenheim and dictated to her his life experiences—in particular, his Holy Land travels, which by then had taken place five decades before.[14] Hugeburc made notes of Willibald's narrative, changed them into the third person, and added an introduction and a conclusion, producing a text known as the *Vita Willibaldi*, or 'The Life of Willibald.'[15] The respective contributions of Willibald and Hugeburc are self-evident owing to the divergent styles of their Latin. Whereas the recorded dictations of Willibald are simple and straightforward, Hugeburc's Latin is in the flamboyant style of Aldhelm of Malmesbury, which is

---

[11] On Willibald's arrival and early years in Eichstätt, see *VW*, ed. Holder-Egger, chap. 104.29–105.11.

[12] On questions of the initial years of Willibald's episcopacy, see *Der hl. Willibald, Klosterbischof oder Bistumsgründer*, ed. H. Dickerhof, E. Reiter, and S. Weinfurter (Regensburg, 1990).

[13] On the date of Willibald's death, see H. Wagner, "Zum Todesjahr des hl. Willibald," *Sammelblatt des Historischen Vereins Eichstätt* 83 (1990): 13–20.

[14] See Bauch, *Quellen zur Geschichte der Diözese Eichstätt*, 88 at n. 10. *VW*, ed. Holder-Egger, chap. 87.20–23 specifies that the occasion took place on Tuesday, 23 June. Tuesday fell on 23 June three times—767, 772, and 778—between Hugeburc's arrival in Heidenheim in 761 and the death of Willibald in 778. Scholars agree on 778 as the most likely year of the text's composition. On the name of Hugeburc, see B. Bischoff, "Wer ist die Nonne von Heidenheim?," *Studien und Mitteilungen zur Geschichte des Benediktinerordens und seiner Zweige*, Neue Folge 18 (1931): 387–88.

[15] The *Life of Willibald* also appears under the title *The Hodœporicon of St Willibald*. The reticence in using the Latin term *vita* is related to the fact that the genre of saints' lives—and sainthood in general—necessitates the death of the subject, whose role as saint is related not so much to his or her earthly virtues but more to the role he or she plays as a mediator between heaven and earth, a credential which Willibald was obviously lacking when the text was composed. The *Vita Willibaldi*, therefore, does not belong to the genre of saints' lives, even though the person of Willibald was later recognized as a saint. Curiously, the text was never amended after his death.

characterized by a creative vocabulary and lengthy sentences full of alliteration.[16] Notwithstanding Hugeburc's essential role in the composition, the text encapsulates the authentic voice of Willibald from the perspective of an elderly bishop looking back upon his adventures as a young man.

4. The Image of Jerusalem: Willibald's Description of the Holy Sites

Willibald's Holy Land itinerary comprised four separate sojourns in the city of Jerusalem. In addition to his initial approach to Jerusalem and his final departure, Willibald's travels in the Holy Land consisted of three circuits of the region. Save for a single comment, which will be discussed below, Willibald's entire description of Jerusalem appears in the narrative of his first sojourn in the city. In addition to the sites associated with the Holy Sepulchre, Willibald describes six other places: Holy Sion, the pool of Bethesda, a column associated with the funeral of Mary, the Church of St. Mary in Gethsemane, a church on the Mount of Olives where Jesus prayed before his passion, and the Church of the Ascension. Along with the sites related to Jesus, Willibald's attention to the places associated with the death of Mary is immediately apparent. It is also worth noting that Willibald is one of the first known Latin pilgrims to have visited Jerusalem after the construction of the Dome of the Rock and the Al-Aqsa Mosque, yet he mentions neither building nor does he make any reference to the Islamic presence in Jerusalem.[17]

4.1. The Church of the Holy Sepulchre: The Place where the Holy Cross was Found

Willibald's description of Jerusalem begins with a reference to the place where the Holy Cross was found.[18] While this commemoration is associated with the basilica of Constantine, Willibald mentions the place before he introduces the church itself, which occurs in the following line: "there is now a church on

---

[16] On the style of Hugeburc's Latin, see E. Gottschaller, *Hugeburc von Heidenheim: Philologische Untersuchungen zu den Heiligenbiographien einer Nonne des achten Jahrhunderts* (Munich, 1973).

[17] For a discussion of the topography of Jerusalem in the Early Islamic period, see Dan Bahat, "The Physical Infrastructure," in *The History of Jerusalem: The Early Islamic Period, 638–1099*, ed. J. Prawer and H Ben-Shammai (New York, 1996), 38–100, and M. Gil, *A History of Palestine, 634–1099*, trans. E. Broido (Cambridge, 1992), 90–104, 430–89.

[18] On the first part of Willibald's description of the Holy Sepulchre, see *VW*, ed. Holder-Egger, chap. 97.10–16.

the place that is called the place of Calvary."[19] Although he does not provide
any physical description of Calvary nor clearly specify its location vis-à-vis the
church, he offers a rather peculiar statement about the place: previously, it was
outside Jerusalem but Helena put the place inside the city when she found the
Cross. Notwithstanding the logic of the statement, it is sufficient to underscore
Willibald's need to explain the intramural location of the sites of Jesus' passion.
He then refers to three crosses placed outside the church, which will be discussed
further below.

Willibald makes a second reference to the place where the Holy Cross was
found in the short narrative of his second sojourn in Jerusalem. During a circuit
of southern Palestine, Willibald was afflicted with a curious blindness, which
occurred during Mass at St. Matthias near Gaza and subsequently lasted for
two months.[20] The severity of the blindness and its implications for his travels
are rather unclear. In any case, his vision was not restored until he returned to
Jerusalem, where, upon entering the church where the Holy Cross was found, his
eyes "were opened, and he received his sight."[21]

It is important to consider two allusions to the image of the cross in the *Vita
Willibaldi* before further discussing Willibald's references to the Jerusalem commemorations associated with the Holy Cross. The first is a story from Willibald's
childhood.[22] In response to an illness which threatened Willibald's life at the age
of three, his parents made a vow pledging their eldest-born son to the monastic
life. Hugeburc notes that the vow was made not in a church but rather at the foot
of a large outdoor cross, typical of the Anglo-Saxon village landscape. Willibald
recovered from his illness and was subsequently placed by his parents in the monastery of Bishop's Waltham. For a number of reasons, the central elements of the
story are credible, and it should be assumed that Willibald grew up reinforced by
a personal narrative that emphasized an intimate association between his life and
the image of the cross.[23] Secondly, Hugeburc twice refers to Willibald as a *crucicolus*, or 'lover of the cross.'[24] The terms of endearment indicate that the image

---

[19] *VW*, ed. Holder-Egger, chap. 97.11–12.

[20] On Willibald's Holy Land blindness, see *VW*, ed. Holder-Egger, chap. 99.11–16.

[21] *VW*, ed. Holder-Egger, chap. 99.15–16.

[22] On Willibald's childhood illness, see *VW*, ed. Holder-Egger, chap. 88.13–43.

[23] Since the text was written during the lifetime of Willibald for a readership that was
intimately familiar with the details of the bishop's life, it is unlikely that Hugeburc would
have included a fictitious story. Moreover, the story provides a credible explanation of why
Willibald, the eldest child, was raised in a monastery. Furthermore, the veracity of the story
is supported by Hugeburc's detailed references to the setting of the village cross.

[24] Hugeburc describes Willibald as "inclitus crucicolus" (*VW*, ed. Holder-Egger,
chap. 87.34) and as "inluster clarusque Christi crucicolus." These phrases have been
translated respectively as "the renowned lover of the Cross" and "that illustrious lover of
the Cross of Christ" by W. R. Brownlow, "The Hodœporicon of Saint Willibald," *Palestine Pilgrims' Text Society*, vol. 3 (London, 1895), 3, 9.

of the cross was an important and consistent theme in Willibald's understanding and practice of the Christian life.

In considering Willibald's references to the place where the Holy Cross was found, it is important to note that the legend of Helena's finding of the True Cross contains two central events, both of which were marked upon the Christian topography of Jerusalem.[25] The first event is Helena's discovery of the three crosses used in the crucifixion. It took a second event, however—a miraculous healing—to discern which of the three was the True Cross of Christ. According to variations of the legend, the crosses were placed upon a sick or recently-deceased person, who, in each case, was restored to perfect health when touched by the True Cross. The locations of the miracle are variously placed in a neighboring house, in the context of a passing funeral procession, and at the place where the crosses were originally discovered.

During the Byzantine period, the place where the Holy Cross was found was associated with the apse of the basilica of Constantine. The *Breviarius A* describes a silver and gold altar marking the spot, which was surrounded by twelve columns of marble surmounted by silver bowls.[26] Given the ornate decorations of the apse, the area was, no doubt, a focus of the looting of the Holy Sepulchre during the Persian conquest of 614.[27] While the finding of the cross continued to be associated with the basilica, the damage of the early seventh century meant that the commemoration had to be restored, if not redesigned, in connection with Heraclius' return of the Cross from its Persian captivity in 631. The texts of the Early Islamic period, while associating the legend with the basilica, do not provide any physical descriptions or specific locations of the commemoration itself.[28] While there is no *prima facie* reason why the place of the commemoration

---

[25] On the legend of the Holy Cross, see S. Borgehammar, *How the Holy Cross was Found* (Stockholm, 1991), and J. W. Drijvers, *Helena Augusta: The Mother of Constantine and the Legend of Her Finding the True Cross* (Leiden, 1992).

[26] *Breviarius A*, chap. 1, ed. R. Weber, *Itineraria et Alia Geographica,* CCSL 175 (Turnhout, 1965), 105–12. Also in Wilkinson, *Jerusalem Pilgrims Before the Crusades,* 117. The columns and silver bowls were originally described by Eusebius, *Vita Constantini,* 3.38, ed. F. Winkelmann (Berlin, 1975), who, while omitting any reference to the cross, describes the apse as the "crowning part" of the basilica.

[27] For a summary of the Persian destruction of 614, see R. Schick, *The Christian Communities of Palestine from Byzantine to Islamic Rule: A Historical and Archaeological Study* (Princeton, 1995), 33–39.

[28] For examples of texts from the Early Islamic period, see Adomnán, *De locis sanctis,* 1.6, ed. L. Bieler, in *Itineraria et Alia Geographica,* 185–234; Epiphanius the Monk, *Account of the Holy City and the Holy Places,* chap. 3, ed. H. Donner, "Die Palästinabeschreibung des Epiphanius Monachus Hagiopolita," *Zeitschrift des Deutschen Palästina-Vereins* 87 (1971): 42–91; Bernard the Monk, *Itinerary,* chap. 11, ed. T. Tobler and A. Molinier, *Itinera Hierosolymitana* (Geneva, 1879), 309–20. Also see Wilkinson, *Jerusalem*

would have been changed, it is not inconceivable that it assumed a different location within the church.

The miraculous healing, according to the *Breviarius*, was associated with the place of the crucifixion during the Byzantine period.[29] But at some point, the commemoration of the miraculous healing assumed a different location, as is indicated by two seventh-century sources. Adomnán states that a tall column, described as being in the middle of the city and to the north of the holy places, was set up at the location where the Lord's cross had been placed upon a dead young man who was restored to life.[30] According to Epiphanius, a four-columned structure marked the place where a dead young woman came to life when similarly touched by the cross.[31] This structure was below the house of Joseph which was on the left, or north, side of the basilica of St. Constantine.[32] Despite variations in the description of the marker, Adomnán and Epiphanius appear to refer to the same location—the column was located in the area to the north of Calvary and the basilica of Constantine but still within the general precinct of the Holy Sepulchre.[33]

The pilgrim Daniel the Abbot visited Jerusalem in the early twelfth century, about a hundred years after the destruction of the basilica of Constantine in 1009. His description of the Holy Sepulchre provides an example of how Christian

---

Pilgrims, 173–74, 208, 266. All references to Epiphanius and Bernard the Monk will follow the section divisions of Wilkinson.

[29] The *Breviarius B*, 2, ed. R. Weber, in *Itineraria et Alia Geographica*, 107–12 describes an exedra near Golgotha that commemorated the miraculous healing. See Wilkinson, *Jerusalem Pilgrims*, 118.

[30] Adomnán, *De locis sanctis*, chap. 1.11, in Wilkinson, *Jerusalem Pilgrims*, 177. Adomnán's column is also identified with the center of the world, a tradition that Christians associated with Calvary.

[31] Epiphanius, *Account of the Holy City*, chap. 4, in Wilkinson, *Jerusalem Pilgrims*, 208.

[32] Wilkinson, *Jerusalem Pilgrims*, 208. The commemoration of the house of Joseph, spouse of Mary, is based upon the second-century *Proto-Evangelium of James*, which places the house and, consequently, the Annunciation in the city of Jerusalem. Epiphanius' reference, though otherwise unknown, must refer to a liturgical space in the immediate vicinity of the basilica of Constantine. On recent excavations on the north side of the Holy Sepulchre, which have uncovered a church from the Early Islamic period, see G. Avni and J. Seligman, "New Excavations at the Church of the Holy Sepulchre Compound," in *One Land—Many Cultures*, ed. G. Claudio Bottini, L. Di Segni, and L. D. Chrupcała (Jerusalem, 2003), 153–62.

[33] Adomnán's description of the column being north of the holy places is compatible with Epiphanius' location of it as being to the left, or north, of the basilica, as is clear from the context of Epiphanius' description, which starts at the tomb and proceeds towards the eastern entrance of the basilica. See Wilkinson, *Jerusalem Pilgrims*, 177 at n. 26, who places Adomnán's column just inside the Damascus Gate.

memory ascribed commemorations to the ruined basilica and, in particular, to the great eastern façade of the church. He writes: "Here to the East is the great door . . . and near this door is the place where St. Helena discovered the true cross of the Lord, instantly restoring a dead virgin to life!"[34] Daniel locates both the discovery and the miraculous healing in the same place, and his description further qualifies the evidence of Adomnán and Epiphanius. During the early Islamic period, the commemoration of the miraculous healing appears to have been located near but slightly north of the eastern façade of the basilica.[35]

It is also possible that the three wooden crosses mentioned by Willibald were somehow associated with the Holy Cross legend. The crosses are described as standing against the wall of the eastern side of the church, suggesting a place near its front entrance. The crosses, he adds, were previously inside the church. However, they now stood outside the church under a roof.[36]

The motif of the three crosses also appears in Adomnán's drawing of the Holy Sepulchre in the rectangle identified as the basilica of Constantine, which Adomnán describes as being built on the site where the three crosses were discovered.[37] As with Willibald, the crosses clearly do not represent Calvary, which is marked on the drawing with a single cross and is described in the text as being made of silver.[38] In short, the collective evidence of Adomnán and Willibald may indicate that after the Persian destruction of 614 the legend of the Holy Cross was marked in the basilica with the motif of three large crosses, which were then moved outside the church prior to Willibald's visit in the early eighth century.[39]

---

[34] Daniel the Abbot, *Abt Daniil: Wallfahrtsbericht*, ed. K. D. Seeman (Munich, 1970), trans. W.F. Ryan in J. Wilkinson, *Jerusalem Pilgrimage, 1099–1185* (London, 1988), 131.

[35] While very little is known of the space to the north of the former basilica of Constantine, see the plans of the complex of the Holy Sepulchre given in V. C. Corbo, *Il Santo Sepolcro di Gerusalemme: Aspetti archaeologici dalle origini al periodo crociato*, 3 vols. (Jerusalem, 1981–1982), 2: plate 3, and C. Coüasnon, *The Church of the Holy Sepulchre in Jerusalem* (London, 1974), plate 8.

[36] See Bauch, *Quellen zur Geschichte der Diözese Eichstätt*, 102 at n. 117. Willibald's description of the three crosses is problematic. While the wording indicates a location near the front eastern entrance of the basilica, the description's context, in which the crosses appear after his references to the place of Calvary and before his description of the tomb of the Savior, may suggest a location in the area of the inner atrium.

[37] On Adomnán's drawing, see Wilkinson, *Jerusalem Pilgrims*, 371–86. The three crosses, which appear in the drawings, are not explicitly mentioned in Adomnán's text.

[38] On the description of Calvary, see Adomnán, *De locis sanctis*, chap. 1.5, in Wilkinson, *Jerusalem Pilgrims*, 173.

[39] The reasons for this movement of the crosses, as described by Willibald, are unclear. If, in fact, the crosses were associated with the Holy Cross legend, they may have been used as temporary markers and were then moved outside when the place where the Holy Cross was found underwent further restorations inside the basilica.

To summarize the evidence, it has been noted that twice in his life, Willibald, 'the lover of the cross,' was the recipient of a miraculous healing that was linked to the image of the cross. The first healing was associated with a large outdoor cross and took place during his childhood, while the second healing took place in Jerusalem as he was entering the church where the Holy Cross was found. The setting of Willibald's second healing has raised questions regarding the commemorations of the legend in Jerusalem at the time of his visit. The descriptions of Adomnán and Epiphanius and the reference by Daniel the Abbot suggest that the miraculous healing was commemorated to the north but near the door of the basilica, while the three crosses of Willibald and Adomnán may be commemorative markers also related to aspects of the same legend. It is possible that Willibald's crosses were located in the front atrium of the basilica, providing a second possibility of a commemorative marker associated with the legend that was positioned near the front entrance of the basilica. It is worth recalling that in Willibald's initial description of Jerusalem, he mentions the place where the cross was found before introducing the basilica itself, perhaps suggesting that he passed one of the sites of the commemorations associated with the legend of the Holy Cross prior to actually entering the church. At the very least, it can be affirmed that Willibald's healing—or, in any case, his attribution of the event—occurred within the immediate context of a commemorative landscape associated with two events of the Holy Cross legend, the second of which, the miraculous healing, had pronounced parallels with Willibald's own experiences with the 'life-giving' qualities of the Holy Cross.

4.2. The Church of the Holy Sepulchre: The Tomb of the Savior

Despite Willibald's personal association with the place where the Holy Cross was found, his description of the tomb of the Savior, characterized by its attention to the original biblical setting, is far more detailed.[40] Willibald refers to the tomb's garden setting, its rock-cut character, the shelf on which Jesus' body was laid, the tomb's entrance, and the stone which was rolled away by the angels.[41] Willibald also portrays the tomb as a place of devotion, as indicated by his twofold reference to prayer and his description of fifteen continually-burning golden lamps inside the tomb. By contrast, his mention of the marvelous dome above the tomb is his only reference to the setting's ecclesiastical grandeur.[42]

---

[40] See *VW*, ed. Holder-Egger, chap. 97.16–25 for Willibald's description of the tomb of the Savior.

[41] Compare Willibald's description with Matthew 27:57–28:10, Mark 15:42–16:8, Luke 23:50–24:12, and John 19:38–18.

[42] For a recent study on the tomb of Christ, see M. Biddle, *The Tomb of Christ* (Stroud, 1999).

4.3. The Other Sites of Jerusalem

Willibald next turns his attention to Holy Sion, which he twice refers to as being in the middle of Jerusalem.[43] This statement must be read in the context of Willibald's reference to the place of Calvary.[44] Whereas Calvary was formerly outside the city, Willibald understood Sion to be the area of 'biblical' Jerusalem. Moreover, Willibald identified Sion as the place of Mary's death.[45] The reference is significant in light of the numerous commemorations that Willibald omits, which include the column of scourging, the room of the Last Supper, the setting of Pentecost, and the place of the stoning of St. Stephen.

Willibald also visited a pool that he identifies as the porch of Solomon. His paraphrase of John 5—Jesus' healing of the Paralytic—curiously rendered in the present tense, establishes the identity of the site as the pool of Bethesda, or the Sheep Pool.[46] Perhaps the most interesting aspect of Willibald's description is the fact that he fails to identify the area as the birthplace of Mary, even though his Jerusalem itinerary takes special note of the events of Mary's death.

Willibald then describes a giant column in front of the city gate that marked the place of the confrontation between the Jews and the Apostles during the funeral procession of Mary. The location of Willibald's column can be securely identified in light of two seventh-century texts that describe the same commemoration. The *Armenian Guide* locates the marker outside the city, two hundred and fifty steps above the tomb of St. Mary, while Epiphanius refers to the marker as being outside the eastern gate of the city.[47] Willibald's column, therefore, was outside the eastern gate of the city, or, following his Jerusalem circuit, between the pool of Bethesda and the tomb of St. Mary.[48] Willibald next mentions the Church of St. Mary in the Jehoshaphat valley. The church contained Mary's tomb, which, Willibald stresses, was merely for commemorative purposes, as her body was not buried there.

---

[43] *VW*, ed. Holder-Egger, chap. 97.28–29 and 98.5–6.

[44] *VW*, ed. Holder-Egger, chap. 97.12–13.

[45] For a recent study on the traditions of Mary's death and assumption, see S. J. Shoemaker, *Ancient Traditions of the Virgin Mary's Dormition and Assumption* (Oxford, 2002).

[46] In the early twelfth century, Daniel the Abbot similarly identifies the Sheep Pool with the porch of Solomon. See Daniel the Abbot, *Abt Daniil*, chap. 16, in Wilkinson, *Jerusalem Pilgrimage*, 132.

[47] The *Armenian Guide*, 6–7, in *Movsisi Kalankatuspwoy Patmutiwn Aluanip asxarhi*, ed. M. Emin (Moscow, 1860) and Epiphanius, *Account of the Holy City*, chap. 24, in Wilkinson, *Jerusalem Pilgrimage*, 166, 212.

[48] Despite the evidence of the *Armenian Guide* and Epiphanius, the location of Willibald's column has frequently been misidentified. See Wilkinson, *Jerusalem Pilgrims*, 242, map 43; Bahat, "The Physical Infrastructure," 46 at note 52; Bauch, *Quellen zur Geschichte der Diözese Eichstätt*, 103 at n. 124.

Willibald then refers to the church on the Mount of Olives where Jesus prayed before his passion. Here, Willibald notes, Jesus told his disciples, "Stay awake and pray, so that you do not enter into temptation."[49] The identity of this church has been debated in light of the Persian destruction of 614 and the question of which sites were subsequently rebuilt. The present-day sites of Pater Noster, Dominus Flevit, and the Church of All Nations have all been proposed.[50] The site's specific identification, however, has little importance for the analysis of Willibald's image of Jerusalem. It is sufficient to note that Willibald associated the area of the Mount of Olives with the events surrounding Jesus' passion.

While Willibald rarely provides physical descriptions of the churches he visited, the Church of the Ascension clearly caught his imagination, and his description of the church highlights the interaction between the church's architecture and the ascension narrative.[51] The round church had no roof and was open to the sky. In the middle of the church, surrounded by a square brass banister, was a perpetually-burning lantern symbolizing Jesus' ascension and expected return. Willibald also refers to two columns against the church walls, which represented the heavenly witnesses of the ascension.[52] Those who could creep between the wall and the columns were freed from their sins.

4.4. Conclusions: The Holy Sites of Jerusalem

The preceding discussion has briefly summarized Willibald's descriptions of the holy sites of Jerusalem with primary attention being given to the place where the Holy Cross was found. The discussion has emphasized the fundamental importance of the image of the Holy Cross in the life of Willibald, while highlighting his personal encounter with the healing powers associated with one of the city's holy places. Furthermore, the brief summary of Willibald's description of Jerusalem has revealed his interest in the places associated with Mary's death as well as those related to the life, death, and ascension of Christ. Willibald notably describes the tomb of Christ in its biblical setting, while all but ignoring its ecclesiastical surroundings. On the other hand, his description of the Church of the Ascension embraces the interplay between architecture and the biblical narrative. Despite the half century that separated the elderly bishop from his days in Jerusalem, a number of images remained firmly fixed in his imagination. While Willibald's descriptions often invoke the biblical setting—which is apparent in his reference to the place

[49] Matthew 26:41.
[50] On the Church of the Agony and the identity of Willibald's church, see C. Kopp, *The Holy Places of the Gospels*, trans. R. Walls (New York, 1963), 345–50; L. Vincent, *Jérusalem nouvelle* (Paris, 1914), 301–27, 328–36, 407–9; Bauch, *Quellen zur Geschichte der Diözese Eichstätt*, 104 at n. 128; Bahat, "The Physical Infrastructure," 94 at n. 328.
[51] Compare with Adomnán, *De locis sanctis*, chap. 1.23, in Wilkinson, *Jerusalem Pilgrims*, 180–81.
[52] Acts 1:11.

of Calvary, in his description of the tomb of the Savior, and in his use of scriptures in regards to the pool of Bethesda and the church where Jesus prayed before his passion—this tendency seems due less to his inability to remember concrete details than to a conscious attempt to reinforce the biblical imagination of his audience. In the end, despite the Islamic presence in the city, Willibald portrays eighth-century Jerusalem as a Christian city, the setting of the biblical past and the place of God's ongoing miraculous wonders.

5. The Image of Jerusalem: The View from Eichstätt

Notwithstanding these images of Jerusalem, which were based upon his first-hand experiences, the elderly Willibald viewed the city as a far and distant place. This image is explicitly expressed in the account of Willibald's motive for leaving Rome, in which Jerusalem is described as a "more remote and less well-known place."[53] While the reference may accurately describe Willibald's initial motives, its appearance in the text indicates that the phrase also reflected the view from Eichstätt.

5.1. The Impact of Culture, Religion, and Politics on Willibald's Image of Jerusalem

The remoteness of Jerusalem was perceived in terms of the number—and the qualitative differences—of cultural and political spheres through which Willibald had to travel en route to Jerusalem. In this regard, a distinct contrast appears in Willibald's respective attitudes towards the Greeks and the Saracens. Despite Willibald's encounter with the Greek world, including a two-year stay in Constantinople, he makes only four explicit references to the Greeks. Three of these are linked with references to the Saracens and occur in his description of Cyprus.[54] The fourth is a reference to a Greek bishop who lived near the coast of Syria, just inside what Willibald refers to as the "region of the Saracens."[55] It is noteworthy that all four references appear precisely in the context of the Greek and Saracen border. By contrast, Willibald's transitions between the Latin and Greek cultural spheres are not noted, and he essentially treats the two worlds as a common religious and political unit. In other words, Greek cultural and political identity notably emerges vis-à-vis the Saracens rather than in contrast to the Latin West.

---

[53] *VW*, ed. Holder-Egger, chap. 92.18–26.

[54] Willibald describes the island of Cyprus as lying between the lands of the Greeks and the Saracens (*VW*, ed. Holder-Egger, chap. 93.4–5). Furthermore, the Cypriots live between the Greeks and the Saracens, and the relations on Cyprus between the Saracens and the Greeks were peaceful (*VW*, ed. Holder-Egger, chap. 95.15–16).

[55] *VW*, ed. Holder-Egger, chap. 94.8–10.

Willibald's de-emphasis of the differences between the Latin and Greek
worlds must be viewed in light of his encounters with the Saracen world, which
by comparison was far more difficult to negotiate and whose religion was other
than Christian.[56] Besides Willibald's imprisonment in Emesa, the narrative of
his final departure from the port of Tyre is marked by numerous references to
issues of security.[57] The episodes collectively reveal a rather distinct feature of
Willibald's mental map: a ring of Saracen authority circumscribed the Christian
holy places. With the appropriate papers, Willibald had been able to travel extensively throughout the Saracen-controlled territories, and he describes a Christian
Holy Land with but a single reference to the "pagan Saracens."[58] However, there
was a distinct zone of Saracen authority which had to be successfully negotiated
in order to enter and exit the Holy Land. Decades later, Willibald would remember that the Holy Lands were under the rule of a people as culturally, religiously,
and politically distinctive as any he had ever known.

5.2. The Impact of Hardships on Willibald's Image of Jerusalem

Willibald's image of Jerusalem as a remote and distant place was also affected by
the number and degree of hardships that he experienced during his pilgrimage
travels. Although the interview between Willibald and Hugeburc took place for
the explicit purpose of recording his reflections on the holy sites, Willibald made
numerous references to the sufferings and deprivations that he endured, which
included:

1. the death of his father in Lucca;
2. a lengthy illness in Rome;
3. the necessity of begging for bread in Phygela;
4. the long, cold winter endured in Patara;
5. the threat of starvation near Mons Gallianorum;
6. his arrest and imprisonment as a suspected spy in Emesa;
7. a five-week illness upon arrival in Jerusalem;
8. a lengthy illness during the season of Lent in Salaminias.[59]

---

[56] See *VW*, ed. Holder-Egger, chap. 94.14, 95.24. Willibald twice refers to the Saracens as pagan.

[57] *VW*, ed. Holder-Egger, chap. 100.3–16.

[58] *VW*, ed. Holder-Egger, chap. 95.22–24. In his description of Nazareth, Willibald
refers to the ransom that the Christians were paying the 'pagan Saracens' to keep them
from destroying their church.

[59] On Willibald's hardships, see the following references in the *Vita Willibaldi*: ed.
Holder-Egger, chap. 91.14–22 (Lucca); chap. 92.2–16 (Rome); chap. 93.17–19 (Phygela);
chap. 93.20–22 (Patara); chap. 94.1–4 (Mons Gallianorum); chap. 94.13–95.15 (Emesa);
chap. 97.25–29 (Jerusalem); chap. 99.9–16 (Palestine); chap. 100.2–12 (Salaminias).

The episodes highlight the degree to which the toil of the earthly life was central to Willibald's memories of his pilgrimage experiences, and his recognition of the numerous obstacles that separated the western pilgrim from the Holy City underscores his image of Jerusalem as a remote and distant destination.

5.3. Jerusalem as the Center of the World

In Willibald's view from Eichstätt, Jerusalem was located at the far end of a continuum of cultural barriers and physical obstacles. This image of Jerusalem contrasts significantly with the view of the Holy City as the center of the world. This idea emerges in Jewish writings of the post-exilic period, particularly in the book of Ezekiel, which describes Jerusalem as the "center of the nations, with countries all around her."[60] In particular, the Temple was understood to be the center of the world and the meeting place of heaven and earth. Christian tradition appropriated the idea of Jerusalem's centrality, shifting the Temple traditions to the sites of Jesus' passion.[61] Adomnán gives an account of a high column in the middle of the city, which was identified with the center of the world.[62] In the ninth century, Bernard the Monk describes chains stretching from each of four churches within the complex of the Holy Sepulchre. The point at which the chains intersected was recognized as the center of the world.[63] While Willibald was undoubtedly cognizant of the tradition, Jerusalem's cosmological centrality failed to make an imprint upon the bishop's image of the city. The firsthand experience of hardships and struggles had taught him that Jerusalem was not in the center of the earth but was rather a far and distant place, which lay on the eastern fringe of the world.

5.4. Perseverance and the Christian Life

Implicit in the numerous anecdotes of hardships is the bishop's advocacy of the virtue of perseverance, which functions as a subtext to Willibald's narrative. This subtext finds expression in the story of Willibald's encounter with a lion which took place while his party was crossing the olive plains of Samaria.[64] An Ethiopian, who was traveling with them, told them not to be afraid and to proceed towards the lion. As they moved closer, the lion disappeared, leaving the pilgrims alone. Moreover, explicit references to perseverance occur in the narrative of the illness from which both Willibald and his brother suffered while in Rome.[65] The two brothers took turns caring for one another, and in spite of their

---

[60] Ezekiel 5:5, 38:12.
[61] R. L. Wilken, *The Land Called Holy* (New Haven, 1992), 11.
[62] Adomnán, *De locis sanctis,* chap. 1.11, in Wilkinson, *Jerusalem Pilgrims*, 177.
[63] Bernard the Monk, *Itinerary*, chap. 11, in Wilkinson, *Jerusalem Pilgrims*, 266.
[64] *VW,* ed. Holder-Egger, chap. 100.20–101.1.
[65] *VW,* ed. Holder-Egger, chap. 92.3–16.

illness, they continued to persevere in their observation of the monastic life. The episode is punctuated by a verse from the Gospels, Matthew 10:22 — "The one who perseveres to the end will be saved" — a verse which embodies Willibald's understanding of the Christian life.[66]

6. Conclusion: Willibald and the City of Jerusalem

When the seventy-eight-year-old bishop dictated his life and travels, the expressed purpose was to record his descriptions of the holy sights which he had seen with his own eyes.[67] However, the interpretation of his Holy Land experiences could not be separated from his view of the Christian life and his advocacy of the virtue of perseverance — an emphasis on the conditions of the earthly life and the necessity of perseverance concerned Willibald as much as a faithful rendering of the holy places of Jerusalem. Instead of championing his exclusive knowledge of the holy places, Willibald, in effect, reminded his followers that while numerous obstacles separated the western pilgrim from the distant and essentially inaccessible walls of Jerusalem, the virtue of perseverance was accessible to everyone. In the end, the goal of the Christian pilgrim was not the earthly city of Jerusalem. Rather, for Willibald and for those who persevered to the end, the day would come when the bishop and his faithful companions would enter Jerusalem together, this time by the gates of the new and heavenly city.[68]

---

[66] Willibald's personal identity with Matthew 10:22 is further suggested by the references to the pilgrim life found throughout the tenth chapter of Matthew.

[67] *VW*, ed. Holder-Egger, chap. 86.2–23.

[68] This research has been supported by the W. F. Albright Institute of Archaeological Research in Jerusalem and the Educational and Cultural Affairs Division of the U. S. Department of State.

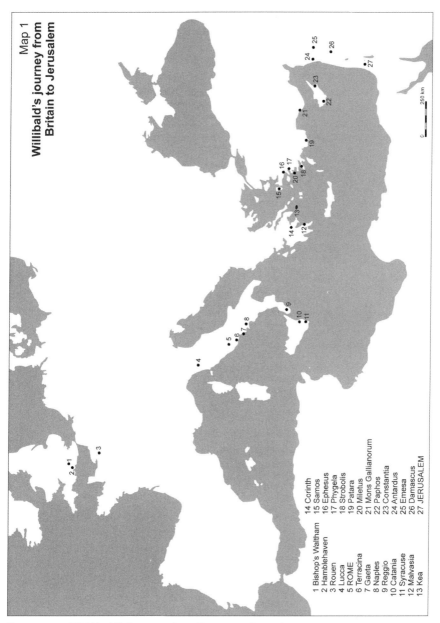

Map 1
Willibald's journey from
Britain to Jerusalem

250 km

1 Bishop's Waltham
2 Hamblehaven
3 Rouen
4 Lucca
5 ROME
6 Terracina
7 Gaeta
8 Naples
9 Reggio
10 Catania
11 Syracuse
12 Malvasia
13 Kea

14 Corinth
15 Samos
16 Ephesus
17 Phygela
18 Strobolis
19 Patara
20 Miletus
21 Mons Gallianorum
22 Paphos
23 Constantia
24 Antardus
25 Emesa
26 Damascus
27 JERUSALEM

FIGURE 9.1. Willibald's Journey from Britain to Jerusalem.

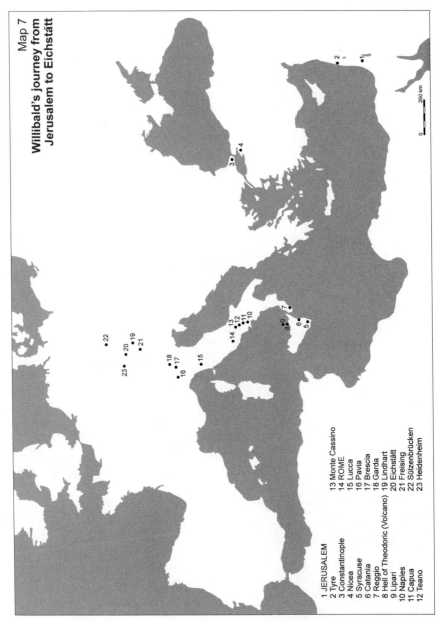

FIGURE 9.2. Willibald's Journey from Jerusalem to Eichstätt.

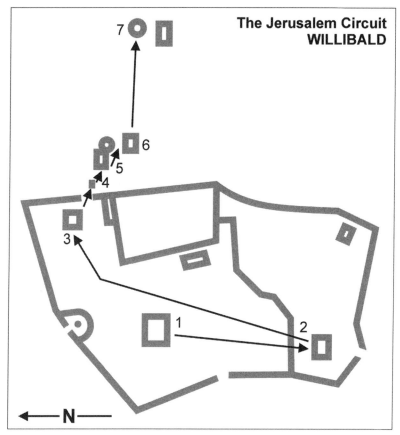

The Jerusalem Circuit
WILLIBALD

1 Church of the Holy Sepulchre   5 Church of St Mary
2 Church of Holy Sion   6 Church of the Agony
3 Pool of Bethesda   7 Church of the Ascension
4 Jephonias Monument

FIGURE 9.3. Willibald's Circuit of Jerusalem.

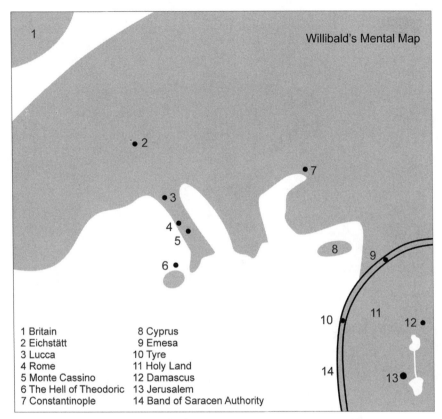

FIGURE 9.4. Willibald's Mental Map.

Rudolf of Fulda's *Vita S. Leobae*: Hagiography and Historical Reality

Barbara Yorke

1. Introduction

As an Anglo-Saxon who spent the greater part of her adult life in Germania, Leoba was a particularly appropriate person to be included in the ISAS conference on "Anglo-Saxon England and the Continent," but her dual spheres of activity mean that there are problems in how to categorize what we know about her. She was an Anglo-Saxon who died probably in 782.[1] Our main source for her life is the *Vita* written shortly before her translation to Petersberg in 837 or 838 by Rudolf of Fulda, a native German, who drew on, among other sources, reminiscences of Anglo-Saxon women in Germania who had served under her.[2] There is therefore some uncertainty in modern secondary literature about whether her *Vita* belongs to the Frankish world of her hagiographer or to the Anglo-Saxon milieu to which she, and the women whose recollections Rudolf used, belonged. One specific example where such problems of categorization have arisen concerns Rudolf's descriptions of the nunnery of Wimborne (Dorset) where Leoba spent much of her early life and where she received her ecclesiastical training.

> Here two monasteries were of old founded by kings of that race, surrounded with high and stout walls, and supplied with a sufficiency of income by a reasonable provision; one a monastery of clerics (*clericorum*), and the other of women. From the beginning of their foundation, each of them was regulated by that rule of conduct, that neither of them was entered by the opposite sex. For a woman was never permitted to enter the congregation of men, or any man the house of the nuns (*virginum*), except priests only,

---

[1] The question of the date of Leoba's death is discussed below.

[2] Rudolf of Fulda, *Vita Leobae Abbatissae Biscofesheimensis*, ed. Georg Waitz, MGH Scriptores 15.1 (Hannover, 1887), 118–31 (hereafter Rudolf, *V. Leobae*); translated in C. H. Talbot, *Anglo-Saxon Missionaries in Germany* (London, 1954), 205–26. For Rudolf's sources of information see below.

Hans Sauer and Joanna Story, eds., *Anglo-Saxon England and the Continent*. With the assistance of Gaby Waxenberger. Essays in Anglo-Saxon Studies, vol. 3. MRTS 394. Tempe: ACMRS, 2011.   [ISBN 978-0-86698-442-3]

who used to enter the churches solely to perform the office of the Mass, and when the service was solemnly concluded, immediately to return to their own dwelling . . . Moreover, the mother of the congregation herself, when she had to make arrangements or give orders about any outside affairs for the profit of the monastery, spoke through the window, and from there decided whatever expediency required to be arranged or commanded.[3]

Rudolf's account of the strict enclosure of two separate foundations for women and men at Wimborne has sometimes been taken as a reflection of Anglo-Saxon reality,[4] though it has also been seen as a portrayal of Carolingian ideals as enacted in Frankish church councils that Rudolf has projected on to an institution of which he had no personal knowledge.[5] Excavation at sites such as Hartlepool and Whitby suggests that they were sufficiently spacious to have allowed separation of the living and working areas of different groups within the communities, though they have not provided evidence of high walls separating such spaces.[6] That clerics rather than monks might serve communities of nuns is confirmed from Anglo-Saxon sources: Guthlac initially joined the *clerici* attached to the nunnery of Repton.[7] On the other hand, one does not receive the impression from the accounts of Hild or Ælfflaed of Whitby that they conducted their affairs solely through a window in their own monastic enclosure. Bishop Cuthbert joined Ælfflaed of Whitby for a feast at one of her halls on an outlying property, and Ælfflaed dealt directly not only with other male clerics, but also with the

---

[3] Rudolf, *V. Leobae*, chap. 2 (123); translated in *English Historical Documents c. 500–1042*, ed. Dorothy Whitelock, 2nd edn. (London, 1979), no. 159 (782–86).

[4] Mary Bateson, "Origin and Early History of Double Monasteries," *Transactions of the Royal Historical Society*, 1st ser., 13 (1899): 137–98, at 180–81; Rosemary Cramp, "Monastic Sites," in *The Archaeology of Anglo-Saxon England*, ed. David Wilson (Cambridge, 1976), 201–52, at 204 and 206; Patricia Coulstock, *The Collegiate Church of Wimborne Minster* (Woodbridge, 1993), 59–61.

[5] Jane Schulenberg, "Strict Active Enclosure and its Effects on the Female Monastic Experience (ca. 500–1100)," in *Medieval Religious Women I: Distant Echoes*, ed. John A. Nichols and Lilian Thomas Shanks (Kalamazoo, 1984), 51–86; Catherine Wybourne, "Leoba: A Study in Humanity and Holiness," in *Medieval Women Monastics*, ed. Miriam Schmitt and Linda Kulzer (Collegeville, MN, 1996), 81–96, at 84–85; Stephanie Hollis, *Anglo-Saxon Women and the Church* (Woodbridge, 1992), 274–80.

[6] Robin Daniels, *Anglo-Saxon Hartlepool and the Foundations of English Christianity: An Archaeology of the Anglo-Saxon Monastery*, Tees Archaeology Monograph Series 3 (Hartlepool, 2007); Rosemary Cramp, "A Reconsideration of the Monastic Site of Whitby," in *The Age of Migrating Ideas*, ed. R. Michael Spearman and John Higgitt (Edinburgh, 1993), 64–73.

[7] Felix, *Life of Saint Guthlac*, ed. Bertram Colgrave (Cambridge, 1956), 84–87; Catherine Cubitt, "The Clergy in Early Anglo-Saxon England," *Historical Research* 78 (2005): 273–87.

tenants on her estates.[8] Whitby was not so much a "double monastery" in the way that Rudolf appears to depict Wimborne, but a nunnery which included clerics among its varied personnel who were following a range of activities, even on its main headland site which, recent excavations suggest, may also have included a trading center.[9]

While one need not assume that all major Anglo-Saxon female religious houses were identical, consideration of the evidence discussed above suggests that, although there may be some genuine traditions about early eighth-century Wimborne behind Rudolf's account, there is also the likelihood of a certain degree of idealization of the arrangements of the community that reflects concerns about the intermingling of male and female religious at the time he was writing. In the absence of any complete Lives for female saints from Anglo-Saxon England written in the seventh or eighth centuries, it has naturally proved tempting to use Rudolf's portrayal of Leoba and her German foundation at Tauberbischofsheim as a guide to the roles played by nunneries in Anglo-Saxon England; but is one justified in doing so? One has to take into account not only that Leoba was working outside her homeland where circumstances were not necessarily identical with those in which nunneries operated in Anglo-Saxon England, but, above all, that Rudolf's portrayal was not a simple reflection of reality, but one based on certain models and written within a specific context.

All hagiographies pose problems for historians because of the conventions of the genre,[10] and, not surprisingly, a number of commentators have expressed reservations about using the *Vita* of Leoba as a historical source. Wilhelm Levison identified passages applied by Rudolf to Leoba presenting her as a model monastic leader which came from earlier writings including Sulpicius's *Life of St Martin*, Pope Gregory's *Dialogues*, and the late fifth-century *Life of St Germanus of Auxerre*.[11] Commenting on such borrowings, Julia Smith has written that it is "unclear how much relationship, if any, this image of Leoba bore to the real story

---

[8] *Two Lives of Saint Cuthbert*, ed. Bertram Colgrave (Cambridge, 1940), 126–29, 261–65; Barbara Yorke, *Nunneries and the Anglo-Saxon Royal Houses* (London, 2003), 13–17, 162–65.

[9] The recent excavations have yet to be published. Interim accounts are available at http://www.eng-h.gov.uk/projects/whitby/wahpsae.

[10] Felice Lifshitz, "Beyond Positivism and Genre: 'Hagiographical' Texts as Historical Narrative," *Viator* 25 (1994): 95–113; idem, "Demystifying the Role of Sanctity in Western Christendom," in *The Cult of Saints in Late Antiquity and the Early Middle Ages*, ed. James Howard-Johnston and Paul Antony Hayward (Oxford, 1999), 115–42; Ian Wood, "The Use and Abuse of Latin Hagiography," in *East and West: Modes of Communication*, ed. Evangelos Chrysos and idem (Leiden, 1999), 93–109.

[11] Wilhelm Levison, *England and the Continent in the Eighth Century* (Oxford, 1946), 76 at n. 2.

of her life" and that Rudolf "submerged her within a traditional male texture."[12] She suggests that Rudolf drew upon these male role-models in the absence of any suitable female ones on which to base his subject. Stephanie Hollis has also argued that Rudolf has distorted aspects of the life of Leoba and her relationship with her kinsman Boniface in part because of the inherent misogyny of medieval churchmen, but also to ensure that his subject conformed to the reforming ideals of the Carolingian Renaissance.[13] What such observations indicate is the necessity of contextualizing the writing of Leoba's *Vita* in order to understand the circumstances behind its composition and to assess Rudolf's attitude towards his subject.

2. Fulda and the Cult of St. Leoba

The immediate circumstance in which the *Vita* was written was the renewed interest in Leoba's cult during the abbacy of Hraban Maur which culminated in the translation of her remains on 28 September 837 or 838 from the south porticus of the abbey church at Fulda to the crypt of a new church on the Petersberg overlooking the main settlement and some four kilometres from the abbey church.[14] This was the second time that Leoba's body had been translated. Boniface's request that she should be buried in the same tomb as him had not been followed, and she had initially been buried close to his tomb, on the north side of the altar dedicated by Boniface to Christ and the Twelve Apostles.[15] Her body had been transferred subsequently, in the time of Abbot Eigil when the abbey church was rebuilt, to the southern porticus.[16] Hollis has seen in the treatment of Leoba's remains embarrassment on the part of successive abbots of Fulda at having a woman buried in their midst.[17] It is certainly the case that access to sacred space could be carefully controlled in ninth-century Francia, and that entry to the central areas of monastic

---

[12] Julia M. H. Smith, "The Problem of Female Sanctity in Carolingian Europe c.780–920," *Past and Present* 146 (1995): 3–37, at 16–17. See also Walter Berschin, "Biographie im Karolingischen Fulda," in *Kloster Fulda in der Welt der Karolinger und Ottonen*, ed. Gangolf Schrimpf (Frankfurt am Main, 1996), 315–24, at 319–20.

[13] Hollis, *Women and the Church*, 271–300.

[14] Rudolf of Fulda, *Miracula Sanctorum in Fuldenses Ecclesias Translatorum*, ed. Georg Waitz, MGH Scriptores 15.1 (Hannover, 1887), 328–41, at 339 (hereafter Rudolf, *Miracula*).

[15] Rudolf, *V. Leobae*, chap. 21 (130).

[16] Werner Jacobsen, "Die Abteikirche in Fulda von Sturmius bis Eigil — kunstpolitische Positionen und deren Veränderungen," in *Kloster Fulda*, ed. Schrimpf, 105–29. Talbot, *Anglo-Saxon Missionaries*, 224, wrongly translates this as "western porch" thus creating some confusion on this point in anglophone secondary literature.

[17] Hollis, *Women and the Church*, 283–88.

foundations by lay people, and especially lay women, might be refused.[18] But there is also a more positive way in which translations of saints out of monastic enclaves can be viewed. The translations of Leoba's body and, in particular, the commissioning of her *Vita* can be seen as indications that her cult was of some significance to Fulda, though the lack of any reference to Leoba in any of the biographies of the Fulda abbots from Boniface to Eigil may suggest that her cult was deemed of greater importance during the abbacy of Hraban Maur than in the abbacies of his predecessors.[19] The translation to Petersberg can be seen not so much as banishment, as rather part of a policy followed by Abbot Hraban Maur to develop the cults of Fulda saints and to open up new religious foci for processions and pilgrimages as occurred at many other major Carolingian abbeys in the ninth century.[20] It is surely significant that Rudolf ended his account of Leoba's life with a joint miracle by Boniface and Leoba in which intervention from both saints and a visit to both their tombs was necessary to achieve a result.[21] The church at Petersberg also contained the relics of St. Felicitas and other female martyrs, and, with the addition of the burial of Leoba's remains in the crypt before the altar dedicated to the Virgin Mary, may have been intended to provide a new focus for female pilgrims.[22] Leoba had evidently developed this speciality by the early modern period when mothers would place sick children to sleep in Leoba's empty tomb so that she might heal them.[23]

It is possible to suggest various reasons why the cult of Leoba was of particular importance to Fulda in the years immediately following her demise. Her death is entered for 28 September 780 in the Fulda necrology,[24] but an original charter in favor of Lull's monastery at Hersfeld implies that she was still alive

---

[18] Julia M. H. Smith, "Women at the Tomb: Access to Relic Shrines in the Early Middle Ages," in *The World of Gregory of Tours*, ed. Kathleen Mitchell and Ian Wood (Leiden, 2002), 163–80.

[19] Berschin, "Biographie im Karolingischen Fulda," for overview of these Lives.

[20] A pilgrimage route from Fulda cathedral to Petersberg is part of the Roman Catholic ceremonies in Fulda today: Maria-Regina Broj, *Ein Liebling Gottes und der Menschen: Die heilige Lioba. Andachts- und Wallfahrtsbuch* (Fulda, 1994).

[21] Rudolf, *V. Leobae*, chap. 23 (130–31); though this miracle occurred when Leoba was still buried in the abbey church at Fulda. For a miracle performed by Leoba with the aid of salt blessed by Boniface see below.

[22] Rudolf, *Miracula*, chap. 14 (339).

[23] As depicted in woodcuts and *ex voto* offerings: Broj, *Die heilige Lioba*, 75–78. The corporeal relics of Leoba were moved back to the abbey church of Fulda at the time of a Hungarian attack in 915; see Gisela Muschiol, "Königshof, Kloster und Mission — die Welt der Lioba," in *Bonifatius — Apostel der Deutschen: Mission und Christianisierung vom 8. bis ins 20. Jahrhundert*, ed. Franz J. Felten, Mainzer Vorträge 9 (Stuttgart, 2004), 99–114, at 112.

[24] *Annales Necrologi Fuldenses*, ed. Georg Waitz, MGH Scriptores 13 (Hannover, 1881), 167.

when the grant was made on 28 July 782, and living on an estate at Schornsheim which formed part of the benefaction.[25] It is therefore more usually suggested that she died in September 782. By the time of her death what Ian Wood has characterized as "the competition for Boniface's aura" among the various religious communities with which he had been associated was well under way.[26] Fulda had asserted its claims through its eventual acquisition of Boniface's body, and Eigil in his *Vita* of Abbot Sturm had demonstrated how Boniface had delegated his authority over the monastery he had founded to him and his successors.[27] Leoba had a major role to play as well in cementing and parading the links of Boniface with Fulda. Rudolf presents Boniface's decision to invite Leoba from England to assist him as occurring at about the same time that he sent Sturm to Monte Cassino in 748 to study the monastic life there.[28] In fact, Leoba may have come to Germany at a somewhat earlier date in the 730s,[29] and her surviving letter to Boniface suggests it was she who took the initiative in contacting Boniface to suggest that she joined him.[30] Rudolf's presentation of events allowed him to show Boniface choosing at the same point two close associates, who would become his spiritual heirs, and who exemplified the best of contemporary monasticism, Sturm through his training at the monastery in which the Benedictine Rule had been nurtured and Leoba through hers in the exemplary traditions of Wessex in which Boniface himself had been raised and had worked as a monastic teacher.

Leoba was Boniface's heir by blood and spiritual kinship. Rudolf states that the latter was the most significant, and it is symbolized in the *Vita* by Boniface's gift of his cowl to Leoba before he departed for his martyrdom, and his instructions to Lull and the senior monks of Fulda to treat her with respect and reverence.[31] His final request was that she should be buried in the same tomb as him. Rudolf is careful to explain why this had not actually happened, how the alternative arrangements that had been made did not imply any disrespect and

[25] *Urkundenbuch der Reichsabtei Hersfeld*, ed. Hans Weirich, Veröffentlichungen der Historischen Kommission für Hessen und Waldeck 19.1 (Marburg, 1936), no. 17 (29–31). The charter is discussed in more detail below.

[26] Ian Wood, *The Missionary Life: Saints and the Evangelisation of Europe, 400–1050* (Harlow, 2001), 55–78.

[27] *Die Vita Sturmi des Eigil von Fulda, literarkritisch-historische Untersuchung und Edition*, ed. Pius Engelbert (Marburg, 1968); Wood, *Missionary Life*, 68–72.

[28] Rudolf, *V. Leoba*, chap. 11 (126).

[29] Barbara Yorke, "The Bonifacian Mission and Female Religious in Wessex," *Early Medieval Europe* 7 (1998): 145–72, at 171.

[30] *Die Briefe des heiligen Bonifatius und Lullus*, ed. Michael Tangl, MGH Epistolae Selectae I (Berlin, 1916), no. 29; the letter is discussed in further detail below.

[31] Rudolf, *V. Leobae*, chap. 17 (129); Hollis, *Women and the Church*, 283–97.

had been validated by the performance of miracles.[32] Leoba's burial at Fulda was a visible testimony of Fulda's right to her inheritance, which presumably included her nunnery at Tauberbischofsheim and perhaps other nunneries that had been founded under her authority. No wonder Fulda continued to treat Leoba with respect, for she not only reinforced its connection to Boniface, but also extended its sphere of influence. As she had outlived Boniface by almost thirty years, there would have been people still alive in the 830s who had known her. Her tomb at Fulda and the ceremonies surrounding her final translation provided opportunities for Fulda to reinforce its links with those who had a personal attachment to her, particularly those who had been her own followers and those patrons of Fulda from the area of Hesse where she had been based.[33]

Leoba had much more than a local significance for the monks of Fulda in the 830s. When Boniface gave Leoba his cowl it was with instructions "to extend the scope of the good work she had begun." As heirs of Leoba and Boniface, monks of Fulda had done this by founding around 780, and so at about the time of Leoba's death, a missionary outpost at Brunshausen in eastern Saxony.[34] In the era of church reform in ninth-century Francia there was an issue of how appropriate such activity was for monks. Rudolf handles very carefully instances where Leoba might appear to be acting contrary to monastic ideals such as *stabilitas*. Her departure from Wimborne to join Boniface was foretold to her in a dream in which her body produced purple thread. An older nun in whom she confided explained that many "will profit by her words and example, and the effect of them will be felt in other lands afar off whither she will go."[35] It was this revelation of divine providence that had persuaded Abbess Tetta to grant her permission to leave, and which also validated her active supervisory role in Hesse.[36] The validation of Leoba's departure from Wimborne to fulfil a preordained destiny may have helped to authorize similar activities by Fulda monks

---

[32] Rudolf, *V. Leobae*, chaps. 21–23 (130–31), though his explanation that the monks did not wish to open the tomb of the martyred Boniface seems singularly unconvincing.

[33] Matthew Innes, *State and Society in the Early Middle Ages: The Middle Rhine Valley, 400–1000* (Cambridge, 2000), 21–29, for patrons of Fulda.

[34] Paschasia Stumpf, *Die Benediktinerklöster in Niedersachsen, Schleswig-Holstein und Bremen* (Munich, 1979), 100. However, the question of the exact date and the circumstances in which Fulda acquired Brunshausen has been the subject of some debate; see Klaus Nass, "Fulda und Brunshausen: Zur Problematik der Missionsklöster in Sachsen," *Niedersächsisches Jahrbuch für Landesgeschichte* 59 (1987): 1–62, and Johannes Fried, "Fulda in der Bildungs- und Geistesgeschichte des frühen Mittelalters," in *Kloster Fulda*, ed. Schrimpf, 3–38, at 37–38.

[35] Rudolf, *V. Leobae*, chap. 8 (125); Talbot, *Anglo-Saxon Missionaries*, 212–13.

[36] Hollis, *Women and the Church*, 277–79; Muschiol, "Königshof, Kloster und Mission," 106–7. See also the dream of Leoba's mother of her unborn daughter as a bell, and more generally Paul Dutton, *The Politics of Dreaming in the Carolingian Empire* (Lincoln, NE, 1994).

who were following her example in aiding the Christianization of a recently-converted area. It may not have been only because of the ubiquity of male Saints' Lives that Leoba acquired her "male texture," for Rudolf was presenting Leoba, at least in part, as a monastic who transcended gender and was a model for men as well as women in the church.

However, Leoba's position as abbess and nun may have had a particular relevance for the development of Fulda's wider interests at the time Rudolf composed her Life, for its involvement in the Christianization of Saxony was to bring Fulda into close association with another female religious community. It was already apparent by the 830s that the Saxon lay elite, like that of the Anglo-Saxons before them, were favoring the foundation of religious houses led by women from their own families as major cult centers in the regions they controlled.[37] The patron of the Fulda foundation at Brunshausen was the family of Count Liudolf (whose grandson was King Henry I).[38] One manuscript of Rudolf's *Vita* of Leoba carries a dedication to Hadamout, generally believed to be Liudolf's daughter Hathumod who was the first abbess of Gandersheim, founded as an "Eigen-kloster" of the Liudolfings.[39] If so, the dedication to Hadamout must be secondary as Rudolf wrote his Life of Leoba ca. 836, before her body was translated to Petersberg, and Hathumod was not born until 840. The survival of the dedication in only one manuscript of the *Vita* could be the result of a copy being made especially for Hathumod ca. 852 when the twelve-year-old abbess and accompanying nuns came to live at Brunshausen while the nunnery at Gandersheim was being built. Although Hathumod had not been born when Rudolf wrote his Life of Leoba, the trend for such family foundations had begun in Saxony by that date. The *Vita* of Leoba had laid down an ideal relationship for monks of Fulda and a prestigious abbess living nearby, whose potential was there for them to utilize when the time was right. It may be relevant to note that Abbess Hathumod was apparently buried not at Gandersheim, but at Brunshausen, perhaps following the precedent set in Leoba's *Vita* in which she was buried not in her own foundation, but in the male community which was her ultimate spiritual home. Ultimately, of course, Gandersheim was to outpace Brunshausen in importance when it became one of the major imperial nunneries of the Ottonian *Reich*, but the nature of future developments could not have been anticipated in the 830s

---

[37] Karl Leyser, *Rule and Conflict in an Early Medieval Society: Ottonian Saxony* (London, 1979), 63–73.

[38] Patrick Corbet, *Les Saints ottoniens: sainteté dynastique, sainteté royale et sainteté féminine autour de l'an Mil*, Beihefte von Francia 15 (Sigmaringen, 1986), 41–50.

[39] Rudolf, *V. Leobae*, 121; Agius, *Vita Hathumodae Abbatissae Gandersheimensis primae*, ed. G. H. Pertz, MGH Scriptores 4 (Hannover, 1841), 165–89, 754–82; Ludger Körntgen, "Gandersheim und die Ottonen," in *Das Gandersheimer Runenkästchen*, ed. Regine Marth (Braunschweig, 2000), 121–38; Eva Schlotheuber, "Die Äbtissinnen Hathumod von Gandersheim und Clara von Assisi," *Damals* 37 (2005): 28–33.

when Fulda was cultivating leading Saxon families and seeking to establish a foothold in recently Christianized eastern Saxony.

There are therefore several reasons not only for Fulda promoting the cult of Leoba through the translation of her body to Petersberg in 837 or 838 and the commissioning of the *Vita*, but also for Rudolf wanting to give a certain slant to his portrait of Leoba. Rather than playing down her relationship with Fulda, as some commentators have suggested, it is more likely that he would have wanted to build it up and to present Leoba as an ideal monastic leader who could take her place alongside those male religious leaders who had established Fulda as one of the leading monastic centers of Francia. The attributes assigned to her from earlier male Lives could be seen as a deliberate choice for a particular purpose rather than borrowings made because no more appropriate models were available. But these literary borrowings and the uses to which Rudolf may have put them are only one aspect of Leoba's *Vita*. Rudolf had other sources for her life which had a very different origin and may bring us closer to biographical reality.

3. Oral Tradition and Rudolf's *Vita S. Leobae*

Rudolf's *Vita* of Leoba belongs to a relatively small group of saints' lives the authors of which were in a position to draw upon the reminiscences of people who had actually known their subject. Such near-contemporary authorship is rare for all saints, but is exceptionally unusual in the Lives of female saints, whether Anglo-Saxon or Frankish.[40] In his prologue Rudolf was concerned to show that he could marshal witnesses to her life as he might have done for a legal case.[41] He carefully describes how he made use of the notes that the priest Mago and other men had taken from four of her nuns, including her kinswoman Thecla,[42] and complains about the unsatisfactory nature of Mago's material "jotted down on odd pieces of parchment in a kind of shorthand."[43] In addition to these written accounts of the remembrances of the women, various members of the Fulda community were also able to provide verbal accounts of aspects of Leoba's life, some

---

[40] Barbara Yorke, "'Carriers of the Truth': Writing the Biographies of Anglo-Saxon Female Saints," in *Medieval Biographies: Essays in Honour of Frank Barlow*, ed. David Bates, Julia Crick, and Sarah Hamilton (Woodbridge, 2006), 49–60.

[41] Rudolf, *V. Leobae*, chap. 1 (121–22); Elisabeth van Houts, *Memory and Gender in Medieval Europe 900–1200* (Basingstoke, 1999), 44–46.

[42] It has sometimes been suggested that the Thecla who gave testimony to Mago was a different person from Leoba's kinswoman Thecla, but this seems an unnecessary assumption.

[43] Talbot, *Anglo-Saxon Missionaries*, 205–6; Berschin, "Biographie im Karolingischen Fulda," 319–20 suggests that Mago's work amounted to a first *Vita* of Leoba and was completed about 831.

of which confirmed the nuns' recollections, while others furnished new material. These latter authorities are said to be drawing upon what they had heard from their own predecessors. Although, as we have seen, it was quite possible that some people who had known Leoba were still alive in the 830s, Rudolf does not specify that he had communicated with anyone who had known her personally. His accounts came at second hand, but he traces the descent of his evidence back to her lifetime.

The type of information that came from memories of Leoba originally transmitted orally are obviously different in form from Rudolf's borrowings from extant *Vitae*, and included various anecdotes and miracles concerning Leoba that are hard to parallel in the Lives of other saints.[44] Many of these accounts have a vividness to them that encourages the belief that they are based on actual events. Many incidents are not so much miraculous, but were resolved by Leoba's strength of character and ostentatious use of Christian display in prayer and processions. But it would be mistaken nevertheless to treat these accounts as straightforward narratives of Leoba's life. All Rudolf's informants had received ecclesiastical training, and his and their accounts of Leoba would be mediated through their knowledge and expectation of the behavior manifested by saintly individuals. So although the material had been passed by word of mouth, and often seems to retain traces of what one might see as oral as opposed to literary story-telling, both Rudolf and his informants are likely to have shaped it in consciousness of biblical and established hagiographical traditions. This is particularly apparent in the account of Leoba's suppression of a fire that threatened to destroy the settlement at Tauberbischofsheim.[45] This is a very common miracle in hagiographical sources,[46] but an individual touch in Rudolf's account is that it was salt blessed by Boniface "which she always kept by her" that quelled the fire. However, it would also have been the case that Leoba would have been brought up in the same traditions, and so may have shaped her own actions and sayings to those she knew to be appropriate to a religious leader who had to establish her authority over those dependent upon her.[47]

It is possible to recognize different types of oral tradition and transmission within Rudolf's *Vita* of Leoba. There are classic examples of monastic

[44] Janet Nelson, "Women and the Word in the Earlier Middle Ages," in *Women and the Church*, ed W. J. Sheils and D. Wood, Studies in Church History 27 (Oxford, 1990), 53–78, at 65–66.

[45] Rudolf, *V. Leobae*, chap. 13 (127–28); Talbot, *Anglo-Saxon Missionaries*, 218–19.

[46] See, for instance, Bede, *HE* 3.10 and 3.17, ed. Colgrave and Mynors, 244–55, 262–63.

[47] For discussion of awareness of such precedents in the writings of Boniface see Catherine Cubitt, "Memory and Narrative in the Cult of the Saints," in *The Uses of the Past in the Early Middle Ages*, ed. Yitzhak Hen and Matthew Innes (Cambridge, 2000), 29–66, at 37–39.

reminiscences being associated with objects that had a special connection with a saint.[48] The objects include "the little spoon which she usually used at table" with which she personally fed milk which she had blessed to a sick nun,[49] and the small cup from which she used to drink that "was called by the sisters 'the Beloved's little one' (*dilectae parvus*)."[50] It is possible that some of the salt blessed by Boniface which suppressed the fire and which "she always kept by her" had also been preserved. Such items were probably kept at Tauberbischofsheim as associated relics which also carried memories of circumstances in which they had been utilized. The cowl which Boniface had given her was presumably kept at Fulda.

Other accounts preserved by Rudolf do not have obvious biblical or hagio-graphical precedents, and can be seen to have some affinities with traditional story-telling. Their contextualization in a monastic setting takes us into the thought-world of Wimborne, Tauberbischofsheim, and Fulda. Particularly striking is the account of the happenings at the grave of the unpopular prioress of Wimborne.[51] The young nuns were so incensed by the memory of her strict discipline that they climbed upon her *tumulus* and cursed her dead body. Subsequently the *tumulus* was found to have subsided some six inches below the ground, which was taken to reflect the severity of God's judgement upon her. Three days of fasting, prayer, and the recitation of the psalms by the nuns who had reviled her, and the intervention of Abbess Tetta, saw the *tumulus* return to its original level, and it was presumed that her soul had been saved from further torment. It seems likely that this story can be seen as preserving 'popular' beliefs about burial places that may have their origin in the pre-Christian past,[52] but have been given an interpretation here com-patible with Christian beliefs on the fate of the soul and provided with a resolution involving Christian ritual. It invites comparison with the even more remarkable foundation story of Minster-in-Thanet,[53] where the evil advisor Thunor was swal-lowed up by the ground and the place where it had happened was marked by the barrow known as "Thunores hlaew." (Among the intriguing possibilities of the Wimborne story is that the *tumulus* of the prioress of Wimborne also took the form

---

[48]   Van Houts, *Memory and Gender*, 93–120.

[49]   Rudolf, *V. Leobae*, chap. 15 (128); Talbot, *Anglo-Saxon Missionaries*, 220–21.

[50]   Rudolf, *V. Leobae*, chap. 11 (126); Talbot, *Anglo-Saxon Missionaries*, 215.

[51]   Rudolf, *V. Leobae*, chap. 4 (123–24); Talbot, *Anglo-Saxon Missionaries*, 208–9.

[52]   Valerie J. Flint, *The Rise of Magic in Early Medieval Europe* (Oxford, 1991), 213–16, 269–73; Sarah Semple, "A Fear of the Past: The Place of the Prehistoric Burial Mound in the Ideology of Middle and Later Anglo-Saxon England," *World Archaeology* 30 (1998): 109–26.

[53]   David Rollason, *The Mildrith Legend: A Study of Early Medieval Hagiography in England* (Leicester, 1982); Stephanie Hollis, "The Minster-in-Thanet Foundation Story," *Anglo-Saxon England* 27 (1998): 41–74; Charlotte Behr, "The Origins of Kingship in Early Medieval Kent," *Early Medieval Europe* 9 (2000): 25–52.

of a burial mound or barrow, a form of burial in vogue among the Anglo-Saxon élite at the time of their conversion.)[54] Further adaptation of traditional story-telling to a monastic context is provided by the second story concerning Abbess Tetta in which her lost keys are returned by a fox.[55] There seems no reason to doubt that these were stories that originated in Anglo-Saxon England, and were recounted by Leoba and her nuns in memory of their spiritual mother Tetta. They are entertaining stories, no doubt polished in the telling, and enjoyed in the communities of both Tauberbischofsheim and Fulda.

A certain element of traditional story-telling may also be apparent in the account of the dead baby found in the mill-pool and which the local people believed was evidence of infanticide by one of the nuns.[56] Like Tetta before her, Leoba used Christian ritual to resolve the situation through recitation of the psalter and a procession around the monastic buildings three times a day behind a crucifix until sufficient psychological pressure had been brought upon the real culprit, a crippled beggar-girl who confessed. There is little of the miraculous in this account. Leoba achieved her results through the ordeal of the cross, a ritual of proof attested in Frankish lawcodes.[57] A second very public display of Christian authority was the incident of the storm where Leoba impressed her lay neighbors by venturing out at its height and quelled it after invoking the intercession of Christ and Mary.[58] Leoba can be perhaps seen in this incident as providing a Christian alternative to the traditional Frankish specialists who raised and calmed storms.[59]

These two accounts are given on the authority of two of the nuns whose reminiscences Rudolf acknowledges that he used: the first is associated with Agatha and the second with Leoba's kinswoman Thecla. Both women are said to have been present when the events took place, and to have urged Leoba to act. It is quite feasible that these accounts preserve a record of events that actually took place, though it is difficult to assess the degrees to which the story has been refined in its retelling by Agatha and Thecla, by the men who took down their accounts, and by Rudolf who wrote the version that we have. However, the fact that the ordeal of the cross had been banned in a decree of Louis the Pious by the time Rudolf wrote his account makes it more likely that the description of its performance originated in the time in which Leoba lived rather than the period

---

[54] Sally Crawford, "Anglo-Saxon Women, Furnished Burial and the Church," in *Women and Religion in Medieval England*, ed. Diana Wood (Oxford, 2003), 1–12; John Blair, *The Church in Anglo-Saxon Society* (Oxford, 2005), 230–33.

[55] Rudolf, *V. Leobae*, chap. 5 (124); Talbot, *Anglo-Saxon Missionaries*, 209–10.

[56] Rudolf, *V. Leobae*, chap. 12 (126–27); Talbot, *Anglo-Saxon Missionaries*, 216–18.

[57] Innes, *State and Society*, 138–39.

[58] Rudolf, *V. Leobae*, chap. 14 (128); Talbot, *Anglo-Saxon Missionaries*, 219–20.

[59] Flint, *Rise of Magic*, 108–16, 188.

in which he was writing. [60] These two records of Leoba's activity as abbess of Tauberbischofsheim vividly evoke the circumstances in which a religious community had to establish its credentials and authority in a converted, but not fully Christianized, area of Germany. [61]

4. Additional Sources for a Biography of Leoba

What is really needed to establish Rudolf's credibility and his methods of working is a comparison of what he says with some independently surviving material. There are not many opportunities to do this, as most of the additional sources in which Leoba is recorded are also connected with her commemoration at Fulda, but such sources as do survive provide an insight into how Rudolf dealt with the factual material with which he was presented. The only piece of writing by Leoba herself which survives is the letter that she sent to Boniface requesting to join him in Germania. [62] The letter has been preserved with other surviving correspondence of Boniface as part of the letter-collection that was put together after his death. Copies of Boniface's letters were presumably available to Rudolf at Fulda, and he refers to letters known to him that Boniface sent to Tetta. [63] Rudolf does not refer to the letter Leoba sent to Boniface from Wimborne in his *Vita Leobae*, but it is possible that it was known to him and was one of the sources he utilized. Material to be found both in the *Vita* and in Leoba's letter includes reference to Leoba's kinship with Boniface being on her mother's side, the names of her parents, and the fact that she was born to them when they were relatively elderly. However, it is also conceivable that Rudolf could have acquired the same information from alternative sources. It would all presumably have been known to Thecla who was herself related to Leoba. What is of particular interest about Leoba's letter to Boniface is that it provides a different interpretation of the circumstances in which she came to Boniface in Germany from that provided by Rudolf. The chief difference is that Rudolf implies that the initiative lay with Boniface, but Leoba's letter makes it clear that it was she who had sought Boniface out. In her short but eloquent letter she reminds Boniface of his obligations towards her as her closest surviving kinsman: when so many of our sources were written by men, it is particularly interesting that we have this letter penned by a woman using kinship ties to put pressure on an older, more

---

[60] Innes, *State and Society*, 138.

[61] Yitzhak Hen, "*Milites Christi Utriusque Sexus*: Gender and the Politics of Conversion in the Circle of Boniface," *Revue Bénédictine* 109 (1999): 17–31.

[62] *Die Briefe*, ed. Tangl, no. 29 (52–53); Talbot, *Anglo-Saxon Missionaries*, 87–88.

[63] Rudolf, *V. Leobae*, chap. 10 (125–26); Talbot, *Anglo-Saxon Missionaries*, 214. These evidently were not included in the exemplar of the surviving letter-collection.

distinguished kinsman.[64] Rudolf's account is not necessarily incorrect, but rather provides a different emphasis in which he implies that Boniface took the initiative in requesting that Leoba be released to assist him when he had learnt of her reputation for learning and holiness. It is highly likely that Boniface did send a formal letter to Abbess Tetta of Wimborne requesting that Leoba join him, a letter that no longer exists, and it is apparent from the extant correspondence that many more letters were exchanged between Boniface and his correspondents in England than have survived. Rudolf has carefully edited his evidence so that matters are presented as occurring as close to Benedictine ideals as possible, and this is probably indicative of a more general way in which he has shaped his evidence for Leoba.[65] His statement that Boniface held Leoba in great affection "not so much because she was related to him on his mother's side as because he knew that by her holiness and wisdom she would confer many benefits by her word and example" is a further example of the same approach. Leoba's letter suggests that their kinship was in fact crucial to the formation of their professional relationship.[66] However, Leoba's letter also helps to confirm other characteristics of her that emerge from Rudolf's portrait—her Latin learning, and also a strong and determined character. One can believe that the author of the letter became the person that Rudolf portrayed.

A further example of Rudolf's care in presenting difficult material that he did not want to suppress altogether comes in his account of Leoba's relations with the royal court. Rudolf recounts Leoba's friendship with Hildegard, the wife of Charlemagne from 771 to 783. According to Rudolf, Leoba was summoned several times to the royal court by Charlemagne and Hildegard and received generous gifts from them.[67] Rudolf assures his readers that "Leoba detested the life at court like poison," and stayed there as little as possible. Her deeper concern was for the various foundations under her supervision, but the patronage of the king and queen, indeed the whole court, was a tribute to Leoba's sagacity and virtue. Here is a good example of Rudolf having his cake and eating it. Leoba's monastic and saintly credentials are upheld, and the possibly questionable visits to the royal court are justified so that this significant information about her influence in the highest circles can be relayed. It is another area in which Leoba acts as heir of Boniface, continuing his influence at the royal court, and in which Fulda might want to stress its position as heir of both of them in the reign of Hildegard's son

---

[64] It is not known exactly how Leoba was related to Boniface. He seems to be of the same generation as her parents, so some such relationship as first cousins once removed may be indicated.

[65] Hollis, *Women and the Church*, 270–300.

[66] On this topic see Lutz von Padberg, *Heilige und Familie: Studien zur Bedeutung familiengebundener Aspekte in den Viten des Verwandten- und Schülerkreises um Willibrord, Bonifatius und Liudger*, 2nd edn. (Mainz, 1997).

[67] Rudolf, *V. Leobae*, chap. 18 (129); Talbot, *Anglo-Saxon Missionaries*, 222–23.

Louis the Pious.[68] Confirmation of Leoba's good standing with the royal court comes from a charter of 782 in which Charlemagne granted to Lull's monastery of Hersfeld the entail of an estate at Schornsheim "infra fisco nostro," which had previously been granted to Leoba for her lifetime by royal gift and on which she was still living at the time that the grant was made.[69] Rudolf refers to Leoba living at Schornsheim in her later years, and that she died on the estate, but says only that she had moved there on the advice of Bishop Lull of Mainz (whose agreement that she should continue to live on the estate at Schornsheim until her death is referred to in the Hersfeld charter).[70] However, as the reference to her removal there is sandwiched between two accounts of her friendship with Hildegard, one suspects that Rudolf knew very well that the grant had been one result of this friendship, and that perhaps behind it was a desire that Leoba should have an estate more conveniently placed for access to Mainz and other royal residences in the region.[71]

In the Bonifacian letter collection three letters survive that were sent to Leoba. There is a general letter from Boniface that addresses her alongside Thecla and other religious women active in Germany,[72] and a short letter to her in which he grants permission for her to give instruction to a certain girl and which mentions the priest Torhthat who is also named by Rudolf.[73] A rather enigmatic letter from Lull assures her of his affection for her, and perhaps hints at some difficulties in the relationship between these two followers of Boniface.[74] Even though these additional sources provide scant material for a biography of Leoba, collectively they give an insight into how Rudolf treated potentially difficult material in his *Vita* of Leoba. They also demonstrate that Rudolf did not necessarily suppress such material, but rather neutralized or adapted it to his overall purposes. Aspects of Leoba's personality, learning, and high standing at the Frankish court in these additional sources seem to confirm the overall impression of her as given by Rudolf.

---

[68] Possibly a parallel with the contemporary role of Hraban Maur is intended: Muschiol, "Königshof, Kloster und Mission," 107–8.

[69] *Urkundenbuch der Reichsabtei Hersfeld*, ed. Weirich, no. 17 (29–31). The original charter survives as well as a later cartulary copy.

[70] Rudolf, *V. Leobae*, chap. 20–21 (130); Talbot, *Anglo-Saxon Missionaries*, 223–24.

[71] Innes, *State and Society*, 185, though Leoba must have been quite elderly when she died, perhaps approaching eighty.

[72] *Die Briefe*, ed. Tangl, no. 67 (139–40).

[73] *Die Briefe*, ed. Tangl, no. 96 (216–17); Rudolf, *V. Leobae*, chap. 21 (130).

[74] *Die Briefe*, ed. Tangl, no. 100 (223). For the rather difficult personality of Lull, see James Palmer, "The 'Vigorous Rule' of Bishop Lull: Between Bonifatian Mission and Carolingian Church Control," *Early Medieval Europe* 13 (2005): 249–76.

5. Leoba and Anglo-Saxon Female Monasticism

Leoba's activities as abbess of Tauberbischofsheim appear unusual in the wider context of the role of women in the Carolingian church and have been seen as more typical of the Anglo-Saxon traditions in which she was raised.[75] The abbesses about whom we are best informed for Anglo-Saxon England tend, like Hild and Ælfflaed of Whitby, to have been of royal birth and connected with Northumbria. The majority of the most prestigious and longer-lived nunneries were royal foundations, and as there were a number of different kingdoms and competing lineages within those kingdoms, all of whom wanted their own foundations run by female relatives, there were a large number of royal nunneries.[76] But women of the nobility might also be heads of religious communities. For instance, when King Æthelbert of the South Saxons granted land to Diosza to found a minster at Wittering, Diosza then transferred the land to his sister, presumably with the intention that she would supervise the foundation.[77] The closest parallel from Anglo-Saxon England for an abbess of a major religious community who was the kinswoman of a bishop is Æthelburh of Barking, who was the sister of Bishop Eorcenwald of London and known to us principally from Bede's excerpts from a lost *libellus* of the nuns of Barking.[78] It is nevertheless probably true to say that as a member of the nobility in royal service, Leoba had greater opportunities to develop her ecclesiastical career by traveling to Germany than by staying in England, and especially if she had stayed at Wimborne whose abbesses (as far as we can tell) were recruited from the West Saxon royal house.[79] The same was probably also true for Boniface, to whose trajectory the fortunes of Leoba were, of course, inseparably linked, as it was probably apparent to him by the time he decided to work in Germany in 716 that he was unlikely to be promoted to the position of bishop in Wessex in the near future.[80]

The question of whether Leoba's activities as a religious leader for the lay inhabitants of the area surrounding Tauberbischofsheim reflects what might have been expected of her Anglo-Saxon counterparts forms part of a wider debate about how pastoral care was managed in Anglo-Saxon England ca. 700–ca. 900

---

[75] Hollis, *Women and the Church.*

[76] Yorke, *Nunneries*, 17–46.

[77] *Charters of Selsey*, ed. Susan Kelly, Anglo-Saxon Charters 6 (London, 1998), no. 7 (37–40).

[78] Bede, *HE* 4.6–10, ed. Colgrave and Mynors, 354–65.

[79] Yorke, "Bonifacian Mission."

[80] Barbara Yorke, "Boniface's Insular Background," in *Bonifatius—Leben und Nachwirken: Die Gestaltung der christlichen Europa im Frühmittelalter*, ed. Franz J. Felten, Jörg Jarnut, und Lutz E. von Padberg, Quellen und Abhandlungen zur mittelrheinischen Kirchengeschichte (Mainz, 2007), 23–37.

and whether monastic communities were involved in its provision.[81] At the very least, all religious communities are likely to have had some responsibility for the spiritual welfare of the tenants on their often extensive estates.[82] The closest parallels for the pastoral activities of Leoba are provided in the accounts of Abbess Ælfflaed of Whitby, the daughter of King Oswiu of Northumbria, whom we see in the Lives of St. Cuthbert intervening in the affairs of peasant tenants on her estates.[83] However, in England there were probably always more priests available and so less need for abbesses to be involved in lives of the laity in ways which might have been deemed inappropriate for nuns by Christian authorities such as Bede and for women of the highest social class by their families, if not by the women themselves.[84] The impressive displays of Christian ritual which Leoba is said to have organized to combat difficult circumstances provide an insight into how a religious community might seek to edify and influence a partially-converted lay community. They provide a possible guide to what could have happened in England as well, but they occur in a specific Frankish context that may not be transferable in all its details. For instance, there is no certain evidence that the ceremony of the ordeal of the cross was utilized in eighth-century England.

By her coming to Germany, Leoba's role in the church had developed in ways that it probably would not have done if she had stayed in Wessex, but the western part of Britain that she came from did have some parallels to the situation she and Boniface experienced in Germany. Western Wessex was an area taken under Anglo-Saxon control relatively recently, where Anglo-Saxon settlers were in the minority and so particularly dependent on one another. It is likely that kinship relations and obligations became particularly important in such circumstances.[85] The British (i.e. Celtic) majority had been Christians for centuries, but, in the eyes of Anglo-Saxon churchmen, some of their practices were aberrant and in a need of 'correction,' which was, of course, one of Boniface's specialities in his Continental career. As far as we can tell, a number of the major religious houses, including Wimborne and the one in which Lull had been trained (which cannot be precisely located), were controlled by women.[86] Therefore both Boniface and

---

[81] Catherine Cubitt, "The 747 Council of *Clofesho*," in *Pastoral Care Before the Parish*, ed. John Blair and Richard Sharpe (Leicester, 1992), 193–211; Eric Cambridge and David Rollason, "The Pastoral Organization of the Anglo-Saxon Church: A Review of the 'Minster Hypothesis'," *Early Medieval Europe* 4 (1995): 87–104; John Blair, "Ecclesiastical Organization and Pastoral Care in Anglo-Saxon England," *Early Medieval Europe* 4 (1995): 193–212; idem, *Church in Anglo-Saxon Society*, 153–56.

[82] Alan Thacker, "Monks, Preaching and Pastoral Care in England," in *Pastoral Care Before the Parish*, ed. Blair and Sharpe, 137–70.

[83] See n. 8 above; Blair, *Church in Anglo-Saxon Society*, 212–13.

[84] Yorke, *Nunneries*, 123–27, 130–31, 187–96.

[85] Yorke, "Boniface's Insular Background."

[86] Yorke, "Bonifacian Mission."

Leoba would have come to Germany with an expectation that women religious might play a significant role in Christianizing a newly subjugated area. One can note that the willingness to draw upon the services of their kinswomen is a feature of the West Saxon missions to Germania that was apparently not found among those of their Northumbrian contemporaries.

6. Conclusion

Like all works of hagiography, Rudolf's *Vita Leobae* was the product of a particular time and place. There were a variety of reasons why the cult of Leoba was of particular importance for Fulda in the first half of the ninth century, and her contemporary relevance when the *Vita* was composed is reflected in the way she has been presented. But Leoba had died only fifty years before Rudolf wrote, and her activities were well within the reach of a living oral tradition. Rudolf's careful marshaling of his witnesses, although in itself something of a hagiographical topos, is nevertheless specific and demonstrates that he could call ultimately on the testimonies of people who had known her. These memories of Leoba were themselves refracted through various literary and oral traditions of storytelling that had their origins in particular Anglo-Saxon and Frankish contexts. They nevertheless appear to take us close to various aspects of Leoba's life and to the circumstances in which religious might find themselves when living among partially Christianized lay people.[87] If Rudolf sometimes does present Leoba as "an honorary man"—to use Carol Clover's phrase for how we should visualize influential women in the early medieval world[88]—this may be apt, since her position as Boniface's closest kin gave her unusual opportunities and significance that were shared by few religious women who were not of royal or comital birth. The 'real' Leoba will always be elusive, but preserved in Rudolf's Life of her are glimpses of the impact she had made on those who lived and worked with her.

---

[87] Hen, *"Milites Christi."*
[88] Carol Clover, "Regardless of Sex: Men, Women and Power in Early Northern Europe," *Speculum* 69 (1993): 363–87.

AMIATINUS IN ITALY: THE AFTERLIFE
OF AN ANGLO-SAXON BOOK

RICHARD MARSDEN

1. Introduction

One of the great achievements of the twin monastery of Wearmouth-Jarrow under Abbot Ceolfrith at the end of the seventh and beginning of the eighth centuries was the production of three large single-volume Latin Bibles. Two were for use in the monastic churches at Monkwearmouth and at Jarrow; one of these disappeared without trace, but a dozen leaves of the other are extant in the British Library.[1] The third pandect (and almost certainly the most sumptuous of the three) survives complete, having been exiled to the relative safety of Italy in 716, soon after completion.[2] It had been made especially as a gift for St. Peter's in Rome, and seems to have been delivered as planned, but it did not stay there. By at least the early eleventh century, and perhaps sooner, it was at the Tuscan monastery of San Salvatore, Monte Amiata, where it remained for another seven hundred years, until the suppression of the monastery at the end of the eighteenth century. It was then taken to Florence, where today it is shelved in the Biblioteca Medicea Laurentiana, as Amiatino 1 — the Codex Amiatinus. It is the oldest complete Latin Bible extant, and scholarly interest has naturally

---

[1] For a detailed account of the production of Ceolfrith's pandects and of their texts, see R. Marsden, *The Text of the Old Testament in Anglo-Saxon England*, CSASE 15 (Cambridge, 1995), chaps. 3–5. A valuable bibliography for Amiatinus, to 2001, is in Michael Gorman, "The Codex Amiatinus: A Guide to the Legends and Bibliography," *Studi Medievali*, 3rd ser., 44 (2003): 863–910, at 897–910. A CD-ROM of the manuscript (made after disbinding) is available from Sismel: *La Bibbia Amiatina/The Codex Amiatinus* (Florence, 2000), and a half-size facsimile from La Meta (Florence, 2002).

[2] All the evidence suggests that Amiatinus was the third to be made, despite the doubts raised (on very flimsy grounds) by Barbara Apelian Beall, in "The Codex Amiatinus and the Significance of a Production Error," *Manuscripta* 40 (1996): 148–56.

Hans Sauer and Joanna Story, eds., *Anglo-Saxon England and the Continent*. With the assistance of Gaby Waxenberger. Essays in Anglo-Saxon Studies, vol. 3. MRTS 394. Tempe: ACMRS, 2011.   [ISBN 978-0-86698-442-3]

been focused on its historical importance as a witness to the earliest forms of the Vulgate text. But manuscript Bibles rarely escape later tampering, and Amiatinus was no exception. Many emendations, additions, and annotations were made over a long period, perhaps as late as the sixteenth century. This textual afterlife of Amiatinus has received scant attention, and here I offer a preliminary, exploratory survey, set against an account of the Italian history of the codex. Parts of that history remain opaque, and parts are obscured by the layers of myth which Amiatinus has always attracted. As Michael Gorman has observed, "it is difficult to think of another important Latin manuscript of which so much pure fiction has been written by so many for so long."[3]

2. Early Years in Italy

How, why, and exactly when Amiatinus reached San Salvatore are among the questions which have yet to be answered. The monastery lies in the province of Siena at Monte Amiata, some 5000 feet up (= ca. 1600 m) in the Apennines, about 100 miles (= ca. 160 km) northwest of Rome and a more or less equal distance southeast of Florence. It is close by the Via Francigena, the road which most travelers from the north would have passed along to get to Rome. The last definite early medieval sighting we have of the huge codex (weighing some 75 pounds or 34 kilos) is in the south of France, at Langres. The anonymous author of the *Vita Ceolfridi* records that Abbot Ceolfrith, though old and ill, had accompanied the eighty monks who set out from Northumbria in the spring of 716, with Rome as their goal, but he died at Langres.[4] "Nevertheless," the chronicler tells us, "some [of the party] accomplished the planned journey to Rome in order to deliver the gifts which [Ceolfrith] had sent, among which was the pandect, as we mentioned, translated from the Hebrew and Greek by the blessed Jerome."[5] This assertion must have been based on the report of the monks who eventually returned home to Northumbria. Furthermore, the chronicler tells us that the monks brought a letter from Pope Gregory, in which Ceolfrith's 'gift' (*munus*) was acknowledged 'as an everlasting memorial' (*ad aeternam sui memoriam*) to St. Peter.[6] The exact nature of the gift is not spelled out, but in the context it can scarcely be doubted that the Bible is meant.

---

[3] Gorman, "A Guide," 875.

[4] For the whole narrative, see *Vita Ceolfridi*, chaps. 22–39, in *Venerabilis Baedae Opera Historica*, ed. C. Plummer, 2 vols. (Oxford, 1896), 1: 395–404, with Ceolfrith's death in chap. 36 (at 402).

[5] *Vita Ceolfridi*, ed. Plummer, 402: "[Q]uidam uero dispositum Romam iter peregere, delaturi munera quae miserat. In quibus uidelicet muneribus erat Pandectes, ut diximus, interpretatione beati Hieronimi presbiteri ex Hebreo et Greco fonte transfusus."

[6] *Vita Ceolfridi*, ed. Plummer, 403.

However, a tradition at San Salvatore itself, assiduously promoted to this day by the monastery's incumbents, insists that the codex in fact never reached Rome at all. According to the account given in a local guidebook, one of the Bibles of Cassiodorus had reached Wearmouth-Jarrow from Italy, and Abbot Ceolfrith had decided to have copies made to distribute to all the dioceses of England.[7] But he wanted pontifical approval of the text, and so a special copy was entrusted to an English monk, who was to take it to Rome in order that its text might be authenticated against that of Jerome's original; this, Ceolfrith believed, was still preserved in the pontifical archives. On the journey, while staying at San Salvatore, the English monk died, and the astute abbot of the house hid the codex to thwart a plan by some of his own monks to take it on to Rome.[8] He had Ceolfrith's name erased from the dedication at the front of the volume and replaced with his own—"Peter of the Lombards." It is a nice story, but, even if we ignore the words of the English chronicler cited above, there is another, more troublesome, problem with it. The monastery at San Salvatore appears to have been founded, at the earliest, in the 740s, far too late to shelter travelers in 716. Legend attributes its foundation to the Lombard king Ratchis in 745, though in fact a nobleman called Erfo, collaborating with Ratchis' brother, may have been responsible, a few years before this date.[9]

There is thus no reason to doubt that Amiatinus reached Rome, but what happened then is a mystery. Gorman surmises that the book would have been placed for safekeeping in the sacristy of St. Peter's Basilica, rather than in the papal archive at the Lateran Palace, but nothing in the book itself or in surviving documents gives any clues.[10] Whatever the reasons for the removal from Rome, it is not in itself surprising that such a fine codex should have ended up at San Salvatore, for this was one of the wealthiest and most important Benedictine abbeys in Italy in the early Middle Ages. Given over to the Cistercians in 1230, it functioned continually until its suppression in 1782.[11] As Gorman's work has now shown, at least by the eleventh century, and probably before this, it had an active scriptorium, and its library of manuscripts rivaled those of Bobbio and

---

[7] Roberto Corvini, *Guida e storia: Abbazia del SS. Salvatore al Monte Amiata in Abbadia San Salvatore Siena*, 3rd edn. (Monte Amiata, 1997), 47–48.

[8] "It may be said in his defense," suggests the guidebook (48), "that in all probability he knew how useless it would be to seek the original at Rome, where everything had been destroyed by the barbarians."

[9] See M. Gorman, "Manuscript Books at Monte Amiata during the Eleventh Century," *Scriptorium* 56 (2002): 225–93, pl. 11–18, at 226. The Monte Amiata guidebook conveniently omits a date for the arrival of the English monk carrying the codex.

[10] Gorman, "A Guide," 874–75.

[11] In the seventeenth century, the early history of the abbey was chronicled by Ferdinando Ughelli (1595–1670), in the twentieth by Wilhelm Kurze; see Gorman, "Manuscript Books," esp. 225–34.

Monte Cassino.[12] We know for certain only that Amiatinus was at Monte Amiata by the early eleventh century, for at this point Ceolfrith's dedication, written
on the verso of the first leaf of the volume, was copied by a scribe called Bonizo
into a manuscript of Gregory's *Moralia in Iob*, now in the Vatican Library.[13] By
this time the most famous Italian emendation to the codex—a modification of
the dedication, on fol. 1v, alluded to above—had already been made. Originally
the elegiac distichs had read:

> *corpus* ad eximii merito
>   uenerabile *petri*
> quem caput ecclesiae
>   dedicat alta fides
> *ceolfridus anglorum*
>   extremis de finib[us] abbas
> deuoti affectus
>   pignora mitto mei
> meque meosq[ue] optans
>   tanti inter gaudia patris
> in caelis memorem
>   semper habere locum

['To the body of the illustrious Peter, justly to be honored, whom lofty faith
consecrates head of the church, I, Ceolfrith, abbot from the farthest ends
of England, send tokens of my devoted feeling, desiring for me and mine
that we may have for ever a remembered place in the heavens, among the
joys of so great a father.']

In a blatant act of appropriation, however, an Italian scribe targeted the four
words italicized above, thereby quite destroying the original scansion. *Corpus*
was changed to *cenobium* and *Petri* to *saluatoris*, thus giving 'To the monastery
of the illustrious Savior [i.e., San Salvatore]', and *Ceolfridus Anglorum* became
Petrus Langobardorum, giving 'Peter of the Lombards '.[14] There was a 'Peter' who

---

[12] Gorman's invaluable "Manuscript Books" identifies a score of volumes copied
there, and more are likely to be found. Interestingly, one of the most popular writers
represented was Bede. What remains of the great library is now widely scattered. As early
as the eleventh century, many of the books went into the Bandini collection, now in the
Vatican Library. After the suppression of the monastery, most of those remaining went to
libraries in Rome, Perugia, and of course Florence.

[13] Vatican City, Biblioteca Apostolica Vaticana, Barb. lat. 573, fol. 1v; see Gorman, "A
Guide," 864, 875, 890. Before Gorman drew attention to this entry, the earliest cited record
showing the presence of Amiatinus at Monte Amiata was from the fifteenth century.

[14] To cope with the awkward syntax of the new version, Gorman translates, "From
the farthest ends of the earth, I, Peter of the Lombards . . .": Gorman, "Manuscript
Books," 255, n. 100.

became abbot of San Salvatore towards the end of the ninth century, and A. M. Bandini, the late-eighteenth-century prefect and cataloger of the Biblioteca Laurenziana, repeating the theory of Ferdinando Ughelli, postulated that the great Bible had been presented at this time by Theobold, archbishop of the Chiusi diocese, in which San Salvatore stood.[15] There is no specific evidence for this, however, and in fact there were at least four abbots by the name of Peter in the ninth and tenth centuries: the one mentioned, who took office in 886 or 887, and others who succeeded in 830, 916, and 991. As Sabina Magrini has noted, there is no good reason to prefer any of them.[16] Gorman has suggested that the codex could have been acquired by Abbot Winizo for the consecration of the monastery's new church in 1035.[17] It was under the abbacy of Winizo (ca. 996–1035) that San Salvatore reached the peak of its power. Gorman speculates that Amiatinus may have been among the many relics displayed at the consecration, though it is not mentioned in the official account of the event.[18] However, even if it were indeed on display, it could of course have been acquired much earlier in the monastery's history.

The replacement words in the dedication are easy enough to detect, for they were added in an uncial less monumental than the original and in a very different (now yellow-brown) ink. Yet they effectively hid the origin of the Bible for many centuries. Indeed, so successful had been Ceolfrith's desire to emulate all things Roman — including scribal habits — that the book was assumed to be Italian, and a tradition arose associating it with Gregory the Great, who some believed might have written it himself. Bandini, on the other hand, assigned it to the mid-sixth century and associated it with an abbot called Servandus.[19] It was not until the end of the nineteenth century that the English origin of Amiatinus was recognized — by an Italian, G. B. De Rossi, who identified the codex as the pandect which Ceolfrith had taken to Italy, as recounted by Bede in chap. 5 of his *Historia abbatum*.[20] It took a few more years for the exact original wording of the dedication to be established, but finally F. J. A. Hort drew attention to the

---

[15] *Bibliotheca Leopoldina Laurentiana seu catalogus manuscriptorum qui iussu Petri Leopoldi . . . in Laurentianam translati sunt quae in singulis codicibus continentur*, 3 vols. (Florence, 1791–1793), 1: 701–32, at 701–3 and 708–11.

[16] S. Magrini, "*Per difetto del legatore. . .* : storia delle rilegature della Bibbia Amiatina in Laurenziana," *Quinio* 3 (2001): 137–67, at 149.

[17] Gorman, "A Guide," 875.

[18] An assertion to the contrary by Ughelli in the seventeenth century is unreliable; see Gorman, "Manuscript Books," 228 and n. 11.

[19] *Bibliotheca Leopoldina*, 1: 704–5; and see Marsden, *Text of the Old Testament*, 89.

[20] 'De origine historia indicibus scrinii et bibliothecae sedis apostolicae commentatio', in *Codices Palatini Latini Bibliothecae Vaticanae*, ed. H. Stevenson and G. B. De Rossi (Rome, 1886), 1: lxxv–lxxviii; and *Venerabilis Baedae Opera Historica*, ed. Plummer, 1: 379.

anonymous *Vita Ceolfridi*, with its copy of the dedication, which removed the remaining uncertainties.[21] Apart from a brief return to Rome in the sixteenth century, described below, Amiatinus stayed at San Salvatore until the monastery was suppressed in 1782. Its books were apparently left mouldering for several years, until the pious Emperor Leopold I (1765–1790) heard about them and gave orders for a rescue mission, as a result of which Amiatinus and other books duly arrived in Florence.[22] After a brief stay in the convent of San Frediano in Cestello, they were deposited in the library attached to the beautiful church of Laurenziana.[23]

3. Intervention in the Text

Italian interventions in the text of Amiatinus consist of emendations of the text itself (by correction or addition), liturgical additions (lections and musical notation), and other miscellaneous additions (including chapter numbers and Greek letters).

3.1. The Emendation Process

The overall impression given by the two thousand written pages of Amiatinus (with its 1016 leaves) is of an immaculately produced manuscript, copied with extreme care and great accuracy. For the most part, the exemplar texts used by the Northumbrians (serving also as script models) were Italian and were of a high standard, although in the three hundred years since Jerome's day textual variation had become widespread.[24] Nevertheless, those pages carry many hundreds of emendations, ranging from the alteration of single letters to the addition or substitution of words or even of whole verses. Original scribal errors of all sorts averaged between one and two per page, in both the Old and the New Testaments.[25] Many of the minor errors (mostly misspellings or the omission of syllables) were put right straightaway by the copyists. Most of the others were

---

[21] F. J. A. Hort, *The Academy* 773 [26 February 1887], 148–49. For a fuller account of the discovery process, see Marsden, *Text of the Old Testament*, 87–90.

[22] *Bibliotheca Leopoldina*, 1: 704–5.

[23] *Novelle lettararie per l'anno mdcclxxxv*, I [Florence, 7 January 1789], 1, and Gorman, "Manuscript Books," 261. The two other identified Amiatinan manuscripts in the Laurenziana are Amiatino 2 (a collection of hagiographical texts) and Amiatino 3 (mainly the works of Hrabanus).

[24] A few exemplars were non-Italian, such as the Irish one used for Psalms, in Jerome's 'Hebrew' version, and it was of rather poor quality. The exemplar for Wisdom, too, seems to have been poor, though its origin is not known.

[25] For a survey of errors and Northumbrian corrections, see Marsden, *Text of the Old Testament*, 184–89.

spotted and corrected before the codex left Northumbria, in a process of check-ing which testifies to the extreme care lavished on the pandect project. The script used for the majority of the 'in-house' corrections made to the main uncial text was a variation on the smaller, less formal uncial used in the manuscript for *capit-ula* and other ancillary material; sometimes it has a distinctive sloping aspect, as found in the text of the canon diagrams in the opening quire. The ink, like that of the main text, is dark brown to black.

Amiatinus left England in 716, calligraphically and textually in prime con-dition. The majority of the subsequent alterations to the text—most of them occur in the Old Testament—were thus emendations, not corrections. The cal-ligraphic variety shown in both corrections and emendations, and the diversity of textual traditions on which the latter seem to be based, bear witness to a cumula-tive process spread over a considerable period of time, probably some six or seven hundred years. There are a few cases where it is not possible to be certain whether minor corrections are Northumbrian or Italian. One such is the conversion of the first *e* to *i* in *oreretur* on fol. 11v (Gen. 2:5), by a process of erasure and faint over-writing. The original Amiatinan form of the word occurs in one or two other early manuscripts, and it is perfectly feasible that it was in the Northumbrian scribe's exemplar and that the change was a later, Italian, one.

An interesting illustration of the problems of assessing the emendation pro-cess is given by the reconstruction of some words in 1 Kgs. 19:18–19, which seem to have become destroyed, perhaps progressively, by a hole which had developed in the parchment on fol. 239r, at the bottom of the left-hand column, after the initial copying. The damage may have distorted some remaining letters, which would account for the fact that part of the restoration is written, apparently, on erasures; it seems unlikely that the latter were part of a deliberate emendation process. The affected passage is given below. The first column shows the text as it probably appeared originally, with the letters which were eventually lost given in italics; the second column shows the text with all the reconstruction, given in bold, completed. The spacing approximates to that in the manuscript (Fig. 11.1, fol. 239r).

*et nu*ntiauit ei omnia quae	n untiauit ei omnia quae **fece**
*fece*rat sibi Saul	rat sibi Saul **ueni**
*et abieru*nt ipse et Samuhel	unt ipse et Samuhel **&**
*et mora*ti sunt in Nahioth	**pfec**ti sunt in Nahioth
*nuntia*tum est autem	**dictum** est autem

The uneven fading of the inks used and the general untidiness of the additions make judgments difficult, but restoration was probably done in two stages, at widely different times. The additions on the first line (*nu*, which is squeezed just above the hole in the parchment, and *fece*) seem to belong to the first stage. They are in brown-black ink and in an uncial which mimics that of the original script, though it is not one of the Northumbrian corrector's scripts (despite its slightly sloping aspect). The other additions vary in their ink color and size: *Ueni, &* and *u* are large and very pale; *p[ro]fecti* and *Dic* are somewhat smaller and appear to have been originally in brown-black ink, but in the case of *Dic* this is partly faded. All the letters are in minuscule, and *Dic* has a capital *D*. Unidentifiable fragments of letters are visible between the hole in the parchment and *p*, and, on the same line, just before the hole.

The most logical interpretation of this evidence is that a smallish hole first destroyed the start of the fourth and fifth lines up from the bottom of the column, and that a comparatively early Italian restorer, at stage one, supplied the lost text, though omitting *et* and supplying *ueniunt* for *abierunt*. Then the hole expanded further downwards, and the start of the next three lines was affected, necessitating the restoration at stage two, much later, when *profec[ti]* was supplied for *mora[ti]* and *dic[tum]* for *nuntia[tum]*.[26] This new text is of great interest. The variants *ueniunt* for *abierunt*, *p[ro]fecti* for *morati*, and *dictum* for *nuntiatum* are not paralleled in any other collated Old Latin or Vulgate manuscript, nor in patristic citations. Reference may have been made by the restorers to exemplars which followed textual traditions no longer extant, but it is also possible that the words were simply chosen because they were appropriate in the context and, in the case of *dictum*, because it fitted in the available space. The change from *morati* to *profecti* is just about acceptable, though it produces a tautology. These modifications are a useful reminder of the arbitrary mechanisms by which new Vulgate textual traditions may arise.

At least two phases of Italian emendation are confirmed by this example, but in fact, as already indicated, we must think in terms of a manuscript in more or less continuous use over many centuries, with alterations being made intermittently during much or most of that time. Consideration of ink color (as it appears to us today) allows crude distinctions to be made between different corrections or emendations, and the varied use of uncial and minuscule scripts adds another dimension. Certain groups of emendations can certainly be identified as being contemporary with each other, and perhaps by one hand, but at no time did a single corrector or emendator work his way systematically through the manuscript.

3.1.1. Corrections

There are about one hundred corrections of simple errors which had been missed by the Northumbrian revisers; they are distributed throughout the codex. On fol. 491r, for instance, *tifica* has been supplied to *bea[tifica]bit* (Sir. 45:8) and, on fol. 754r, *ma* to *ani[ma]bus* (1 Macc. 2:40), this error having occurred at the end of a line. In both cases a corrector imitates informally the original uncial script; the

---

[26] On the verso of the leaf, the damage affected only the *m* of *sententiam* (1 Kgs. 20:12), a loss made good with a suspension mark, probably added at stage two.

ink is pale brown. On fol. 31r (Gen. 29:33), omitted *que* has been added above the line in a dark brown ink, using a finely-written *q* with a long descender and a semi-colon as suspension mark.[27] On fol. 533v, *dero* is emended to *dedero* by the addition above of *de*, in which the ascender of the uncial *d* is horizontal and the loop of the *e* almost invisible. Possibly the same hand added a required extra *f* above *efuderis* on fol. 131r. However, on the same page, the correction of *liberit* to *liberabit* (Isa. 58:11), by the addition above of *ab*, is in caroline minuscule, written in a mid-brown ink. Minuscule is used also, but by a different hand and in darker ink, to add omitted *facit* after *habitare* (1 Esd. 5:12) on fol. 734v.[28] On fol. 341v, eight words from 1 Chron. 14:11–12 had been omitted by homoeoteleuton (*ibi David et dixit diuisit D[eu]s inimicos meos*); they are supplied in a neat uncial resembling that of the Northumbrian scribes but different in several ways. Notable are the use of a capital *D* in each case and an uncial *M* in which the first two minims form a completely closed circle and the third is correspondingly round. This may be the same hand which, as will be seen below, was responsible for several additions in Amiatinus.

The rationale for some alterations is not clear. On fol. 91v, for instance, an already misspelled *superlectili* (Lev. 8:10, for *supellectili*) has been supplied with an extra *p* (in an apparent minuscule form) above the first one, while the absence of a second *l* is ignored, but the erroneous *r* in the word has been marked for omission with two dots beneath (presumably at the same time). It seems to be the same hand, on the same page, which has corrected *uasi* to *basi* (Lev. 8:11), by the superimposition of a minuscule *b* on the *u*. Some orthographical emendations must have been made to bring the Amiatinan readings in line with other traditions which were being compared. In Num. 4:6–14, for example, where *ianthinarum* occurs six times (on fol. 115v), *ci* has been added above in four cases (in a fairly pale ink and possibly by the scribe of a big addition, noted below, on fol. 131r) to produce *iacinthinarum* (Num. 4:10, 11, 12, and 14), a version otherwise known only in two eleventh-century manuscripts from Monte Cassino and, as a correction, in the Tours Octateuch (ca. 800).[29] In Num. 4:14, the original reading in Amiatinus was in fact *iantinarum*, but an *h* had been added above, while

---

[27] It may be contrasted with the same addition made on fol. 53v (Exod. 3:2), where a Northumbrian uncial *q* and a short dash as suspension mark indicate the work of the original scribe or at a contemporary corrector.

[28] The form of the verb, *facit*, reflects the usage in the eighth-century Maurdramnus Bible (Amiens, Bibliothèque Municipale, 6; *CLA* 6: no. 707) and in some tenth- to twelfth-century Spanish Bibles. The perfect tense *fecit* is more common and more correct.

[29] Monte Cassino, Biblioteca del Monumento Nazionale di Monte Cassino, 520 and 531, and Tours, Bibliothèque Municipale, 10. There is much variation in the spelling of the word among the collated manuscripts; see *Biblia Sacra iuxta latinam vulgatam versionem ad codicum fidem*, ed. H. Quentin et al., 18 vols. (Rome, 1926–1995) [hereafter *Biblia Sacra*], 3 (*Libri Numerorum–Deuteronomii*), 92–94.

the manuscript was still in Northumbria. Oddly, two earlier occurrences of *ian-thinarum*, in Num. 4:6 and 8, were ignored by the Italian corrector.

3.1.2. Additions

Additions to the text, some of them extensive, constitute the most prominent aspect of the emendation of Amiatinus. An interesting one has been made in pale ink to the first colon of Eccles. 2:16 on fol. 438r, whose original text is *non enim erit memoria sapientis similiter ut stulti in perpetuum* (Fig. 11.2, fol. 438r). A scribe began to write his addition immediately to the right of *in perpetuum*, getting as far as *par obit*, but changed his mind, partly erased what he had written, and superimposed a crudely drawn cross as an omission mark. He then entered the whole addition, *par obitus memoria dispar*, marked by another cross, at the bottom of the column. Notable in the curiously untidy but basically uncial script are a minuscule *b* with very tall ascender, prominent wedges on some letters, the 9-shaped suspension mark for the syllable *us*, a capital *D* in *dispar*, and the use, in *memoria*, of first a capital *M* and then an uncial of the sort noted above, in which the first two minims form a closed circle. The four-word addition, following on from the statement that 'there shall be no remembrance of the wise, any more than of the fool,' seems to say (somewhat subversively), 'equal in death, [but] unequal in memory'. Its origin has not been traced, and it appears to have no Greek, Old Latin, or patristic precedents. It does, however, occur in four other Vulgate manuscripts, in three cases integrally and once as an addition. All are from northern France or Germany, and date from the later eighth or early ninth centuries.[30] This may indicate an early date also for the addition to Amiatinus.

The same hand seems to have been responsible for a twenty-three-word addition to Num. 20:6, above the first column on fol. 131r. It is signaled, both in the text (after *corruerunt proni in terram*) and before the added words, by a vertical chain of three tight circles with a short straight stroke hung below, a *signe de renvoi* used nowhere else in the codex. The ink is again pale, and a capital *D* alternates with two uncial forms of the letter. The addition appeared first in the eighth-century predecessors of the Theodulfian and Alcuinian Bibles, and then in those Bibles themselves.[31] Thereafter it spread almost universally, reaching

---

[30] They are the Maurdramnus Bible; Stuttgart, Württembergische Landesbibliothek, HB. II. 35 (*CLA* 9: no. 1358); Sankt Gallen, Stiftsbibliothek, 28; and Metz, Bibliothèque Municipale, 7 (*CLA* 6: 786), where the words were added by a second hand. The latter three Bibles have known textual inter-connections: Bonifatius Fischer, *Lateinische Bibelhandschriften im frühen Mittelalter*, Vetus Latina: Aus der Geschichte der lateinischen Bibel 11 (Freiburg, 1985), 183.

[31] There are small variations between the various witnesses (see *Biblia Sacra*, 3, 189). The Amiatinus version is: "clamaueruntque ad dominum atque dixerunt domine deus exaudi clamorem populi huius et aperies thesaurum tuum fontem aque uiuae ut satiati cesset murmuratio eorum."

the Bibles of Monte Cassino, for instance, by the late tenth century. The scribe responsible for the additions to Eccles. 2:16 and Num. 20:6 may also be the one who both supplied omitted words in 1 Chron. 14:11–12, noted above, and wrote at least some of the interpolations in Kings, which are discussed below.

There are a number of additions to the text of Amiatinus made in minuscule scripts. On fol. 499r, *alba* has been added above and to the right of *lana* in the third colon of Isa. 1:18 (*et si fuerint rubra quasi uermiculus uelut lana erunt*), in very black ink and in a minuscule which I have not noted anywhere else in the manuscript. The amplification, which originated in the Septuagint, is rare in the earlier medieval period, though it was used by Jerome in his commentary on Isaiah and by Gildas in his *De excidio Britanniae*.[32] Its earliest recorded Vulgate use, as an integral part of the text, is in two manuscripts of the mid-eighth century.[33] Subsequently it was in all the Alcuinian Bibles but occurred only intermittently in others before the thirteenth century, after which it spread widely and eventually became standard in the printed editions of the Vulgate.

A minuscule script whose angularities suggest distinct protogothic tendencies was responsible for a pair of additions in mid-brown ink on fols. 542r and 542v, where *uidue* has been added to Jer 5:28 and *et dixi* to 5:17. The addition of *uidu(a)e* is characteristic of a number of Spanish manuscripts of the tenth to twelfth centuries (including the Codex Toletanus), but that of *et dixi* appears not to be paralleled.

3.1.3. Old Latin Interpolations in Kings

In its original form, Amiatinus had none of a series of more than one hundred Old Latin interpolations which were established, to varying extents, in the Vulgate text of 1–2 Kings (i.e., 1–2 Samuel) from the sixth century.[34] A majority of them eventually became 'naturalized' and they remain in the received Vulgate today. The fact that the original text of Amiatinus had none attests to the age of the textual tradition used in the Italian exemplar of Kings used at Wearmouth-Jarrow for Ceolfrith's pandects. However, eight of the interpolations, of between four and twenty-two words, were added to Amiatinus later. They were

---

[32] Jerome, *Commentarii in Isaiam*, ed. M. Adriaen, vol. 1, CCSL 73 (Turnhout, 1963), 119; *Gildas: The Ruin of Britain and other Works*, ed. M. Winterbottom (London and Chichester, 1978), 108.

[33] Munich, Bayerische Staatsbibliothek, Clm. 14080, containing Isaiah and Jeremiah and written after 750, apparently at Regensburg (*CLA* 9: no. 1289; Fischer, *Lateinische Bibelhandschriften*, 186), and Sankt Gallen, Stiftsbibliothek, 40, containing the same two books and written before 781 at St Gall (*CLA* 7: no. 898; Fischer, *Lateinische Bibelhandschriften*, 182).

[34] See Robert Weber, "Les interpolations du livre de Samuel dans les manuscrits de la Vulgate," in *Miscellanea Giovanni Mercati*, vol. 1, *Bibbia, Letteratura, Cristiana Antica*, Studi e Testi 121 (Vatican City, 1946), 19–39.

written either immediately adjacent to the text being supplemented, where space allowed, or at the top or bottom of the appropriate column. Robert Weber made an extensive study of all the interpolations, and in his classification those added to Amiatinus are no. 2 (1 Kgs. 5:6a, fol. 224v), no. 3 (1 Kgs. 5:6b, fol. 224v), no. 4 (1 Kgs. 5:9, fol. 225r), no. 8 (1 Kgs. 9:25, fol. 2208r), no. 9 (1 Kgs. 10:1, fol. 228r), no. 19 (1 Kgs. 14:22, fol. 232r), no. 59 (2 Kgs. 4:5, fol. 254r), and no. 70 (2 Kgs. 6:21, fol. 256r).[35] All but one of these eight interpolations were later to become an integral part of the text of the Bibles of the Cassinian, Toletanus, and Theodulfian groups, as well as a twelfth-century Italian recension associated with Rome[36] and the thirteenth-century Paris Bibles. But these were only a few interpolations among many others: for instance, the Theodulfian Bibles eventually carried a total of 100, the Cassinian Bibles 51, and the Paris Bibles 70. The one interpolation among the Amiatinan eight which did not achieve wide circulation is no. 3, *percussit eos passione quam Greci sirigi uocant*, which was added to the second colon of 1 Kgs. 5:6 (Fig. 11.3, fol. 224v). It expands a passage telling of the punishments brought on the men of Ashdod as a consequence of their treatment of the ark of the covenant: 'he afflicted them with a disease which the Greeks call *suriggion* [i.e., ulcers].' The addition is rare; it occurs, in the margin, in one of the later Alcuinian Bibles,[37] but appears to have circulated as an integral part of the Vulgate text only in the twelfth-century Italian manuscripts carrying a textual tradition associated with Rome, noted already above.[38] It also occurs among a series of extracts from the books of Kings in a manuscript written at St. Gall in the last quarter of the eighth century.[39] It is worth noting that, in the other seven interpolations in Kings, where there are small textual variations between witnesses, it is with those of the Italian group that Amiatinus consistently concurs. Now we may easily assume that a manuscript of this group, or a derivative, was the source of the addition of number 3 and the other seven interpolations in Amiatinus. Yet the manuscripts in question also carried up to forty-three others, and there is no obvious reason why only the eight would have been chosen for copying. It may be noted also that, in Amiatinus, the rare

[35] Weber, "Interpolations," 22–29. For texts and variations, see also *Biblia Sacra*, 5 (*Liber Samuhelis*).

[36] Vatican City, Biblioteca Apostolica Vaticana, Vat. lat. 10510, 10511, and 12958.

[37] Rome, Biblioteca Vallicelliana, B. 6 (early ninth century), where the variations *passionem* and *siritigrum* occur. This and one other late product of Tours are the only Alcuinian manuscripts to carry any of the Old Latin interpolations.

[38] See n. 36. They have the variation *siringium*.

[39] Sankt Gallen, Stiftsbibliothek, 11 (*CLA* 7: 896). Among the varied contents of this manuscript (written in part by the scribe Winithar) are Jerome's hexaplaric versions of several Old Testament books; see Fischer, *Lateinische Bibelhandschriften*, 180–81.

interpolation no. 3 has been crossed out by a single line through it, an occurrence which I discuss further below.[40]

One scribe was responsible for the six additions in 1 Kings, and the resemblance of his script to that used for the additions in Ecclesiastes and Numbers noted above is at once obvious. He uses a small uncial, which keeps close to a two-line aspect but is less formal than that of the main script, with inconsistency in the letter forms and a tendency to diminution. Notable are an *M* whose first two minims form a closed bowl, a capital *D*, alternating with an uncial form, a capital *E* to start a line, a *P* whose descender barely breaks out of the two-line format, and rather exaggerated serifs on some letters, such as *R*. In two of the interpolations, both of them written in the limited space available alongside the original text, rather than above or below columns, the Tironian symbol is used for *et* (on fols. 225r and 228r). The interpolations in 2 Kings, on fols. 254r and 256r, seem to have a rather different aspect, with even more variation in the sizes of the letters; ascenders and descenders more often break the two-line format. They use an uncial *q*, where in an earlier interpolation (on fol. 232r) a capital was used, and two forms of uncial *d*, and not, as earlier, sometimes a capital. It may be that two different, though very similar, hands wrote the Kings interpolations. If that is the case, the second hand seems to have been responsible also for the addition to Numbers on fol. 131r, noted above.

Abbreviations used in the interpolations include *q* for *qui* and *qa* for *quia*, both of which Lindsay associated particularly with Italy, the less common *ei'* for *eius*, and a semicolon for *us* in *quibus*.[41] Although the Tironian symbol for *et* used in interpolations nos. 4 and 8 is a characteristically insular abbreviation, its independent Continental use is well attested also, and there seems no reason to use this as evidence that the interpolations were made while the codex was still in England.[42] Two different *signes de renvoi* are used in connection with two of the interpolations, a symmetrical cross with a dot in each of the four angles (no. 1) and a pair of rounded brackets, back to back and with a dot within the arc of each (no. 5). Neither is used for any of the certain Northumbrian corrections. The

---

[40] In his edition of the Amiatinan Old Testament, *Biblia Sacra Latina Veteris Testamenti Hieronymo interprete ex antiquissima auctoritate in stichos descripta* (Leipzig, 1873), 258, Friedrich Constantin von Tischendorf notes the rejection of the addition but wrongly describes it as being effected by subpuncting, rather than crossing out.

[41] W. M. Lindsay, *Notae Latinae: An Account of Abbreviation in Latin MSS. of the Early Minuscule Period (c. 700–850)*, with a Supplement (Abbreviations in Latin MSS. of 850 to 1050) by D. Bains (Hildesheim, 1963), 235–36 and 240 and appendix, 37 (*qui*), 245 (*quia*), and 36 (*eius*).

[42] On *et*, see Lindsay, *Notae Latinae*, 74–77. Recording the occurrence of a Tironian *nota* in Amiatinus, Lindsay (at 75) implies that it is part of an insular correction, though he gives no reasons. It is worth noting that Bede shows no knowledge of any of the interpolations in his commentary on the first book of Samuel.

additions in Kings—like the others noted above—do seem to have been made in Italy, but the use of the formal script suggests an early date for them, perhaps in the later eighth or the ninth centuries.[43] Why only eight of the Old Latin interpolations are in Amiatinus, out of a possible one hundred or more, remains a puzzle. It may simply be that the copy of Kings used in Italy as the source for them contained only the eight used. If so, this may be further evidence of a comparatively early date for their copying, before a far higher number of them became established generally in Italian manuscripts.

3.2. Liturgical Additions

Two annotations highlighting liturgical readings had already been added to Amiatinus in Northumbria, one in the Old Testament (*in s[an]c[t]i ioh[annis] bap[tistae]*), beside Isa. 49:1 on fol. 526r, one in the New (*in assumtione s[an]c[t]i iohan[is] euang[elistae]*), next to John 21:19 on fol. 903v. Both may have been derived from the examplars used for copying.[44] Five more notes of liturgical readings were added in Italy, though not all at the same time; three are in the Old Testament (two relating to Lent, one to Holy Week), three in the New (all relating to Holy Week). In addition, three passages—in Lamentations, Daniel, and Jonah—were marked with musical notation in Italy, which can probably be dated to the later tenth or the eleventh centuries. Giacomo Baroffio considers it evident that the musical notation was not inserted in Amiatinus for the benefit of a cantor, who would have known it well, but as "the written memory of a living tradition handed down orally."[45] In the case of the marking of reading passages, the same general principle might apply, although, as we shall see, several passages are at least partly punctuated, suggesting that some reading may actually have been done from the codex.

3.2.1. Lections

The first two Italian liturgical annotations are written by one hand, in an untidy caroline minuscule in mid-brown ink. On fol. 37v, *Dom[enica] iii. i[n] quad[ragesima]. iosep cu[m] sedeci[m]* appears above the right-hand column. To judge from the placing of some punctuation in the text (consisting mainly of large

---

[43] On fol. 256r, it is possible to compare directly a Northumbrian corrector's hand (which makes good a six-word omission) and the hand responsible for an interpolation in Kings on the same page. Among obvious differences are those seen in the forms of *T* (which has clubs at each end of the cross-piece in the latter hand but only on the left in the former) and of *N* (in which the descending diagonal meets the right-hand upright about two-thirds of the way down in the latter but at the base in the former). Distinct features of the interpolation script include also the 'looped' *m*.

[44] See Marsden, *Text of the Old Testament*, 189–90.

[45] Giacomo Baroffio, "Music in the Codex Amiatinus," *La Bibbia Amiatina* (CD-ROM).

commas at the end of cola), which was presumably added at the same time, this identifies a passage, beginning at Gen. 37:2 (*hae sunt generationes*) and extending to the end of 37:22, to be read on the third Sunday in Lent. Detailed records of early liturgies are scarce, and our only complete witness to the 'standard' Roman liturgy is the tenth-century *Liber comitis*, from Corbie. There, Gen. 37:6–22 is assigned for the second Sunday in Lent.[46] The proper noun in the Amiatinan note is spelled *Iosep*—not *Ioseph*, the form in the Genesis text in Amiatinus and most Vulgate manuscripts. Second, on fol. 52v, *Dom[enica] iiii. i[n] xl* is written immediately to the left of the opening of the passage to which it draws attention, Exod. 3:1–6 (*Moses autem pascebat oues Iethro*), which is indeed the first lesson in Matins for the fourth Sunday in Lent in later liturgies but is not in the *Liber comitis*. Again, some punctuation has been added to the text, and it extends as far as the end of Exod. 4:8, on fol. 53r.

The third Italian Old Testament annotation, above the second column of text on fol. 636v, is in red ink, now very faded, and reads *lectio danihel p[ro]ph[et]e cu[m] cantico*. The script is a characteristic Beneventan minuscule, notable for its inclusion of half-uncial letters, such as the 'oc' *a* and round *d*, and for idiosyncratic forms, such as *t* with a descending bow on the left of the head-stroke. The specimen of script is small, but, using E. A. Lowe's dating criteria, it seems clear that it is not from the earliest formative phases of Beneventan minuscule (i.e., the eighth and ninth centuries), though it does not perhaps have the maturity characteristic of the eleventh and twelfth centuries (after which use of the script declined rapidly).[47] The note appears to be associated with the beginning of Dan. 3, a third of the way down the second column, to the first verse of which has been prefixed, in a Beneventan script as well, *in diebus illis*. This addition is witnessed also in two Visigothic liturgical manuscripts.[48] Much of the highlighted Daniel passage carries musical notation, too, which is described below. In the *Liber comitis*, Dan. 3:1–23 is among lections added for Easter, and 3:35–45 is assigned for the fifth week in Lent.[49]

In the New Testament, two of the additions, relating to consecutive days in Holy Week, are made in the same, curiously repetitive, manner. First, on fol. 956r, *F[e]r[ia] v i[n] cena d[omi]ni* is written next to 1 Cor. 11:20 (*Conuenientibus ergo*) in a large and fairly informal uncial, using, however, a capital *D*; the note

---

[46] W. H. Frere, *Studies in Early Roman Liturgy*, 3 vols., Alcuin Club Collections 28, 30, 32 (Oxford, 1930–1935), vol. 3, *The Roman Epistle-Lectionary*, 6, no. XXXVIII.

[47] E. A. Lowe, *The Beneventan Script: A History of the South Italian Minuscule*, 2nd edn. prepared and enlarged by Virginia Brown, 2 vols., Sussidi Eruditi 33–34 (Rome, 1980), vol. 2, *Hand List of Beneventan Mss.*, 44. According to Gorman ("A Guide," 876), the scriptorium at Monte Amiata never indulged in what he calls "idiosyncratic experiments" such as the Beneventan script.

[48] *Biblia Sacra* 16 (*Liber Danihelis*), 58 and xv.

[49] Frere, *Roman Epistle-Lectionary*, 9, no. LXVI, and 8, no. LVIII, respectively.

is then more or less repeated at the bottom of the column, but this time in rustic capitals, though the *A* of *cena* remains uncial: *F[e]r[ia] v hoc est cena d[omi]ni*).[50] The ink appears to be the same for both notes and a single hand is likely to be involved, though the reason for the repetition, and the change of script, is not clear. In the *Liber comitis*, the reading assigned for 'the Lord's supper,' on Maundy Thursday, is 1 Cor. 11:20–32.[51] Second, on fol. 996v, *F[e]r[ia] vi. In parasceue* is written next to Heb. 4:11 (*Festinemus ergo*); again, this is repeated at the bottom of the column in rustic capitals, though this time the *E* of *est* is uncial: *F[e]r[ia] vi hoc est parasceue* (see Fig. 11.4, fol. 996v). *Parasceue* is Good Friday and later liturgies duly assign Heb. 4:11–16 for the mass that day, though it is not in the *Liber comitis*.[52] The third New Testament annotation, on fol. 1000r, adds another lection for Holy Week but seems to have been made much later than the previous pair; certainly it is in a very different hand, a large and untidy minuscule, in a pale brown ink. It is next to Heb. 9:11 (*Christus autem adsistens*) and reads: *sabb[atum] s[an]c[t]o l uii*. In the *Liber comitis*, Heb. 9:9–11 is assigned for Palm Sunday.[53] There is no added punctuation in any of the highlighted New Testament passages.

3.2.2. Musical Notation

In Italy also, three sections of the Old Testament in Amiatinus were annotated, or partly so, for chanting during the liturgy of the mass at various points during Holy Week.[54] The first is the Lamentations of Jeremiah, which follow the main text of the prophet in Amiatinus without a break but whose first word, *quomodo*, is given a capital *Q*. Amiatinus is the oldest of eleven Vulgate manuscripts (from the forty collated by the editors of the Rome *Biblia Sacra*) to have musical notation added to Lamentations;[55] the verses were sung at Matins during the paschal

---

[50] The first note on fol. 996r has many resemblances to the Northumbrian correctors' hands (including a slight sloping aspect), but there are dissimilarities also, and the size and the untidy manner of presentation are quite uncharacteristic of Northumbrian additions.

[51] Frere, *Roman Epistle-Lectionary*, 9, no. LXV.

[52] Frere, *Roman Epistle-Lectionary*, 56, notes this lection as being assigned, in developments of the standard liturgy, for an extra Wednesday celebration in 'Septuagesima IV.'

[53] Frere, *Roman Epistle-Lectionary*, 7, no. LIV.

[54] For a brief survey of the topic, see Baroffio, "Music in the Codex Amiatinus." A nineteenth-century musicologist, Oskar Fleischer (see Baroffio's n. 4), maintained that the neums had been added in Northumbria, but the study by Ludwig (specifically of the notation in Lamentations: see following note) confirmed their status as fairly late, Italian, additions. The practice of musical notation is not apparent in England until the period following the Benedictine Reform, at the latter end of the tenth century; see Susan Rankin, "Chant," in *BEASE* (Oxford, 1999), 96 (and personal communication).

[55] A short study by Paul Ludwig has been devoted to the subject: "Lamentations notées dans quelques manuscrits bibliques," *Études Grégoriennes* 12 (1971): 127–30.

triduum sacrum, i.e., the three days from from Maundy Thursday to Easter Saturday. The first four of the five chapters (which are on fols. 586r–590r) are each divided into twenty-two verses, prefixed in sequence by the names of the letters of the Hebrew alphabet, *aleph* to *thau*, written in the margin in red ink (which seem to have been added in Northumbria). Neums were added to each letter as far as *nun* of the second chapter (Lam. 2:14, fol. 587v). Ludwig associates their fine, fluid outline with Beneventan work of the tenth to eleventh centuries.[56] An apparently different hand, but still associated by Ludwig with the area of Rome or Monte Cassino, added the notation above the verses themselves, but this is complete only in the first chapter; thereafter it is intermittent, except on the cadences. In Lam. 5, where the verses are numbered not in the Hebrew but in the Greek alphabet, only the cadences are notated (fols. 589v–590r).

As noted above, the musical notation in Daniel begins on fol. 636v above *in diebus illis*, which was added before Dan. 3:1, presumably at the same time as the neums. The notated passage is long, and includes the "prayer of the three youths" (Dan. 3:24–45), the most heavily notated section, with its beginning and end marked by crosses, and the "song of the three youths" (Dan. 3:52–90), which is notated only on the first four and last two lines. Daniel was sung during the Easter Eve liturgy, on the night of Holy Saturday.

The most complete notation in Jonah is on the canticle *Clamaui de tribulatione mea* (Jon. 2:3–11), on fol. 664v (a passage prefaced probably by the original Northumbrian copyist with the heading *CANTICUM* in red), but it begins before this, at Jon. 1:3, and extends beyond, as far as the end of the book (Jon. 4:11), on fol. 665r.[57] One hand seems to have been responsible for the notation in Daniel and Jonah, and may be contemporary with that used for the notation in Lamentations. The canticle *Clamaui* does not feature in the *Liber Comitis*, but Jon 3:1–10 is among lections added there for Easter and is also assigned for Monday in the penultimate week of Lent.[58]

3.3. Miscellaneous Additions

Characteristically for a medieval Vulgate Bible, most of the books of the Old Testament in Amiatinus are divided into *capitula*, whose numbers, in Roman numerals, are given in the margin, often in red. (Some books, such as Chronicles, Ruth, and most of the sapiential books, never had divisions.) They seem to be part of the original production of the codex. However, while it was in Italy, modern chapter divisions (which usually amount to far fewer per book than the *capitula*) were entered throughout the Old Testament, written in the left margin in Roman numerals, more often than not within an angled bracket. Where the

---

[56] Ludwig, "Lamentations notées," 127.

[57] The Jonah notation is not discussed by Baroffio, "Music in the Codex Amiatinus," but is recorded in Tischendorf et al., *Biblia Sacra Latina*, 915.

[58] Frere, *Roman Epistle-Lectionary*, 9, no. LXVI*, and 7, no. LV.

new divisions coincide with old ones, the new number is written below or adjacent to the old, with the latter sometimes crossed out. It looks as though at least two different scribes were responsible. Some numerals are written with thick black lines, with stylized and often sloping figures, some with lighter and simpler lines, and some of the latter are unusually large and very untidy; the *i* is usually dotted in all cases. Yet sometimes both bold and light numerals are found within a single book, apparently at random, which seems to indicate either that two (or more) people worked somewhat haphazardly to complete the numbering, or that one annotator varied his style at will. As for the date of the added numbers, a clear *terminus a quo* is the first quarter of the thirteenth century, for the modern system of division, attributed to Stephen Langton (d. 1228), was first current in the thirteenth-century Bibles of Paris.[59] No modern chapter numbers were given to the New Testament books in Amiatinus.

Capital Greek letters have been added, in reddish-brown ink (very faded in some cases), to the inner margins of sections of Exodus, Leviticus, and Deuteronomy. In Exod. 20:3–17 (fols. 67r–67v) and Deut. 5:6–12 (fol. 151r), they mark the laws of the decalogue, while in Lev. 19:11–16 (fols. 101v–102r) they highlight ten of the thirty ordinances presented in the chapter (which are similar in structure and purpose to those of the decalogue). In Exodus and Leviticus, each Greek letter is topped by a bar resembling a suspension mark, clubbed at each end. The letters in Deuteronomy lack the bar, and the forms differ a little (in theta, for instance, the cross-stroke is barely visible) and they may have been added later than the others and by a different hand. In each of the three biblical books appears a sequence of the Greek numerals for '1' through '10'. Thus, after capital alpha to delta (1–4) comes an uncial e to represent epsilon (5), then what appears to be a small zeta (actually a 'stigma' or s-t digraph, the numeral '6'), and then capital zeta to iota (7–10): i.e., A, B, Γ, Δ, e, ϛ, Z, H, Θ, I.[60] It is hard to know when these Greek numeral-letters were added, but, to judge from a similarity of ink, it may be wondered whether some (at least those in the first two books) are contemporary with the added chapter-numbers, i.e., mid-thirteenth century or later. However, it was during the period from the ninth to the eleventh centuries, according to Gorman's observations, that the quality of writing

---

[59] See P.-M. Bogaert, "La bible latine des origines au moyen âge: Aperçu historique, état des questions," *Revue théologique de Louvain* 19 (1988): 137–59, and 276–314, at 286–87; and Marsden, *Text of the Old Testament*, 35.

[60] Tischendorf, *Biblia Sacra Latina*, reads the small zeta as a sigma, printing it for the three books as, respectively, ϛ, S (*sic*), and S (*sic*). The editors of the Rome *Biblia Sacra*, 2 (*Liber Exodi-Leuitici*) and 3 (*Libri Numerorum-Deuteronomii*) concur with my interpretation, though in each of the three occurrences of zeta, both small and large, the form is irregular, and in one case resembles a *yogh*. The forms of alpha and beta are exactly like their uncial equivalents, A and B, in the main text.

in Greek at Monte Amiata was particularly high.[61] Contemporary with the addition of the Greek letters could be transliterations of the two Greek words used in Jerome's prologue to the Pentateuch on fol. 9r: *iporaspist[es]* (last letters illegible) and *sintaigma*. They are written in an untidy minuscule and a pale ink.

4. The Second Adventure in Rome

Finally, I turn to the later history of Amiatinus in the sixteenth century—and to the crossing out of one of the eight interpolations in Kings, noted above.[62] As early as April 1546, the Council of Trent had declared the Vulgate to be authentic and demanded that a corrected edition be prepared, in view of the known problems of corruption of the text. However, a projected commission to undertake the work failed to materialize at once, apparently through lack of direction from Rome. Little interest was shown there until the pontificate of Pius IV (1559–1565), when a revision of sorts was prepared (with Cardinal Sirleto among the scholars involved) but, for obscure reasons, never printed. Then, in 1566, Pius V set up a commission, consisting of five cardinals, including Sirleto and Carafa, and twelve other scholarly advisers. There was initial enthusiasm, but progress had stalled even before the death of Pius in 1572, owing probably to the difficulty of such a varied body of scholars reaching an informed consensus about variant readings. Only Sirleto remained dedicated to the revision, and it is now that Amiatinus enters the story.

The cardinal had become aware of the antiquity and potential importance of the codex and he tried, in 1572, to have it sent to Rome. The monks of Monte Amiata, however, refused to let their treasure go, and the new pope, Gregory XIII, preoccupied with a revision of the Septuagint, did not lend his support. Sirleto therefore dispatched Spinello Benci, bishop of Montepulciano, to Monte Amiata, to make a collation of Amiatinus, and Benci duly sent this to Sirleto early in 1574.[63] Although the collation does not survive, it was always supposed that Sirleto had entered its readings (along with those of four other main witnesses) in the margins of his working exemplar, a copy of the printed Bible of Louvain of 1547 which is still extant.[64] Some variants there are indeed marked *Lan* or

[61] Gorman, "Manuscript Books," 273.

[62] For the following account I have relied mainly on Fridolin Amman, *Die Vulgata Sixtina von 1590: eine quellenmässige Darstellung ihrer Geschichte, mit neuem Quellenmaterial aus dem venezianischen Staatsarchiv* (Freiburg im Breisgau, 1912); Henri Quentin, *Mémoire sur l'établissement du texte de la Vulgate* (Rome, 1922), 160–69, and A. Mercati, "Per la storia del codice Amiatino," *Biblica* 3 (1922): 324–28. Amman is especially interesting on the personalities and politics of the long revision process.

[63] For further details see Mercati, "Per la storia del codice Amiatino."

[64] Vatican City, Biblioteca Apostolica Vaticana, Vat. lat. 9517.

Lang for *Langobardus*, which seems apt enough, considering the naming of "Peter of the Lombards" in the dedication of Amiatinus. Yet Henri Quentin eventually showed that these are not Amiatinan readings after all.[65] Either Sirleto did not use Benci's collation, and the *Langobardus* readings are from another source altogether, or they are indeed Benci's readings but the Bible he collated was not Amiatinus. On balance, the latter seems to be the most likely explanation; that is, Benci had been fobbed off by the monks of San Salvatore with another Bible. He himself had written to Sirleto about the difficulty of reading what he called the 'semi-longobardic script' (*lettera meza langobarda*) of the supposed Amiatinus, even though one of the most obvious aspects of the codex is its astonishing legibility. Furthermore, Benci had reported that Amiatinus (coveted still as the supposed autograph work of Gregory the Great) was preserved with such reverence among the relics of the monastery of San Salvatore, not only by the monks but also by the local populace, that if it was not treated with respect there was "danger of uproar and insurrection."[66]

The succession of Sixtus V to the pontificate in 1585 gave a fresh impetus to the Vulgate revision project. The pope set up a new commission, with six members under the presidency of Cardinal Carafa. It was now, with pressure from the pope himself, that the monks of Monte Amiata were finally persuaded to send their precious book to Rome. A fascinating record of the deliberations of the council of the monks of San Salvatore was preserved by a later abbot of the abbey, Giancolombino Fatteschi (1770–1775).[67] On 26 June 1587, after lengthy discussion, they decided to send a deputation to Rome to argue against the request, pointing out the great veneration in which the ancient Bible was held by monks and local people alike. But at a meeting on 6 July they capitulated. They did insist, however, on sending the abbot and one or two other monks along with the codex, to ensure that it was looked after and to get it back as soon as possible or, even at this stage, to see whether Rome could be persuaded to let them bring it straight back and make do with copies. On the verso of the front fly-leaf of Amiatinus is fixed a contemporary note recording that the volume was taken to Cardinal Carafa on 12 July 1587.[68]

---

[65] Quentin, *Mémoire*, 168–69.

[66] Mercati, "Per la storia del codice Amiatino," 326 ("pericolo di rumori et di sollevationi"), citing from the account of Fatteschi (see next note).

[67] His *Memorie Istorico-Diplomatiche dell'antichissimo Monastero di San Salvatore del Monte-Amiato nell'Agro Senese in Toscana* survives in two manuscripts, copied in 1811. See Gorman, "Guide," 898. Parts of it are printed in Carlo Vercellone, *Dissertazioni accademiche di vario argomento* (Rome, 1864), 90.

[68] The following transcription of the note, which is hard to read, is based on the version in Carlo Vercellone, *Variae lectiones Vulgatae Latinae Bibliorum editionis*, 2 vols. (Rome, 1860–1864), 1: xxvi, n. 1: "La presente Bibia A dì 12 di luglio 1587 fu portata al illustrissimo Card. Antonio Carafa per l'opera dell'emendatione della Bibia latina vul-

The commission already had other important Bibles (such as the Codices Paulinus, Vercellianus, and Ottobonianus) and had arranged for collations of more to be sent to them. Although the documentary evidence of their work does not survive (as it does for the earlier commission), what appears to be the exemplar presenting their considered suggestions for emendation does; known as the Codex Carafianus, it is an edition of the Louvain Bible issued by Christopher Plantin in 1583, with corrections and emendations written in the margins.[69] The aim of the Sixtine commission was to restore Jerome's text as far as possible, and so the authority of the oldest Latin manuscripts became their benchmark. As for the importance of Amiatinus, Quentin has shown that it does seem to have been the authority which more often than not was chosen, in both Old and New Testament books, to support suggested emendation of the Louvain text; sometimes the readings adopted were unique to Amiatinus, and its authority is especially notable in Exodus, the Gospels, and Acts.[70] Nevertheless, its readings were by no means always accepted; alternatives were adopted from other old and good texts.

Carafa's commission, however, had not reckoned with the personality of Sixtus himself. A man with an inflated belief in his own qualities as an editor, he insisted that all potential corrections and emendations be presented to him for approval, and then proceeded to reject most of them.[71] It appears that he was angry that too often they parted from the Vulgate with which he was so familiar, a *textus receptus* which was essentially a version deriving from the Paris Bibles. The commission's own failure to take the trouble to show the pope the usually very sound justification for their changes may have exacerbated the problem.[72] Sixtus also insisted on considerable alterations to the commission's system of verse division, which was based on that established by Robert Estienne. In the last months of his life, the impatient pope rushed out his edition, and some copies had already been distributed before his death in August 1590. But within little more than a week, the Congregation of Cardinals had suspended its sale; shortly after that, it was officially suppressed and copies were recalled.

There was tacit acknowledgement by all concerned that the Sixtine text should be revised and reissued as quickly as possible, and thus only essential

---

gata per ordine di S. Santità Sixto V in Roma e fu restituita alli 19 di gennaro 1590 alli Reverendi Padri D. Marcello Vanni et D. Stefano Bizzotti Monaci di Monastero di S. Salvatore in Montamiata. Io Arturo de' conti d'Elci."

[69] Now Vatican City, Biblioteca Apostolica Vaticana, Vat. lat. 12959. For an illustration, see Quentin, *Mémoire*, 172.

[70] Quentin, *Mémoire*, 172–80. See also Amman, *Die Vulgata Sixtina*, 171–80.

[71] See especially Quentin's scathing account of Sixtus as an editor, *Mémoire*, 181–83. The pope had produced an abysmal edition of Ambrose, which he ordered should be the only source for all future citation of this father.

[72] Thus Quentin, *Mémoire*, 183.

changes could be made. Many of Carafa's readings were restored, the punctuation and verse division were emended, and as many as three thousand changes were in fact made. Yet the stamp of Sixtus remained and the revised edition was far from satisfactory from a textual point of view. Though finished by 5 July 1591, it was not issued until some months later, under the pontificate of Clement VIII (elected in January 1592, after the deaths of both Gregory XIV and his immediate successor, Innocent IX), and hence it would become known as the "Clementine" Vulgate. However, it was still ascribed on the title-page to Sixtus, an economy with the truth made necessary by the fact that the late pope had attached a bull to the 1590 edition, declaring it unalterable.

It remains to return briefly to the eight Old Latin interpolations made to the text of Kings in Amiatinus. All but one of the additions were used for the new edition prepared for Sixtus. Their authority, however, will have been established, not just from Amiatinus, but from one of the many other manuscripts or printed editions which the Rome revisers used, and which carried, not just the Amiatinan eight, but the dozens more which were also accepted by the revisers. The one of the Amiatinan eight which did *not* appear in the new edition was Weber's no. 3 (1 Kgs. 5:6, *percussit eos passione quam Greci sirigi uocant*), the one which is crossed out in Amiatinus, as noted above. It is tempting, though nothing can be proved, to surmise that it was at the point when Cardinal Carafa was collating Amiatinus with all the other sources in Rome, and found no. 3 to be anachronistic, that this crossing-out took place—conceivably executed by Carafa himself.

Whatever the case, after two and a half years, Amiatinus was allowed home from Rome, though with some reluctance, according to the account of Vercellone. Citing Fatteschi, he reports that only the mediation of the illustrious Medici family secured the codex's release "dalle unghie dei romani."[73] It is intriguing to wonder whether even that would have been enough, had those Romans known that the great Bible had originally been a gift to St. Peter's. It was given back to its reverend guardians for return to Monte Amiata on 19 January 1590, as recorded again in the note preserved on the front flyleaf.[74] If my supposition is correct, another small change in its textual character—probably the last—had been completed.

5. Conclusions

This short survey of the textual afterlife of Amiatinus has been impressionistic, rather than systematic. Varieties of ink and script make it abundantly clear that interventions in the text which had left Northumbria were many and various, and spread over a considerable time, but the details are hard to establish. The

---

[73] *Dissertazioni accademiche*, 90 ("from the clutches of the Romans").
[74] See n. 68.

sometimes lengthy additions made in a neat uncial—including the interpolations in Kings—may have been among the earliest (and most substantial). If so, where they were made becomes an intriguing question. If Amiatinus did not reach Monte Amiata before the start of the eleventh century, as suggested by Gorman, then it must have been at another center (perhaps still in Rome) that the uncial additions were made. Alternatively, this could be seen as an argument for an earlier arrival of the codex at Monte Amiata (considerably before the opening of the eleventh century) and the making of these particular alterations there. Later additions and emendations to the Bible, usually in forms of minuscule, are various. Some are rather untidy, and there is no sign of any systematic revision or checking of the text. The musical notation and associated Beneventan annotations are comparatively easy to date: most likely they were made in the later tenth or eleventh centuries. The chapter numbers, and perhaps some at least of the Greek notation, must be rather later than this, from the second quarter of the thirteenth century onwards. In respect of Vulgate textual history, while some amplifications and variations are paralleled in other Italian textual traditions (including that of Monte Cassino), what is most interesting is a number whose origins are obscure and which have not been noticed in any other biblical manuscripts or patristic citations of scripture. They remind us how little we know about the early textual history of the Vulgate, and presumably they are traces of textual traditions which have not otherwise survived.

Much of the above assessment is inevitably conjectural, but now that Michael Gorman has effectively opened up the great library of Monte Amiata, or what survives of it (and in fact there is plenty), an obvious desideratum in Amiatinan studies is a systematic examination of the library's books, both those written in-house and those collected from elsewhere and worked on there. Comparison of the scripts used in the copying, correction, and annotation of these manuscripts with those used for the interventions in Amiatinus may yield some interesting results and enable a few more of the details of the eventful life of one of the greatest of English books to be ascertained.

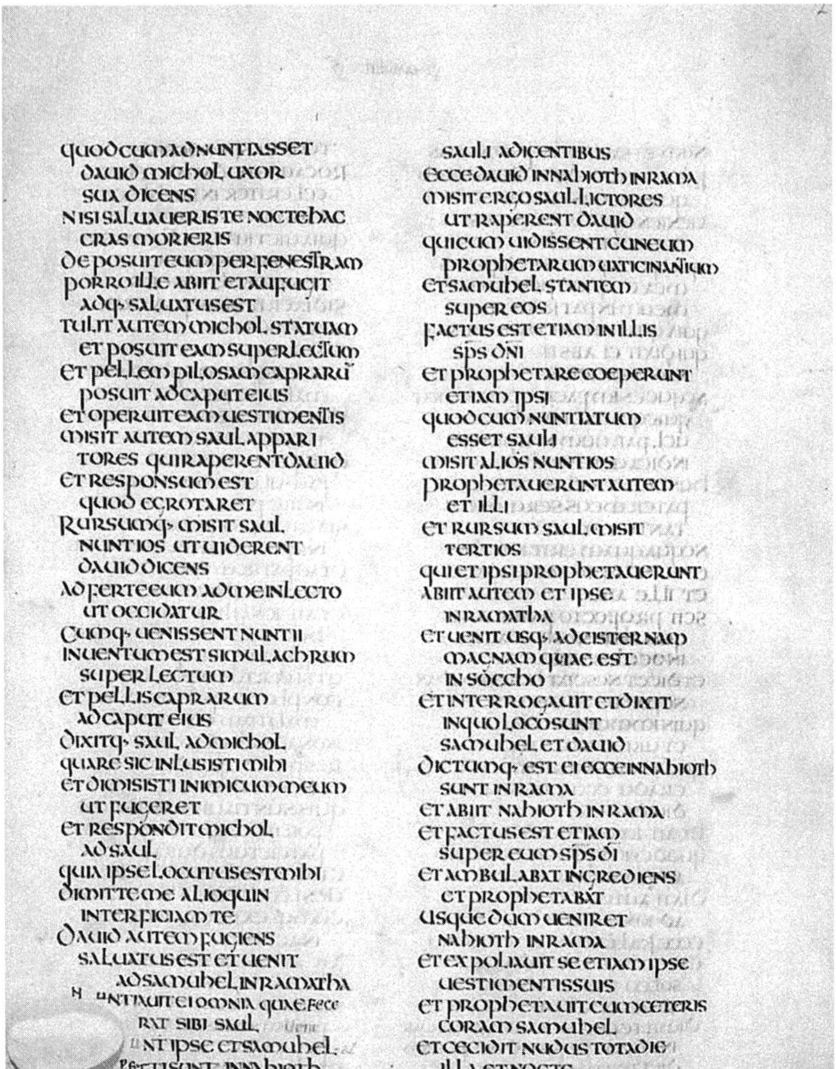

quod cum adnuntiasset
dauid michol uxor
sua dicens
nisi salvaveris te nocte hac
cras morieris
deposuit eum per fenestram
porro ille abiit et aufugit
adq(ue) salvatus est
tulit autem michol statuam
et posuit eam super lectum
et pellem pilosam caprarum
posuit ad caput eius
et operuit eam vestimentis
misit autem saul appari
tores qui raperent dauid
et responsum est
quod aegrotaret
rursumque misit saul
nuntios ut viderent
dauid dicens
adferte eum ad me in lecto
ut occidatur
cumque venissent nuntii
inventum est simulacrum
super lectum
et pellis caprarum
ad caput eius
dixitque saul ad michol
quare sic inlusisti mihi
et dimisisti inimicum meum
ut fugeret
et respondit michol
ad saul
quia ipse locutus est mihi
dimitte me alioquin
interficiam te
dauid autem fugiens
salvatus est et venit
ad samuhel in ramatha
nuntiavit ei omnia quae fece
rat sibi saul
nt ipse et samuhel
erunt in nabioth
tum est autem
sauli adicentibus
ecce dauid in nabioth in rama
misit ergo saul lictores
ut raperent dauid
qui cum vidissent cuneum
prophetarum vaticinantium
et samuhel stantem
super eos
factus est etiam in illis
sps dni
et prophetare coeperunt
etiam ipsi
quod cum nuntiatum
esset sauli
misit alios nuntios
prophetaverunt autem
et illi
et rursum saul misit
tertios
qui et ipsi prophetaverunt
abiit autem et ipse
in ramatha
et venit usque ad cisternam
magnam quae est
in socho
et interrogavit et dixit
in quo loco sunt
samuhel et dauid
dictumque est ei ecce in nabioth
sunt in rama
et abiit in nabioth in rama
et factus est etiam
super eum sps di
et ambulabat ingrediens
et prophetabat
usque dum veniret
nabioth in rama
et expoliavit se etiam ipse
vestimentis suis
et prophetavit cum ceteris
coram samuhel
et cecidit nudus tota die
illa et nocte
unde et exivit proverbium

FIGURE 11.1. Florence, Biblioteca Medicea Laurentiana, Amiatino 1, fol. 239r, showing damage to the parchment and a two-stage restoration of the text of 1 Kgs. 19.

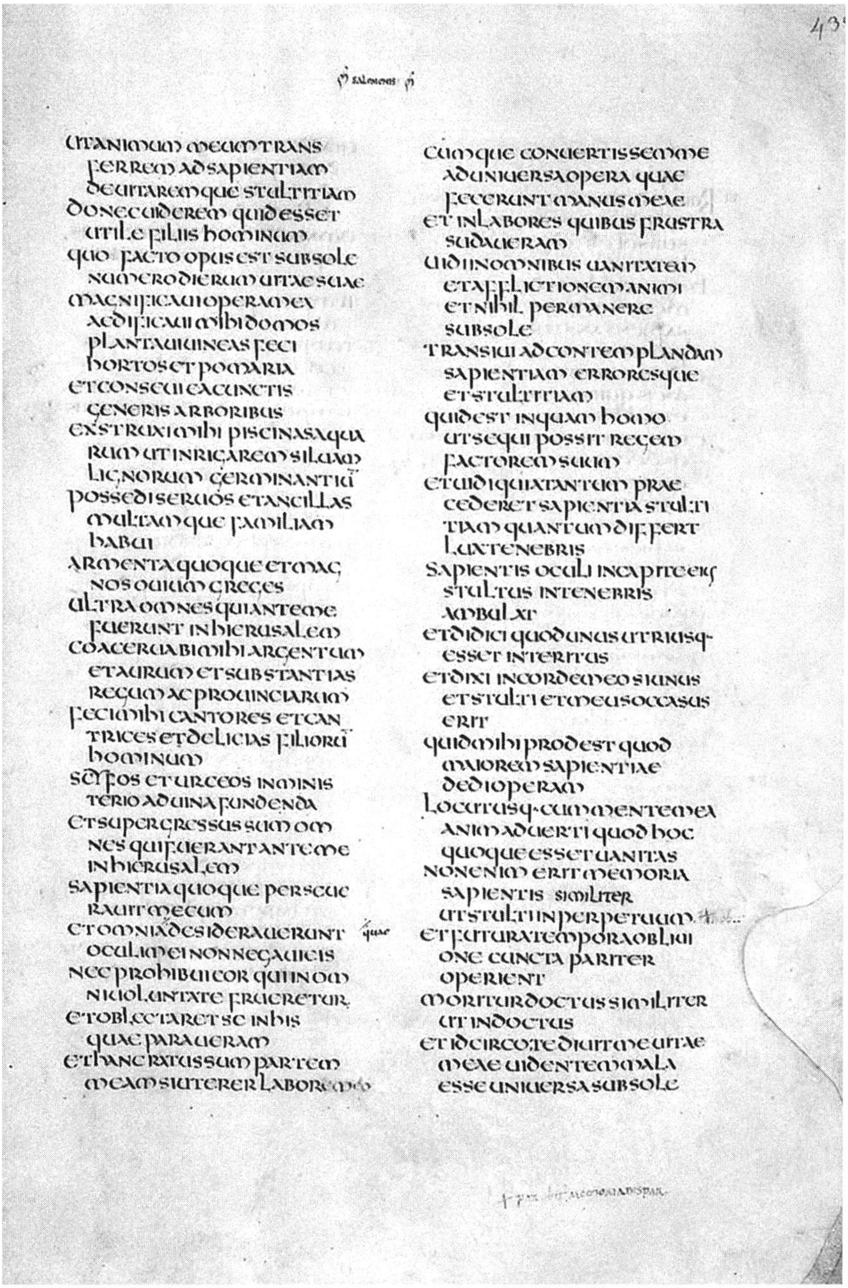
uitanimum meum trans
ferrem ad sapientiam
deuitaremque stultitiam
donec uiderem quid esset
utile filiis hominum
quo facto opus est sub sole
numero dierum uitae suae
magnificaui opera mea
aedificaui mihi domos
plantaui uineas feci
hortos et pomaria
et conseui ea cunctis
generis arboribus
exstruxi mihi piscinas aqua
rum ut inrigarem siluam
lignorum germinantiū
possedi seruos et ancillas
multamque familiam
habui
armenta quoque et mag
nos ouium greges
ultra omnes qui ante me
fuerunt in hierusalem
coaceruaui mihi argentum
et aurum et substantias
regum ac prouinciarum
feci mihi cantores et can
trices et delicias filiorū
hominum
scyfos et urceos in minis
terio ad uina fundenda
et supergressus sum om
nes qui fuerant ante me
in hierusalem
sapientia quoque perseue
rauit mecum
et omnia desiderauerunt quae
oculi mei non negaui eis
nec prohibui cor quin omni
uoluptate frueretur
et oblectaret se in his
quae parauerā
et hanc ratus sum partem
meam si uterer labore meo

cumque conuertissem me
ad uniuersa opera quae
fecerunt manus meae
et in laboribus quibus frustra
sudaueram
uidi in omnibus uanitatem
et adflictionem animi
et nihil permanere
sub sole
transiui ad contemplandam
sapientiam erroresque
et stultitiam
quid est inquam homo
ut sequi possit regem
factorem suum
et uidi quia tantum prae
cederet sapientia stulti
tiam quantum differt
lux tenebris
sapientis oculi in capite eius
stultus in tenebris
ambulat
et didici quod unus utriusq;
esset interitus
et dixi in corde meo si unus
et stulti et meus occasus
erit
quid mihi prodest quod
maiorem sapientiae
dedi operam
locutusq; cum mente mea
animaduerti quod hoc
quoque esset uanitas
non enim erit memoria
sapientis similiter
ut stulti in perpetuum
et futura tempora obliui
one cuncta pariter
operient
moritur doctus similiter
ut indoctus
et idcirco taeduit me uitae
meae uidentem mala
esse uniuersa sub sole

Figure 11.2. Florence, Biblioteca Medicea Laurentiana, Amiatino 1, fol. 438r, showing a rare addition made to Eccles. 2:16.

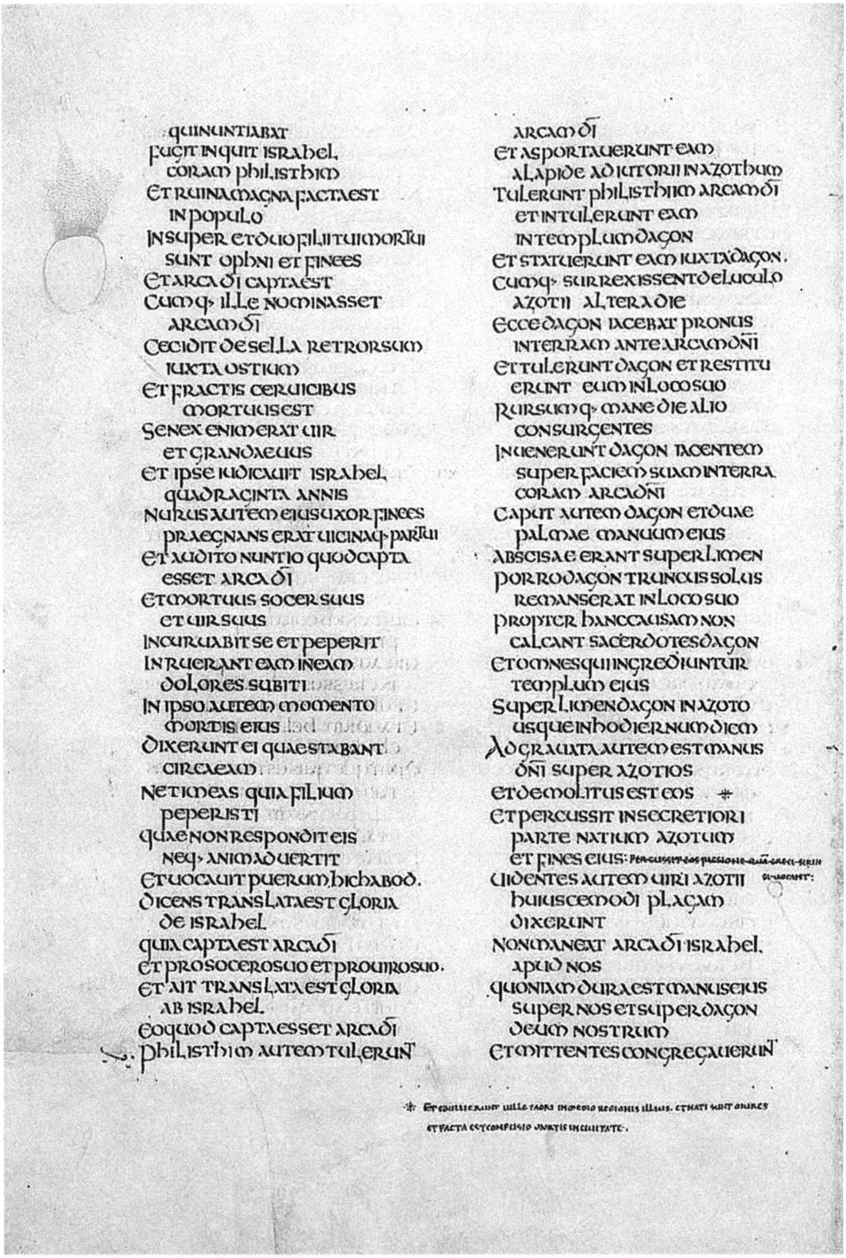

:quinuntiabat
fugit inquit israbel.
   coram philisthim
et ruina magna facta est
   in populo
insuper et duo filii tui mortui
   sunt ophni et finees
et arca dī captaest
cumq· ille nominasset
   arcam dī
cecidit de sella retrorsum
   iuxta ostium
et fractis ceruicibus
   mortuus est
senex enim erat uir
   et grandaeuus
et ipse iudicauit israbel.
   quadraginta annis
nurus autem eius uxor finees
   praegnans erat uicinaq· parti
et audito nuntio quod capta
   esset arca dī
et mortuus socer suus
   et uir suus
incuruabit se et peperit
in ruerant eam ineam
   dolores subiti
in ipso autem momento
   mortis eius
dixerunt ei quae stabant
   circa eam
ne timeas quia filium
   peperisti
quae non respondit eis
   neq· animaduertit
et uocauit puerum hichabod.
   dicens translata est gloria
   de israbel
quia captaest arca dī
et pro socero suo et pro uiro suo.
et ait translata est gloria
   ab israbel
eo quod captaesset arca dī
philisthim autem tulerun'

arcam dī
et asportauerunt eam
   a lapide ad iutorii in azothum
tulerunt philisthim arcam dī
   et intulerunt eam
   in templum dagon
et statuerunt eam iuxta dagon.
cumq· surrexissent de luculo
   azotii altera die
ecce dagon iacebat pronus
   interram ante arcam dōni
et tulerunt dagon et restitu
   erunt eum inloco suo
rursumq· mane die alio
   consurgentes
inuenerunt dagon iacentem
   super faciem suam interra
   coram arca dōni
caput autem dagon et duae
   palmae manuum eius
abscisae erant super limen
porro dagon truncus solus
   remanserat inloco suo
propter hanc causam non
   calcant sacerdotes dagon
et omnes qui ingrediuntur
   templum eius
super limen dagon in azoto
   usque inhodiernum diem
ad grauata autem est manus
   dōni super azotios
et demolitus est eos   ✣
et percussit insecretiori
   parte natium azotum
et fines eius: percussit eos passione a.... a..... s....
uidentes autem uiri azotii   a...unt:
   huiuscemodi plagam
   dixerunt
non maneat arca dī israbel.
   apud nos
quoniam dura est manus eius
   super nos et super dagon
   deum nostrum
et mittentes congregauerun'

✣ Er ebullierunt uille ragas in medio regionis illius. et nati sunt omnes
   et facta est confusio mortis in ciuitate.

Figure 11.3. Florence, Biblioteca Medicea Laurenziana, Amiatino 1, fol. 224v, showing two interpolations in 1 Kgs. 5:6, with one subsequently crossed out.

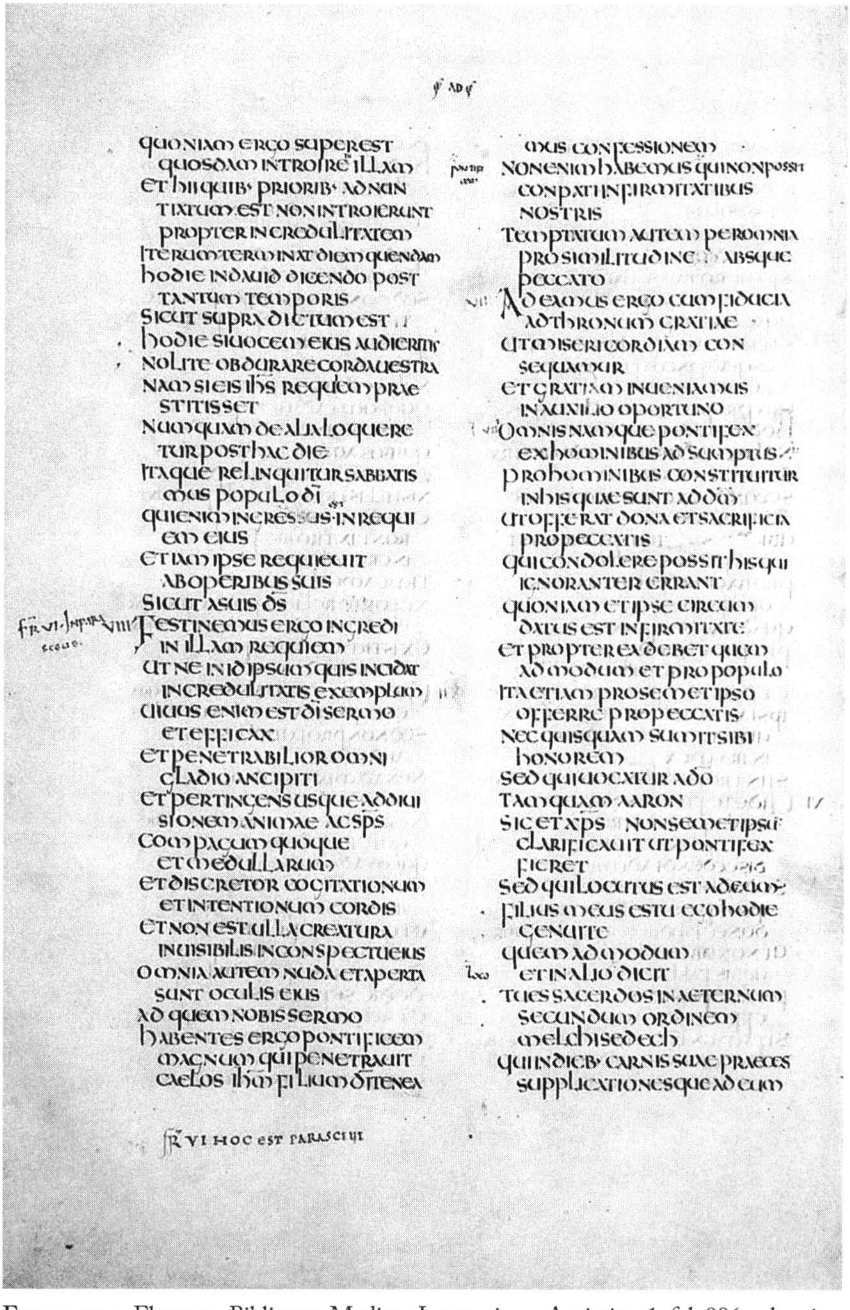

FIGURE 11.4. Florence, Biblioteca Medicea Laurentiana, Amiatino 1, fol. 996v, showing a liturgical annotation, duplicated, designating a Good Friday lection from Hebrews.

Travel between England and Italy in the Early Middle Ages

David A. E. Peltaret

Travel between Anglo-Saxon England and Italy might seem to be a subject that has been thoroughly investigated.[1] To the general surveys of Wilhelm Levison, Veronica Ortenberg, and W. J. Moore[2] may be added the specialist studies by Simon Keynes on the entries containing Anglo-Saxon names in the *Liber Vitae* of San Salvatore, Brescia, and by Veronica Ortenberg on Archbishop Sigeric's itinerary from Rome to England in 990.[3] New evidence, however, has come to light in recent decades and old evidence can still be examined anew to learn more about the practicalities of travel. A grand survey of the whole Anglo-Saxon period, investigating all the evidence and the impact on England and on Italy of

---

[1] This paper is dedicated to the memory of René Derolez, philologist and runic specialist and first president of the International Society of Anglo-Saxonists.

[2] Wilhelm Levison, *England and the Continent in the Eighth Century* (Oxford, 1946); Veronica Ortenberg, *The English Church and the Continent in the Tenth and Eleventh Centuries: Cultural, Spiritual, and Artistic Exchanges* (Oxford, 1992); W. J. Moore, "The Saxon Pilgrims to Rome and the Schola Saxonum" (Docteur ès Lettres diss., University of Fribourg, 1937); see also Joanna Story, *Carolingian Connections: Anglo-Saxon England and Carolingian Francia, c. 750–870*, Studies in Early Medieval Britain (Aldershot and Burlington, VT, 2003). Stephen Matthews, *The Road to Rome: Travel and Travellers between England and Italy in the Anglo-Saxon Centuries*, BAR International Series 1680 (Oxford, 2007) appeared after this paper was completed. Norbert Ohler, *Reisen im Mittelalter*, 4th edn. (Düsseldorf, 2004), provides much practical information; the 1986 edition has been translated into English under the title *The Medieval Traveller*, trans. Caroline Hiller (Woodbridge, 1989). I have been unable to see G. Ferraresi, "Viaggi e viaggiatori dall'Inghilterra a Roma nel periodo anglosassone" (tesi di laurea in storia medievale, Università degli Studi di Bologna, 2000); my thanks to Peter Jackson for the reference.

[3] Simon Keynes, "Anglo-Saxon Entries in the 'Liber Vitae' of Brescia," in *Alfred the Wise: Studies in Honour of Janet Bately on the Occasion of her Sixty-Fifth Birthday*, ed. Jane Roberts and Janet L. Nelson with Malcolm Godden (Cambridge, 1997), 99–119; Veronica Ortenberg, "Archbishop Sigeric's Journey to Rome in 990," *Anglo-Saxon England* 19 (1990): 197–246.

Hans Sauer and Joanna Story, eds., *Anglo-Saxon England and the Continent*. With the assistance of Gaby Waxenberger. Essays in Anglo-Saxon Studies, vol. 3. MRTS 394. Tempe: ACMRS, 2011.   [ISBN 978-0-86698-442-3]

travel between the two countries (including the migration of manuscripts and of ideas), would be of monograph length. This brief paper, therefore, will concentrate on the period from the seventh to the mid-tenth centuries and will focus on evidence that has been overlooked or which can be discussed from a different perspective. Its purpose will be to act as a stimulus to further specialist investigations and, in the spirit of the International Society of Anglo-Saxonists, to provide an incentive for international collaboration.

We might start by looking at the experience of a specific traveler in a particular place and at a particular time to illustrate the ramifications of such an investigation. In ca. 704 while returning to England from Rome, Bishop Wilfrid, sometime bishop of York, fell desperately ill.[4] Perhaps eager to convey a sense of humility in support of his appeal to the pope against his deposition from office, Wilfrid and his party had traveled to Rome on foot.[5] When Wilfrid became sick on his return journey, we are told that he was placed on a horse (perhaps one of the pack animals that must have been an essential part of the entourage of any Anglo-Saxon party traveling overland through the Continent) and eventually was carried on a litter. After four days he was brought to Meaux, northeast of Paris, where he had a vision.

"[E]cce! angelus Domini in ueste candida sancto pontifici nostro apparuit, dicens: 'Ego sum Michael summi Dei nuntius, qui misit me ad te indicare, quod tibi adduntur anni uitae pro intercessione sanctae Mariae genetricis Dei semperque uirginis et pro subditorum tuorum lacrimis, ad aures Domini peruenientibus; et hoc tibi erit signum, quod ab hac die in dies melioratus sanaberis et ad patriam tuam peruenies, tibique substantiarum tuarum carissima quaeque redduntur, et in pace uitam consummabis. Paratus quoque esto, quia post IIII annorum spatium iterum uisitabo te. Iam enim memento quod in honore sancti Petri et Andreae apostolis domos aedificasti, sanctae uero Mariae semper uirgini intercedenti pro te nullam fecisti. Habes hoc emendare et in honorem eius domum dedicare.'"

["[L]o! an angel of the Lord in shining raiment appeared to our holy bishop and said, 'I am Michael, the messenger of the most high God, who sent me to tell you that years of life have been added to you by the intercession of St Mary, Mother of God and ever Virgin, and by the lamentations of your followers, which have reached the ears of the Lord; and this shall be a sign to you: from this day you will begin to grow better day by day, and you will reach your native land; and all the most precious of your possessions will be

⁴ *Vita Wilfridi I. episcopi Eboracensis auctore Stephano*, ed. W. Levison, in *Passiones vitaeque sanctorum aevi Merovingici*, ed. B. Krusch and W. Levison, MGH, SS rer. Merov. 6 (Hannover and Leipzig, 1913), 193–263; Stephanus, *Vita sancti Wilfridi*, in *The Life of Bishop Wilfrid by Eddius Stephanus*, text, trans. and notes Bertram Colgrave (Cambridge, 1927). All subsequent references will be to the latter edition.
⁵ Stephanus, *Vita sancti Wilfridi*, chap. 50, ed. Colgrave, 102.

returned to you, and you will end your life in peace. Also be prepared; for after the space of four years I will visit you again. Now remember that you have built churches in honour of the Apostles St Peter and St Andrew; but you have built nothing in honour of St Mary, ever Virgin, who is interceding for you. You have to put this right and to dedicate a church in honour of her.'"] (Stephanus, *Vita sancti Wilfridi*, chap. 56, ed. Colgrave, 122 (text) and 123 (translation)).

Today we do not have to invoke divine intervention to explain Wilfrid's vision. Rome was notorious for its malaria: even Garibaldi could not succeed in eradicating it and it was not until well into the twentieth century that the disease was conquered in Italy.[6] The parasite can take effect quite some time after its victim has been bitten by a mosquito; high fever and attendant hallucinations are a natural consequence. A malarial fever would be as good a diagnosis as any for those who might choose not to suggest a divine source for what Wilfrid saw.

The account prompts many questions, and during this paper there will be occasion to ask a few of them; some may even be answered. The first and most natural of these questions, "Why Meaux?," is not strictly germane to our topic and can be disposed of quickly. At the Synod of Whitby Wilfrid had spoken on behalf of the Frankish bishop Agilbert and he himself had subsequently been consecrated as a bishop by Agilbert, who was later to be buried at Jouarre in the diocese of Meaux.[7] This is not the place to dip our toes into the murky waters of Merovingian politics, but suffice it to say, western Francia, i.e., the area then incorporated in Merovingian Neustria, had not proved to be particularly friendly territory for Wilfrid. Because of his past links with Agilbert, he or his party may have considered that he would receive a welcome in Meaux—and perhaps a decent burial there if he died. This question does, however, prompt one more relevant to our purposes: "What route did Wilfrid take to get to Meaux?"[8]

---

[6] The credit is usually given to Mussolini but "Fascism's anti-malarial achievements were largely confined to the Pontine Marshes [south of Rome]": see Daniel Pick, *Rome or Death: The Obsessions of General Garibaldi* (London, 2005), 214–17, esp. 216.

[7] On Agilbert see Jacques Dubois, "Les évêques de Paris: des origines à l'avènement de Hugues Capet," *Bulletin de la Société de l'Histoire de Paris et de l'Île-de-France* 96 (1969): 33–97, at 64–67. See also C. I. Hammer, "Arbeo of Freising's 'Life and Passion' of St Emmeram: The Martyr and his Critics," *Revue d'Histoire Ecclésiastique* 101 (2006): 5–36, at 11–15, and references mentioned there.

[8] It is a mark of the lack of interest of English historians in the *practicalities* of medieval travel that one has to go back to the old prize-winning university essay by J. E. Tyler, *The Alpine Passes: The Middle Ages (962–1250)* (Oxford, 1930) to learn more about medieval Alpine passes. Fortunately, for Italy itself, several Italian scholars have taken an intense interest in the medieval topography of their own country and have published detailed guides to medieval routes, notably Renato Stopani, *La via Francigena: una strada europea nell'Italia del medioevo* (Florence, 1988) and idem, *La via Francigena del sud: L'Ap-*

By 704 Wilfrid was a seasoned traveler to Rome. On his first trip there as a young teenager in ca. 653 he had accompanied the devout bibliophile Benedict Biscop, from Kent down to Lyons.[9] Lyons, a former Roman *civitas* and seat of a metropolitan bishop, with its numerous stone-built churches and monasteries, must have been an overwhelming sight for the young Wilfrid.[10] Benedict, on the first of his six trips to Rome, had been eager to reach his destination and left Wilfrid behind there. The latter did, however, eventually also make his way to Rome. Both Benedict Biscop and Wilfrid might have traveled on south through Provence and then crossed the sea to a port such as Ostia: certainly Benedict took this route home after his third trip, when he escorted Theodore and Hadrian back to England via Marseilles in 668.[11] But the sea route presents navigational complexities involving the prevailing winds and currents;[12] Benedict and later Wilfrid might equally have crossed by the pass at Mont Cenis, after which a variety of Italian towns would have lain below, offering a choice of routes down to Rome.

We can rule out the route that Wilfrid probably took after he went missionizing in Frisia. He had then visited Dagobert II, king of Austrasia, who offered him the bishopric of Strasbourg, which Wilfrid declined.[13] His most likely route to Rome on that occasion was via the Rhine valley, then to Lake Geneva, thereafter via Martigny over the Great St. Bernard Pass or via Chur to the Septimer, and thence to Italy.[14]

pia Traiana nel medioevo (Florence, 1992). For further literature see the useful *Bibliografia sulla Via Francigena: Prima stesura aggiornata al 31 agosto 1995*, ed. Fabrizio Vanni and Luciano Bassini, intro. Renato Stopani, De Strata Francigena: Studi e ricerche sulle vie di pellegrinaggio del medioevo 3 (Poggibonsi, 1995).

[9] Stephanus, *Vita sancti Wilfridi*, chap. 3, ed. Colgrave, 8.

[10] On the topography of Lyons at this period see Jean-François Reynaud, *Lugdunum Christianum: Lyon du IVᵉ au VIIIᵉ s.: topographie, nécropoles et édifices religieux*, Documents d'archéologie française 69 (Paris, 1998).

[11] *Historia abbatum auctore Bedae*, chap. 3, in *Venerabilis Baedae Historiam ecclesiasticam gentis Anglorum, Historiam abbatum, Epistolam ad Ecgberctum una cum Historia abbatum auctore anonymo*, ed. Charles Plummer, 2 vols. (Oxford, 1896), 1: 364–87, at 366 (text); *The Age of Bede*, trans. J. F. Webb, ed. with intro. D. H. Farmer, rev. repr. (Harmondsworth, 1998), 189; Bede, *HE* 4.1, ed. Colgrave and Mynors, 130.

[12] For an introduction to the difficulties of navigation in the western Mediterranean and further bibliography on its climate, sea currents, and prevailing winds see John H. Pryor, *Geography, Technology, and War: Studies in the Maritime History of the Mediterranean, 649–1571*, Past and Present Publications (Cambridge, 1988, repr. with additional preface, 1992), 12–24, 87–101.

[13] Stephanus, *Vita sancti Wilfridi*, chap. 28, ed. Colgrave, 24.

[14] The St. Gotthard Pass was not available because it seems not to have been opened up until early in the thirteenth century. See further Tyler, *Alpine Passes*, chap. 9, esp. 96–100.

We can also rule out the route that would later have appealed to Anglo-Saxon missionaries in Bavaria, which required crossing several lines of Alps via the Brenner Pass, because it simply lay too far to the east.[15]

It is possible, however, that in 704 Wilfrid aimed at returning home to England by an alternative to the Mt Cenis–Lyons route. By traveling over the Great St. Bernard Pass he could have proceeded in an almost straight north-north-westerly direction through Neustria, as Sigeric's detailed late-tenth-century itinerary from Rome through Francia back to Kent shows.[16] Wilfrid's great enemy, Ebroin, the Neustrian *major domus*, was long dead and so Neustria might no longer have seemed so hazardous.[17] This was probably the route taken from England just twelve years later by Abbot Ceolfrith of Monkwearmouth-Jarrow, who died just short of the Alps at Langres.[18]

When writing about medieval travelers, scholars frequently fail to discuss the daily practicalities of a journey. When Wilfrid decided to undertake his first trip to Rome, his path was eased by a social network. Eanflæd, wife of Oswiu and queen of the Northumbrians, commended the young man through her messengers to her family in Kent,[19] just as Gregory the Great had written letters of introduction to various dignitaries in Gaul in order to smooth Augustine's path in 597;[20] similar letters of commendation from Alcuin penned two centuries later survive in the latter's letter collections.[21]

---

[15] On the Brenner Pass see Tyler, *Alpine Passes*, chap. 11, 111–17.

[16] See the map of Sigeric's itinerary in Ortenberg, "Archbishop Sigeric's Journey to Rome," 320.

[17] On Ebroin see Paul Julian Fouracre, "The Career of Ebroin Mayor of the Palace c.657–680" (Ph.D. diss., University of London, 1981), esp. 285, where he states that there seems to be no objection to summer/autumn 680 as the date of his death. Ebroin's relationship with Wilfrid is illuminatingly discussed by Hammer, "Arbeo of Freising's 'Life and Passion' of St Emmeran," 10–15, 32–33.

[18] Bede, *Historia abbatum*, chap. 21, ed. Plummer, 1:385 (text); *The Age of Bede*, 208–10 (translation); *Historia abbatum auctore anonymo*, chaps. 31–32, in *Venerabilis Baedae*, ed. Plummer, 1: 388–404, at 400 (text); *The Age of Bede*, 224–25 (translation). See also the essay by Richard Marsden in this volume.

[19] Stephanus, *Vita sancti Wilfridi*, chap. 3, ed. Colgrave, 8; Bede, *HE* 5.19, ed. Colgrave and Mynors, 518.

[20] Gregory, *Epistulae* 6.51, 6.52, 6.54, 6.55, and 6.60, in *S. Gregorii Magni Registrum epistularum libri I-VII*, ed. Dag Norberg, CCSL 140 (Turnhout, 1982), 423–25, 427–28, 433, now conveniently translated in *The Letters of Gregory the Great*, trans., with intro. and notes John R. C. Martyn, Mediaeval Sources in Translation 40, 3 vols. (Toronto, 2004), 2: 438–41, 444.

[21] For example, Alcuin, *Epistolae*, nos. 11, 103, and 259, ed. Ernst Dümmler, in *Epistolae Karolini aevi* 2, MGH, Epistolae 4 (Berlin, 1895), 37, 149–50, 417. Cf. also the contribution by Lucia Sinisi in this volume.

We may assume that Wilfrid had traveled to Kent in the company of Ean-flæd's messengers. He had then had to wait a year before he could find a guide in the person of Benedict. After Benedict left him, he did not travel alone but journeyed from Lyons to Rome with companions.[22] Since his biographer had told us that he was "fleet of foot,"[23] we may assume that, as on his final journey from Italy, he was walking rather than traveling on horseback.

On the Continent as in Britain any medieval traveler had to deal with the roads. The Romans had regularly repaired and upgraded their highways but, as Bryan Ward-Perkins has noted, "there is no evidence that this continued in any systematic way beyond the early sixth century."[24] The breakdown of central authority meant that the highways deteriorated, tolls sprang up (ostensibly to repair the roads, though this may frequently be doubted), and the old system of posting stations largely fell into abeyance.[25] We should not be surprised that during Wilfrid's second trip to Rome in 679 Dagobert II gave him a guide in the person of the bishop of Toul, Deodatus, who led him to Perctarit, the king of the Lombards, in northern Italy.[26] We can only speculate why Wilfrid was taken to Perctarit. The latter clearly had ties with England: Paul the Deacon reports that he was en route from Gaul to Britain when a divine messenger told him of the death of Grimoald, who had seized the throne; he returned to Pavia, where he ousted Grimoald's small son and gained the kingdom.[27]

Now that the necessary matter of choosing a route has been discussed, it is worthwhile considering some of the daily practical aspects of traveling to Italy. What happened at nightfall, for instance? Here we can only piece together evidence from sources widely scattered in place and time. But the answer seems simple: travelers camped if lodging was not available. Nowhere does Stephen of Ripon discuss this aspect of Wilfrid's trips. But when Willibald and his brother Wynnebald persuaded their father to travel with them to Rome in 721, we learn

---

[22] "cum sociis suis": Stephanus, *Vita sancti Wilfridi*, chap. 5, ed. Colgrave, 10.

[23] "pedibus uelox": Stephanus, *Vita sancti Wilfridi*, chap. 3, ed. Colgrave, 8.

[24] Bryan Ward-Perkins, *The Fall of Rome and the End of Civilization* (Oxford, 2005), 133.

[25] This conclusion is qualified because one seems to have remained in use on the Augsburg-Salzburg highway in ca. 680: see Hammer, "Arbeo of Freising's 'Life and Passion' of St. Emmeran," 8 (location), 29 (date). One might suppose that others survived in Italy and possibly southern Gaul.

[26] So Stephen of Ripon: see Stephanus, *Vita sancti Wilfridi*, chap. 28, ed. Colgrave, 54. Stephen's account is a partial one. Deodatus presumably accompanied Wilfrid all the way to Rome: they both attended the synod of 679, where they were the 48th and 49th signatories of the fourth session respectively. (In the latter document Deodatus is called "Adeodatus" in both the Greek and Latin versions.)

[27] Paul the Deacon, *Historia Langobardorum* 5.33, ed. L. Bethmann and G. Waitz, MGH, Scriptores rer. Lang. (Hannover, 1878), 45–187, at 155 (text); Paul the Deacon, *History of the Langobards*, trans. William Dudley Foulke (Philadelphia, 1907), 236–37.

that they camped near Rouen.[28] Two types of tent are depicted in manuscripts, though as any art historian knows, illustrations are treacherous material. The ninth-century Utrecht Psalter, whose provenance is from near Rheims, includes a cone tent in its depiction of Psalm 60. This picture was replicated in the Harley Psalter in the twelfth century in Canterbury by the eighth of the artists who had provided illustrations for it over the course of a hundred years or so. Artist H rearranged the position of the tent and converted it into what appears to be a wedge tent. It has been suggested that the art in the Utrecht Psalter mostly derives from a lost late-antique illustrated psalter.[29] But our illustrators preserved a vital detail that suggests that they and their sources were familiar with the realities of camping. Anyone who has pitched a tent in windy, stormy weather knows that a complete supply of a small accessory object is needed to ensure a peaceful night's sleep. Although not mentioned in Ohlgren's iconographical index, the two sets of tents in the illustrations depict a full complement of tent pegs.[30]

After his first trip, Wilfrid's ecclesiastical status and political contacts may have enabled him to obtain lodgings en route. Not all would have been so fortunate. As the zest for travel to Rome grew in the eighth century, there would obviously have been a need for accommodation, especially in the treacherous Alpine passes. Here it is instructive from several points of view to examine somewhat later evidence about housing for travelers in a monastery on the pilgrim route to Rome that was visited by Cenwald, bishop of Worcester, while on a diplomatic mission to Germany in 929: namely St. Gall, in modern-day Switzerland.[31] The

---

[28] Hugeburc of Heidenheim, *Vita Willibaldi episcopi Eichstetensis*, ed. O. Holder-Egger, MGH, Scriptores 15.1 (Hannover, 1887), 86–106, at 91 (text); *The Anglo-Saxon Missionaries in Germany*, trans. and ed. C. H. Talbot (London, 1954), 157 (translation).

[29] For the dating of the artists in the Harley Psalter see William Noel, *The Harley Psalter*, Cambridge Studies in Palaeography and Codicology 4 (Cambridge, 1995), 167, figs. 77 and 78. On Artist H see 115–20 and 164. For an introduction to the Utrecht Psalter see Koert van der Horst, William Noel, and Wilhelmina C. M. Wüstefeld, *The Utrecht Psalter in Mediaeval Art: Picturing the Psalms of David* (Utrecht, 1996) and on its putative late-antique origin see Suzy Dufrenne, *Les illustrations du Psautier d'Utrecht: Sources et apport carolingien*, Association des publications près les Universités de Strasbourg 161 (Paris, 1978). Tents are listed in the index to *Insular and Anglo-Saxon Illuminated Manuscripts: An Iconographic Catalogue, c. A.D. 625 to 1100*, comp. and ed. Thomas H. Ohlgren, Garland Reference Library of the Humanities 631 (New York, 1986).

[30] The illustration to Psalm 131 (132) even more clearly shows the presence of tent pegs: see *Anglo-Saxon Textual Illustration: Photographs of Sixteen Manuscripts with Descriptions and Index*, comp. and ed. Thomas H. Ohlgren (Kalamazoo, 1992), 237, no. 2.91.

[31] The evidence is preserved in St. Gallen, Stiftsbibliothek, 915, p. 5, printed in *Libri Confraternitatum Sancti Galli Augiensis Fabariensis*, ed. Paul Piper, MGH, Necrologiae Germaniae, Supplementband (Berlin, 1884), 137; for a text and translation and entries concerning Anglo-Saxons in other Continental confraternity books see Simon Keynes, "King Athelstan's Books," in *Learning and Literature in Anglo-Saxon England:*

plans of the monastery are well known, especially since the sumptuous edition of them by Horn and Born in 1979.[32] These plans display no fewer than seven separate building-complexes devoted to monastic hospitality and its attendant administration. There was a lodging for visiting monks; a hospice for pilgrims and paupers, complete with an annexe containing a kitchen, bake-, and brew-house; the lodging for the Master of the hospice for pilgrims and paupers, an office that was subordinate to the Porter, who himself had a separate lodging. A fifth complex was for distinguished guests, which also had its own kitchen, bake-, and brewhouse. A sixth building housed servants of the monastery visiting from outlying estates and other servants such as those that might be traveling with the Carolingian emperor's court. Finally, a damaged part of the plans contains what Horn has argued was a house for vassals and knights traveling in the emperor's entourage.[33]

Grand architectural plans often fail to be translated into buildings that accord with the architect's vision—or even into buildings at all. It must also be acknowledged that the plans date, most likely, from the 820s, more than a hundred years after pilgrims had started regularly traveling from England and Francia to Rome. Whether the plans resulted in buildings or not, they do at least present an idealized picture of what was thought *should* be provided for visitors to the monastery. When we examine the plans in detail, we find that the accommodation was modest: there was provision for only sixteen persons in the hospice for pilgrims and paupers, a figure that is not out of line with the extant statutes of Adalhard from Corbie in France, which date from 822. The latter show that the normal number of the poor staying overnight in Corbie would be twelve.[34]

The plans are instructive about the realities of a pilgrim's life. Those who were dependent on charity were presented with housing where the heat in the accommodation portion of the building, which was a lean-to on either side of the hall, had to drift across the partitions at the side from a central fireplace in the middle of the hall; the architect, furthermore, has not bothered to plan for a privy. The house for distinguished guests, on the other hand, had two double

---

Studies Presented to Peter Clemoes on the Occasion of his Sixty-Fifth Birthday, ed. Michael Lapidge and Helmut Gneuss (Cambridge, 1985), 143–201, at 198–201 and pls. 13–16.

[32] Walter Horn and Ernest Born, *The Plan of St. Gall: A Study of the Architecture and Economy of, and Life in a Paradigmatic Carolingian Monastery*, California Studies in Art, 3 vols. (Berkeley, Los Angeles, and London, 1979).

[33] The buildings are described in Horn and Born, *Plan of St Gall*, 2: part 5.8; see especially 2: 166 for an interpretation of the damaged section of the manuscript.

[34] "duodecim pauperes qui supra noctem ibi manent": *Consuetudines Corbeienses* 10, ed. Joseph Semmler, in *Initia consuetudinis Benedictinae: Consuetudines saeculi octavi et noni*, ed. Kassius Hallinger, Corpus consuetudinum monasticarum 1 (Siegburg, 1963), 355–422, at 372. There is a convenient translation by Charles W. Jones in Horn and Born, *Plan of St Gall*, 3: Appendix 2, 103–23, at 105.

rooms with fireplaces at both narrow gable-ends of the building. A lean-to on the long side of the building housed servants, while on the other side there were stables for the animals, beyond which were the latrines, situated well away from aristocratic noses and conveniently placed for the ordure from the animals to be mucked out. The *Consuetudines Corbeienses* laid down that each pilgrim was to receive a daily ration of a loaf of mixed wheat and rye bread weighing 3.5 pounds and two tankards of beer, with a further half a loaf to be issued on departure. There was special consideration for sick pilgrims and those from abroad. Given the superior accommodation provided for distinguished guests in the St. Gall plans, we might well imagine that the latter were provided with more lavish and varied fare.

Some aspects of human behavior thus never change. The indigent were treated with charity, but it was much better to be rich and powerful. Marcel Mauss's insight into the reciprocity of most human relations as described in his *Essai sur le don* no doubt applied to the latter.[35] We may fairly assume that accommodation was expected to be matched by a counter-gift, and other monastic benefactions, such as inclusion of one's name in a *Liber Confraternitatis* as at St. Gall or Pfäfers,[36] are unlikely to have come cheaply.[37]

It is natural to consider the speed of travel overland to and from Rome. Ceolfrith, who was traveling on horseback, landed in Gaul on 12 August and died in Langres on 25 September: presumably had he been in good health he could have made better time.[38] Unfortunately, Sigeric's itinerary does not record how long he took on his journey back home. On the basis of two itineraries by Frenchmen made from France to Rome in 1254 and 1350 Yves Renaud has estimated that a senior prelate such as a bishop and his entourage would, in the course of a long journey, cover only thirty to forty kilometers a day (i.e., nineteen to twenty-five miles), whereas ordinary travelers such as pilgrims could travel more than fifty

---

[35] Translated as *The Gift: Forms and Functions of Exchange in Archaic Societies*, trans. Ian Cunnison (London, 1954).

[36] The entries in the confraternity book of Pfäfers seem to date from 941 x 946: it has been speculated that they reflect a visit by Oda, archbishop of Canterbury (941–958), and his retinue, perhaps on a journey to or from Rome to collect his *pallium*. See further Keynes, "King Athelstan's Books," 201 and pl. 16.

[37] One may suspect that the "reliquary of remarkable craftsmanship, English work (*Anglico opere*), decorated subtly and most beautifully with silver, gold, and gems, sent [to Monte Cassino] by a certain Englishman of rank" (*a quodam nobili Anglo transmissus*) in the second decade of the eleventh century was a gift prompted by a prior visit to the monastery: see *Die Chronik von Montecassino*, ed. Hartmut Hoffmann, MGH, Scriptores 34 (Hannover, 1980), 230, lines 22–26.

[38] Anonymous, *Historia abbatum*, chap. 32, ed. Plummer, 1: 400 (arrival in Gaul); Bede, *Historia abbatum*, chaps. 21 and 23, ed. Plummer, 1: 385–86 (arrival and death in Langres).

kilometers (31 miles) *per diem*.[39] It is possible that the couriers (*hleaperas*) sent by King Alfred with documents to Rome in 880 might have been able to travel even more rapidly, especially if they were furnished with the means to hire horses:[40] in the mid-fifteenth century professional couriers in Italy were able to cover sixty to seventy kilometers a day on average.[41]

Travel is an inherently dangerous activity, and, sadly, for some the trip to Rome was a terminal experience. This applies to more than just various Anglo-Saxon kings such as Cædwalla who deliberately retired to Rome, especially in the late sixth and early seventh centuries, in order to die near the saints.[42] As we have seen, Ceolfrith died in Langres, north of the Alps, in 716. Two centuries later, in 921 and again in 923 Anglo-Saxons were killed by Saracens in the Alps.[43] Others just did not make it there. The father of Willibald and Wynnebald crossed the Alps, but then died in Lucca, where he was buried.[44] A priest called Hunwine, who was deputed by Cuthbert, the abbot of Wearmouth-Jarrow, to take a variety of gifts to Lull in the late 750s, was aiming to reach Rome, but died, evidently

---

[39] Yves Renouard, "Routes, étapes et vitesses de marche de France à Rome au XIIIᵉ et au XIVᵉ siècles d'après les itinéraires d'Eude Rigaud (1254) et de Bartélemy Bonis (1350)," in *Studi in onore di Amintore Fanfani*, 3 vols. (Milan, 1962), vol. 3: *Medioevo*, 403–28, at 428.

[40] *The Anglo-Saxon Chronicle MS A*, ed. Janet M. Bately, *The Anglo-Saxon Chronicle*: A Collaborative Edition, ed. David Dumville and Simon Keynes, 3 (Cambridge, 1986), 54, s.a. 889.

[41] Renouard, "Routes, étapes et vitesses," 428.

[42] Clare Stancliffe, "Kings who Opted Out," in *Ideal and Reality in Frankish and Anglo-Saxon Society: Studies Presented to J. M. Wallace-Hadrill*, ed. Patrick Wormald, Donald Bullough, and Roger Collins (Oxford, 1983), 154–76, at 156–57. For Cædwalla's epitaph see Richard Sharpe, "King Ceadwalla's Roman Epitaph," in *Latin Learning and English Lore: Studies in Anglo-Saxon Literature for Michael Lapidge*, ed. Katherine O'Brien O'Keeffe and Andy Orchard, 2 vols. (Toronto, 2005), 1: 171–94, at 176–77.

[43] Could one of these entries be a doublet? *Les annales de Flodoard*, ed., intro., notes Ph. Lauer (Paris, 1905 [1906]), 5, 19 (texts); *English Historical Documents c. 500–1042*, ed. Dorothy Whitelock, English Historical Documents 1, 2nd edn. (London, 1979), 344, no. 24 (translations). Alfred's sister Æthelswith, who had been married to Burgred, ousted king of the Mercians, died en route to Rome and was buried in Pavia in 888, though this was presumably a return visit, as Burgred had gone to Rome in 874 after his abdication: see *Anglo-Saxon Chronicle MS A*, ed. Bately, 49, s.a. 874.

[44] Hugeburc, *Vita Willibaldi*, chap. 3, ed. Holder-Egger, 91 (text); Talbot, *Anglo-Saxon Missionaries*, 158 (translation); and Hugeburc, *Vita Wynnebaldi abbatis Heidenheimensis*, ed. O. Holder-Egger, MGH, Scriptores 15.1 (Hannover, 1887), 106–17, at 107–8. Andreas Bauch reproduces Holder-Egger's editions of the Lives of Willibald and Wynnebald with translations by him into German on the facing pages, together with extremely useful introductions and notes, in *Quellen zur Geschichte der Diözese Eichstätt*, vol. 1: *Biographien der Gründungszeit*, 2nd edn., Eichstätter Studien, Neue Folge, 19 (Regensburg, 1984).

without fulfilling his commission, south of the city in Benevento.[45] Wigheard went to Rome in 668 to receive his *pallium*; he reached his destination, but died in Rome of the plague, leaving a vacancy in Canterbury that was to be filled subsequently by Theodore.[46]

Benedict and Wilfrid were the forerunners of what was to become a veritable flood of Anglo-Saxon visitors to Rome from the late seventh century onwards. A demand for accommodation in the Eternal City was an inevitable consequence, which was eventually met. Around the time when Ine, king of the West Saxons, retired to Rome in 726 the so-called *Schola Saxonum*, the Saxon quarter of Rome, came into being,[47] which is where most Anglo-Saxon travelers thereafter are likely to have stayed. The evidence for the *Schola* has long been assembled and need not be rehearsed here.[48]

On his first visit to Rome Wilfrid, we are told, visited the shrines of the saints. At this time there was still something of the old Roman horror of having dead bodies interred in urban areas and so the places he visited would have been the various catacombs on the roads leading out of Rome. It was not until the ninth century that the bones of the martyrs were to be brought within the walls of Rome and placed in various churches (some built for that purpose). We are not told how Wilfrid located these sacred sites, but it was natural that pious tourists, like most visitors to a foreign place, would find a *vade mecum* to places of especial interest in Rome to be very useful. Guidebooks were composed to meet the need: several were compiled in the seventh century, suggesting that religious tourism was already becoming significant. One of these guides, a now-lost *Itinerarium urbis Romae*, may have been brought back to England by an Anglo-Saxon visitor: in the twelfth century William of Malmesbury draws on it in his *Gesta regum Anglorum*.[49]

---

[45] *Die Briefe des heiligen Bonifatius und Lullus*, ed. Michael Tangl, MGH, Epistolae Selectae (Berlin, 1916), 251, no. 116 (text); Whitelock, *English Historical Documents* 1: 832, no. 185 (translation).

[46] Bede, *HE*, 3.29 and 4.1, ed. Colgrave and Mynors, 318 and 328.

[47] This has been extensively covered in the literature: see, for example, Moore, "Saxon Pilgrims," 90–125, and Ortenberg, "Archbishop Sigeric's Journey to Rome," 204–6.

[48] Moore, "Saxon Pilgrims"; see also G. J. Hoogewerff, "Friezen, Franken en Saksen te Rome," *Mededeelingen van het Nederlandsch Historiaat Instituut te Rome*, 3rd ser., 5 (1947): 1–70 and 4 plates and a map of the various *scholae* in Rome opposite 70, esp. 9–11, 32, 36–38, 60–61.

[49] *Notitia ecclesiarum urbis Romae* may be the earliest extant guide, being written in the period 625 x 649. Vying with it is *De locis sanctis martyrum quae sunt foris ciuitatis Romae et ecclesiae quae intus Romae habentur*, compiled ca. 635 x 645. Sharing features in common with the latter is the *Itinerarium Malmesburiense* (compiled 648 x 672), so called because it survives embedded in William of Malmesbury's *Gesta regum Anglorum*, chap. 352, in William of Malmesbury, *Gesta regum Anglorum / The History of the English Kings*, vol. 1, ed. and trans. R. A. B. Mynors, completed R. M. Thomson and M. Winterbottom, Oxford Medieval Texts (Oxford, 1998), 614–20, an English provenance that prompts

Having touched on aspects of travel experienced by Anglo-Saxons journeying to Italy, we might now ponder why they chose to go there. Our travelers may be classified into three broad categories: those engaged in some form of ecclesiastical business, pilgrims, and those involved in trade. As will become apparent, the categorization is not watertight or exclusive, and is merely a convenient way of assembling a large amount of information in a concise and orderly fashion.

We have already seen that Wilfrid on his second and third trips engaged in appeals to the papal court. A more common reason for ecclesiastical trips to Rome was for an archbishop to collect his *pallium*. This is a well-known reason for archbishops of Canterbury and, later, York to go to Rome: it need not be discussed further here.[50]

Perhaps inevitably there were some Anglo-Saxon ecclesiasts who pursued a religious career in Italy. For instance, after Willibald, the later bishop of Eichstätt, had returned to Italy following his trip to Jerusalem (described in such detail in Hugeburc's Life of the saint), he traveled to the recently refounded abbey of Monte Cassino, where in the course of a residency lasting some ten years from 729 onwards he reformed the monastery on Benedictine principles.[51]

Not everyone followed Benedict's rule, however. For eleven months, probably between 769 and 770, a bishop called Wigbert, "who was from the people of the Angles in origin," held the office of abbot of Farfa, just northeast of Rome.[52] Poor Wigbert was unfortunate in his biographer. Gregory of Catino compiled his history of the monastery at a time of ecclesiastical reform around 1100. Because Wigbert's predecessor had declared him his successor on the day

---

the suggestion that it was brought back by an English pilgrim. The *Anonymus Einsiedelensis* followed, being compiled in the mid-eighth century. For the dating and the texts see *Codice Topografico della Città di Roma*, vol. 2, ed. Roberto Valentini and Giuseppe Zucchetti, Fonti per la Storia d'Italia 88 (Rome, 1942), 72–99 (*Notitia*), 101–31 (*De locis sanctis*), 141–53 (*Itin. Malmes.*), and 155–207 (*Itin. Einsied.*), all reprinted with minor emendations in *Itineraria et alia geographica*, ed. F. Glorie, CCSL 175 (Turnhout, 1965), 305–11, 315–22, 325–28, and 331–43, respectively. For some brief comments on the *Itinerarium Malmesburiense* see William of Malmesbury, *Gesta regum Anglorum / The History of the English Kings*, vol. 2: *General Introduction and Commentary* by R. M. Thomson in collaboration with M. Winterbottom, Oxford Medieval Texts (Oxford, 1999), 308–9.

[50] See *Prosopography of Anglo-Saxon England*; http://www.pase.ac.uk, Event Terms, s.v. "Pallium-receipt," "Pallium-despatch," and "Pallium-request" (accessed 22 September 2006).

[51] Hugeburc, *Vita Willibaldi*, chap. 5, ed. Holder-Egger, 102 (text); Talbot, *Anglo-Saxon Missionaries*, 172–73 (translation). On Willibald's visit to Jerusalem, see the contribution by Rodney Aist in this volume.

[52] Richard Ring kindly first drew my attention to Wigbert, whom he discusses in "The Lands of Farfa: Studies in Lombard and Carolingian Italy" (Ph.D. diss., University of Wisconsin, 1972), 207–10. My thanks to him for supplying me with copies of extracts from the editions cited in n. 53–54 below.

he died, contrary to the Benedictine Rule, Gregory excluded him from the list of abbots, damned him for his bad behavior, and reported his deposition by a Lombard *gastaldus* from a neighboring town, who was acting under the orders of King Desiderius.[53] Some ten years later "Guigpertus aepiscopus"—surely the same man—with the support of Charlemagne, who had deposed the Lombard monarchy, and Hildebrand, the duke of Spoleto, donated to Farfa the monastery of the Holy Angel situated between the two rivers at the broken bridge near Rieti, so we may suspect that the story was rather more complex and that Wigbert may have fallen foul of the politics of the last days of the Lombard kingdom.[54] Because there are so many other Anglo-Saxons who attained high ecclesiastical office in various Continental polities north of the Alps, we might be reasonably optimistic that a search of Italian church records will reveal more Anglo-Saxon clerics who did likewise in Italy.

The second category of visitors to the the Eternal City is perhaps most likely to attract our attention, namely, the pilgrims. One pilgrim story may be taken as representative of the experience of many. A pupil of Aldhelm's, Æthilwald, composed a poem no later than 705 about three men who had made a pilgrimage to Rome. It is written in a rather recherché form of Latin[55] and does not name its central characters, which provide two very good reasons as to why the account has not fired the imagination of scholars.

The fate of one of the three pilgrims must have been sadly common: he died in Rome. The two surviving pilgrims eventually returned to their fatherlands (*patrias*), presumably two different Anglo-Saxon kingdoms. What is particularly instructive is the goods that accompanied them. They returned home with volumes of monastic rules, silks and cloth dyed in purple, relics of the saints, and images of the Virgin. Given our scanty sources, it is instructive to find that all these objects can be paralleled from other sources. Benedict Biscop brought

---

[53] "quendam episcopum, Wigbertum nomine, Anglorum gente exortum": *Constructio monasterii Farfensis*, Lectio 2, and *Chronicon Farfense*, in *Chronicon Farfense di Gregorio di Catino: Precedono La constructio farfensis e gli scritti di Ugo di Farfa*, ed. Ugo Balzani, vol. 1, Fonti per la Storia d'Italia pubblicate dall'Istituto storico italiano, Scrittori secoli IX–XII (Rome, 1903), 18–19 and 155, respectively. In the latter source he is called "Guicbertum nomine." The spelling *Wigbert* suggests that Gregory had access to an early source preserving the Anglo-Saxon spelling of the name.

[54] "concedimus . . . monasterium sancti angeli quod est positum inter duo flumina ad pontem ante ciuitatem reatinam": *Il regesto di Farfa compilato da Gregorio di Catino e pubblicato dalla Società romana di Storia patria*, ed. I. Giorgi and U. Balzani, 5 vols. (Rome, 1879–1914), 2: 109, no. 142. Wigbert's name has here been influenced by the spelling of Lombard names. The "Holy Angel" is presumably the archangel Michael, whose interest for Anglo-Saxons is discussed further below.

[55] See now Brent Miles, "The *Carmina Rhythmica* of Æthilwald: Edition, Translation, and Commentary," *Journal of Medieval Latin* 14 (2004): 73–117, at 77–83 (introduction and text), 92–93 (translation), and 96–109 (commentary). For the date see 77.

home not merely books with him from his six journeys to Rome; he also introduced a monastic rule that was a blend of no fewer than seventeen rules that
he had encountered on his travels.[56] When Wilfrid built his church at Ripon
sometime between 671 and 678, he adorned it with "gold and silver and varied
purples."[57] Since the purple was derived from a Mediterranean shellfish, it ultimately had to have traveled from there. As for the relics of the saints (perhaps at
this time still contact-relics rather than actual mortal remains), Wilfrid returned
from all three of his visits to Rome with relics.[58] Likewise, Benedict Biscop on
his fifth trip to Rome had brought back "an abundance of relics of the blessed
apostles and martyrs of Christ," as well as paintings of the saints and "an image
of the blessed mother of God and ever-Virgin Mary" together with representations of the twelve apostles to adorn the walls of the church of St. Peter at
Wearmouth.[59]

Fortunately the sources are not so reticent about the identity of other pilgrims. Moore lists fifty-four named pilgrims from England, from Benedict Biscop in the mid-seventh century to visitors in the late eighth century. Moore concentrated on traditional literary sources and thus denied himself the opportunity
to encounter more direct evidence of Anglo-Saxons in Rome. In 1935, two years
before Moore published his study, Angelo Silvagni recorded in the *Inscriptiones
Christianae urbis Romae* a collection of names incised in the Catacomb of Commodilla. Silvagni commented: "Litterae forma capitali sunt, uncialibus uel potius
anglo-saxonicis permixtae . . ." ('The letters are capitals, mixed with uncials or
rather Anglo-Saxon [script] . . .').[60] Unfortunately, Silvagni's transcription seems
to have been overlooked by Anglo-Saxonists. In 1975 Antonio Ferrua published
in another volume of the *Inscriptiones* some names that are preserved in the Catacomb of Marcellinus and Peter, including someone with the seemingly Anglo-
Saxon name of *Ceolbert*.[61] In 1994 as a contribution to the report on the frescoes

---

[56] Anonymous, *Historia abbatum*, chap. 6, ed. Plummer, 1: 390 (text); *The Age of Bede*,
215 (translation).

[57] "auro et argento purpuraque uaria mirifice decorauit," in Stephanus, *Vita sancti
Wilfridi*, chap. 17, ed. Colgrave, 34.

[58] Stephanus, *Vita sancti Wilfridi*, chaps. 5, 33, and 55, ed. Colgrave, 12, 67, and
121.

[59] Bede, *Historia abbatum*, chap. 6, ed. Plummer, 1:369 (text); *The Age of Bede*, 192
(translation).

[60] *Inscriptiones Christianae urbis Romae septimo saeculo antiquiores*, nova series, vol.
2: *Coemeteria in Viis Cornelia Aurelia, Portuensi et Ostiensi*, ed. Angelus Silvagni, Inscriptiones Christianae Italiae saeculo XVI antiquiores, Pars Prior: Roma 1.2 (Rome, 1935),
369, no. 6449.

[61] *Inscriptiones Christianae urbis Romae septimo saeculo antiquiores*, nova series, vol.
6: *Coemeteria in Viis Latina, Labicana et Praenestina*, ed. Antonius Ferrua, Inscriptiones
Christianae Italiae saeculo XVI antiquiores, Pars Prior: Roma 1.6 (Rome, 1975), 92, no.
15966 B 7 (hereafter cited as *ICVR*, n.s. 6, ed. Ferrua).

in the Catacomb of Commodilla, Professor Carlo Carletti published a series of graffiti, identified by him as including Anglo-Saxon names, which are incised on the full-length fresco depiction of St. Luke.[62] Carletti noted that one of the names, *Eadbald*, is in runic script. Since then he has identified another inscription, conjecturally transcribed by Ferrua as "Fir(mina) filia,"[63] to be, in fact, the runic form of an Anglo-Saxon name *Fajhild*. Yet another inscription transcribed by Ferrua as *Firmina* has been read by A. E. Felle as *æpelferþ*, a relatively common Anglo-Saxon name, here also written in runic script.[64]

Carletti has located some 370 names of persons in fourteen catacombs in Rome that date from the end of the seventh to the beginning of the ninth centuries, with up to a dozen of them being Anglo-Saxon. From a human angle, this is a very exciting finding because here we can encounter records made by Anglo-Saxons from perhaps thirteen centuries ago. The last word on this material has certainly not yet been said, however. For instance, Carletti claims that one of the inscriptions, apparently written in a minuscule script, represents an Anglo-Saxon named *cedilomi*. It is difficult to recognize this as an Anglo-Saxon name. From the transcription it might plausibly be suggested that the first element is *aedil*, an early form of *æthel-* 'noble,' though it is difficult to suggest what the second element might be. The text is badly in need of re-examination by an Anglo-Saxon palaeographer.[65]

Professor Carletti was able to move beyond Silvagni and Ferrua in his interpretation of the Roman epigraphic material because of another dramatic discovery he had made over a decade before at Gargano on the Adriatic coast southeast of Rome, a discovery which proves that Anglo-Saxon pilgrims moved well beyond Rome when they visited Italy.

In ca. 787 a deaf and mute man of English ethnic origin came with his companions to the shrine of St. Benedict at Monte Cassino. Praying at the shrine of the saint, not an hour later he regained his powers of speech—and proved to be

---

[62] Johannes Georg Dekkers, Gabriele Mietke, Albrecht Weiland, mit einem Beitrag zu Geschichte und Topographie von Carlo Carletti, *Die Katakombe "Commodilla": Repertorium der Malereien*, Roma Sotterranea Cristiana 10 (Vatican City, 1994).

[63] *ICVR*, n.s. 6, ed. Ferrua, 92, no. 15966 B 6.

[64] *ICVR*, n.s. 6, ed. Ferrua, 94, no. 15972. Felle's article was promised as forthcoming in *Romanobarbarica* 17 (2002–2004), though it is not in that volume and I have been unable to trace it; his interpretation was reported in advance of publication by Ute Schwab, "Weitere angelsächsische Runen in Rom," *Nytt om Runer: Meldingsblad om runeforskning* 17 (2002 [2004]): 17–18, at 17.

[65] So far there has only been a preliminary examination of the Roman uncial script of some of the catacomb inscriptions: see Carlo Tedeschi, "L'onciale usuale a Roma e nell'area romana in alcune iscrizioni graffite," *Scrittura e civiltà* 16 (1992): 313–29 and plates 1–10.

bilingual in both English and Latin.[66] W. J. Moore mentioned the incident in passing. What he failed to record was that the disabled man and his companions were pilgrims who were en route to St. Michael of Gargano.

Gargano is the location of a remarkable cave on the Adriatic coast. It became in the sixth century the site of a shrine to St. Michael the Archangel, a cult brought to Italy by the Byzantines. At a conference in 1978 Professor Carletti revealed that there were Anglo-Saxon names to be found incised there, including no fewer than four runic inscriptions, to which a fifth, **leofwini** *Leofwini*, has more recently been recognized.[67] The four inscriptions have now been the object of a thorough runological and philological examination by René Derolez and Ute Schwab;[68] their readings of three of them may be taken as definitive, all being

---

[66] *Die Chronik von Montecassino*, chap. 13, ed. Hoffmann, 48–49. For an analogue and a possible source of the story see 48, n. 1 to chap. 13.

[67] Carlo Carletti, "Iscrizioni murali," in *Il santuario di S. Michele sul Gargano dal vi al ix secolo: Contributo alla storia della Langobardia meridionale: Atti del convegno tenuto a Monte Sant'Angelo il 9–10 dicembre 1978*, ed. idem and Giorgio Otranto, Vetera Christianorum, Scavi e ricerche 2 (Bari, 1980), 7–158 and 21 plates, with photographic reproductions of the physical setting and three of the inscriptions in figs. 1–4, opposite 332. The four inscriptions are discussed by Maria Giovanna Arcamone in "Le inscrizioni runiche di Monte Sant'Angelo sul Gargano," *Vetera Christianorum* 18 (1981): 157–71 and figs. 1–3, repr. verbatim in *Puglia paleocristiana*, Vetera Christianorum, Sezione Apuliae res 1–6, 6 vols. (Bari, 1970–1991), 4: 107–22 (vols. 4–6 were published under the title *Puglia paleocristiana e altomedievale*). The latter has now published the fifth inscription: "Una nuova inscrizione runica da Monte Sant'Angelo," *Vetera Christianorum* 18 (1992): 405–10, repr. verbatim in *Culto e insediamenti Micaelici nell'Italia meridionale fra tarda antichità e medioevo: Atti del Convegno Internazionale, Monte Sant'Angelo 18–21 novembre 1992*, ed. Carlo Carletti e Giorgio Otranto, Scavi e ricerche 7 (Bari, 1994), 184–89. Arcamone's 1992 paper (which accurately transliterated the runes) elicited an important response from Ute Schwab and René Derolez, "More Runes at Monte Sant'Angelo," *Nytt om Runer: Meldingsblad om runeforskning* 9 (1994): 18–19. Arcamone has another discussion of the runic inscriptions at Rome and Gargano, together with photographs and transcriptions, in "Iscrizioni runiche in Italia," in *I Germani e la scrittura: Atti del XXXIII Convegno dell'Associazione Italiana di Filologia Germanica, Pescara, 7–9 giugno 2006*, ed. Elisabetta Fazzini and Eleonora Cianci (Alessandria, 2007), 127–49. The inscriptions at Rome and Gargano are also briefly discussed and catalogued in Elisabeth Okasha, "Anglo-Saxon Inscriptions Found Outside the British Isles," in *West Over Sea: Studies in Scandinavian Sea-Borne Expansion and Settlement before 1300: A Festschrift in Honour of Dr. Barbara E. Crawford*, ed. Beverley Ballin Smith, Simon Taylor, and Gareth Williams, The Northern World 31 (Leiden, 2007): 69–80, at 72–73, 78–79.

[68] R. Derolez and U. Schwab, "The Runic Inscriptions of Monte S. Angelo (Gargano)," *Mededelingen van de Koninklijke Academie voor Wetenschappen, Letteren en Schone Kunsten van België, Klasse der Letteren*, Jaargang 45, Nr. 1, Academiae Analecta (Brussels, 1983), 96–112. (For those who might seek to obtain this volume by inter-library loan, it is important to specify "Klasse der Letteren"; it is distinct from the series "Klasse der

clearly identifiable as names in English runic script: **wigfus** *Wigfus*, **herræd** *Herræd*, and **hereberehct** *Hereberehct* (= *Herebreht*).[69] The fourth set of runes is damaged and can be read either as [. . .]**mægu**[. . .] *mægu* or [. . .]**mægy**[. . .] *mægy*.

There are also other names incised in the shrine at Gargano. One inscription of particular interest reads: "+ EADRHID SAXSO V(IR) H(ONESTUS)." Though the form of the second element of the personal name is puzzling, the spelling of the first element and the ethnic designator seems clearly to denote someone of Anglo-Saxon origin, though the location of the inscription and the honorific "uir honestus" suggests that he was in the employ of the Lombard ducal court, probably around 706.[70]

The other non-runic inscriptions at Gargano have been subject to little or no palaeographic or onomastic analysis.[71] Just as Derolez and Schwab have been

---

Schone Kunsten." My thanks to Dr. Francesca Tinti for obtaining a copy of this article for me.)

[69] The use of the arc ⌢ indicates that the letters beneath it form a single bind rune. (A bind rune is a ligature of two or more runes that have the main stave in common. For an introduction see Mindy MacLeod, "Ligatures in Early Runic and Roman Inscriptions," in *Runes and their Secrets: Studies in Runology*, ed. Marie Stoklund, Michael Lerche Nielsen, Berte Holmberg, and Gillian Fellows-Jensen [Copenhagen, 2006], 183–99, and further literature there cited.) It is regrettable that later publications still perpetuate errors. The names **wigfus** *wigfus*, **herræd** *herræd*, and **hereberehct** *hereberehct* are all mistranscribed in Carlo Carletti, "Testimonianze scritte del pellegrinaggio altomedievale in Occidente Roma e l'Italia," in *"Los muros tienen la palabra": Materiales para una historia de los graffiti*, ed. F. M. Gimeno Blay and Mª Luz Mandigorra Llavata, Publicaciones del Seminario internacional de estudios sobre la cultura escrita "Jose Trenchs Ódena" 3 ([Valencia], 1997), 73–102, at 99, pl. 4; also in idem, "Roma e il Gargano: Testimonianze scritte di visitatori altomedievali," in *Libri, Documenti, Epigrafi medievali: possibilità di studi comparativi: Atti del Convegno internazionale di studio dell'Associazione italiana dei Paleografi e Diplomatisti, Bari (2–5 ottobre 2000)*, ed. Francesco Magistrale, Corinna Drago, and Paolo Fioretti, Studi e ricerche 2 (Spoleto, 2002), 547–63, at 562; and in idem, "Iscrizioni murali del santuario garganico," in *Culte et pèlerinages à saint Michel en Occident: les trois monts dédiés à l'archange*, ed. Pierre Bouet, Giorgio Otranto, and André Vauchez, Collection de l'École française de Rome 316 (Rome, 2003), 91–103, at 102, fig. 5.

[70] Derolez and Schwab devoted an appendix to this (non-runic) inscription in "Runic Inscriptions of Monte S. Angelo," 125–30, in 1983. In spite of this, Antonio Enrico Felle in "Testimonianze epigrafiche del pellegrinaggio Garganico in età altomedievale: la memoria e la scrittura," *Mitteilungen zur christlichen Archäologie* 7 (2001): 60–77, mistranscribes the name *Eadrhid* reproduced in the photograph on 75, fig. 17, and reprints Carlo Carletti's inaccurate apograph in fig. 18. (Felle's paper is a revision of a paper published two years before in *L'angelo, la montagna, il pellegrino: Monte Sant'Angelo e il santuario di San Michele del Gargano: archeologia, arte, culto, devozione dalle origini ai nostri giorni*, ed. Pina Belli D'Elia [Foggia, 1999], 30–41.)

[71] The complexities can be illustrated from the name *TATO*, which appears in majuscule script at Gargano, and a second name in minuscules that has been transcribed

able to suggest a date of between 700 and 750 for the Gargano runic inscriptions on the basis of their letter forms, so it might be possible to provide a closer dating than "late seventh to early ninth centuries" for the names in non-runic scripts. Furthermore, close attention to the inscriptions might identify other Anglo-Saxons whose presence has been overlooked, either because they employed a Latinate or biblical name or because their names have been confused with others of Germanic origin. All this will be tricky work and it should be performed by scholars possessed of an intimate knowledge of insular and other contemporary European scripts, and also with the necessary philological and onomastic knowledge. Fortunately, considerable advances have been made in recent years in the understanding of the development of insular script, especially through an analysis of inscriptions of various kinds.[72] The names offer a precious increment to this small corpus of inscriptions, though, as already indicated, analysis will not be easy: apart from the difficulty of reading the inscriptions themselves accurately, one cannot automatically assume that the names are all autographs. Investigators will need also to explore whether there could be Frisians included amongst the

---

as *tato*, though the latter inscription as reproduced in a color photograph in *L'angelo, la montagna, il pellegrino*, ed. Belli D'Elia, 41, could be read as *tate*. Carletti has assumed without discussion that these are Beneventan, presumably in script as in name. Tato is certainly a known Beneventan name (see Wilhelm Bruckner, *Die Sprache der Lango-barden*, Quellen und Forschungen zur Sprach- und Culturgeschichte der germanischen Völker 75 [Strassburg, 1879], 240, s.v. *Tàdo*), but the final majuscule "O" is characteristic of the quadrangular display script found in certain Anglo-Saxon manuscripts such as the Lindisfarne Gospels and *Tate* is an attested female Anglo-Saxon hypocoristic name (Mats Redin, *Studies on Uncompounded Personal Names in Old English*, Inaugural Dissertation [Uppsala, 1919], 114, s.v. Tate). Carletti may well be right in his assessment, but his assumption is worth testing by someone familiar with both insular and Beneventan scripts.

[72] See, for example, G. Charles-Edwards, "The Springmount Bog Tablets: Their Implications for Insular Epigraphy," *Studia Celtica* 36 (2002): 27–45; eadem, "A Reconsideration of the Origins of Early Insular Monumental Lettering of the Mixed Alphabet Type: The Case of the 'Lapis Echodi' Inscription on Iona," *Proceedings of the Society of Antiquaries of Scotland* 134 (2004): 173–81; Carlo Tedeschi, "Osservazioni sulla paleografia delle iscrizioni britanniche paleocristiane (V–VII sec.): contributo allo studio dell'origine delle scritture insulari," *Scrittura e civiltà* 19 (1995): 67–121; idem, *Conge-ries lapidum: Iscrizioni brittaniche dei secoli V-VII*, 2 vols. (Pisa, 2005); Gifford Charles-Edwards, "Insular Display Capitals and their Origins," in *Making and Meaning in Insular Art: Proceedings of the Fifth International Conference on Insular Art held at Trinity College Dublin, 25–28 August 2005*, ed. Rachel Moss, TRIARC Research Studies in Irish Art 1 (Dublin, 2007), 228–41. Further work on this subject will now be greatly facilitated by the volumes of *A Corpus of Early Medieval Inscribed Stones and Stone Sculpture in Wales*, vol. 1: *South-East Wales and the English Border*, ed. Mark Redknap and John M. Lewis (Cardiff, 2007); vol. 2: *South-West Wales*, ed. Nancy Edwards (Cardiff, 2007); and vol. 3: *North Wales*, ed. Nancy Edwards (forthcoming).

names: one of the two dedicatees of the church in the *Schola Frisonum* in Rome was St. Michael, and so it is not unreasonable to suggest that Frisians too may have visited Gargano.[73]

The presence of Anglo-Saxon names inscribed in two quite different scripts, Roman and runic, at holy sites in both Rome and Gargano invites further consideration. The association of runes with magic and with religious monuments, such as the Ruthwell Cross, might suggest one explanation. To attach one's name in a powerful script to a holy site or image could be seen as mystically transferring some of that religious power to oneself, a means of securing one's future—if not in this world, then certainly in the next. On the other hand, the presence of names in Roman script rather undermines that conjecture. The names perhaps suggest instead that in the early centuries of the Anglo-Saxon era both alphabetical systems were in common use. This helps explain the presence of runes on coins. For about a hundred years from the late sixth century on, runes appear on coins from the southeast of England; coins from East Anglia bear runes throughout the eighth century, the name of the mysterious King Beonna from ca. 760 being inscribed in a mixture of runes and Roman script; runes continue to appear on some Northumbrian coins as late as the first half of the ninth century.[74] One might even go further and suggest that at first texts in the vernacular might have been written in runes, which would explain why they were used to incise the Old English *Dream of the Rood* on the Ruthwell Cross. On that hypothesis, Roman script would have been the province of Latin texts, the preserve of more formal writings, including writings from the classical past and legal documents such as land charters. Coins literally bore mixed messages: they proclaimed the status of the ruler in whose name they were issued, yet they had the everyday function of exchange. The mixed alphabet on the Beonna coinage helps explain how the runic letters eth, thorn, and wynn could become incorporated into the Roman alphabet that eventually became the normal script for recording the Old English vernacular. We should not necessarily interpret the Roman and runic alphabets as having equal standing: the Roman alphabet was too closely associated with Rome and the Christian religion. We might even interpret the preservation of some names in runic script, therefore, as signifying humility. Derolez and Schwab have suggested that the names in runes at Gargano date from no later than the eighth century, which might point to the origins of our pilgrims as lying

---

[73] The *schola* is first mentioned in the sources in 799. See further Sible de Blaauw, "The Medieval Church of San Michele dei Frisoni in Rome," *Mededelingen van het Nederlands Instituut te Rome/Papers of the Netherlands Institute in Rome* 51–52, *Antiquity* (1992–1993), 151–221, esp. 157.

[74] Philip Grierson and Mark Blackburn, *Medieval European Coinage: With a Catalogue of the Coins in the Fitzwilliam Museum, Cambridge*, vol. 1: *The Early Middle Ages (5th–10th Centuries)* (Cambridge, 1986), 158.

in Northumbria or East Anglia, though this may be a conjecture too far. There is the potential here for further fruitful speculation.

Charlemagne had complained to Offa about Anglo-Saxon merchants who masqueraded as pilgrims in order to avoid paying tolls on their goods. Travel is an expensive activity, and the boundaries between pious pilgrims and our third category of traveler, traders, were not always clear-cut. In 747 Archbishop Boniface inveighed against women traveling to Rome: "For there are very few cities in Lombardy, Francia, or Gaul in which there is not an English adulteress or prostitute. This is a scandal and a disgrace to your whole church."[75] We may suspect that here Boniface is guilty of rhetorical excess. We know of a sufficient number of mishaps that occurred to Anglo-Saxon travelers not to believe that some women were driven to prostitution when a husband died en route or they were robbed. One should certainly not make light of the tragedies that lay behind the occupation followed by such women. It should be recorded here, however, because medieval sources are remarkably coy about prostitution: for a moment a veil of silence has been briefly lifted. An alternative for women who had fallen on hard times was begging. Again, the evidence is slight: Asser has a (no doubt much-embroidered) story about Eadburg, the widow of Beorhtric, king of the West Saxons, who died a beggar in Pavia.[76]

There is plenty of evidence for persons from England engaged in more acceptable economic transactions. It is clear that at all periods there were Anglo-Saxons willing to travel great distances to engage in trade. We know of two important Anglo-Saxon trade treaties, one involving Rome and the other Pavia. Sometime between 882 and 884 Alfred the Great concluded a treaty with Pope Marinus that released the *Schola Saxonum* from tolls.[77] Its effect was likely to have fostered trade in Rome and ultimately benefited Alfred through the tolls that could be exacted from the merchants returning home with Italian goods to sell. Less well known is the so-called *Honorantiae Civitatis Papiae*.[78] Apparently dating from ca. 900, it is an agreement between an unnamed Anglo-Saxon king and his Lombard counterpart.[79] The contents of the agreement reveal the range of goods

---

[75] *Die Briefe des heiligen Bonifatius und Lullus*, ed. Tangl, no. 98 (169, lines 22–25). The translation is mine. See also *The Letters of Saint Boniface*, trans. with intro. Ephraim Emerton, Records of Civilization, Sources and Studies (New York, 1940), 140, no. 62.

[76] Asser, "De rebus gestis Ælfredi," c. 15, in *Asser's Life of King Alfred, together with the Annals of Saint Neots erroneously ascribed to Asser*, ed. with intro. and comm. William Henry Stevenson; new impression with article on recent work on Asser's Life of Alfred by Dorothy Whitelock (Oxford, 1959), 14.

[77] *Anglo-Saxon Chronicle MS A*, ed. Bately, 53, s.a. 885.

[78] *Honorantiae* means 'fundamental rights': the title, in fact, dates from the fourteenth century.

[79] *Die "Honorantie Civitatis Papie": Transkription, Edition, Kommentar*, ed. C. Brühl and C. Violante (Cologne and Vienna, 1983). The agreement could, in fact, have been

for which Anglo-Saxon traders might expect to find a market. The Anglo-Saxon king agreed to make a triennial payment of refined silver, shields, spears, and swords. In addition he agreed to send long- and short-haired greyhounds, which proves that the English attachment to dogs has a long ancestry. A darker side of trans-Alpine trade is revealed in the clause that states that the tithes payable on goods entering Lombardy by certain routes included slaves.

If large numbers of people start traveling abroad over an extended period of time, however, inevitably some of them will get up to no good. The *Honorantiae* mentions that Anglo-Saxon merchants had been participants in affrays resulting from the imposition of tolls on them, a factor that had prompted the drawing up of the treaty. In Lucca an unnamed Briton was reported in a court action over the disputed ownership of a church to have burnt a charter that evidently did not support the claimant's case. Maddeningly, as so often happens, we know nothing more about him: he could well have been a Celt rather than an Anglo-Saxon.[80] An Irish abbot, Indrechtach úa Fínnachta, was killed by Anglo-Saxon robbers in 854 when he was traveling to Rome, though the source is silent as to whether this murder took place in England or on the Continent.[81]

The economic impact of Anglo-Saxon visitors and traders on Italy is likely to have been considerable. Some of the goods brought into the country by merchants have already been outlined in the discussion of the trade treaty with Pavia. What might have appealed most to Italians, however, was English currency. English coins have been found in widely scattered places in Italy, from Aosta to Rome. At least six hoards have been identified. In the absence of banks, it was a natural precaution to bury one's specie; mortality can easily account for why the hoards were not recovered by their owners. An intriguing find made near Rome was a gold ring with the legend "+ AVFRET," said to have been found with a "considerable number" of Alfredian coins.[82] Sadly, the hoard cannot now

---

made by a cleric acting on behalf of the king, such as Plegmund, archbishop of Canterbury from 890 to 923. In Alfred's reign he had been in communication with Fulk, the archbishop of Rheims, and with Pope Formosus; in 909 he took the alms of King Edward the Elder and the people to Rome, whence he returned with relics. He is not recorded as receiving a *pallium* in Rome, though he possibly could have gone there for this purpose in Alfred's reign. Archbishops of Canterbury traveled to Rome to receive the *pallium* from at least 927 on: see Levison, *England and the Continent*, 242. I have briefly discussed this treaty in D. A. E. Pelteret, *Slavery in Early Mediaeval England* (Woodbridge, 1995), 74–76. See also Keynes, "Anglo-Saxon Entries," 99 and note 4.

[80] Simon Young, "A Britto in Eighth-Century Tuscany," *Studia Celtica* 31 (1997): 281–82.

[81] *Fragmentary Annals of Ireland*, chap. 242, ed. Joan Newlon Radner (Dublin, 1978), 96.

[82] [Communication by Edmund Waterton], in "Proceedings at the Meetings of the Archaeological Institute," *Archaeological Journal* 16 (1859): 183–96 (7 January 1859), at 194; C. E. Blunt, "Anglo-Saxon Coins Found in Italy," in *Anglo-Saxon Monetary History:*

be identified. It is a pleasing flight of fancy to imagine that this might have been part of a consignment of Peter's Pence of the kind that the *Anglo-Saxon Chronicle* relates was sent by Alfred the Great. Two hoards give us an insight into how much in the way of coinage might be taken abroad. One hoard found in Vatican City consisted of 517 Anglo-Saxon coins, as well as six Continental deniers and three silver ingots; it was probably deposited in ca. 927, early in the reign of Æthelstan.[83] The second, found in the Forum at Rome, was even larger, consisting of eight hundred Anglo-Saxon coins as well as four deniers of Pavia, Regensburg, and Limoges, a gold solidus of Theophilus, and a pair of niello fibulae inscribed to the "Lord Marinus the pope"; it was probably deposited in ca. 945.[84] Some late-eighth-century single-coin finds are consonant with the kinds of places that an Anglo-Saxon might have visited: three pennies of Offa found near Modena, and an East Anglian penny from Tivoli. The chronological range of these coins is wide, extending from early sceattas to six unprovenanced coins of Edward the Elder to ones as late as Edward the Confessor and Harold II.

To my mind, what is much more significant is that some Italian coins have been found that imitate English ones. Two coins of Charlemagne that were struck in Lucca are imitations of coins of Offa; a papal coin in the name of a Pope John is derived from a coin of Edward the Elder, and another possibly from a coin of Æthelstan.[85] This surely speaks to the scale and financial importance of Anglo-Saxons who came to Italy, whether as religious tourists or as merchants.

Their interactions with the locals may well have been financially complex, thereby fostering economic growth. One may take as an example Adaltruda (i.e., Æthelthryth), "a Saxon handmaiden of God, the daughter of Adelwald, who was a king of the Saxons overseas." She bought the church of San Dalmazio in Lucca[86] for seven hundred gold solidi in 782.[87] Her payment was not in her

---

Essays in Memory of Michael Dolley, ed. M. A. S. Blackburn (Leicester, 1986), 159–69, at 162–63 (Hoard no. 6).

[83] Blunt, "Anglo-Saxon Coins Found in Italy," 160–61, and, more generally, Grierson and Blackburn, *Medieval European Coinage*, vol. 1.

[84] Blunt, "Anglo-Saxon Coins Found in Italy," 161 (Hoard no. 4).

[85] Blunt, "Anglo-Saxon Coins Found in Italy," 166.

[86] Isa Belli Barsali helps one visualize Lucca at this time: see "La topografia di Lucca nei secoli VIII–XI," in *Atti del 5° Congresso internazionale di studi sull'Alto Medioevo: Lucca 3–7 ottobre 1971* (Spoleto, 1973), 461–554 and 18 figs. and 5 maps (at 481 and 528, n. 10, for San Dalmazio), and also Hansmartin Schwarzmaier, *Lucca und das Reich bis zum Ende des 11. Jahrhunderts: Studien zur Sozialstruktur einer Herzogstadt in der Toskana*, Bibliothek des Deutschen Historischen Instituts in Rom (Tübingen, 1972), 18–70, 335–411 (at 32 for San Dalmazio).

[87] "auri sol*edo*s num*er*o septinientos": *Chartae Latinae antiquiores* 37: *Italy XVIII*, ed. Albert Bruckner and Robert Marichal (Dietikon-Zurich, 1990), no. 1082, at 48, line 32.

native coinage but in the local currency, so the resources she brought with her from England must have been traded.[88]

In particular, Anglo-Saxon economic influence in Rome may have been extremely powerful in shaping the economic development of that city in the seventh and eighth centuries. It has been something of a puzzle as to what fueled the growth of Rome at that time. How was Sergius, pope from 687 to 701, able to afford to provide a gold image of St. Peter and six silver lights weighing 170 lbs. at St. Peter's? Where did John VII, who succeeded to the papal see in 705, just the year after Wilfrid left following his third visit to Rome, find the resources to build an oratory to St. Mary within St. Peter's with walls of colored mosaic and decorated with a large amount of gold and silver? This must surely have been the consequence of visits from men of status and means, such as Cædwalla, who retired to Rome after his short period of conquest as king of the West Saxons; the aristocratic Benedict Biscop, whose assiduous collections for his monastic establishments of Wearmouth and Jarrow must have demanded considerable expenditure; and the ecclesiastical entrepreneur, Wilfrid, with his desire for relics. We must never underrate the wealth of Anglo-Saxon England and how much of its wealth was expended abroad over the centuries. Just as we might envisage the early emporia of Ipswich, London, Southampton, and York as kick-starting the English economy, we might see that steady stream of English

---

[88] Schwarzmaier, *Lucca und das Reich*, 32, states that Adaltruda was 'apparently' (*anscheinend*) a daughter of Æthelwold Moll, sometime king of the Northumbrians from 758 to 765, for which he provides supporting conjectural evidence. This interpretation is also adopted by Ortenberg, *English Church and the Continent*, 103 (her n. 37, however, conflates Æthelwold Moll and his son Æthelred; she also claims that the charter refers to "Aethelbald of Mercia" and that Æthelwold Moll was King of Mercia), and by Story, *Carolingian Connections*, 184. Young, "A Britto," 282, also refers to Æthelwold Moll. Æthelwold married an Æthelthryth in 762 and Æthelwold's son, Æthelred, was king of the Northumbrians from 774 to 778 x 779 and from 790 to his murder in 796. The identification is not impossible, especially if Æthelred and Æthelthryth were the products of a prior union. But before this hardens into an orthodoxy it is worth considering whether it might not refer instead to Æthelbald, king of the Mercians up to his assassination in 757. A daughter of Æthelbald might not have been welcome in the Mercia of Offa and may well have felt safer abroad. *Adaluuald* is attested several times in early Lombard sources; the element *–bald* appears only once in a late transcription by Gregorio di Catino: see Bruckner, *Die Sprache der Langobarden*, 217, s.vv. *Adaluuald* and *–bald: Aldebaldus*. In northern Italy the Anglo-Saxon name *Æthelbald* could thus easily have been assimilated into the more familiar Lombard name *Adaluuald*: especially as the letters <b> and <uu> probably represent voiced bilabial sounds, even if articulated slightly differently.

pilgrims (supplemented by pilgrims of other origins) as having the same effect in Rome.[89]

Anglo-Saxons may have influenced Italian life in more subtle ways than simply contributing to the economic sphere of existence. For example, the manuscript that is now Modena, Archivio Capitolare O.I.11, dated by its recent editor, Loretta Piccinini, to the early part of the ninth century, contains what René Derolez has termed a "runic alphabet," i.e., a list of runic characters that follow the order of the Latin alphabet rather than that of the *fuþorc*.[90] Noting that there are two manuscripts in that collection from St. Gall, Piccinini suggests that it might have been the product of a monk from St. Gall or a scribe from Bobbio, though inevitably this is conjectural.[91] Since runes could have a talismanic as well as a communicative function, there is particular interest in her observation that the alphabet is in a manuscript containing medicinal recipes, and that there might be an association here between magic and medicine, found both in England and on the Continent, following from the decline of Roman schooling in medicine.[92] One should not interpret this manuscript as indicating the direct influence of a specific Anglo-Saxon who might have written the alphabet; rather it suggests the kind of indirect influence that persons traveling abroad can have on the countries they visit.

Much has been made of the impact on English life of the goods and ideas brought back from Italy. More can yet be said, though one example must suffice. Theodred, bishop of London, who died sometime between 951 and 953, left in his will a yellow chasuble (which is specifically distinguished from an unornamented yellow vestment) as well as a white one, both bought in Pavia. Anglo-Saxon embroidery was famous, but clearly Theodred treasured his Italian imports.[93] Could not these imports in turn have influenced the native products?

---

[89] This is essentially the conclusion reached by Paolo Delogu, "The Rebirth of Rome in the 8th and 9th Centuries," in *The Rebirth of Towns in the West AD 700–1050*, ed. Richard Hodges and Brian Hobley, CBA Research Report 68 (London, 1988), 32–42, at 37, where he draws attention to the greater availability of silver for gifts during the eighth century. One might suggest, however, that the earliest seventh-century Anglo-Saxon pilgrims still could bring gold with them to Rome.

[90] Loretta Piccinini, "Rune anglosassoni in un codice latino (Archivio Capitolare di Modena, O. I. 11)," *Romanobarbarica* 12 (1992–1993): 173–88 and fig. 4. See also Giulio Garuti Simone, "*Runica manuscripta* e dintorni: l'Alfabeto runico di Modena," in *I Germani e la scrittura*, ed. Fazzini and Cianci, 151–59.

[91] Piccinini, "Rune anglosassoni," 187–88.

[92] Piccinini, "Rune anglosassoni," 186.

[93] *Anglo-Saxon Wills*, ed., with trans. and n. Dorothy Whitelock, Cambridge Studies in English Legal History (Cambridge, 1930), no 1, 4 (text) and 5 (translation) = P. H. Sawyer, *Anglo-Saxon Charters: An Annotated List and Bibliography* (London, 1968), no. 1526.

Less easy to evaluate is the intellectual impact of these encounters with Italy on the realms touched by Anglo-Saxon missionaries and intellectuals. Boniface, who had visited Rome, sent the Bavarian Sturm to study regular discipline at Monte Cassino, with results that are difficult to assess.[94] Alcuin relates how, when traveling to Rome as a young man, he had heard a Jew, Lullus, debating with a Christian, Peter, in Pavia. It obviously had a lasting impression on him, as he wrote about it in a letter rather late in life.[95] There is much more work to be done here.

Nagging away at the back of the mind must still lurk several questions begged by Wilfrid's vision recounted at the start of this paper. Why did the absence of a church dedicated to St. Mary the Mother of God feature so prominently? Why was St. Michael the Archangel the divine messenger? Even if one wishes to accept that this was a miraculous vision, where did Wilfrid learn about these sainted figures? And did he actually construct a church dedicated to Mary?

The last question is easiest to answer. He did indeed build one in Hexham, southeast of the church of St. Andrew, the latter being on the site of the present cathedral. Richard of Hexham reports that the church of St. Mary was circular in shape with four projecting portions.[96] By the seventeenth century it was in ruins, but parts survived at least into the nineteenth century in the buildings across the market-square from the cathedral.

As for St. Mary herself, it is important to realize that certain changes had taken place in Rome between Wilfrid's second visit in 679 and his third and final one in 703. Sergius had occupied the papal see from 687 to 701, and during that long reign had enlarged the liturgy, so that, as the *Liber Pontificalis* recounts, "on the days of the Lord's Annunciation, of the Falling-asleep and Nativity of St. Mary the ever-virgin mother of God, and of St Simeon . . . , a litany should go out from St. Hadrian's and the people should meet up at St. Mary's."[97] Wilfrid was keenly attuned to ecclesiastical developments: he had been schooled in Roman calendrical practices on his first trip to Rome, which had stood him in such good stead in his defence of the Roman Easter at Whitby in 664, and

[94] *Eigilis vita sancti Sturmi abbatis Fuldensis*, chap. 14, ed. Georg Heinrich Pertz, MGH, Scriptores 2 (Hannover, 1829), 371–72 (text); Talbot, *Anglo-Saxon Missionaries*, 191–92 (translation); and cf. Levison, *England and the Continent*, 79, 103.

[95] Alcuin, *Epistolae*, no. 172, ed. Dümmler, 285.

[96] Richard, prior of Hexham, *The History of the Founding of the Church of Hexham, and of the Bishops of that Place*, chap. 4, in *The Priory of Hexham: Its Chroniclers, Endowments, and Annals*, ed. J. Raine, Surtees Society 44 (Durham, London, and Edinburgh, 1864), 1–62, at 14–15 and n. x, and 18.

[97] Translation from *The Book of Pontiffs* (Liber Pontificalis): *The Ancient Biographies of the First Ninety Roman Bishops to AD 715*, trans. with intro. Raymond Davis (Liverpool, 1989), 87. See Andrew J. Ekonomou, *Byzantine Rome and the Greek Popes* (Lanham, MD, 2007), 260–61.

he probably learnt more about Roman customs from his second visit there in 679. He must have been troubled to find that, though he had followed good Roman practice in having churches dedicated to Saints Andrew and Peter, he had ignored the Mother of God.

Does the presence of St. Michael in Wilfrid's vision suggest that he had traveled to Gargano? Probably not: there is no evidence in Stephen of Ripon's account that he ever visited there. Bertram Colgrave in his edition of Stephen's *Life of Wilfrid* suggested that perhaps his round church in Hexham was influenced by San Lorenzo in Milan.[98] But this is misguided: the conjecture accounts neither for St. Mary nor for St. Michael, nor for Wilfrid's presence in Milan. Instead one might look to Pavia for the explanation of Wilfrid's vision. Situated as it was on a river crossing over a tributary of the Po and on a major road, it was ideally placed as a stopping point for Anglo-Saxons traveling to and from Rome.[99]

Throughout his career Wilfrid had fostered international contacts amongst the powerful, both lay and ecclesiastical. Wilfrid had good reason to revisit Pavia during his third Italian trip to nurture ties, direct and indirect, that he had formed with the ruling elite there. As already mentioned, during his second visit to Italy in 679 he had received hospitality and protection from Perctarit, king of the Lombards, who had by then transferred his capital from Milan to Pavia. Subsequently, Wilfrid and Anastasius, bishop of Pavia, were two of the 125 bishops who signed a lengthy record (preserved in both Latin and Greek) of a papal synod in Rome in 679, where they affirmed their rejection of the Monothelite heresy.[100] Wilfrid was not in Italy during the reign of Perctarit's son and successor, Cunincpert, who reigned from 688 to 700. Cunincpert married an Anglo-Saxon woman called, according to Paul the Deacon, Hermelinda, of whom one wishes more were known.[101] The first part of her name is equivalent to Old English *Eormen-*, a name-element borne by ruling families in both Northumbria and Kent, kingdoms with which Wilfrid had had close ties. Cunincpert's reign is significant in this context because he had a particular devotion to St. Michael, who had played a part, he believed, in the overthrow of a usurper who had formerly sworn fealty to him in a church in Pavia dedicated to St. Michael. He

[98] *Life of Bishop Wilfrid*, ed. Colgrave, 183.

[99] For an introduction to the early medieval topography of Pavia see D. A. Bullough, "Urban Change in Early Medieval Italy: The Example of Pavia," *Papers of the British School at Rome* 34 (N. S. 21) (1966): 82–130 and plate 20.

[100] The proceedings, which are little known to most Anglo-Saxonists, are printed as "Actio quarta," in *Concilium universale Constantinopolitanum tertium: Concilii actiones I–XI*, ed. Rudolf Riedinger, Acta conciliorum oecumenicorum, Series secunda, 2.1 (Berlin, 1990), 46–159 (with Greek and Latin texts on facing pages).

[101] Paul the Deacon, *Historia Langobardorum* 5.37, ed. Bethmann and Waitz, 157 (text); *History of the Langobards*, trans. Foulke, 240 (translation).

introduced the figure of St. Michael on the reverse of his gold coinage, a practice that continued after his reign. [102] By the time of Wilfrid's third visit to Italy, there were several churches and monasteries in Pavia dedicated either to St. Mary or to St. Michael. Of course, there were many churches that by this time must have been dedicated to Mary or Michael, but what gives particular strength to my conjecture that Wilfrid's dream drew its *dramatis personae* from a visit to Pavia is that, like his church dedicated to St. Mary in Hexham, Santa Maria *in pertica* in Pavia was a round building. [103] Wilfrid had reason to visit it because it had been

---

[102] For a good illustration of a gold tremissis of Cunincpert with St. Michael on the reverse with shield and lance see *Il santuario di S. Michele arcangelo sul Gargano dalle origini al X secolo*, ed. Giorgio Otranto and Carlo Carletti, Scavi e ricerche 4 (Bari, 1990), 46, fig. 19.

[103] The church in Pavia, Santa Maria in Pertica, unfortunately was demolished in 1815: see Bullough, "Urban Change," 104. Richard of Hexham (died 1178) provides a description of the Church of St Mary at Hexham and states that it is one of three churches there that were believed to have been started by Wilfrid and completed by his successor, Acca: "Sunt autem, praeterea, in eadem uilla duae adhuc aliae ecclesiae, una haud procul a muro matris ecclesiae mirandi operis, et ipsa, scilicet, in modum turris erecta, et fere rotunda, a quatuor partibus totidem porticus habens, in honorem Sanctae Mariae semper Uirginis dedicata. . . . Has uero tres ecclesias Sanctus Wilfridus incepisse creditur, sed beatae memoriae Acca pontifex, successor eius, illas consummauit; unam, ut supradictum est, ad honorem Sanctae Mariae semper Uirginis. . . ." ("There are, furthermore, in the same town a further two churches, one of remarkable construction not far from the wall of the mother church, and that one, indeed, built in the form of a tower and almost round, having on its four sides as many chapels, is dedicated in honour of St Mary ever Virgin. . . . St Wilfrid is believed to have begun these three churches, but Bishop Acca of blessed memory, his successor, completed them, the one, as has been mentioned above, in honour of St Mary ever Virgin. . . .") Aelred of Rievaulx (died 1167) credits the building of the church of St Mary at Hexham to Wilfrid alone and provides a description of its exterior form similar to Richard's: "Construxerat quondam beatus Wilfridus in eodem uico ecclesiam in honore beatissimae uirginis Mariae opere rotundo, quam quatuor porticus, quatuor respicientes mundi climata, ambiebant." ("The blessed Wilfrid had once constructed in the same town a church in honour of the most blessed Virgin Mary with a round form, which four chapels, facing the four quarters of the world, surrounded.") See Richard of Hexham, "Historia Haugustaldensis ecclesiae," chap. 4, and Aelred of Rievaulx, "De sanctis ecclesiae Haugustaldensis et eorum miraculis libellus," chap. 5, in James Raine [the younger], *The Priory of Hexham*, 2 vols, Publications of the Surtees Society 44 and 46 (Durham, 1864–1865), 1: 1–62, at 14–15 and 18, and 1: 173–203, at 183, respectively. The translations are mine. For the meaning of *porticus* see Éamonn Ó Carragáin, "The Term *Porticus* and *Imitatio Romae* in Early Anglo-Saxon England," in *Text and Gloss: Studies in Insular Learning and Literature Presented to Joseph Donovan Pheifer*, ed. Helen Conrad O'Briain, Anne Marie D'Arcy, and John Scattergood (Dublin and Portland, OR, 1999), 13–34.

founded by Rodelinda,[104] the wife of his host during his second trip, Perctarit.

Certain towns have recurred in this paper, especially Pavia and Lucca; an Anglo-Saxon presence has also been noted in some monasteries such as Monte Cassino and Farfa. There were many other towns on the Via Francigena that Anglo-Saxons were likely to have visited, such as Turin if they crossed at the Alps at Mont Cenis, and, if they used the Great St. Bernard Pass, Vercelli (already known to all Anglo-Saxon literary historians because the Vercelli Book of Old English poetry fetched up there).[105] A careful search of early written sources for various Italian towns and for significant monasteries might reveal other Anglo-Saxon links.[106] The presence of Anglo-Saxons at Gargano, only hinted at in written sources, suggests that Anglo-Saxon visitors might have left physical evidence of their presence elsewhere in the form of graffiti, some perhaps unrecognized because they were incised in runic script. Here the catacombs of Naples, a city already with links to England in the person of Abbot Hadrian and the writings that must have migrated there as a result of his relocation to England in 669,[107] might be a good place to start.[108]

---

[104] Paul the Deacon, *Historia Langobardorum* 5.34, ed. Bethmann and Waitz, 156 (text); *History of the Langobards*, trans. Foulke, 238 (translation).

[105] The Vercelli Book probably did not arrive in its current home until the eleventh century, but a funerary inscription from Vercelli was transmitted to England several centuries before: see Éamonn Ó Carragáin, "Rome, Ruthwell, Vercelli: 'The Dream of the Rood' and the Italian Connection," and Patrizia Lendinara, "Un'iscrizione di Vercelli nell'Inghilterra anglosassone," in *Vercelli tra Oriente ed Occidente tra tarda Antichità e Medioevo: Atti delle Giornate di Studio, Vercelli 10–11 aprile 1997, 24 novembre 1997*, ed. Vittoria Dolcetti Corazza, Bibliotheca Germanica, Studi e testi 6 (Turin, 1998), 59–100 and 4 figs., at 94, and 183–219, respectively.

[106] Willibald, for instance, traveled through Fondi, Gaeta, Naples, Reggio Calabria, Catania, and Syracuse on his way to the Holy Land, and after his stay at Monte Cassino visited Rome, Lucca, Pavia, Brescia, and Garda: Hugeburc, *Vita Willibaldi*, chaps. 4 and 5, ed. Holder-Egger, 92–93 and 103–104 (text); Talbot, *Anglo–Saxon Missionaries*, 159–60 and 173–74 (translation).

[107] The Northumbrian Lindisfarne Gospels could have drawn on such a manuscript. St. Januarius (S. Gennaro), a martyr bishop who is patron saint of Naples, is commemorated in this Gospel-book, so the saint certainly was known in England at the end of the seventh century. This could have prompted Anglo-Saxon pilgrims when in Italy to visit Naples as the center of his cult. On the Neapolitan pericope-lists in the Lindisfarne Gospels and the possible link with Hadrian see Bernhard Bischoff and Michael Lapidge, *Biblical Commentaries from the Canterbury School of Theodore and Hadrian*, Cambridge Studies in Anglo-Saxon England 10 (Cambridge, 1994), 155–60.

[108] For an introduction see Umberto M. Fasola, *Le catacombe di S. Gennaro a Capodimonte* (Rome, 1975), with a bibliography, 237–39.

This paper has not aimed at closing off an area of research by reaching definitive conclusions, but at revealing vistas to those working in a range of disciplines that have long enriched Anglo-Saxon studies. Both the vision of Wilfrid and the pilgrim names incised on the walls at Gargano suggest, for instance, that scholars in a number of fields could well go back to their respective sources and see what evidence there might be for the cult of St. Michael the Archangel in England, for it can now be placed in a wider geographic context.[109] Indeed, further examination of written sources may show Anglo-Saxons fostering the cult on the Continent: not only did Bishop Wigbert fund a church dedicated to the "Holy Angel" at Farfa, but also another "very holy man" of English origin, Philip, after being inspired to leave his homeland for Rome, subsequently settled in the middle of the eighth century in Chelles, where he dedicated an oratory in honor of St. Michael.[110] The presence of Anglo-Saxon names on the fresco of St. Luke in the Catacomb of Commodilla and on St. Miles in the Catacomb of Pontianus[111] prompts the question as to whether these two saints might have had influence in England. The patient exploration of such archaeological and historical material will take researchers well beyond the accumulation of factual evidence about the practical aspects of travel into the realm of ideas; ultimately it will have a bearing on Anglo-Saxon architecture, art, hagiography, liturgy, and literature.[112] In spite of the valiant efforts of a limited number of scholars to work with sources

---

[109] There is, for instance, an early tympanum depicting St. Michael (though possibly not of Anglo-Saxon date) at Kingswinford, near Stourbridge, in the West Midlands: see Charles E. Keyser, "Notes on a Sculptured Tympanum at Kingswinford Church, Staffordshire, and Other Early Representations in England of St. Michael the Archangel," *Archaeological Journal* 62 (1905): 137–46 and pl. facing 137.

[110] "uir sanctissimus Philippus genere Anglus, transmarinis insulis ortus": *Vita Philippi presbyteri Cellensis*, chaps. 1–2, ed. A. Hofmeister, MGH, Scriptores 30.2 (Leipzig, 1934), 798–801, at 798, and cf. Levison, *England and the Continent*, 168 and n. 2.

[111] See, for instance, "healfred p(res)b(yter)," in Silvagni, *Inscriptiones christianae*, 2.97, no. 4533 III e, mentioned by Alan Thacker, "In Search of Saints: The English Church and the Cult of Roman Apostles and Martyrs in the Seventh and Eighth Centuries," in *Early Medieval Rome and the Christian West: Essays in Honour of Donald A. Bullough*, ed. Julia M. H. Smith (Leiden, 2000), 249–77, at 261.

[112] Richard F. Johnson, who briefly mentions the work of Carletti, Derolez, and Schwab on the Gargano inscriptions and those in the catacomb of Commodilla, has made an excellent start on this by examining the literary influence of the cult in *Saint Michael the Archangel in Medieval English Legend* (Woodbridge, 2005), to which he appends a brief study, "St. Michael in Medieval English Iconography," 140–48.

from both sides of the English Channel, there is still need for more researchers to bring the Anglo-Saxons closer to mainland Europeans.[113]

[113] I wish to express my thanks to Francesca Tinti for first drawing my attention to the Italian inscriptions and for saving me from several errors (though she is not responsible for any that remain), to Nicholas Brooks and Gaby Waxenberger for facilitating my access to several recent publications, and to the British Academy for providing funding towards my travel expenses to Munich.

From York to Paris: Reinterpreting Alcuin's Virtual Tour of the Continent

Lucia Sinisi

Of Alcuin's overall literary output, just under three hundred prose epistles have been preserved,[1] along with over a hundred and fifty poems,[2] not to mention his well-known theological, exegetical, and grammatical treatises, all of which amounts to an unusually large extant production for a medieval writer.[3] His letters have been widely studied because of the enormous importance they undoubtedly have both from a literary point of view, as an example of the epistolary style of writing used in the eighth and ninth centuries in northern Europe, and also from a purely historical perspective thanks to the great wealth of information that they contain. His poems, in contrast, have enjoyed less critical favor, with interest focusing mainly on a small number of them, particularly his "York Poem," or *Versus de patris regibus et sanctis Eboracensis Ecclesiae*, written to celebrate the

---

[1] According to Bullough, "The total number of these still extant is impressive, compared with collections of previous and immediately succeeding centuries. The standard modern edition contains at least two hundred and eighty-one letters written by Alcuin, even after the exclusion of eight or nine letter-prefaces to longer works, the elimination of those written by him in the king's name as well as of ones addressed *to* Alcuin, and the rejection of a few letters wrongly attributed to him": Donald A. Bullough, *Alcuin: Achievement and Reputation* (Leiden and Boston, 2004), 35. They were collected and edited by Ernst Dümmler in MGH, Epistolae 4 (Berlin, 1895), 1–481.

[2] Alcuin's poems were collected first in 1617 on the basis of a manuscript, now lost, that belonged to the abbey of Saint-Bertin: André Duchesne, *B. Flacci Albini sive Alchuini, Karoli Magni Regis, ac Imperatoris magistri, Opera quae hactenus reperiri potuerunt . . .* (Paris, 1617). This was followed by Frobenius Forster's edition, *Beati Flacci Albini seu Alcuini Abbatis Caroli Magni Regis ac Imperatoris Magistri Opera . . .* 4 vols. (Regensburg, 1777) which constitutes the basis of Migne's collection in PL. The standard critical edition is by Ernst Dümmler, MGH, *Poetae Latini Aevi Carolini* 1 (Berlin, 1881), 160–351.

[3] For a complete bibliography of Alcuin's works (up to 1999) see *Clavis scriptorum Latinorum Medii Aevi: Avctores Galliae 735–987, tomvs II: Alcuinus*, ed. Marie-Hélène Jullien and Françoise Perelman (Turnhout, 1999).

Hans Sauer and Joanna Story, eds., *Anglo-Saxon England and the Continent*. With the assistance of Gaby Waxenberger. Essays in Anglo-Saxon Studies, vol. 3. MRTS 394. Tempe: ACMRS, 2011.   [ISBN 978-0-86698-442-3]

school of York with its vibrant cultural life,[4] and his famous, heartfelt lament
on the appalling news of the destruction of Lindisfarne in 793, *Postquam primus
homo paradise liquerat hortos*, which remains emblematic of the outrage expressed
by the Christian community in Europe at the act of sacrilege committed by the
pagan Vikings.[5]

In 1970, Dieter Schaller published an analysis of another of Alcuin's poems,
known as *Cartula perge cito trans pelagi aequora cursu*, an exquisite *carmen* written
in hexameters in the guise of a poetic epistle.[6] In his analysis of Alcuin's short
work, Schaller argued that within the court of the Frankish king "the necessity
of communication by letter on the part of poets who were not in direct contact with one another and who frequently lacked a fixed point of focus for their
activities in the court" made it necessary to find new ways of divulging information so as to keep up the network of contacts established by the members of
the Palatine school around the figure of the sovereign patron and protector of
the arts.[7] Thus, within this restricted cultural circle of the Carolingian court,
a literary genre developed which corresponded exactly to this particular need:
that of the "Vortragsdichtung," "to be read aloud to his many eminent friends" in
each of the itinerant courts of Charlemagne; or of the "Zirkulardichtung," which
presupposed that the poem was delivered to each of the "Stationen" or places of
residence of the various addressees. In this paper I intend to show that this poem
corresponds to criteria different from those outlined by Schaller and, by examining it in the light of the tradition of the canon of the poet's apostrophe to his book
or poetic composition, to argue that it should not be considered as belonging to
the "Zirkulardichtung" genre, despite the structural division of the brief *carmen*
into "Stationen."

The poem *Cartula perge cito trans pelagi aequora cursu* is preserved *sine titulo*
in a single, well-known manuscript, Paris, BN, lat. 528, at fol. 132r-v, the history of which can be traced back to the eleventh century when we know it was
in the library of the monastery of Saint-Martial of Limoges, with the signature
145. Saint-Martial is not, however, the scriptorium that produced the manuscript

---

    [4] Recently edited in *The Bishops, Kings and Saints of York*, ed. P. Godman (Oxford,
1982).

    [5] Also in P. Godman, *Poetry of the Carolingian Renaissance* (London, 1985), 126–38.

    [6] D. Schaller, "Vortrags- und Zirkulardichtung am Hof Karls des Großen," *Mittel-
lateinisches Jahrbuch* 6 (1970): 14–36, repr. in idem, *Studien zur lateinischen Dichtung des
Frühmittelalters*, Quellen und Untersuchungen zur Lateinischen Philologie des Mittelalters 11 (Stuttgart, 1995), 328–29. Alcuin, *Carmina*, no. 4, ed. Dümmler, 220–23; see also
Stephan Lebecq, *Marchands et navigateurs frisons du haut Moyen Age*, 2 vols. (Lille, 1983),
1: 218 and, with an Italian translation of the poem, F. Stella, ed., *La poesia carolingia*
(Florence, 1995), 152–57, 399–401.

    [7] P. Godman, *Poets and Emperors: Frankish Politics and Carolingian Poetry* (Oxford,
1987), 44.

because, on the basis of its palaeographical characteristics, its origin is commonly attributed to Saint-Denis where, according to Bischoff, it was assembled during the abbacy of Fardulf (793–806).[8] It was transferred to the Bibliothèque Nationale de France only in 1730 to allow Abbot Lebeuf to prepare the first edition of Paulus Diaconus' epistles and *carmina* contained in it.[9]

The manuscript is very complex and heterogeneous, both from a palaeographical point of view and for its content which includes, along with the works of Paulus Diaconus and Peter of Pisa for which it is renowned, a great variety of items, from lives of saints, like the *Vita Audoeni*, to the anonymous *Quaestiones in Genesim* and the *De Schematibus Scripturae* of Bede. Like another famous manuscript, the Codex Vindobonensis 795 (*olim* Salisburgensis 140) which preserves the vast majority of the letters by Alcuin, it also contains samples of a Gothic alphabet. On the whole it can be said that the interests of the compiler tended mostly towards aspects of grammar and rhetoric.[10] Among all these various items, Alcuin's text stands out because the short *carmen* is the only work by our English-born poet in that manuscript.

As is usual with texts extant in only a single manuscript, with this *carmen* we are implicitly faced with a series of editing problems that we do not find in texts preserved in more than one codex; moreover, the fact that it stands alone within the manuscript, without any apparent connection to the other works contained in it, prevents us from removing some of the doubts as to the underlying conceptual

---

[8] D. Nebbiai-Dalla Guarda, *La bibliothèque de l'abbaye de Saint-Denis en France du IXe au XVIIIe siècle* (Paris, 1985), 33. B. Bischoff, "Ein karolingisches Denkmal des Gotischen (Zweite Hälfte des neunten Jahrhunderts)," in idem, *Anecdota Novissima: Texte des vierten bis sechzehnten Jahrhunderts*, Quellen und Untersuchungen zur lateinischen Philologie des Mittelalters 7 (Stuttgart, 1984), 256. It was dated to the ninth century by Ernst Dümmler, "Die handschriftliche Überlieferung der lateinischen Dichtungen aus der Zeit der Karolinger, I," *Neues Archiv der Gesellschaft für ältere deutsche Geschichtskunde* 4 (1879): 87–159, at 104, and in MGH, 31, and by K. Neff, *Die Gedichte des Paulus Diaconus: Kritische und erklärende Ausgabe* (Munich, 1908), xix, and also by Nebbiai-Dalla Guarda, *La bibliothèque de l'abbaye de Saint-Denis*, 298. It was dated to the first half of the ninth century by L. Delisle, *Histoire générale de Paris: Le cabinet des manuscrits de la Bibliothèque Nationale*, 3 vols. (Paris, 1881), 3: 258, whereas Bourgain considers it as having been written shortly after the composition of Paulus Diaconus' poems, i.e. the beginning of the 9th century: P. Bourgain, "Les recueils carolingiens de poésie rythmique," in *De Tertullien aux Mozarabes, II: Antiquité tardive et christianisme ancien (VIe-IXe siècles)*, ed. L. Holtz and J.-C. Fredouille, Moyen Âge et Temps Modernes 26 (Paris, 1992), 117–27, at 121.

[9] Ed. Dümmler, 31.

[10] For a list of contents, see *Catalogue Général des Manuscrits Latins, Bibliothèque Nationale, Tome Ier (Nos 1–1438)*, ed. Ph. Laurel (Paris, 1939), 184–86. For the presence in the codex of a Gothic alphabet, see A. Zironi, "I *Gotica Parisina* nel codice Bibliothèque Nationale de France, lat. 528," in *Il plurilinguismo in area germanica nel Medioevo*, ed. L. Sinisi (Bari, 2005), 301–39.

framework in which it was written, since we do not know the circumstances of its transmission. So, everything that follows is valid insofar as we take its *lectio* for granted.

According to Dümmler, Alcuin's *carmen* must be dated around the year 780, and it was probably written in York, not long before Charlemagne invited him to his court.[11] This opinion is widely upheld thanks to the chronological references in the text which, as we shall see, confirm this hypothesis.[12] The *carmen* has been defined a "poetic epistle,"[13] and it is construed according to a model that was widespread in European literature, that of "the poet's apostrophe to his own work or his own book."[14] The sources of this model can be traced back to the dawn of European literature, to the famous exhortation of Pindar to his song to go by any available ship to spread the good news of Pytheas' victory; most examples come from the classics, particularly the Latin poets Horace, Ovid, and Martial, who gave it a configuration that was to remain exemplary.[15]

In his *carmen* Alcuin describes how his small "Schriftstück" (*cartula*) undertakes an exhausting *itinerarium*, presumably setting out from England and ending up, in the final stage of the journey, at Saint-Denis, with detailed descriptions of each part of the journey and the various stops along the way. It follows a path that becomes, in practice, a great journey of devotion and homage to the places where the epic story of the Anglo-Saxon missions to the Continent occurred, and which is enlivened by the lay and religious characters met along the way. As has already been noted, the pattern adopted by Alcuin in this poem is by no means original but follows a model that had already been used by past poets from Horace, Ovid, and Martial to Statius and Ausonius. In this respect, particularly surprising is the degree of analogy between Alcuin's *carmen* and the well-known *Propempticon ad libellum* by Sidonius Apollinaris, *carmen* 24, which ends his book of *nugae*. In Sidonius' poem, the author takes leave of the book (*liber*) he has just completed, exhorting it to go on from his home in *Aviticum*, near Clermont, to Narbonne, to reach the *sodales* or comrades of the poet who dwell at different places along the way. As in Sidonius' *Propempticon*, the description of the route

---

[11] Dümmler reports Frobenius' opinion: "Scriptum esse suspicamur (hoc carmen) post Alcuini Roma reditum in Britannia anno 780, in quo itinere cum viris illustribus, quos hic nominat, familiaritatem contraxerit": in MGH, 220.

[12] Schaller, "Vortrags- und Zirkulardichtung," 19; Godman, *Poets and Emperors*, 45.

[13] Schaller, "Vortrags- und Zirkulardichtung," 14; Godman, *Poets and Emperors*, 44.

[14] On the tradition of the canon of the apostrophe to the book and the contact with the dedicatee, see the fundamental study by M. Citroni, "Le raccomandazioni del poeta," *Maia* n.s. 2 (1986): 111–46; see also V. Sivo, "L'apostrofe al proprio libro di un grammatico medievale," *Pan* 18–19 (2001): 469–79.

[15] Although — Citroni points out — its documentation in Greek poetry is not very frequent and only a few traces are extant before Horace: see Citroni, "Le raccomandazioni," 112.

that Alcuin's *cartula* must follow is divided up into a series of 'frames' by means of which the *itinerarium* is structured, in accordance with a predilection that had developed in the Latin poetry of the late classical era for "'fragmenting' the narrative into independent pictures (a legacy of the Alexandrine technique of 'Kleinwerk')."[16] Each frame—which can very often be easily identified through the presence of the anaphoric adverbs *hic* and *hinc*—constitutes a stage in the journey and is therefore set in a different place. Each character is greeted using a different formula, according to a rigid etiquette, generally preceded by the verbal forms *dic* or *dicito*, which had also by then become widely-used formulae in that type of poetry.

In the introductory line Alcuin, directly apostrophizing his *cartula*, urges it to take to the sea and head towards the mouth of the mighty river Rhine, teeming with fish, "piscosi Rheni," where the first frame of the *carmen* is set. Here, to stop the boat being pushed out to sea again a strong rope must be tied to the stern from the land, probably drawn by draught animals, according to a custom already described by Horace in his famous "iter brundusinum":[17]

> Cartula, perge cito pelagi trans aequora cursu
> Ostia piscosi flabris pete fortia Rheni
> Ingrediens rapidis pontum qua volvitur undis[18]
> Tum tua prelongo ducatur prora remulco,
> Ne cito retrorsum rapiatur flumine puppis.
> (lines 1–5)

The second frame is set in Utrecht (ancient *Trajectum*), which—as the poet observes—is 'no further than a night's walk' from where the boat landed ("nocte non amplius una"). Here the *cartula* will meet the first of the many historical characters mentioned in the poem, Alcuin's friend Alberic,[19] nephew of and successor to Gregory, who in turn had succeeded the great missionary Willibrord at the diocese of Utrecht. It is recommended that Alberic should be addressed with the deferential title "Vaccipotens presul," which indicates that he had already been consecrated bishop of the diocese of Utrecht at the time of the composition of the poem; because it is known that the consecration took place in 777, this reference constitutes a *terminus post quem* for the dating of our *carmen*.[20]

---

[16] Sidonius Apollinaris, *Carme 24: Propempticon ad libellum*, ed. Stefania Santelia (Bari, 2003), 21, at n. 15.

[17] *Q. Horati Flacci Opera*, ed. D. R. Shackleton Bailey (Stuttgart, 1985), *Sermones* 1. 5, at 11–23.

[18] The end of this line, according to Dümmler, is reminiscent of Ovid, *Met.* 1. 570, "spumosis volvitur undis": Dümmler, in MGH, 220.

[19] Bishop Alberic had been a pupil of Alcuin's at the school of York. He had later left for the Continent, where he was consecrated bishop of the diocese of Utrecht.

[20] Bullough, *Alcuin*, 316.

To the exhausted traveler, Prior Hadda will make sure that a good meal consisting of honey, butter, and a soup made from pulses ("cumpultim") will be served because 'neither oil nor wine are expected to be found in Frisia' ("non oleum nec vinum Fresia fundit"):

> Si meus Albricus veniens occurrat in amne
> "Vaccipotens praesul!," properans tu dicito, "salve,"
> Nam tibi Hadda prior nocte non amplius una
> In Traiect mel cumpultimque buturque ministrat:
> Utpote non oleum nec vinum Fresia fundit.
>
> (lines 6–10)

The third frame is set in the rich city of Dorestad, at that time a flourishing center of trade with England and Scandinavia.[21] The city's mercantile environment is embodied by the merchant Hrotberct, described here as "niger" and inhospitable, and as someone who does not appreciate poetry ("tuum carmen").[22] Alcuin suggests leaving Dorestad as soon as possible and recommends heading towards the "litora" of the river Rhine, where the poet Ionas lives,[23] and where the tired traveller is sure to find a place to rest and plenty of vegetables, fish, and bread:

> Hinc tua vela leva, fugiens Dorstada relinque:
> Non tibi forte niger Hrotberct parat hospita tecta,
> Non amat ecce tuum carmen mercator avarus.

---

[21] For the navigation and commerce on the Rhine see Lebecq, *Marchands et navigateurs*, 215–22.

[22] For the name Hrotberct see S. Lebecq, "On the Use of the Word 'Frisian' in the 6th–10th Centuries' Written Sources: Some Interpretations," in *Maritime Celts, Frisians and Saxons*, ed. Seàn McGrail, Council for British Archaeology Research Report 71 (London, 1990), 85–90, at 87. In this context it is highly unlikely that the adjective *niger* refers to the colour of Hrotberct's skin; possibly it is used with the Horacian meaning of "full of *livor*" (i.e. livid with envy) which the poet from Venosa adopts when referring to the denigrators of his poetry.

[23] There are no references as to the identity of Ionas; even Szövérffy, who is careful to list all the people cited in the short *carmen*, identifying their status and place of residence, fails to mention him, although he must undoubtedly have been a major figure, since Alcuin mentions him again in line 42, when he lists the people that the *cartula* should be able to find at the Carolingian court: J. Szövérffy, *Weltliche Dichtungen des Lateinischen Mittelalters: Ein Handbuch*, 1: *Von den Anfängen bis zum Ende der Karolingerzeit* (Berlin, 1970), 445, at n. 63. But see also Bullough, *Alcuin*, 316 and n. 202, where it is suggested he may be the then abbot of the monastery founded by the missionary Swithberht on the islet given to him by King Pipin and his wife Plectrud, where Kaiserswerth (Düsseldorf) now lies, which, according to Dresden, may be identified with the place-name *Litora*, mentioned by Bede (*Historia Ecclesiastica* 5.11); see A. Dresden, "Beda Venerabilis und der älteste Name von Kaiserwerth," *Düsseldorfer Jahrbuch* 28 (1916): 211–18.

Sed diverte mei vatis tu litora Ione:
Est nam certa quies fessis venientibus illuc
Hic holus hospitibus, piscis hic, panis abundat.
(lines 11–16)

Cologne, the hospitable town of Agrippina, constitutes the scenario for the fourth frame, where it is recommended to pay a visit to the bishop of the diocese, Ricwulf (772–794), greeting the praiseworthy prelate with 'a humble voice' ("humili voce"):

Urbs Agrippina tibi pandit, scio, tecta benigne:
Hic humili patrem Rievulfum voce saluta
Dic: "Tua laus mecum semper, dilecte, manebit."
(lines 17–19)

A swift boat will leave from there, down the river, passing all the villages along it, until it reaches the confluence of the Moselle; after crossing the wide river by using oars ("remigio"), the boat will pull up at the bank and from there they will arrive on foot at the "loca sancta" of St. Willibrord, whose *vita* Alcuin wrote in 796 or 797:[24]

Hinc castella petes currenti nave per undas,
Donec ad optatae pertingas flustra Musellae.
Remigio postquam spatium sulcaveris amnem,
Hic tum siste ratem, puppis potiatur harena,[25]
Et pete Wilbrordi patris loca sancta pedester
(lines 20–24)

At Echternach, the idealized *peregrinatio* to the revered places which constituted the stage of the great epic of the English missionaries on the Continent is coming to an end; the *cartula* is approaching the *loca* where men of ecclesiastical and lay power live, where admission is not always granted: with frame six the *cartula* is approaching the residence of the influential bishop Beornrad (776–798), at whose request Alcuin wrote the *Vita Willibrordi*.[26] In the *carmen* Beornrad is

---

[24] "Vita Willibrordi archiepiscopi Traiectensis auctore Alcuino," ed. B. Krusch and W. Levison, MGH, SS rer. Merov. 7 (Hannover and Leipzig, 1920), 113–41; a modern English translation in C. H. Talbot, *The Anglo-Saxon Missionaries in Germany: Being the Lives of SS. Willibrord, Boniface, Leoba and Lebuin together with the Hodoeporicon of St. Willibald and a Selection from the Correspondence of St. Boniface* (London and New York, 1954), 3–22.

[25] Virgil, *Aeneid* 1. 172: "potiuntur Troes harena."

[26] Alcuin, *Epistolae*, no. 120, ed. Dümmler, MGH, Epistolae 4, 175. Beonrad is also the dedicatee of Alcuin's poem *Est mihi scriptulus dicione*: Alcuin, *Carmina*, no. 8, ed. Dümmler, 228.

called by his pseudonym "Samuel," an example of Alcuin's extravagant fancy for giving nicknames to members of the court and to his beloved students.[27] When addressing the young deacon who will open the door of the bishop's residence, the *carmen* recommends the use of an Apollinean tone of voice, and to say that the invitation came from Alcuin ("Puplius Albinus") from the faraway land of the Britons ("ab orbe Britanno"). The poet warns that the possibility of being received in the presence of the high prelate is by no means certain but, should the occasion arise, Alcuin suggests lying down at his feet and proffering a gift of copies of the grammars by Priscian and Phocas, both of which—we know from the list of manuscripts that Alcuin cites in his York Poem—could be found in York's well-stocked library, provided, that is, that they have not been swallowed up by Neptune's waves.[28] This last comment highlights the fear of the medieval traveler of undergoing a journey by sea, the dangers of which were a constant worry for Alcuin himself, as expressed in the initial verses of a *carmen* dedicated to his disciple Corydon, where the poet declares that he escaped by a divine miracle from the fury of the waves:[29]

> Atque sacerdotis Samuhelis tecta require.
> Castalido portas plectro pulsare memento
> Constanter puero Pithea dic voce ministro:
> 'Puplius Albinus me misit ab orbe Britanno
> Predulci dulcem patri perferre salutem'.

---

[27] This aspect of Alcuin's personality has been analysed by Mary Garrison, "The Social World of Alcuin: Nicknames at York and at the Carolingian Court," in *Proceedings of the Third Germania Latina Conference held at the University of Groningen*, ed. L. Houwen and A. MacDonald, Germania Latina 3 (Groningen, 1998), 59–79.

[28] See line 1555 of the York Poem, Alcuin, *Carmina* 1, ed. Dümmler, 204. Anglo-Saxon literature of that period abounds with references to *codices* as gifts and their often tragic end during the journey. One example is the Codex Amiatinus, the highly-esteemed gift that Ceolfrith wanted to give to the pope but was unable to deliver because of his untimely death during the journey (see the essay by Richard Marsden in this volume). Further examples are given in the many letters sent by Anglo-Saxon missionaries working on the Continent and requesting books, such as the letter from St. Boniface addressed to Abbess Eadburga to thank her for the books she had sent, or the entreaty made to the pupil Duddo to send him a copy of the Holy Scriptures and the texts of the Fathers of the Church, or the other missive sent to Abbess Eadburga written to encourage her to continue her work of copying the letter of St. Paul, using gold lettering, as she had promised (Talbot, *The Anglo-Saxon Missionaries in Germany*, 735–36).

[29] "En tuus Albinus, saevis ereptus ab undis / Venerat, altithrono nunc miserande deo": Alcuin, *Carmina*, 32, ed. Dümmler, 249–50; Godman, *Poetry of the Carolingian Renaissance*, 122–23. According to Bullough, the mention in our poem of the gift of Phocas' and Priscian's grammars represents "the earliest evidence of York's supplying copies of Antique secular works to a Continental centre": Bullough, *Alcuin*, 317.

Si tibi praesentis fuerit data copia verbi[30]
Fusa solo supplex plantas tu lambe sacratas,
Dicque "Valeto, pater Samuhel," dic: "Vive sacerdos."
Detege iam gremium, patres et profer honestos
Prisciano e Foca, tali quia munere gaudet
Si non Neptunus pelago demersit illos.

(lines 25–35)

Through Beornrad's intercession, admission may be granted to the court of Charlemagne—where the next frame (no. 7) is set—although the precise location of the court (which was itinerant until 796 when Aachen was chosen as a fixed residence) is difficult to establish at the moment of the composition of the *carmen*.[31] At the court one must forthwith greet the "proceres," "patres," and "fratres," then lie down at the sovereign's feet and, with a highly deferential tone and resorting to all one's poetic skills, offer a ceremonious and laudatory greeting, asking for protection and imploring him not to listen to the words, inspired by deep envy, of the eminent intellectuals who surround the king of the Franks, above all Paulinus of Aquileia,[32] Peter of Pisa, Alberic, Beornrad, and Ionas who, as rivals of Alcuin's in the art of poetry and rhetoric, might conspire to deprive him of the king's favors.[33] Particular deference is to be shown towards the two fearful Italians, Peter and Paulinus, while towards the evidently less influential prelates, Ricvulf, Raefgot, and Rado,[34] a simple courteous greeting should be adequate:

---

[30] As Dümmler notes, "Si tibi . . . fuerit data copia verbi" recalls Virgil's "coram data copia fandi" in *Aeneid* 1. 250: ed. Dümmler, 221.

[31] According to Schaller, "Vortrags- und Zirkulardichtung," 19, it might refer to the city of Düren, Eifel, but see also Bullough, *Alcuin*, 318, where the connotation of the adverb *forte* is stressed.

[32] There are several extant letters sent by Alcuin to Paulinus of Aquileia over the years, which indicate a constant relationship between the two eminent intellectuals: Alcuin, *Epistolae*, nos. 28, 60, 86, 95, 96, 99, 139, ed. Dümmler, 69–71, 103–4, 128–31, 139–40, 143–44, 220–22.

[33] Dieter Schaller devotes a paper to this far from sublime aspect of court patronage, characterizing the relationships between the major personalities of Charlemagne's entourage, an aspect which emerges clearly in our *carmen:* see D. Schaller, "Poetic Rivalries at the Court of Charlemagne," in *Classical Influences on European Culture, 500–1500*, ed. R. R. Bolgar (Cambridge, 1971), 151–57.

[34] The first of the three prelates mentioned in line 49, Ricvulf, bishop of Cologne, has already been mentioned (line 18), while the identity of the second, Raefgot, remains obscure because there is no other reference to him. The last of the three, Rado, chancellor of Charlemagne from 776 till 794 and later abbot of Saint-Vaast (790–807), is the recipient of a letter (Alcuin, *Epistolae*, 74, ed. Dümmler, 115–17) from Alcuin, in which it is announced that the author is sending a "vita sancti Vedasti emendata." He is also the dedicatee of some versicles by Alcuin himself: "In aecclesia Sancti Vedasti in pariete scribendum": Alcuin, *Carmina*, 88, ed. Dümmler, 308–13.

Si te forte velit regis deducere ad aulam,
Hic proceres patres fratres percurre, saluta.
Ante pedes regis totas expande camenas,
Dicito multoties: "Salve, rex optime, salve.
Tu mihi protector, tutor, defensor adesto,[35]
Invida ne valeat me carpere lingua nocendo
Paulini, Petri, Albrici, Samuelis, Ione,
vel quicumque velit mea rodere viscera morsu;[36]
te terrente procul fugiat, discedat inanis."
Murmure dic tacito: "Cathegita Petre valeto!
Herculeo sevus claro[37] ferit ille, caveto!"
Paulini gaudens conplectere colla magistri,
Oscula melligeris decies da blanda labellis.
Ricvulfum, Raefgot, Radonem rite saluta,
Auriculas horum peditemptim tange canendo,
Dic: "Socii fratres laeti salvete valete."

(lines 36–51)

The instructions as to how Alcuin's *cartula* should greet the king of the Franks ("ante pedes regis totas expande camenas"), the most influential man in western Christendom, and the men of power who will be visited en route, are reminiscent of the best-known passages from the preface to Ovid's *Tristia* where the poet goes into detail as to how his book should behave in the presence of Augustus, an echo of passages by Horace, in particular of *Epistle* 1:13 in which Horace addresses Vinnius Asina, encharged with taking the book of Odes to Augustus; and it is precisely as a result of the reworkings carried out by Ovid here and elsewhere that these passages come to be configured as the prototypes of a certain courtly manner of approach by the poet towards the high and mighty.[38]

The following frame (no. 8) sees the *cartula* in the illustrious city of Mainz, where it is exhorted to pay homage to Lull, "doctor" and "specimen ecclesiae,"

---

[35] "The traditional epithets of royal power—*protector, tutor, defensor*—are transposed into a literary context which makes of Charlemagne not only the supreme authority in matters political but also the ultimate arbiter in critical discrimination": Godman, *Poets and Emperors*, 45.

[36] Carena underlines the Horatian use of the verb *rodere* to indicate the act of criticising the poet's work by envious colleagues, as in *Sermones*, 1.4.81 and 6.46: C. Carena, *Carmi dalla corte e dal convento* (Florence, 1995), 64, at n. 15.

[37] Schaller proposes changing "claro" in line 46 to "clava": Schaller, "Vortrags- und Zirkulardichtung," 19, at n. 18: "Eine Waffe, mit der man zuschlagen (*ferire*) kann, und noch dazu eine für Hercules charakteristische, ist die Keule! Es ist also zu lesen: *Herculea servus clava* . . . Das richtet sich gegen grobschlächtige Methoden des Italieners in der geistigen Auseinandersetzung."

[38] Citroni, "Le raccomandazioni," 129.

since he was the direct successor to St. Boniface in Mainz and an important pro-tagonist in the Christianization of Frisia and Germany, but above all because he was involved personally in the translation of the saint's remains from Dokkum, the place where he was martyred, to the monastery of Fulda:

> Egregiam forsan venies Maggensis ad urbem
> Perpetuumque vale doctori dicito Lullo,
> Ecclesiae specimen, sophiae qui splendor habetur,
> Moribus et vita tanto condignus honore.
>
> (lines 52–55)

The penultimate frame (no. 9) is set in Speyer, where Bassinus was bishop until 782.[39] To the noble prelate Alcuin recommends that he should be remembered to "Paulo," evidently referring to Paulus Diaconus who had become a powerful member of the Carolingian court's entourage immediately after the conquest by the Frankish king of the Lombard kingdom of northern Italy in 774:

> O Bassine bone, Spirensis gloria plebis,
> Me, rogo, commenda Paulo, pater alme, patrono,
> Cuius et alma domus fratres nos fecerat ambos.
>
> (lines 56–58)

The last frame (no. 10) sees the *cartula* at Saint-Denis, the seat of Abbot Fulrad until 784. Alcuin praises his great skill in composing *carmina*:

> Quis, Fulerade pius, lyrico te tangere plectro
> Audebit? Meritis Musarum carmina vincis
> Nunc tamen hanc ederam circum sine tempora sacra
> Serpere,[40] summe pater, tibimet bonitate sueta,
> Vel demitte semel memet tibi dicere salve.
>
> (lines 59–63)

After outlining the journey this piece of paper should undertake and after indulg-ing in the memory of a journey already undertaken, Alcuin exhorts the *carta* (as the "instrumentum" to which he has entrusted his poetical composition is now named) to set out on the homeward journey, and the recurrence of the adverb *cito*,

---

[39] The last year of Bassinus' bishopric (782), together with the year of Fulrad's death (784), is decisive in terms of dating the composition of the *carmen*, since it constitutes the *terminus ante quem*. On Fulrad and the date of our *carmen* see A. Stoclet, *Autour de Fulrad de Saint-Denis (v. 710–784)* (Paris, 1993), 148–54.

[40] Carena compares "Nunc tamen hanc ederam circum sine tempora sacra serpere" with Virgil's "hanc sine tempora circum / inter victricis hederam tibi serpere laurus" (*Eclogae* 8. 12–13): Carena, *Carmi dalla corte*, 64, at n. 19.

already used at line 1, would seem to suggest, according to the structure of the *Ringkomposition*, that the composition is formally about to end:

> Heia age, carta, cito navem conscende paratam
> Oceanum Rhenum sub te natet unca carena.
>   (lines 64–65)

The exhortation to set out on the return journey is expanded and takes on a more urgent tone over the next few verses, with the poet inviting the *cartula* to hurry without stopping to see the gold that the inhabitants are extracting from the earth, or to see the villages, the houses, or the flowery countryside:

> Materies auri non te, rogo, fulva retardet
> Accula quem fesses profert de viscere terrae
> Non castella domus urbes nec florida rura
> Deteneant stupidam spatio nec unius horae
> Sed fuge, rumpe moras,[41] propera, percurre volando:
>   (lines 66–70)

After having made assurances that his *cartula* will not linger in the places encountered on the way back, in the following verses Alcuin expresses the wish that his *Schriftstück* may find all his friends in good physical and mental state and the invocation that God may allow them to live long in good health and that they will be welcomed into the heavenly kingdom on their death:

> Incolumes sanos gaudentes atque vigentes
> Inveniens utinam nostros gratanter amicos.
> Det deus omnipotens illis per secla salutem,
> Postea caelestem laetos deducat in aulam.
>   (lines 71–74)

Bearing in mind the canons that this model of the apostrophe to the book generally follows, the *carmen* would seem to have ended at this point, not only from a conceptual point of view, since the *cartula* has carried out its task, but also from a formal point of view. I am referring to the pattern used that was widespread within the "Ringkomposition" genre of writing, which, as Sidonius Apollinaris in his *Propempticon* observes, for example, could be considered the final section or *explicit*. Alcuin, however, unexpectedly adds a further section of seven verses in which he expresses the ardent wish that the instrument that he had entrusted his composition to, the *cartula*, may return to him in the spring, and he makes a heartfelt plea that it should return to its homeland ("certa reverte"),

---

[41] Carena, *Carmi dalla corte*, 64, at n. 21, notes that the exhortation *rumpe moras* may derive from Mercury's incitation to the hesitant Aeneas, at Aeneid 4. 569.

without neglecting to mention everything it had been told during its pilgrimage; then—the poet hopes—he will be able to hear again "te ludere tectis, atque novas iterum nobis adferre camenas" ('singing under the roof, bringing to us again new songs'); then he can weave golden garlands with the new flowers, "tum tibi serta novis de floribus aurea fingam" and, he adds, "sociata mihi pratis pausabis amoenis" ('you will lie at my side in lovely meadows') :

> Omnibus his actis patriam tu certa reverte
> Et quod quisque tibi dicat narrare memento
> Ut cum vere novo rubrae de cortice gemmae
> Erumpant, nostris videam te ludere tectis
> Atque novas iterum nobis adferre camenas
> Tum tibi serta novis de floribus aurea fingam
> Et sociata mihi pratis pausabis amoenis
> (lines 75–81)

The model followed by Alcuin so far presupposes a poetic artifice which consists of an exhortation to the book that has just been completed or to the instrument on which the message has been written (a *cartula* or, as in Catullus' *carmen* 35, a "papyrus")[42] to reach the addressee of the work, to bring the poet's greetings or to recommend the work. On the contrary, in this *carmen* the *cartula* must come back; and it is to the *cartula* that Alcuin promises to weave golden garlands.

This is not the only work of this genre in which the instrument on which the poetic work was written is exhorted to return; for example, for Ausonius, in *Epistle* 19b to his friend Paulinus, "the 'winged' iambus is exhorted to send the poet's greetings to the addressee and then to return home immediately."[43] In our *carmen*, however, there are some extra lines, the last five, where the poet hopes to hear again "novas camenas" ('new songs') in the spring when the *cartula* comes back, which, when compared to the model, would seem to be transgressively redundant.

We must therefore reconsider the situation. The poetic epistle does not fit the traditional model; certainly it is quite different in form and function from the stylistically formal poetic epistles written by Alcuin's contemporary intellectuals belonging to the Carolingian circle, examples being Angilberct's *Cartula, curre modo per sacra palatia David*[44] and Hibernicus Exul's *Carta, Christo comite, per telluris spatium / Ad Caesaris splendidum nunc perge palatium*,[45] the latter an epigone

---

[42] "Poete tenero, meo sodali, velim Caecilio, papyre, dicas Veronam veniat . . . ": *Q. Valerii Catulli Veronensis Liber*, ed. K. Lachmann (Berlin, 1829), 18–19.

[43] Santelia, *Carme 24*, 30–31.

[44] See the *Ecloga ad Carolum* (794/95), in which Alcuin's disciple puts the invitation to the *cartula* within the eclogue, at line 72.

[45] *Versus Karoli Imperatoris*, no. 4, ed. Dümmler, in MGH, *Poetae Latini Aevi Carolini* 1, 399–400.

of the Ovidian tradition of exile written by an author who, like so many other Carolingian poets, suffered in exile as Ovid had done.[46] Almost all of them are dedicated to Charlemagne with panegyric or encomiastic intents; some of them can be classified as belonging to the "Vortragsdichtung" postulated by Schaller as responding to the poet's intention of being remembered at court. Nor does our *carmen* fit—or at least not fully—into the models of "apostrophe of the poet to his poetical composition," classified by Citroni according to their functions into three types: 1) that of Ovidian derivation, which presupposes the sending of a poem or a book just finished to a faraway dedicatee; 2) that derived mainly from Martial, which represents the offering of a book just finished to an authoritative person who will become its patron; or 3) the ostentation of modesty or reverential awe, which has its sources both in Horace and in Martial, towards the patron to whom the poet is sending his work.[47] All of these models were variously combined by later authors, like Statius in his epistle to Victorius Marcellus inserted into his *Silvae*, where the apostrophe is directed to the "epistula" (*Curre per Euboicos non segnis, epistola, campos*),[48] which is exhorted to follow the road from Naples to Rome, according to an itinerary minutely described by its author, or Ausonius who writes an "epistula" (Epist. 9b) that will accompany two books,[49] where a *carmen* is inserted containing an apostrophe to the book, which is entreated to go to Sirmio to greet the addressee Petronius Probus.[50]

Returning to Alcuin's *carmen*: even if there are hints of the elements that would allow us to classify it according to the types indicated by Citroni, such as the fact that the *cartula* is not traveling alone but carries with it the burden of books by two grammarians (line 34), valued gifts for "sacerdos Samuhel," and perhaps also the *carmen* that the "niger" Hrotberct will not appreciate (line 13: these may be different verses to our *carmen*), above all there is a situation of fear of *livor*, 'malice,' causing the poet to express his worry that critical opinions of his work may arise from his colleagues, and ask for the protection of a particularly authoritative person, the king himself. The poem thus eludes any definitive classification, particularly in the light of the seven 'redundant' final verses.

If we compare it to the *Propempticon* by Sidonius, the structure of which it closely resembles, it is apparent that the function of the two poetical compositions is quite different: in the *Propempticon* we are in the presence of a process of *ecdosis* by which the poet Sidonius, taking leave of the book of "nugae" he has just

---

[46] Citroni, "Le raccomandazioni," 141.

[47] Citroni, "Le raccomandazioni," 140.

[48] Statius, *Silvae*, 4.4. See also the apostrophe to the whole *Thebaid*, which closes the last book of the work, where Statius is sure that it will not be the object of *livor*; Santelia, *Carme 24*, 29.

[49] One is the *Apologi* by Julius Titianus, the other the *Chronica* by Cornelius Nepos.

[50] "Perge, o libelle, Sirmium / et dic ero meo ac tuo / ave atque salve plurimum"; for other examples by Ausonius, see Santelia, *Carme 24*, 30–31.

completed, exhorts it to reach his "sodales" in order to gather a series of impressions or suggestions about the finished work; in Alcuin's *carmen* this situation is not clearly expressed. Even Godman, who does not show any doubts in classifying it according to Schaller's definition, cannot help remarking on the absolute originality of the poem:

> Stylistically as well as thematically a spirit of experimentation informs this text. The direct address to the personified epistle as *cartula*—unprecedented, as to its opening, in extant Latin poetry—and the neologistic diction (exemplified by the ironical, perhaps self-parodic, coining of one of the compound adjectives which are a characteristic feature of Alcuin's lexicon) contribute to create an effect whose originality is not diminished by the existence of literary models. [51]

Moreover, the term *cartula* itself, used in this form for the first time by the poet to define the means—the instrument—on which his text is traveling, would seem to offer the possibility of a new interpretation. The term is used generically to indicate the material on which a brief piece of writing (*scriptum* or *Schriftstück*) is actually written, just as in Catullus' *carmen* 35 the apostrophe is addressed to the "papyrus." According to the *Mittellateinisches Wörterbuch*, only *stricto sensu* can this be seen as referring to a letter and, moreover, where certain citations can be interpreted as being an *epistula*, they are in most cases referring to *epistulae rogationis* 'begging letters,' not strictly as private missives, or *epistulae*. [52]

Furthermore, if we take into account the technical details linked to the production and dispatch of *epistulae* at this time, we realize that letters were written in most cases on a single parchment sheet (or sometimes a bifolium or even a whole *libellus*, according to the length of the text), fastened with a strip and then sealed with a *sigillum* 'seal'; "and the name of the addressee, occasionally with an additional form of identification or even greeting, was written on the outside." [53] An example of this practice is to be found in a private *epistula* that Alcuin addressed to Angilbert, in which the sender begs the addressee to make sure it is handed to Adalhard (here called "Antonius"), abbot of Corbie, still tied to the document to which it is attached, because it would be offensive to present the prelate with an opened letter:

---

[51] Godman, *Poets and Emperors*, 45–46.

[52] See *Mittellateinisches Wörterbuch bis zum ausgehenden 13. Jahrhundert* (Munich, 1971), s. v. *chartula*. In citing the passage from Alcuin, the same dictionary offers for the term *cartula* the metonymic meaning of *carmen*. Du Cange, *Glossarium Mediae et Infimae Latinitatis* (repr. Graz, 1954) 2: 292–297 gives *instrumentum, contractus, conventio* and so on (conventionally), with many lemmata.

[53] Bullough, *Alcuin*, 42.

Antonio itaque filio meo, fratri vestro, has litteras alias deprecor, ut quam citissime clausa cartula sicut est deprecor ut dirigas; quia si distincta veniat in praesentiam illius vilescit apud eum

['I insist that these documents be immediately handed to Antonius, my son and your brother, with the cartula as it is, absolutely sealed; as, if presented to him separately, he might be offended'][54]

although Alcuin would like Angilbert to read it "eo dirigente iterum." The same situation is described in the distich *Discingat chartam mitis, rogo, dextera David* which was copied just before the beginning of an *epistula* written by Alcuin to Charlemagne, in which he apologizes for not having gone to see him when requested to do so.[55] Another example is to be found in the lines "Nulla manus [cartam] discingat ni tua, praesul," which, Bullough argues, "must belong to another letter, now lost (or unidentifiable)."[56] But the most relevant example for our purpose is in the lines "Curre velox carta, plures fer cincta salutes / Dic: tua me queso discinge dextera illi," which accompany and were "originally on the outside" of a letter written this time by Alcuin's disciple Candidus to his master.[57] From just these two lines, it is evident that these verses closely resemble, on the whole, the style of our *Cartula, perge cito pelagi trans aequora cursu*. Not only does the poet begin his poem with an apostrophe to the actual instrument which will carry his message to the dedicatee, but also the imperative form "dic" in the following line, addressed to the parchment sheet, reminds us of the intimate tone that Alcuin uses in his *carmen*.

In the light of these reflections, bearing in mind the obsessive interest on the part of the poet in the journey the *cartula* must undertake and his concentration on finding the right words to address the persons to be met—elements that strongly characterize the work—and above all the absence of any clear mention of who the work's dedicatee is, I believe that we can put forward the hypothesis that the *carmen* is meant to be a small document, halfway between an *hodoeporicon* and an ironic *vade-mecum* which Alcuin has drafted to be used by someone, perhaps a student, who is about to undertake an *itinerarium* that is well known to the erudite man of York.[58] In my opinion, this small work was not "a real letter

---

[54] Alcuin, *Epistolae*, no. 221, ed. Dümmler, 365.

[55] Bullough, *Alcuin*, 42, at n. 95.

[56] Alcuin, *Carmina*, no. 29.2, ed. Dümmler, 248; Bullough, *Alcuin*, 42.

[57] *Epistolae variorum Carolo Magno regnante scriptae*, ed. Dümmler, in MGH, *Epistolae* 4, no. 39 (557–61); Bullough, *Alcuin*, 42.

[58] Unfortunately there are no references to this hypothetical journey in Alcuin's extant letters which belong mostly (if not wholly) to the period after his years spent in York: Dümmler, in MGH, *Epistolae* 4, 2. See also Bullough, *Alcuin*, 317 where he notes that, "Like a majority of commentators, I believe that Alcuin's journey precedes that to

designed to be read aloud to his many eminent friends at each of these locations"[59] and was not addressed to Fulrad, as was upheld after it had been found at Saint-Denis;[60] rather, the addressee is to be found among the young scholars of the York school where Alcuin was working. It would not be too hazardous, at this point, to interpret the poem as a sort of *vade-mecum* that the Northumbrian deacon wrote on a strip of parchment to accompany an official *epistula*, or a *libellus* to be submitted to the scrutiny of his newly-acquired *sodales* on the Continent, and which gave detailed instructions to the carrier on the things to say, do, and see during the journey. Probably the student was about to undertake a journey of study, or perhaps some diplomatic mission, or perhaps more simply he was a courier of the missives sent from the bishopric of York to the Continent, since "the form and address-clauses of a few of the 'epistolae' indicate that their carrier was expected to take them to several destinations successively."[61] In loving tones the master provides him with a series of geographical facts relating to his *itinerarium* that are familiar to him and, not without a hint of irony, he also includes suggestions about the proper behavior to adopt towards the great dignitaries along the Rhine and the Moselle, as Alcuin himself experienced with such fruitful results in the course of his brilliant career. These instructions take a poetic form, that of the *carmen*, which came naturally to this highly-skilled poet. This reading might explain the "effervescent familiarity with which Alcuin, at a similar date, advertises his apparently effortless entrée to court" which is in stark contrast to the attitude of Paulus Diaconus who, interceding with Charlemagne for the safety of his brother taken prisoner by the Frankish army in Italy, "never moves beyond a poised and distant correctness."[62]

It is obvious that the official *epistula*, or perhaps the newly-written book, which is attached to the *cartula*, will be read by all the high-ranking characters mentioned in the *carmen*, while the *portitor* will be the sole dedicatee of the delightful verses that accompany the document. We might consider it as a present for the *missus*, someone dear to his master, before he sets out on his journey; the triviality of the gift is clearly apparent to its author, since from the beginning of his poetical composition he uses the word *cartula*, a diminutive of *carta*, just as *epistiuncula* is a diminutive of *epistula*.[63] This interpretation might help to explain the light tone—sometimes tongue-in-cheek—that pervades Alcuin's little poem, thus explaining Godman's puzzled remark on the "effervescent familiarity" that characterizes it.

Rome to obtain the pallium, ending somewhere in the middle-Rhine region or in a place with easy access to it."

[59] Godman, *Poets and Emperors*, 44.
[60] Schaller, "Vortrags- und Zirkulardichtung," 19.
[61] Bullough, *Alcuin*, 40.
[62] Godman, *Poets and Emperors*, 50.
[63] Bullough, *Alcuin*, 39.

At the end of the *carmen* Alcuin manifests the hope of seeing his young and inexperienced *missus* safely back home (*certa reverte*) in York in the following spring, when he will narrate in detail all the things he heard on the Continent ("et quod quisque tibi dicat narrare memento"); then they will compose new *carmina* again and the master will weave golden garlands, resting on "pratis amoenis" which, as Schaller has pointed out and demonstrated with many examples, is a widely-used metaphor in Carolingian times for poetical activity.[64]

Certainly, the *portitor* reached the final destination, Saint-Denis, delivering the missive to its last addressee, Fulrad, according to the instructions he had been given, as testified by the presence of the poem in the manuscript, Lat. 528. But, in contrast to Candidus's apostrophe to his *carta* to Alcuin, mentioned above, where the accompanying letter survives, with *Cartula, perge cito trans pelagi aequora cursu* we have lost trace of the official *epistula* or *libellus* to which it was attached.[65]

---

[64] Schaller, "Vortrags- und Zirkulardichtung," 33–35.
[65] My thanks to Stefania Santelia for her invaluable suggestions and kind help.

Panegyric and Reflection in a Poem by Abbo of Fleury to Ramsey Abbey

Catherine A. M. Clarke

Despite a steadily increasing number of his works in modern editions, Abbo of Fleury remains a relatively peripheral figure for many scholars working in Anglo-Saxon and medieval Latin studies. In particular, although several recent studies have attempted to resolve questions of authorship and to provide workable modern English translations of some of his difficult and complex pieces, Abbo's literary output has received little attention in terms of its interest and quality as poetry. This article will examine one poem by Abbo of Fleury: the panegyric to Ramsey included within the *Vita Oswaldi*, as well as in other manuscript locations. This difficult and deliberately obscure poem presents us with a fascinating variation on the medieval literary convention of the monastic *locus amoenus* or 'delightful place', playing with imagery of light and reflection to mythologize and celebrate the abbey of Ramsey and its setting. The poem exhibits Abbo's sophisticated knowledge of astronomy, and addresses an ideal audience familiar with the constellations and their mythical connotations. Beyond the imagery of light and mirrored light in the skies and waters around Ramsey, the poem reflects upon its own status as panegyric and its participation in literary processes of reflection and mirroring.

Abbo's poem to Ramsey Abbey is incorporated into Book I of Byrhtferth's *Vita Oswaldi*, as preserved in the London manuscript. It also appears with Abbo's *Quaestiones Grammaticales* in London, BL, MS. Additional 10872. In addition, it occurs in Andrew of Fleury's eleventh-century *Vita Gauzlini*, and alongside excerpts from the *Quaestiones Grammaticales* in Erfurt, Wissenschaftliche Allgemeinbibliothek, Amplon. 4º. 53.[1] The version of the poem used here is that edited

---

[1] The final line of the poem varies, occurring in the Continental manuscripts as "Quos, Benedicte pater, iure tuere pares." For example, see *Vie de Gauzlin, abbé de Fleury*, ed. and trans. Robert-Henri Bautier and Gillette Labory (Paris, 1969). I am grateful to Michael Lapidge for these manuscript references, and for sharing with me his edition and translation of the Abbo poems discussed in this paper prior to their publication. Any mistakes or misapprehensions in this interpretation are my own.

Hans Sauer and Joanna Story, eds., *Anglo-Saxon England and the Continent.* With the assistance of Gaby Waxenberger. Essays in Anglo-Saxon Studies, vol. 3. MRTS 394. Tempe: ACMRS, 2011.　　[ISBN 978-0-86698-442-3]

and translated by Michael Lapidge.[2]

   1 O Ramesiga cohors, amplis que claudere stagnis,
         purior obrizo niteris esse Deo.
     Vasta palus, piscosa nimis, sua dindima pandit,
         ut noua sint heremi claustra reperta tibi.
   5 Nam qua coruifere consurgit proditor Hidre,
         insula siluoso gurgite pulchra nitet;
     et qua splendentis se mergunt lora Bootis,
         pons est inde suis peruius Angligenis:
     qua Cynosura poli fixum regit undique girum,
 10   anguillosa palus nescit habere modum.
     Inde refert umbras uaga lux Phebea sinistras,
         terra patet nullo continuata uado.
     Qua me sorte dedi ignotis, ignotus, alumnis:
         quos Christus semper saluet, honoret, amet!

[1 'O noble throng of Ramsey, secluded by spreading waters,
     You strive to be purer than gold for God's sake.
    The vast fen, abounding in fish, yields its secrets
     So that new confinements of the wilderness may be found for you.
 5 For where the destroyer of the raven-bearing Hydra arises,
     There gleams an exquisite island with its woodland waters;
    And where the reins of gleaming Boötes sink,
     There is a land-bridge accessible to all the English;
    Where the Lesser Bear rules its fixed orbit of the sky,
10   There the eel-filled waters know no bounds.
    From there the sun's unsteady light draws back its sinister shadows;
     The earth lies open linked up by no shallows.
    In this place I, a stranger, luckily gave myself over to unknown students:
     May Christ always save, honor and love them!']

The multiple copying of this text suggests a sense of its literary worth and importance beyond its local connections with Ramsey, and invites us to look more closely at its qualities as a poem. Certainly, the poem provides us with excellent evidence of the developing and strengthening intellectual relationships between England and the Continent in the late tenth century, attesting to the reciprocity of cultural influence and exchange. Abbo's period away from Fleury at Ramsey Abbey dates to around 985–987, and although his references to his time in England are often ambivalent (the experience is described as his "exile"),[3] this poem offers an unequivocal panegyric to Ramsey.

---

    [2] *Byrhtferth of Ramsey: The Lives of St Oswald and St Ecgwine*, ed. and trans. Michael Lapidge (Oxford, 2009), 92, 93.
    [3] For example, see *Quaestiones Grammaticales*, ed. A. Guerreau-Jalabert (Paris, 1982), chap. 3.

Although such a close reading of any text can inevitably entail the dangers of over-interpretation, Abbo's poem to Ramsey seems to be a deliberate intellectual puzzle or game, challenging the reader to disentangle allusions and layers of meaning. The Latin itself is difficult and reminiscent of the late tenth-century "hermeneutic style."[4] The ostentatiously bookish vocabulary includes in line 2 *obrizo*, a term for a kind of purified gold (the gold refined for Byzantine currency standard). In line 3 *dindima* is appropriated from the vocabulary of classical mythology: Dindymus was a mountain in Phrygia sacred to the goddess Cybele and associated with cult and secrecy. The poem displays a real enjoyment of language for its own sake, revelling particularly in multivalency and word play. *Cohors* in line 1 evokes both the company of men and the architectural structure of Ramsey—both monks and cloister—and its military connotations contribute to the impression of silvery shining which is cultivated throughout the poem. *Niteris* in line 2 (from *nitor*, to strive) resonates with *nitet* (from *niteo*, to shine) in line 6, setting up verbal echoes across the poem which parallel its descriptions of visual reflection and mirroring. The poem may also include an early exploitation of the pun on *angligens–anguilla*, echoing across lines 8 and 10 and suggesting an association between Englishness and these abundant fenland assets.[5]

As with many other panegyric texts associated with fenland or levels monastic houses in late Anglo-Saxon England and the post-Conquest period, Abbo's poem to Ramsey exploits and mythologizes the abbey's topographical setting. Ramsey is presented as a cultivated island *locus amoenus* set amid the wilderness of the fens. The poem's description of the island of Ramsey, "amplis que claudere stagnis" (l. 1), emphasizes the inaccessibility of the abbey. This physical inaccessibility parallels the inaccessibility of the poem's language, imagery, and allusions, which are open only to an intended, invited audience. In line 4 the phrase "Ut noua sint heremi claustra reperta tibi" has resonance both in terms of the physical landscape cultivation at Ramsey and the constant reclamation of more land from the fen marshes, and also in terms of the pursuit and refinement of the Benedictine life within the abbey. Although the poem's exploitation of landscape, and particularly the island monastery setting, is typical of many texts celebrating marshland houses, Abbo's choice of focus and imagery is strikingly

---

[4] See Michael Lapidge, "The Hermeneutic Style in Tenth-Century Anglo-Latin Literature," *Anglo-Saxon England* 4 (1975): 67–111.

[5] I am grateful to Mary Carruthers for this suggestion. For a later example of this pun, see Thomas Bradwardine, "De memoria artificiale adquirenda," ed. Mary Carruthers, *Journal of Medieval Latin* 2 (1992): 25–43, at 40: "Si bene noveris ullum regem . . . ponas eum ibi et teneat in dextra sua manu anguillam se plurimum agitantem, que 'Angliam' tibi dabit." ['If you should know well any king . . . place him there and let him hold in his right hand an eel wriggling about greatly, which will give you 'England'.'] Translation from *The Medieval Craft of Memory*, ed. Mary Carruthers and Jan M. Ziolkowski (Philadelphia, 2002), 213–14.

unusual. The monastic island *locus amoenus* is conventionally described through imagery of fertility and agriculture, verdure and pastoral beauty. The much later, thirteenth-century Ramsey Chronicle includes a far more conventional description of Ramsey as an island *locus amoenus*.

> Hæc autem insula duobus ferme millibus in longum extensa, egena latitudine paulo strictior habetur. Quæ tam alneto quidem quam arundineto cum virore calami et juncti pulchre in girum coronata, multo antequam inhabitaretur arborum genere . . . Nunc vero longiore temporis tractu nemoribus ex parte demolitis, terra ubere gleba arabilis cernitur et opima, fructibus et frugibus jocunda, hortis consita, pascuis opulenta, nonnullis adhuc arboribus nemorosa, et pratorum gratia verno tempore spectantibus et arridente velut depicta floribus tota insula vario coloratura colore.[6]

> ['This island extends nearly two miles in length, although it lacks somewhat in width, being a little narrower across. It is beautifully crowned all around with as much alder as reed, with green canes and bulrushes, and before it was inhabited it was full of all sorts of trees . . . But now, after a long period of time, the woods are partly gone. The land is fit for the plough with its rich, fertile earth; it is pleasant with crops and fruits, filled with gardens, rich with pastures, and still leafy with many trees. In springtime the meadows are delightful to behold, and the whole island seems to smile, as if embroidered with many flowers.']

Abbo's poem, however, includes little sense of a pastoral setting, and strikingly omits the visual imagery of pastoral verdure. Indeed, Abbo's depiction of Ramsey is free of any real color—certainly not the green of a *locus amoenus*—playing instead with ideas of light and shade and the shining brightness of starlight, moonlight, fish, eels, and water.[7] The martial connotations of *cohors* (l. 1) and the purity of refined gold, *obrizo* (l. 2), also contribute to this effect of metallic shimmering. Rather than focusing on the greenness of the cultivated land at Ramsey, Abbo chooses to center his poem on the spaces which surround the island: the wide fenland sky and the waters of the marshes.

The poem focuses on a depiction of the stars visible in the night sky over Ramsey, and their reflections in the waters surrounding the island. The poem itself is structured around a series of couplets which balance mirrored glimpses of sky and water. Line 5, "Nam qua coruifere consurgit proditor Hidre" is balanced with line 6, "insula siluoso gurgite pulchra nitet." Line 7, "et qua splendentis se

---

[6] *Chronicon Abbatiæ Ramesiensis*, ed. W. Dunn Macray (London, 1886), Book 1, 7–8.

[7] As well as fitting within this scheme of silvery shining, the fen 'abounding in fish' may implicitly allude to the monastic community at Ramsey, with the fish as a familiar biblical symbol for the Christian individual or the soul.

mergunt lora Bootis" is coupled with line 8, "pons est inde suis peruius Angligenis." Line 9, "qua Cynosura poli fixum regit undique girum" pairs with line 10, "anguillosa palus nescit habere modum." Finally, in lines 11 and 12, the receding light of the sun ("Inde refert umbras uaga lux Phebea sinistras") is linked to a glimpse of the vast marshes below ("terra patet nullo continuata uado"). The constellations of Hercules (the 'destroyer of the raven-bearing Hydra'), Boötes, and Cynosura or the Lesser Bear can indeed all be seen together in this configuration in the spring sky over Ramsey. Hercules would indeed appear to be emerging (*consurgit*) from beneath the horizon, while Boötes appeared to sink (*se mergunt*). So Abbo is describing a realistically possible view of the stars from Ramsey Abbey. However, his choice of this particular configuration and of these particular constellations seems motivated by a desire to link the imagery of the heavens with the features and values of life at the Benedictine monastery at Ramsey.

First, Abbo exploits the technicalities of early medieval astronomical knowledge to link the movements of the stars with their setting over the fenland waters. The poem describes the constellations as 'emerging' (*consurgit*, l.5) and 'sinking' (*se mergunt*, l.7). This vocabulary expresses the medieval idea that when stars 'set' below the horizon they are submerged in the watery 'underworld' section of the zodiac beneath the equator. Of course, as these constellations appear and disappear over the fens at Ramsey, they do indeed seem to emerge from and sink into water. Abbo also seems to have focused upon constellations which have particularly relevant mythological associations and connotations for their place above the monastery. The constellation Hercules is the legendary slayer of the Hydra, the constellation also known as Draco or Anguis. This constellation, representing a serpent or water snake, certainly links well with the imagery of the eel-filled waters around Ramsey, and Hercules is a powerful—if rather grandiose—emblem for the 'conquest' and exploitation of the fens and their eely abundance. This reading may seem fanciful, but a twelfth-century poem in the Ely *Libellus* provides an interesting analogue, comparing the Ely subsidiary site of 'Little Downham' to a transported Garden of the Apples of the Hesperides, again raising connotations of the Herculean labor and struggle involved in cultivating and defending a fenland island location.[8] Boötes is the constellation of the herdsman or shepherd—evidently appropriate in this monastic context and particularly relevant to the late Anglo-Saxon Benedictine monasticism which so stressed imagery of the spiritual shepherd in key documents such as the *Regularis Concordia*.[9] Cynosura, or the Lesser Bear, has no particular mythological

---

[8] See *Liber Eliensis*, ed. E.O. Blake (London, 1962) Book 2, chap. 2, 398.

[9] For example, Edgar and his abbots follow the example of the "Pastorum Pastor": *Regularis Concordia*, ed. and trans. Thomas Symons (London, 1953), chap. 3. L. Kornexl, *Die Regularis Concordia und ihre altenglische Interlinearversion, mit Einleitung und Kommentar*, Münchener Universitätsschriften, Texte und Untersuchungen zur Englischen Philologie 17 (Munich, 1993).

associations, but, as a Northern Hemisphere star which never sets, its fixed orbit around the Pole made it crucial for medieval navigation. As a constellation, therefore, it would seem to have connotations of constancy and order—again, a fitting symbol for life under the Benedictine monastic rule.

At this point the question arises of Abbo's audience and the extent to which they may have been alert to these astronomical allusions and mythological associations within the poem. Abbo's own proficiency in astronomy is amply evidenced by the scientific work produced earlier in his career.[10] However, the interest of the Anglo-Saxons in astronomy has tended to be dismissed as purely functional and little developed beyond the needs of *computus*. In Old English poetry, Jennifer Neville finds "a reflection of a general disregard for cosmology," and Gopa Roy observes Anglo-Saxon attention to astronomy and cosmology "only in connection with other [more practical] areas of interest."[11] Abbo's teaching at Ramsey certainly contributed to a growth of interest in astronomy, influencing in particular his pupil Byrhtferth of Ramsey, and we can probably assume that Abbo's own pupils would have had the background knowledge necessary to access and unravel the allusions within the poem. Beyond this, manuscript evidence demonstrates not only the status of Abbo's home abbey of Fleury as a major center for the production and circulation of astronomical works, but also the direct transmission of astronomical texts and knowledge from Fleury to southeast England in the late tenth century. In his recent work on manuscripts of the *Cicero-Aratea* and the appropriation of their iconography in the Bayeux Tapestry, Cyril Hart examines the manuscript London, BL, Harley 647, a ninth-century Carolingian manuscript of the *Cicero-Aratea* "which reached Canterbury from the great abbey of Fleury-sur-Loire in the last quarter of the tenth century."[12] Harley 647 is well annotated, and Hart suggests that these annotations may have been made by Abbo himself.[13] Harley 647 arrived at Canterbury along with another manuscript from Fleury, London, BL, Harley 2506, which includes astronomical works by Abbo of Fleury alongside a version of the *Cicero-Aratea*.[14] This manuscript also contains line drawings of constellation motifs by an English artist, the

---

[10] See R. B. Thomson, "Two Astronomical Tractates of Abbo of Fleury," in *The Light of Nature: Essays in the History and Philosophy of Science Presented to A. C. Crombie*, ed J. D. North and J. J. Roche (Dordrecht, 1985), 114–33, and idem, "Further Astronomical Material of Abbo of Fleury," *Medieval Studies* 1 (1988): 671–73.

[11] Jennifer Neville, *Representations of the Natural World in Old English Poetry* (Cambridge, 1999), 156. Gopa Roy, "The Anglo-Saxons and the Shape of the World," in *Essays on Anglo-Saxon and Related Themes in Memory of Lynne Grundy*, ed. Jane Roberts and Janet Nelson (London, 2000), 455–81, at 455.

[12] Cyril Hart, "The *Cicero-Aratea* and the Bayeux Tapestry," in *King Harold II and the Bayeux Tapestry*, ed. Gale R. Owen-Crocker (Woodbridge, 2005), 161–78, at 162.

[13] Hart, "The *Cicero-Aratea*," 174.

[14] Hart, "The *Cicero-Aratea*," 174.

"Ramsey Master," who was working at Fleury-sur-Loire.[15] The arrival of these manuscripts in southeast England in the late tenth century raises the intriguing possibility that they may have traveled with Abbo to England—tangible proof of Abbo's transmission of astronomical learning to the Anglo-Saxons.[16] Certainly, these manuscripts provide clear evidence of the cultural exchange between Ramsey and Fleury in the tenth century, and the developing interest in astronomical science in late Anglo-Saxon England. The iconography of these *Cicero-Aratea* manuscripts also illuminates Abbo's panegyric to Ramsey. Harley 647, for example, includes an elaborate Planisphere (fol. 21 verso), which features detailed representations of constellation motifs described in Abbo's poem to Ramsey (Hercules, the 'raven-bearing Hydra', Boötes).[17] The Planisphere's image of the Hydra, for example, certainly bears a convincing resemblance to an eel! This map of the heavens gives us an invaluable visual guide to Abbo's conceptualization of Ramsey in his panegyric poem, as well as an insight into frameworks of interpretation for its early readers.

Abbo's apparent choice of constellations appropriate to his subject of Ramsey in "O Ramesiga cohors" is certainly a powerful device for celebrating and elevating the status of the abbey. Night sky and fenland water appear to be mutually reflecting: Ramsey seems to mirror aspects of the myth and legend displayed in the heavens, but the heavens can also be seen to reflect, celebrate, and immortalize aspects of the monastic life at Ramsey. Nevertheless, although the constellations which Abbo chooses to describe do have particular relevance in the context of a poem to an English fenland monastery, it may be that their specific associations are less important than the overall impression of classical and astronomical knowledge. The constellations, with their connotations of classical learning and authority, shine in the sky and are reflected in the waters around Ramsey, suggesting that this is a place where classical learning shines on for the English.

Interestingly, this imagery of reflection recurs as a panegyric motif in the much later thirteenth-century Ramsey Chronicle. Recalling this period of the Benedictine foundation and flourishing of the abbey in the tenth century, the Chronicle includes within its foundation myth an exchange between the reformer Dunstan and the benefactor Æthelwine. Dunstan speaks:

> Hic est . . . alter Elysius, viris summo Paradiso destinatis ab æterno provisus. In hoc loco fidei tuæ et devotionis speculum, O amice [Æthelwine],

---

[15] Hart, "The *Cicero-Aratea*," 174.

[16] Hart suggests this possibility, but comments that "it is perhaps more likely that they formed part of the exchanges of manuscripts between the three houses [Fleury, Ramsey, Canterbury] which followed Abbo's visit": "The *Cicero-Aratea*," 175.

[17] See Hart, "The *Cicero-Aratea*," 163, fig. 12.

viventem æternæ memoriæ tuæ imaginem speculantibus exhibens, per successive futuræ generationis secula resultabit.[18]

['Here is a second Elysium, provided in eternity for men destined for the
highest place in Paradise. In this place a mirror of your faith and devotion,
O friend, reflecting the living image of your eternal memory, will shine
back throughout the ages of successive generations.']

Dunstan's speech in the Chronicle presents the foundation of Ramsey as a mirror of Æthelwine's faith and devotion, again perhaps deliberately exploiting the
reflecting waters of the abbey's actual topography. It would not be surprising for
a post-Conquest text such as this to look back deliberately to the heritage and
authority of earlier writings, and this passage from the Chronicle may represent
a self-conscious participation in the same tradition as Abbo's panegyric. Alternatively, it may be that these instances are entirely independent exploitations of the
symbolic potential of Ramsey's island location. However, certainly each example
shows participation in literary traditions which associate panegyric with the idea
of reflection. Of course, in the early medieval period we can look far beyond
Abbo's poem to Ramsey to find panegyric texts which center upon images of
light and reflection. Yet Abbo's own panegyric style offers some other prominent
examples.

Abbo's acrostic poem to Dunstan, also embedded within the *Vita Oswaldi*
(Part 5), includes prominent imagery of reflection to celebrate virtue. The poem
begins:

SVMME SACER, TE SVMMA SALVS TVEATVR AMICIS,
Virtutis uerae speculo sub carnis amictV
Mundo fulgentem, qui magnus culmine moruM . . .

['GREAT BISHOP, MAY HEAVENLY SALVATION PROTECT
YOU FOR YOUR FRIENDS, / shining on the world with a mirror of
true virtue from beneath the cloak / of the flesh, you who are a great man
through the loftiness of your merits . . .'[19]]

Later, the refrain recurs:

SVMME SACER, TE SVMMA SALVS TVEATVR AMICIS!
Angelicam qui fers faciem de luce supernA,
Lacteolus uultu, pollens ex ordine presuL . . .

---

[18] *Chronicon*, ed. Macray, chap. 1, 38.
[19] Text and translation from Lapidge, *The Lives of St Oswald and St Ecgwine*, 166,
167 (poem lines 1–3).

['GREAT BISHOP: MAY HEAVENLY SALVATION PROTECT YOU
FOR YOUR FRIENDS! / You who offer an angelic face reflecting heavenly
light, / milk-white in visage, you are a bishop mighty in station . . .'[20]]

The poem depicts Dunstan's virtue in terms of the reflection of heavenly grace.
Again, it seems that Abbo has chosen a careful combination of form, subject, and
content: the panegyric imagery of reflection seems particularly appropriate in an
acrostic poem which is based on mirrored letters. As with the poem to Ramsey,
there seems to be a sense of the text participating in the process of reflection
which it describes.

The imagery of starlight also occurs in another panegyric context in Abbo's
work. A poem to Emperor Otto presents his glory through celestial metaphors.

> Otto ualens caesar, nostro tu cede coturno!
> Tot felix atauis, quot cẹlo sydera lucent.
> Te dominum sibi saxo tulit, te roma notauit,
> Orbis & ipse cupit solo contentus alumno.
> Virtutum titulis & uir cognosceris actu
> Ac domitor patrię, [p]acis sectator in aula,
> Lumen ubique micans, solus lucendo uelud sol,
> Ergo dei solito reddentur sancta benigne
> Nec deerit uirtus, omnis qua gratia culmen
> Scandit & occultis secedit nenia causis.

> ['Powerful Emperor Otto, yield to our plaintive song! (You are) fortunate
> in as many ancestors as stars shine in the sky. The Saxon took you as his
> lord; Rome glorified you, and the very world, content with its only child,
> desires you. In the titles of your honours, as well as in deed, you are recog-
> nized as a man, a ruler of your nation, a promoter of peace in the courts, a
> beacon shining everywhere, alone in your brilliance like the sun. Therefore,
> let God's sanctities kindly be restored as a matter of course. Your power, by
> which all grace mounts to the heavens and sorrow departs through hidden
> causes, will not fail.'][21]

While Abbo depicts Dunstan's Christian virtue as a more humble reflected
light, Otto is compared to the sun itself, shining powerful and alone. Though
Abbo seems to enjoy using astronomical metaphors in his panegyric—a motif
which links his roles and expertise as poet and scientist—the use of celestial
and star imagery is, of course, far more widespread. The poem to Otto recalls
the Carolingian tradition of 'star mantles' which display the constellations as a

---

[20] Text and translation from Lapidge, *The Lives of St Oswald and St Ecgwine*, 166,
167 (poem lines 18–20).

[21] Text and translation from Scott Gwara, "Three Acrostic Poems by Abbo of
Fleury," *Journal of Medieval Latin* 2 (1992): 203–36, at 228–29 (poem lines 1–10).

representation of royal power and authority.[22] Abbo's poem to Ramsey fits within these panegyric conventions of astronomical imagery and motifs of reflection. More broadly, in classical, late antique, and medieval literature, we find the familiar association between panegyric and reflection, and the general concept of art as the mirror of reality. In *European Literature and the Latin Middle Ages* Ernst Robert Curtius catalogs many of the biblical, classical, and patristic precedents for medieval uses of the mirror metaphor, including Plato and Cicero, as well as Cassiodorus and Notker Balbulus.[23] This association is most obvious in relation to specific genres such as the medieval 'Mirrors for Princes' and other literary *specula*, and panegyric forms. Abbo's poem to Ramsey celebrates the abbey as the realisation of an ideal and an exemplum—a mirror—for the monastic life.

Abbo's poem to Ramsey, therefore, fits within a series of medieval panegyric conventions involving the imagery of reflection, mirrors, and light. Conventionally for a poem addressed to an English fenland monastery, Abbo celebrates Ramsey as an island *locus amoenus* in the marshes, yet we are not presented with the fertile, pastoral place typical of later Chronicle texts. Instead, for Abbo, the *locus amoenus* of Ramsey is one of learning and knowledge, represented through the constellations shining in the skies above. The poem displays the astronomical imagery so characteristic of Abbo's poetry (as well as his scientific work) and can be read in the context of the developing interest in astronomy in late Anglo-Saxon England and the exchange of astronomy-related manuscripts between England and the continent in the late tenth century. Abbo's poem also aligns itself with broader early medieval panegyric traditions which use stars as symbols of power and glory. The poem to Ramsey suggests a dual process of reflection, with the waters around Ramsey mirroring the constellations and the classical learning they represent, and the heavens themselves mirroring aspects of life in the Benedictine monastery. As in his more conspicuously artful acrostic poems, Abbo's poem to Ramsey displays a complex and thorough connection of form and content. Word-play and erudite puns set up aural parallels and echoes through the text, just as the poem's couplets describe the visual echoes of mirrored light and reflection between water and sky. With the imagery of reflection and mirroring at its very center, the poem also draws attention to its own status as panegyric and its place within the literary tradition of the mirror or exemplum. This poem is as much as celebration of Abbo's own literary skill, and a reflection upon panegyric form, as it is an address to Ramsey Abbey. The poem does seem to invite rather a self-regarding reader: one who can hold up this difficult poem as a kind of glass to reflect his own classical, astronomical, and literary learning. A fitting gift indeed for Abbo's circle of pupils at Ramsey Abbey.

---

[22] Stephen C. McCluskey, *Astronomies and Cultures in Early Medieval Europe* (Cambridge, 1998), 141–43.

[23] Ernst Robert Curtius, *European Literature and the Latin Middle Ages*, trans. Willard R. Trask (London, 1953), 336.

Was Cathedral Reform at Christ Church Canterbury in the Early Ninth Century of Continental Inspiration?

Nicholas Brooks

In the Latin West it was common throughout the Middle Ages for reforming bishops to seek to regulate the life of their cathedral clergy by introducing elements of monastic discipline and of communal living. Such efforts normally had to be mediated in such a way as to secure the support of the local élites, from whom both the bishops and leading members of the chapter tended to be drawn.[1] Our most detailed information on the composition of cathedral communities in early Anglo-Saxon England concerns Canterbury and Lindisfarne and has been transmitted by Bede, whose priorities were, of course, those of the monk.[2] It is disputed how far the creation of such episcopal sees by missionary monks gave to English cathedrals—and thence to the clergy of early medieval England—a distinctively monastic character in which the normal contrast between contemplative monks and pastoral clergy was blurred.[3] The debate complicates any assessment of the

---

[1] M. Zacherl, "Die *vita communis* als Lebensform des Klerus in der Zeit zwischen Augustinus und Karl dem Grossen," *Zeitschrift für katholische Theologie* 92 (1970): 385–424; Josef Semmler, "Le monachisme occidental du VIIIe au Xe siècle: formation et réformation," *Revue Bénédictine* 103 (1993): 68–89, at 86–89; idem, "Mönche und Kanoniker im Frankenreich Pippins III. und Karls des Grossen," in *Untersuchungen zu Kloster und Stift,* Veröffentlichungen des Max-Planck-Instituts für Geschichte 48 (Göttingen, 1980), 78–111; Rudolf Schieffer, *Die Entstehung von Domkapiteln in Deutschland*, Bonner historische Forschungen 43 (Bonn, 1976), 250–60; John C. Dickinson, *The Origins of the Austin Canons* (London, 1950), 7–25.

[2] Bede, *HE*, ed. Colgrave and Mynors, 1.23–27 and 1.33 (for Canterbury), 4.4, 4.27, and 5.12 (for Lindisfarne), 68–102, 114–16, 346–48, 430–34; Nicholas Brooks, *Early History of the Church of Canterbury* (Leicester, 1984), 87–91; for Alcuin's usage in relation to York and other sees, see Donald A. Bullough, *Alcuin: Achievement and Reputation* (Leiden, 2004), 165–76.

[3] Among those minimizing the distinction are Sarah Foot, "Anglo-Saxon Minsters: A Review of Terminology," in *Pastoral Care before the Parish*, ed. John Blair and Richard

Hans Sauer and Joanna Story, eds., *Anglo-Saxon England and the Continent*. With the assistance of Gaby Waxenberger. Essays in Anglo-Saxon Studies, vol. 3. MRTS 394. Tempe: ACMRS, 2011.   [ISBN 978-0-86698-442-3]

extent to which Anglo-Saxon ecclesiastical reforms were inspired by contemporary reform movements on the Continent. In particular it affects our comprehension of contacts between Canterbury and the major Frankish churches in the early ninth century.[4] This paper seeks to answer a fundamental question. Was the reform of the Canterbury cathedral community by Archbishop Wulfred (805–832) inspired either by the reforms of Bishop Chrodegang of Metz (742/7–766) or by the efforts of Charlemagne, Benedict of Aniane, and Louis the Pious to adopt those reforms in cathedral churches throughout the Frankish world? Or was the Canterbury reform rather a parallel independent effort, drawing inspiration from similar roots, but essentially an insular achievement?

Chrodegang's *Regula Canonicorum* for his community at Metz, which drew heavily but selectively upon the Benedictine Rule and a range of other patristic and monastic authors, seems to have been promulgated in connection with the Frankish synod of Ver (Verneuil) of 755, over which Chrodegang had presided.[5] Chrodegang was happy to draw upon his monastic sources when regulating the observance of the canonical hours in his cathedral and when prescribing arrangements for communal eating in a refectory and sleeping in a dormitory. But he departed from both letter and spirit of the *Rule of St. Benedict* in authorizing the bishop to permit suitable 'canons' (*canonici*) to retain their private property and even to sleep in their own 'lodgings' (*mansiones*) within the *claustra* ('the precinct'):

> We decree that the canonical clergy, who live under the ordinance with the help of God, ought to live within the precinct. They should all sleep in the same dormitory, except for those given special permission by the bishop, as he may think fit, to have lodgings of their own and to sleep separately,

---

Sharpe (Leicester, 1992), 212–25; eadem, *Monastic Life in Anglo-Saxon England* (Cambridge, 2006), 48–72, and John Blair, "Debate: Ecclesiastical Organization and Pastoral Care in Anglo-Saxon England," *Early Medieval Europe* 4 (1995): 193–212; John Blair, *The Church in Anglo-Saxon Society* (Oxford, 2005), 3–4, 68–71, 112–13. Among those emphasizing its importance are Catherine Cubitt, "Pastoral Care and Conciliar Canons: The Provisions of the 747 Council of *Clofesho*," in *Pastoral Care before the Parish*, ed. Blair and Sharpe, 193–211; eadem, "The Clergy in Early Anglo-Saxon England," *Historical Research* 78 (2005): 273–87, and Eric Cambridge and David Rollason, "Debate: The Pastoral Organization of the Anglo-Saxon Church: A Review of the 'Minster Hypothesis'," *Early Medieval Europe* 4 (1995): 87–104. There is a convenient overall survey in Julia Barrow, "Cathedral Clergy," in *BEASE* (Oxford, 1999), 84–87.

[4] For a survey of these relations see Joanna Story, *Carolingian Connections: Anglo-Saxon England and Carolingian Francia, c. 750–870* (Aldershot, 2003), 199–211.

[5] M. A. Claussen, *The Reform of the Frankish Church: Chrodegang of Metz and the "Regula Canonicorum" in the Eighth Century* (Cambridge, 2004), esp. 114–206; Julia Barrow, "Review Article: Chrodegang, his Rule and its Successors," *Early Medieval Europe* 14 (2006): 201–12.

though within the enclosure and each in his individual bed. . . . And in the lodgings within the precinct, neither cleric nor layman should presume to drink, to eat, or to sleep, save for the clerics who are members of the congregation, or those clerics who at the bishop's command look after the older ones within that precinct.[6]

It is uncertain whether or how widely Chrodegang's *Rule* was disseminated beyond his diocese after the Council of Ver. Certainly Charlemagne's great reforming "General Admonition" of 789 (now known to have been extensively influenced by Alcuin) insisted that those who entered the canonical life should live in all respects as 'canons' in accordance with their *Rule* and that the bishop was to regulate their 'life'—just as an abbot did that of monks.[7] This fits the statement from the report—perhaps also drafted by Alcuin—of the papal legates, Bishops George of Ostia and Theophylact of Todi, concerning the episcopal councils they held in England in 786. The legates had enjoined the English bishops to ensure that "canons should live canonically and monks and nuns conduct themselves according to rule (*regulariter*), so that there should be a differentiation between a canon, a monk, and a layman."[8] The implication must be that the distinction was already widespread among the Franks.

A renewed effort to establish the reform of Frankish cathedral clergy as 'canons' was begun in the last years of Charlemagne's reign and continued early in that of his son. In the summer of 813 successive provincial reforming synods were held at Arles, Rheims, Mainz, and then at Tours. They put emphasis on the

---

[6] Chrodegang, *Regula canonicorum*, chap. 3, ed. J.-B. Pelt, *Études sur la cathédrale de Metz: la liturgie, 1: la liturgie, Vᵉ-XIIIᵉ siècles* (Metz, 1937), 11: "Ita instituimus ut in illo claustro ille clericus canonicus qui sub ordine, Deo adiuvante, vivere debet, omnes in uno dormiant dormitorio, preter illos quibus episcopus licentiam dederit, secundum quod ei rationabiliter visum fuerit; ut in ipso claustro per dispositas mansiones dormiant separatim; et per singula lecta singuli dormiant. . . . Et per illas mansiones ipsi clerici canonici nullum clericum eorum habeant sine precepto episcopi sui. Et si permiserit ut habeant, sic sit conversatio illorum cum humilitate et Dei timore, qualiter nec Deo nec episcopo displiciant, nec illis qui sub manu sua ipsam congregationem regunt. . . . Et in ipsas mansiones infra ipsa claustra nec clericus nec laicus bibere nec manducare non praesumet nisi ipsi clerici qui in ipsa congregatione sunt, aut illi clerici qui ibidem in ipsa claustra per iussionem episcopi sui seniores suos deserviunt . . . ." My translation is adapted from that of Jerome Bertram, *The Chrodegang Rules* (Aldershot, 2005), 56–57.

[7] *Admonitio Generalis* 789, chap. 73; ed. Alfred Boretius, MGH, Capitularia Regum Francorum 1 (Hannover, 1883), no. 22 (60). For Alcuin's influence on the *Admonitio*, see Bullough, *Alcuin*, 379–86.

[8] The Legates' Synod of 786, chap. 4, in *Alcuini Epistolae*, ed. Ernst Dümmler, MGH, Epistolae 4 (Berlin, 1895), no. 3 (22). Alcuin's assistance to the author, George of Ostia, is argued most fully by Catherine Cubitt, *Anglo-Saxon Church Councils c. 650–c. 850* (Leicester, 1995), 153–90.

'canonical' life: on eating in a refectory and sleeping in a dormitory, in order that cathedral clergy might be better able to celebrate the canonical hours together and to pursue the clerical way of life.[9] Then, some three and a half years later, Louis the Pious provided a normative text, the *Institutio Canonicorum*, which was intended to be adopted in cathedrals throughout his empire and to implement the reforms agreed by the 813 councils. This text comprised a preface with a much-extended selection of patristic, conciliar, and papal pronouncements on the requirements of the clerical life, followed by a revised version of Chrodegang's *Rule*. Thus, for example, the *Institutio* clarifies that the bishop should provide a *mansio* within the precinct, where those members of the cathedral community who did not have their own lodgings, or who through age, infirmity, or imbecility could no longer look after themselves, would live and be cared for together.[10] Finally—for the sake of completeness—mention should be made of the so-called *Enlarged Regula Canonicorum*, seemingly produced in the mid-ninth century in the Loire valley and reaching England (perhaps from Fleury?) with the tenth-century monastic reform movement. It was to be translated into Old English at Winchester and incorporated material both from the original *Rule of Chrodegang* and from the *Institutio canonicorum* with a view to providing fuller guidance for bishop and clergy. The Latin *Enlarged Rule* and the Old English translation were both, of course, composed too late to have influenced the reforms carried out at Canterbury by Archbishop Wulfred in the second decade of the ninth century.[11]

Our knowledge of Wulfred's reforms does not derive from comparable rules or ordinances for English cathedrals, disseminated at synods of the English church. It comes rather from charters, which begin to be preserved in numbers

---

[9] Council of Arles (10/11 May), chap. 6; Council of Rheims (mid-May), chap. 8; Council of Mainz (May–June, 813), chap. 9: "In omnibus igitur . . . decreuimus ut canonici clerici canonice vivant, . . . ut simul manducent et dormient . . . ."; Council of Tours (summer 813), chap. 23: "Canonici clerici civitatum, qui in episcopiis conversantur, consideravimus ut in claustro habitantes simul omnes in uno dormitorio dormiant, simulque in uno reficiantur refectorio, quo facilius possint ad horas canonicas celebrandas occurrere ac de vita et conversatione sua admoneri et doceri"; *Concilia Aevi Karolini* 1/1, ed. Albert Werminghoff, MGH, Concilia 2.1 (Hannover and Leipzig, 1906), 251, 254, 262–63, 289. For the program of these councils, see Rosamond McKitterick, *The Frankish Church and the Carolingian Reforms, 789–895* (London, 1977), 12–15, 21–24, 50–56, 83–89.

[10] Council of Aachen, 816, *Institutio canonicorum*, chap. 142, ed. Werminghoff, in *Concilia*, 417: "Quamvis canonicis proprias licitum sit habere mansiones, debet tamen a praelato mansio infirmorum et senum intra claustra canonicorum fieri, ut qui suam forte non habent in eadem suam possint aptissime tolerare inbecillitatem, quatenus ibidem et subsidiis ecclesiasticis, quibus indigent, et fratrum adminiculis misericorditer sustententur."

[11] *The Old English Version of the Enlarged Rule of Chrodegang, with Latin Text and English Translation*, ed. Brigitte Langefeld, Texte und Untersuchungen zur Englischen Philologie 26 (Munich, 2003).

from Canterbury from the last years of the eighth century.[12] The crucial document is a charter or privilege of Archbishop Wulfred purporting to record his
revival and rebuilding of his cathedral minster (Appendix, no. 1).[13] The witnesses
are the archbishop, a priest abbot (Wernoth, probably of St. Augustine's), eight
priests, two deacons, and a *prepositus* or 'provost'. No medieval manuscript of
this charter survives. Its text is known only from William Somner's *Antiquities
of Canterbury*, first published in 1640. Somner, who was librarian and archivist
at the cathedral from 1635 until his death in 1669, was a fine scholar, renowned
as the author of the first Dictionary of Old English.[14] Unfortunately the charter
has a problematic date, since its incarnation year, 813, is not consistent with the
given indiction (iii) or the episcopal year (iiii). The figures given in **bold** type in
the table below are those in Somner's text of the charter, with the figures that
should correspond to each alongside.

Incarnation year	Indiction	Wulfred's episcopal year
dcccxiii	indictione vi	viii episcopatus < *or* viiii>
dcccx	**indictione iii**	v episcopatus <*or* vi>
dcccviii	indictione i	**iiii episcopatus**

Fortunately we can deduce from this table that 813 is likely to have been the correct date, since common copying errors will explain how the recorded dates could
have arisen from the first line (iii for vi, iiii for viii), but not from the subsequent
ones. Moreover, the 813 date is confirmed by the links in formulation between
this privilege and documents of nearby years. Thus, its rare verbal invocation
"In nomine sancti saluatoris Dei et Domini nostri Iesu Christi" recurs in three
Canterbury charters of the following year, one of which survives in authentic and
contemporary form.[15] Its phrase "pro intimo cordis affectu" is also matched by
their "pro intimo caritatis affectu." Wulfred's unusual title *archipontifex* had been

---

[12] A new scholarly edition of the entire corpus of *Anglo-Saxon Charters* is in progress
under the auspices of the British Academy. *The Charters of Christ Church Canterbury*, ed.
Nicholas Brooks and Susan Kelly, is forthcoming (2011). Charters are cited here both
from that edition and from BCS. Reference is also made to their number in S, which is
available in an electronic and updated form on the Anglo-Saxon Charters website (or
"Kemble") at http://www.trin.cam.ac.uk/chartwww.

[13] Brooks and Kelly, *Charters of Canterbury*, no. 47 (BCS 342; S 1265).

[14] William Somner, *Dictionarium Saxonico-Latino-Anglicum* (London, 1659). A
brief biography of Somner by White Kennett was included in the second edition of William Somner, *A Treatise of Gavelkind* (London, 1726), and there is a modern assessment
by William Urry in the facsimile reprint of the 1703 edition of Somner's *Antiquities of
Canterbury* (Wakefield, 1977), v–xxiv.

[15] Brooks and Kelly, *Charters of Canterbury*, nos. 48 (BCS 348; S 177), 49 (BCS 346;
S 175), and 50 (BCS 344, S 176).

used twice for him in an original charter two years previously.[16] The right of individual members of the community to bestow their properties ("liberam habeant facultatem in eodem monasterii donandi") may be compared with a clause in a Worcestershire charter to the abbot of Kempsey of 799 for 802.[17] The mandatory clause ("precipio omnibus successoribus meis . . . hanc donationem . . . inconcussam et inuiolatum") is a rare feature of Anglo-Saxon diplomatic, but finds a close parallel in an authentic charter to Archbishop Wulfred of the year 831.[18] Such examples do much to establish that Wulfred's charter was printed from an authentic privilege of the year 813. What then does it say?

First, Wulfred declares: "I have revived (*refici*) with the helping love of God, by renewing and restoring (*renouando et restaurando*) for the love and honor of God, and by rebuilding (*reædificando*), the holy monastery of the church of Canterbury, with the help of the priests and deacons and all the clergy of the same church, serving the Lord God together." Wulfred's revival and reconstruction of the *monasterium* (or minster) of the church of Canterbury may have been primarily directed towards rebuilding the monastic buildings and the communal life, though the wording certainly cannot be taken to exclude a rebuilding of the cathedral church as well.[19] Second, Wulfred then goes on to grant that the *familia Christi* are to have and to enjoy "with a perpetual right of inheritance" the houses which they have built by their own labor. They may give or bequeath them in their lifetimes, or at death, to whoever they might wish, and all are individually to have the free power of giving them within the same monastery, but not to anyone outside the community (*congregatio*). Third, these benefits have been bestowed on certain conditions. The brethren were to be "more humble to God and more grateful for all his benefits," to "attend with diligent regularity in the church at the canonical hours and to pray for the remission of sins, their own and others'." They were also to use the refectory (*domus refectionis*) and the dormitory and to observe all this "according to the rule of the life of monastic discipline" (*iuxta regulam monasterialis disciplinae uitae*). Any who threatened or damaged this "constitution," in particular by holding gatherings (*conuiuia*) "for feeding,

---

[16] Brooks and Kelly, *Charters of Canterbury*, no. 44 (BCS 335; S 168) of 811.
[17] BCS 295 (S 154): "post se suis heredibus cuicumque uoluerit liberam donandi habeat facultatem."
[18] Brooks and Kelly, *Charters of Canterbury*, no. 60 (BCS 400; S 188): "Omnibusque successoribus meis . . . hanc donationem libertatemque . . . fixam incontaminatamque obseruare precipio."
[19] For the substantial westward extension and enlargement of the pre-Conquest cathedral to give it a basilical form ("the second Anglo-Saxon cathedral"), possibly to be associated with Wulfred's reform, see Kevin Blockley, Margaret Sparks, and Tim Tatton-Brown, *Canterbury Cathedral Nave: Archaeology, History and Architecture*, Archaeology of Canterbury, n.s. 1 (Canterbury, 1997), 5–8.

drinking, or even sleeping in their own cells" would be liable to the power of the archbishop, and their houses would be at his disposition.

Since the work of Margaret Deanesly in 1925 this attempted reform and revival of the Canterbury cathedral community has been associated with the contemporary reforms of Frankish cathedral chapters along the lines promulgated in Chrodegang's *Regula canonicorum.*[20] Certainly it is at least a remarkable coincidence that Archbishop Wulfred's charter can be assigned to 813, the very year that a series of Frankish provincial synods decreed that sleeping and eating in common and observance of the Office at the canonical hours were obligatory for cathedral clergy. For these are the very issues that Wulfred's privilege of that same year emphasised. Moreover, not only had both Chrodegang's *Rule* and the *Institutio Canonicorum* of 816–817 drawn heavily upon the Benedictine Rule in their attempt to improve the quality of the communal life and worship of cathedral clergy, but the *regula monasterialis uitae*, to which Wulfred's charter refers, is indeed the, or a, title by which the *Rule of St. Benedict* refers to itself.[21]

But in 1996 Brigitte Langefeld in an important article, the conclusions of which she has largely repeated in her edition of the *Enlarged Regula canonicorum* in 2003, challenged this view.[22] She pointed out that despite the close parallels in the objectives of Wulfred's reforms and those of Chrodegang and later of Benedict of Aniane and Louis the Pious in the *Institutio canonicorum*, the Carolingian reformers had consistently insisted that cathedral clergy were 'canons' (*canonici*) living a communal life according to a rule, the purpose of which was to make the canonical life distinct from the regular cloistered life of monks. Monks in the Carolingian territories were to follow the Benedictine Rule, but canons the canonical rule. The language of Wulfred's reform privilege of 813 and of his later Canterbury charters is certainly different. He never refers to 'canons' or to any 'canonical rule' at Canterbury, but instead repeatedly associates his cathedral clergy with the 'rule of monastic life' or with 'monastic discipline.'[23] Indeed the Canterbury documents do not quote either from Chrodegang's *regula canonicorum* or from the 816–817

---

[20] Margaret Deanesly, "The *familia* at Christ Church, Canterbury, 597–832," in *Essays in Medieval History Presented to Thomas Frederick Tout*, ed. A. G. Little and F. M. Powicke (Manchester, 1925), 1–13; Brooks, *Church of Canterbury*, 155–64; Cubitt, *Anglo-Saxon Church Councils*, 201.

[21] For Chrodegang's use of the *Rule*, see F. Grimme, "Die Kanonikerregel des hl. Chrodegang und ihre Quellen," *Jahrbuch der Gesellschaft für lothringische Geschichte und Altertumskunde* 27/28 (1917): 1–44, and Claussen, *Reform of the Frankish Church*, 114–65.

[22] Brigitte Langefeld, "*Regula canonicorum* or *regula monasterialis uitae*? The Rule of Chrodegang and Archbishop Wulfred's Reforms at Canterbury," *ASE* 25 (1996): 21–36; *OE Enlarged Rule of Chrodegang*, ed. Langefeld, 16–17.

[23] "iuxta regulam monasterialis disciplinae uitae" (Brooks and Kelly, *Charters of Canterbury*, no. 42; BCS 342; S 1188); "monasterialisque uitae regulam" (Brooks and Kelly, no. 59; BCS 384; S 1436); "regula monasterialis uitae" (Brooks and Kelly, no 69; BCS 421; S 1438).

Institutio. Moreover, the evidence of manuscript transmission suggests that when Chrodegang's *Rule* did become known in England, it was the version known as the *Enlarged Rule of Chrodegang*, which was composed too late to have influenced Wulfred. That text seems to have reached England only with the monastic revival of the tenth century, when several leading English monk-bishops may have needed norms for the clergy in major churches in their dioceses.[24]

Thus far we may certainly accept Langefeld's revision. The terminology of the Wulfredian reform is distinct from that of the Frankish church in the late eighth and early ninth century. It belongs to an older European tradition less concerned to distinguish the monastic way of life sharply from the clerical. If Wulfred had known and been inspired by the contemporary Frankish reforms (as the coincidence of enactments in the year 813 might suggest), he must have used them selectively. He avoided their contrast of 'canonical' and 'monastic' regimes. In Wulfred's Canterbury a 'monastic' (or minster) life remained the ideal for his cathedral clergy. The idea of a 'secular clergy', separate from monks, was therefore not appropriate. Wulfred's emphasis on the use of the dormitory and refectory suggests that he was indeed concerned to ensure both the celibacy and the communal spirit of his cathedral community. But, *pace* Langefeld, there is no sign that Wulfred planned the adoption of a fully monastic regime with a significant proportion of the Christ Church community comprising a corps of monks at its heart.[25] On the contrary, the *familia Christi* in Wulfred's 813 privilege is defined as "the priests, deacons, and all the clergy serving God together," without reference to any monks at all. That suggests instead that the archbishop, like so many cathedral reformers of the previous three or four centuries (including indeed Chrodegang and Benedict of Aniane), was concerned to strengthen the communal life of his clergy by selective use of guidance from the *Rule of St. Benedict*.

Where both Chrodegang and Wulfred departed decisively from the Benedictine prescription was, of course, over private property. Chrodegang had openly admitted in chapter 31 of his *Rule* that his canons could not be persuaded to renounce their private property and to share everything in common, after the example of the Apostles. They should rather be permitted to enjoy the income (*stipendium*) from their properties, but not to bequeath them after death to any earthly heirs or kin, but only to the particular church or within its 'congregation' of canons. Those joining the community were expected to donate their lands to God and to the clergy there, but could receive them back from the bishop as *precaria*—conditional leases—which would revert fully to the cathedral at their

---

[24] The earliest manuscript of English provenance would seem to be Brussels, Bibl. Royale, 8558–63, fols. 1r–38v of saec. x¹. See M. Drout, *How Tradition Works*, MRTS 306 (Tempe, 2006), 179–217.

[25] Langefeld, "*Regula canonicorum?*," 30–36.

death.[26] Although this explicit Chrodegangian provision was to be dropped in 816–817, the *Institutio* still envisaged that some canons would have their own property (*facultates*) and therefore be less dependent on the communal shares of food, clothing, and offerings. It also still allowed such canons to have their own lodgings within the precinct.[27] There was therefore little real difference here in the canonical regime that Louis the Pious and Benedict of Aniane prescribed for general adoption from Chrodegang's provisions at Metz. Aristocrats could enter cathedral congregations, enjoy the income of their private landed possessions, and have their own quarters or *mansiones* within the precinct. The cathedral church would ultimately benefit when such property reverted to it. Not surprisingly, such arrangements ensured aristocratic domination of cathedral chapters throughout the Carolingian age and long thereafter.

Two remarkable documents from the end of Wulfred's pontificate and another from just after it show how his reform had worked in practice in relation to his clergy's private property. They show how similar were the attitudes of English cathedral clergy to those of the canons of Continental chapters. The first is a grant made to Christ Church by Archbishop Wulfred towards the end of his life.[28] It survives in contemporary form, with the text on the face written by one known Christ Church scribe; but with a different contemporary Christ Church scribe adding the witnesses on the dorse on a later occasion. It should be observed that there would have been room to write the witnesses on the face and that the first two witnesses are said to be Archbishop Wulfred (who died on 24 March 832) and his successor but one, Archbishop Ceolnoth (elected 27 July 833). Evidently some form of polite fiction is involved here. It may best be explained by supposing that the charter had been drawn up on Wulfred's deathbed, but completed only after the difficulties that had attended the succession to the see in 832–833 had been resolved by the eventual consecration of Ceolnoth (27 August 833).[29] Wulfred grants "a certain part of his hereditary lands" (i.e. of his personal property), namely four 'sulungs' (*aratrorum*) at *Sceldesforda*, to the community after

---

[26] *Regula canonicorum*, chap. 31, ed. Pelt, *Études*, 24–25: ". . . Et precaria, si ita ei placuerit, exinde ab episcopo accipiat in ea ratione, ut, dum advivet, ipsas res usufructuario ordine habent: et post obitum eius cum omni integritate omnique superposito ad ecclesiam cui data fuerint vel ipsius congregationis ipsas res absque ullius consignatione vel expectata traditione revertantur."

[27] *Institutio canonicorum*, chap. 120, ed. Werminghoff, in *Concilia*, 408: ". . . studeat necesse est clerici in accipiendis ecclesiasticis sumptibus suum vitare periculum. Proinde qui et suas et ecclesiae habent facultates et utilitatem ecclesiae, aut interius aut exterius conferunt, accipiant in congregatione cibum et potum et partes elemosinarum et his contenti sunt . . ."; for chap. 142 (ed. Werminghoff, in *Concilia*, 417), see above n. 10.

[28] Brooks and Kelly, *Charters of Canterbury*, no. 62 (BCS 380; S 1268), printed below in Appendix, no. 2.

[29] For the archiepiscopal dates and the disputed succession of Swithred and Feologeld in 832, see Brooks, *Church of Canterbury*, 142–43.

his death "for his soul and in the hope of a heavenly reward." The donation was
never to be alienated or sold by the community, but was to remain forever in that
congregatio's possession. After the bounds of the property have been detailed and
"in return for the munificence of this land and all the benefits he had obtained
for them since their *communis congregatio* had been formed," Wulfred will seek
from them (*flagitabo*) that "they should commemorate him . . . and provide as
much help for his soul through almsgiving, psalm-singing, and the celebration of
masses as they can perform." He then reminds them that the grant is conditional
upon the maintenance of all the acts and statements that "we" have previously
agreed (*ante condicta*) unchanged and upon each one of them striving to increase
what we have agreed for the good, with God's help. The reference here is seemingly not only to the charter of 813, but also to oral agreements that had been
reached to reinforce it at various moments in Wulfred's pontificate.

The deathbed charter then changes tack by recording two other bequests
that tell us much about how Wulfred's clergy had held land. He bequeaths to the
community on his death 85 *segetes* (perhaps acres, or rather 'rods') of land that
had been given to him (with the landbook) by Cyneheard, the deacon, who had
received them from the West Saxon kings, Egberht and Æthelwulf, as a personal
inheritance (*in propriam hereditatem*). This bequest is made "for both our souls"
(Cyneheard's and Wulfred's?) and on condition that every morning and evening,
when the brethren enter the church of St. Peter for the accustomed chant, they
should say the Lord's Prayer for his soul (Wulfred's?)—a provision that implies
liturgical collaboration between St. Augustine's (= St. Peter's) and Christ Church
in the city of Canterbury.

Third and finally, Wulfred bequeathed to the community a *curtis* or *uilla*
within the 'monastery' or minster which had been owned by Dodda 'the monk'
(*monachus*). Presumably this 'court' (*curtis*) was one of the *domus*, the building of
which within the precinct had been sanctioned in the 813 agreement. It is comparable to the *mansiones* within the *claustra* that Chrodegang's canons had been
allowed but which could not be alienated from the *congregatio*. Wulfred intended
Dodda's 'court' for whatever use the *familia* might wish. But he suggests that it be
either used to feed the citizens "when there was opportunity and need" or, when
a priest or deacon became infirm, he might repose therein with fitting honor. The
inspiration for such provisions are of course to be sought in the requirement of the
Rule of St. Benedict that infirm brethren should be assigned a special cell.[30] But
we surely come closer to Wulfred's arrangements in Chrodegang's provision that
cathedral clergy too infirm to carry out their pastoral duties should be assigned
by the archdeacon or *primicerius* special lodgings within the precinct where they
could recover and, more particularly, in the *Institutio Canonicorum*'s injunction to

---

[30] *Regula Sancti Benedicti*, chap. 36, ed. J. McCann (London, 1952), 90: "Quibus
fratribus infirmis sit cella super se deputata, et servitor timens Deum et diligens ac soli-
citus."

the bishop to institute a *mansio* for the elderly sick and infirm within the canons' precinct, where they could be tended by the brethren.[31] Dodda is one of only two known 'monks' at Christ Church in the ninth century, and profession as a monk seems to have been a rare act of personal asceticism by very senior members of the community.[32] Langefeld's contrary suggestion that a body of monks may have escaped detection because they were restricted from serving as witnesses[33] could scarcely apply to internal transactions regulating the community's constitution and the living arrangements within the precinct.

Wulfred's deathbed charter thus shows us transfers of private property not only between senior members of the community, but also between the archbishop and the community as a whole. Retention of estates within the community was in accord with the reforms that Wulfred had agreed with them in 813 and closely parallels the contemporary canonical regimes of Frankish cathedrals. The next document in the Appendix (no. 3) is a tiny but fascinating fragment from an Old English bequest or will of Archbishop Wulfred.[34] The passage was quoted by Somner in the course of a discussion of the meaning of bookland. He described the document as "the gift of certain houses to his (i.e. Wulfred's) successors in the see of Canterbury." It may, however, be that the *aefreweardum* of this fragment were Wulfred's chosen heirs within Christ Church, rather his successors as archbishop. Since Somner understands *min wic* in the fragment as a *mansio*, we should probably conclude that the document had granted a number of *wicu* ('dwellings') within the precinct to particular Canterbury clerks of his choice. Certainly the fragment's message—namely that these properties were not Christ Church property, but Wulfred's bookland and therefore his to dispose as he wished—is clear. It reads like a riposte to Christ Church's hopes that the community would immediately receive the bulk of the archbishop's great wealth.

What actually happened to the archbishop's wealth seems to be revealed in a fascinating charter (Appendix, no. 4), which is unfortunately known only from an unsatisfactory Latin version found in the manuscripts of the main Christ Church

---

[31] Chrodegang, *Reg. can.*, chap. 28, ed. Pelt, *Études*, 22: "Si aliquis ex clero infirmatur qui ad hunc ordinem se peculiaris iunxerint et non habuerint unde in infirmitate necessitatibus suis possint implere, post episcopum habeat de illis maximam curam archidiaconus et primicerius et caveant ne neglegantur infirmi; . . . et . . . archidiaconus vel primicerius . . . prevideat ut . . . quibus infirmis sint mansiones deputatae super se rationabiliter dispositae, condignae et aptae, ubi esse possint dum de infirmitatibus suis convalescant." Council of Aachen, 816, *Inst. can.*, chap. 142, see above, n. 10.

[32] The other monk at Canterbury is Sefreð *monachus*. He appears as the owner of landed property in the community's land at Kingston or Barham (Kent) in a charter of 873 and as a witness in a list perhaps of 874 (Brooks and Kelly, *Charters of Canterbury*, nos. 93, 82; BCS 536, 538; S 344, 319). He had earlier witnessed successively as subdeacon, deacon, and priest. See Brooks, *Church of Canterbury*, 161 and n. 35.

[33] Langefeld, *"Regula canonicorum?,"* 34

[34] Brooks and Kelly, *Charters of Canterbury*, no. 63 (S 1622).

cartulary.[35] That source regularly but arbitrarily altered the formulation of Latin documents, recorded Old English documents as Latin ones (often giving them erroneous dates in the process), and frequently rewrote grants to lay beneficiaries as if they had been donations to the 'monks.' Here it records bequests purportedly made by the Christ Church priest Werhard, a kinsman of Archbishop Wulfred, at some date between 833 and ca. 845—perhaps near the start of that period. Werhard, here styled 'priest' (*presbiter*), had risen rapidly in the community: he had been a deacon in 824, but rose to be 'priest-abbot' near the start of Ceolnoth's pontificate.[36] As testator, Werhard says that he 'restores' (*reddo*) to Christ Church after his death the estates within Kent and beyond, which he had held by gift of Archbishop Wulfred and by the consent of the community. In 'restoring' them he claimed to be obeying the command of the archbishop, who had accumulated them with great effort in the hope of eternal salvation. The listed lands comprised a huge lordship. Many were to be the principal manors of the church of Canterbury for the rest of the Middle Ages. There were said to be 104 hides at Harrow (Middlesex), 100 at Otford (Kent), 32 at Graveney, 44 at Bishopsbourne, 10 at Easole, and 36 at Barham, plus a number of smaller properties, including one by the north wall of Canterbury. Werhard then repeats that he was following instructions given by Wulfred in a *scriptum* drawn up before the archbishop fell sick. There Wulfred had made provision for daily alms from these manors to feed fixed numbers of paupers and for annual payments for clothing. The archbishop had also ordered a daily mass for his soul and for other benefactors and had arranged that 1200 paupers should be fed on bread with cheese or lard, and be given a penny annually on his anniversary. Finally, Werhard goes on to dispose of a series of substantial estates, mostly in Middlesex, from his own patrimony and acquisitions.

It is impossible to know how far to trust this document. We may doubt the hidage assessments, particularly for Kentish estates, where assessment in 'sulungs' (*aratra*) was normal by that time. And the document's tendency to make every bequest into a gift to the monks of Christ Church certainly arouses suspicion. Five of the manors (Otford, Bishopsbourne, Northwood in Whitstaple, all in Kent, and Harrow and Hayes in Middlesex) did indeed become Canterbury estates, but as major archiepiscopal estates, not 'manors of the monks.' It is likely that Wulfred's and Werhard's bequests had more varied beneficiaries than is here admitted. But the particular estates mentioned and the provisions for almsgiving and for commemoration ring true. It is certainly likely that the priest Werhard had come to enjoy a huge landed inheritance, probably in part in his own right, but chiefly through the nepotism of Archbishop Wulfred. This wealth would surely have contributed to his rise to become priest-abbot of the Christ Church community. If Werhard had hoped that it might help propel him to the archi-

---

[35] Brooks and Kelly, *Charters of Canterbury*, no. 64 (BCS 402, S 1414)
[36] For his career, see Brooks, *Church of Canterbury*, 141–42.

episcopal throne, he was to be disappointed, for it was Archbishop Ceolnoth (833–870) who eventually succeeded Wulfred and who long outlived Werhard.

Werhard's huge personal landed wealth and the testamentary arrangements within the *congregatio* that we can glimpse in all these four documents are of course utterly against the spirit and letter of the Benedictine Rule's prohibition of private property for monks. They fit very well, however, with the arrangements that Chrodegang and Benedict of Aniane established for cathedral chapters in the Frankish world. Though Wulfred did not quote the Frankish texts, it is surely unlikely that he was ignorant of the main drift of the Carolingian reforms. As Joanna Story has reminded us, links between the English and Frankish churches at this time were close.[37] Archbishop Wulfred himself twice traveled to Rome: in 805 to collect the *pallium* and then again in 814 in the midst of his dispute over the control of the Kentish minsters with the Mercian king, Coenwulf. On both journeys he is likely to have become acquainted with several cathedrals of the Frankish realm and therefore with their concerns and their internal arrangements. Moreover, Wulfred's great reforming synod of Chelsea in 816 has a specific link with another of the Frankish provincial synods of 813, that of Chalon-sur-Saône, which is the source for the prohibition of the ministry of Irish priests, on the grounds that their ordinations were irregular since they had no rank or honor of metropolitan.[38] Such links make it very unlikely that it is a coincidence that Wulfred's reform of his cathedral clergy was enacted in 813, the very year that comparable but 'canonical' regimes were being advocated in Frankish synods. One might therefore conclude by suggesting that in the reform of cathedral chapters, as so often in more recent European history, England and the Continent were consciously moving along parallel lines of development, but were using a distinct vocabulary. That was a difference of nomenclature rather than of substance, but one which may have aided the acceptance of the reforms in England. It should not obscure the reality of cross-Channel influence.

---

[37] Story, *Carolingian Connections*, 206–9.

[38] Synod of Chelsea, 816, chap. 5, in *Councils and Ecclesiastical Documents Relating to Great Britain and Ireland*, ed. Arthur W. Haddan and William Stubbs, 3 vols. (Oxford, 1871), 3: 581; Council of Chalon, July 813, chap. 43, ed. Werminghoff, in *Concilia*, 282.

Appendix

[The documents printed here are drawn from the forthcoming *The Charters of Christ Church Canterbury*, ed. Nicholas Brooks and Susan Kelly (Anglo-Saxon Charters, British Academy, London 2011), but with a reduced apparatus. Previous and partial editions are not fully listed here.]

1

Archbishop Wulfred's privilege for the rebuilt Christ Church, Canterbury, establishing a common dormitory, refectory, and worship for the community. A.D. 813 (? for 808 × 813)

A. Lost original
Ed.:   a. Somner, *Antiquities of Canterbury* (1640), 477–78, from A
        b. BCS 342
        c. Brooks and Kelly, *Charters of Canterbury* (forthcoming), no. 47
Listed: S 1265
Edited from Somner, *Antiquities*

+ In nomine sanctæ[a] salvatoris Dei et Domini nostri Iesu Christi. Anno ab incarnatione ejusdem Dei et redemptoris mundi .dcccxiii. indictione .iii[a].[b] præsidente Christi gratia archipontifice Wlfredo metropolitano sedem ecclesiæ Christi quæ sita est in Dorovernia civitate anno .iiii°.[c] episcopatus eiusdem archiepiscopi, divina ac fraterna pietate ductus, amore Deo auxiliante, renovando et restaurando pro honore et amore Dei sanctum monasterium Dorovernensis ecclesiæ reædificando refici,[d] auxiliantibus eiusdem ecclesiæ presbiteris et diaconibus cunctoque clero Domino Deo servientium simul. Ego Wlfredus misericordia Dei archisacerdos pro intimo cordis affectu dabo et concedo familia Christi habere et perfruere domos quas suu[e] proprio labore construxerunt iure perpetuo hereditatis munificentia, illis viventibus seu decedentibus cuicunque relinquere vel donare voluerint unusquisque liberam habeant facultatem in eodem monasterio donandi sed nec alicui foras extra congregationi. Ita etiam in Christi caritate obsecrans præcipio omnibus successoribus meis hanc predictam donationem inconcusse[f] et inuiolatam salua ratione seruandam sine fine semper in euum: Hac tamen conditione, ut Deo humiliores et gratiores omnium beneficiorum Dei semper existant, seduloque frequentatione canonicis horis ecclesiam Christi visitent orantes ac deprecantes pro seipsis propriis piaculis et pro aliorum remissione peccatorum misericordiam Domini implorent. Necnon domum refectionis et dormitorium communiter frequentent iuxta regulam monasterialis disciplinæ vite observant, ut in omnibus honorificetur Deus et vita nostra et bona conversatio nobis nostrisque proficiat in bonum. Si quis illorum per audaciam suæ malæ voluntatis hanc prædictam constitutionem inritam habere et in oblivionem deducere et congregare convivias ad vescendum et bibendum seu etiam dormiendum in propriis cellulis, sciat se quisquis ille sit reatum se esse propriæ domi et in potestate archiepiscopi ad habendum et cuicunque ei placuerit donandum l'g̅ manentem itaque hanc kartulam in suæ nihilominus firmitate. Ego Wlfred gratia Dei archiepiscopus signo sancte crucis Christi confirmans subscripsi.

+ Ego Wernoth presbyter abbas consensi et subscripsi.
+ Ego Wulfheard presbyter consensi et subscripsi.
+ Ego Heamund presbyter consensi et subscripsi.
+ Ego Oswulf presbyter consensi et subscripsi.
+ Ego Ceolstan presbyter consensi et subscripsi.
+ Ego Tudda presbyter consensi et subscripsi.
+ Ego Diornoth presbyter consensi et subscripsi.
+ Ego Guthmund presbyter consensi et subscripsi.
+ Ego Cuthberht presbyter consensi et subscripsi.
+ Ego Coenhere diaconus consensi et subscripsi.
+ Ego Brunheard diaconus consensi et subscripsi.
+ Ego Hehferth prepositus consensi et subscripsi.

a *Error for* sancti b *Indiction incorrect for 813* c *Incorrect for 813* d *For* refeci e*For* suo f *For* inconcussam g *Abbreviation for* vel; *but that is unintelligible, so some scribal error may have occurred.*

2

Archbishop Wulfred grants to Christ Church, Canterbury, after his death, four sulungs (aratra) at Sceldesforda (*i.e. Staple*), *Kent, with thirty acres* (iugera) *of pasture, together with eighty-five* segetes *formerly belonging to Cyneheard the deacon and land in Canterbury formerly belonging to the monk Dodda.* [ca. A.D. 825 × 832]

A. London, BL, Cotton Augustus ii. 72: original, s. ix[1], parchment, 214 × 530 mm
    Endorsements: (1) *by the scribe of the charter*: Sceldes fordæs boec ⁊ ðeara pica on byrg; (2) *in a hand of s. xii*: Wluredus archiepiscopus dedit Scealdeford ecclesie Christi Cantuarie . \conuentus/ (*added in a later hand*); (3) *in another hand of s. xii*: Ⅎluredus archiepiscopus dedit Scealdeuorde \fratribus/ ecclesie Christi et prata .xxx. iugerum que ab ipsis antea habebat . et agellum .lxxxv. segetum quem Ⅎigardus diaconus ei donauit . et curtem Dodde monachi; (4) *in another hand of s. xii*: latine; (5) *in a hand of s. xiii*: anno dccc.xxiiii
Ed.:   a. *Facsimiles of Ancient Charters in the British Museum*, ed. E. A. Bond, 4 vols. (London, 1873–1878), 2: 17 (facsimile and transcript of A)
        b. BCS 380
        c. Brooks and Kelly, *Charters of Christ Church*, no. 62
Listed: S 1268

+ In nomine altithroni Regis aeterni Ego Uulfred gratia Dei archiepiscopus . de meis multifariis necessitatibus frequenti meditatione mentis meae cogi-
tans . quapropter pro remedio et salute animae meae speque et amore futuræ
aeternique[a] remunerationis in caelis . illa deuota familia quae Deo omnipotenti
seruitura est[b] in Dorouernia ciuitate . aliquam partem meae propriæ hereditariæ
terrae hoc est .iiii. aratrorum quod ab incolis terre illius nominatur æt Sceldes
forda cum illa prata quae mihi ab eadem familia ante tradita fuerat hoc est .xxx.
iugerum post obitum meum dabo et concedo siuimet[c] ipsis habendum feliciterque perfruendum in propriam possessionem posterisque suis semper derelin-
quendum qui cum gratia Dei ad eandem[d] famulatum futuri sunt . Et numquam
hæc mea donatio huius terræ ab ista prædicta familia tradatur nec pro alia com-
mutatur nec pecunia uenundatur . sed semper in posterum ad necessitatem istius
congregationis cum omnibus usis eius in propria possessione permaneat.

His notis terminibus circumiacentibus . in oriente terra regis quæ pertinet ad
Eastrege . in meridiae Osberhting lond . iterum in meridiæ et in occidente terra
quæ pertinet ad Uuigincgga ham . in aquilone uero Sceldesford et dimidium
riuuli paludis.

Seu etiam cum illa munificentia huius terrae omnibusque bonis quas illis
fecerim . postquam nostra communis congregatio per Dei gratiam facta est ad
istam meam familiam flagitabo ut me cum diuinis spiritalibusque bonis semper memorare concedant . talemque adiutorium pro refrigerio anime meae in
elemosynis salmodiisque ac celebratione missarum faciant qualem illis uidetur
quod perficere possint . Acque[e] condicione interposita . hanc praedictam[f] agel-
lum donabo . ut omnia nostra acta et dicta a nobis ante condicta firma inmu-
tataque perpetualiter maneant et semper ad meliora quod ad bonum condictum
habuimus Deo auxiliante unusquisque augescere contendat.

Insuper etiam illam terram quod Cynehard diaconus habuit et ille mihi don-
auit . siuique[g] in propriam hereditatem a regibus Ecgberhto et Aeðeluulfo donata
fuerat . hoc est .lxxxv. segetum cum libello eiusdem agelli . ista prædicta familia
in Dorouernia post dies meos pro nostrorum amborum animarum salute donabo
. hacque condicione ut semper uespere matutinaque tempore quando fratres ad
ecclesiam beati Petri apostoli ad consuetam[h] canticum ingrediuntur pro suppli-
catione animæ illius illud dominicum orationem pater noster decantent.

Seu etiam illum curtem quem Dodda monachus in monasterio habuit et
siui[i] in propriam possessionem optinebat[j] post migrationem spiritus mei ae[k]
seculo pro nostre animarum salute hoc est mei Cynehardi et Doddan huic eadem
familiae ad proprium usum liberaliter feliciterque perfruendum concedo . ad
quacumque utilitate ei placuerit uel necesse fuerit sua propria bona intus condere
ualeant . uel ad refectionem ciuorum[l] quando alicui oportunitas uel necessitas
temporis contigerit . Seu etiam quando presbyter aut diaconus familiae illius
corporali infirmitate grauatus fuerit congruo honore ibi requiescere possit . pro
hancquem[m] donate commoditate huius uillæ istam meam deuotam familiam
rogabo . quod fideles remuneratores intercessoresque animarum nostrarum apud

omnipotentem Deum existere concedatis . Hoc ipsumque posteris uestris obseruare perpetualiter praecipite.[n]

+ Ego Uulfred gratia Dei archiepiscopus
+ Ego Ciolnoth diuina gratia archiepiscopus
+ Ego Beagmund presbyter abbas
+ Ego Uuerhard presbyter abbas
+ Ego Aeðelhun presbyter
+ Ego Abba presbyter
+ Ego Hunred presbyter
+ Ego Osmund presbyter
+ Ego Ƿigmund presbyter
+ Ego Badanoð diaconus
+ Ego Heaberht diaconus
[+ Ego No]ðpulf diaconus
+ Brunhard presbyter
+ Hysenoð presbyter
[+ Dae]gmund presbyter
[+ Bior]nferð presbyter
[+ . . .]e
[+ Eard]pulf
[+ Oba]
+ Cichus
+ Ealhheard
+ Osmod
[+ Fr]ioðgeard
[+Ƿi]ting
[+ ..]elered

a For aeternaeque *b Probably for* seruitur *c For* sibimet *d For* eundem *e For* Hacque *f For* hunc praedictum *g For* sibique *h For* consuetum *i For* sibi *j A spelling for* obtinebat *k For* a *l For* ciborum *m For* hacque *n The subscriptions are written on the dorse. Places which are worn and cannot be made out are noted by square brackets.*

3

Fragment of a bequest by Archbishop Wulfred to his successors. [A.D. 805 × 832]

A. Lost exemplar
Ed.:   a. William Somner, *A Treatise of Gavelkind* (London, 1726), 88 (with translation, 88–89), from A
          b. Brooks, *Church of Canterbury*, 353 n. 37, from Somner (in part)

c. Katherine Lowe, "William Somner, S 1622 and the Editing of Old English Charters," *Neophilologus* 83 (1999): 291–97, at 293–95, from Somner; 295, revised text, with translation

d. Brooks and Kelly, *Charters of Canterbury*, no. 63
Listed: S 1622
Edited from Somner, with emendations proposed by Lowe

. . . Gif ðonne huelc mon ðæt uord cpæðe ðæt ne me siae min wic ðon alefedran[a] ðon oþrum higum to brucenne ne minum aerfrepeardum. ðonne þite he ðæt hit naes nefre Cristes cirican land ne nenges monnes boclond ær min. ⁊ ðonne se monne[b] ieond ðence ⁊ asmeaie be oðerra monna boclondum ie in friþstolum ie butan. huader hio megen hiora agen sellan oððe on hiora lif <a>gan[c] sue him leof siae oððe for huðu[d] min scyle beon unie[. . .]lðenre[e] ðon oðrum monnum hiora.

a *Somner notes*: Quære; 'for the writing is not clear' b *For* mon c gan *Somner*
d ? *For* forhuon e *Somner was unable to read his source here; probably for* unie[pea]ldenre

Translation
If then any man should utter the statement that it is not more permissible for me or my heirs to enjoy my property than other members of the community, then he should know that it was never Christ Church land nor any man's bookland before it was mine. And then that person should consider and think about other people's bookland, both in consecrated places and outside, whether they are able to give away their own [bookland] or possess [it] during their lifetime as may be pleasing to them, or why mine ought to be more restricted[a] than that of other people.[b]

a *Literally 'less under control, less disposable at will'*
b *Translation adapted from Lowe, "Editing".*

4

Werhard, priest, bequeaths land to Christ Church, Canterbury, partly in fulfillment of the will of Archbishop Wulfred. A.D. 830 [for 833 × ca. 845]

F. Cambridge, Corpus Christi College, 189, fols. 198v–199r: copy, s. xii
G. Canterbury, Dean and Chapter, Register P, fols. 18v–19r: copy, s. xii
H. London, Lambeth Palace, 1212, p. 319: copy, s. xiii
Ed.:   a. BCS 402, from H
         b. Brooks and Kelly, *Charters of Canterbury*, no. 64
Listed: S 1414; Margaret Gelling, *Early Charters of the Thames Valley* (Leicester, 1979), no. 208
Edited from H, with variants from F and G

[A]nno dominice incarnationis .dcccxxx. Ego Werhardus[a] gratia Dei[b] presbiter hiis litteris[c] intimare cupio quomodo uolo post obitum meum substanciam meam[d] et terras diuidere quas, donante Deo et Wlfredo archiepiscopo propinquo meo auxiliante, adquisiui. Inprimis autem cum magna humilitate et humili deuocione reddo ecclesie Christi et monachis [e]fratribus meis[e] ibidem Deo[f] seruientibus omnes terras infra Canciam et extra quas hactenus tenui, donante prefato archiepiscopo et consenciente predicta familia[g] Christi. Precepit enim hoc michi idem archiepiscopus ita facere, eo quod easdem terras ad opus iam [h]sepedicte familie[h] emisset et cum magno labore adquisisset, pro remuneracione eterne salutis.[i]

Hec autem sunt nomina terrarum quas reddo: Hergas .c. et .iiii. hidas;[j] Otteford[k] .c. hidas; Grauenea[l] .xxxii. hidas; Burnan .xliiii. hidas; Oesuualun[m] .x. hidas; Bereham[n] quam idem archiepiscopus et monachi[o] ecclesie Christi michi dederunt pro commutacione terre de Cliue .xxxvi. hidas; unum iugum quod iacet in australi parte Limene et ab incolis nominatur Lambaham[m],[p] pertinet autem ad Burnan[q] et reddit[r] .xl. pensas casei et agnos et lanam absque caseo; aliud iugum apud Northuuda et reddere debet .cxx. mensuras quas Angli dicunt ambres de sale; marascos[s] omnes in australi parte Limene et in aquilonali[t] cum prefatis terris deuote reddo; mansionem quoque [u]que est[u] in aquilonali[v] parte Dorobernie muris[w] et clausulam quod Angli dicunt teage, que pertinet ad predictam mansionem.

Hanc autem reddicionem ideo ex parte reddo, quia ipse[d] dominus meus archiepiscopus ita precepit michi et in scripto quod ipse scribere fecit [x]antequam infirmaretur,[x] de diuisione rerum suarum, hoc idem notari precepit. In quo etiam scripto constituit elemosinam quam cotidie fieri precepit in illis terris quas ipse adquisiuit pro anima sua et pro animabus omnium illorum qui ecclesie Christi aliquid auxilii impendissent. Et hoc intentissime fieri precepit ita ut diceret: 'Inter Deum et sequentes nos archiepiscopos sit de facienda aut negligenda [y]istam elemosinam a me ordinatam.[y] Apud Hergan quinque[z] pauperes; apud Otteford[a2] quinque;[z] apud Cliue .ii.; apud Grauenea[b2] .ii.; apud Oesuualun unus;[z] in ciuitate Dorobernia[c2] sex.[z] Unicuique detur cotidie ad manducandum quod conuenienter sit satis et per annum cuique pauperi ad uestitum .xxvi. denarii.' Cotidie quoque precepit missam celebrari pro anima sua et pro animabus supra memoratorum. In anniuersario suo precepit dari mille .cc. pauperibus ad manducandum, cuique panem unum[z] et caseum aut lardum et denarium unum.[z] Hoc est preceptum archiepiscopi Wlfredi.[d2]

Ego quoque[d2] Werhardus presbiter concedo ecclesie Christi prenominate in ciuitate[e2] Dorobernia,[c2] pro salute anime mee et Wlfredi archiepiscopi, .xxxii. hidas de patrimonio meo quas dare possum cui uolo, nomine Hyse. Aliam quoque terram nomine Megeldeuurthe,[f2] quam Ceolnothus archiepiscopus et monachi[g2] sepe nominate ecclesie Christi mihi[h2] dederunt eidem ecclesie redono. Adhuc addo terram[d2] octo hydarum nomine Cuniland; super hoc .xxx. hidas cum uilla nomine Tuicham[i2] in prouincia Middelsexan.[j2] Uideant ergo fratres et domini mei monachi[g2] ecclesie Christi, ut memores sint anime mee, quia libenti animo reddidi quod reddere[k2] debui, et quod meum fuit deuotissimo animo Christo contuli.

[a] Wernardus F, G [b] Dei gratia G [c] literis G [d] *Word omitted* F [e...e] *Omitted* F [f] Deo ibidem F [g] predicte familie H [h...h] sepe <...> ecclesie G [i] salutis eterne G [j] hydas G (*passim*) [k] Otheford G; F *omits* Otteford .c. hidas [l] Grauenea' F [m] Oesuualunn F, G [n] Berham F, G [o] mo' H [p] Lambeham G; Lambaha'm H [q] Burneham G [r] reddet G [s] *A spelling for* mariscos [t] aquilone H [u...u] *Omitted* F [v] aquiloni H [w] muri F [x...x] *Omitted* F [y...y] ista elemosina ... ordinata F [z] F *and* G *have numerals here* [a2] Octoford F; Ottheford G [b2] Gravena F; Graueneia G [c2] Dorobernie G [d2] *Word omitted* G [e2] urbe F [f2] Mecgelduurthe F; Mecgeldeuurthe G [g2] modo H (*incorrect expansion of abbreviation* mo') [h2] *Word omitted* H [i2] Tuuicham F, G [j2] F *ends here* [k2] redere G

An Anglo-Saxon Wall Painting
at St. Mary's Church, Deerhurst,
and its Context

Michael Hare

1. Introduction

The church of St. Mary at Deerhurst might at first sight seem an unlikely candidate for the discovery of an Anglo-Saxon wall painting.[1] It is well documented that in 1861–1862 the church was stripped of all its internal plaster with some loss of wall paintings of unknown date, and then replastered.[2] However, there has been a growing appreciation in recent years of the quantity of early painted remains on dressed stone surfaces at Deerhurst. For instance, Richard Gem has

---

[1] I am extremely grateful to my two colleagues, Steve Bagshaw and Richard Bryant, for their major contributions to the project described in this paper and for allowing me to use some of their material here. At Deerhurst, Will and Shelagh Morris have regularly provided much logistical support with characteristic good nature and good humor. The Friends of Deerhurst Church gave significant financial support without which the project would not have been possible. The visit of ISAS to Munich provided an opportunity to meet Matthias Exner of the Bayerisches Landesamt für Denkmalpflege (the leading German authority on early medieval wall painting); he made a number of valuable comments. Other scholars who have made useful observations include Klaus Gereon Beuckers, Lawrence Butler, Richard Gem, Gale Owen-Crocker, Philip Rahtz, Jo Story, and Lorna Watts.

[2] For a detailed architectural description of St. Mary's, Deerhurst, see Harold M. Taylor and Joan Taylor, *Anglo-Saxon Architecture*, 3 vols. (Cambridge, 1965–1978), 1: 193–209. For the results of subsequent investigations, see Philip Rahtz and Lorna Watts with Harold Taylor and Lawrence Butler, *St Mary's Church, Deerhurst, Gloucestershire: Fieldwork, Excavations and Structural Analysis, 1971–1984*, Reports of the Research Committee of the Society of Antiquaries of London 55 (Woodbridge, 1997). For the loss of wall paintings in 1861–1862, see Steve Bagshaw, Richard Bryant, and Michael Hare, "The Discovery of an Anglo-Saxon Painted Figure at St Mary's Church, Deerhurst, Gloucestershire," *Antiquaries Journal* 86 (2006): 66–109, at 66–67 and 102–3.

Hans Sauer and Joanna Story, eds., *Anglo-Saxon England and the Continent*. With the assistance of Gaby Waxenberger. Essays in Anglo-Saxon Studies, vol. 3. MRTS 394. Tempe: ACMRS, 2011.   [ISBN 978-0-86698-442-3]

drawn attention to the paint on the beast-head label-stop on the north side of the chancel-arch, and he has argued for a ninth-century date for this paint.[3]

In September 1993, just a few weeks after the ISAS outing from Oxford to Deerhurst, the interior of Deerhurst church was redecorated, the contractor working from long ladders. The opportunity arose to have a quick look at the triangular-headed panel at high level on the north side of the east wall (fig. 16.1). It was evident that there was a considerable quantity of paint on the panel, though the viewpoint (just below the panel at the top of a swaying ladder) did not allow proper examination. It was not until 2002 that it was possible to get together a small team to investigate further. Our detailed initial report appears in the *Antiquaries Journal*.[4] This paper is an abbreviated version of that report, with the intention of making the discovery known to Anglo-Saxonists.

The great height of the panel is doubtless the reason why the painting has not previously been noticed (the base of the panel is about 8.5m above the floor of the church below).[5] It is expensive to work at this height, and safety has been a major consideration. So far we have had the opportunity only of making two short inspections of the painted panel; an initial examination was carried out from a scaffolding tower, while a second, very brief, examination was subsequently made from a high-level hoist. Neither platform proved sufficiently stable to take photographs that do full justice to the painted remains, and this paper is therefore illustrated by Richard Bryant's drawn record (fig. 16.2). No technical study has yet been made.

2. Description

The triangular-headed panel, of oölitic limestone from the Cotswolds, is 0.87m wide and 1.38m high from the base to the apex of the triangular head. The surviving remains are painted in dark red line. Setting-out lines, inscribed in the

---

[3] Richard Gem, "Church Architecture," in *The Making of England: Anglo-Saxon Art and Culture AD 600–900*, ed. Leslie Webster and Janet Backhouse (London, 1991), 185–88. The polychromy on the chancel-arch has recently been the subject of further study: Richard Gem, Emily Howe, and Richard Bryant, "The Ninth-Century Polychrome Decoration at St Mary's Church, Deerhurst," *Antiquaries Journal* 88 (2008): 109–64. The painted remains at Deerhurst should also be considered in conjunction with the carved and painted angel of *c.* 800 discovered recently at Lichfield Cathedral: Warwick Rodwell, Jane Hawkes, Emily Howe, and Rosemary Cramp, "The Lichfield Angel: A Spectacular Anglo-Saxon Painted Sculpture," *Antiquaries Journal* 88 (2008): 48–108.

[4] Bagshaw et al., "Anglo-Saxon Painted Figure."

[5] In normal lighting the painting is to all intents and purposes invisible from ground level. Occasionally favorable lighting conditions are found in which at least some of the detail can be seen; the optimum conditions so far noted occurred on a bright and clear mid-February morning at around 9:45 a.m.

FIGURE 16.1. The interior of St. Mary's Church, Deerhurst, looking east, taken from a high-level hoist at the west end of the nave in November 2003. The panel with the painted figure is to the left of the high-level window in the eastern wall. Photograph by Richard Bryant and Steve Bagshaw.

Figure 16.2. St. Mary's Church, Deerhurst: the painted panel. Recorded and drawn by Richard Bryant (see fig. 16.1. for its position).

stone, define the sides of the pillars. Much of the image has clearly been lost; we suspect that a post-medieval covering of limewash was scraped off the stone during the restoration of 1861–1862, probably taking early paint with it.[6]

The painting depicts a standing figure within an architectural frame consisting of a triangular-headed arch supported by piers with stepped capitals and bases. The most obvious feature of the figure is the halo, painted in a bold, wide curve and resting upon the shoulders. The face is delicate, and much of the right eye can be seen, together with the nose, the nostrils, and most of the upper lip. The hair on the left side of the face seems to cover the ear and could be braided. The crown of the head survives, as does part of the neck on the right side. The figure's right cheek is rounded, but none of the chin could be discerned. The figure holds a rectangular object, presumably a book, in his draped left hand. Little

---

[6] Bagshaw et al., "Anglo-Saxon Painted Figure," 67–69.

of the right arm and none of the right hand survive, but the remains of the folds of the sleeve indicate that the arm is raised, perhaps in blessing.

The figure is clothed in a long tunic and an over-garment that is gathered in above the waist. The folds of the over-garment are drawn in fine, flowing lines, with delicate detailing and a lightness of touch which suggests that this is the work of an artist of some quality. The draperies fly out on either side of the figure in the style found in many manuscript illustrations of tenth-century date.

The lower part of the figure is more fragmentary, and we are not certain whether the original painting represented a long, attenuated figure filling most of the frame or a shorter figure with some feature(s) beneath it (for instance the figures of patrons or donors). To the figure's left, about halfway down, there is a narrow, horizontal rectangular painted shape with a rather broken outline. This may be the remains of a table or stand. Across the center of the image, at the level of the rectangular feature described above, there are three irregular, vertical ovals of solid paint. One is on the left side of the rectangular object, one lies below the garment folds that fall from the draped left hand, and one lies to the right of the figure. None of these seem to have anything to do with the design. They are probably blobs of paint caught, perhaps, on something like a modern sign painter's rest (a fabric-covered pad on the end of a long stick) and then transferred across the image as the rest was moved to support the painter's brush hand. These errors may originally have been masked out with detailed application of gesso.

We have also examined the triangular-headed panel at the same level on the south side. Here there are now no painted remains visible to the naked eye. There are, however, grounds for thinking that the design of any painting on this panel may have been different. There are no incised setting-out lines for pillars, but there is a horizontal incised line forming the base line of the triangular head. There are also faint traces of a second incised horizontal line running across the panel 30–40mm from the bottom.

3. Discussion

The image of a standing figure, holding a book in a draped and shrouded hand (most commonly the left hand), was widespread in Christian Europe from late antiquity through to the later Middle Ages; indeed such figures are still commonly found in icons produced in the Orthodox world today. Numerous examples from Anglo-Saxon England could be cited, for instance Christ on the

Ruthwell Cross, the apostles on the Hedda Stone in Peterborough Cathedral, or the prophet Nahum on the Cuthbert Stole in Durham Cathedral.[7]

Before discussing the date and identity of the figure, a few words should be said about the intended final appearance of the Deerhurst painted figure. Most of the known wall paintings of early medieval date in Europe north of the Alps were polychrome. The normal first step in the production of a polychrome image was a preparatory drawing in red (or occasionally yellow) brush strokes; this preparatory drawing is sometimes all that has survived to the present day, with no trace — or only very slight traces — of the full polychrome image. We consider it probable that what survives at Deerhurst is just such a preparatory drawing and that the final image is likely to have been polychrome. Details such as the three blobs of paint across the center of the image and the erratic layout of the capitals of the architectural frame are best explained as *pentimenti*, that is to say errors and trials which were not intended to be visible in the finished painting, but which have subsequently emerged into the light of day.

At the time of the discovery of the painted figure in 2002, we initially inclined to the view that it represented Christ, possibly Christ trampling the beasts. However, we now reject this interpretation after considering the context. The existence of two panels, one on the north side and one on the south side, seems likely to imply a coherent program, and it is difficult to envisage a coherent program with Christ on the north side. The figure must therefore represent a saint. The drapery seems likely to indicate a male saint,[8] but at the moment there is insufficient information to enable us to suggest a specific identity, though the high brow might conceivably correspond to the iconographical type of St. Paul.[9] But beyond that slight possibility, we can say no more, for both universal and local saints could be represented in the pose of the Deerhurst figure.

The closest English parallels for the Deerhurst figure, with its delicate detailing and floating drapery, can be found in several well-known line-drawings from manuscript art of the second half of the tenth century. On the page of St. Dunstan's Classbook that shows Dunstan at the feet of Christ, the figure of Christ shows many similarities to the Deerhurst figure. Christ holds a tablet or book in his left hand and wears an over-garment over a long tunic. The over-garment is light and delicate, and the cloth floats away from the body as if moving in the breeze. This work seems likely to date to the middle of the tenth century, probably before Dunstan left Glastonbury in 957, though a later date cannot be excluded.[10]

---

[7] David M. Wilson, *Anglo-Saxon Art from the Seventh Century to the Norman Conquest* (Woodstock, NY, 1984), pl. 70 (Ruthwell) and pl. 93 (Hedda Stone); *The Relics of St. Cuthbert*, ed. C. F. Battiscombe (Durham, 1956), pls. 33–34 (Cuthbert Stole).

[8] I am grateful to Gale Owen-Crocker for advice on this point.

[9] I am grateful to Matthias Exner for suggesting this possibility.

[10] Oxford, Bodleian Library, MS. Auct. F.4.32, fol. 1r; see Mildred Budny, "'St Dunstan's Classbook' and its Frontispiece: Dunstan's Portrait and Autograph," in *St

An even closer parallel is offered by the figure of Christ in a copy of Gregory the Great's *Regula Pastoralis*, written at St. Augustine's, Canterbury, in the third quarter of the tenth century. The *Regula Pastoralis* is bound in with some earlier material that includes several outline drawings. One is of Christ who carries a book in his left hand, which is draped in a fold of his light over-garment. His right hand is raised and holds a cross, but the folds of his right sleeve are again similar to the surviving folds on the Deerhurst figure.[11]

Further parallels can be found in the three late tenth-century illustrations of Christ as King, God, and Man from the Sherborne or Dunstan Pontifical. Here both Christ as God and Christ as Man are depicted as standing figures wearing light over-garments over long tunics. Both figures hold a book in the draped left hand. The image of Christ as King from this series is very similar, except that he is crowned and his hand, in which he holds a book, is not draped by his over-garment.[12] It is worth noting that in one particular the Deerhurst figure does differ from these figures in manuscript art. The book carried by the Deerhurst figure is square, whereas the manuscript figures all carry tall, narrow books.[13]

It is of course very uncertain how far we should rely on manuscript art to date a figure in the different medium of wall painting. One can illustrate the difficulty of dating wall paintings by comparison with manuscript art with reference to the wall paintings of late tenth-century date in the outer crypt at St. Emmeram in Regensburg. These paintings bear little resemblance to contemporary Regensburg

---

Dunstan: His Life, Times and Cult, ed. Nigel Ramsay, Margaret Sparks, and Tim Tatton-Brown (Woodbridge, 1992), 103–42, pl. 4 and color pl. I, and Francis Wormald, *English Drawings of the Eleventh and Twelfth Centuries* (London, 1953), pl. 1; Helmut Gneuss, *Handlist of Anglo-Saxon Manuscripts: A List of Manuscripts and Manuscript Fragments Written or Owned in England up to 1100*, MRTS 241 (Tempe, 2001), no. 538.

[11] Oxford, St. John's College, MS. 28, fol. 2r, illustrated in *St. Dunstan*, ed. Ramsay et al., color pl. II; also Wormald, *English Drawings*, pl. 2, and Bagshaw et al., "Anglo-Saxon Painted Figure," fig. 8; Gneuss, *Handlist of Anglo-Saxon Manuscripts*, no. 684.

[12] Paris, BN lat. 943, fols. 5v, 6r and 6v; see Jane Rosenthal, "The Pontifical of St. Dunstan," in *St. Dunstan*, ed. Ramsay et al., 143–63, pls. 1–3; also Wormald, *English Drawings*, pls. 4a, 4b, 5a, and Bagshaw et al., "Anglo-Saxon Painted Figure," fig. 9. Gneuss, *Handlist of Anglo-Saxon Manuscripts*, no. 879. Richard Gem (oral communication) has pointed out that if the figure on the Deerhurst panel had the tall, attenuated proportions of the figures in the Dunstan Pontifical, the figure would fill the panel.

[13] I am grateful to Jo Story for the suggestion that the tall, narrow books found in manuscript art from the second half of the tenth century may derive from the late antique diptych and allude to the Book of Life; see Kim Bowes, "Ivory Lists: Consular Diptychs, Christian Appropriation and Polemics of Time in Late Antiquity," *Art History* 24 (2001): 338–57.

manuscript art, but are quite close in style to manuscripts of ninth-century date from Regensburg.[14]

There is, moreover, very little wall painting art with which the Deerhurst painted figure can be compared; the other wall painting still *in situ* known from Anglo-Saxon England is at Nether Wallop near Winchester, probably to be assigned to a late tenth- or early eleventh-century date in view of the similarities to art in Winchester manuscripts of the late tenth century.[15] We should also bear in mind that there is comparatively little manuscript art from England during the century from 850 to 950.

Light, floating draperies such as are found in the Deerhurst figure occur in the art of the later Carolingian period, for instance in an initial of mid-ninth-century date depicting the Ascension in the Drogo Sacramentary from Metz.[16] It is at least worth considering the possibility that Carolingian influences made themselves felt in England rather earlier in the field of wall painting than they did in manuscript art. The possibility of a date for the Deerhurst painted panel that is earlier than the manuscript illustrations of the second half of the tenth century is supported by an important discovery from Winchester. A large fragment of a wall painting, bearing parts of three figures, was found during archaeological excavations in 1966. The painting was on one face of a limestone block that was reused in a stratified archaeological context dated to "the years around 900."[17] The date of the context means that the reused wall painting fragment must be, at the latest, late ninth century.

There is insufficient evidence to suggest a precise date for the Deerhurst painted figure. The comparisons with manuscript art suggest that a date in the second half of the tenth century is most likely, but a date in the first half of the tenth century cannot be excluded. An early eleventh-century date might also be considered possible if the style of the draperies occurred at a later date in the medium of wall painting than in the medium of manuscript art.

---

[14] Matthias Exner, "Denkmäler frühmittelalterlicher Wandmalerei in Bayern: Bestand, Ergebnisse, Aufgaben," in *Wandmalerei des frühen Mittelalters*, ed. idem (Munich, 1998), 99–118, at 109–11.

[15] Richard Gem and Pamela Tudor-Craig, "A 'Winchester School' Wall-Painting at Nether Wallop, Hampshire," *Anglo-Saxon England* 9 (1981): 115–36.

[16] Paris, BN lat. 9428, fol. 71v, illustrated in C. R. Dodwell, *The Pictorial Arts of the West 800–1200* (New Haven and London, 1993), 60 (pl. 46).

[17] Martin Biddle and Birthe Kjølbye-Biddle, "The Dating of the New Minster Wall Painting," in *Early Medieval Wall Painting and Painted Sculpture in England*, ed. Sharon Cather, David Park, and Paul Williamson, BAR British Series 216 (Oxford, 1990), 45–63, at 62.

4. The Structural Context of the Panel

Steve Bagshaw's work on the petrology of the building stones of Deerhurst church has enabled him to argue that the masonry of the nave is of a single build from a height of about 1.80m above the floor of the nave to the top of the walls. The detailed reasoning is set out in our paper in the *Antiquaries Journal*, and there is not space here to consider the evidence more closely.[18] The work of this period corresponds broadly to Phase IV as defined by Philip Rahtz and Lorna Watts in their account of the excavations and examination of the standing building at Deerhurst in the 1970s.[19] For the dating of this phase we follow Richard Bailey's recent assessment of the sculpture integral to the building; he argues convincingly for a date in the ninth century, probably in the first half of the century.[20]

We do not consider the two panels to have been an integral part of the east wall when first constructed, but rather to be insertions of slightly later date. We have reached this conclusion partly because the art-historical evidence points to a later date for the panel with surviving paint, but also because there are good reasons for thinking that the two panels blocked earlier openings, traces of which can be seen on the exterior of the wall. Detailed measurement has shown that the two interior panels fit precisely over the remains of the blocked openings. It should also be noted that there seems to have been a rather larger opening in the center of the wall; as a result of the insertion of a late medieval window, only the external sill of this opening survives, and its exact character is uncertain.

On the exterior face of the wall, preliminary analysis of all three openings (the two smaller openings and the central opening of which only the sill now remains) suggests that they were integral with the construction of the wall at that level. The explanation favored here is that the blocked features, behind the panels, represent openings created with the construction of the wall at that level, and blocked internally with painted triangular-headed panels during a subsequent episode of refurbishment and rebuilding. The openings appear to connect a proposed high-level floor above the chancel with the upper level of the apse. Access, at least visually, to this space at this level implies that it had a liturgical function and, therefore, a floor.

---

[18] Bagshaw et al., "Anglo-Saxon Painted Figure," 84–97.

[19] Rahtz et al., *St Mary's Church, Deerhurst*, 166–75.

[20] Richard N. Bailey, *Anglo-Saxon Sculptures at Deerhurst*, Deerhurst Lecture 2002 (Deerhurst, 2005).

5. The Painted Figure and its Liturgical Context

It is not easy to interpret the Deerhurst painted figure in the context of the liturgical life of Deerhurst church. An initial problem is that, although Deerhurst
was evidently a minster church, the nature of the community which it served at
different times in the Anglo-Saxon period is unknown. The earliest reference is
found in a document from the Worcester archive dated in or shortly after 804
by which Æthelric, son of Æthelmund, granted four estates "to the place (*locus*)
which is called Deerhurst for me and for my father Æthelmund, if it should
happen that my body rests there"; the lands were granted "on condition that the
community (*congregatio*) carries out their vows as they have promised me."[21]

There is no further evidence for the ninth century, while the tenth century
presents even greater problems. Not long before 1100 the hagiographer Osbern,
precentor of Canterbury, wrote a *Passion of St. Ælfheah* (St. Alphege), the archbishop of Canterbury who was murdered at Greenwich in 1012. Osbern placed
the origin of Ælfheah's monastic career at Deerhurst, commenting that "inasmuch
as the place was sparsely inhabited, virtue made those who did live there most
admirable."[22] It is likely that Ælfheah did indeed begin his ecclesiastical career at
Deerhurst, but it is a moot point whether Osbern had reliable information about
the quality of religious life there. Osbern's remarks have led to the suggestion that
Deerhurst was a fully monastic community living under the Benedictine rule in
the late tenth century. As Patrick Wormald has shown, there could indeed have
been a Benedictine community at Deerhurst in the last third of the tenth century,
but there are also other possible explanations for Osbern's treatment of Ælfheah's
early career; it is perhaps more probable that Deerhurst was served by secular clergy
at this period.[23] The uncertainty is frustrating. The parallels in manuscript art were
produced at centers closely associated with the leaders of the Benedictine reform.
Does this style occur at Deerhurst because it was itself a Benedictine establishment, or was such art more widespread in the late Saxon period? How far should
we see the influence of the diocesan center of Worcester, itself Benedictine, or of
such monasteries as Evesham, Gloucester, Pershore, and Winchcombe, all within
a twenty-mile radius of Deerhurst? The monasteries of the diocese of Worcester do not seem to have been especially notable in the production of illuminated

---

[21] P. H. Sawyer, *Anglo-Saxon Charters: An Annotated List and Bibliography*, Royal
Historical Society Guides and Handbooks 8 (London, 1968), no. 1187; Walter de Gray
Birch, *Cartularium Saxonicum*, 3 vols. (London, 1885–1893), 1: no. 313 (text); *English
Historical Documents c. 500–1042*, ed. Dorothy Whitelock, 2nd edn. (London, 1979), no.
81 (translation).

[22] Osbern, *Vita vel passio S. Ealphegi*, printed in *Anglia Sacra*, ed. H. Wharton, 2
vols. (London, 1691), 2: 122–42, at 123–24.

[23] Patrick Wormald, *How Do We Know So Much About Anglo-Saxon Deerhurst?*,
Deerhurst Lecture 1991 (Deerhurst, 1993), 7–9.

manuscripts in the later tenth and eleventh centuries, but the position may have been different in the field of wall painting.[24]

A further problem arises from the fact that the figure at Deerhurst is painted on a panel projecting from the face of the wall. It is assumed that the companion panel on the south side was painted, as also the projecting rectangular panel at the west end (in this case an inscription rather than an image might be considered). The Deerhurst painted panel cannot easily be paralleled, and it is unclear how far the Deerhurst examples should be seen as part of a wider tradition of painted panels. What can surely be said is that the projection from the wall face is intended to emphasize the importance of the painted image. Likewise, the placing of the figure between two columns surmounted by an arch is an antique device long used to enhance the dignity of important figures.

We do not consider it likely that the painted panel and its southern counterpart were designed to be seen from the floor of the church, some 8.5m below. There is a significant collection of features (outlined briefly above and discussed in detail in our paper in the *Antiquaries Journal*) which incline us to believe that there was a high-level floor above the arch leading into the apse.[25] The level of the floor of such a space is in all likelihood indicated by two short stretches of string-course in the east wall adjacent to the north and south walls of the church; these string-courses, which seem to be decorative rather than structural, are about 1m below the base of the triangular-headed panels, perhaps suggesting a floor about 0.7m below the panels, after allowing for the thickness of the joists.

There would seem to be three possibilities for the extent of such an upper floor. First, there could have been a high-level eastern gallery, as suggested by Harold Taylor.[26] Second, the floor could have covered the central space defined by the present east wall and the former cross-wall. Both the foundations and the scars left by this cross-wall were seen in the restoration of 1861–1862, and the scars are stated to have extended to the top of the nave walls.[27] Third, it is possible that the floor covered not only the central space but also the nave, effectively constituting an upper church.

We tend to favor the third explanation, though we do so only after very careful consideration, as we realize that an upper floor of this nature is hard to

[24] For a discussion of book production at Worcester itself, see Richard Gameson, "Book Production and Decoration at Worcester in the Tenth and Eleventh Centuries," in *St Oswald of Worcester: Life and Influence*, ed. Nicholas Brooks and Catherine Cubitt (Leicester, 1996), 194–243.

[25] Bagshaw et al., "Anglo-Saxon Painted Figure," 97–101.

[26] Harold M. Taylor, "Tenth-Century Church Building in England and on the Continent," in *Tenth-Century Studies*, ed. D. Parsons (London and Chichester, 1975), 141–68, 237–41, at 163 and figs. 17 and 18.

[27] G. Butterworth, "The History of Deerhurst Church, Gloucestershire," *The Ecclesiologist* 23 (1862): 89–101, at 94–95.

parallel in the pre-Romanesque period. Indeed, even in the Romanesque period there are few known survivals of churches with upper floors above the main body of the building, despite the existence of many thousands of churches across Europe north of the Alps.[28] In England, Harold and Joan Taylor suggested the former existence of an upper floor at the Anglo-Saxon church of Wing, though the evidence is by no means compelling.[29] There are other possible hints in the written sources. One would, for instance, like to know more of the character of the upper floor (*upfleringe*) of the stone church at Wilton in which a gathering of some thirty people took place in 1072 under the presidency of Edith, the widow of Edward the Confessor.[30]

The high-level panels at Deerhurst are unusual features, and unconventional thinking may not be entirely out of order. Externally the level of the floor would have been marked by the great molded string-course which ran from the west tower along the nave to the north and south porticus. The floor would also have been at the same level as the elaborate second-floor chapel in the tower which opens towards the nave through a double triangular-headed opening (fig. 16.3).[31] The projecting rectangular panel that is set above this opening in the west wall of the nave seems likely to have been part of the same (or at least an analogous) scheme of decoration as the triangular-headed panels in the east wall of the church. It is, moreover, legitimate to ask from what level the painted ornament—which it presumably once bore—was intended to be viewed. The base of this panel is at a height of a little over 10m above the floor of the nave; it must be highly doubtful whether the panel was designed to be seen from ground level. It is possible that it was intended to be viewed from the western gallery in the nave (the floor of which would have been about 5m above the floor of the nave), but the simplest interpretation may be that it was designed to be seen from an upper floor.

The northern aperture of the double triangular-headed opening was cut down to form a doorway, presumably at an early date. The doorway could have provided

---

[28] For a brief survey of chancels with chambers above them, see Eric Fernie, "The Church of St Magnus, Egilsay," in *St Magnus Cathedral and Orkney's Twelfth-Century Renaissance*, ed. Barbara E. Crawford (Aberdeen, 1988), 140–61, at 148–52.

[29] Taylor and Taylor, *Anglo-Saxon Architecture*, 2: 670–71.

[30] The reference to the *upfleringe* of the stone church at Wilton is found in a charter of 1072, most recently edited and translated by Simon Keynes, "Giso, Bishop of Wells (1061–88)," *Anglo-Norman Studies* 19 (1997): 203–71, at 262–63. This stone church, which had been built by Edith and dedicated in 1065, is reported to have been on a more modest scale than Edward's Westminster: see *Vita Ædwardi Regis qui apud Westmonasterium requiescit*, 1.6–7, printed in *The Life of King Edward Who Rests at Westminster*, ed. and trans. Frank Barlow, 2nd edn. (Oxford, 1992), 70–74.

[31] For this chapel see Taylor and Taylor, *Anglo-Saxon Architecture*, 1: 194–98 and 2: pls. 445–48; Rahtz et al., *St Mary's Church, Deerhurst*, 97–118.

FIGURE 16.3 The double triangular-headed opening in the west wall of the nave at St. Mary's Church, Deerhurst, taken from a high-level hoist in November 2003. This view is taken from the same position as fig. 16.1, but looking west. The base of the projecting rectangular panel above the double opening can also be seen.
Photograph by Richard Bryant and Steve Bagshaw.

access to the chapel via a timber stairway from the west gallery in the nave, but it might also have communicated between the chapel and an upper floor over the nave. If a complete upper floor once existed, then there were presumably openings in the former cross-wall at two different levels, an arch at ground level and a further arch or doorway(s) at the level of the upper floor. Whether or not a floor once extended over the nave, it is possible that further painted panels may once have existed on both faces of the cross-wall. The answers to at least some of these issues are likely to survive behind the plaster of the restoration of 1861–1862. In particular, it seems likely that future archaeological work might one day be able to define the extent of the upper floor.

The elaborate character of the second-floor chapel in the tower is noteworthy. In addition to the double triangular-headed opening in the east wall, the north and south walls each have a window and an aumbry, while a doorway opens west into space. Just beneath this high-level doorway, Rahtz and Watts (following Harold Taylor) drew attention to features which were interpreted as the blocking of former holes designed for beams to support an external timber gallery.[32] A number of similar features can be detected at the same height in the north and south walls of the tower and in the west wall of the nave. There are grounds for reconstructing an external timber gallery round three sides of the tower formed from a complex network of interlocking timbers.[33] A parallel for such an arrangement is provided by a timber gallery (rebuilt in the early eighteenth century) round three sides of the west tower at the church of St. Peter, Beho in the Belgian Ardennes (fig. 16.4). At Beho, which dates from ca. 1100, it is documented that, in the eighteenth century, the gallery was used for the display of relics.[34] A similar explanation seems likely at Deerhurst, and it is possible that the upper chapel at Deerhurst was connected with the cult of whatever relics Deerhurst may have possessed.

Upper chapels in western towers can be paralleled extensively on the Continent. However, what was happening at high level at the east end at Deerhurst remains elusive and is difficult if not impossible to parallel. It is suggested above that there were early openings from the east wall into the roof-space of the apse. The two smaller openings can never have been more than viewing points, or perhaps additional sources of light for the apsidal space. The sill of the central opening was positioned well above the postulated floor-level, and this may indicate that this opening was also designed primarily for viewing rather than for access (fig. 16.5). When the two smaller openings were blocked and covered by the stone panels, the bottoms of the panels were set on exactly the same level as the top of the sill of the central opening, which suggests that, at least by this time, the ensemble was conceived as a whole. One possibility is that the high apsidal space contained a major shrine or reliquary sited directly above the principal altar of the church in the apsidal sanctuary. Such a relationship would effectively be a reversal of the spatial relationship often found between shrines sited in crypts directly beneath the high altar.[35]

---

[32] Rahtz et al., *St Mary's Church, Deerhurst*, 101, 130 n. 74.

[33] The evidence is discussed in detail in Michael Hare, "The 9th-Century West Porch of St Mary's Church, Deerhurst, Gloucestershire: Form and Function," *Medieval Archaeology* 53 (2009): 35–93.

[34] Beho is considered in more detail in the study mentioned in the previous note. The evidence for the use of the gallery at Beho for the display of relics is set out in the useful guidebook by J. Jakobs, *Beho* (Beho, 1957); the church is also briefly discussed by E. den Hartog, *Romanesque Architecture and Sculpture in the Meuse Valley* (Leeuwarden, 1992), 174.

[35] John Crook, *The Architectural Setting of the Cult of Saints in the Early Christian West c. 300–1200* (Oxford, 2000), 65–67, 80–82, 93–95, and 136–38.

FIGURE 16.4. The west tower of St. Peter's Church, Beho (Gouvy, Luxembourg, Belgium), showing the external western gallery used for the display of relics in the eighteenth century.

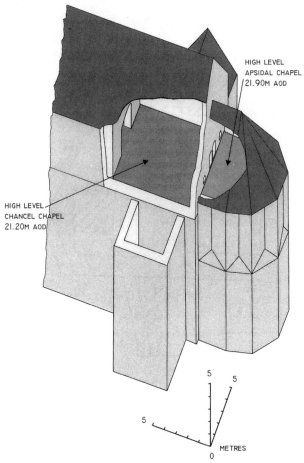

HIGH LEVEL
APSIDAL CHAPEL
21.90M AOD

HIGH LEVEL
CHANCEL CHAPEL
21.20M AOD

5

5

5

METRES

0

FIGURE 16.5. Axonometric reconstruction of the suggested high-level floors at the east end of St. Mary's Church, Deerhurst in the ninth century. AOD means above Ordnance Datum. Drawn by Steve Bagshaw.

There are thus straws in the wind which lead us to suggest that one facet of the high-level activity at Deerhurst may have been related to the cult of Deerhurst's relics. As to the specific function of the painted image, a few possible lines of thought can be put forward for further consideration. In 1993 Richard Gem suggested that the high-level panels at Deerhurst were perhaps examples of what was intended by Canon 2 issued by the Council of Chelsea in 816; it was prescribed that a consecrating bishop was required to see "that there is *depictum* on the wall of the oratory, or on a tablet, or even on the altar, to which saints both are dedicated." The passage is not as clear as one might wish, and Gem expressed uncertainty as to whether an inscription or an image was intended.[36]

The possible context outlined above for the Deerhurst panels may, however, indicate a rather less public function. Arnold Klukas argued that Deerhurst church was remodelled to conform with the liturgical observances of *Regularis Concordia*,[37] but we would suggest a ninth-century date for many of the features considered by Klukas to belong to the later tenth century. However, Klukas did make the interesting proposal that some of the high-level spaces at Deerhurst might represent the *secreti oratorii loci* mentioned twice by *Regularis Concordia*; these "secret places of the oratory" were reserved for private devotions and private masses. Such *secreti oratorii loci* are unlikely to have been unique to Benedictine monasteries. For instance, in the mid-twelfth century, Prior Richard of Hexham, describing the seventh-century church at Hexham, mentions that Wilfrid "Oratoria quoque quam plurima, superius et inferius, secretissima et pulcherrima, in ipsis porticibus cum maxima diligentia et cautela constituit": 'Moreover, he arranged with great diligence and care many oratories above and below in those porticus, of much secrecy and much beauty.'[38] Hexham had of course been monastic at the time of Wilfrid's foundation, but had ceased to be so long before the Norman Conquest; Richard's remarks seem to be based, at least in part, on evidence which had survived to his own day. It may be that the images on triangular-headed panels at Deerhurst were intended to be the focus of private devotions, perhaps in association with a shrine and/or an altar or altars.

There is so much that we do not know about Deerhurst that hard and fast conclusions would be premature. At this stage it is perhaps more productive to think in terms of the intended audience of the painted image. At high level at the east end of the church, it is surely unlikely that the painted panel was intended to have a popular audience; in this respect one might contrast it with the sculpture of the Virgin and Child over an archway in the west tower, which would have been seen by all those who entered through the principal entrance.[39] Rather, it

---

[36] Richard Gem, "Architecture of the Anglo-Saxon Church, 735 to 870: From Archbishop Ecgberht to Archbishop Ceolnoth," *Journal of the British Archaeological Association* 146 (1993): 29–66, at 48, 51–55. The text reads, "Seu etiam praecipimus unicuique Episcopo, ut sciat depictum in pariete oratorii, aut in tabula, vel etiam in altaribus, quibus sanctis sint utraque dedicata": *Councils and Ecclesiastical Documents Relating to Great Britain and Ireland*, ed. A. W. Haddan and W. Stubbs, 3 vols. (Oxford, 1869–1878), 3: 580.

[37] Arnold W. Klukas, "Liturgy and Architecture: Deerhurst Priory as an Expression of the *Regularis Concordia*," *Viator* 15 (1984): 81–106.

[38] Richard of Hexham, *Historia Hagustaldensis ecclesiae*, chap. 3, *The Priory of Hexham*, ed. J. Raine, 2 vols., Surtees Society 44, 46 (Durham, 1864–1865), 1: 1–106, at 12–13.

[39] Bailey, *Anglo-Saxon Sculptures at Deerhurst*, 7–11.

the eleventh century contain mainly Old English texts. With the exception of the *Lacnunga*, which has mixed Latin and English contents, the only Latin text known was the *Herbarius*.[3] From the mid-eleventh century onwards, Latin texts are more numerous and various, and in fact no more Old English medicine exists in surviving manuscripts until well into the twelfth century.

TABLE 17.1. Manuscripts containing medical material in Old English (*), or deriving from England before the end of the eleventh century.

1	Herrnstein, Bibliothek der Grafen Nesselrode, s. ix/x, South England or N.W. Germany (destroyed)	*Herbarius*
2	British Library, Royal 12.D.xvii, s. xᵐ, Winchester?	*Bald's Leechbook; *Leechbook III*
3	British Library, Harley 585, s. xi¹, South England?	*Herbarius; *Lacnunga*
4	British Library, Cotton Vitellius C.iii s. xi¹ ᵒʳ ᵐᵉᵈ, Canterbury, Christ Church?	*Herbarius*
5	Oxford, Bodleian Library, Hatton 76, s. xiᵐᵉᵈ, Worcester?	*Herbarius*
6	Cambridge, University Library Gg 5.35 after 1039, Canterbury, St. Augustine's	medical verses, *Practica Petrocelli* (extracts), pseudo-Soranus, *In artem medendi isagoge* (extracts)
7	Cambridge, Peterhouse 251 s. xi² (post-Conquest) or xi/xii, Canterbury, St. Augustine's?	Galen, *Ad Glauconem, Liber tertius, Liber Aurelii, Liber Esculapii*

ten or Owned in England up to 1100, MRTS 241 (Tempe, 2001), with idem, "Addenda and Corrigenda to the 'Handlist of Anglo-Saxon Manuscripts'," *ASE* 32 (2003): 293–305. Gneuss's work has enabled me to do an enormous amount that would not have otherwise been possible. I have also used Richard Gameson, *The Manuscripts of Early Norman England* (Oxford, 1999). The table is based upon that published in D. Banham, "A Millennium in Medicine? New Medical Texts and Ideas in England in the Eleventh Century," in *Anglo-Saxons: Studies Presented to Cyril Roy Hart*, ed. Simon Keynes and Alfred P. Smyth (Dublin, 2006), 230–42, but sharp-eyed readers will notice the omission of Durham, Dean and Chapter Library A.III.31, which Alan Piper tells me is Italian, and of Oxford, St. John's College, 17, which is not discussed here.

[3] On the *Lacnunga* see the edition by Edward Pettit, *Anglo-Saxon Remedies, Charms and Prayers from British Library MS Harley 585: The Lacnunga*, 2 vols. (Lampeter, 2001). The *Herbarius* is printed from a variety of manuscripts by Hubert Jan de Vriend, parallel with his edition of *The Old English Herbarium and Medicina de quadrupedibus*, EETS o.s. 286 (Oxford, 1984).

8	Cambridge, Trinity College R.14.50, s. xi³/⁴, South England	*Passionarius Galieni*
9	British Library, Sloane 1621, s. xi, Bury St. Edmunds?	Medical prayers, *antidota*, recipes, *De urinis* (unfinished)
10	Cambridge, Trinity College R. 14.31, s. xiˣ, Canterbury, St. Augustine's	Medical recipes and extracts
11	British Library, Sloane 475, fols. 125–231, s. xiˣ or s. xi/xii, England	*Liber tertius?* (fragment), *De urinis*, Egyptian days, recipes, glosses
12	Oxford, Bodleian Library, Bodley 130, s. xi/xii, Bury St. Edmunds?	*Herbarius*
13	Oxford, Bodleian Library, Ashmole 1431, s. xi/xii, Canterbury, St. Augustine's	*Herbarius*
14	Cambridge, Trinity College O.7.37, s. xi/xii, Westminster	Medical recipes and extracts
15	British Library, Sloane 2839, s. xi/xii or s. xiiⁱⁿ, England?	Medical texts, inc. recipes; *Petrocellus*, cauterization tract
16	British Library, Harley 6258B, s. xiiᵐᵉᵈ ᵒʳ ², South England?	**Herbarius; *Peri didaxeon*

Presumably Old English continued to be used, perhaps even written, but alongside it was a whole group of new texts that differ from it not only in language, but in a number of other characteristics as well. Exactly when these new texts started to arrive is less than clear, but the earliest English manuscript containing this new type of medicine would seem to be Cambridge, University Library Gg.5.35, the "Canterbury classbook," or "Cambridge Songs manuscript." Frustratingly, this is not a precisely datable manuscript, despite all the work that has been done on it, but it does seem likely that it was made before the Norman Conquest.[4]

Let us turn then from the thorny question of date to the texts themselves. Many of the new texts are related, and many travel together, both in England and on the Continent. The *Ad Glauconem de methodo medendi*, an apparently genuine work of Galen, is usually followed by the pseudo-Galenic *Liber tertius* (named in relation to the two books of the *Ad Glauconem*, so closely were they identified) and frequently by the *Liber Esculapii*.[5] These two latter texts have

---

[4] Gneuss, *Handlist*, commits himself only to s.xi med.; Gameson, *Manuscripts of Early Norman England*, omits CUL Gg.5.35, presumably on the grounds that it dates from before 1066.

[5] *Ad Glauconem* is listed in Galen's *De libris propriis*, translated by P. N. Singer in *Galen: Selected Works* (Oxford, 1997), 3–22, at 13. The *Liber tertius* is edited by Klaus-Dietrich Fischer, "Galeni qui fertur ad Glauconem Liber tertius ad fidem codicis

The *materia medica* of the new texts is also much more like that of the Continent and the later Middle Ages. Work on the Old English texts suggests that their compilers deliberately adapted or selected their recipes to suit English conditions: a high proportion of the recipes use herbs easily grown in Britain, or herbs and spices relatively easily obtainable from the western Mediterranean, and vehicles such as water, beer, or lard, rather than imports like wine or olive oil.[16] The new texts, by contrast, use exotic ingredients like mastic and petroleum, and their *materia medica* is generally much more Mediterranean; beer and lard are absent. The recipes are also much more polypharmic: most Old English recipes (even in the *Herbarius*) have no more than two or three herbs and a vehicle, but those of the "new medicine" often have long and elaborate lists of ingredients, including some that are themselves compounds.[17]

Measurements, and the symbols used for them, are another feature of the new texts. Anyone who studies the Old English recipes is soon struck by their almost total lack of precise measurements.[18] The *Herbarius*, apart from the first chapter, "De herba vettonica," originally a separate work, has just as few. This is in complete contrast to the recipes in the new texts, which look much more like those of the later Middle Ages, with their extensive use of scruples, drams, and ounces, and the standard symbols for them.[19]

The vocabulary of the new texts is also much more sophisticated than that of Old English medicine. To some extent this is a function of the difference in language, since even quite homely words can look scholarly in Latin, but the new texts also use an extensive Greek-derived technical vocabulary for diseases (*scotomia, melancholia*), their cures (*trociscus, cataplasma*), parts of the body, physiological processes, and so on.

Overall, it can be seen that these new medical texts which arrived in England in the eleventh century belonged not only to an international medicine, but a much more sophisticated one than had been known before. The most important aspect of this sophistication, in terms of intellectual history, is their use and understanding of medical theory, but their citation of authorities, their more exotic *materia medica*, their polypharmacy, their use of measurements and symbols, and their technical vocabulary are all symptomatic.

It will be immediately apparent that more work on the manuscripts, both English and Continental, of these new texts is needed to shed light on the routes

---

[16] This information comes from my *Materia medica Anglo-Saxonica* project, although the general observation is hardly original.

[17] For both these aspects, see Banham, "Arestolobius, the Patriarch of Jerusalem and the Bark that Comes from Paradise."

[18] Pettit, *Anglo-Saxon Remedies*, xxviii–xxix, has a list of those used in the *Lacnunga*.

[19] For an example, see the "Prescription of Arestolobius" from BL, Sloane 1621 printed in the Appendix below, where words in curled brackets are represented in the manuscript by symbols.

by which they arrived in England. Most of the texts had already been circulating on the Continent from the ninth century, and in some cases earlier.[20] We have no reason to suppose that the English copies are more closely related to each other than to Continental ones, or indeed that the English ones all have similar Continental affinities. It would not even be justifiable to assume that these affinities will necessarily point in the direction of eleventh-century cross-Channel links that are already known from other sources. Nevertheless, it would seem perverse to ignore such links completely in our search for mechanisms that may have brought new medical knowledge to England.

Turning then to known links between England and the Continent, those established by the monastic reformers of King Edgar's reign were probably no longer of great importance by the date of our first 'new medicine' manuscripts. Those established by the Norman Conquest would seem to be too late (depending on the date of CUL Gg.5.35), although, given Norman attitudes to Anglo-Saxon libraries in other subject areas, the newcomers may well have felt that they needed modernizing in the medical field, too.[21] Be that as it may, if our new medicine started to arrive before the Conquest, we might look instead at the 'little conquest' of Edward the Confessor's reign. In contrast to the Conquest proper, this earlier group of immigrants consisted mainly of ecclesiastics, among them Baldwin, formerly a monk of Saint-Denis, the Confessor's physician. Baldwin was made abbot of Bury St. Edmunds in 1065, and after the Conquest continued as royal physician under the Conqueror and William Rufus, dying in 1097/98.[22] Given his professional interest, Baldwin seems a very likely candidate to have brought medical books to England, or to have imported them after his arrival.[23]

There is thus a strong temptation to attribute medical manuscripts of the relevant period to Bury, and thus to associate them with Baldwin. Fortunately,

---

[20] Augusto Beccaria, *I codici di medicina del periodo presalernitana (secoli ix, x e xi)*, Storia e letteratura, Raccolta de studi e testi 53 (Rome, 1956), soon to be supplemented by the work of Monica Green and Eliza Glaze.

[21] See R. M. Thomson, "English Libraries and the Norman Conquest," in *The Role of the Book in Medieval Culture: Proceedings of the Oxford Symposium, 26 September–1 October 1982*, ed. P. Ganz, 2 vols., Bibliologia 3, 4 (Turnhout, 1986), 1: 27–40.

[22] Not an enormous amount is known about Baldwin's life and career apart from this; see Antonia Gransden, "Baldwin, Abbot of Bury St. Edmunds, 1065–1097," *Anglo-Norman Studies* 4 (1982): 65–76, 187–95.

[23] Unfortunately it is not known how long he was in England before his appointment to Bury. On his book acquisitions more generally, see now Rebecca Rushforth, "The Eleventh- and Early Twelfth-Century Manuscripts of Bury St Edmunds Abbey" (Ph.D. diss., Cambridge, 2003), 99–104, 178–97, as well as Teresa Webber, "The Provision of Books for Bury St. Edmunds Abbey in the 11th and 12th Centuries," in *Bury St. Edmunds: Medieval Art, Architecture, Archaeology and Economy*, ed. Antonia Gransden, British Archaeological Association Transactions 20 (Leeds, 1998), 186–93.

Rebecca Rushforth's comprehensive study of the Bury scriptorium in the eleventh century has been able to establish that none of the medical manuscripts sometimes attributed to Bury, such as the "Bury Herbal" (Oxford, Bodleian Library, Bodley 130, at Bury later in the Middle Ages) or Cambridge, Peterhouse 251, contains hands resembling those she has identified as belonging to that house.

In London, British Library, Sloane 1621, however, Rushforth has identified a scribe from Bury. Following Michael Gullick's identification of this manuscript (no. 498.8.1 in Gneuss's "Addenda and Corrigenda") as English, Rushforth found a hand on fols. 32v and 62v–63r which also occurs in Cambridge, University Library Ii.6.5, which was certainly written at Bury.[24] This hand, belonging to the end of the eleventh century, made additions to Sloane 1621 after the main text was written, consisting of fourteen lines written in a blank space on fol. 32v, and several recipes on an added bifolium, fols. 62–63. It is not yet clear how long after the original collection was written these additions were made, nor just how late in the century this scribe was active, but it is perfectly possible that in Sloane 1621 we have a medical book that was at Bury, and which was added to there during Baldwin's lifetime. It is theoretically possible that the whole book, or at least Part 2, was written there under Baldwin, but Rushforth does not think that any of the main hands belong to the Bury scriptorium. This presumably means that Baldwin (if it was he) had the book copied elsewhere, possibly from a Continental manuscript belonging to another English house, or alternatively acquired it by gift or purchase. In either case, there must have been other people in England in Baldwin's time with the means and inclination to commission or acquire manuscripts of the new medicine. This is of course perfectly possible: Baldwin may not have been the only medical practitioner to arrive in England in the Confessor's reign, and there is no inherent reason why only practitioners should have been interested in medical books.[25]

To return to the manuscript, I should now like to make some more detailed remarks about the contents of Sloane 1621, which are summarized in the Appendix below. It actually consists of at least two different codices, or, rather, parts of codices. Written entirely in Latin, they are apparently of similar date, although additions have been made to Part 2, and they were presumably bound together, at some unknown date (the present binding is modern), because of the links between their content. Part 1 is partly medical and partly musical, but Part 2 is entirely medical. It contains largely recipes rather than any substantial texts attributed to major figures in the history of medicine, and so, in that respect, it resembles earlier English medical manuscripts, but it is the character and content of those recipes that differ.

[24] Rushforth, "The Eleventh- and Early Twelfth-Century Manuscripts," 58–59 and (for CUL Ii.6.5), 57–58.
[25] There is scant evidence for any others, but see Banham, "A Millennium in Medicine?" 239–40, for some speculation on this score.

Part 2 begins with a substantial group of recipes written in two hands to fol. 38r, and then a number of hands. The collection starts part way through a recipe (perhaps a quire has been lost), and all the complete ones begin with the word *antidotum*, which has led to the collection being described as an antidotary. However, the word is not being used here in its technical sense, but seems to be just a fancy synonym for *recipe*, or *remedy*. They deal with a wide range of disorders, and range from very simple recipes to elaborate ones with long lists of ingredients, including exotica. Many of them have specific names, the antidote of so-and-so, *sancti Pauli*, for instance, or *dia-* something-or-other, like *diamargariton* (a common Greek or pseudo-Greek form of designation for such learned medicines); all of them measure in drams, scruples, and/or ounces, and all use the standard symbols, or at least a version of the standard symbols. All the various scribes who contributed to Part 2 use different forms of the symbols, and some are not even internally consistent, but seem to follow the usage of different exemplars. This group of recipes thus has five of my criteria for identifying this 'new medicine': they are written in Latin, but use Greek vocabulary and exotic ingredients, along with precise and standardized measurements, and the use of symbols. There is also a substantial degree of polypharmacy.

All these characteristics also apply to the other recipes, whether single or in groups, that make up the rest of Sloane 1621, Part 2. We have *electuaria*, *sales*, *trocisci*, *unguenta*, including an "Ointment of precious *nardipisticus* which the Romans brought back from Jerusalem after our Lord Jesus Christ suffered for us," and the famous "Prescription of Arestolobius," or "Aristobolus" as he is named (probably correctly) here. This last is also found (in Old English) in the *Lacnunga* and, unattributed, in *Leechbook* III (the collection following Bald's *Leechbook* in British Library, Royal 12.D.xvii, s. x^m, Winchester?), and in various later recipe collections.[26] The *Lacnunga* version is the earliest attributed version I know of, and *Leechbook* III the earliest overall, but presumably their source was an as-yet unidentified Latin version. Sloane and the Old English versions are not particularly close, and are unlikely to have the same immediate source. The Prescription must therefore have a quite complex prehistory, but whether any of it is to be found in surviving manuscripts remains to be seen. As for the "Unguentum . . . quod Romani adtulerunt," this is otherwise unknown to me, but it may well have an equally interesting story. Finally, there is the beginning of a text *De urinis mulierum*. This particular text is not found in any earlier English manuscript, but it is not unusual to find short texts on urines or bloodletting (in Latin or Old English) in earlier books, including otherwise non-medical ones.

---

[26] This recipe seems to go back at least to the eighth century on the Continent. The *Leechbook* III version is printed by Cockayne, *Leechdoms, Wortcunning and Starcraft*, 2: 314, 316. The *Lacnunga* text and translation is at Pettit, *Anglo-Saxon Remedies*, 1: 116–19, and discussion of this and variant English versions (but not Sloane) at 2: 341–45.

In overall terms, however, Sloane 1621 is a good example of what I have termed 'the new medicine', new, that is, to England in the mid-eleventh century, and an international medicine which was much more learned than had been available in England before. This is not, however, to cast aspersions on Anglo-Saxon medicine, which is an extremely interesting body of work. One of the most interesting things about it is that it appears to have developed largely in isolation from Continental Europe before the mid-eleventh century, despite the large number of known contacts between England and the Continent. The explanation for this must be that those crossing the Channel during most of the Anglo-Saxon period had priorities other than medicine (the healing of the soul rather than the body, the reform of the Church, escaping with their lives, and so on); only in (probably) the Confessor's reign did people start coming to England for whom the care of the sick was a central interest. Baldwin of Bury is the clearest example of such a person; since he owed royal favor and appointment to high office to his medical knowledge, his motivation for keeping that knowledge up to date is clear; in fact we are driven to question why there are not more medical books associated with his name. Other practitioners, such as Faricius of Arezzo, later abbot of Abingdon, are known to have come to England in the second half of the century, but their numbers hardly seem large enough to account for the quantity of 'new medicine' appearing in England at this time. Did medicine just become a more fashionable subject of study in England in the second half of the eleventh century than it had been before?

Appendix
London, British Library, Sloane 1621:
provisional summary contents

Part 1:
1. 2r: medical prayers
2. 2v–4v: *Monocordi diuisio* etc.

Part 2:
3. 5r–32r and 33r–52r (acephalous): *antidota*, ca. 92 items
4. 32v: 2 added *electuaria*
5. 53r–55r (acephalous): 11 recipes, mostly *sales*
6. 56r (added folio): *Confectio salis sacerdotalis* [How to make priests' salt] (unfinished):

   Recipe haec. Salis communis .xvij. ysopi. Pulegi. ameos. Colene zinziberi. ana. {dragmam} j. Siler .xij. Timu {uncias}. iiij. Satureia. {dragmam} j. Cinnamu. {uncias} .iiij. piper .{dragmam} j.

   [Take these: 17 [units omitted] of common salt, 1 dram each of pennyroyal, ammi, Colene ginger, 12 [units omitted] of siler, 4 ounces of timu, 1 dram of savory, 4 ounces of cinnamon, 1 dram of pepper.]
7. 58r–61v and 64r–67r: 33 recipes, mostly *trocisci*
8. 62r–63r (added bifolium): 9 recipes
9. 67r: added recipe
10. 67v: 3 added *electuaria*
11. 68r–107v: ca. 127 recipes
12. 107v–108r: (added) *Unguentum nardipistici preciosi quod adtulerunt romani de hierusalem. postquam dominus noster iesus christus passus est pro nobis* [The ointment of precious *nardipisticus* that the Romans brought back from Jerusalem, after our Lord Jesus Christ suffered for us] and *Unguentum gyras*
13. 108v: (added) "Prescription of Arestolobius":

    Confectio qui utebatur aristobolus rex omni corpori/ dans sanitatem ad reumam capitis. ad uertiginem. ad ca/liginem oculorum. ad cauculum. ad splen. ad lumbos ad san/guinem superhabundantem. ad genua. ad paraliticum./ podagram. leprosos. et qui uigilias patiuntur. et ad ele/fantiosos. Recipe hec appii seminis. {uncias} ii. fenuculi seminis. {uncias} ii. leuisitici/ seminis. {unciam} i. aneti seminis. [*]Centaurie. Betonice. Rute seminis.[*]/ an<a> {unciam} i. piper {uncias} iii. Cauli seminis. pastinace seminis. fenugreci farina/ ana {unciam} i. folio. {uncias} ii. et si folium non habueris; uulgagine/ sicco. {uncias} iiii. mastice {uncias} iii. iuquiam[i] {unciam} i. [*]Bacas lauri {uncias} ii. [*] Hec omnia puluerem facias temperabis in uino.

    [*] corrected by another hand over erasure
    [The confection that King Aristobolus used, for the whole body, giving health to rheum in the head, to vertigo, to mistiness of the eyes, to the

stone, to the spleen, to the loins, to a superabundance of blood, to the knees, to the paralytic, gout, the leprous and those who suffer sleeplessness, and to those with elephantiasis. Take these things: 2 ounces of celery seed, 2 ounces of fennel seed, 1 ounce of lovage seed, 1 ounce each of dill seed, centaury, betony, rue seed, 3 ounces of pepper, 1 ounce each of cabbage seed, parsnip seed, fenugreek flour, 2 ounces of folium, and if you have no folium, 4 ounces of dry asarabacca, 3 ounces of mastic, 1 ounce of henbane, 2 ounces of bay berries. Make all these into a powder, temper in wine.]

14. 108v: added *electuarium*
15. 110r–v: ca. 5 added recipes
16. 111r: (added) *De urinis mulierum* (unfinished)

I. General Index[1]

A

Aachen, 283, 306

Abbo of Fleury (*c*. 945–1004), spent two years at Ramsey Abbey (985–987), xiv, xx, 6, 293–302

 Panegyric in praise of Ramsey, xx, 288, 293–302

Acculturation, 132, 135–38

Acrostic, 69, 300–2

Adam of Bremen, cleric and historian (d. *c*. 1085), 144–51

Adomnán or Adamnan, abbot of Iona (*c*. 624–704), 185–87, 190–93

Ælfheah or Alphege, Saint, archbishop of Canterbury (d. 1012), 163, 332

Ælfric, abbot of Eynsham (*c*. 950– *c*. 1010), 4–14, 99, 120–29, 130, 171, 175

 Catholic Homilies, 4, 9–10, 13

 Grammar, 4

Æthelric, son of Æthelmund (fl. 804), 332

Æthelstan, king of England (893/4–939), 166–67, 171, 266

Æthelweard, ealdorman (d. *c*. 998), xviii, 46, 163–78

 Chronicon Æthelweardi, xviii, 163–68, 171–78

Æthelwulf, king of Wessex (839–858), xviii, 46, 67, 165, 312

Agency, agent, 22, 140

Alchred or Alhred, king of Northumbria (fl. 765–774), 150

Alcuin of York, scholar and poet (*c*. 735– 804), xiv, xix, 143, 152, 156, 159, 160–61, 231, 249, 269, 275–92, 303–5

 Cartula perge cito, xix, 275–92

Alfred, King of Wessex (871–899), xiii, xvi, 4, 10, 15, 36, 45–46, 51, 63–68, 84, 104–5, 131, 165, 176, 245, 254, 264–66

 Cura pastoralis, 9–10; *see also* Index II, Oxford, Bodleian Library, Hatton, 20

Alfredian translations, 103–4, 125

Alfredian coins, 256

Altfrid, bishop of Münster (*c*. 800–874), xvii, 140

 Vita Liudgeri, xvii, 140–49, 151–52, 158, 160–61

Aluberht, Anglo-Saxon preacher (fl. 765– 782), 145–56

Angels, fall of, illustrated, 65, 72, 81, 188

Anglo-Latin texts, 3, 5–6; *see also* Æthelweard; Abbo of Fleury; Alcuin; Bede; Byrhtferth of Ramsey; Durham, *Liber vitae*

Anglo-Saxon Conquest, 113–9, 122, 129, 132, 134

Anglo-Saxon Chronicle, xviii, 6, 46, 125–28, 134, 163, 167, 171–76, 254, 264, 266

Anglo-Saxon mission, 17, 140, 152, 155, 158, 181, 278

---

[1] The index is selective and only the more important persons, places, texts, ideas etc. are listed. The dates of the persons mentioned sometimes refer to their entire lifespan and sometimes just to their period of reign or rule. d. = died; fl. = floruit.

K

Kentish. *See* Old English dialects
Kinship, kindred, kin-group, 32, 49, 204, 211–12, 215; *see also* Family

L

Lacnunga, 342, 346, 349
Landscape, xv, 21–41, 46, 52–53, 56, 184, 188, 295
Langefeld, Brigitte, scholar, 309–10, 313
Language, linguistics, xiv, xvii, 1, 5–6, 8–17, 19, 32, 63–64, 67–70, 73, 94, 113–39, 295, 341, 343, 346; *see also* Contact linguistics; Grammars; Imperfect learning
Language contact, 15, 115–20, 122, 138
Language shift, xvii, 114, 117–18, 121–23, 127, 132, 134, 137. *See also* Borrowing; Lexicon, lexical; Old English, Old English dialects; Old Saxon
Progressive aspect, 122–26, 137
Standardization, standard language. *See* Old English: Standard Old English; Substratum, substratal, substrate; Superstratum, superstratal, superstrate
'to be' 120–22; *see also* Word-formation
Latin, xiv, xv, xviii–xxi, 3–21, 24, 29, 32, 42, 55, 60, 66, 69, 94, 115–39, 151, 163, 182–83, 191–92, 212, 217, 224, 226–30, 237–38, 250, 257, 260, 263, 268, 270, 278–79, 289, 293, 295, 303, 306, 314, 341–42, 344–50; *see also* Anglo-Latin texts; Cicero; Donatus; Martial; Ovid; Priscian; Sidonius Apollinaris
Leechbook III. *See* Bald's *Leechbook*
Lejre, xv–xvi, 41–62
Leoba, Anglo-Saxon missionary in Germany, founder and first abbess of Tauberbischofsheim (*c.* 710–782), xiv, xviii, 199–217
Vita S. Leobae. See Rudolf of Fulda
Leopold I, emperor of the Holy Roman Empire (1765–1790), 222

Letters, xviii, 17, 99–100, 146, 155, 160, 165–67, 176–78, 211–13, 222–29, 233–35, 249, 258, 261, 263–64, 267, 275–77, 282–83, 289–90, 301
Lexicon, lexical, 72, 116, 118, 121, 136, 289
Liber Aurelii, 342, 344
Liber Esculapii, 342–44
Liber tertius, 342–45
Lichfield cathedral, angel (Staffordshire), 324n.3
Life-span, life expectancy, xv, 28
Light (as opposed to darkness), xv, xvii, xx, 10, 16, 50, 77–78, 85–86, 151, 174, 180, 190, 192, 234, 245, 264, 267, 276, 288, 290–91, 293–94, 296–97, 300–2, 336, 340, 346
Lindisfarne, 8–9, 128, 262, 273, 276, 303
Lindisfarne Gospels. See Index II, London, British Library, Cotton Nero D.IV.
Linguistic, xv, 11, 14, 16, 31, 34, 37, 47, 59, 62, 68–69, 81, 85, 89, 94, 116–38; *see also* Language
Liturgy, liturgical texts and books, xv, 5, 13, 230–35, 269, 274, 332
Liudger, Frisian missionary, first bishop of Münster, (*c.* 742–809), xvii, 142–44, 146–55, 159-62, 212; *see also* Altfrid, *Vita Liudgeri*
Liudolf, duke of Swabia, son of Edith and Otto I, father of Matilda (d. 956), 165, 206
Locus amoenus, xx, 293, 295–96, 302
Louis the Pious, king of the Franks and emperor (778–840), xx, 66–67, 148–49, 153, 155, 210, 213, 304–9, 311
Low German, 69–70, 74, 113, 119, 122
Lucca, xix, 180, 192, 254, 265–67, 272
Lull or Lullus, Anglo-Saxon missionary in Germany, archbishop of Mainz (*c.* 710–786), 139, 146, 149, 156, 203–4, 213, 215, 254, 264, 269, 284

II. Index of Manuscripts and Inscriptions